Textbook on
International Human Rights

Textbook on
International Human Rights

Fourth edition

Rhona K. M. Smith

OXFORD
UNIVERSITY PRESS

OXFORD
UNIVERSITY PRESS

Great Clarendon Street, Oxford ox2 6DP

Oxford University Press is a department of the University of Oxford.
It furthers the University's objective of excellence in research, scholarship,
and education by publishing worldwide in

Oxford New York

Auckland Cape Town Dar es Salaam Hong Kong Karachi
Kuala Lumpur Madrid Melbourne Mexico City Nairobi
New Delhi Shanghai Taipei Toronto

With offices in

Argentina Austria Brazil Chile Czech Republic France Greece
Guatemala Hungary Italy Japan Poland Portugal Singapore
South Korea Switzerland Thailand Turkey Ukraine Vietnam

Oxford is a registered trade mark of Oxford University Press
in the UK and in certain other countries

Published in the United States
by Oxford University Press Inc., New York

© Rhona Smith, 2010

The moral rights of the author have been asserted
Database right Oxford University Press (maker)

Crown copyright material is reproduced under Class Licence Number
C01P0000148 with the permission of OPSI
and the Queen's Printer for Scotland

This edition 2010

All rights reserved. No part of this publication may be reproduced,
stored in a retrieval system, or transmitted, in any form or by any means,
without the prior permission in writing of Oxford University Press,
or as expressly permitted by law, or under terms agreed with the appropriate
reprographics rights organization. Enquiries concerning reproduction
outside the scope of the above should be sent to the Rights Department,
Oxford University Press, at the address above

You must not circulate this book in any other binding or cover
and you must impose this same condition on any acquirer

British Library Cataloguing in Publication Data

Data available

Library of Congress Cataloging in Publication Data
Smith, Rhona K. M.
Textbook on international human rights / Rhona K. M. Smith. — 4th ed.
p. cm.
Includes index.
ISBN 978-0-19-956118-6
1. Human rights. I. Title.
K3240.S55 2009
341.4'8—dc22

Typeset by Macmillan Publishing Solutions
Printed in Great Britain
on acid-free paper by
Ashford Colour Press, Gosport, Hampshire

ISBN 978-0-19-956118-6

3 5 7 9 10 8 6 4

OUTLINE CONTENTS

DETAILED CONTENTS

5   The United Nations organizational structure   51

6   Regional protection of human rights   84

7   Europe   94

8 The Organization of American States 116

9 The African Union 134

10 Monitoring, implementing, and enforcing human rights 149

11 Substantive rights—general comments   176

12 Equality and non-discrimination   189

13 The right to life   210

22 Group rights   347

23 Looking to the future   371

PREFACE

This text is intended to serve as a broad introduction to International Human Rights Law. Human Rights is a fascinating subject which pervades all aspects of life and all levels of society. In the last fifty years it has developed into a discipline in its own right, distinct from Public International Law. Given the breadth of human rights this text cannot address all aspects of the topic, nor even cover exhaustively those areas most commonly taught in courses, as every course follows a different pattern depending on the interests of those involved.

The approach taken is to introduce the reader to the scope of the subject in preparation for further study and research. To this end, primary sources have been employed as far as possible. Suggestions for further reading and appropriate website references are provided at the end of each chapter to provide a starting point for further study. The non-primary texts referred to are commonly found in university libraries and often available to subscribers online. A cross-section of substantive rights provides an indication of the scope of some of these rights (civil, political, economic, social, cultural, and collective) combining jurisprudence from the regional and international systems. An understanding of those covered in this book should facilitate study of any other rights and freedoms.

The basic documents, full references for which are given in the Table of Instruments, are usually accessible through websites as well as in compilations of documents (for example, Ghandhi, PR, *International Human Rights Documents*, 5th edn (Oxford; OUP Blackstone, 2006) and Brownlie, I, and Goodwin-Gill, GS, *Basic Documents on Human Rights*, 5th edn (Oxford: OUP, 2006)). Cases, on the other hand, can be traced through websites and the official annual reports of the organization concerned. For example, the Treaty Bodies Database Search function of the site of the Office of the High Commissioner for Human Rights (www.ohchr.org) facilitates access to the jurisprudence of the conventional mechanisms of the United Nations while the official sites of the European Court of Human Rights and the Inter-American Court of Human Rights have specific search engines. In addition to the websites cited (the emphasis being on the official websites), there are detailed human rights' virtual libraries with links to jurisprudence through the University of Minnesota (www1.umn.edu/humanrts), through the SIM Document Centre at the University of Utrecht (www.sim.law.uu.nl) and through Bayefsky.com (www.bayefsky.com) which was established by Professor Ann Bayefsky. The information in the present text for the cases allows searches to be conducted on these and other search engines. Appropriate links and more information on this can be found in the companion website to this textbook. Web links in the text have been updated to July 2009.

Inevitably with a work like this, there are those people without whom it would not have been possible and those in spite of whom it appears. I wish to publicly record my gratitude to the former, to those whose support and assistance made this possible. My interest in Human Rights started at the University of Strathclyde during my doctoral studies and through teaching on the then undergraduate introductory course on European Human Rights, though international issues increasingly appeared in the programme to appease student interest (and indulge personal preference). More recently, I have benefited from the experience of teaching International Human Rights at Northumbria University and the feedback thereon from the students. For resource facilities, staff at the Council of Europe and the United Nations in Geneva kindly answered queries and I was lucky enough to visit the Corte Interamericano de Derechos Humanos and its associated library in San José, Costa Rica. Various anonymous reviewers generously read and commented on the text, many other academics completed and returned book evaluation forms, and several students emailed me. From the preparation period of the first edition, I remain indebted to my family and friends, particularly N Busby, K Davidson, M Muir, S Grant, L Stevenson, L Swigciski, and R Webster. For the gestation period of subsequent editions, additionally S Buckley, J Core, E Duff, S Schnitzer, and the Blue Max & Jazz Co. I have also been fortunate to be invited to teach in China, Indonesia, and Canada over the last few years which has greatly developed my understanding of international issues. I would like to formally thank CASS, RWI, PUSHAMUII, NCHR, PULS, and UWO for these opportunities. Finally I wish to credit those I have been fortunate enough to meet during my travels all over the world who have heightened my interest in and understanding of international human rights' issues.

This book is dedicated *til far, mor og Lorna, tusind tak og karlig hilsen* and, in the spirit intended, to my godchildren, Gray, Ryan, Kahlia, and Duncan (in Australia) and Alistair.

The law contained in this text is correct as at 4 June 2009.

TABLE OF CASES

AmCHR—American Court of Human Rights

AfCHR—African Commission on Human Rights

CAT—Committee Against Torture

CERD—Committee on the Elimination of Racial Discrimination

ECHR—European Court of Human Rights

ECJ—European Court of Justice

HRC—Human Rights Committee (ICCPR)

ICJ—International Court of Justice

ICTR—International Criminal Tribunal for Rwanda

ICTY—International Criminal Tribunal for Yugoslavia

PCIJ—Permanent Court of International Justice

In general, the texts of the cases and opinions can be located online as well as in specialist libraries. Cases can be accessed from the general site of each instrument/body, and/or from online human rights libraries and document centres. They may also be found annexed to the annual reports of the bodies concerned.

TABLE OF INSTRUMENTS

Page numbers in **bold** indicate that the text is reproduced in full.

1

Introduction

Human rights and fundamental freedoms are the birthright of all human beings; their protection and promotion is the first responsibility of Governments

(Vienna Declaration and Programme of Action 1993)

The period since the formation of the United Nations in 1945 has witnessed an unprecedented expansion in the internationally recognized rights of all people with acceptance of a human rights dimension to the quest for international peace and security. In a comparatively short period of time, the United Nations has styled itself as protector of the internationally proclaimed rights of all.

In some ways, there is nothing new about prescribing inalienable rights of people—national and international laws have long recognized that there are inherent limits on the powers of States. Some of these limitations will be considered in Chapter 2 which provides a brief historical background to international human rights. Human rights traditionally embody elements of the rule of law—recognition that States should act in accordance with 'higher' norms of behaviour. This will be touched upon, though the focus will be on examples of other restraints on State treatment of individuals—the fear of reprisals, for example. Early human rights such as the evolving prohibition on slavery will also be detailed. To many, modern international human rights law was pioneered in the inter-war period by the work of the League of Nations in developing minority rights through minority protection guarantees while the International Labour Organization sought to set standards on the protection of workers.

The principal focus of this text, however, is on modern international human rights law. Accordingly, there will be a detailed consideration of the creative development of the concept by the United Nations. Chapter 3 will introduce the reader to the work of the United Nations in the field of human rights. It will provide an overview of the main achievements of the organization. This will be followed, in Chapter 4, by a more detailed examination of the so-called 'International Bill of Rights', a tabulation of the universally accepted human rights and freedoms to which all are entitled without distinction. The work of the United Nations in the field of human rights is supported by a number of institutions, agencies, and organs. The principal bodies will be examined in Chapter 5, with a particular focus on the main treaty-monitoring bodies. The aim is to achieve comprehension of the international agenda on human rights and the methods by which these rights can be achieved.

Since developments on the international level have not been in isolation, the contribution of regional organizations will also be considered. Chapter 6 will introduce the rationale behind developing regional protection of human rights. It will also introduce those regional systems which are essentially declaratory and not supported by any implementation mechanism. Attention will then turn to the three leading regional human rights systems—Europe, the Americas, and Africa. Regional organizations in all three have adopted detailed tabulations of rights and freedoms. The realization of these regional rights is supported by the establishment of bodies that have responsibility for overseeing the efforts made by States in this respect. The most developed, oldest, and arguably the most effective regional system, is that of the Council of Europe. The work of the Council of Europe and developments within other European regional organizations will be examined in Chapter 7. Chapter 8 will then turn the attention of the reader to developments in the Americas, under the auspices of the Organization of American States. The American human rights system has a long history and many successes. Finally, the newest regional system—that of Africa—will be examined in Chapter 9. It has many innovative features and employs one of the most comprehensive human rights instruments in scope.

Naturally, the tabulation of human rights, be it at the international or regional level, is of little use to the individual without an effective means of implementation. Chapter 10 will thus examine the methods available for securing international and regional human rights. The focus will primarily be on the United Nations, but cross-references will be made to the work of the regional organizations which have already been discussed. The main criticisms levied at the system will be addressed with reference to current proposals for change.

The remainder of the text seeks to provide the reader with a flavour of the substance of international human rights. Chapter 11 provides a general overview of substantive rights and the various limitations thereto. A number of salient issues will be discussed including State discretion in selecting and applying rights: derogations, reservations, declarations, and denunciations will be reviewed.

The following chapters examine individual rights and freedoms. A reflective cross-section of rights are depicted with reference to the work of both international and regional organizations. Examples drawn from the jurisprudence of the various supervisory bodies illustrate the application and scope in each case. Given the diversity of sources employed, the survey of each right is, by necessity, indicative rather than definitive. Further reference should be made to the instrument concerned, the views of the monitoring bodies and associated literature for specific information thereon.

Within the space constraints, it was necessary to isolate certain rights for consideration. The rights selected reflect the breadth of modern international human rights law. The comparative proliferation of jurisprudence from the Human Rights Committee and the European Court of Human Rights influenced the selection of rights with the emphasis on rights most commonly claimed by individuals. This also accounts for a balance in favour of individual civil and political rights though elements of economic, social, and cultural rights and collective rights are considered where possible. Inevitably there are overlaps between different rights and conflicts of rights which must be balanced. The scope of the present text does not facilitate a detailed discussion thereof.

In terms of the Charter of the United Nations, the concept of equality of peoples' rights is paramount. Reference to equal rights is made in the Preamble, Article 1(2), Article 13 (1)(b), and Article 55(c), for example, reinforcing the founding of a system of universal human rights by the United Nations. Few, if any, human rights instruments do not include a non-discrimination clause, seeking to ensure the rights enshrined therein are guaranteed for all. As such clauses underpin all other human rights, they are examined first in Chapter 12.

Turning to more specific rights, the right to life is clearly the most fundamental of all rights—all other rights add quality to that life. Chapter 13 draws together African, American, European, and international jurisprudence on the right to life as well as detailing the international measures on genocide. Preventing genocide was of particular concern to the United Nations in its early years, given the atrocities of the Second World War. It continues to be relevant today as the work of the Ad Hoc International Criminal Tribunals for Rwanda and the former Yugoslavia testify.

Chapter 14 seeks to provide an introduction to the prohibition on torture and similar forms of treatment and punishment. Torture has been singled out by both international and regional bodies with specific instruments and monitoring systems solely designed to combat such practices.

Slavery is first mentioned in Chapter 2 as international action against it has a long history. The contemporary law on slavery and analogous practices is grouped in Chapter 15 alongside wider issues of liberty of person. The circumstances in which international and regional bodies permit deprivation of liberty will be reviewed.

Chapter 16 addresses issues of equality before the law and the right to a fair trial. The Statute of the new International Criminal Court reflects the basic guarantees for a fair trial which are considered. More than in other chapters, there is reliance on jurisprudence of the European Court of Human Rights due to the volume of cases it has decided on this, one of the most prolific grounds of challenge to date.

Self-determination is a right which transcends categorization. It is, in contrast to the foregoing, essentially a collective right exercisable not by an individual, but only by a group. Although the principle is enshrined in the United Nations Charter and the first Article of both the International Covenants, it remains controversial. There is little consensus on its application outwith 'classic' decolonization. As Chapter 17 illustrates, it has not been successfully claimed before the international or regional bodies.

Chapter 18 focuses on freedom of expression, one of the civil and political rights which is viewed as a key indicator of democracies. It is often remarked that human rights fail when the beneficiaries have no voice and cannot make their claims heard. The chapter surveys both the right and the principal legitimate limitations—for example propaganda for war.

The right to work is reviewed in a very broad approach (Chapter 19). An example of economic, social, and cultural rights, it is also an area in which other organizations, hitherto not addressed in detail, have exerted an influence. The work of the International Labour Organization has contributed extensive standard setting provisions while the Council of Europe's Social Charters provide evidence of the shift in such standards over the years.

Ultimately, a key to securing universal human rights is education. Chapter 20 thus concludes the survey of selected substantive rights with a discussion of the right to education and human rights education, an especially apt chapter as the United Nations Decade for Human Rights Education ends.

Chapter 21 considers the return to acceptance of the need for minority rights despite the planned deviation therefrom in light of the problems of the League of Nations (Chapters 2–3). Minority rights are essentially collective in nature. The increased protection of minority groups under the international regime provides an introduction to the modern law in this area. The discussion on minority rights leads neatly on to Chapter 22, which presents a brief overview of the growing phenomenon of group rights. Indigenous peoples, women, children, and refugees are considered.

The final chapter seeks to draw together the main themes which have permeated the text, outlining the future agenda for international human rights. Human rights have a major role to play in the new world order, not least in their contribution to the maintenance of peace and security. In little over 50 years, international human rights has developed as a distinct branch of public international law. Its importance cannot be underestimated.

Returning once more to the Vienna Declaration adopted by the World Conference on Human Rights: 'All human rights are universal, indivisible and interdependent and interrelated. The international community must treat human rights globally in a fair and equal manner, on the same footing, and with the same emphasis' (Declaration 5). At the end of this text, the reader should be better placed to make an informed decision on the veracity of this.

2

Historical background

Human rights have roots deep in the mists of time yet the term itself dates back barely sixty years to international discussions preceding the founding of the United Nations. Since 1945, the scope of human rights has been elaborated and the concept now permeates the fabric of international society. The origins of international human rights lie in philosophical discussions evolved through the centuries. Indeed, human rights represents the modern interpretation (and an expansion of) the traditional concept of the rule of law. A detailed discussion of such philosophies is beyond the scope of the current text. However, this chapter will provide a basic introduction by placing international human rights in a historical context with an emphasis on developments to the eve of the foundation of the United Nations.

2.1 Origins of international human rights

There are divergent views as to the origins of human rights: the existence of a body of basic rights can be traced back to the early thirteenth century in Europe and has featured in various predominantly European schools of thought since that time. In many respects its origins lie in philosophical discourse with concepts such as liberty and even 'rights'. It is linked to the constitutional concept of the rule of law—the inherent limitations on the exercise of absolute power by a sovereign or Parliament. The rule of law in turn links to theories of natural law and religious doctrines. Accordingly, some would argue earlier religious scripts embodying rules and regulations governing the conduct of society are the foundation of human rights. The basic tenets of all faiths prescribe boundaries of conduct, often norms of religious law. Many aspects of such laws are still applied today—the Shari'a laws of many Islamic States, for example. Although such sources tend to emphasize duties, political and religious traditions worldwide proclaimed certain 'rights' for peoples: the right to expect their rulers to be fair and reasonable, with limited authority in respect of the private lives and property of their subjects. An example can be found in England: Magna Carta of 1215 enshrined a number of principles which now fall within the broad ambit of human rights, including the principle of equality before the law, a right to property and an element of religious freedom, albeit such rights extended only to nobles. The Declaration of Arbroath (Scotland) in 1320, in contrast, spoke of the profound right to liberty, rating it above glory, honour, and riches. Some minimal rights were mentioned in the 1688 Bill of Rights of England and Wales though with little substance.

There are two principal origins of theories: the liberty-based theory prevalent in common-law jurisdictions and the rights-based theory of civil legal systems. Both address the relationship between the individual and the State, attempting to regulate interference by the State in an individual's private life. In essence, the liberty theories demand that the individual is free from arbitrary State interference while the rights theories are based on the inherent rights of peoples, which the State must respect.

2.2 The eighteenth century: Revolutions and rights

Some of the great philosophers of eighteenth- and nineteenth-century Europe focused on the idea of a body of so-called 'natural rights', rights which should be enjoyed by all human beings. These great thinkers developed a corpus of basic rights to be afforded to mankind. Many of those rights found legal expression at the close of the eighteenth century. The United States and France, respectively, adopted statements on rights when proclaiming the independence of the former British North American colonies and when establishing the first French Republic following the 1789 revolution. The French Declaration of the Rights of Man (1789) and the United States' Declaration of Independence (1776) and Bill of Rights (ie the first ten amendments which were ratified in December 1791) articulate various rights to be enjoyed by all citizens including liberty and equality.

The French Declaration was inspired by the United States' Declaration of Independence (though predates the Bill of Rights). It begins by stating that 'Men are born and remain free and equal in rights'. The concept of liberty is defined in Art 4—'Liberty consists in being able to do anything that does not harm others'. Other Articles relate to the exercise of the rule of law, including fair trial processes (Arts 6–10). Inevitably, given the nature and origins of the French revolution, the right to free communication of ideas and opinions and the right to manifest such opinions subject only to the limitations of established Law and Order are guaranteed (Arts 10–11) while matters of taxation are also addressed (Arts 13–14). The Declaration remains a cornerstone of the French Constitutions including the present 1958 version. The French Declaration had considerably wider impact, serving as a guide for constitutions of other European and former colonial countries as well as the European Convention on Human Rights itself (Council of Europe).

The American Bill of Rights refers to freedom of religion (Amendment I), various requirements relating to due process and the right to a fair trial (Amendments V, VI, VII, VIII) and freedom of person and property (Amendment IV). These rights all have modern equivalents in human rights instruments. Perhaps more controversial in modern society is the right to bear arms (Amendment II) although the text refers to it for the purpose of civil defence, 'necessary to the security of a free State'. These rights remain the foundation of the United States Constitution today, applied regularly in the national courts.

2.3 The role of international law

Originally, international law was, literally, the law of nations. It was exclusively concerned with the interaction of States—diplomatic relations and the laws of war.

Individuals were considered the property of the State in which they lived. Until comparatively recently, the manner in which a State treated its own nationals was thus an issue within the exclusive competence of that State, subject to neither external review nor international regulation. The multilateral treaties discussed in this section were the exceptions.

Since time immemorial, customary international law has recognized that some individuals deserved protection, often greater protection than that afforded to the nationals of a State. For example, States have long recognized a duty of care to strangers traversing over their land—for over two thousand years, it has been recognized that emissaries and official State messengers enjoy a right of passage through territories other than their own. This was essential in the days before international post, telephones, and the Internet. Similarly, customary international law has decreed the parameters within which wars should be conducted, and the treatment to be accorded to non-combatants. This is now referred to as international humanitarian law. The other principal area of law to be discussed in this chapter is the protection of minorities. The work of the League of Nations and the provisions of the Peace Treaties concluded after the First World War were crucial in developing this area of law. In each of these areas, custom and practice has been codified and consolidated into a written tabulation of rights.

International law has undoubtedly shaped human rights. The legal statement of rights is, in some respects, a codification of the rule of law by lawyers and legal draftsmen. International human rights, however, goes beyond the boundaries of general international law. There is an overlap between the traditional effect of international law (relations between States) and the traditional effect of national and constitutional law (relations between the State and individuals) with human rights allowing the international community to determine some limits to what a State may do to its nationals.

The traditional approach, basing the individual's 'rights' on the proprietorial rights of the State, is best illustrated by reference to the law of aliens which prescribed a certain standard of treatment States were obliged to accord nationals of other States.

2.4 **The law of aliens**

Hersch Lauterpacht, reworking Oppenheim's seminal *Treatise on International Law*, analyses the law of aliens, concluding that international law essentially imposes an obligation on States to 'grant certain privileges' to foreign heads of States and diplomatic personnel in return for which each State has the right to expect its citizens to be granted certain rights by foreign States when on their territory. International law imposes the duty on States; it is the internal laws of the State which realize the rights. The law of aliens facilitated international trade and travel, promoting the development of the global economy. There are obvious similarities to diplomatic law (discussed infra).

2.4.1 **Reparations and reprisals**

With the growth of the nation State and the consequential migration of man, the position of the alien underwent a fundamental change: an alien became perceived as representing a facet of the international persona of his or her State of origin.

Consequently, an injury to an alien would be construed as an indirect injury to the State of origin for which reparation (in the form of reprisals) could and would be sought. There are a number of cases originating from this. This principle of a wrong to a person being equitable to a wrong to the State is the basis of the nationality ground of jurisdiction in international law—a State has the right to take up any claim on behalf of one of its nationals at the international level.

This theory has also received judicial cognition: in the *Panevezys Railway Case (Estonia v Lithuania)* a precise formulation was provided at p 16: 'in taking up the case of one of its nationals ... a State is in reality asserting its own right to ensure, in the person of its nationals, respect for the rules of international law'. As the decision as to whether to bring an international claim lay solely within the discretion of the State, an individual could not compel a State to act on his or her behalf. Before the individual submitted his or her claim to the government, the injured person must have exhausted the local remedies available in the host State, thereby affording that State an opportunity of redressing the injury sustained. (The same requirement is found in modern law—an individual claiming a violation of a right enshrined in a human rights instrument is usually required to take reasonable steps to exhaust all domestic remedies before bringing the matter to the attention of the international/regional bodies.)

The growing number of international commissions and tribunals established to adjudicate in such matters further evidenced the institutionalization of the treatment of disputes of this nature. The Jay Commissions, constituted pursuant to the 1794 Jay Treaty concluded by the United States and Great Britain, are an early example of this. National and international claims commissions became the accepted modus operandi of settling such international disputes. However, with the advent of the Industrial Revolution, a codification of acceptable State responses to attacks on their nationals was required.

2.4.2 The two schools of thought

The increase in inter-State communications and relationships prompted the development of a corpus of law on the status of aliens. There are two recognized schools of thought as regards the treatment of foreigners by a host State: the national or equality treatment standard and the International Minimum Standard of Treatment.

2.4.2.1 *The national or equality standard of treatment*

Many developing countries, particularly in Latin America, adhered to this school of thought. In essence, a foreigner should be accorded only the same rights, however few or great in number, as a citizen of the host State. In other words a visitor to a State should not expect to be afforded more protection than a national of that State—ie there should be no positive or negative discrimination towards the alien. To quote a leading exponent of this school of thought, Carlos Calvo: 'aliens who established themselves in a country are certainly entitled to the same rights of protection as nationals, but they cannot claim any greater measure of protection' (Calvo, C (in trans), at p 231).

Calvo's doctrine was accepted by the First International Conference of American States and later encapsulated in the Montevideo Convention on the Rights and Duties of States 1933, Art 9: 'nationals and foreigners are under the same protection of the law and the national authorities, and foreigners may not claim rights other than or more extensive than those of nationals'.

This view poses one main problem: it negates public international law in that it deprives a State of the right to protect its nationals outside of her territorial boundaries. Consequently, it would be justifiable for a State to deprive a foreigner of all human rights if its own nationals were similarly deprived. This theory has never been universally accepted. Indeed, judicial disapproval of the Calvo Clause is reported as early as 1926 (*North American Dredging Company Case* (US/Mexico)).

2.4.2.2 *The International Minimum Standard of Treatment*

Adherents to this school of thought, on the other hand, believed that there was a minimum universal standard of treatment which must be observed by all States in their treatment of foreigners. This minimum standard applied irrespective of the treatment accorded to a State's own nationals.

In many regards, this theory is an expansion of that proposed by Emmerich de Vattel. As Elihu Root states:

'each country is bound to give to the nationals of another country in its territory the benefit of the same laws, the same administration, the same protection, and the same redress for injury which it gives to its own citizens, and neither more nor less: provided the protection which the country gives to its own citizens conforms to the established standard of civilisation.' [Root, E, p 521]

A minimum standard of treatment, 'the established standard of civilisation', was thus identified. Concepts of 'civilisation' are, of course, rarely part of international law due to the imperialistic, paternalistic overtures. The Permanent Court of International Justice recognized the International Minimum Standard of Treatment in the *Case Concerning Certain German Interests in Polish Upper Silesia (Merits)*, noting the existence of a generally accepted international law respecting the treatment of aliens which applied irrespective of any adverse or contrary domestic legislation.

2.4.2.3 *Recognition of the International Minimum Standard*

The doctrine of an International Minimum Standard is also articulated in various international instruments. An early example is the Convention respecting the Conditions of Residence and Business and Jurisdiction, concluded between Britain, France, Italy, Greece, Japan, and Turkey in Lausanne on 24 July 1923.

By virtue of the International Minimum Standard of Treatment, a foreigner may enjoy a greater degree of protection than a national of the State in which he or she is either visiting or temporarily resident—effectively there may be positive discrimination. Indeed the individual in the capacity of an alien enjoys a larger measure of protection under international law than would be accorded to a mere national of a State.

This recognition of a basic standard of treatment to be accorded to foreigners predates international recognition of the corpus of law known today as human rights. The International Minimum Standard comprises, inter alia, the right to personal liberty and the right to equality before the law—today both are recognized as fundamental human rights.

2.4.3 **Contemporary law on aliens**

It is interesting to note that the Declaration on the Human Rights of Individuals Who Are Not Nationals of the Country in Which They Live 1985, adopted by a consensus of the General Assembly, was intended to prescribe the basic rights of aliens which would, by custom, become binding international law. In accordance with the provisions of international law, declarations of the General Assembly are not legally binding though naturally they enjoy considerable moral force. The Declaration purports to considerably extend the International Minimum Standard of Treatment which perhaps is inevitable given that by 1985 international human rights were entrenched in law.

Although the law of aliens may be considered a distant relation of human rights, insofar as it recognizes the right of aliens to a certain standard of treatment, it does so solely because of the designation of an alien as a part of that State. Thus a violation of the rights of an alien is viewed as a wrong against a State. The individual has no right of action. Moreover, it must be remembered that the law of aliens, by definition, only applies to an individual in a State other than that of nationality. Human rights, in contrast, apply equally to all individuals without distinction, and can usually be enforced against one's State of nationality/residence.

2.5 Diplomatic laws

The other related situation in which individuals were accorded some rights under international law on the basis of being viewed as a part of the State is diplomatic law. The law of aliens is a close relative of the law relating to diplomatic status. Kings and emperors traditionally corresponded by messenger—their emissaries and couriers have always been subject to special protection. In Ancient Egypt, the pharaoh's messengers and diplomatic envoys carried with them the seal of the pharaoh, production of which guaranteed the carrier free and unhindered passage throughout the region. Later, in the Roman Empire, the emperor's certificate of free passage would be carried by all messengers and would likewise guarantee safe passage.

2.5.1 The development of diplomatic law

Heads of State have always enjoyed a degree of freedom. They effectively 'owned' the territory concerned. As a consequence, they could bind the State at the international level, accepting and denouncing obligations. The very root of international law is the relationship between States. As the human manifestation of the State, fair treatment of Heads of State was not so much a courtesy as essential. International relations function in part on the basis of reciprocity, fair treatment of a Head of State by another State assured such fair treatment of that State's representatives in the host State in return. Diplomatic law functioned initially as an extension of this—diplomatic personnel clearly represent the sovereign and thus should enjoy some of the freedoms and rights accorded to the sovereign. An injury to a State representative was taken to be an injury to the head of State and thus to the State. States were immune from prosecution in other States thus diplomatic personnel should enjoy the same level of immunity. The 1920s marked the apex of the rule of absolute State immunity. As representatives of the State, diplomatic personnel require to be free to act without undue pressure from the receiving State. They effectively embody the State and thus should be entitled to carry out the State's will without hindrance.

2.5.2 **Modern diplomatic law**

In contemporary international law, the law on diplomatic and consular immunity is codified in the Vienna Convention on Diplomatic Relations 1961 and the Vienna Convention on Consular Relations 1963. It represents the culmination of one of the International Law Commission's greatest attempts at consolidation and progressive development of customary international law. Modern thought has veered away from the theory that diplomatic personnel enjoy certain rights and privileges by virtue of a territoriality principle to the current approach, as adopted by the International Law Commission, of 'functional necessity'—ie, individuals require rights and privileges in order to perform unhindered the functions expected of them.

By providing a set of rules for the conduct of diplomatic affairs, the international community has acknowledged that a certain group of people requires certain rights in order to perform their functions. It is for this reason some authors allude to diplomatic law as related to modern human rights.

2.6 **The laws of war—international humanitarian law**

An individual's rights are most likely to be compromised when States engage in armed conflict. Such conflicts are clearly within the discretion of States. However, the exercise of powers of war and peace inevitably impact on individuals within the State, both those involved in fighting and civilians. As international conflict (war) was a characteristic of international relations, it was perhaps inevitable that a distinct body of law developed to regulate conduct in such times. Many ancient religious texts advocate respect for adversaries in time of battle. St Augustine, writing in the fourth century, referred to a 'just war'. By the late thirteenth century, the Viqayet of Spain enshrined a code of conduct for warfare. Bilateral treaties increasingly governed armed conflict, albeit frequently on a war-by-war case-specific basis. Contemporary law on the matter is part custom and part codification in a number of bilateral and multilateral treaties. International humanitarian law aims at protecting individuals during and after hostilities. It is based on centuries of customary international law. In articulating rights to be accorded to all individuals, it clearly has an impact on human rights.

The law in this area comprises two sets of law: the law of war as codified by the Hague Conventions, which articulate the rights and obligations of belligerents and humanitarian law; and the Geneva Conventions, which strive to safeguard the basic rights of non-combatants and civilians. In all circumstances, international humanitarian law represents a balance between the exigencies of combat situations and the generally accepted laws of humanity.

2.6.1 **The laws of war**

The primary codification of the laws of war appears in the seminal work of Hugo Grotius, *De jure belli ac pacis*, in the early seventeenth century, whilst the first legal instrument (the Lieber Code of 1863) applied to Union combatants in the American Civil War. It was not until the turn of the century that the first multilateral Convention on the subject was concluded. The year 1899 marked the first International Peace Conference. Czar Nicholas II invited representatives from major European and global States to convene at The Hague. Unfortunately, the Conference was an unqualified disaster—no agreement was reached on the primary objective of securing a real and lasting peace. On a more positive note, a Permanent Court of Arbitration was agreed upon to facilitate the peaceful settlement of inter-State disputes and, perhaps more importantly, international humanitarian law was born. The plenipotentiaries agreed on various texts which established the parameters for the conduct of warfare. The Convention with respect to the Laws and Customs of War on Land and associated regulations codified and developed existing law on the conduct of hostilities.

In 1907, the Hague Convention and Regulations were adopted, remaining in force to the present day. The laws of The Hague (the laws of war) establish the rights and obligations incumbent on belligerents. All military personnel are expected to know and to act in accordance with these principles. Some attempts were made in the Hague Conventions to protect the civilian population, though the Geneva Conventions expanded this.

2.6.2 Humanitarian law

In 1864, the Swiss government convened a diplomatic conference, chaired by Henry Dunant and attended by sixteen States, including the founders of the International Red Cross Committee. The participants adopted the Geneva Convention for the amelioration of the condition of the wounded in armies in the field. This Convention enshrined rules to protect the victims of war and wounded military personnel as well as introducing a system for identifying medical personnel, lodgings, and transport by means of the now-famous red cross emblem.

Following the First World War, the 1929 Geneva Convention relating to the treatment of prisoners of war provided some elements of protection for such prisoners. However, these provisions were found lacking during the Second World War. Civilians and military personnel were killed in equal numbers. The Geneva Conventions of 1949 sought to articulate a code of international humanitarian law which would ensure no repeat of this human devastation.

There are four Geneva Conventions which have since been supplemented by two 1977 Protocols. The Conventions relate to the amelioration of the condition of wounded and sick armed forces in the field and at sea, the treatment of prisoners of war, and the protection of civilians in time of war. The Protocols purport to strengthen the protection of victims of international and non-international armed conflicts. This represented a response to the increasingly violent national struggles for liberation which characterized international relations. The Geneva Conventions of 1949 and the two Protocols, over 500 Articles in total, remain in force today and are the central instruments of international humanitarian law.

Certain principles underpin humanitarian law: persons who are not involved in any hostilities should be treated humanely and cared for without discrimination; captured combatants must be treated humanely and must not be tortured or treated violently; should they be tried before a court of law, regular judicial procedures must be employed; no superfluous injury should be inflicted during the course of hostilities; the civilian population should not be the subject of military attacks. These principles remain fundamental to humanitarian law, according to

Discussion topic

International criminal law

The killing fields of Rwanda, Cambodia and the Balkans stand silent witness to the brutality that passed unchecked by an international system lacking both the will and the vision to act. We can and must do better. [Ki-Moon Ban, from http://www.un.org/reform/responsibility.shtml]

International criminal law has developed considerably since the trials in Nuremberg and Tokyo after the Second World War. Ad hoc tribunals have brought some of the perpetrators of the atrocities in Rwanda and the Balkans to justice, while the Extraordinary Chambers in the Courts of Cambodia are commencing proceedings against indicted members of the Khmer Rouge regime. Each body is acting after the events. Similarly, the International Criminal Court exercises jurisdiction over those implicated in current atrocities when the State in question has ratified the Rome Statute and the person can be brought to trial. However, is the will and vision to act to pre-empt atrocities, mentioned by Ki-Moon Ban, evident?

the International Court of Justice (*Case concerning Military and Paramilitary Activities in and against Nicaragua*).

To guarantee the securement of the rights incorporated into the Geneva framework, signatory States must ensure these general principles are taught to all members of their armed forces. Those failing to comply with their duties face prosecution and even extradition to face trial. The Tribunals established to try war criminals involved in hostilities in Rwanda and the former Yugoslavia apply many Articles of the Geneva Conventions.

2.6.3 Modern humanitarian law and laws of war

The Geneva Conventions and the two Protocols thereto remain the cornerstone of contemporary humanitarian law. However, a number of other Conventions and Protocols have added to and updated the law. For example, cultural property is protected by the 1952 Hague Convention for the protection of cultural property in the event of armed conflict. Biological and toxic weapons are prohibited by a 1972 Convention. This theme is followed by the 1980 Convention on prohibitions or restrictions on the use of certain conventional weapons which may be deemed to be excessively injurious or to have indiscriminate effects: mines, booby traps, non-detectable fragments, incendiary weapons, and laser weapons are covered. The year 1997 saw the high-profile adoption of a Convention on the prohibition of the use, stockpiling, production, and transfer of antipersonnel mines and on their destruction.

The United Nations Charter is clear in its condemnation of recourse to the use of force in international relations (Art 2(4)), following on from the Kellogg–Briand Pact of 1928 (the General Treaty for the Renunciation of War). However, hostilities are a sad reality of the new global order, with civil wars, violent national liberation movements, and United Nations-sanctioned interventions ensuring that there is a continuing need for laws governing conduct in combat situations.

Those aspects of humanitarian law which articulate rights for individuals clearly are related to human rights, as are those protecting of cultural property. However, human rights afford protection to all individuals in peace and war whilst humanitarian law strives to protect individuals in combat situations, governing the conduct of hostilities and the treatment of both civilians and captured combatants (prisoners of war). Most human rights' documentation acknowledges that certain human rights are inviolable whilst the enforcement of others may be suspended during emergency situations (discussed in Chapter 11). International humanitarian law 'fills the gap', providing a minimum standard of treatment for all during hostilities. As such, it is human rights law for application in the most extreme situations.

2.7 Slavery

From the early nineteenth century, international moves have been made to eliminate slavery. In a comparatively short period of time, customary international law condemned slavery. This arguably demonstrates a degree of recognition of State responsibility for individual safety and security. Moreover, they demonstrate an inherent recognition that the right to liberty and personal freedom is fundamental to individuals. Freedom from slavery remains an inalienable human right today— see Chapter 15.

2.7.1 The development of the law

In 1772, Lord Mansfield gave his seminal judgment in the *Somerset* case that no man could be a slave on British land: '[slavery is] so odious, that nothing can be suffered to support it' (p 19). Internationally, the 1815 Congress of Vienna declared the slave trade as repugnant to both morality and humanity. During the early nineteenth century, the British government entered into a series of bilateral treaties to secure the right to search vessels on the High Seas which were suspected of being involved in slave trading. Treaties were concluded with, inter alia, Spain, Sweden, the Netherlands, Russia, Prussia, France, and the United States. The Brussels Conference of 1890 reached agreement on the searching of suspected vessels within designated areas of African seas. This work was continued by the League of Nations which developed further multilateral conventions on the subject. A Slavery Commission was established by the League Council in 1924. Members were asked to eradicate slave trade practices through sale, exchange, and gifts. Situations of forced labour and 'coercive' adoptions were also condemned. It must be recalled that the jurisdiction of the League extended to a number of mandated and colonized territories, including large tracts of Africa. Even as late as 1937, the League was reporting incidences of slave dealings.

The customary international law was codified in 1926 by the Slavery Convention with the 1956 Supplementary Convention on the Abolition of Slavery, the Slave Trade and Institutions and Practices Similar to Slavery expanding the law, clearly prohibiting slavery. It should be noted that other ad hoc Conventions strove to suppress trafficking in women and children.

2.7.2 **The modern law of slavery**

Today the international community, deeming it an international crime, officially abhors slavery, and slave trading is aggressively condemned. The modern law pertaining to slavery and liberty of persons is considered in Chapter 15.

2.8 **Minority rights**

While the laws prohibiting slavery provide one example of recognized rights of individuals against the deprivation of human dignity, the evolution of minority rights goes further, providing a more comprehensive set of rights. Minority rights provide groups of individuals who are a minority in a State with certain rights enforceable against the State exercising power over them. Minority rights represent early recognition of the need for individuals to be protected against State interference as opposed to alien and diplomatic law, which were based on a reciprocity of the exercise of State powers, the individuals almost incidentally benefiting therefrom.

The idea of a specific body of law to protect minorities found favour in nineteenth-century Europe, home to a large number of ethnic, religious, and linguistic groups. Minority rights are a precursor to international human rights. The reason for the shift in focus from minority rights to universal rights is discussed infra.

2.8.1 **The treaty approach to minorities**

At the Congress of Vienna in 1815, Austria, Prussia, and Russia declared their intentions of respecting the nationality of their respective Polish subjects: 'The Poles, who are respectively subjects of Russia, Austria and Prussia, shall obtain a Representation and National Institutions regulated according to the degree of political consideration, that each of the Governments to which they belong shall judge expedient and proper to grant them' (Final Act of the Congress of Vienna, Art 1). The declaration was a statement of intent thus binding only morally. No State or organization had the power to supervise the action of the States; thus enforcement was within the discretion of each State. The Treaty of Berlin of 1878 is similar—it imposed on the disintegrating Ottoman Empire and its Balkan successors a duty to respect the lives, properties, and religious liberties of their populations.

Most of the major treaties of the time worked on the principle that the Great Powers could implement such guarantees in their agreements with the weaker States by dint of their perceived strength. However, with respect to, inter alia, these provisions, Inis Claude has written that:

'[t]he system could have worked satisfactorily only if the great Powers had acted together; in practice, each power concerned itself primarily with its own material or political interests, and the Concert of Europe seldom functioned as an instrument for the protection of the collective protection of minorities. [p 8]'

2.8.2 **The link to nationalism**

Minority protection before the two world wars may be linked to the contemporaneous rise of nationalism. Individuals began to appreciate the uniqueness of their national, cultural, and social identity. Accordingly, national groups developed individual concepts of nationality based on their unique traits. Karl Marx considered nationalism a 'characteristic of bourgeois society' which had outlived its usefulness. However, through time, these identifying characteristics formed the basis of distinction between ethnic groupings in the State. Those groups which possessed different characteristics from the majority of the population came to be regarded as 'minorities' and were, in general, proud of their distinctive cultural heritage.

Thus the idealistic goal was not always achieved; the polyglot empires of Central and Eastern Europe tended to respond to the challenge of nationalism by striving to eradicate the distinctive characteristics of their subjects, establishing a common pattern of nationality upon their heterogeneous population. Such attempts to impose an artificial uniform nationality upon all groups (irrespective of their cultural and ethnic origins) in a territory proved, ultimately, unsuccessful.

Indeed, State-imposed oppression of nationalistic expression frequently had the opposite effect from that desired—strengthening the determination of the minority to preserve all aspects of its cultural identity. Nationalism became a major factor in European politics escalating the deterioration of the international order, which culminated in the outbreak of the First World War. Nationalistic propaganda became a weapon in the fight for power.

Contributory to the outbreak of the hostilities in the First World War, nationalism remained prominent as an international problem between the wars. Distinct protection of ethnic/national groups first crystallized into law during the closing stages of the First World War. At the Peace Conference many nationalist aspirations were settled as the 'Big Four' sought to give some substance to the 'One Nation, One State' concept of statehood.

2.8.3 After the First World War

Europe's internal frontiers were essentially redrawn following the conclusion of the First World War. Many potential and actual minority problems were alleviated at this time. However, the seeds of other problems were, as time was sadly to corroborate, sown. The Allied statesmen were faced with a daunting task at the Peace Conference. In the main, the object of the protection of minorities instituted by the treaties was political not humanitarian. The aim was to avoid the many inter-State frictions that had occurred as a result of the frequent ill-treatment of national minorities. By internationalizing the problem of minorities via the treaties, the Allied and Associated Powers sought to secure the guarantee of minority rights in States, thus alleviating the possibility of neighbouring States intervening in domestic affairs. The rationale was sound: national minorities could not disturb international peace and security if their national problems were resolvable in an established international forum (the League of Nations) and thus neighbouring States did not require to resort to covert or open hostilities in defence of a minority group.

This was the first time that nationalist aspirations were considered in the drawing of State boundaries. It was the normal practice, as evidenced at the Vienna Conference of 1815, for the views of rulers to be regarded as paramount. In 1919, at Versailles, the views of the population were considered, with plebiscites being held as deemed appropriate and beneficial to the interests of the population in question.

2.8.4 **The Peace Conference**

The Peace Conference settlement effectively encapsulated the 'mood of the moment' with a near-total restructuring of Central Europe. Such was the general antipathy towards Germany and Austria, and the 'superpower' status assumed by the victorious Allies, that redrawing the European boundaries was approached with vigour, not trepidation. The objectives of rendering the Central Powers politically and economically impotent, while settling many of the nationalist aspirations declared by groups throughout Europe (thereby lessening the threat of further international strife), were realized only to an extent.

Two main systems were established with a view to alleviating Europe's nationalistic problems: transfers of groups from one State to another and reorganizing boundaries. Part of the aim of the Peace Settlement was to decimate the large powers whose actions had been at the root of the war and who were deemed to be the aggressors as well as losers. By reducing the size of these State-empires, their power was considered diminished and the likelihood of future transgressions minimized due to the umbrella supervision of the Allies over the new States. The enforcement of the imposed minority guarantees by the organs of the League of Nations will be examined later.

2.8.4.1 *Plebiscites*

Plebiscites enabled the population to decide under which State's rule they wished to live. Where a group was unavoidably renationalized, minority Treaties were drawn up or minority rights enshrined in the relevant treaty in an attempt to protect the group from majority oppression. The break-up of the Austro-Hungarian, Turkish, and German Empires resulted in large areas of Europe being 'up for grabs'—these areas were either given to the Allied States or combined and enlarged to form new States such as Yugoslavia and Czechoslovakia. Various schemes were implemented to alleviate the human problems caused by this reorganization. For example, the plebiscite held in Schleswig (an area lying north of the Kiel Canal of Germany and at the southern end of mainland Denmark) resulted in Humptrup being granted to Germany and Saed going to Denmark in reflection of the majority wishes of the residents of the area.

2.8.4.2 *Forced transfers*

Forced transfers of minority groups have been hailed as 'the most radical means of preventing national minorities.' (De Azcarate, P, p 16). As a remedy for specific problems, this method may be justified. However, as a general remedy for ailing nations, the liberal use of forced population transfers exhibits the failing of society to organize itself in such a way that people may live together in harmony irrespective of race, language, or religion. The very diversity of attitudes and ideas which forced transfers of populations might suppress is often a rich source of vitality and strength in a State. Homogeneity never has been, nor ever can be, an ideal for the organization of human societies.

2.8.4.3 *Transfers of populations*

Transfers of populations were effected in areas where the new boundaries resulted in substantial numbers of ethnically separate people residing in a State other than that of their nationality. Population transfers were effected, for example, between the Greeks and Bulgarians. Concluded under the auspices of an impartial international commission of four members, this was an exemplary transfer. The commission guaranteed the prevention of State pressure on those eligible to change nationality and provided an unbiased body for effecting the change of nationality for those who so elected. Assistance in transferring material possessions and selling, transferring, and registering property and land was provided.

Exchanges also occurred between Germany and Poland: West Prussia and Posen were transferred to Poland, with control of strategically important Danzig being assumed by the League of Nations. The object of giving the State of Poland access to the sea was thus achieved at the expense of dividing East Prussia from the rest of Germany. Some provisions were made for the transfer of German populations in the Polish Corridor to Germany. However, the success of this scheme was limited—indeed, the anomaly of Germans living in the Polish corridor subsequently precipitated the Second World War.

2.8.4.4 *Problems associated with these approaches to minorities*

It is perhaps indicative of the changing values of the international community that minority transfers were not as prominent a tool for resolving nationality conflicts in the aftermath of the Second World War. Redrawing international frontiers is fraught with potential pitfalls. A declared boundary between any two States will only operate when the separated States are on cordial terms. A breakdown in the transfrontier relations generally results in a break in the territorial integrity of one or other State.

2.8.5 **The League of Nations and minorities**

The idea of including general provisions on minority protection in the Covenant of the League of Nations was mooted but rejected in 1919. Contrary to popular belief, there is no specific mention of national minorities or the enforcement of the minority clauses in the Covenant of the League of Nations. Consequently, the issue, along with the concerns of the people in the Balkans and certain Poles, was remitted to the New States Committee which imposed minority protection guarantees as a condition of recognition by the Allied and Associated Powers of their new independence or State frontiers. In spite of this, protection of minorities was also stipulated as a precondition to membership of the League itself. Minority protection was of a specialist and limited character under the auspices of the League of Nations—it was a method of ensuring international supervision of new States. The role of the League of Nations in supervising minority rights paved the way for the United Nations' development and enforcement of universal human rights after the Second World War.

Protection of minority groups under the auspices of the League of Nations was twofold: guarantees embodied in mandates/trust territory treaties and guarantees imposed on States (primarily the defeated States) in the Peace Treaties.

2.8.5.1 *Minority guarantee clauses*

In entrusting the League with the protection of minorities in the new Europe, a special clause was inserted in the Peace Treaties of Versailles, Neuilly, St Germain, and Trianon by which Poland, Czechoslovakia, Greece, Romania, or Yugoslavia agreed to protect minorities within their new borders. For example, by Art 93 of the Treaty of Versailles, Poland: 'agrees and accepts to embody in a Treaty with the Principal Allied and Associated Powers such provisions as may be deemed necessary by the said Powers to protect the interests of inhabitants of Poland who differ from the majority of the population in race, language, or religion'. Such clauses were the basis of the minority system of the League of Nations and the foundation of the subsequent special minority protection treaties drawn up at the Peace Conference. Later, Declarations professing minority protection were recorded by the League of Nations in respect of Albania, Estonia, Latvia, Lithuania, and Finland (the Aaland Islands).

The special-minority chapters in these peace treaties contained what became known as the 'guarantee clause'. In each instance, identical terms were used. The terminology of the clause indicates the nature of the guarantee and indeed the treaties—part retributive, part supervisory. The Allied and Associated Powers were imposing 'rules' on the defeated powers which were in a poor bargaining position and had little option but to accede to the treaties and the guarantees therein.

2.8.5.2 *Enforcing the guarantee clauses*

The League developed an elaborate enforcement mechanism for the minority-protection guarantees. However, the system enjoyed only a short lifespan—it was never fully or successfully effective. A special 'minorities section' was established within the framework of the League to consider minority complaints before remitting them to a tripartite committee of the Council of the League: the president of the League sat with two colleagues in each case. No Council member with an interest in the case or with ethnic origin similar to either the State or the minority concerned could hear the case. Ultimately, a rapporteur on minority questions would examine an admitted case and make a report to the Council with recommendations for remedial action. Given the chaotic state of Europe, the League's systems arguably were never given a fair chance to work. In 1929, about 300 petitions reached Geneva. Approximately half of these were admitted but only eight reached the Council. In only two instances did the Council eventually propose any action to be taken, requesting an undertaking from the State concerned that it would cease the offending behaviour.

2.8.5.3 *The Permanent Court of International Justice*

The Permanent Court of International Justice acknowledged the desirability of minority protection. Deciding the *Case Concerning the Question of Minority Schools in Albania*, the Court held that the treaties for the protection of minorities were designed to ensure the equality of minorities and majorities. The Court also had to adjudicate on the application of the various conventions and treaties adopted in pursuance of the objectives discussed *supra*. The *Advisory Opinion on the Greco–Bulgarian Convention* is an example of the Court defining minorities who would benefit from the provisions of the Convention. The definition proposed by the Court remains indicative of legal thought in the formative years of minority protection.

2.8.5.4 *The success of the League*

The League of Nations had limited success enforcing the minority guarantee clauses. Ultimately, the enforcement of any aspect of international law is dependent on the will of the contracting parties. As fervent nationalism reared its head, the international organization was powerless to prevent State action. When Germany withdrew from the membership of the Council of the League of Nations, following

---

Key case

Advisory Opinion on the Greco-Bulgarian Convention,
1930 PCIJ Rep Series B, No 17, p 19

This opinion was sought in connection with the peace treaties drawn up after the First World War. Clarification was sought over the scope and application of various aspects of the Convention of Neuilly which facilitated reciprocal emigration between Greece and Bulgaria with the aim of defusing potential tension in the region and securing peace. Of particular relevance to minorities is the question on whether Greco-Bulgarian communities possessed the characteristics of minorities even although they shared the same racial origin as the majority. For identifying these communities, the Court suggested the following criterion:

a group of persons living in a given country or locality, having a race, religion, language and traditions of their own, and united by the identity of such race, religion, language and traditions in a sentiment of solidarity, with a view to preserving their traditions, maintaining their form of worship, securing the instruction and upbringing of their children in accordance with the spirit and traditions of their race and mutually assisting one another.

Hitler's denunciation of the Locarno Treaty and the reoccupation of the Rhineland by the German army on 7 March 1936, the time bomb began ticking for the Second World War. The League of Nations was rendered impotent by the lack of an effective enforcement mechanism for its guarantees. An epidemic of world lawlessness was spreading. Many international obligations were broken without retribution (not least that of Munich). The League was flouted with impunity. Germany invaded Czechoslovakia in March 1939, Italy invaded and annexed Albania the following month, then Abyssinia and, on 1 September 1939, Germany invaded Poland. The international response was, by then, inevitable.

2.8.6 The modern law on minorities

A degree of minority protection is still present in contemporary law. 'National minorities', a term employed in the post-war era to refer to the ethnic groups of Europe, is reincarnated in the 1994 Council of Europe Framework Convention for the Protection of National Minorities. At the international level, in 1995, the United Nations adopted a Declaration on the Rights of Persons belonging to National or Ethnic, Religious and Linguistic Minorities. The contemporary law relating to minorities will be addressed in more detail in Chapter 21. Work under the auspices of the International Labour Organization and latterly the United Nations addresses the related but distinct issues surrounding the rights of indigenous peoples.

2.9 The International Labour Organization

Article 23 of the Covenant of the League of Nations comes closest to a provision on human rights. It imposes an obligation on Members of the League to 'secure and maintain fair and humane conditions of labour for men, women, and children' and 'to secure just treatment of the native inhabitants of territories under their control'. The former was addressed in more detail by the International Labour Organization while the latter relates to the mandates and guarantees for trust territories (minority protection—ibid).

The participants in the peace conference created the International Labour Organization (ILO) in 1919. It is a survivor of the Treaty of Versailles, the peace treaty signed with Germany. The idea for such an organization had first been mooted in the nineteenth century (by a Welshman and a Frenchman) with the consequent International Association for Labour Legislation (Basel, 1901) a dry run for the new organization. The ILO was motivated by many factors, humanitarian concerns included—working conditions of the early twentieth century were often exploitative and detrimental to health and well-being; there was little regulation of vulnerable groups, such as children. This was giving rise to increasing concern. Moreover, given history (eg, the Russian Revolution), it is no surprise that the threat of social unrest and even workers' revolutions unbalancing the new world order was also a consideration. Regulating working conditions should pacify the workers and even, in a way, recognize their contribution to the ensuing peace. The Preamble to its Constitution states that 'universal and lasting peace can be established only if it is based upon social justice'. The purposes of the Organization were outlined in the Preamble and now also in the attached Declaration of Philadelphia 1944 (annexed to the Constitution).

Naturally, the Allies supported international regulation, as it would prevent a less scrupulous State from ignoring any guidelines, exploiting their workforce, and undercutting costs. The ILO was the first international organization on which individuals were represented. Half the executive body comprised government representatives, a quarter employers' representatives, and the final quarter, employees' representatives.

The first set of Conventions adopted by the organization addressed various issues of concern including working hours and working conditions for women (including maternity protection) and for children (including minimum-age requirements). Some of these are discussed in Chapter 19 on the right to work. In the last eighty years, the ILO has continued to set standards and supervise the application thereof throughout Member States. It retains a dominant presence in international labour standard setting today. For its efforts, the ILO was even awarded the Nobel Peace Prize in 1969, its fiftieth anniversary.

2.10 **After the Second World War**

The Second World War brought with it the persecution of minorities on a scale unprecedented in modern Europe. Genocidal practices became a facet of life in the Third Reich. At the conclusion of the war, Europe was in complete disarray with vast numbers of displaced persons, refugees, and escapees in all States. It was essential that control was exercised over the situation and the slow process of recovery instigated. Within Europe, it was essential to strive for normality in an area stunned with horror at the atrocities perpetrated and devastated by despair and disillusionment with governments.

2.10.1 **The Potsdam Conference**

The 1945 tripartite Conference of Berlin—the Potsdam Conference—with the 'Big Three' States of the United Kingdom, the Union of Soviet Socialist Republics, and the United States of America was the foundation of the central leadership pillar of the post-war period. While Europe remained in turmoil, the 'Big Three' helped bridge the gap of transition from the old order through to the construction of the new one, thereby contributing substantially to the framework of the new Europe.

Europe was in a constant state of turmoil and upheaval, with a constant flux of populations through transfers, both forced and voluntary. Aid organizations sought to repatriate displaced persons and reunite families separated during the events of the previous decade. Displaced persons, refugees, and internees were gradually repatriated though it remained impossible to obtain accurate population/census figures. Many States were left with severe labour shortages, others with economic shortfalls. The influx of refugees and displaced persons taxed the already stretched resources of States.

2.10.2 **Towards international protection of human rights**

In the years following the two world wars, under the guidance of the Allied and Associated Powers, national homogeneity was the declared aim, chaos the result. The original humanitarian principles were often sidestepped and even deliberately ignored. In Czechoslovakia, for example, months of embittered wrangling on both sides preceded the expulsion of minorities such as the Magyars. Minorities and their treatment became a matter for bilateral negotiation, not general international concern. Many pre-war boundaries were simply re-established as the accepted frontiers. The only survivor of the League-style period of minority protection is the Swedish–Finnish agreement concerning the preservation of the culture, language, and traditions of the Swedish population of the Aaland Islands which remain under Finnish jurisdiction.

The tumultuous problems experienced in Europe at this time prompted the new world order to 'change tack': minority and sectoral protection was replaced by a concerted global attempt to secure basic rights for all, without distinction. Both the Council of Europe (discussed infra) and the United Nations were established at this time. These organizations are known today for their advanced systems aimed at protecting human rights.

2.10.3 **On the brink of the United Nations**

Before the foundation of the United Nations, the human rights protection which existed was clearly sporadic. As particular problems were identified by the dominant political and economic powers of the day, remedies were sought. Treaties thus protected specified minority groups and addressed specific problems of perceived vulnerable groups.

However, the advent of a truly global international community created in the shadow of mass violations of human rights and serious infringements of territorial sovereignty, with ensuing catastrophic suffering, provided an appropriate platform for the launch of contemporary human rights. In many respects, the development of international human rights is an example of the principle of subsidiarity—the international community only steps in when the State cannot or will not deal with the problem. When the national system does not protect the fundamental rights of the individual, then, by necessity, the needs of those peoples becomes a matter for international law. Today, a substantial body of international law recognizes universal human rights. The system of human rights protection developed by the United Nations will be discussed in the next chapter.

CASES

Advisory Opinion on the Greco-Bulgarian Convention, 1930 PCIJ Rep Series B, No 17, p 19.

Case Concerning Certain German Interests in Polish Upper Silesia (Merits), 1926 PCIJ Rep Ser A, No 7.

Case Concerning Military and Paramilitary Activities in and against Nicaragua, 1986 ICJ Rep 14.

Case Concerning the Question of Minority Schools in Albania, 1935 PCIJ Series A/B, No 64, p 17.

North American Dredging Company Case (US/Mexico) (1926) 4 RIAA 26 at 29.

Panevezys Railway Case (Estonia v Lithuania), 1939 PCIJ Rep Ser A/B, No 76.

Somerset v Stewart (1772) Lofft I.

READING

De Azcarate, P, *League of Nations and National Minorities: An experiment* (trans EE Brooke) (Washington, DC: Carnegie, 1945).

Bartolomei, H et al (eds), *The International Labor Organization* (Conn: Westview, 1996).

Calvo, C, *Le Droit International*, 5th edn (Paris, 1885) (In French, expanding on and translated from original Spanish *Derecho internacional teórico y práctico* (Paris 1868))

Clark, G, 'The English practice with regard to reprisals by private persons' (1933) 27 American Journal of International Law 694–723.

Claude, I, *National Minorities: An international problem* (Cambridge, Mass: Harvard University Press, 1955).

Gill, G, *The League of Nations from 1929 to 1946* (New York: Avery, 1997).

Gray, C, *International Law and the Use of Force* (Oxford: Oxford University Press, 2001).

Grotius, H, *De jure belli ac pacis*, Barents and Douma (eds) (Dordecht: Martinus Nijhoff, 1952).

Hersch Lauterpacht, reworking Oppenheim's seminal *Treatise on International Law*, now published as Jennings and Watts (eds) *Oppenheim's International Law*, 9th edn (England: Longman, 1996).

ICRC, *Human Rights and the ICRC: International humanitarian law* (Geneva: ICRC, 1993).

——, *Respect for International Humanitarian Law: Handbook for Parliamentarians* (Geneva: ICRC/Inter-Parliamentary Union, 1999).

ILO, *International Labour Standards: A worker's manual*, 4th edn (Geneva: ILO, 1998).

Ishay, M, *The History of Human Rights From Ancient Times to the Globalization Era* (Berkeley: University of California Press, 2008).

Martinez, J, 'Anti-slavery courts and the dawn of international human rights law' (2008) 117(4) The Yale Law Journal 550–641.

Meron, T, *Human Rights and Humanitarian Norms as Customary Law* (Oxford: Clarendon Press, 1989).

Ostrower, G, *The League of Nations from 1919–1929* (New York: Avery, 1997).

Root, E, 'The basis of protection to citizens residing abroad' (1930) 24 American Journal of International Law 517.

Scott, G, *Rise and Fall of the League of Nations* (London: Hutchinson, 1973).

United Nations, *The League of Nations 1920–1946: Organization and accomplishments* (New York: United Nations, 1996).

Wright, Q, *Mandates under the League of Nations* (London: Greenwood, 1969).

WEBSITES

www.gpoaccess.gov/coredocs.html—US Government Printing Office.

www.archives.gov—US National Archives and Records Administration.

www.elysee.fr/elysee/elysee.fr/anglais/the_institutions/founding_texts/the_declaration_of_ the_human_rights/the_declaration_of_the_human_rights.20240.html—documents estab- lishing the French Republic.

www.icrc.org—International Committee of the Red Cross (humanitarian law).

www.ilo.org—The International Labour Organization.

3

The United Nations

The League of Nations was replaced by a new international organization—the United Nations. In addition to assuming some of the functions of its predecessor, the United Nations was compelled to address the problems of mass violations of human rights and serious infringements of territorial sovereignty, events which had precipitated the two world wars and caused great suffering. The unprecedented devastation of two world wars within thirty years had so demoralized accepted political thinking, that a plausible mechanism for protecting future generations from such trauma was essential. For this, an international response was considered appropriate. With the prevailing mood, consensus was forthcoming. Consequently, the Charter of the United Nations (hereinafter referred to as 'the Charter') was adopted in San Francisco in 1945, entering into force on 24 October 1945.

3.1 The United Nations Charter

The stirring preambular paragraphs of the Charter state:

We the peoples of the United Nations determined to save succeeding generations from the scourge of war, which twice in our lifetime has brought untold sorrow to mankind, and to reaffirm our faith in fundamental human rights, in the dignity and worth of the human person, in the equal rights of men and women and of nations large and small ... have resolved to combine our efforts to achieve these aims ...

There is a clear emphasis on the notion of equality and on the inherent dignity and worth of each and every person.

The aims of the United Nations, as stated in the Preamble to the Charter, reflected contemporary world opinion. The primary function of the United Nations is the maintenance of international peace and security (Art 1(1)). However, it was, and is, accepted that achievement of a general respect for human rights and fundamental freedoms is a condition favourable to the maintenance of such peace and to respect for law in general. Consequently, references to human rights were made in the constituent document (the Charter) of the new organization.

The aim of developing human rights protection is reinforced in the declared purposes of the organization, as postulated in Art 1 of the Charter:

[t]he Purposes of the United Nations are:

...

2. To develop friendly relations among nations based on respect for the principle of equal rights and self-determination of peoples, and to take other appropriate measures to strengthen universal peace.
3. To achieve international co-operation in solving international problems of an economic, social, cultural or humanitarian character, and in promoting and encouraging respect for human rights and for fundamental freedoms for all without distinction as to race, sex, language or religion ...

Allusion to the link between international peace and security and the protection of human rights is intentional. As more recent developments by, for example, the Organization for Security and Cooperation in Europe demonstrate, protection and promotion of human rights (especially of ethnic and religious minorities) is still a major factor is ensuring stability in potentially volatile areas (the work of the OSCE is addressed in the context of regional protection in Europe—Chapter 7).

The inclusion of references to human rights in the Charter was radical in its time. It represents acknowledgement of the role of international law in protecting the rights of individuals and effectively marks the beginning of the end of the exclusivity of State jurisdiction over nationals. In the aftermath of war in Europe, imposing positive human rights obligations on all States was unthinkable although imposing constitutional guarantees on the 'defeated' States was, on the other hand, viewed as creating a firm foundation of national law, albeit through treaties, and thus acceptable (as considered in Chapter 2).

3.1.1 The influence of the Nuremberg Criminal Tribunal

The trial and judgments of the International Military Tribunal at Nuremberg of major war criminals added further fuel to the embryonic international human rights movement. Expanding individual liability under international law from 'universal crimes', such as piracy on the high seas to war crimes and 'crimes against humanity' (Art 6, Charter of the International Military Tribunal for the Trial of War Criminals), irrevocably changed the nature of international law. Suddenly, it was no longer the preserve solely of nations. The Tribunal found individuals liable for crimes against humanity and war crimes, sentencing them accordingly. The Tribunal considered that crimes against international law are committed by men, not by abstract entities, and only by punishing individuals who commit such crimes can the provisions of international law be enforced. Individuals had been catapulted onto the international stage where they remain. (The International Criminal Tribunals for Rwanda and the former Yugoslavia indicated a return to the Nuremberg approach, with individuals being held to account for serious contraventions of international (criminal) norms. Article 5 of the 1998 Statute of the International Criminal Court lists those crimes within the jurisdiction of the now permanent court.)

The new United Nations drew on the early potential for individual responsibility, and its corollary, individual rights, progressively elaborating on the tentative references to human rights incorporated into the Charter of the organization.

3.1.2 **Developing international human rights law**

The human rights provisions of the United Nations Charter have been described as 'scattered, terse, even cryptic' (Steiner, H, Alston, P, and Goodman, R, p 135). No comprehensive system for protecting human rights was enshrined in the Charter. Rather, the goal of securing respect for human rights was specified with States pledging to encourage the promotion and observance of rights within their territories. There was no real definition or articulation of 'human rights' although reference was made to the concept of equality and the notion of the dignity and worth of the human person. It is unlikely that the drafters of the original Charter could have foreseen the development of international human rights law to its present form based on the Charter's references. It is even less likely that they would have condoned the developments, given the inevitable clash with traditional notions of State sovereignty and the then prevailing theoretical basis of international law. With respect to the actual provisions of the Charter, the final text represents a considerable expansion on the original Dumbarton Oaks Proposals, largely at the behest of the smaller States and the non-governmental organizations which lobbied the conference delegates. Initially, the Soviet Union objected to broadening the scope of the embryonic organization to include economic and social cooperation and both the British and the Soviet delegations at Dumbarton Oaks had reservations on the inclusion of human rights in the Charter. However, majority opinion at San Francisco favoured some mention of respect for human rights and fundamental freedoms though the decision was taken not to annex a Bill of Rights.

From the outset, the United Nations has placed great emphasis on the promotion of economic and social progress and development of all States. This has positive repercussions for international human rights, introducing political and economic stability, conditions more conducive to the realization of human rights. The need for this has been heightened by the growing membership of the organization and the acknowledgement of the growing gap between the more advanced and the developing nations of the world. With originally 51 members, now 192, cooperation and consultation have been key words in the development of United Nations' social policy, with financial and technical assistance also playing a prominent role.

The failure of national laws to protect citizens had been cruelly demonstrated; the responsibility thus lay with the global community, the new United Nations Organization. As the League of Nations had proven unsuccessful in its attempts to protect minorities from the States in which they find themselves, the new organization sought to approach the question of human rights from a different angle—adopting the concept of equality for all in place of the idea of protection of minorities. The new organization was anxious to avoid the problems associated with minorities which had beset its predecessor, ultimately leading to its collapse. The United Nations system is based on a fundamental and irrevocable belief in the dignity and worth of each and every individual. Realization of this should, ipso facto, obviate the need for minority protection; every individual is entitled to the same fundamental rights and freedoms. The protection of the basic rights of all citizens of the world has evolved to surpass national law; it is an integral part of 'being' and thus neither nationality nor State opinion are determinant factors.

Having pledged to promote universal observance of and respect for human rights, the United Nations required an institutional framework to exercise responsibility therefor. Accordingly, Chapter IX of the Charter, International Economic and Social Co-operation, elaborates on the economic and social foundations of peace. Article 55 of the Charter aims at creating 'conditions of stability and well-being which are necessary for peaceful and friendly relations among nations based on respect for the principle of equal rights and self-determination of peoples'. In furtherance thereof, the Charter then lists economic and social aims which the United Nations shall promote 'without distinction as to race, sex, language or religion' (Art 55(c)). Article 61 of the Charter created the Economic and Social Council, a body with 18 (now 54) members. One of the functions of this body is making recommendations for the purpose of promoting respect for, and observance of, human rights and fundamental freedoms for all (Art 62(2)). To assist in this task, the Economic and Social Council was to establish a Commission for the protection of human rights. This Commission (since superseded by the Human Rights Council) was supplemented by a number of other bodies. Today, there is a comprehensive network of institutions, organs, and committees which oversee the implementation and realization of human rights at the international level. Seven committees, created by the principal human rights treaties, monitor the implementation of each treaty: these treaty-monitoring bodies are the Committee on Economic, Social and Cultural Rights; the Human Rights Committee; the Committee against Torture; the Committee on the Elimination of Racial Discrimination; the Committee on the Elimination of Discrimination against Women; the Committee on the Rights of the Child; and the Migrant Workers' Committee. These committees work with and report through the Economic and Social Council and the General Assembly of the United Nations. The institutional infrastructure of the United Nations vis-à-vis the protection and promotion of human rights, including these committees, are examined in more detail in Chapter 5.

The new international organization very quickly established itself as a body which would actively fulfil its commitment under Art 55 of the Charter, prompting universal respect for, and observance of, human rights and fundamental freedoms. Progress in this area has been achieved in a number of ways: drafting Conventions and resolutions, applying political pressure to States, preparing and disseminating relevant information, and internationally condemning serious human rights violations.

3.2 Building international human rights law

As has been observed, the Charter did not specify in detail what was covered by 'human rights', neither did it define State responsibility for the promotion of these rights. Today, there is a cocktail of international instruments aimed at securing the promotion and respect of human rights. The law relating to human rights is highly prescriptive though there remain many grey areas and the realization of rights is still, in many respects, dependant on the will of States.

The first step taken by the United Nations with respect to human rights was the affirmation of the existence of a body of international human rights. The articulation of the Universal Declaration of Human Rights in 1948 and the two subsequent International Covenants of 1966 (on Civil and Political Rights and on Economic, Social and Cultural Rights) form the foundation of international human rights protection, as advocated by the United Nations. Often referred to as the International Bill of Rights, these instruments embrace a truly global membership and remain the starting point of any examination of modern international human rights. The Universal Declaration tabulates what was to become the accepted standard of rights which inalienably attach to all human persons while the International Covenants elaborate on these rights in a more detailed, legally enforceable manner. International committees acting under the auspices of the United Nations have responsibility for monitoring the implementation of the Covenants. The International Bill of Rights will be considered in more detail in Chapter 4.

However, these instruments represent only the starting block for an examination of international human rights. The United Nations has subsequently adopted a number of other international instruments which add further clarity and definition to the provisions of the Universal Declaration. A detailed discussion of these instruments is outwith the scope of the present text; however, their importance justifies an overview to illustrate the scope of contemporary human rights protection.

3.2.1 War crimes and crimes against humanity

> ### Discussion topic
>
> **Heads of State and International Criminal Law**
>
> On 4 March 2009, the Office of the Prosecutor of the International Criminal Court issued a warrant for the arrest of Omar Hassan Ahmad Al Bashir, the president of the Republic of Sudan. He is charged with five counts of crimes against humanity (torture, murder, forcible transfers, rape, and extermination) and two counts of war crimes (pillaging and intentionally directing attacks against civilian population/those not involved in hostilities). He is the first Head of State to be cited by the International Criminal Court and the warrant is proving divisive and controversial. Other Heads of States have been prosecuted in national and international fora once they have left office. Examples include Charles Taylor (former Liberian president now before the Sierra Leone Special Court), Slobodan Milosevic (former Yugoslavian president who died during trial before the ad hoc International Criminal Tribunal for the Former Yugoslavia), Augusto Pinochet Ugarte (former Chilean president prosecuted in Chilean courts who died before any trials were completed). In contrast, the ad hoc International Criminal Tribunal for Rwanda rejected a bid to indict President Paul Kagame on counts of being complicit in the assassination of his predecessor, an event which precipitated the genocide.
>
> The issues raised concern command responsibility, sovereign immunity, and international criminal law.

There has been considerable progress since the Nuremberg Tribunal found individuals guilty of violating war crimes and crimes against humanity. Pursuant to a United Nations' General Assembly Declaration in 1946 that genocide was an international crime, the United Nations adopted the Convention on the Prevention and Punishment of the Crime of Genocide in 1948. The Convention defines genocide and provides for the trial of individuals charged with it either in the State in which the act was committed or before any competent international penal tribunal

(Art VI). Contracting States pledged to facilitate the extradition of those indicted for genocide. Although originally intended to be in effect for ten years, the commitment of States to eradicating genocide has been such that it remains in force today (Art XIV). Sadly, as the International Criminal Tribunals for Rwanda and the former Yugoslavia demonstrate, genocide and war crimes are still perpetrated today. Indeed, as the twentieth century drew to a close, concern over the number of instances of genocide and 'unimaginable atrocities that deeply shock the conscience of humanity' prompted the international community to adopt the Statute of the International Criminal Court (Rome, 1998, Preamble). The Rome Statute, which entered into force on 1 July 2002, established a permanent International Criminal Court which functions alongside the United Nations system, exercising jurisdiction over the most serious crimes considered of concern to the international community as a whole: the crime of genocide, crimes against humanity, war crimes, and the crime of aggression (Art 5). Each crime is further defined in the Statute. Unlike the International Court of Justice, the International Criminal Court has jurisdiction over individuals. It is the only international adjudicatory body before which individuals have *locus standi*. A prosecutor investigates situations referred by a State or *proprio motu* on the basis of information received (Arts 14–15, 53–5). Following trial and conviction, the Court may impose a range of penalties including imprisonment, fines and forfeiture of assets (Art 77). There is a right of appeal against decisions of the Court (Arts 81 et seq).

The salient international criminal law is prescribed in the Statute as are the procedural safeguards accorded to any accused person which ensure that the trial will be conducted in accordance with the now universally accepted principles of equality before the law, fairness to the accused, and the right to a fair trial. The rights protected include *ne bis in idem* (not being tried twice for the same crime), *nullum crimen sine lege* (a prohibition on retroactive application of the Statute), a minimum age of criminal responsibility (eighteen years), a pretrial within a reasonable time following surrender of the person to the Court, trial in the presence of the accused, the presumption of innocence, and, in Art 67, a full tabulation of the rights of an accused person.

The Court is constituted in The Hague, the Netherlands. The establishment of the International Criminal Court is, in many ways, a logical conclusion to the development of the detailed rights of the individual by the United Nations. Just as contemporary international human rights began with the Nuremberg Tribunal and the acknowledgement of the duties of individuals, so it is reasonable to respond to fifty years of development of international human rights with the establishment of a permanent court with jurisdiction over individuals. For many, the only regret is that there is no real equivalent court with jurisdiction for systematic violations of other human rights, the treaty-monitoring bodies (discussed *infra*) exercising no real judicial function. Only at the regional level can States be held accountable (in a judicial setting) for infringements of human rights (see Chapters 7–9).

3.2.2 Protection of vulnerable groups

While universal rights have indeed been a major feature of the United Nations Organization, the system in place to secure their realization is flawed. Many peoples remain inherently vulnerable to exploitation and abuse. Infringements of human rights may not be actioned due to issues of legal standing or simply through lack of access to the necessary legal resources. Creating discrete instruments aimed at promoting protection of the rights of vulnerable groups has punctuated the work of the United Nations, strengthening the universalism of human rights. A brief overview of key groups follows in the current context; a more detailed consideration of the rights of indigenous people, women, children, and refugees appears in Chapter 22.

3.2.2.1 *Refugees*

As the Second World War demonstrated, refugees and displaced people are vulnerable, with their rights frequently ignored. Refugees transcend national boundaries, thus an international response is required. The United Nations adopted the Convention relating to the Status of Refugees in 1951. Although the instrument was created solely in response to population displacement in Europe, its ambit has now been extended both geographically and in time to all refugees. History sadly attests to the ongoing vulnerability of the growing number of refugees and internally displaced people. The strengthened code of rights adopted in 1951 remains the key instrument for refugees.

3.2.2.2 *Migrant workers*

Alongside refugees, an increasing number of people elect to leave their State of nationality to seek work elsewhere. As travel becomes commonplace and knowledge and skills transfer more readily, it becomes apparent that migrant workers have also been suffering from human rights abuses. The International Labour Organization developed guidelines for migrant workers. Its 1949 Convention No 97 Migration for Employment and the 1975 Migrant Workers (Supplementary Provisions) Convention (No 143) were supported by Recommendations. However, ratification has been slow. The pervasive reluctance of States to embrace migrant workers is further evidenced by the United Nations Convention on the Rights of Migrant Workers which finally secured the necessary ratifications to enter into force in July 2003, thirteen years after being opened for signature. The United Nations estimates that there are more than 150 million migrant workers, some 2 per cent of the global population (though note this figure includes refugees and asylum seekers). The breadth of the convention is notable as it covers seasonal workers, those who commute to work across international borders, self-employed workers, seafarers on vessels of a different registration to that of the worker, and itinerant workers (Art 2). States ratifying the Convention include Azerbaijan, Bolivia, Cape Verde, Egypt, El Salvador, Ghana, Morocco, the Philippines, Senegal, Seychelles, and Uganda. Even now, the most industrialized States, with large migrant populations, have proven reluctant to sign up.

Rights accruing to migrant workers and their families encompass a range of universal rights from healthcare to culture as well as comprehensive employment rights. Migrant workers also enjoy rights to leave and return. Guiding principles for dealing with issues of migration are decreed: international migration of workers is to be considered in accordance with sound, equitable, and humane conditions (Art 64).

3.2.2.3 *Women*

From the outset, equality of rights between men and women was enshrined in the United Nations Charter. However, this was an aspirational goal with a substantial gulf between the status of men and women. As Chapter 12 discusses, significant efforts have been made to promote the elimination of inequality of opportunity between the sexes. The United Nations continued the pioneering work of the International Labour Organization in addressing the rights of women. In furtherance thereof, concern extended beyond non-discrimination to strategies for promoting the rights of women. A Commission on the Status of Women and the Division for Advancement of Women works towards ameliorating the position of women in society.

3.2.2.4 *Children*

Children are unique insofar as they are inherently dependent on others for their early survival and rights. Refugees, migrant workers and women may be similarly vulnerable but the duration of vulnerability is variable and treatment is geographically inconsistent. Human rights abuses against children have long been the subject of international concern. From the 1924 Declaration on the Rights of the Child during the era of the League of Nations, children retained a presence on the United Nations agenda. Ultimately sufficient political consensus was found to ensure children's rights could be tabulated in the 1989 United Nations Convention on the Rights of the Child. Comprehensively including civil, cultural, economic, political and social rights, the indivisibility and universality of the United Nations human rights system is at the heart of children's rights.

3.2.2.5 *Indigenous peoples*

Protecting indigenous peoples, in some respects, develops the work of the League of Nations on minority rights. Like minorities during the League era, indigenous peoples are subjected to abuses of their human rights by those controlling the State in which they find themselves geographically placed. Frequently, they are of a different ethnic background from the ruling powers. While in the era of the League, traditional colonial powers undertook protection of basic rights of intra-State minorities and colonized groups, the United Nations found itself facing a different problem. Self-determination (Chapter 17) secured the end of colonization but failed many First peoples, those indigenous populations living in areas colonized centuries previously. In such cases, decolonization removed the colonizing power but did not remove the generations of descendents from the original occupying/conquering/colonizing force. Progress towards agreeing a Declaration on the Rights of Indigenous Peoples was hastened by the adoption of the Draft text by the Human Rights Council at its inaugural session in June 2006.

3.2.3 **Slavery, torture, forced labour, and trafficking**

Not only did the United Nations adopt standard-setting treaties enshrining international human rights (the International Bill of Rights) and treaties aimed at deemed vulnerable groups (women, children, refugees), it also adopted instruments on specific fundamental rights. Genocide and war crimes have already been considered *supra*. The United Nations is based on respect for human dignity: the ancient practice of slavery, the modern-day forms of forced labour and trafficking of persons, and the use of techniques of torture are clear affronts to human dignity. Attempts had to be made to eradicate such practices in the new world order. This would create an environment conducive to the culture of respect for human rights and freedoms.

The origins of the law on slavery have been considered in Chapter 2, the modern law being considered in Chapter 15. Suffice for now to highlight that the gravity of the offence prompted the United Nations to adopt the 1949 Convention for the Suppression of the Traffic in Persons and of the Exploitation of the Prostitution of Others and the 1956 Supplementary Convention on the Abolition of Slavery, the Slave Trade, and Institutions and Practices Similar to Slavery. According to Interpol, smuggling people is now the third most profitable activity for organized crime worldwide. The Trafficking in Human Beings Branch of the International Criminal Police Organization is currently trying to chart known smuggling routes. These trafficking activities are covered by international instruments though often the State is not directly responsible. Associated activities include forced and compulsory labour (Convention Concerning the Abolition of Forced Labour 1957) while those failing to pay the required fee for being smuggled may be tortured and abused.

Torture is another activity which has long been the subject of international regulation. In 1984, the United Nations adopted its Convention against Torture and other Cruel, Inhuman or Degrading Treatment or Punishment (Chapter 14 deals with torture in more detail). A Committee against Torture was established by the Convention with responsibility for the implementation thereof in the territory of Contracting States.

3.2.4 **Other human rights instruments**

The United Nations has adopted many other declarations and instruments on human rights. Some elaborate on rights and freedoms, others address specific instances of violations, for example, calling on particular States to protect certain categories of rights. The United Nations often adopts declarations as a precursor to the drafting of a detailed binding instrument—this has been seen with, inter alia, children's rights, the International Bill of Rights, racial discrimination, and discrimination against women. Other areas of law have been the subject of Declarations which have not yet metamorphosed into binding conventions.

The Declaration on the Elimination of All Forms of Intolerance and of Discrimination Based on Religion or Belief was adopted in 1981. Religion was one of the original grounds for discrimination identified by the United Nations. However, given the nature of religion, it proved difficult to obtain agreement on any text which could apply to all of the world's major religions. The Declaration on the Rights of Persons Belonging to National or Ethnic, Religious and Linguistic Minorities 1992 evidences a return to minority protection, albeit within narrowly defined limits. Both these instruments can derive authority from the concept of equality which was included in the United Nations Charter.

3.3 **The impact of the United Nations on international human rights**

The standards have been set, international human rights law exists in theory, the ball is now in the court of the States and other international players to ensure its effective realization and implementation. The United Nations works to protect international human rights in a number of different ways. As States may seek assistance from the United Nations in order to realize their human rights obligations under the various instruments, the United Nations has developed a Technical Co-operation Programme in the Field of Human Rights. Through this programme, States may request and receive technical assistance in the promotion and protection of human rights. The support available ranges from advisory services to training courses, sometimes necessitating the presence 'in the field' of United Nations' personnel. Training programmes may include those set up for the benefit of lawyers, judges, the armed forces, and the legal enforcement agencies (eg, the police) in the State concerned. Many of these programmes are financed by independent voluntary contributions.

Undoubtedly, the creation of a treaty-based body of international human rights law has been one of the successes of the organization. In little over fifty years, international human rights law has become a documented reality. The United Nations Charter and the family of international instruments which it spawned provide a concrete basis for the protection of the individual under international law. In the words of the International Law Association:

The United Nations inspires the hope of so many of the world's downtrodden. Every year thousands of individuals and groups appeal to UN bodies for help. On their behalf a myriad of non-governmental organizations attempt to place their cases on the international agenda. When national institutions fail, when governments are unresponsive, millions of the tortured, the repressed, the hungry, turn to the UN. [Bayevsky, A, pp 681–99]

The United Nations system will now be examined in more detail. Focus will first centre on the International Bill of Rights before shifting to the United Nations institutional structure—ie, those organs and bodies involved in the promotion and protection of international human rights.

READING

Baehr, P, *Human Rights: Universality in practice* (Basingstoke: Palgrave, 2001).

Bayefsky, A, *Report on the UN Human Rights Treaties: Facing the implementation crisis*, first report of the Committee on International Human Rights Law and Practice, International Law Association, Helsinki Conference 1996, reproduced in A Bayefsky (ed), *The UN Human Rights Treaty System in the 21st Century* (The Hague: Kluwer, 2000).

van Boven, T, 'Human rights and the rights of peoples' (1995) 6 European Journal of International Law 461–76.

Buergenthal, T, Skelton, D, and Stewart, D, *International Human Rights in a Nutshell*, 3rd edn. (St Paul, Minn: West Group, 2002).

Cassesse, A, *International Criminal Law* (Oxford: Oxford University Press, 2003).

Donnelly, J, *Universal Human Rights in Theory and Practice* (Ithaca, Cornell University Press, 2002).

Goodhart, M (ed), *Human Rights: Politics and practice* (New York/Oxford: Oxford University Press USA/Oxford University Press, 2009).

Hannum, H (ed), *Guide to International Human Rights Practice*, 3rd edn (New York: Transnational, 1999).

Humphrey, J, *Human Rights and the United Nations: A great adventure* (New York: Transnational, 1984).

Kittichaisaree, K, *International Criminal Law* (Oxford: Oxford University Press, 2001).

McGoldrick, D, Rowe, P, and Donnelly, E (eds), *The Permanent International Criminal Court: Legal and policy issues* (Oxford: Hart Publishing, 2004).

Meron, T, *Human Rights Law-Making in the United Nations: A critique of instruments and processes* (Oxford: Oxford University Press, 1986).

Schabas, W, *An Introduction to the International Criminal Court*, 3rd edn (Cambridge: Cambridge University Press, 2007).

Shelton, D (ed), *International Crimes, Peace and Human Rights: The role of the International Criminal Court* (New York: Transnational, 2000).

Sieghart, P, *The International Law of Human Rights* (Oxford: Oxford University Press, 1994).

Steiner, H, Alston, P, and Goodman, R, *International Human Rights in Context: Law, politics, morals*, 3rd edn (Oxford: Oxford University Press, 2008).

De Than, C, and Shorts, E, *International Criminal Law and Human Rights* (London: Sweet & Maxwell, 2003).

Tomuschat, C (ed), *Human Rights: Between idealism and realism* (Collected Courses of the Academy of European Law) (Oxford: Oxford University Press, 2003).

United Nations Division of Public Information, *Basic Facts about the United Nations* (New York: United Nations, 2001 (republished annually)).

WEBSITES

www.un.org/english—The United Nations.

www.un.org/rights/index.shtml—United Nations Human Rights.

www.un.org/rights/HRToday/—Briefing paper on Human Rights (UN).

www.ohchr.org—United Nations High Commissioner for Human Rights.

www.un.org/ha/—United Nations Humanitarian Affairs.

www.unhcr.ch—United Nations High Commissioner for Refugees.

www.unicef.org—United Nations Children's Fund.

www.un.org/ga/children—May 2002 United Nations Special Session on Children.

www.un.org/womenwatch/index.html—United Nations Internet Gateway on the Advancement and Empowerment of Women—Womenwatch.

www.interpol.int/Public/THB—Interpol site on Children and Human Trafficking.

www.un.org/law/icc/index.html—International Criminal Court.

www.un.org/icty/index.html—International Criminal Tribunal for the former Yugoslavia.

www.ictr.org—International Criminal Tribunal for Rwanda.

4

The International Bill of Human Rights

Since its inception, the United Nations has strived to secure the promotion and protection of human rights worldwide. The first, and possibly the singularly most important, step taken by the United Nations in furtherance of the incumbent obligation to promote respect for human rights and fundamental freedoms was the General Assembly's adoption, on 10 December 1948, of the Universal Declaration of Human Rights. Although not technically legally binding, the effect of the Universal Declaration has far surpassed the expectations of the drafters and it is widely accepted as the consensus of global opinion on fundamental rights. The original intention that it would be followed swiftly by a binding enforceable tabulation of rights was not to be realized; it was to be eighteen years before consensus was reached on the text of the International Covenants and a further ten years before the instruments attracted sufficient ratifications to enter into force.

The International Bill of Human Rights consists of the Universal Declaration of Human Rights, the International Covenant on Civil and Political Rights and two Optional Protocols annexed thereto and the International Covenant on Economic, Social and Cultural Rights. It has been referred to by the United Nations as 'the ethical and legal basis for all the human rights work of the United Nations ... the foundation upon which the international system for the protection and promotion of human rights has been developed' (OHCHR, *Fact Sheet No 22*, p 3). This Chapter will examine each of these instruments with reference to the scope and enforceability of each. Selected rights contained in the instruments are considered in more detail in the latter part of this book.

The International Bill of Human Rights has been described as 'a milestone in the history of human rights, a veritable Magna Carta marking mankind's arrival at a vitally important phase: the conscious acquisition of human dignity and worth' (OHCHR, *The International Bill of Rights Fact Sheet 2, Rev 1*). The creation of an international Bill of Human Rights is sometimes considered implicit in the United Nations Charter. Indeed, following on from the work of the League of Nations, setting minimum standards of rights was always on the agenda. In its very first session the General Assembly transmitted a draft Declaration on Fundamental Human Rights and Freedoms to the Economic and Social Council (ECOSOC) for consideration by it and by its new sub-organ, the Commission on Human Rights. The International Bill of Human Rights was originally to be drafted by three working groups—one on a general declaration of international human rights standards, one on more specific elaboration of the rights (a covenant of rights), and the third on the implementation mechanism. Due to time constraints, only the declaration was redrafted to an appropriate standard in time for the General Assembly's Paris meeting. In Resolution 217A (III) of 10 December 1948, the General Assembly of the United Nations adopted the Universal Declaration of Human Rights. The first bold step towards creating an International Bill of Human Rights had been taken.

4.1 The Universal Declaration of Human Rights

The forces of moderation, tolerance and understanding that the text represents will probably in future history-writing be seen as one of the greatest steps forward in the process of global civilization. [Alfredsson, G, and Eide, A, p xxvii]

The Universal Declaration was adopted without a dissenting vote, although eight States (Byelorussian SSR, Czechoslovakia, Poland, Saudi Arabia, Ukrainian SSR, USSR, Union of South Africa, and Yugoslavia) abstained. The passage of time, in concert with the increasing reliance on the Universal Declaration by the global community, has largely negated the impact of these abstentions testifying to the veracity of the statement by the then president of the General Assembly that the Universal Declaration was a remarkable achievement, a step forward in the great evolutionary process. It was the first international instrument in which rights to be accorded to all peoples were articulated. Accordingly, its importance cannot be underestimated. In spite of this, debate continues over the enforceability of it and its legal status in contemporary international law.

4.1.1 Is the Universal Declaration binding?

A Declaration of the General Assembly is not, by definition, legally binding, though it has strong moral force. Moreover, it is arguable that many of the rights enunciated in the Charter are now so widely accepted that they form part of the general principles of law, although they may not have crystallized into customary international law. However, see the *dicta* of Judge Ammoun in his separate opinion on the *Namibia Case* that the provisions of the Universal Declaration of Human Rights 'can bind States on the basis of custom ... whether because they constituted a codification of customary law ... or because they have acquired the force of custom through a general practice accepted as law'. Whichever, undoubtedly no State can avoid the impact of the Universal Declaration. In the last fifty years, it has increasingly lived up to its proclaimed goal as being 'a common standard of achievement for all peoples and all nations'. It is frequently referred to in international, regional, and national human rights instruments and jurisprudence.

Arguably, not all rights in the Universal Declaration have crystallized into custom: decisions should be based on an analysis of the status of the right in question. The American case of *Filartiga v Pena-Irala*, is one instance of a major court—the United States' Circuit Court of Appeals—pronouncing on whether torture was a breach of customary international law. Circuit Judge Kaufman offered the view that the prohibition on torture 'has become part of customary international law, as evidenced and defined by the Universal Declaration of Human Rights'. Slavery has undoubtedly achieved similar status, being denounced as a crime against humanity at the 2001 World Conference Against Racism, Racial Discrimination, Xenophobia and Related Intolerance in Durban.

The Universal Declaration is claimed to represent 'the conscience of the world—[to be] a synthesis, a profession of faith, a common philosophy of human rights—and ipso facto a part of general international law' (Haksar, U, p 36). The Universal Declaration enshrines a consensus on the content of internationally recognized rights owed to humankind. The rights articulated therein are sufficiently broad they can span all cultures and religions with a minimum of difficulty hence the near unanimity of adoption. Some commentators argue that the Universal Declaration is paternalistic in overtones though, unlike the minority clauses concluded by the League, it has weathered the test of time. Both the International Court of Justice and a multitude of national courts have employed the Universal Declaration either as an interpretative tool or as customary law. It is often used as a point of reference for constitutional questions, especially in newer States. NGOs rely on the Universal Declaration as the standard of human rights; some such as Article 19, the international NGO on freedom of speech, even takes their name from the Universal Declaration.

The status of the Universal Declaration is variable. It is clear that it can, however, freely be employed as an interpretative aid with respect to the Charter and as a policy guide to accepted international practice. The substance of some of the rights enunciated in the Universal Declaration render any kind of enforcement provision ineffective as they are articulated in a vague and non-legalistic style (a deficit the Covenants were intended to remedy).

4.1.2 **The importance of the Universal Declaration**

Many States have not signed and/or ratified the International Covenants. Consequently, the Universal Declaration may be the only applicable international human rights instrument. The Universal Declaration has been used as the basis for the constitutive documents of many new, emerging, and newly decolonized States. It is widely perceived as, although not originally intended to be, the definitive statement on human rights in contemporary society. Most international human rights instruments subsequently adopted by the United Nations have a basis in the Universal Declaration and give further definition and cognizance to those rights. Indubitably, it provides a valuable framework of human rights which many subsequent documents expand into legally binding texts. As will be seen, the two International Covenants expand the Universal Declaration while other instruments such as the International Convention on the Elimination of All Forms of Racial Discrimination, the Convention on the Elimination of All Forms of Discrimination Against Women and the United Nations Convention on the Rights of the Child draw on the scope and content of the Universal Declaration. The importance of the Declaration may be gauged by the many international, regional, and national statements which indicate its universal applicability as an international standard: for example, the Helsinki Declaration, adopted as the Final Act by the 1975 Conference on Security and Co-operation in Europe, includes the following statement: 'In the field of human rights and fundamental freedoms, the participating States will act in conformity with the purposes and principles of the Charter of the United Nations and with the Universal Declaration of Human Rights' (1(a), Declaration on Principles Guiding Relations between Participating States). All the basic instruments on human rights adopted by the regional organizations refer to the Universal Declaration in preambular paragraphs. More recently, the Vienna Declaration and Programme of Action drawn up by the World Conference on Human Rights in 1993 states that the Universal Declaration is 'the source of inspiration and has been the basis for the United Nations in making advances in standard setting' (Preamble).

In light of the foregoing, it is fitting that the United Nations and many Member States, now celebrate the day on which the Universal Declaration was adopted, 10 December, as Human Rights Day. The fiftieth anniversary of the Universal Declaration (1998) was commemorated worldwide as Human Rights Year.

4.1.3 **The content of the Universal Declaration**

The Preamble to the Universal Declaration of Human Rights recognizes the inherent dignity and the equal and inalienable rights of all members of the human family as being the foundation of freedom, justice, and peace in the world. It also reiterates the pledge that Member States of the United Nations take to achieve the promotion of universal respect for and observance of human rights and fundamental freedoms. The Declaration was presented in realization of these aims—it seeks to articulate a common understanding of the rights and freedoms involved.

Although the General Assembly proclaimed the Universal Declaration to be 'a common standard of achievement for all peoples and all nations', the standard enshrined in the Universal Declaration is one to be achieved progressively, a goal to be aimed at, indeed a mountain to climb for some of the States concerned. This explains why some of the rights are inalienable, their realization instantaneous, while other rights are in a weaker position, being more aspirational.

The Universal Declaration is unequivocal in the guarantee of equality to all peoples:

Article 1. All human beings are born free and equal in dignity and rights. They are endowed with reason and conscience and should act towards one another in a spirit of brotherhood.

Article 2. Everyone is entitled to all the rights and freedoms set forth in this Declaration, without distinction of any kind, such as race, colour, sex, language, religion, political or other opinion, national or social origin, property, birth or other status. Furthermore, no distinction shall be made on the basis of the political, jurisdictional or international status of the country or territory to which a person belongs, whether it be independent, trust, non-self-governing or under any other limitation of sovereignty.

Equality, and thus a prohibition on discrimination on any ground, is at the foundation of the human rights policy of the United Nations. The principle of non-discrimination is expanded upon in Chapter 12. Several Articles of the Universal Declaration reiterate and, in some instances, reinforce this prohibition on discrimination, extending the ambit of the Declaration to the promotion of understanding, tolerance, and friendship among all nations and all racial or religious groups, thereby furthering those activities of the United Nations which seek to secure the maintenance of international peace and security. (The maintenance of international peace and security is, of course, the overriding purpose of the Organization itself (Art 1(1) Charter)). The approach of the new world order to human rights has been without doubt characterized by constant reiteration and reinforcement of the premise that all people are created equal.

The Declaration commences with the notion that all peoples are born free and equal in dignity and rights (Art 1) and thus should be entitled to enjoyment of the rights enshrined in the Convention without distinction or discrimination (Art 2). Article 3 then encapsulates the most fundamental of all rights—'Everyone has the right to life, liberty and security of person.' The right to liberty is further clarified and expanded in succeeding Articles of the Universal Declaration with slavery and the slave trade prohibited and all persons entitled to freedom from torture and similar treatment (Arts 4–5). All people are entitled to freedom of movement and residence throughout their State, the right to a nationality and the right to seek asylum from persecution (Arts 13–15). Many rights in the Universal Declaration govern the rights of persons in detention and rights to a fair trial (Arts 7–11). The family is entitled to respect and protection as the natural and fundamental group unit of society— States are obliged not to interfere arbitrarily with the individual's privacy, home, correspondence, family, and reputation and men and women are entitled to marry and found a family (Arts 12 and 16). Freedom of thought, conscience, and religion, opinion and expression are protected, as is freedom of assembly and association (Arts 18–20). In an attempt to secure democracy, the right to participate in government and public service is included in Art 21. To ensure individuals are ensured an adequate standard of living, health, and well-being, the right to work, social security, rest and leisure periods, education and cultural life are prescribed (Arts 22–7). The universality and indivisibility of rights is emphasized by the breadth and scope of the rights in the Universal Declaration.

However, the Universal Declaration is not merely a statement of rights. There is an element of reciprocity: Article 29 provides that 'Everyone has duties to the community in which alone the free and full development of his personality is possible.' The African Charter on Human and Peoples' Rights, and to a lesser extent the American Convention on Human Rights, go much further, articulating a number of duties the individual owes the community and State.

4.1.4 Minority protection and the Universal Declaration

The Universal Declaration creates a new species of rights—universal human rights which are the inalienable birthright of each and every person—though throughout the deliberations on the Universal Declaration, the inclusion of an Article dealing with minorities was favoured. The new underlying premise of universal human rights should have rendered specific minority protection superfluous. Everyone was accorded the basic human rights (freedom of religion and freedom from discrimination) which previously had been the prerogative of minorities. The incompatibility of a term protecting minority groups in the same document as a profession of the equality of all overrode the concerns that national minorities were the victims of some of the worst crimes against humanity perpetrated during the Second World War. In the end, political considerations outweighed pure humanitarian idealism and the proposed minority clause was excluded from the final document. However, the third part of the resolution of the General Assembly through which the Universal Declaration was adopted was entitled 'Fate of Minorities' and refers the question of minority protection to the Commission on Human Rights and the Sub-Commission. The result of these discussions, contemporary minority protection, is addressed in more detail in Chapter 21.

4.1.5 **The importance of the Universal Declaration**

The Universal Declaration attracts and deserves accolades of superlatives. Without doubt, it was an unprecedented step for the world—State acknowledgement that individuals were no longer solely subject to the whims of the State. Rather individuals were entitled as a birthright to equality and to fundamental rights. These rights were specified by international law but had origins predating the Universal Declaration. As the embodiment of a set of accepted universal human rights, the Universal Declaration is unparalleled. It is the first example of such a universal document transcending culture and traditions to prescribe a global standard. As has been noted, the principal failing of the Universal Declaration is perhaps its legal status or lack thereof. It is legally unenforceable, except insofar as it is accepted as enshrining 'general principles of law' or aspects of custom. The General Assembly agreed that Member States, in conformity with their obligations under Articles 55–6 of the United Nations Charter, should 'solemnly publicise the text of the Declaration and ... cause it to be disseminated, displayed, read and expounded principally in schools and other educational institutions, without distinction based on the political status of countries or territories' (UN GA Resn 217). The Secretary-General is given the responsibility of publishing and disseminating the text in as many languages as possible. Nine States abstained from approving this part of the Resolution 217, none objected. Human rights education is considered along with the right to education in Chapter 20.

The advent of computerization and the Internet has furthered these objectives. The Universal Declaration is now available online through the website of the UN High Commissioner for Human Rights in over three hundred language versions including Akuapem Twi, Asante, Catalan, Corsican, Czech, Kurdish, Nepali, Quechua, Samoan, Scots Gaelic, Tongan, Turkish, and Zulu as well as Latin and Esperanto. Indeed, the Universal Declaration holds the world record as the most widely translated document—it is truly universal. In many countries, events such as independence from colonial powers or the fiftieth anniversary of the Universal Declaration itself were celebrated with constitutions, even monuments incorporating the Universal Declaration. Observation of Human Rights Days should further promote the Universal Declaration. The only instrument since the Declaration which has came close to achieving such prominence is the Convention on the Rights of the Child which has been translated, often in a simplified, more accessible form, into a number of different languages. Multimedia packages are available online and through UNICEF, Save the Children, and regional bodies for teaching the convention to children.

1968 was designated the International Year of Human Rights and culminated in a World Conference on Human Rights, held in Tehran, Iran. The conference adopted a Proclamation reviewing the progress made in the twenty years since the Universal Declaration was adopted. The Conference proclaimed that illiteracy was a barrier to the promotion of education (Proclamation 14) and it was imperative that all States fulfil their solemn obligations to promote and encourage respect for human rights and fundamental freedoms for all (Proclamation 1) before affirming its faith in the principles of the Universal Declaration of Human Rights and urging all peoples and governments to dedicate themselves to the principles enshrined therein, redoubling their efforts to 'provide for all human beings a life consonant with freedom and dignity and conducive to physical, mental, social and spiritual welfare' (Decision 1). Starting in 1968, prizes for outstanding contributions to the protection and promotion of human rights have also been awarded.

The fortieth anniversary of the adoption of the Universal Declaration was commemorated with a high profile campaign 'Know your human rights' with local, national, regional, and international events and activities in furtherance of this goal. Many of these activities provided an impetus for further development of human rights and helped set the scene for the World Conference in Vienna some four years later.

The World Conference on Human Rights held in Vienna in 1993 further affirmed the views of the international community (a community which had more than trebled in membership): 'All human rights are universal, indivisible and interdependent and interrelated' (Declaration 5). The basic tenet of equality which underpinned the Universal Declaration was thus endorsed and the new global community expressed its recognition of the equal importance of all the rights enshrined in the Universal Declaration.

Yet more recently, the United Nations General Assembly Millennium Declaration (UN Doc A155/L.2) para 25 articulates the resolve of the Member States to 'respect fully and uphold the Universal Declaration of Human Rights'. No doubt similar sentiments will be expressed during the forthcoming sixtieth anniversary celebrations (2008).

4.2 **The United Nations International Covenants of 1966**

It was the hope of the drafters that the Universal Declaration would be swiftly followed by a more detailed tabulation of rights and freedoms in a legal format (Part E, GA Resn 217(III), 1948). The original idea, as proposed by the Human Rights Commission at its second sitting, was for an International Bill of Rights comprising a Declaration, a Covenant, and Measures of Implementation. After protracted discussion, the General Assembly agreed to the drafting of two distinct instruments rather than a single legally binding covenant expanding upon the whole litany of rights enshrined in the Universal Declaration. The two covenants were requested to be presented to the General Assembly at the same time in an attempt to highlight the 'unity of the aim' (GA Resn 543(VI), 1952). The series of negotiations and consultations, which shaped the drafting of the two covenants, was lengthy and comprehensive, involving State, specialized agency, and NGO participation.

The intended alacrity of the drafting proved unattainable in reality. It was not until 16 December 1966 that the Economic and Social Council succeeded in presenting satisfactory draft proposals to the General Assembly for approval and adoption as annexes to resolutions of that day. The International Covenants are intended to supersede the Universal Declaration insofar as they provided a legally binding option. However, although they have relatively high numbers of contracting parties, their acceptance is by no means universal. Consequently, the continuing value of the Universal Declaration cannot be underestimated.

The Economic and Social Council finally settled upon a dual approach to human rights protection. This may only partly be attributable to the difficulties encountered in expanding the entire Universal Declaration in one text. The provisions of the

Universal Declaration became two international instruments: the International Covenant on Civil and Political Rights (ICCPR) and the International Covenant on Economic, Social and Cultural Rights (ICESCR). The former essentially concerns those rights and freedoms detailed in Arts 3–21 of the Universal Declaration while the latter codifies the provisions of Arts 22–7. In the resolution of the General Assembly which adopted the two Covenants, the hope was expressed that 'the Covenants and the Optional Protocol [to the ICCPR] will be signed and ratified or acceded to without delay and come into force at an early date' (GA Resn 2200A, 1966). Once more, the General Assembly was attempting to unite the two Covenants. To an extent, it was a successful ploy. History attests that the numbers of ratifications and accessions to each is comparable (ratification of the Optional Protocol is a different issue). Many States thus view the two Covenants as a unit although obviously there are political considerations with States wishing to be seen on the international stage to profess adherence to the International Bill of Human Rights.

The Covenants were hailed as the International Bill of Human Rights and introduced amid a wave of international and popular support. However, this was, perhaps, an idealistic aspiration and it was not to be. It took almost ten years for the Covenants to enter into force: the Economic, Social and Cultural Covenant on 3 January 1976 and that of Civil and Political Rights on 23 March 1976. Even today, the status of the Covenants (with respect to accessions and ratifications) does not fully reflect their universal importance. Approximately three-quarters of the membership of the United Nations is bound by the Covenants. The International Bill of Human Rights maybe has not been as swift and overwhelming a success as initially envisaged by the drafters of the Universal Declaration 1948.

The emphasis in each of the Covenants varies to reflect the perceived nature of the rights addressed therein. It was deemed politically unacceptable and impractical to replicate the Universal Declaration with all the now expanded rights in one document. With the adoption of two distinct covenants, the difference has perpetuated

Discussion topic

Twin Covenants born of one Universal Declaration

Each State Party to the present Covenant undertakes to take steps, individually and through international assistance and co-operation, especially economic and technical, to the maximum of its available resources, with a view to achieving progressively the full realization of the rights recognized in the present Covenant by all appropriate means, including particularly the adoption of legislative measures. [Art 2(1) International Covenant on Economic, Social and Cultural Rights]

Where not already provided for by existing legislative or other measures, each State Party to the present Covenant undertakes to take the necessary steps, in accordance with its constitutional processes and with the provisions of the present Covenant, to adopt such laws or other measures as may be necessary to give effect to the rights recognized in the present Covenant. [Art 2(2) International Covenant on Civil and Political Rights]

For many observers, this is the key difference between the two covenants. With reference to the rights and freedoms enshrined therein, evaluate the necessity for this distinction.

the belief that human rights exist in a hierarchy of different 'generations' of rights. It was many years before the indivisibility of rights was once again emphasized in the Convention on the Rights of the Child at the United Nations, the African Charter on Human and Peoples' Rights, and the EU Charter on Fundamental Rights.

4.2.1 A family of universal rights?

In essence, the International Covenant on Civil and Political Rights details what some commentators regard as first-generation human rights. That is to say, the fundamental basic human rights required to be exercisable by everyone in any fair democratic society. These rights are essentially those which evolved in the eighteenth century with the French and American Declarations. Such rights are reasonably universally recognized and accepted. They should be realized immediately in all Member States of the United Nations. First-generation rights include the right to life, the right to liberty, and the right to a fair trial before an independent and impartial tribunal or court as well as fundamental freedoms such as those of expression and of conscience.

The International Covenant on Economic, Social and Cultural Rights, on the other hand, is concerned with so-called second-generation human rights. These rights evolved in the latter stages of the nineteenth century with social reform in Europe. More 'idealistic' in nature, such rights may be less readily realizable, especially by developing States. The right to education, the right to appropriate housing, the right to social security, and the right to a safe and healthy working environment and adequate leisure and rest time are examples of second-generation rights. Some commentators maintain these rights in fact have the earliest origin.

So-called third-generation rights are a comparatively new phenomenon, hence their designation. They are, effectively, group rights: rights which may be exercised collectively. Rights of peoples or solidarity rights as they are sometimes known are gaining increasing prominence—for example, the right to self-determination or the right to an environment conducive to development. In 1986, the General Assembly of the United Nations adopted the Declaration on the Right to Development. Including the right to development as a human right aims at the creation of the conditions necessary for the full realization of all other human rights of both first and second generations. It stresses the interdependence, indivisibility, and universality of the two Covenants (see Chapter 23). The Declaration constitutes a significant step by the United Nations in the direction of conceptualizing third-generation human rights. Neither Covenant encapsulates this section of human rights although both instruments include identical provisions on the right to self-determination. Arguably, States viewed the inclusion of self-determination as a reflection on the decolonization process rather than a foray into collective rights (see Chapter 17).

The key to the academic debate on the different generations of rights lie in the recognition that human rights are indivisible. The generational differences may reflect the chronological development of the rights but it must be remembered that the genus is the family of rights. Like any family, the different generations may be viewed as combined into a single solitary unit, in this case, the universal rights of all human beings.

4.2.2 **The International Covenant on Economic, Social, and Cultural Rights**

4.2.2.1 *Overview*

The International Covenant on Economic, Social and Cultural Rights charges contracting parties to:

take steps, individually and through international assistance and co-operation, especially economic and technical, to the maximum of its available resources, with a view to achieving progressively the full realization of the rights recognised in the present Covenant by all appropriate means, including particularly the adoption of legislative measures. [Article 2]

An evolving programme of realization, depending on the goodwill and resources of States, is clearly envisaged. Given the nature of some of the rights, such an approach is essential. A variety of technical cooperation and a range of specialized agencies can provide further backup for States in this process: needs are often identified through the reports system and met through the processes which are discussed in the following chapters.

The Covenant itself is divided into five parts and runs to thirty-one Articles. As of July 2009, 160 States have ratified the Covenant.

4.2.2.2 *The rights*

The ICESCR is the first international instrument to deal extensively with economic, social, and cultural rights. (For accuracy, it should be noted that the European Social Charter of 1961 (Council of Europe) predates the ICESCR with various economic and social rights. Naturally its jurisdiction is, however, limited to Europe.) The right to self-determination is provided in Article 1 and is the sum total of Part 1 of the Covenant. It is identical to that of the International Covenant on Civil and Political Rights though some commentators have suggested that it may be construed differently, 'giving recognition to a right to economic, rather than political, self-determination' (Craven, M, p 25). The remaining rights are found in Part 3 of the Covenant.

According to the Covenant, everyone is entitled to a right to work and earn a living (Art 6). The realization of this right is dependent of the establishment of appropriate training and vocational programmes. Provision of work is not the sole requirement. The working conditions must be fair. Here, some reference can be made to the provisions of the International Labour Organization which began the process of delineating the minimum standards of work which every individual is entitled to. The ILO is focused on vulnerable groups, the ICESCR applies to everyone although nursing mothers and children are singled out in Art 10. Trade Union membership and activities are also covered. Minimum standards of work are addressed further in Chapter 19 on the right to work.

Other rights in the Covenant on Economic, Social and Cultural Rights include an adequate standard of living, food, physical and mental health, education, and a rich cultural life including the protection of the moral and material interests of an author of any scientific, literary, or artistic work.

4.2.2.3 *Implementation*

Implementation of the International Covenant on Economic, Social and Cultural Rights is by reports. States are required to send periodic reports to the Committee on Economic, Social and Cultural Rights of the Economic and Social Council. No supervisory body was established by the Covenant, thus the periodic reports were originally transmitted to the Secretary-General of the Economic and Social Council (Art 16). These reports detail the advances made by the State in the realization of the goals set for them in furtherance of the progressive achievement of the rights and freedoms embodied in the Charter for their entire population. However, in 1986, the Committee on Economic, Social and Cultural Rights was set up to consider the compliance of States parties with that Covenant. The Committee on Economic, Social and Cultural Rights may transmit the report, or part thereof, to the Human Rights Council for study and general recommendations (Art 19). The Economic and Social Council may then bring to the attention of other organizations and subsidiary, specialized agencies of the United Nations any matters arising out of the reports with which they may be able to assist, for example, by providing technical assistance. Assistance and cooperation are the key words with respect to this Covenant—the fostering of international cooperation as a by-product contributing to the maintenance of friendly relations among States.

4.2.2.4 *Concluding observations*

The rights enshrined in the Covenant have in many respects been slow to achieve international prominence, partly due to their conception as lesser or secondary rights. The African Charter, in its preamble, reverses this view, stating that economic and social conditions are necessary for the realization of civil and political rights. The recent return to emphasizing the universality and indivisibility of rights should bolster the Covenant as will the development of the work of the Committee in the future.

4.2.3 **The International Covenant on Civil and Political Rights**

4.2.3.1 *Overview*

The International Covenant on Civil and Political Rights, on the other hand, is unequivocal on the obligations incumbent on contracting parties: Article 2 provides:

1. Each party to the present Covenant undertakes to respect and to ensure to all individuals within its territory and subject to its jurisdiction the rights recognised in the present Covenant ...

2. Where not already provided for by existing legislative or other measures, each State Party to the present Covenant undertakes to take the necessary steps, in accordance with its constitutional processes and with the provisions of the present Covenant, to adopt such legislative or other measures as may be necessary to give effect to the rights recognised in the present Covenant ...

This Covenant becomes effective following ratification by a State. Realization of the rights and freedoms enshrined in the Covenant is immediate. To an extent, this suggests that more importance should be attached to this Covenant. However, the discrepancy is not attributable to the importance of the rights and freedoms concerned, rather it was the perceived ease with which the rights can be enforced and given true effect within a State. Rights pertaining to civil and political freedoms were deemed easier to legislate for, whereas those on social, economic and cultural rights require, in general, a long-term approach and the injection of financial and technical aid to the economy of the State concerned. By its very nature, the Economic, Social and Cultural Covenant is restricted by the resources available in a State. However, it is submitted that many civil and political rights also require considerable financial resources on the part of States. Thus, this distinction is arguably artificial.

4.2.3.2 *The rights*

Essentially, the International Covenant on Civil and Political Rights expands those rights enshrined in Arts 1–21 of the Universal Declaration on Human Rights. The right to life is stated, with the Second Protocol to the Covenant seeking the abolition of the death penalty, reinforcing the sanctity of life. The prohibition on slavery and torture is detailed (Arts 7–8). Deprivation of liberty through detention and the rights of an accused to a fair trial are tabulated in considerably more detail than the Universal Declaration. The status of the alien should be determined in accordance with the law and all residents of a State have the right to move freely throughout the territory (Arts 12–13). Naturally, the freedom of thought, conscience, and religion is secured as is the freedom of expression and holding opinions, with particular reference made to the prohibition of propaganda of war and advocacy of racial hatred in Art 20. This clearly reflects on the events of the Second World War and other conflicts since. Assembly and association is prescribed with restriction only possible in accordance with the law and where necessary in a democratic society (Arts 21–2). Children are to be protected as befits their minor status (Art 24)—this Article is itself expanded on considerably by the United Nations Convention on the Rights of the Child 1989. Democratic rights of participation in government are also included. Finally, Art 27 provides for the right of ethnic, religious, or linguistic minorities to enjoy their culture, profess and practise their religion, and use their own language in a partial return to the concept of minority rights as advocated by the League of Nations.

4.2.3.3 *Implementation*

Implementation of the Civil and Political Covenant is, as with its twin, a matter primarily of reports. However, unlike the Economic Social and Cultural Covenant, a Human Rights Committee was established by the Covenant (in terms of Art 28). State Parties submit reports to the Committee on the measures they have adopted which give effect to the rights recognized in the Covenant and on the progress made in the enjoyment of those rights within their jurisdiction (Art 40). However, Art 41 of the Covenant enables States to declare, at any time, their recognition of the competence of the Committee to receive and consider any communications to the effect that the State concerned is not fulfilling its obligations under the Covenant. This system of inter-State complaints operates on the basis of reciprocity as do the regional systems. More controversial is the First Optional Protocol to the Covenant which, in Art 1, provides for individual petition to the Committee. The Protocol has not proven as popular as was intended (112 ratifications as of July 2009). Indeed, many of the larger developed States have not acceded to it-the United Kingdom and the United States of America, for example. The Human Rights Committee is also empowered with making recommendations and issuing comments on any matter within its competence.

The Human Rights Committee is an active body based in Geneva. Concluding observations adopted following consideration of State reports and its views adopted pursuant to individual communications are final but not binding. However, its independent reports on alleged violations of the Covenant are annexed to its annual report to the General Assembly. Consequently, they have strong moral force and, to date, with a few notable exceptions, States have acted in accordance with the reasoned opinion of the Committee.

4.2.3.4 *Concluding observations*

Despite the significant number of signatory parties, 164 as of July 2009, the civil and political rights included in the Covenant are still regularly violated worldwide. A perusal of the concluding observations of the Human Rights Committee adopted pursuant to State periodic reports reveals many gaps between the written constitutional guarantees of many States and the reality of human rights abuses. The annual and State-specific reports of Non-Governmental Organizations (NGOs) are particularly instructive in this respect.

4.3 **Conclusions on the Bill of Human Rights**

Does the Bill of Human Rights live up to the expectations of the original proponents? Undoubtedly, the length of time it took to complete the Bill is a negative factor. Similarly, the length of time it has taken to secure ratifications for the two International Covenants is derisory. On the other hand, the fact that so many States have signed up to the Bill and, on paper at least, are attempting to conform with its standards is commendable. However, as is the case with other aspects of public international law, States will always try and justify their actions in terms of the salient standards. Hence, there are many reservations and derogations in respect of the Covenants. Note, though, that the 1993 World Conference on Human Rights, held in Vienna, declared that States should not resort to reservations, a wholesale embrace of the Articles being preferred. In general, those States reluctant to be held publicly accountable do not ratify the Optional Protocol to the ICCPR and barely comply with the requirements to submit periodic reports.

The Covenants permit States to declare themselves legally as well as morally bound by the terms of the Universal Declaration. Principles contained in the International Bill of Human Rights have occasionally been invoked before the International Court of Justice. Throughout the world, national judges apply the rights articulated in, or the principles underlining, the Universal Declaration and Covenants either directly or by applying national law which is modelled on components of the International Bill of Human Rights.

Many would argue that the implementation branch of the International Bill of Human Rights is a greenstick: it is pliable and though there may be fractures in a State's performance, the breaks are rarely absolute. State reports are the primary means of implementing the human rights contained in the International Bill of Human Rights. As is discussed in Chapter 10, a reporting system is often considered to 'lack teeth'. The First Optional Protocol to the International Covenant on Civil and Political Rights does enable the Human Rights Committee to receive individual complaints alleging violations of human rights though only against those States who have recognized the competency of the Committee for this purpose.

All three principal regional human rights instruments (discussed in more detail later) acknowledge the Universal Declaration in preambles. Nothing in any regional instrument is ever to be taken as compromising the Universal Declaration on Human Rights and international law. The instruments themselves testify to the interdependence and indivisibility of all rights: respect for civil and political rights inevitably involves elements of economic, cultural, and social rights whilst full and active enjoyment of economic, social, and cultural rights requires the enjoyment of civil and political freedoms.

Together, the United Nations Declaration and the two International Covenants form the foundation of international human rights protection, as advocated by the United Nations. Many organs and bodies within the United Nations Organization are involved with the protection and promotion of human rights. It is now necessary to examine the organizational structure of the United Nations in respect of human rights.

CASES

Filartiga v Pena-Irala (1980) F 2d 876 (2d Cir 1980); (1980) 19 International Legal Materials 966, noted in (1981) 75 American Journal of International Law 149.

Namibia Case (Legal Consequences for States of the Continued Presence of South Africa in Namibia (South West Africa) Notwithstanding Security Council Resolution 276 (1970) Advisory Opinion) 1971 ICJ Reps 16.

READING

Alfredsson, G, and Eide, A (eds), *The Universal Declaration of Human Rights: A common standard of achievement* (The Hague: Martinus Nijhoff, 1999).

Arambulo, K, *Strengthening the Supervision of the International Covenant on Economic, Social and Cultural Rights: Theoretical and procedural aspects* (Antwerp: Intersentia, 1999).

Baderin, M, and McCorquodale, R (eds), *Economic, Social and Cultural Rights in Action* (Oxford, Oxford University Press, 2007).

Boerefijn, I, *The Reporting Procedure under the International Covenant on Civil and Political Rights* (Antwerp: Intersentia, 1999).

Buergenthal, T, Shelton, D, and Stewart, D, *International Human Rights in a Nutshell*, 3rd edn (St Paul, Minn: West Group, 2002).

Craven, M, *The International Covenant on Economic, Social and Cultural Rights: A perspective on its development* (Oxford: Clarendon Press, 1995).

Donnelly, J, 'The relative universality of human rights' (2007) 29(2) Human Rights Quarterly 281–306.

Eide, A et al, (eds), *The Universal Declaration of Human Rights: A commentary* (Oslo: SUP, 1992).

Eide, A, Krause, K, and Rosas, A, *Economic, Social and Cultural Rights: A textbook*, 2nd edn (Dordecht: Martinus Nijhoff, 2001).

Goldewijk, BK, Contreras, B, and Carbonari, PC, *Dignity and Human Rights: The implementation of economic, social and cultural rights* (Antwerp: Intersentia, 2002).

Haksar, U, *Minority Protection and the International Bill of Rights* (Bombay: Allied, 1974).

Harland, C, 'The status of the International Covenant on Civil and Political Rights (ICCPR) in domestic law of State Parties: An initial global summary through United Nations' Human Rights Committees' documents' (2000) 22(1) Human Rights Quarterly 187–260.

Johnson, MG, and Symonides, J, *The Universal Declaration of Human Rights: A history of its creation and implementation 1948–1998* (Pan: UNESCO, 1998).

Joseph, S, Schultz, J, and Castan, M, *The International Covenant on Civil and Political Rights: Cases, materials and commentary* (Oxford: Oxford University Press, 2000).

Kabasakal Arat, Z, 'Forging a global culture of human rights: Origins and prospects of the International Bill of Rights' (2006) 28(2) Human Rights Quarterly 416–37.

Kirkup, A, and Evans, T, 'The myth of Western opposition to economic, social and cultural rights? A reply to Whelan and Donnelly' (2009) 31(1) Human Rights Quarterly 221–38.

Meron, T, *Human Rights and Humanitarian Norms as Customary Law* (Oxford: Clarendon Press, 1989).

Morsink, J, *The Universal Declaration of Human Rights: Origins, drafting and intent* (Philadelphia: University of Pennsylvania Press, 2000).

Nowak, M, *UN Covenant on Civil and Political Rights, CCPR Commentary*, 2nd edn (Kehl: Engel, 2005).

Office of the High Commissioner for Human Rights (OHCHR), *The International Bill of Rights Fact Sheet 2*, Rev 1 (Geneva: OHCHR, 1996).

OHCHR, *Fact Sheet No 22, Discrimination against Women* (Geneva: OHCHR).

Whelan, D, and Donnelly, J, 'The West, economic and social rights and the global human rights regime: Setting the record straight' (2007) 29 Human Rights Quarterly 908.

—— and ——, 'Yes, a myth: A reply to Kirkup and Evans' (2009) 31(1) Human Rights Quarterly 239–55.

WEBSITES

www.ohchr.org—United Nations High Commissioner for Human Rights.

www.unhchr.ch/udhr—UNHCHR Universal Declaration site.

5

....

The United Nations organizational structure

Having discussed the International Bill of Rights, the organizational structure of human rights bodies and organs under the auspices of the United Nations will now be explained to facilitate an understanding of the implementation and enforcement mechanisms applied by the United Nations in furtherance of its obligation to promote and preserve human rights. Attention will focus briefly on other organizations and other sub-organs of the United Nations which play a role in the protection and promotion of human rights.

5.1 An overview of the United Nations organizational structure

Virtually every body of the United Nations is involved to some extent in the protection of human rights. However, the United Nations human rights organizational structure is reasonably straightforward with responsibility for human rights being focused primarily in a few key bodies. Embodying a wide variety of approaches, the United Nations has the goal of securing the universality of human rights with full recognition of the equality, dignity, and worth of all mankind (see Figure 5.1).

The General Assembly is probably still at the top of the list of United Nations organs, although the Security Council also has some responsibility for human rights issues—indeed primary responsibility when international peace and security is threatened. Most formal reports on human rights are eventually channelled to the General Assembly of the United Nations, often via the Economic and Social Council (ECOSOC).

Alongside the United Nations High Commissioner for Human Rights, based in Geneva, the Human Rights Council obviously has an important role under its terms of reference, not least with its special procedures mechanisms (the Country and the Thematic Rapporteurs), and the various Working Groups reporting to it. Eight Committees, created by the principal human rights treaties, monitor the implementation of each treaty: these treaty-monitoring bodies are the Committee on Economic, Social and Cultural Rights, the Human Rights Committee, the Committee against Torture, the Committee on the Elimination of Racial Discrimination, the Committee on the Elimination of Discrimination against Women, the Committee on the Rights of the Child, the Committee on the Protection of the Rights of All Migrant Workers and Members of Their Families and the Committee on the Rights of Persons with Disabilities (the Committee on Enforced Disappearances has

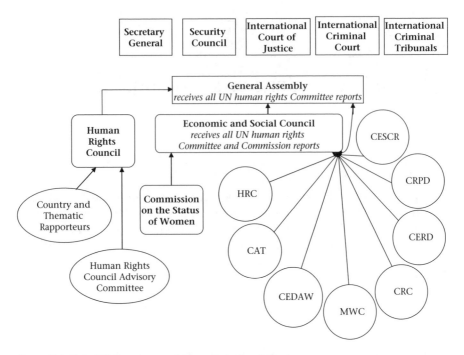

Figure 5.1 United Nations human rights organizational structure.

not yet been established as that core treaty has not yet attracted sufficient ratifications to enter into force). These Committees work with the Economic and Social Council and the General Assembly of the United Nations. Each will be discussed in turn, focusing first on the principal organs of the United Nations: the Security Council, the General Assembly, and the International Court of Justice.

5.2 The Security Council

The Security Council has primary responsibility for the maintenance of international peace and security. It also operates a fairly stringent non-intervention policy as regards the internal affairs of States (Art 2(7) UN Charter). Accordingly, the Security Council was initially reluctant to be drawn into human rights discussions. The de facto separation of powers between the General Assembly and the Security Council compounded this—essentially the two organs do not share concurrent jurisdiction over issues, the General Assembly ceasing involvement once the Security Council is seized of a matter.

As history attests, many international disputes are precipitated by violations of human rights—minority rights are a particularly obvious example—and thus non-observance of human rights may constitute a threat to international peace. Support for this can be drawn not only from history but also from the United Nations Charter. Indeed, in terms of the Charter, Art 1(2), the purpose of developing friendly relations between nations is firmly based on a mutual respect for the principle of equality and is second only to the maintenance of international peace and security in the stated purposes of the organization. Where human rights are contributing to friction between States, the Security Council may take action to restore the peace under the terms of the Charter. This is the most obvious situation in which the Security Council will involve itself in human rights.

5.2.1 Self-determination

The Security Council, as an integral part of its decolonization strategy, advocated self-determination of all peoples. The realization of this has involved issues of human rights violations. In Southern Rhodesia, the 1965 unilateral declaration of independence by the Smith regime was not recognized by the United Nations though was later held to constitute a threat to peace and thus brought within Chapter VII of the Charter. Various resolutions called on the United Kingdom to observe human rights within the territory and, eventually, sanctions were imposed. Elsewhere, the Security Council has endorsed various plebiscites and action has been forthcoming, if not necessarily swift, to secure and realize acts of self-determination of colonized people. The tragic case of East Timor and the recent declaration of independence by Kosovo are examples. Self-determination is considered in more detail in Chapter 17.

5.2.2 United Nations interventions

Since the formation of the United Nations, there have been numerous acts of aggression, civil wars, and international uses of force. Where international peace and security is threatened or violated, the Security Council can take enforcement action. Korea in 1950 is an early example. Alongside the development of peacekeeping actions, the Security Council has been involved increasingly in international humanitarian work. International humanitarian law, with non-derogable human rights, was discussed in Chapter 2. The massive humanitarian operation sanctioned in territories of the former Yugoslavia from 1992 to date, Somalia in 1992, and the ongoing struggle between the Palestinians and Israelis in Israel/ Palestine are examples of the United Nations becoming involved in humanitarian aid and human rights issues. In the former, there was deemed to be a threat to peace, thus justifying intervention. The United Nations has had a presence in Israel and surrounding States for some forty years in the form of peacekeepers, truce observers, and relief workers. They work with the consent of the host State.

5.2.3 Other situations

The Security Council will often condemn violations of certain human rights, though action may be less forthcoming—for example, slavery and practices analogous thereto have been condemned. The approach of the Security Council to international terrorism is, perhaps, somewhat chequered despite the loss of civilian life which may ensue but then, the old adage can be adapted: one person's terrorist is another's freedom fighter. Perhaps the right to life, particularly when denied through the crime of genocide, is the main human right breach of which the Security Council is overtly seen to condemn on a regular basis—resolutions adopted with respect to Rwanda and the former Yugoslavia illustrate this. There are many United Nations Security Council resolutions which call upon States to conform to international standards of human rights. This is a little more insipid than condemning violations of human rights but is politically more successful as such calls from the Security Council are viewed gravely by many States.

5.2.4 Sanctions

The United Nations Security Council has the power to impose the ultimate penalty against States failing to conform to international legal obligations—sanctions. Until 1990, the United Nations had only imposed sanctions on two States, Southern Rhodesia and South Africa. Since then, sanctions have been applied to several more. The most comprehensive set of sanctions imposed to date was those against Iraq although the effect of the sanctions was subsequently ameliorated by the implementation (in 1995) of the aid for oil programme. The resolution on the DPR Korea in October 2006 was notable for the emphasis on ensuring humanitarian aid was not impeded, yet the political and diplomatic impact on the DPRK government was debatable in light of the controversy over its rocket test in April 2009. Reports by United Nations' and other bodies have questioned the effect of sanctions, given their negative effect on the life of much of the civilian population: infant mortality has risen and pubic health has deteriorated as a consequence of sanctions, for example. General Comment No 8 of the Committee on Economic, Social and Cultural Rights discussed further the relationship between economic sanctions and respect for economic, social, and cultural rights, concluding that 'lawlessness of one kind should not be met by lawlessness of another kind which pays no heed to the fundamental rights that underlie and give legitimacy to any such collective aim' (para 16). The popularity of unilateral sanctions, favoured by the United States of America, has also increased in recent years, despite the increasing discomfort with which the United Nations seems to regard such action.

5.2.5 Conclusions

The most serious complaint raised against the Security Council is that it is less likely to take action against its permanent members. This has been particularly notable in the case of the People's Republic of China and alleged abuses of human rights, particularly in Tibet (and was aptly demonstrated in protracted discussions over US-instigated military action against Iraq and Afghanistan). In spite of this, the Security Council has carved out a role for itself in preserving and promoting human rights, especially when serious violations are involved. The response of the Council to the apartheid system in South Africa shaped the future of the organ with respect to human rights violations. Systematic violations of human rights are frequently a contributor to, and symptomatic of, armed conflict between States and, increasingly, civil unrest and disturbances. Iraq, Haiti, and Kosovo are recent examples. The Security Council will thus find itself continually drawn into discussions on human rights.

5.3 The General Assembly

The General Assembly has considerable competency to deal with human rights. In terms of Art 13 of the Charter, it 'shall initiate studies and make recommendations for the purpose of … (b) promoting international co-operation in the economic, social, cultural, educational, and health fields, and assisting in the realization of human rights and fundamental freedoms for all without distinction as to race, sex, language, or religion'. Resolution 60/149 (2005) calls for intensified efforts to achieve universal ratification of the international covenants and emphasizes that national measures to combat terrorism must be in accordance with international law with States avoiding resort to derogation (Art 4 ICCPR) which erodes human rights. Studies have been undertaken on a variety of human rights issues: Resolution 43/115 (1988), for example, appointed Professor Philip Alston as independent expert to review the work of the treaty-monitoring bodies with a view to increasing their long term efficiency; Resolution 62/171 (2007) declared the year commencing on 10 December 2008 (the sixtieth anniversary of the adoption of the Universal Declaration of Human Rights) the International Year of Human Rights Learning; Resolution 63/171 (2008) drew attention to the growing problems of defamation of religions; Resolution 56/116 (2001) proclaimed 2003 the start of the United Nations Literacy Decade; Resolution 59/113 (2004) proclaims the World Programme for Human Rights Education; and Resolution 58/234 (2003) designated 7 April, 2004 the International Day of Reflection on the Genocide in Rwanda. Such resolutions are not legally binding though they may have considerable effect on, for example, the functioning of the treaty-monitoring bodies or the profile of certain issues. They may also shape the future of human rights policy in certain areas. On a country basis, the General Assembly may elect to discuss human rights abuses in any given State and examine the situation therein—Resolution 63/18 (2008) expresses concern over the humanitarian consequences of the deteriorating security situation in Afghanistan; while Resolution 63/199 (2008) focuses on human rights in the Islamic Republic of Iran; and Resolution 63/205 (2008) addressed the human rights situation in Myanmar. In terms of General Assembly Resolution 60/251, the new Human Rights Council was established, the status of which will be considered after five years (2011) at which time the Council may become a full organ of the United Nations (para 16).

5.3.1 Declarations on human rights issues

Declarations of the General Assembly are not legally binding but have moral force, being indicative of majority global opinion. This is especially true when adopted unanimously or without a dissenting vote. Statements of intent (soft law) may lead to subsequent adoption of legally binding measures. The Universal Declaration on Human Rights is one of the greatest achievements of the General Assembly, subsequently being translated into 'hard' law by the International Covenants (Chapter 4). However, other notable successes are the Declaration on the Rights of the Child 1959, the Declaration on the Elimination of all Forms of Racial Discrimination 1963, the Declaration on the Elimination of Discrimination Against Women 1967, the Declaration on the Elimination of All Forms of Intolerance and of Discrimination based on Religion or Belief 1981, the Declaration on the Rights of Persons belonging to National or Ethnic, Religious and Linguistic Minorities 1992 and the Declaration on the Protection of All Persons from Enforced Disappearances 1992. Many of these Declarations subsequently manifested themselves in binding international instruments.

5.3.2 **Logistical support**

The General Assembly will coordinate logistical support and technical support reacting to the needs of State in realizing their obligations under the International Bill of Rights. It can authorize work of United Nations specialized agencies—for example training has regularly been provided in furtherance of the right to a fair trial. In some States, the United Nations may send observers to assist in national elections (East Timor is one example). These activities are normally approved by the General Assembly. Special Emergency Sessions of the General Assembly facilitate discussions on specific problems and countries in an attempt to decide remedial action. Most recently, an emergency special session was convened by Qatar to consider Occupied East Jerusalem and other Occupied Palestinian Territory. The session ran on various dates from April 1997 to present (UN Doc A/RES/ES-10/2–9).

5.3.3 **Receiving reports**

The General Assembly receives and considers reports made by all the treaty-monitoring bodies and through the Economic and Social Council. The element of publicity which this entails, for example naming States which fail to submit periodic reports, raises the profile of human rights and emphasizes the importance placed by the international community on compliance therewith. Indeed, the Economic and Social Council is responsible to the General Assembly (Art 60) and its members are elected by it (Art 61). The Secretary General of the United Nations acts as a depository for instruments of ratification and signatory to most major treaties. Any public emergencies considered by a State Party to justify derogation from any of the instruments must be notified to the Secretary General.

5.3.4 **General debates**

General debates of the General Assembly play an important role in raising the profile of universal human rights. Certain serious human rights situations have been the subject of debate with the General Assembly deploring abuses of human rights and calling on the State or States involved to conform to international standards. A plethora of relevant issues can be debated on the floor of the General Assembly in addition to discussion generated by submissions of human rights related declarations and instruments. Where necessary, Special Rapporteurs and other experts may be sanctioned by the General Assembly to investigate and report on specific issues.

5.3.5 **Conclusions**

The General Assembly has a major role to play in the implementation of human rights treaties. Like all organs of the United Nations, it must act within the powers conferred on it by the United Nations Charter. However, the reality is the General Assembly enjoys rather broad powers and frequently delegates human rights issues to specialized bodies as will be seen.

5.4 **The International Courts**

There are two international courts operating within the United Nations organization: the International Court of Justice, the original world court established by the United Nations Charter and the International Criminal Court established by a separate statute in 2002.

5.4.1 **The International Court of Justice**

Established by Article 92 of the United Nations Charter, the International Court of Justice suceeded the Permanent Court of International Justice (the judicial organ of the League of Nations). Fifteen judges, drawn from different States, are elected by a majority of both the General Assembly and Security Council. Ad hoc judges may be selected by States involved in a dispute before the Court may be appointed for the duration of that particular case where there is no national judge already in the Court. The Court sits as a chamber or full court and can hear contentious cases and deliver advisory opinions. Any State can recognize the competence of the Court to deal with any case.

The International Court of Justice is not however, competent to adjudicate on disputes raised by individuals or on substantive issues raised under any international human rights instrument. But, as with the Permanent Court of International Justice which defined much of the early law on minorities, the International Court of Justice may contribute to the subject by defining and interpreting conventions and duties incumbent upon States.

Bosnia-Herzegovina instituted proceedings against Yugoslavia (Serbia and Montenegro) before the International Court of Justice in 1993 alleging violations of the Genocide Convention and international human rights law. A provisional measure was granted in 1993 prohibiting Yugoslavia from committing further acts of genocide. The adoption of provisional measures indicates a perceptible change in policy of the International Court of Justice with provisional measures being used to limit serious abuses of human rights pending a decision on merits. On 26 February 2007, the Court found Serbia (the appropriate respondent State) had violated the provisional measures by failing to prevent genocide in Srebenica in July 1995 but was not guilty of committing genocide in any form. This judgment was deemed to be 'appropriate satisfaction' in the case.

The application of the Genocide Convention is still being considered in *Croatia v Serbia and Montenegro*, an application filed in July 1999. Race discrimination is also at issue before the Court, as Georgia filed an application against the Russian Federation following the hostilities in border territories in August 2008. By October 2008, provisional measures had been ordered to prevent escalation of racial discrimination in South Ossetia, Abkhazia and adjacent areas in Georgia, the emphasis being firmly on ensuring 'without distinction as to national or ethnic origin, security of persons; the right of persons to freedom of movement and residence within the border of the State; [and] the protection of the property of displaced persons and of refugees' (para 149). These proceedings are an attempt to enforce treaty obligations (under the International Convention for the Elimination of All Forms of Racial Discrimination) between the two parties. This is the first instance in which the Court has been called upon to exercise such jurisdiction in respect of a core human rights treaty.

In addition, advisory opinions of the court may contribute to jurisprudence—the *Reservations to the Genocide Convention Case* is a prime example.

5.4.2 The International Criminal Court

With an ever-greater awareness of those subjected to heinous war crimes and other crimes against humanity, and following on from the ad hoc International Criminal Tribunals for Rwanda and the Former Yugoslavia, the calls for a permanent World Criminal Court gained momentum. After protracted negotiations, the Rome Statute creating the International Criminal Court was opened for signature in 1998. The overt objective of the Statute is that 'the most serious crimes of concern to the international community as a whole must not go unpunished' (preamble).

Taking a lead from the Nuremberg and Tokyo Tribunals and the success of the ad hoc Criminal Tribunals, the International Criminal Court has jurisdiction over persons. This jurisdiction complements national criminal jurisdictions, hence the ongoing indictments in Rwanda, Sierra Leone, etc. The Court is permanent and sits in The Hague in the Netherlands.

According to the Rome Statute, the International Criminal Court has jurisdiction over genocide, crimes against humanity, war crimes and the crime of aggression (Art 5). Crimes against humanity (Art 6) include enslavement, torture, sexual slavery, enforced disappearances of persons, and apartheid, all of which are covered by human rights. Many aspects of war crimes are also covered by contemporary instruments on human rights although obviously there is an overlap with humanitarian law, the Statute draws on the provisions of the Geneva Convention (Art 8).

5.5 The Economic and Social Council

The Economic and Social Council has fifty-four members, elected for three-year terms by the General Assembly. It meets throughout the year with its principal session in July (New York or Geneva). The Economic and Social Council (ECOSOC) has a broad remit to initiate studies and reports with respect to 'international economic, social, cultural, educational, health, and related matters' (United Nations Charter, Art 62(1)). It may also 'make recommendations for the purpose of promoting respect for, and observance of, human rights and fundamental freedoms for all' (Art 62(2)). ECOSOC assists in the organization of human rights conferences and has worked with other United Nations and associated bodies in furtherance of the promotion of universal human rights. The treaty-monitoring bodies (conventional mechanisms) established under the auspices of the United Nations report to the Economic and Social Council and thence to the General Assembly. In addition, ECOSOC coordinates various United Nations programmes, including the United Nations Development Programme, and receives annual reports from specialized agencies such as the United Nations Educational, Scientific and Cultural Organization, the International Labour Organization, and the World Health Organization. The mandates of the foregoing impact on human rights.

Given the workload of the Economic and Social Council, it frequently works through delegation to sub-organs. ECOSOC supports ten commissions, five regional commissions, various specialist committees, and expert bodies. One of ECOSOC's original substantive commissions was the Commission on Human Rights, established in 1946 in furtherance of its obligations under Art 68 of the United Nations Charter. The work of this Commission has now been subsumed by the new Human Rights Council. The Commission ceased operation in 2006.

5.5.1 **The Commission on the Status of Women (CSW)**

The Commission on the Status of Women was established as a functional commission of the Economic and Social Council by Resolution 11(II), 1946. Its primary function is to prepare recommendations and reports to the Council on promoting women's rights in political, economic, civil, social, and educational fields. It may also put forward recommendations on areas requiring immediate attention. Following the Beijing Conference and Platform for Action, the General Assembly mandated the Commission with preparing for the 2000 follow up to the Beijing Conference, undertaking regular reviews of the specified critical areas of concern. Women and education, training, the environment, decision-making, and health are all areas currently being reviewed with gender mainstreaming and ageing women more recent additions. The Commission's membership has grown considerably since its inception with fifteen members. Its forty-five members meet for approximately eight working days every year. Some of the servicing of the Commission is carried out by the Division for the Advancement of Women.

5.5.1.1 *Division for the Advancement of Women (DAW)*

The Division for the Advancement of Women is part of the Department of Economic and Social Affairs within the United Nations Secretariat. Its mission is to ensure the participation of women as equal partners with men in all aspects of human endeavour. Accordingly, it seeks to promote women as equal participants and beneficiaries of sustainable development, peace, and security, governance and human rights, stimulating a mainstreaming of a gender perspective within and outside the United Nations system (DAW's mission statement). The Division has three broad functions: analysing gender issues; promoting women's human rights; and coordinating policies. Its current director is Carolyn Hannan. The Division services the Commission on the Status of Women and has serviced the Committee on the Elimination of Discrimination against Women.

5.6 **The Human Rights Council**

In June 2006, the Human Rights Council met for the first time. It replaces the Commission on Human Rights and, at least initially, takes over many of its functions. As many of the Commission's powers are subsumed by the Council, note that some relevant instruments still refer to the Commission, not the Council: thus this text retains references to the Commission (where appropriate). A brief overview of the Commission follows, before the structure and powers of the new Council are examined. The Council instituted a comprehensive review of its new powers, adopting resolutions concerning the status of each aspect of the Commission's work consonant with the new Council's powers.

5.6.1 **The Commission on Human Rights**

The Commission on Human Rights was created in 1947 with the goal of drafting the Universal Declaration of Human Rights. After achieving this, it focused on setting standards for international human rights though had no authority to consider violations of human rights until 1967. Since then, it established and administered a number of extra-Conventional mechanisms for enforcing human rights. Its fact-finding capacity was also expanded with the introduction of special rapporteurs and working groups on particular countries/issues. Further to the Vienna Declaration and Programme of Action 1993, the Commission on Human Rights focused more on being a conduit for technical assistance and cooperation with a general shift towards promotion of economic, social and cultural rights and the rights of vulnerable groups.

The Commission was long the subject of criticisms and was highlighted as requiring attention by the Secretary-General in his seminal report 'In Larger Freedom: Towards development, security and human rights for all'. Kofi Annan considered that 'the Commission's capacity to perform its tasks has been increasingly undermined by its declining credibility and professionalism' (para 182). This report was a follow up to the United Nations Millennium Summit and lays down a blueprint for the future of the organization. It also drew on the High Level Panel on threats, challenges and change, a body appointed by the Secretary-General to consider existing and recent threats to international peace and security, to evaluate the response of the international community, and make recommendations for strengthening the capacity and capability of the United Nations. Ultimately the result (as impacts on human rights) was General Assembly Resolution 60/251 on establishing a Human Rights Council and terminating the Commission on Human Rights.

5.6.2 **Creating the Council**

By General Assembly Resolution 60/251, the Assembly decided to establish, as a subsidiary organ, a Human Rights Council in Geneva, to replace the Commission on Human Rights. The status of the Council will be reconsidered by late 2011 and it is possible at that time that it will become a full organ of the United Nations. This would elevate human rights further in the United Nations structure, creating three Councils for the three principal areas of work of the organization: the Security Council for international peace and security, the Economic and Social Council for world development and the Human Rights Council for human rights. At present, however, the Council remains a subsidiary of the General Assembly, though this in itself is a higher status than the Commission (a functional commission of the Economic and Social Council) enjoyed. The Council consists of forty-seven members—States tendered expressions of interest through to May 2006, with countries elected by secret ballot thereafter. The terms of Resolution 60/251 seek to ensure a geographical balance of Member States (para 7). Interestingly, elections to the Council should take into account the human rights contribution and commitments of States. Moreover, any State committing gross and systematic violations of human rights can be suspended from membership by a two-thirds majority vote of the General Assembly (para 8)! In contrast to its predecessor, the Council is mandated to meet at least three times a year and for a minimum of ten weeks in total. It also has the power to hold special sessions, and has regularly availed itself of this option, meeting several times each year, discussing a variety of human rights situations in, inter alia, Israel and Palestine, Sudan (especially Darfur), the Democratic Republic of Congo, and Myanmar (Burma).

5.6.3 The functions of the Council

In terms of Resolution 60/251, the functions of the Council are to:

(a) Promote human rights education and learning as well as advisory services, technical assistance and capacity-building, to be provided in consultation with and with the consent of Member States concerned;

(b) Serve as a forum for dialogue on thematic issues on all human rights;

(c) Make recommendations to the General Assembly for the further development of international law in the field of human rights;

(d) Promote the full implementation of human rights obligations undertaken by States and follow-up to the goals and commitments related to the promotion and protection of human rights emanating from United Nations conferences and summits;

(e) Undertake a universal periodic review, based on objective and reliable information, of the fulfilment by each State of its human rights obligations and commitments in a manner which ensures universality of coverage and equal treatment with respect to all States; the review shall be a cooperative mechanism, based on an interactive dialogue, with the full involvement of the country concerned and with consideration given to its capacity-building needs; such a mechanism shall complement and not duplicate the work of treaty bodies; the Council shall develop the modalities and necessary time allocation of the universal periodic review mechanism within one year after the holding of its first session;

(f) Contribute, through dialogue and cooperation, towards the prevention of human rights violations and respond promptly to human rights emergencies;

(g) Assume the role and responsibilities of the Commission on Human Rights relating to the work of the Office of the United Nations High Commissioner for Human Rights, as decided by the General Assembly in its resolution 48/141 of 20 December 1993;

(h) Work in close cooperation in the field of human rights with Governments, regional organizations, national human rights institutions and civil society;

(i) Make recommendations with regard to the promotion and protection of human rights;

(j) Submit an annual report to the General Assembly. [Para 5]

Perhaps the most interesting function is that of universal periodic review ((e) above). The process for this is detailed in Human Rights Council Resolution 5/1 on Institution-building of the United Nations Human Rights Council. Each UN Member State will be reviewed over a four-year period, irrespective of which human rights treaties each State has ratified. Human Rights Council Resolution 5/1 notes that Universal Periodic Review is based on the Charter of the United Nations, the Universal Declaration of Human Rights, Human Rights instruments to which a State is party and voluntary pledges and commitments by States to human rights. The review will address international human rights law and, perhaps more controversially, international humanitarian law.

The Council appoints a 'troika' of Council Member States to review each State's report, taking into account the available documentation: reports submitted by the Office of the High Commissioner on Human Rights (one a compilation of treaty body reports on those treaties the State has ratified, the other a compilation of additional credible information on the human rights situation prevailing in the country under review). Questions (from the Council) and answers (from the State) follow before the outcome document is drafted and published. The first outcomes were published in 2008. To date (July 2009), most focus on selected issues (eg, women and children in Indonesia's review) rather than provide a full overview of the prevailing human rights situation. After completion of a full cycle, universal periodic review will be reviewed to evaluate its efficacy as a mechanism for monitoring and reviewing human rights and humanitarian law compliance.

5.6.4 Individual complaints

Given that the Commission on Human Rights declared in 1947 that it had no jurisdiction to action individual complaints, remarkable progress has been made reversing this. ECOSOC Resolution 75(V), endorsing the view of the Commission, was eventually reversed by Resolution 1503 (XLVIII) in 1970. This confidential communications procedure was revised by the Commission on Human Rights in 2000 (ECOSOC Resolution 2000/3 (entitled procedure for dealing with communications concerning human rights)), creating a procedure which remained operational until Human Rights Council Resolution 5/1 (2007) set the parameters for the current process.

The process has three stages: a Working Group on Communications, comprising of independent experts drawn from the new Human Rights Council Advisory Committee, will conduct an initial review of communications for admissibility; the Working Group on Situations (drawn from the Council members) will consider admissible communications and, if it considers it appropriate, will prepare reports thereon for the Council; the Human Rights Council receives reports and recommendations and may take appropriate action. The admissibility criteria remain virtually unchanged from that employed by the former Commission and no information on the nature of the complaints or the discussions of the Council will be made public unless, of course, the State consents.

5.6.5 Special procedures

The Human Rights Council also assumed responsibility for the special procedure mechanisms of the Commission on Human Rights and is currently reviewing their operation, in accordance with General Assembly Resolution 60/251. The Council has followed the Commission in mandating a number of rapporteurs to investigate and monitor the human rights situations in defined countries/areas and assess specified human rights and vulnerable groups. Human Rights Council resolution 5/1 also introduced procedures for reviewing, rationalizing and improving the system of thematic and country rapporteurs; each mandate was individually reviewed to determine its fate, while the entire process of appointment and nomenclature was unified to minimize repetition in furtherance of enhancing the promotion and protection of all human rights. Now thematic mandates will run for three years, country mandates for one year. To clarify the role and responsibilities, Human Rights Council Resolution 5/2 (2007) adopted a Code of Conduct for Special Procedures Mandate-holders of the Human Rights Council. Rapporteurs are drawn from practitioners and academics with considerable expertise in human rights. They can undertake visits with the consent of the State concerned and report back to the Human Rights Council (preciously the Commission). At present there are country mandates for Cambodia, the Democratic People's Republic of Korea, Haiti, Myanmar, Somalia, and Sudan among others. Current thematic mandates cover the right to adequate housing, the right to education, arbitrary detention, mercenaries and their impact on self-determination, minority issues, violence against women, torture, and human rights defenders.

Discussion topic

Membership of UN human rights bodies

The Human Rights Council comprises Member States which profess adherence to international human rights standards, treaty-monitoring bodies, the Advisory Committee, and the special procedures of the Human Rights Council and are individuals deemed to have relevant expertise. Human Rights Council Resolution 5/1 (2007) specifies that the paramount criteria for appointing special procedure mandate holders should be '(a) expertise; (b) experience in the field of the mandate; (c) independence; (d) impartiality; (e) personal integrity; and (f) objectivity' with '[d]ue consideration ... given to gender balance and equitable geographic representation, as well as to an appropriate representation of different legal systems' (paras 39 and 40). Similar provisions appear in the various treaties establishing committees to monitor compliance. However, funding for these experts is very limited and the scope of their UN work is dependent, often, on self- or other external funding.

Undoubtedly the level of independence has increased over the years since the first treaty-monitoring bodies were established. However there are still many issues concerning the practicalities of the appointment and work of individuals nominated to serve the UN bodies.

5.6.6 The Sub-Commission on the Promotion and Protection of Human Rights

In 1946, the Sub-Commission on the Prevention of Discrimination and the Protection of Minorities was established as a subsidiary organ of the Economic and Social Council and the Commission on Human Rights. In many respects this committee was a remnant of the League of Nations' focus on minority rights, a focus which was deemed redundant (albeit with misplaced optimism) with the adoption of a universal approach to Human Rights. The twenty-six member Sub-Commission had an advisory role. In 1999, ECOSOC approved a name change; it became the Sub-Commission on the Promotion and Protection of Human Rights. Human Rights Council Decision 1/102, 30 June 2006, mandated the continuation of the Sub-Commission for a year to enable a full examination of its functions to be undertaken. Its last meeting commenced on 31 July 2006 and ran for a month to enable it to address outstanding issues. The Sub-Commission has now been disbanded.

The tasks of the Sub-Commission were firstly to undertake studies and make recommendations to the Human Rights Council concerning the prevention of discrimination of any kind relating to human rights and fundamental freedoms and the protection of racial, national, religious, and linguistic minorities and secondly to perform any other functions which may be entrusted to it by the ECOSOC or by the Human Rights Council. Studies under the auspices of the Sub-Commission include globalisation and its impact on the full enjoyment of human rights (Resolution 1999/8, final report UN Doc E/CN.4/Sub.2/2003/14), the realization of the right to drinking water and sanitation and economic, social and cultural rights (Resolution 2001/2, preliminary report UNDOC E/CN.4/Sub.2/2002/10), and the issue of indigenous peoples' permanent sovereignty over natural resources (Resolution 2001/10, preliminary report UN Doc E/CN.4/Sub.2/2003/20). Although some commentators highlight a perceived overlap in functions of the Sub-Commission and the then Commission, the Sub-Commission remained primarily an independent advisor on human rights issues.

5.6.7 **The Human Rights Council Advisory Committee**

The Human Rights Council Advisory Committee, in effect, replaced the Sub-Commission, retaining some elements of its role as independent advisor on human rights. It was established following Resolution 5/1 of the Human Rights Council and comprises eighteen experts, nominated by dint of their expertise. Its inaugural session was held in August 2008 and it is mandated to meet for up to two sessions each year. The role of Committee is advisory, though note it lacks the implementation powers of its predecessor—it cannot adopt resolutions, for example. The Committee will focus on themes, adopting recommendations to assist the work of the Human Rights Council. Early recommendations were on topics including human rights education and training, discrimination against those with leprosy, gender mainstreaming and the right to food. The constitutive documents for the Advisory Committee reinforce its role as supporting the intergovernmental Council, albeit as an independent 'think-tank' offering expertise on human rights.

5.7 **The High Commissioner for Human Rights**

The mandate of the Office of High Commissioner for Human Rights derives from Arts 1, 13, and 55 of the United Nations Charter. The mission statement is 'to protect and promote human rights for all'. In an attempt to ensure greater efficiency, the Office of the High Commissioner and the Centre for Human Rights merged in 1997. As a consequence, the Office of the High Commissioner provides secretarial support for the treaty-monitoring bodies. The High Commissioner is based in Geneva, Switzerland though maintains an office (and a director) in New York. The post of High Commissioner for Human Rights was created by General Assembly Resolution 48/141 of 20 December 1993 (A/RES/48/141). Article 2 requires the High Commissioner for Human Rights to be of high moral standing and personal integrity with expertise both in human rights and in the understanding of the diverse cultures of the global community. Appointment is by the Secretary-General of the United Nations, approved by the General Assembly and, with due regard for geographical rotation, is in four-year terms. Within the United Nations system, the appointment is at the rank of Under-Secretary-General. The High Commissioner has primary responsibility for United Nations human rights activities under the direction and authority of the Secretary-General. The areas of responsibility include coordinating human rights promotion and protection throughout the United Nations system, providing advisory services, technical and financial assistance in the field of human rights, actively contributing towards the removal of barriers to the realization of human rights, education, and public-information programmes promoting human rights, and streamlining the present system to improve its efficiency and effectiveness. In an attempt to enhance international cooperation for the promotion and protection of human rights, the High Commissioner will also engage in dialogue with governments. Mr José Ayala-Lasso was the first High Commissioner with Mary Robinson taking over responsibility in 1997 followed by Sérgio Vieria de Mello in September 2002. Canadian Supreme Court Justice Louise Arbour was appointed in February 2004 following the death of Sérgio Viera de Mello in an attack on the United Nations Baghdad headquarters in August 2003. She served one term and was succeeded by Navanethem Pillay.

The High Commissioner provides a focal point for human rights activities under the auspices of the United Nations, a 'human face' for international human rights. Through the activities outlined above and through speeches, press briefings, publications, and conferences, the High Commissioner strives to maintain an ever higher public profile for human rights. The work undertaken in support of the Decade for Human Rights Education is one example of this.

The Office of the High Commissioner for Human Rights has also established a major presence on the internet with its website providing a wealth of resources, thereby further publicizing international human rights.

5.7.1 **Others**

A Research and Right to Development Branch works towards the promotion and protection of the right to development. The Support Services Branch, on the other hand, has a more general mandate servicing the Commission on Human Rights, the Sub-Commission and the treaty-monitoring bodies. Finally the Activities and Programmes Branch has responsibility for implementing the United Nations Decade for Human Rights Education, managing the Voluntary Fund for Technical Cooperation in the Field of Human Rights, and supporting human rights fact-finding and investigatory missions, Special Rapporteurs, and other human rights field presences.

5.8 **Treaty-monitoring bodies**

5.8.1 **Introduction**

Many international instruments relating to human rights include some kind of enforcement mechanism. The most common is a reports system whereby States submit a report on their implementation of the rights in the instrument. These reports are studied by a Committee established by the salient instrument concerned. After examining the report and other submitted documents (eg NGO reports, reports from other UN treaty bodies), questions may be put to the State. Then, the Committee issues concluding observations on the report and progress of the State. Reports are submitted within a year or two of accession/succession/ratification then thereafter periodically as per the Convention: often every four or five years. The Committees are typically non-judicial bodies with competency to receive complaints from States and/or individuals alleging violations of human rights. Their opinions and recommendations are usually published. These treaty-monitoring bodies are referred to as conventional mechanisms: their powers are derived directly from the convention in question. Some of these committees only have automatic competency to receive inter-State complaints, the individual complaint procedure, where applicable, being dependent on explicit State consent. In all cases, the powers of the Committee are derived solely from the Convention thus are restricted to that which the High Contracting States are willing to cede. There are inevitably limitations to the jurisdiction of the Committees and the jurisprudence produced by them is incomparable to that of regional human rights courts such as the European Court of Human Rights. Nevertheless, the importance of the Committees should not be underestimated. Each Committee will be considered in turn with the principal treaty provisions governing its operation outlined.

For individual communications, complaints must be in set minimum formats—eg, contain the name and contact details of the complainant, the details of the incidences, and a chronology of domestic action which has been taken to try and remedy the situation. An initial admissibility stage in the proceedings will filter out irrelevant, incomplete, abusive, and inconsistent applications. The full details for admissibility will be found in the rules of procedure for the Committee in question. In general, once a complaint is found admissible, the State against whom the complaint is made will be asked to submit its observations in response. The Committee will then consider the complaint and the observations, possibly in dialogue with the State(s) concerned. After consideration of the merits, a report will be issued containing the conclusions and opinion of the Committee.

5.8.2 **Human Rights Committee**

The Human Rights Committee was established by the International Covenant on Civil and Political Rights (Art 28). It consists of eighteen members of 'high moral character and recognized competence in the field of human rights' (Art 28(2)) with consideration given to legal experience. Members serve in their personal capacity for terms of four years with a staggered system of re-election. The Committee has competency to consider periodic reports, to receive inter State complaints, and, under the Optional Protocol, to receive individual petitions. The practice has evolved whereby the Committee meets thrice a year: New York in late March/early April, then Geneva in July and in late October/early November. The Office of the High Commissioner for Human Rights provides the necessary secretarial support. The workload of the Human Rights Committee is constantly growing with the increase in State Parties and a heightened awareness of the work of the Committee.

5.8.2.1 *Reports*

Contracting parties are bound to submit periodic reports on the measures they have adopted to give effect to the Covenant when requested to do so by the Committee (Art 40(1)). Initial reports should be submitted within a year of the entry into force of the Covenant for the State in point. The Human Rights Committee produced general guidelines for States in 1997; although not legally binding, the Committee encourages States to follow these guidelines in order to expedite the process. It is important in the initial report for the State to outline the salient features of its legal system which protect the specified rights. This should include reference to any constitutional provisions. Jurisdictional measures should be addressed as should the applicable procedures for invoking rights before competent bodies seeking either the enforcement of the right or appropriate remedies for any violation thereof. A more detailed tabulation of the rights covered by the Covenant and their protection at the national level should then follow. All relevant legal provisions should be annexed to the initial report. The Committee considers the report, availing itself of the opportunity to engage in a constructive dialogue with representatives of the State under consideration.

Following on from the initial reports, the 'constructive dialogue' between State and Committee should be continued with the submission and consideration of periodic reports. There is no interval specified in the Covenant. However, the present practice guidelines of the Committee require submission every five years. It is theoretically possible for the Committee to request ad hoc reports from States (Art 40(1)(b)). However, this provision is rarely invoked, the Committee restricting itself to requesting periodic reports. Should a particularly dramatic alleged violation occur, the Committee may request a special report. Clearly, five years can be an inordinately long time in the evolution of human rights, national political and economic situations, though, with the proliferation of delays in the submission of periodic reports, the interval between reports may be considerably longer.

As with all conventional mechanisms, the Annual Report of the Human Rights Committee is ultimately transmitted to the United Nations General Assembly. It summarizes the activities of the Committee and lists defaulting States (ie, those which have not submitted reports on time). The intention is that this naming will produce the desired result of a report in swift course.

5.8.2.2 *Inter-State complaints*

Inter-State complaints may be submitted against a State which has declared its recognition of the competency of the Committee for this purpose (Art 41). Any such complaint is first subject to a system of peaceful resolution with the State notifying the receiving State of the complaint and allowing time for explanation and clarification in writing of the complaint. If there is no satisfaction within six months, the matter may be referred to the Committee which, assuming all available domestic remedies have been exhausted, may consider the matter in closed session. Should no friendly settlement be reached, the Committee will transmit to the States concerned a report on the facts and the written and oral submissions. Note that this is not a judicial process. The Committee acts more as a neutral mediator.

5.8.2.3 *Individual complaints*

The creation of a body competent to receive individual communications was viewed as an essential part of securing universal respect for, and implementation of, the International Bill of Rights. However, conclusion of the text of a clause on individual petition proved almost impossible due to lack of consensus. Individual petition was considered to be an infringement of the national sovereignty of States and contrary to the still prevalent view that only States were subjects of international law. Nonetheless, agreement was eventually reached on the text of an Optional Protocol providing for individual petitions thereby fitting the final piece into the jigsaw of the International Bill of Rights.

Individual communications must satisfy set admissibility criteria—they must be written, must not be anonymous, or an abuse of the right of petition and may only be considered once available domestic remedies have been exhausted (Art 2, Optional Protocol). Naturally, the Committee will not consider any communication which is being examined under another international procedure (Art 5, Optional Protocol). Admissible individual petitions are forwarded to the State concerned by the Human Rights Committee for comment before views are adopted. Examination of such communications is in closed session. Individuals may employ legal representation to assist in the preparation of a communication but the lack of oral hearings obviates the need for a system of legal aid. Once final views are adopted by the Committee, they are communicated to both the State and the individual involved and are then made public.

The individual complaint procedure under the Optional Protocol has developed to the extent that it is sometimes regarded as almost quasi-judicial. However, views of the Committee in these cases are not legally binding. Approximately two-thirds of the State Parties to the Covenant have consented to abide by the Optional Protocol. It has 112 State Parties as of July 2009. Looking at the permanent members of the Security Council, over half (the United Kingdom, the United States of America, and the People's Republic of China) have not even signed the Optional Protocol— perhaps not the best example for new States to follow. As a partial response to the number of communications concerning them, Jamaica (which has already been found to have violated the Covenant in ninety-eight cases) and Trinidad and Tobago (twenty-one violations) have denounced the Optional Protocol (Art 12) though all cases pending at the time the denunciations took effect will continue to be considered. The number of communications received by the Committee has expanded rapidly in the last fifteen years as a consequence of growing public awareness of its work although there have been fewer than 1,500 communications to date.

Due to the nature of many rights covered by the Covenant on Civil and Political Rights, on occasion the Committee has taken the step of securing interim protection for an individual. For example, without prejudice to the merits of the communications and pending a decision on admissibility (which can take up to eighteen months), the Committee may transmit an urgent request to a State for the suspension of a death sentence. Interim measures are, of course, not legally binding on the State.

The Committee has no independent fact finding functions. However, in serious cases (e.g. concerning the right to life, torture, arbitrary arrests, etc), it has adopted the practice of spreading the burden of proof so it is not on the author of the communication alone. In such cases there is thus an onus on the State Party concerned to respond in full to the complaint raised against it. The Committee issues a consensus opinion though individual opinions on the merits may be added if members of the Committee so desire. Like other human rights monitoring bodies, the workload of the Committee has increased considerably—at present there are some 316 cases pending.

Any expressed opinion of the Committee carries with it a normative obligation for States to provide necessary remedies to the author of the communication. This will often mean a change in national law or policy. Since 1990, the Human Rights Committee has monitored State reaction to decisions taken by it. With full cooperation of the State, the Committee will thus seek to verify that the State has remedied the deficiency in law or practice which has been found. To date, the State against which most violations have been found is Jamaica whose subsequent denunciation of the Optional Protocol, though technically legal, is morally questionable and goes somewhat against the idea of effective implementation as envisaged in the International Bill of Rights. Moreover, it sets a dangerous precedent. For the record, Uruguay has the second highest number of confirmed violations (forty-five) though most of them are clustered in the formative years of the Committee's work. There are no cases pending against Uruguay.

5.8.2.4 *General comments*

Article 40(4) of the Covenant authorizes the Committee to adopt 'such general comments as it may consider appropriate'. The nature and scope of these general comments have evolved over the years. General Comments have provided information on the internal procedures adopted by the Committee, issued guidelines to States on completing periodic reports, and have addressed specific provisions of the Covenant, providing guidance on interpretation thereof.

5.8.2.5 *Conclusions*

With over 1,000 individual communications concluded and hundreds of State reports received and considered, the Committee 'has transformed what was a novel and in some ways radical mandate into one that now appears conventional' (Steiner, H, p18).

5.8.3 **Committee on Economic, Social and Cultural Rights**

The first meeting of the Committee on Economic, Social and Cultural Rights was in 1987. Unlike the other Committees, it was not established by its corresponding treaty—the International Covenant on Economic, Social and Cultural Rights 1966. Rather it was established in 1985 by the Economic and Social Council to assist it in monitoring the implementation of the Covenant 'following the less than ideal performance of two previous bodies entrusted with monitoring the Covenant' (*Fact Sheet No 16 (Rev 1)*, p 19). The Committee consists of eighteen members elected by ECOSOC in their private capacity for terms of four years. Elections are staggered every two years. As with other such Committees, the meetings are held in Geneva.

5.8.3.1 *Reports*

The primary function of the Committee is to monitor the implementation of the Covenant by Contracting States. Initial reports are submitted within one year of the entry into force of the Covenant for the State concerned. Given the progressive nature of the realization of rights under the Covenant, the reports should indicate 'factors and difficulties affecting the degree of fulfilment of obligations under the present Covenant' (Art 17(2)). Cross references to information submitted to other United Nations bodies is acceptable. Reports are submitted to the Secretary General who transmits copies to the Economic and Social Council and, where appropriate, to specialized agencies of the United Nations. After the initial report, a system of periodic reports is employed. The Covenant is to be achieved 'progressively' (Art 2(1)) thus the periodic reports are required to detail progress made in achieving the observance of the articulated rights (Art 16(1)) as well as indicating factors and difficulties affecting fulfilment of obligations under the Covenant. Reports are also filed by specialized agencies with competence in relevant matters. In order to assist States in realizing the goals specified in the Covenant, the monitoring bodies may bring to the attention of other organs of the United Nations, subsidiary organs and specialized agencies concerned with furnishing technical assistance any matters arising out of the reports. This enables such bodies to decide on the advisability of international measures which may contribute towards the effective progressive implementation of the Covenant (Art 22). The Committee has drawn up detailed reporting guidelines to assist States preparing periodic reports.

The first General Comment of the Committee (1989) highlighted the advantages of the reports system for monitoring the implementation of the Covenant. States may attend the salient Committee session, answering questions and clarifying issues at that time. Upon completion of examination, the Committee issues its concluding observations and recommendations. Despite the flexible nature of this Covenant, violations can occur. When problems with overdue reports are experienced, it is the habit of the Committee, after due notice to the State Party concerned, to consider the economic, social, and cultural rights in the State on the basis of all the information available to them. This is inevitably a good opportunity for NGOs to inform debate. The practice of considering the human rights situation in any given State in the absence of an overdue report is gaining ground in international and regional organizations. Some States will attend sessions to defend against any circumstantial or uncorroborated evidence on their human rights situation. This allows the Committee to obtain a more balanced viewpoint.

5.8.3.2 *General discussion days*

The Committee on Economic Social and Cultural Rights designates one day per session as a General Discussion day (for example, on the right to education or the effective implementation of the Covenant). Special Rapporteurs, NGOs, specialized United Nations agencies, and others may contribute towards these debates on particular provisions of the Convention, themes, or rights. Sometimes, these discussions will pave the way for the issuing of a General Comment on a particular aspect of the Covenant. The success of these days has prompted suggestions for adoption of such a practice by all monitoring bodies. However, inevitably time is the greatest constraint.

5.8.3.3 *Field trips*

Provision is made for the Committee to visit States for *in situ* investigations and information gathering. The Committee requests an invitation from the State before it will undertake a visit thereby acknowledging the sovereignty and territorial integrity of the State concerned. In the absence of an invitation, no visit will take place. The first mission undertaken by the Committee was to Panama in 1995.

5.8.3.4 *Individual petitions*

The preparation of an Optional Protocol to the Covenant which will enable the Committee to receive individual complaints is ongoing. The Optional Protocol was approved by the General Assembly in December 2008. It will be opened for signature in September 2009 and obviously will enter into force for those States concerned once sufficient ratifications are secured. This is an interesting development and completes monitoring for individual violations of the Universal Declaration (albeit still subject to ratifications).

5.8.4 **Committee against Torture**

The Committee against Torture commenced duties on 1 January 1988 following the entry into force of the Convention against Torture 1984 on 26 January 1987. The Committee consists of 'ten experts of high moral standing and recognised competence in the field of human rights, who shall serve in their personal capacity' (Art 17). Members serve for four years with half the membership being subject to renewal every two years. The Committee meets twice a year in Geneva with secretariat services provided by the United Nations Office of the High Commissioner for Human Rights. The Committee has broad powers of examination and investigation in an attempt to ensure the effectiveness of the Convention in practice.

There are various ways in which the Committee operates including periodic reports, individual complaints, and investigation.

5.8.4.1 *Reports*

The Committee considers periodic reports from High Contracting States which are submitted every four years (Art 19). To improve this process, it has issued general guidelines to States on the completion of reports. States under consideration by the Committee may attend the session at which their report is considered and may clarify issues raised by the Committee. General comments on the report will then be made to which the State may respond.

5.8.4.2 *Inter-State complaints*

Inter-State complaints may be raised before the Committee if both the States concerned have recognized the competence of the Committee in this respect under Article 21. The States must first attempt to resolve the matter between themselves, failing which either State may elect to refer the issue to the Committee. The Committee will attempt to help the States arrive at a friendly settlement whilst drawing up its own version of the facts as found. Should there be a failure to reach a friendly settlement, the Committee will submit a report to those States with comments and suggestions.

5.8.4.3 *Individual complaints*

Individual complaints may also be raised before the Committee against States which have agreed to the procedure articulated in Art 22. There are currently sixty-four states which have acceded to the individual complaint machinery, including some of the permanent members of the Security Council, France and Russia. Complaints are lodged by the claimant victim or, if this is not possible, by relatives or representatives. The State Party against whom the complaint is made is asked to submit written observations within six months. Consideration of individual communications is held in closed meetings. As with other treaty-monitoring bodies, individuals must first exhaust all local remedies (though this requirement is waived where the application of remedies is unreasonably prolonged or is unlikely to bring effective relief to the victim (Art 22(5)(b)). Due to the nature of any violation of the Convention, the Committee may also seek guarantees against irreparable damage to the alleged victim for the duration of the investigation. This form of provisional protection is unusual in international law but some kind of maintenance of the status quo is clearly essential when torture is under consideration. (The process is more formal than that employed by the Human Rights Committee, perhaps more akin to the work of the International Court of Justice and the International Criminal Tribunals.) The final recommendations and conclusions of the Committee are transmitted to the State for observations before the final view is adopted.

So far, the Committee has dealt with over 300 individual complaints against a number of countries. States that have been found to have infringed the Convention include Australia, Austria, France, the Netherlands, Spain, Sweden, Switzerland, Tunisia, and Venezuela. The Eurocentricity of violations is interesting, especially given the almost concurrent jurisdiction of the Council of Europe with its Committee Against Torture in this respect. The geographical spread of violations reflects that of the States which have accepted the Committee's competence. Indeed the countries with the highest number of complaints are Sweden, Switzerland, Canada, France, Australia, and the Netherlands, together accounting for over 80 per cent of communications.

5.8.4.4 *Investigations*

The investigatory powers of the Committee are enshrined in Art 20. The investigatory powers distinguish the Committee against Torture from other United Nations Committees which have little power of initiation of actions. It is a reflection of the seriousness with which torture is viewed by the international community that the Convention enables this. If the Committee receives reliable information indicating that systematic torture is occurring in any given State, then the Committee may invite the State to cooperate in an investigation thereof. The procedure is dependent on State cooperation and may include a visit to the State concerned. Such proceedings are confidential though the Committee and State may agree to include a summary of findings in the Committee's annual report. Although this is a significant power, the major limitation is the need for State acquiescence. It is perhaps questionable how much benefit accrues from a report into serious violations of torture with appropriate recommendations and suggestions which is submitted confidentially to a State. Yet, the gravity of a request for a visit should hopefully spur a State into reconciling its actions with prevailing international standards. The eradication of the practice of torture was one of the major challenges undertaken by the United Nations. It has certainly had some success. However, the comparatively low participation in the individual complaint process has hindered the impact of the Committee. This is balanced by the use of technical support for States identified through the periodic reports. Provision of training of police, for example, helps to minimize infringements of the Convention by reinforcing what treatment is and is not compatible. With torture, more than some other rights and freedoms, prevention is better than cure.

5.8.4.5 *Optional Protocol*

An Optional Protocol to the Convention providing for 'a system of regular visits undertaken by independent international and national bodies to places where people are deprived of their liberty, in order to prevent torture and other cruel, in human or degrading treatment or punishment' (Art 1) entered into force on 22 June 2006. A Sub-committee on Prevention is established to visit places of detention, advise States, facilitate necessary training, make recommendations, and cooperate with the United Nations mechanisms to strengthen the protection of persons deprived of their liberty (Art 11). All States ratifying the Protocol agree to accept Sub-committee delegations to their territory and agree to grant the Sub-committee access to detention centres. They also agree to enter into constructive dialogue on implementing the recommendations of the Sub-committee (Art 12). The forty-eight States currently accepting this mechanism include Albania, Costa Rica, Denmark, Honduras, Liberia, Mauritius, Serbia, the United Kingdom, and Uruguay. The potential impact of this new power is significant as the work of the European Committee for the Prevention of Torture (discussed Chapter 14) demonstrates.

5.8.5 **Committee on the Elimination of Racial Discrimination**

Article 8 of the International Convention on the Elimination of All Forms of Racial Discrimination 1966 established a Committee on the Elimination of Racial Discrimination (CERD) to oversee the enforcement of the terms of the Convention. This was the first body created by the United Nations to monitor and review State compliance with a specific set of treaty obligations. Like many such Committees, CERD now meets in Geneva and is supported by a secretariat provided by the United Nations Office of the High Commissioner for Human Rights.

CERD comprises eighteen 'experts of high moral standing and acknowledged impartiality' (Art 8(1)). This expert panel plays a very important role in the implementation of the Convention. Members are elected for four years with a staggered election of half the membership every two years. As with many United Nations appointments, the membership of CERD should reflect 'equitable geographical distribution and … representation of the different forms of civilisation as well as of the principal legal systems'. Each State nominates one person, a secret ballot of all Contracting States determining the final composition of the Committee. Of course, the CERD is an autonomous body.

Four procedures are used to oversee the Convention's application: reports, inter-States complaints, individual communications, and the examination of petitions from non-self-governing and trust territories.

5.8.5.1 *Reports*

In terms of Art 9 of the Convention, High Contracting States undertake to submit to the Secretary-General of the United Nations (for communication to the Committee) a report on the legislative, judicial, administrative, and other measures taken by the State to give effect to the Convention's provisions. These reports are submitted within one year of the entry into force of the Convention, thereafter every two years and as requested by the Committee. The only action upon these reports which may be taken by the Committee is the making of suggestions and recommendations to the State Parties and the referral of matters to the General Assembly.

The Committee does, however, possess (and exercise) powers to request informa-tion from the State concerned. The Committee is funded privately though little attempt is made to seek back payments from defaulting States.

5.8.5.2 *Inter-State complaints*

The Convention also provides for a compulsory inter-State complaints procedure by which States may raise issues relating to the compliance of other States with the Convention (Arts 11–13). Such provision for inter-State complaints is reasonably uncontroversial in the sphere of international relations—States are rarely willing to instigate an action against another State on the international stage. After a full investigation of the matter, a report is produced for transmission to the State Party concerned and to the Secretary-General of the United Nations.

5.8.5.3 *Individual complaints*

The optional individual complaint process forms an integral part of the Conven-tion as it is enshrined in Art 14 of the Convention, rather than in an Optional Pro-tocol. This perhaps should have made it more attractive to States. Still, out of 173 State Parties, some 53 have recognized the competence of the Committee to receive and process individual communications. Consenting States include Australia, the Russian Federation, Peru, Chile, Bulgaria, and Algeria but not the United Kingdom, People's Republic of China, New Zealand, or the United States of America.

The first-ever communication deemed admissible was against the Netherlands (*Yilmaz-Dogan v Netherlands*). Since then, the Committee has considered communica-tions against Australia, Denmark, France, the Netherlands, Norway, Slovakia, and Swe-den. Only five violations have been upheld (Denmark twice, the Netherlands twice, and Slovakia). In total, only twenty-eight individual complaints have been received.

The Convention does provide that States may nominate (or create *ab initio*) an independent body for the review of individual complaints at the national level prior to the matter being brought before CERD. In such a situation, individuals would have to exhaust domestic remedies and then be considered by the national body before approaching CERD. Although this may appear unduly restrictive on the alleged victim, such a system should encourage States to participate. Due to the consen-sual nature of international law, any initiative that encourages participation should be welcomed. By bringing more States within the ambit of the Convention, the potential for its success increases: more States endorse the views encapsulated in the Convention, thus more of the world's population benefits from the protection the Convention offers. In the Programme of Action adopted by the Second World Conference to Combat Racism and Racial Discrimination 1993, States were encour-aged to create appropriate accessible national bodies for considering complaints at the national level. The hope was expressed that such a body would be open to all with legal aid available when necessary. In general, the Committee receives few indi-vidual reports compared with similar procedures before other Committees.

5.8.5.4 *Examination of petitions and reports from non-self-governing and trust territories in furtherance of the objectives of the Declaration on the Granting of Independence to Colonial Countries and Peoples (Art 15)*

In contrast with the optional individual procedure, the provisions relating to the receiving of individual petitions from United Nations' bodies and inhabitants of trust and non-self-governing bodies are mandatory (Art 15). Naturally, these latter provisions are aimed at securing the fulfilment of the United Nations' objectives in respect of decolonization. CERD gives opinions and makes recommendations on individual and group petitions from these territories as well as giving recommendations on reports from other United Nations bodies on combating racial discrimination in these territories.

The Committee is now operating in a new era, applying the Convention to 'circumstances that were not contemplated in the drafting process', with success dependant on its ability to strictly apply the definition of racial discrimination in the Convention itself to situations and conflicts rather than being drawn into characterization of conflicts as ethnic or political (Banton, M, p 78). The 2001 World Conference on Racism demonstrated how emotive racial discrimination remains for millions of people today.

5.8.6 Committee on the Elimination of Discrimination against Women

Equality of rights between men and women was proclaimed in the Charter of the United Nations. The realization of this is partly devolved to the Committee of the Convention on the Elimination of Discrimination against Women. The Committee began work in 1982 following the entry into force of the Convention on the Elimination of All Forms of Discrimination against Women 1979. The Convention is one of the more widely ratified in the United Nations system (186 State Parties as of May 2009, surpassed only by the Convention on the Rights of the Child). However, its provisions have also been subject to considerable numbers of declarations and reservations. This not only undermines its effectiveness but also has repercussions for the Committee in its work. The Committee is established under Art 17 of the Convention. It consisted of originally eighteen experts, though since attracting thirty-five State Parties, there have been twenty-three experts. Members are elected by secret ballot from nominations by State Parties. In general, unlike other United Nations Committees, the membership of this Committee has almost exclusively been female—Mr Johan Nordenfelt, the first male member, served in the initial sessions. The members of the Committee serve terms of four years and, of course, the elections are staggered. In terms of the Convention, the Committee meets for not more than two weeks annually (Art 20). This is unlike other Committees which have no maximum length of time imposed. With the explosion in United Nations Member States and, accordingly, ratifications of the Convention, it proved increasingly difficult for the Committee to carry out their work in a mere fortnight. Interim exceptional measures, adopted by the General Assembly, facilitate longer and more regular periods of meetings. An amendment to Art 20 will obviate these time restrictions pending ratification by two-thirds of the contracting parties. It was adopted in 1995 but States are somewhat recalcitrant in ratifying it. In the meantime, the Committee meets for around two three week periods, though the General Assembly (A/RES/62/218) has authorized the committee to meet for three three-week sessions from 2010, as an interim measure pending ratification of Art 20. The annual report of the Committee is fed through ECOSOC to the General Assembly. The Division for the Advancement of Women services the Committee which, unlike other treaty-monitoring bodies, does not meet in Geneva. The Committee used to alternate between Vienna and New York but now is based solely in New York. There have been numerous calls for the Committee to meet in Geneva and thus be in a position to interact more freely with the other treaty-monitoring bodies. While this may assist in raising the profile of the Committee, the principal problem lies with the servicing requirements. Tying the Committee to the Division for the Advancement of Women, whilst undoubtedly consolidating the United Nations approach to women's issues by drawing together the relevant bodies thereby highlighting the importance placed by the United Nations on it, undoubtedly has had a negative impact on the profile and even some aspects of the workings of the Committee.

5.8.6.1 *Reports*

State Parties to the Convention agree to submit periodic reports every four years on the 'legislative, judicial, administrative or other measures which they have adopted' to give effect to the Convention (Art 18). The Division for Advancement of Women offers training courses for government officials involved in compiling these reports. It is hoped that this will help render the reports more relevant and useful. States are encouraged to highlight factors and difficulties affecting the degree of fulfilment of the obligations adopted under the Convention. Appropriate assistance may thus be provided to the State in question. The Committee has requested reports be split into background information on the political, legal, and social situation of the State and more detailed specification of the steps taken to realize the goals of the Convention. The Committee will make general observations on the report and any reservations the State has on the Convention. In a spirit of 'constructive dialogue' the Committee will then invite the State to discuss particular Articles of the Convention before the Committee draws up its concluding observations. The final report is usually positive, drawing on the strengths of the State's performance while indicating areas which should be focused on in the next periodic report, providing, as appropriate, practical guidance on the implementation of the Convention.

5.8.6.2 *General recommendations*

The Convention also provides that the Committee can make general recommendations and suggestions (Art 21). These should be based on the reports received from States and its examination of this information. After a weak start, the Committee has decided to copy its fellow treaty-monitoring bodies (CERD, Human Rights Committee, etc) and has drawn up a work programme under which it will examine substantive areas of the Convention on a regular basis. This should contribute considerably towards clarification and interpretation of the provisions of the Convention.

5.8.6.3 *Individual complaints*

Following the recommendation in the 1993 Vienna Declaration and Programme of Action, an Optional Protocol to the Convention on the Elimination of all forms of Discrimination against Women was adopted in 1999. This Protocol seeks to provide for the receipt and consideration of individual communications by the Committee. Concurrent with the Protocol, women have the option of complaining to the Commission on the Status of Women about instances of discrimination. Although the Commission cannot take action on the basis of such a complaint, the information is used as the Commission is charged with discerning trends and patterns of discrimination against women. This information may help shape future policies. For the victim, it may be better to use this avenue rather than meekly accept the State action. NGOs often report to the Commission on relevant matters. There are ninety-seven states party.

The Protocol goes further enabling the Committee to investigate any instances of 'grave or systematic violations by a State Party of rights set forth in the Convention' (Art 8). As with the Committee against Torture, the Committee will cooperate with the State Party in investigating the matter: all available information on the situation will be gathered; inquiries will be undertaken and a report will be submitted urgently to the Committee. With the consent of the State Party, the inquiry process may include a visit to the territory. Such inquiries are conducted in private and, at all times, with the cooperation of the State concerned. The State Party will be invited to address the issues raised in observations to the Committee within a six-month period. States ratifying the Protocol may opt out of the provisions granting the Committee the power to investigate systematic violations of the Convention, consenting only to the proposed system of individual complaints. The Committee considered its first merits communication in 2005 (*A-T v Hungary*). Since then a handful of opinions have been issued.

5.8.6.4 *Grave and systematic violations*

Article 8 of the Optional Protocol enables enquiries to be undertaken if reliable evidence of grave and systematic violations of human rights in any ratifying State is received. The Committee will enter discussions with the State and may undertake a visit; the first enquiry was conducted in Mexico in July 2004 (UN DOC CEDAW/C/2005/OP.8/MEXICO).

Discussion topic

Individual communications to UN Treaty bodies

As of July 2009, four treaty-monitoring bodies have considered individual communications: Committee on the Elimination of Racial Discrimination (CERD); Human Rights Committee (HRC); Committee on the Elimination of Discrimination Against Women (CEDAW); and the Committee Against Torture (CAT). The numbers of violations found are as follows: CERD 10; HRC 480; CEDAW 4; and CAT 45. All other communications were either inadmissible, discontinued, or provided insufficient evidence for a violation of one or more treaty Article to be found. These numbers are comparatively small when one considers that in the first three months of 2009, the European Court of Human Rights (part of the regional human rights mechanism of the Council of Europe) delivered 563 judgments. While obviously not all States accept the individual complaint mechanisms, the small number of international communications resulting in violations are an interesting statistic, when compared to the (admittedly unworkable) volume of complaints before, for example, the European Court of Human Rights.

5.8.7 **Committee on the Rights of the Child**

One of the most popular initiatives of the United Nations has been its work on children. The Committee on the Rights of the Child first met in 1991, commencing monitoring State compliance with the 1989 Convention on the Rights of the Child in 1993 following receipt of the first State Parties' reports. Article 43 of the Convention constitutes a Committee on the Rights of the Child comprising 'ten experts of high moral standing and recognised competence in the field covered by [the] Convention'. Members serve terms of four years, with five being elected every two years. The Committee is required to meet annually but, given the almost universal ratification of the Convention (193 State Parties, including all United Nations' Member States bar the United States of America and Somalia who have signed but not ratified it), the Committee requested an increase in its meetings. The State Parties and General Assembly approved, thus since 1995 the Committee has met for three three-week sessions each year.

5.8.7.1 *Reports*

The Convention on the Rights of the Child is implemented primarily by the reporting system. State Parties undertake to submit reports every five years to the Committee (Art 44). These reports should contain sufficient information to provide the Committee with a 'comprehensive understanding of the implementation of the Convention in the country concerned'. In drafting concluding observations, the best interests of the child (Art 3) and the principle of non-discrimination (Art 2) underpin the realization of the rights. Unlike other reporting systems which have been discussed, the Committee on the Rights of the Child requires that governments publish the reports within their jurisdiction and disseminate the observations of the Committee. The approach taken by the Committee is one of consolidation—the Committee views itself as working alongside developing internal State systems for monitoring and realizing children's rights. The 'comprehensive national approach' adopted by the Committee on the Rights of the Child is to be encouraged according to para 89 of the Vienna Declaration and Programme of Action.

Due to the diverse range of rights enshrined in the Convention, the Committee has a unique position in the United Nations system. It is effectively applying the full myriad of international human rights, civil and political, economic, social and cultural, albeit only to a limited sector of the population. Given the almost universal nature of the Convention, this puts the Committee in a privileged position. Assuming reports are submitted timeously, taking the reports in conjunction with the additional information on each State obtained in pre-sessional meetings from NGOs and specialized agencies allows the Committee to build up what should be a full and accurate picture of the human rights situation in almost every member State of the United Nations.

5.8.8 **Migrant Workers Committee**

The General Assembly adopted the International Convention on the Protection of the Rights of all Migrant Workers and Members of their Families in 1990. It currently has forty-one State Parties, entering into force on 1 July 2003. Article 72 of the Convention provides for the establishment of a Committee on the Protection of the Rights of All Migrant Workers and Members of Their Families with ten expert members (rising to thirty when forty-one States ratify). The Committee, which held its first meeting in March 2004, receives and considers State reports on the implementation of the Convention rights within their jurisdiction. The first report (Mali) was considered in 2006. Following initial reports, States should submit reports every five years (Art 73). An optional system of inter-State complaints and individual communications is envisaged in Arts 76–7, but awaits the necessary ten ratifications. Progress on ratification of the Convention was (and is) slow, although the Programme of Action concluded by the World Conference Against Racism 2001 called for States to legislate for the protection of migrant workers.

5.8.9 Committee on the Rights of Persons with Disabilities

The newest treaty-monitoring body is that monitoring the Convention on the Rights of Persons with Disabilities. The Convention entered into force in May 2008 and currently has sixty-two States Party. Article 34 establishes a Committee of twelve members, each serving a renewable term of four years. Membership increases once a sixtieth State ratifies the treaty. The Committee considers State reports, which are submitted on a four-year cycle. Individual communications can also be considered if brought against one of the forty States which, at present have ratified the Optional Protocol to the Convention. The first session of the Committee was held in February 2009, addressing procedural issues. Once initial State reports are submitted, subsequent sessions will begin consideration thereof.

5.9 Others

5.9.1 Truth Commissions

The United Nations has had occasional cause to institute Truth Commissions in countries which have recently been through a period of turmoil. The most high-profile and longest-running Truth Commission is that of South Africa. The United Nations, however, normally sponsors Truth Commissions which last for six months to a year. The objective of these commissions is to ascertain the facts in an open conciliatory atmosphere following the cessation of hostilities. Truth Commissions can be held under a variety of auspices and operate with diverse mandates and methodologies. In the United Nations, this extreme form of fact-finding may be used to identify individuals responsible for gross and systematic violations of human rights within the region concerned. Protection of witnesses is a key consideration. Fact-finding missions such as that preceding the ad hoc International Criminal Tribunal for Rwanda had a judicial goal in mind. Others, such as the United Nations Commission on the Truth for El Salvador 'sought closure' for the region after a prolonged period (twelve years) of violence and unrest. The people wished to deal with the past then move on to the future with a clean slate. In the Americas, other truth-establishing fact-finding missions were undertaken by the Organization of American States. Guatemala, Chile, and Haiti, for example, hosted similar fact-finding missions after peace was established.

In general, Truth Commissions seek to establish facts. They rarely have criminal jurisdiction, though criminal liability may well arise out the established facts and the salient authorities may pursue legal action at a later date. The Sierra Leone Truth and Reconciliation Commission is expected to focus more on the suffering during the civil war than will the Special Court established to adjudicate on the crimes against humanity committed during that period. (Obviously the International Criminal Tribunals for Rwanda and the former Yugoslavia have dual functions.) An emerging body of academic writing considers truth and reconciliation as having significant roles in nation-rebuilding and human rights promotion (eg, see Clark and Kaufman).

5.10 Conclusions

Problems associated with implementing human rights instruments are considered in more detail in Chapter 10. Focusing solely on the United Nations, one of the main problems is its ad hoc organization. A variety of Committees receive reports from the same States, often at the same time. States who do not sign instruments at the time of opening for signature often accede en masse. This can be unduly oner-ous. As universal human rights have developed with the increasing codification of standards in international instruments, more and more sub-organs have been created. This can cause confusion—for example several of the treaty-monitoring bodies have, in effect, concurrent jurisdiction.

A recent development has been the advent of regular chairpersons' meetings when the chairs of the various treaty-monitoring bodies meet to discuss areas of com-mon interest and concern. These meetings could pave the way for a consolidated approach to the areas of commonality in implementing universal human rights.

The specialist organizations of the United Nations could have a greater role to play, and could be more integrated into the process. They are invited to provide oral information to committees before State periodic reports are considered. In some instances this can be beneficial and inform the work of the Committee. This may be particularly so when the specialist organ can provide specific 'on the ground' infor-mation about the human rights situation in any particular State. Given financial constraints, this is not realistic. The Committee on the Elimination of all forms of Discrimination against Women is making progress in this field. Its representatives sit in meetings of the Commission on the Status of Women. Greater use of recog-nized NGO reports could further inform the work of the United Nations bodies involved in human rights, providing detailed information on conditions.

What many fail to appreciate is the financial and personnel constraints which curb the work of the United Nations. Severe financial problems render much of the system almost ephemeral, dependent on the goodwill of committee members and of Member States for continuation. Personnel is another problem—the secretariat available to the various human rights bodies is drastically smaller than an equivalent size of orga-nization in the private sector or even elsewhere in the public sector. It is undoubtedly a tribute to all those involved that the systems manage to function at all.

CASES

A-T v Hungary, Communication 2/2003, Decision January 2005.
Bosnia-Herzegovina v Yugoslavia (provisional measures), 1993 ICJ Reps, p 24.
Bosnia-Herzegovina v Serbia and Montenegro (merits), 27 February 2007, ICJ (online).

Georgia v Russian Federation, (2008) ICJ (online).

Reservations to the Genocide Convention Case, 1951 ICJ Reps 15.

Yilmaz-Dogan v the Netherlands, UN Doc CERD/C/36/D/1/1984 (1988).

READING

Alfredsson, G, Grimheden, J, Ramcharan, B, andde Zayas, A (eds), *International Human Rights Monitoring Mechanisms: Essays in honour of Jakob Th Möller*, 2nd edn (Leiden: Martinus Nijhoff Publishers, 2009).

Alston, P, and Crawford, J (eds), *The Future of UN Human Rights Treaty Monitoring* (Cambridge: Cambridge University Press, 2000).

Alston, P, 'Neither fish nor fowl: The quest to define the role of the UN High Commissioner for Human Rights' (1997) 8(2) European Journal of International Law 321–35.

Arambulo, K, *Strengthening the Supervision of the International Covenant on Economic, Social and Cultural Rights: Theoretical and procedural aspects* (Antwerp: Intersentia, 1999).

Aznar-Gómez, MJ, 'A decade of human rights protection by the United Nations Security Council: A sketch of deregulation' (2000) 13(1) European Journal of International Law 223–41.

Bailey, S, *The UN Security Council and Human Rights* (New York: St Martin's Press, 1994).

Banton, M, 'Decision-taking in the Committee on the Elimination of Racial Discrimination' in P Alston and J Crawford (eds), *The Future of UN Human Rights Treaty Monitoring* (Cambridge: Cambridge University Press, 2000) 55–78.

Bayefsky, AF, *The UN Human Rights Treaty System* (New York: Transnational, 2001).

Bedi, S, 'The development of human rights law by the judges of the International Court of Justice' (Oxford: Hart, 2007).

Bijnsdorp, M, 'The strength of the Optional Protocol to the United Nations Women's Convention' (2000) 18(3) Netherlands Quarterly of Human Rights 329–55.

Boekle, H, 'Western States, the UN Commission on Human Rights and the "1235 Procedure": The "question of bias" revisited' (1995) 13 Netherlands Quarterly of Human Rights 367–402.

Boerefijn, I, *The Reporting Procedure under the Covenant on Civil and Political Rights* (Antwerp: Intersentia, 1999).

——, 'Towards a strong system of supervision: The Human Rights Committee's role in reforming the reporting procedure under Article 40 of the Covenant on Civil and Political Rights' (1995) 17(4) Human Rights Quarterly 766–93.

Chapman, A, and Ball, P, 'The truth of Truth Commissions: Comparative lessons from Haiti, South Africa and Guatemala' (2001) 23(1) Human Rights Quarterly 143

Christie, K, *The South Africa Truth Commission* (Basingstoke: Macmillan, 2000).

Clark, P, and Kaufman, Z (eds), *After Genocide: Transitional justice, post-conflict reconstruction and reconciliation in Rwanda and beyond* (London, Hurst & Co Publisher, 2008).

Davidson, S, 'Intention and effect: The legal status of the Final Views of the Human Rights Commission' (2001) New Zealand Law Review 125–44.

Evatt, E, 'Reflecting on the role of international communications in implementing human rights' (1999) 5(2) Australian Journal of Human Rights (www.austlii.edu.au/au/journals/AJHR/1999).

Felice, W, 'The UN Committee on the Elimination of All Forms of Racial Discrimination: Race, and economic and social human rights' (2002) 24(1) Human Rights Quarterly 205–36.

Goldewijk, BK, et al, *Dignity and Human Rights: The implementation of economic, social and cultural rights* (Antwerp: Intersentia, 2002).

Hannum, H (ed), *Guide to International Human Rights Practice*, 4th edn (New York: Transnational, 2004).

Ingelse, C, 'The Committee Against Torture: One step forward, one step back' (2000) 18(3) Netherlands Quarterly of Human Rights 307–27.

Lauren, P. '"To preserve and build on its achievements and to redress its shortcomings": The journey from the Commission on Human Rights to the Human Rights Council' (2007) 29(2) Human Rights Quarterly 346–67.

Martin, I, 'A new frontier: The early experience and future of international human rights field operations' (1998) 16(2) Netherlands Quarterly of Human Rights 121–39.

McGoldrick, D, *The Human Rights Committee* (Oxford: Oxford University Press, 1991).

Nowak, M, *Introduction to the International Human Rights Regime* (Leiden: Brill, 2004).

O'Flaherty, M, *Human Rights and the United Nations: Practice before Treaty Bodies* (The Hague: Kluwer, 2002).

Pritchard, S, 'Breaking the national sound barrier: Communicating with the CERD and CAT Committees' (1999) 5(2) Australian Journal of Human Rights (www.austlii.edu.au/au/journals/AJHR/1999).

Sangster, K, 'Truth Commissions: The usefulness of truth-telling' (1999) 5(1) Australian Journal of Human Rights (www.austlii.edu.au/au/journals/AJHR/1999).

Schabas, W. 'First prosecutions at the International Criminal Court' (2006) 27 Human Rights Law Journal 25–40.

Steiner, H, 'Individual claims in a world of massive violations: What role for the Human Rights Committee' in P Alston and J Crawford (eds), *The Future of UN Human Rights Treaty Monitoring* (Cambridge: Cambridge University Press), pp 15–54.

United Nations, *Fact Sheet No 16 (Rev 1) The Committee on Economic, Social and Cultural Rights* (Office of the High Commissioner for Human Rights: Geneva).

WEBSITES

www.un.org/english—The United Nations.

www.un.org/Docs/sc—Security Council of the United Nations information.

www.icj-cij.org—International Court of Justice.

www.ohchr.org—Office of the United Nations High Commissioner for Human Rights.

www2.ohchr.org/english/bodies/treaty/index.htm—United Nations Treaty Body Database.

www.un.org/ga—General Assembly of the United Nations.

www.un.org/docs/ecosoc—Economic and Social Council information.

www2.ohchr.org/english/bodies/hrcouncil—Human Rights Council.

www2.ohchr.org/english/bodies/chr/index.htm—Commission on Human Rights.

www2.ohchr.org/english/bodies/subcom—Sub-commission on the promotion and protection of human rights.

www.un.org/womenwatch/daw/csw—United Nations Commission on the Status of Women.

www.un.org/womenwatch/daw—Division for the Advancement of Women.

www2.ohchr.org/english/bodies/hrc/index.htm—Human Rights Committee.

www2.orhcr.org/english/bodies/cescr/index.htm—Committee on Economic, Social and Cultural Rights.

www2.ohchr.org/english/bodies/cat/index.htm—Committee against Torture.

www2.ohchr.org/english/bodies/cerd/index.htm—Committee on the Elimination of Racial Discrimination.

www.un.org/womanwatch/daw/cedaw—Committee on the Elimination of Discrimination against Women.

www2.ohchr.org/english/bodies/crc/index.htm—Committee on the Rights of the Child.

www2.ohchr.org/english/bodies/cmw/index.htm—Committee on Migrant Workers.

www.un.org/unrwa—United Nations Palestine Refugee Programme.

www.unmikonline.org—United Nations Mission in Kosovo.

www.un.org/ha—United Nations Humanitarian Affairs.

6

Regional protection of human rights

The international system for protecting human rights is not infallible. There are still numerous violations of human rights, many of which appear to go unchallenged at the international level. Moreover, the international community can take limited action to rectify the failure of any given State to file initial and/or periodic reports. Due to the number of Member States, compromises have had to be made: the pluralistic nature of the world today, in concert with the fundamental requirement of human rights that all peoples should enjoy rights free from discrimination, means that differences in cultures should be celebrated not oppressed. As a consequence, reaching a consensus on the scope and content of more detailed rights is almost inevitably doomed to encounter difficulties with conflicting religious and cultural norms. As has been commented, 'the job or providing such [human] rights is more difficult in an ethnically diverse society than in a more homogenous one' (Walker et al, p 263). Moreover, strengthening the enforcement mechanism will be a challenge to the very (consensual) ethos of international law. The system of human rights developed by the United Nations made no possibility for regional human rights systems. Chapter VIII of the Charter of the United Nations only provided for the development of regional systems aimed at securing the maintenance of peace and security (the Organization for Security and Cooperation in Europe is the first example of such a regional initiative). The first regional human rights developments occurred in Europe under the auspices of the Council of Europe though such schemes were met with some distrust and scepticism by the United Nations. Europe adopted a single legally binding instrument of human rights less than two years after the United Nations General Assembly agreed upon the Universal Declaration of Human Rights, more than fifteen years before the adoption of the International Covenants. Perhaps slightly threatened at the prospect of the universality of human rights being undermined by more enforceable and thus effective regional systems, it was 1977 before the General Assembly publicly acknowledged the benefit of regional rights. General Assembly Resolution 32/127 called on States to consider the establishment of regional machinery for the protection and promotion of human rights. Not all regions answered the call.

The following chapter will explore the principal regional organizations in the world today with an outline of their human rights documentation and enforcement mechanisms. To provide a context, a brief overview of regional systems and the advantages therewith will be provided first.

6.1 **The advantages of regional systems**

There are inevitably many advantages to developing regional systems of human rights. Fewer States will be involved thus political consensus should be more forthcoming on both texts and any monitoring/enforcement machinery. Many regions are also relatively homogeneous with respect to culture, language, and tradition, which has obvious advantages. However, all regional systems remain creatures of international law. They are created by treaties, which may be applied and interpreted in accordance with the Vienna Convention on the Law of Treaties, and function purely because of inter-State consensus. Accordingly, regional systems exist under international law and bear witness to many of the same problems as regards, for example, enforcement.

6.1.1 **Drafting and adopting texts**

Regional arrangements can be easier to draft than their international counterparts. A smaller number of States should mean political accord though this theory does not hold up to scrutiny—the membership of the United Nations was considerably smaller than now at the time of drafting the International Bill of Rights yet agreement on texts was neither swift nor easy. Many regions have common linguistic, religious, and cultural traditions, which facilitates the drafting process: the African Charter seeks to embody a uniquely African concept of human and peoples' rights; the Arab League and the Commonwealth of Independent States are regional systems adopted on the basis of a perceived common heritage. The principal regions which operate human rights systems are relatively homogenous insofar as their States have broadly similar political and cultural histories (admittedly very broad similarities in some instances).

The final texts of regional systems should be easier to administer and disseminate. This presupposes a reasonably developed infrastructure and thus a system less unwieldy than that of the United Nations. In this respect, Europe has proven most successful.

6.1.2 **Accessibility**

Regional systems are, by definition, more accessible. It is infinitely cheaper and easier for Americans to go to Washington DC (the Inter-American Commission on Human Rights) or San José (the Inter-American Court of Human Rights) or for Africans to go to an African State (the African Commission has its Secretariat in Banjul, the Gambia, but rotates its meetings throughout the region) than it is for them to participate in United Nations events at Geneva. Obviously Europeans have an advantage as their region is home to both Council of Europe and United Nations mechanisms.

Geographical accessibility is an important factor. In the Americas, the benefit of the Internet revolution has been harnessed with an established procedure for the online submission of complaints to the Commission. (Naturally, this presupposes the existence of the necessary technological infrastructure.) In Africa, the benefit of rotating meetings throughout the region is sometimes outweighed by problems with transport infrastructure. However, at least as many Africans as possible have the opportunity of attending the public sessions of the Commission in a city/State near them. This is a unique approach which, in principle, embodies the very essence of geographical accessibility.

Linguistic accessibility is another potential benefit. Most regional systems publish texts and, where appropriate, receive communications in all the major languages of the region. In contrast, the United Nations has a more limited range of official languages although, as noted, the Universal Declaration of Human Rights is the most widely translated document in the world. For individuals seeking to enforce their rights against States, either domestically or at the regional or international level, the linguistic accessibility of relevant texts, decisions and declarations is crucial. It is, however, conceded that sometimes dissemination in general rather than dissemination in an appropriate language is the main problem to be surmounted.

Greater familiarity with the States involved can produce a more successful system at the implementation stage, too. States may be more willing to accept comments from their regional colleagues than from the international community at large. However, often diplomacy can be a double-edged sword; excessive employment of diplomatic niceties almost rendered the effectiveness of the African system non-existent. In general, commissioners and judges considering State reports and complaints against States at the regional level are more familiar with the issues at stake and the economic and political restraints under which a State operates. The United Nations has highly experienced and qualified Committee members but the ratio of Committee members to State members is considerably greater. Consequently, 'local' specialized knowledge may be lacking.

6.1.3 **Enforceability**

Regional systems can be easier to enforce than international systems. There may be a greater political will to conform to regional texts as they are sometimes seen as being of more immediate concern than the international initiatives. Diplomatic efforts may be more successful when pressure is applied by neighbouring States rather than States from more distant regions. Similarly, there will always be more of an incentive with respect to implementation of decisions of regional bodies. Regional sanctions can be a very real threat though obviously this raises other issues under international law. In the ideal world (probably not this one), regional systems should be mutually supportive and thus solutions to problematic or difficult situations should be more forthcoming.

Clearly, the lack of willingness on the part of States to bring inter-State complaints under international law is amplified at the regional level. In 1978, Ireland became the first State to bring an inter-State complaint (against the United Kingdom) before a regional court for adjudication.

6.2 **The principal regional systems**

There are three main regional systems that aim to protect and promote human rights: the Council of Europe; the Organization of American States; and the Organization of African Unity/the African Union. Of these, Europe has the oldest and most developed system with an established judicial mechanism for

Key case

Inter-State complaints before regional human rights bodies

Ireland v United Kingdom (1978) Series A, No 25 (ECHR)
Ireland instituted proceedings against the United Kingdom concerning a period of violence and alleged terrorist activity involving various groups on the island. Northern Ireland (part of the UK) had imposed a system of internment (detention without trial) and evidence has been amassed of various interrogation techniques (now known as the 'five techniques') being deployed by British forces against detainees. The European Court found that the UK had violated the right to liberty but that the violations were justified due to the prevailing political and security situation which caused the UK to derogate from the salient Article. More controversially, the Court found that the interrogation techniques were inhuman and degrading treatment but fell short of the threshold to constitute torture.

Cyprus v Turkey (2001) ECHR, Application no 25781/94
A Grand Chamber of the European Court of Human Rights found fourteen violations of the European Convention on Human Rights in respect of the situation pertaining in northern Cyprus following Turkish military action in 1974 and the continuing division of the island's territory. These violations were found against Turkey which was deemed to have responsibility for northern Cyprus under Art 1 of the European Convention. The failure of Turkish authorities to provide information on missing Greek-Cypriots thought to be in/last heard of in northern Cyprus and the failure to conduct appropriate investigations of their whereabouts led to violations of the right to life and the prohibition on arbitrary detention. Greek Cypriots living in northern Cyprus were found to be discriminated against to such an extent it constituted degrading treatment.

Communication 227/1999 *Democratic Republic of Congo v Rwanda, Burundi and Uganda*, African Commission on Human and Peoples' Rights 20th report (EX CL/279(IX)), p112
The Congolese government alleged grave and massive violations of human rights perpetrated by the government forces of Rwanda, Burundi and Uganda in the DR Congo. Thousands of people were claimed to have been massacred and women deliberately infected with AIDS by being systematically raped by soldiers with AIDS. Evidence was led of mass transfers of civilian populations. Trade was adversely affected as well as access to natural resources and essential services (healthcare etc).

  Many Articles of the Charter were deemed infringed. Armed aggression was found to violate the right of the Congolese peoples to self-determination, while the activities of the foreign forces infringed a number of additional rights including the rights life, dignity and physical integrity, freedom of movement, and the right to national and international peace and security. Burundi did not participate but was found to have violated the charter provisions too.

No inter-State proceedings have been instituted in the Americas.

determining complaints brought by individuals. The inter-State and individual complaint processes before the European Court of Human Rights are no longer optional. Overall it has proven an effective judicial organ with a high degree of success in the implementation of its decisions. As a consequence of the compulsory jurisdiction over individuals, it represents the logical progression of the recognition of the individual's rights under international/regional law. However, the Court is still an organism of international law and repeatedly asserts its role as supervisory, the primary responsibility for the implementation of the European Convention remaining with States. The European system is outlined in more detail in Chapter 7.

In the Americas, the Organization of American States has a very long history. Its human rights machinery is not as developed as the European system yet the achievements have been remarkable given the political turmoil in the region until comparatively recently. Promoting democracy has been a priority in the region and, indeed, has been its major success. States of emergency were commonplace thus human rights have often been relegated in importance in response to serious problems of political and economic stability. The Commission has documented a number of gross and systematic violations of human rights over the years, using the information to pressurize the State concerned to redress the situation. Individual communications were not anticipated to be the main concern, their use initially restricted to evidencing gross and systematic violations of rights and freedoms. However, the establishment of the Inter-American Court provided a judicial forum for the determination of individual complaints, further developing the pioneering work of the Commission. More discussion of the American system follows in Chapter 8.

The youngest developed regional system is to be found in Africa. Even more than the Americas, Africa has a recent history of oppressive regimes and serious systematic violations of human rights. Against such a violent and often undemocratic background, attempts to consolidate human rights should perhaps have been doomed to failure. However, the African system has succeeded in developing a coherent regional system for the protection of human rights. The Commission has received a number of complaints, particularly, in contrast to the other regional systems, channelled through non-governmental organizations (NGOs). Frequently the communications brought before the African Commission concern very grave violations of rights. Decisions have to be made on torture and the right to life, rather than on the intricacies of the right to privacy as deliberated on by the European Court. Nevertheless, not least by its continued existence, the African system has succeeded in raising many issues in public awareness and developing a distinctively African body of human rights materials. The African system will be examined in Chapter 9.

6.3 Other regional initiatives

The Council of Europe, the Organization of American States and the Organization of African Unity/African Union provide the only effective regional systems for promoting and protecting human rights. However, other regional, transnational, and non-aligned groupings of States have chosen to demonstrate their commitment to universal human rights by adopting instruments enshrining the rights they profess to respect. None of these instruments are yet supported by effective implementation machinery.

6.3.1 **The Arab League**

The League of Arab States was established in March 1945, inter alia, to control the execution of agreements concluded by Member States, further strengthen relations between them, and to generally supervise the affairs and interests of Arab countries (Art 1, the Alexandria Protocol establishing the League, Shawwal 20th 1363 (7/10/44)). From seven founding States (Jordan, Saudi Arabia, Iraq, Syria, the Lebanon, Egypt, and Yemen), it has grown to twenty-two members including most Arab States in the Middle East and Northern Africa. In 1994, the governments of the Member States of the League of Arab States adopted the Arab Charter on Human Rights though no ratifications followed. The Charter sought to articulate human rights in a manner which reflects the historical Islamic Shari'a law and other religious laws, believed to be divinely revealed, common to most of the Member States. It reaffirmed the principles enshrined in the Cairo Declaration on Human Rights in Islam. Like the African Charter, there was an emphasis on condemning foreign occupation and colonization, issues which have been problematic to many Arab States.

As the Charter proved ultimately unsuccessful as a human rights mechanism—ie, it did not attract ratifications—talks began on modernizing the Charter. The revised version was adopted by the Summit of Arab States in May 2004 and has already entered into force. Civil, cultural, economic, political and social rights are included and, reflecting modern human rights, protection for those with a disability (Art 40) is also explicitly included. Many of the provisions reflect the principal international instruments although commentators have raised concerns over the actual wording of some of the substantive rights (eg, Rishmawi, pp 371–6). Although, unlike the other regional systems, no mechanism for reviewing individual complaints is envisaged, there is a monitoring system: Art 45 creates an 'Arab Human Rights Committee' which will receive and consider State reports (Art 48). Reports will be submitted a year after ratification, then every three years, ensuring the potential for a comprehensive review mechanism when operational. Rishmawi considers that the Charter represents the 'best opportunity in a generation to advance protection and promotion [of human rights] in the region' (p 376). Whether it achieves that goal remains to be seen. As with any new system, there may be a period of settlement, before the impact can be accurately assessed.

6.3.2 **The Commonwealth of Independent States**

Following the dissolution of the Soviet Union, in December 1991 a number of the newly independent States agreed to form the Commonwealth of Independent States (CIS). It presently comprises twelve former soviet republics. Political impetus for the CIS States to develop human rights implementation machinery is compounded by aspirations to membership of the Council of Europe (mostly now achieved) and the European Community. Accordingly, the CIS adopted a Convention on Human Rights and Fundamental Freedoms in 1995. The initiatives of the United Nations and the Organization for Security and Cooperation in Europe are recognized in the preambular paragraphs as is the Declaration of the Heads of Participating States of the CIS on international obligations in the field of human rights. Many of the rights contained in the Convention are similar to those of the European Convention adopted under the auspices of the Council of Europe. However, there are a number of differences in the detail. For example, Art 6 of the CIS Convention explicitly provides that an accused should not be forced to testify against himself or plead guilty, a minority clause similar to Art 27 of the International Covenant on Civil and Political Rights is included, and the freedom from forced or compulsory labour explicitly excludes the fulfilment by parents of their duty to create the necessary conditions for their children and, by children above the age of majority, the duty to support parents who require assistance (Art 4(3)(e)). The CIS Convention, moreover, goes considerably further than its European counterpart in articulating a variety of economic and social rights including the right to social security, the right to special protective measures, the right to work, aspects of the right to health, and rights to vocational training.

The CIS created a Human Rights Commission in 1993 by a Decision of the Council of Heads of State of the CIS pursuant to Art 33 of the Statute of the CIS. Art 34 of the Convention gives the duty of enforcing the Convention to the Human Rights Commission. Regulations on the Human Rights Commission were attached. The Commission has a number of members equal to that of contracting parties. There are provisions for inter-State and individual communications. The Commission sits in Minsk.

Following the expression of concern in the Parliamentary Assembly of the Council of Europe over the potential overlap between the Council of Europe and CIS regional mechanisms, the European Court of Human Rights was asked to give an advisory opinion on the matter. On 2 June 2004, the Court delivered its verdict: viz that the question posed by the Committee of Ministers was actually whether the CIS mechanism was 'another procedure of international investigation or settlement' under Art 35 of the European Convention. This was a matter which would be determined if it arose during proceedings and thus was not a matter for a competent advisory opinion. It should be noted that a number of complaints from individuals in the CIS jurisdiction have been brought to the European Court and dealt with in that venue. Given that the CIS mechanism appears not to be fully established and functioning, debate on any potential overlap appears academic.

6.3.3 Asia and the Pacific

The principal omission from this catalogue is Asia and the Pacific. There are proposals for a regional system of human rights protection within Asia but nothing concrete at present. Intra-Asian political and economic support is blossoming beyond the Pan Asian Games with trading developments among South East Asian nations and Asian-Pacific cooperation. The alleged barriers hitherto claimed by the heterogeneity of the region appear to be crumbling. Consensus on a variety of issues is emerging. For example, in 1993, Asian State representatives finalized the Bangkok Declaration on Human Rights which contained the aspirations of the region for the then forthcoming World Summit. More recently (1997), at the behest of the Asian Human Rights Commission and a plethora of NGOs, an Asian Charter on Human Rights was concluded. This instrument calls for all States to establish Human Rights Commissions (para 15.4c) and promotes the notion of developing a regional mechanism which is discussed in more detail below.

Given the geographical breadth of the region, there are inevitably some transnational developments. For example, many States in the region are former colonies of Great Britain and consequently members of the Commonwealth. The meetings of Heads of States of the Commonwealth will sometimes highlight human rights issues. However, the scope of the Commonwealth is considerably wider than just the Asia Pacific region (it has fifty-four members worldwide) and the main thrust of human rights concerns recently has been in Africa (though note the position of Fiji following the coup). The Law Association for Asia and the Pacific (LAWASIA) also seeks to raise the profile of human rights in the region. For example, in October 2001, the Beijing Statement of Principles on the Independence of the Judiciary (1995) was approved in Christchurch.

Throughout the South Pacific, the United Nations can be seen to function at a transnational level though the Pacific Islands Forum seeks to foster political, social, and economic cooperation. Given the vast number of States in the region and the vast difference in economic and political status, the sluggish evolution of regional cohesion is understandable. Achieving agreement between wealthy States such as Japan and Brunei Darussalam and poorer States such as Bangladesh and Kiribati will be problematic. Political ideologies range from Communism in China through to the democracies of Australia and New Zealand. The human rights situation of Mynamar (Burma), Pakistan, and the Democratic Peoples' Republic of Korea, for example, have given rise to international concern but limited regional action.

ⓠ Discussion topic

ASEAN

ASEAN Member states range from Myanmar (Burma) in the north-west to Indonesia in the south-east. The countries are at different stages of development, have different historical backgrounds (eg, colonisation), and have diverse cultural heritages with different predominant religions, languages, and traditions. ASEAN appears to be taking a different approach to human rights protection than other regional bodies, raising interesting issues on the purpose of regional human rights bodies and treaties in an era of near universal ratification of human rights. Electing not to establish (at least initially) a mechanism for individual communications is perhaps shrewd given the problems of backlog and enforcement which beset the existing regional courts.

Persevering with regional human rights systems raises questions on their relevance and role in contemporary society.

6.3.3.1 *Association of South East Asian Nations*

The Association of South East Asian Nations (ASEAN) has made considerable progress in developing a new regional human rights organization. In November 2007, the ASEAN Charter was adopted. It applies to the ten ASEAN members (Brunei Darussalam, Cambodia, Indonesia, Laos, Malaysia, Myanmar, Philippines, Singapore, Thailand, and Vietnam) and is essentially a constitution for the organization although it also notes human rights protection in the region. The Charter entered into force in December 2008 and makes provision, inter alia, for an ASEAN

Human Rights Body to be established (Art 14). At the time of writing (mid 2009) the terms of reference for this body are still in a draft stage. It should be noted that the ASEAN Charter also reinforces respect for territorial integrity and the principle of non-interference in the internal affairs of Member states (Art 2(2)(a) and(e)). It remains to be seen whether this impacts negatively on human rights protection.

Any attempt under the auspices of ASEAN to uphold and maintain principles of international human rights is likely to be welcomed by the international community. Southeast Asia encompasses a diverse range of States at different stages of democratization and 'development' and with varying human rights records. Securing agreement on including human rights in the charter and working towards establishing a human rights body represent considerable achievements.

6.4 Conclusions on regional systems

The regional systems are now part and parcel of the universal system for the protection of human rights and fundamental freedoms, operating under the constraints of international law they cannot take precedence over international human rights. The benefits of the regional systems are manifest: as they operate in harmonious coexistence with the international regime, the individual benefits from enhanced arrangements protecting rights. This, surely, can only be a positive development.

CASES

Ireland v United Kingdom (1978) Series A, No 25 (ECHR).
Decision on the Competency of the Court to give an Advisory Opinion 1, 2/6/2004 (ECHR).

READING

Bauer, J and Bell, D (eds), *The East Asian Challenge for Human Rights* (Cambridge: Cambridge University Press, 1999).

Bielefeldt, H, 'Muslim voices in the human rights debate' (1995) 17(4) Human Rights Quarterly 587–617.

Byre, A, and Byfield, B (eds), *International Human Rights Law in the Commonwealth Caribbean* (Dordecht: Martinus Nijhoff, 1991).

Caballero-Anthony, M, 'The ASEAN Charter: An opportunity missed or one that cannot be missed?' (2008) Southeast Asian Affairs 71–85.

van Dijk, P, and van Hoof, G, *Theory and Practice of the European Convention on Human Rights*, 3rd edn (London: Butterworths, 1998).

Ghai, Y, 'Human rights governance: The Asia debate' (2000) 1(1) Asia-Pacific Journal on Human Rights and the Law 9–52.

Harris, D, and Livingstone, S (eds), *The Inter-American System for Human Rights* (Oxford: Clarendon Press, 1998).

Mayer, A, *Islam and Human Rights: Tradition and Politics*, 3rd edn (Conn: Westview, 1998).

Monshipouri, M, 'The Muslim World half a century after the Universal Declaration of Human

Rights: Progress and obstacles' (1998) 16(3) Netherlands Quarterly of Human Rights 287–314.

Naim, AAA, 'Human rights in the Arab World: A legal perspective' (2001) 23(3) Human Rights Quarterly.

Ramcharan, B, 'Complementarity between universal and regional organizations: Perspectives from the United Nations High Commissioner for Human Rights' (2000) 21(8) Human Rights Law Journal 324–6.

Rishmawi, M, 'The Revised Arab Charter on Human Rights: A step forward?' (2005) 5 Human Rights Law Review 361–6.

Seah, D, 'The ASEAN Charter' (2008) 58 International and Comparative Law Quarterly 197–212.

Umozurike, UO, *The African Charter on Human and Peoples' Rights* (Leiden: Kluwer, 1997).

De Varennes, F, *Asia-Pacific Human Rights Documents and Resources* (The Hague: Kluwer, vol 1, 1998; vol 2, 2000).

Walker, S, and Poe, SC, 'Does cultural diversity affect countries' respect for human rights?' (2002) 24(1) Human Rights Quarterly 237–63.

WEBSITES

www.coe.int—the Council of Europe.

www.oas.org—Organization for American States.

www.africa-union.org—the African Union.

www.arableagueonline.org—League of Arab States (English site being reconstructed).

www.cisstat.com/eng/cis.htm—Commonwealth of Independent States.

www.cis.minsk.by/—Executive Committee of the CIS (in English).

www.aseansec.org – Secretariat of ASEAN.

www.aseanhrmech.org - Working Group for an ASEAN Human Rights Mechanism.

www.forumsec.org.fj—the Pacific Islands Forum.

www.thecommonwealth.org—the Commonwealth Secretariat.

7

Europe

This chapter will examine the regional organizations with jurisdiction over human rights issues in Europe. The primary focus is on the Council of Europe, which has the most developed system of protection for human rights at the regional level. However, cognizance will also be taken of the work of the European Union (European Community) and the Organization for Security and Cooperation in Europe (formerly the Conference for Security and Cooperation in Europe). Both the Council of Europe and the European Union have courts. The Council of Europe created the first international court before which individuals have automatic *locus standi*, while the European Court of Justice (ECJ) is a supranational court with unique jurisdiction. At present, the Organization for Security and Cooperation in Europe remains a political initiative with limited potential for enforcement of human rights. Inevitably there can occasionally be areas of overlap; however, all three bodies tend to interact well. When necessary, the two European courts will cross-refer to each other and thus, by and large, the three organizations coexist to the greater benefit of human rights.

7.1 Council of Europe

Like the United Nations, the Council of Europe was founded in the turbulent period after the cessation of hostilities in the Second World War. Around twenty countries attended the Congress of Europe at The Hague in May 1948 with the goal of exploring options for unification in Europe. Shattered economies needed a focus; the perceived demise of the power of the nation State required a federal response; and the continued security of the region required multinational backing. Among the concluding recommendations were those aimed at developing economic and political integration—ultimately this was addressed by the adoption of various treaties, cumulatively leading to the European Union. The issues regarding defence prompted moves towards founding the Western European Union against the then perceived threat from the East. Perhaps the clearest and most immediate result of the Congress, however, was the impetus for the founding of the Council of Europe.

The Council of Europe was founded in 1949 with ten Member States. By 1989, when Finland acceded, the Council encompassed virtually all of Western Europe. As the Berlin Wall fell and the Iron Curtain disintegrated, the Council of Europe was waiting and ready to expand eastwards. Now, forty-seven countries are members, from Portugal in the west to the Russian Federation in the east: some 800 million people fall within the ambit of the Council. In addition to Member States, there are Observers to the Parliamentary Assembly (Canada, Israel, and Mexico) and Observers to the Committee of Ministers (the Holy See, Japan, and the three North American States—US, Canada, and Mexico). Belarus is currently the only State candidate. All Member States pledge conformity to the rule of law. Accordingly, it is a prerequisite to membership of the Council of Europe that a potential member State actively promotes the enjoyment of human rights and fundamental freedoms within its territory.

7.2 **The development of European human rights protection**

Human Rights were high on the agenda of the new organization. The founding States drew up a convention on human rights and fundamental freedoms which was opened for signature on 4 November 1950, entering into force in September 1953. All Member States of the Council have signed and ratified it. The drafters sought to provide a mechanism for realizing civil and political rights and freedoms as proclaimed in the Universal Declaration on Human Rights. There was remarkable political consensus on this initiative facilitating the speedy adoption of the text. In terms of the Preamble:

The Governments signatory [thereto], being Members of the Council of Europe, … Being resolved, as the governments of European Countries which are like-minded and have a common heritage of political traditions, ideals, freedom and the rule of law to take the first steps for the collective enforcement of certain of the rights stated in the Universal Declaration, Have agreed as follows.

From this initial starting point, the Council of Europe has developed one of the most advanced systems for the protection of human rights anywhere in the world. According to the Court's official statistics, 1,881 judgments were delivered in 2008 and 30,163 judicial decisions (on, eg, admissibility). Of the judgments, a majority concerned the conduct of judicial proceedings. The Council of Europe system has a refined enforcement mechanism and is very effective with almost all States taking the necessary remedial action to conform to the Convention as interpreted and applied by the Court. For the reasons already discussed, human rights protection will almost inevitably be easier to enforce at the regional rather than international level. However, the European system further benefits from the comparatively minor infringements which make up the bulk of the Court's caseload. There are relatively (as compared to the Organization of American States and the African Union) few instances of flagrant violations of the right to life or freedom from torture as most Member States have established democratic institutional frameworks. This by no means lessens the importance of the system. Rather it further justifies the gulf between the European and other regional systems.

7.3 **The Convention and associated instruments**

7.3.1 **The European Convention on the Protection of Human Rights and Fundamental Freedoms (the European Convention)**

The European Convention is the prime instrument on human rights within Europe. The rights enshrined therein are essentially drawn from the first half of the

Universal Declaration. They are the right to life; freedom from torture and other inhuman, or degrading treatment or punishment; freedom from slavery and forced or compulsory labour; right to liberty and security of person; right to a fair trial; prohibition on retroactive penal legislation; right to private and family life, home and correspondence; freedom of thought, conscience and religion; freedom of expression; freedom of assembly and association; right to marry and found a family; right to an effective remedy for a violation of the rights; and freedom from discrimination in respect of the specific rights and freedoms. With a focus primarily on civil and political rights, the Convention did not greatly expand the Universal Declaration. It did provide considerably more detail on many of the rights and, of course, it articulated a binding legal framework to ensure the realization of those rights. The Convention is the first instrument to provide an effective enforcement mechanism for human rights protection though, in keeping with a strict notion of international law, the Convention envisaged the Court as a supervisory body, hearing cases brought by States against States or referred by the Commission pursuant to its decision on an individual application. The compulsory nature of the individual compulsory mechanism only dates to the entry into force of Protocol 11—November 1998.

The greatest success of the Convention can be attributed in part to the pioneering work of the Commission and Court in developing a fairly detailed jurisprudence on the rights. Teleological and dynamic interpretative techniques have facilitated the evolution of rights and freedoms in concert with changing norms of society. Moreover, the use of devices such as the margin of appreciation contributes to the effectiveness of the system by recognizing the discretion accorded to States in determining the scope of application of some rights and freedoms. This enables States to stamp their own societal norms such as morals and security on the generic rights. For example, in one of the earlier cases, *Handyside v UK*, the European Court acknowledged that there was a margin of appreciation given to both the domestic legislators and the judicial bodies that are called upon to interpret and apply the law. The exercise of the margin of appreciation is not unfettered. It goes hand in hand with European judicial supervision—the European Court is the ultimate arbiter of whether the margin of appreciation has been exceeded by a State.

7.3.2 **The Protocols**

The rights contained in the Convention have been amended and augmented over the years by a series of Protocols. The First Protocol added rights to education and free elections as well as entitlement to peaceful enjoyment of possessions. The Fourth Protocol prohibits imprisonment for debt and adds to the law on liberty by providing for freedom of movement, prohibiting the expulsion of nationals and proscribing the collective expulsion of aliens. The Sixth Protocol concerns the abolition of the death penalty and thus adds to the right to life articulated in Art 2 of the Convention. Protocol 13, in force July 2003, aims at a blanket prohibition on the death penalty, removing the Art 2, Protocol 6, exception of the use of the death penalty in time of war or imminent threat of war. The Seventh Protocol establishes certain procedural safeguards for the expulsion of aliens and addresses certain criminal matters such as the right to appeal, double jeopardy, and compensation for wrongful conviction. It also determines that there shall be equality

---

Ⓔ Key case

Handyside v United Kingdom (1976) Ser A, No 24

The applicant published 'the Little Red Schoolbook' in Denmark and, following translation, in a number of other European countries. The book involved a chapter on sex education and was aimed at schoolchildren. Handyside was convicted of violating national laws on obscene publications. A key issue discussed in the European Court of Human Rights was whether the infringement of freedom of expression (Art 10) was justified on the UK's claimed ground of protecting morals, as the book was available in other European countries. Article 10(2) permits interference with the freedom in certain circumstances. The UK was found not to have breached the Convention. The Court noted that:

it is not possible to find in the domestic law of the various Contracting States a uniform European conception of morals. The view taken by their respective laws of the requirements of morals varies from time to time and from place to place, especially in our era which is characterised by a rapid and far-reaching evolution of opinions on the subject. By reason of their direct and continuous contact with the vital forces of their countries, State authorities are in principle in a better position than the international judge to give an opinion on the exact content of these requirements as well as on the 'necessity' of a 'restriction' or 'penalty' intended to meet them.[Para 48]

This discretion is not unfettered: '[t]he domestic margin of appreciation [.] goes hand in hand with a European supervision' (para 49).

This is widely known as the margin of appreciation doctrine.

---

between spouses in private law matters. A Twelfth Protocol enshrining a general principle of non-discrimination entered into force in April 2005.

All of these Protocols are optional. States are not obligated to accept them. (It should be noted that other Protocols have been compulsory as they have changed the implementation and institutional process. The most notable of these exceptions are Protocol 11 which changed the two tier Commission and Court machinery for bringing complaints to a single reformed permanent Court and the new Protocol 14 that will alter the process of human rights complaints once Russia—the final State—has ratified it.)

7.3.3 **Other conventions**

The Council of Europe has adopted a number of other conventions aimed at securing a broader spectrum of human rights within its jurisdiction.

7.3.3.1 *European Social Charter 1961*

The Charter guarantees social and economic human rights. The European Social Charter of the Council of Europe should not be confused with similar sounding documents adopted under the auspices of the European Union/Community. The economic and social rights embodied in the Charter help to redress the imbalance of rights protected in Europe—the Convention being essentially concerned with civil and political rights. However, the use of a variety of instruments does little to emphasize the indivisibility of rights. The original Charter was adopted in 1961. It has since been augmented by three Protocols (1988, 1991, and 1995). Thereafter, in 1996, a revised Social Charter was opened for signature, entering into force on 1 July 1999 a month after receipt of the third ratification. It is intended that this revised Charter will progressively replace the first Charter which it subsumes. The Charter adopts an unusual format. It is divided into parts containing general principles, specific rights, and the obligations incumbent upon States. The first part of both the original and the revised versions lists a number of principles and rights pertaining to social policy which all Contracting States must endorse. States agree to strive for the attainment of economic and social conditions best placed to secure the realization of the specified rights and principles: just conditions of work; freedom of association; collective bargaining; social security; social, legal, and economic protection of young people; equal opportunities and treatment without sex discrimination; social protection for the elderly; and protection from poverty and social exclusion. The second part of the Charter is restricted to a detailed tabulation of rights from which States can pick and choose. In terms of Part III of both versions, States must elect to be bound by a certain number of the provisions, including certain core Articles (selected from the right to work, the right to form organizations and bargain collectively, protection of young persons, the right to social security, social and medical assistance, and various family rights and rights of migrant workers). A 1995 additional Protocol to the initial Charter and Part IV of the revised version enable collective complaints by specified bodies to be submitted to the Secretary General for transmission to the Committee of Independent Experts for consideration.

7.3.3.2 *The European Charter for Regional and Minority Languages 1992*

This instrument adopts a similar format to the European Social Charter with a list of policy aims and objectives followed by a pick and mix list of more specific rights, in this case, each graded to enable compliance at different levels: for example, with respect to the provision of education in minority languages, a State may choose to provide all education, a part of such education, education where parents so demand, or simply cultural education in or related to the minority or regional language. Such education can be provided at either pre-school, primary, secondary, tertiary, further, or adult education levels (Art 8). States thus have the maximum number of options and all States should be able to accede to the Charter (although obviously States should constantly strive to realize more significant rights than those presently on offer). Other rights covered by the Charter relate to the language used in judicial proceedings, by the media, by administrative and public authorities, and the pluralism of languages in cultural activities and general cultural, economic, and social activities.

7.3.3.3 *Framework Convention for the Protection of National Minorities 1995*

The Framework Convention aims to define a system for the protection of national minorities and thus the maintenance of regional peace and stability. It was adopted in 1995 and thus constitutes a partial response by the Council of Europe to the dissolution of the Soviet Union, the democratization of the former Eastern bloc countries and the advances made in the area by the United Nations and the OSCE. Following the entry into force of the Convention, a State has a year to effect implementation before reporting to the Secretary General of the Council of Europe. Rights include guarantees of equality before the law, cultural preservation, religious freedom, minority language usage, and rights to transfrontier contacts between related minority groups. In many respects, the rights resemble the minority guarantees proposed and implemented under the auspices of the League of Nations seven decades previously.

7.3.3.4 *European Convention on the Exercise of Children's Rights 1996*

This 1996 Convention aims at furthering the realization of the United Nations Convention on the Rights of the Child, especially Art 4 on the implementation of the rights, within the jurisdiction of the Council of Europe. The Convention is focused on involving the child in the decision making process and keeping the child informed of relevant judicial proceedings. The best interests of the child is the relevant standard imposed, having regard to the age and level of understanding of the child in question. A Standing Committee is established to review the implementation of the Convention and provide advice and assistance to States wishing to strengthen their laws relating to the promotion and exercise of children's rights.

7.3.3.5 *Convention on Human Rights and Biomedicine 1997*

In 1997, the Council of Europe succeeded in drawing up a Convention that relates to biomedicine, a new area with profound consequences for human rights. The Convention was followed in 1998 by an additional Protocol on the cloning of human beings. These instruments aim at promoting the beneficial use of advancements in biomedicine whilst simultaneously regulating any use of new technology which may impinge on the dignity and worth of the human person. Taking a lead from the United Nations Declaration on Human Rights, it establishes the primacy of the human being which shall prevail over the sole interest of society or science (Art 2). The Convention goes on to deal with rules on patient consent for health care, the protection of private life and the right to information, human genome interventions and discrimination, protection of persons involved in scientific research, organ and tissue removal, and disposal of the human body. The first additional Protocol builds on this by prohibiting 'any intervention seeking to create a human being genetically identical to another human being, whether living or dead' (Art 1(1)), while a further additional Protocol addresses transplantation of organs and tissues of human origin.

7.4 **The institutional framework**

As the most developed regional organization involved in the protection of human rights and fundamental freedoms, it follows that the Council of Europe has a highly developed institutional framework though not all of its bodies are involved directly in the promotion and protection of human rights.

7.4.1 The Secretary-General

The Secretary-General is appointed by the Assembly on the recommendation of the Committee of Ministers (Art 36, Statute of the Council of Europe). The Secretary-General heads the Council's Secretariat. The Secretary-General acts as a depository for ratifications, reservations, and renunciations of the various Council of Europe instruments. As has been noted, collective complaints under the Social Charter are sent in the first instance to the Secretary-General.

7.4.2 The Committee of Ministers

The Committee of Ministers is the primary decision-making body of the Council. It is comprised of the Minister for Foreign Affairs from each member State (members may appoint alternates who may be senior diplomats). The Committee meets biannually—in November and in April/May. The role of the Committee is defined as being threefold: first, as a forum for discussing on equal footing national approaches to problem solving; secondly, to agree pan-European responses to these problems; and thirdly, as a guardian of the tenets by which the Council operates. This latter function includes the monitoring of the compliance of Member States with their obligations under the Human Rights Convention. The Committee liaises with the other bodies of the Council, monitors the compliance of Member States with their international obligations, considers applications by new Member States, drafts and concludes conventions, adopts recommendations, and administers the budget of the organization.

Given the incumbent workload, it is perhaps inevitable that the Committee tends to function through Deputies. The appointment of Deputies was approved by the Committee in March 1952. Each Minister appoints a Deputy who attends plenary session every couple of weeks. They may adopt decisions with the same force of law as the Ministers themselves. These Deputies are usually the Permanent Representative of the States to the Council. The Statute of the Council provides more detail on the functioning of this organ. Essentially, there are three divisions of meetings: A, B, and DH. A-level meetings are full Deputy meetings and B-level meetings are rarely attended by the Deputies, while DH meetings concern the obligations of the Committee under the European Convention on Human Rights. Meetings of the Deputies are governed by their own rules of procedure, with most decisions being taken by majority. The work of the Committee is set by the chair, a position held by each member State in turn (in accordance with the alphabetical order in English): Switzerland assumed responsibility in November 2009, serving until May 2010 when Macedonia will take over until November 2010. The chairmanship should then be assumed by Turkey followed by Ukraine for May–November 2011, followed by the United Kingdom until May 2012.

The Committee of Ministers has exercised a monitoring procedure since 1996. By virtue of this, the Committee can consider questions of implementation of commitments concerning the situation of democracy, human rights, and the rule of law in any member State (Declaration on Compliance with Commitments Accepted by Member States of the Council of Europe, 10 November 1994, 95th Session—Monitor/ Inf(99)3/Monitor/Inf(98)2). The questions are referred to the Committee by Member States, the Secretary-General, or on a recommendation from the Parliamentary Assembly. The monitoring system operated by the Committee is confidential, operating on a spirit of cooperation. Often, selected themes are focused on.

7.4.3 **The Parliamentary Assembly**

The Assembly is representative of the peoples of the Council of Europe sitting in broad political groups. It is headed by a Bureau and operates through a number of committees. During its Strasbourg Sessions, the Bureau, Committees, and Political Groups hold meetings. Outside these Sessions, there are meetings of PACE and the Western European Union (WEU) committees. PACE Committees include Equal opportunities for Women and Men, Culture and Education, and Legal Affairs and Human Rights. There is also a Committee which oversees the honouring of obligations and commitments by Member States of the Council—the Monitoring Committee.

The Committee on Legal Affairs and Human Rights is responsible for a whole variety of activities which promote and defend human rights. It can act as advisor to the Parliamentary Assembly. It rose to prominence following the collapse of communist rule in the former Eastern-bloc countries. The Committee oversees the human rights applications within those territories which have joined the Council. Resolution 1115 (1997) set up a special committee for this purpose. This Committee provides the Political Affairs Committee with materials on which to base reports on any potential Member State. All Member States must comply with the basic human rights standards proclaimed by the Council.

7.4.4 **The European Court of Human Rights**

The European Court is an international institution established by the European Convention to receive complaints from individuals and States alleging violations of those rights protected under the Convention. The Parliamentary Assembly elects judges for a term of six years (Arts 22–3 though this will be amended by Protocol 14). In practice, half the judicial positions are filled by election every three years on a rolling basis. Judges sit in their individual capacity and do not represent their State of origin (Art 21). Obviously judges must be independent and cannot undertake any work or external activity which may compromise their independence or impartiality. From within its numbers, the members of the Court elect a president, two vice-presidents, and chamber presidents. These officials serve for three years.

The Court is governed by its own Rules of Court. It is divided into four sections, each with a composition fixed for three years. Each section should reflect a balance of both geography and gender as well as being a blend of the legal systems operated by Contracting States. Each section has a President, in the case of two of the sections, the President is also a Vice President of the plenary court. Section Vice-Presidents assist section Presidents as necessary.

Each section is divided into Committees of three judges, created for twelve months at a time. Committees carry out some of the tasks previously within the competency of the former Commission. To hear cases, the judges sit in Chambers of seven, appointed on a rotating basis from within each section. In each case, the section President and the judge appointed by the respondent State sit (Art 27(2)). If the respondent State elects a judge from outwith the section, he or she sits *ex officio* in the case. The Grand Chamber comprises seventeen judges—it is reconstituted every three years. Note that Protocol 14 envisages changes to this system. When it enters into force (ie, following Russia's ratification) a single judge will determine admissibility for most applications.

As well as hearing cases, Art 47 provides that the Court may, at the request of the Committee of Ministers, give advisory opinions on legal questions arising from the interpretation of the Convention and its Protocols. Such opinions are given by the Grand Chamber with the potential for separate opinions to be attached.

7.4.5 The European Commissioner on Human Rights

The European Commissioner on Human Rights is a new organ first approved at the Summit of Heads of State and Government in 1997 and created in 1999. The Commissioner is elected by the Parliamentary Assembly, the successful candidate serving a non-renewable term of six years. The purpose of the Commissioner is to promote education and awareness of human rights in the Member States; identify possible shortcomings in the law and practice of Member States with regard to compliance with human rights; and help promote the effective observance and full enjoyment of human rights, as embodied in the various Council of Europe instruments. The Commissioner is neither a judicial organ nor an ombudsman. Essentially, the Commissioner provides advice and information on human rights protection and encourages cooperation with all national ombudsmen and national and international human rights mechanisms. Depending on the circumstances, the Commissioner may have contact with States and other organs of the Council of Europe. The jurisdiction over human rights matters extends throughout the competencies of the Council of Europe, the office may be asked to investigate any area and can issue opinions, recommendations, and reports on any competent area.

7.4.6 The European Commission on Human Rights

The European Commission was abolished in 1999. It was established under the original European Convention to receive complaints being raised by applicants claiming that their human rights were violated. Acting as a 'filter', the Commission dealt with questions of admissibility. However, the Commission also gave an opinion on the case—these opinions were published though they were not binding on the Court. After giving an opinion and having failed to secure a friendly settlement, the Commission could elect whether or not to take a case to the European Court or, in the alternative, to pass the matter to the Committee of Ministers. Cases decided before 2001 may still have an opinion of the Commission. Most cases decided thereafter are decided in accordance with the new provisions of the Convention, as amended by Protocol 11, and thus the Commission has no role to play.

7.5 Implementing human rights

7.5.1 The Strasbourg machinery (original and now)

The Eleventh Protocol to the Convention, which entered into force in 1998, irrevocably altered the procedure for bringing complaints before the European Court of Human Rights by restructuring the entire enforcement machinery. Since inception the Court had handled a growing number of cases. The first case was heard by the Court in 1967, in 1981, 52 cases were referred to the Court, by 1997, 119 cases were pending before the Court. By 1993, the Commission was handing some 2,037 complaints. By 1997, 4,750 complaints were filed with the Commission. The Eleventh Protocol was opened for signature on 11 May 1994. Due to the radical reformation of the human rights control machinery, all Contracting States were required to sign the Protocol before it entered into force. The final ratification was lodged with the Council in October 1997. In terms of the Protocol, the Council then had one year to undertake the necessary organizational and procedural changes to facilitate the establishment of the permanent Court and the creation of new Rules of Court. The current European Court of Human Rights became operational on 1 November 1998 (see Figure 7.1). Under the terms of the Protocol, the Commission continued for one year, until 31 October 1999, to facilitate processing of applications which had been declared admissible prior to the entry into force of the Protocol. Note that the Fourteenth Protocol will result in further changes when it enters into force, reform all the more urgent considering that as at December 2008, some 97,300 applications were pending before judicial bodies (chambers or committees).

7.5.2 Inter-State complaints

Article 33 of the Convention provides that High Contracting Parties may refer to the Court 'any alleged breach of the provisions of the Convention and the protocols thereto by another High Contracting Party'. The first inter-State case considered by the Court was *Ireland v United Kingdom*. The only other one considered by the Court has been *Cyprus v Turkey*.

7.5.3 Individual complaints

Following the entry into force of Protocol 11, the individual complaint process became compulsory for all Contracting States. Under the original system, States could elect whether or not to recognize the jurisdiction of the Court in this respect. The success of the Commission and Court, especially the high level of compliance with their decisions, meant that a compulsory submission to judicial process was acceptable to States. In reality the number of communications received by the Court has continued to increase. According to the Court's latest statistics (2008), there were 49,850 applications allocated, an increase of almost 150 per cent from the 18,164 registered in 1998 and close to the total number of applications registered between 1955 and 1982. Concern at the escalating number of complaints prompted discussions within the Committee of Ministers on the efficacy of a new protocol facilitating the striking off of applications raising no substantial issue under the Convention. Protocol 14 (not yet in force) is the result.

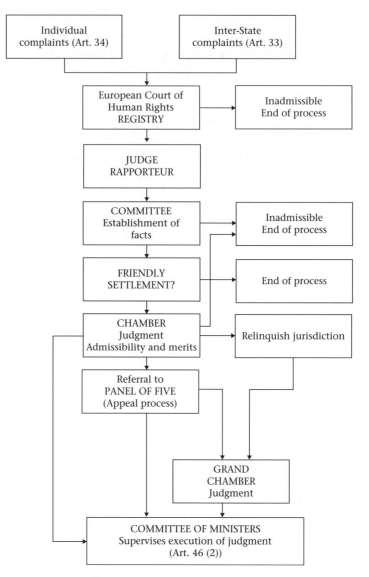

Figure 7.1 Individual and inter-State complaints.

7.5.3.1 *The four stages*

In terms of the Strasbourg machinery, there are at most four stages in the processing of a complaint: the Committee stage; the Chamber; the Grand Chamber; and the Committee of Ministers. Ideally, though not always, these four stages should reflect the admissibility, merits, appeal, and enforcement aspects of the process. A general overview of the process follows. In terms of Article 34 of the Convention, petitions can be received from 'any person, non-governmental organisation or group of individuals claiming to be the victim' of a violation by one of the High Contracting Parties of the rights enshrined in the Convention and/or Protocols. The need for the applicant to be a victim is an essential part of the process.

7.5.3.2 *The Committee*

Committees have competence to declare complaints inadmissible or strike cases off the list. In many respects, the Committee carries out the screening process hitherto the prerogative of the Commission. A case is deemed inadmissible in accordance with the criteria laid down in Article 35 of the Convention: anonymous complaints and non-exhaustion of domestic remedies are two grounds of dismissal. Reasons must always be given for a finding of inadmissibility. Cases are also struck off the list at any stage of the proceedings when it becomes apparent that the applicant does not intend to pursue the application, the matter has been resolved or similar reasons (Art 37). There is no appeal from these decisions although a case which has been struck off the list may be restored if the Court considers that the circumstances so justify. Committees dismiss applications by unanimous vote (Art 28). However, acceptance by the Committee does not mean that the merits of the case will be heard, as a Chamber may also vote to strike out a case or deem it inadmissible. Note that under Protocol 14, a single judge may determine admissibility, and cases may be inadmissible if the applicant 'has not suffered a significant disadvantage' (Art 12).

7.5.3.3 *The Chamber*

Chambers include, *ex officio*, the judge of the State Party concerned. The *ex officio* post or the ad hoc equivalent enables issues of domestic law to be clarified by a recognized and respected expert in the national system concerned. Chambers decide on the admissibility of inter-State complaints and can also decide on the admissibility of individual complaints which come before it from the Committee (Art 29). Decisions on admissibility are usually taken separately from decisions on the merits of the case. The Court will pursue the examination of the case, possibly involving an investigation with the assistance of the State Party concerned. The Court will also attempt to secure a friendly settlement, attaining which means that the case can be struck off the list (Art 39).

Hearings before the European Court are usually held in public with all relevant documents available for public access. Judgments of Chambers become final unless the matter is referred to the Grand Chamber. Should either party wish to refer a case to the Grand Chamber within the specified three-month period, it is referred to a panel of five judges of the Grand Chamber who will accept or reject the referral. If a referral is rejected then the decision of the Chamber becomes final. Otherwise, the Grand Chamber is seized of the matter.

Where a case before a Chamber raises a serious question affecting the interpretation of the Convention or Protocols, or when a Chamber is faced with a situation where it may render a decision apparently inconsistent with previous judgments of the Court, then that Chamber may relinquish jurisdiction in the case to the Grand Chamber (Art 30). Jurisdiction can be relinquished at any time up until the Chamber renders judgment unless one of the parties to the case objects.

7.5.3.4 *The Grand Chamber*

The Grand Chamber includes an *ex officio* judge of the State Party involved in the case, the president of the Court and the presidents of the Chambers. The Grand Chamber exercises jurisdiction in three situations: where a Chamber relinquishes jurisdiction to the Grand Chamber (Art 30); where a party to a case regarding which a Chamber has issued a judgment requests a referral within three months of that judgment (a panel of five judges decides on whether the case raises a serious question affecting the interpretation or application of the Convention and thus should be referred) (Art 43); and where the Committee of Ministers of the Council of Europe requests an advisory opinion though the circumstances in which this can occur are narrowly delineated (Art 47). The Grand Chamber considers the merits of the case and delivers a final binding judgment. Note that there is no appeal from a first instance decision of the Grand Chamber.

7.5.3.5 *The Committee of Ministers*

The Committee of Ministers has responsibility for supervising the implementation of the judgment of either the Chamber or the Grand Chamber of the European Court. The final judgment is transmitted to the Committee of Ministers. As with all international law, enforcement is dependent on the will of States. The Court's decisions are binding on States which undertake to abide by them. Ultimately expulsion is the only sanction available should a State fail to comply with the judgment of the Court. The early series of State complaints against Greece—the initial 'Greek cases' of *Denmark, Norway and Sweden v Greece*—prompted Greece to temporarily withdraw. In contrast, the current run of cases against Turkey involving serious violations of human rights can be viewed as illustrating a failure of law in regions of the country rather than as a failure of Turkey to comply with its obligations in general.

7.6 **Organization for Security and Cooperation in Europe**

Formerly the Conference on Security and Cooperation in Europe, this body is now a comprehensive security organization with fifty-five participating States and a geographical remit stretching from 'Vancouver to Vladivostock' (*OSCE Handbook*, 2007, p 1). It is the biggest regional security organization in the world (and is recognized under Chapter VIII of the United Nations Charter as the European regional arrangement for those purposes). In spite of its emphasis on security—arms control, conflict prevention, and economic and environmental security—the OSCE has also attached increasing significance to the human dimension of security matters. The rationale for this is reminiscent of the United Nations' reasoning: the protection and promotion of human rights and fundamental freedoms is regarded as an important factor in the maintenance of international peace and security. However, unlike the United Nations, the OSCE does not have legal status in international law. It is predominantly a political body. Given that the organization grew out of an ideologically divided Europe with a focus on security and cooperation in Europe, this was inevitable. The process began in 1973 with the formal opening of the Conference on Security and Cooperation in Europe (CSCE) in Helsinki. Even achieving attendance and participation in the Conference was remarkable given the protracted negotiations and difficulties encountered in finding common ground. All of Europe (except Albania) attended along with the USA and Canada. The Final Act of the Helsinki Conference was signed in 1975 by thirty-five Heads of State. It sets out the aims and areas of commonality decided upon by the delegates, underpinned by the premise that participating States have a common interest in the security of

Europe and preventing further conflict in a region already decimated twice in thirty years by war. Participating States pledged to work together to these ends in a series of periodic conferences and meetings. With no infrastructure as such, the meetings in themselves were the sole momentum for developing links between States across the Iron Curtain and, in the political circumstances, it was a surprisingly successful vehicle.

The third set of recommendations adopted in the Final Act of the Helsinki Conference dealt with cooperation in humanitarian and other fields. This broad category covered human rights, education, and culture: Articles addressed the importance of respect for human rights and fundamental freedoms, particularly of thought, conscience, and religion as well as the vexed issue of self-determination.

The main impetus for change was the response of the parties to the collapse of communism. The Charter of Paris 1990 was 'a new beginning' for a whole and free Europe. It marked the formalization of the CSCE (Helsinki) process with a decision to have biennial (every two years) meetings and establish an institutional infrastructure.

In 1994, the new institutional framework and associated developments was reflected in the decision to launch the process as the Organization for Security and Cooperation in Europe (OSCE) in 1995. The OSCE worked in a Europe which was inconceivable in the years leading up to the first Helsinki Conference, and indeed for many years thereafter. However, the dissolution of the Soviet Union and the former Yugoslavia have brought unique challenges to the organization and its emphasis on security. The priorities of the OSCE today include assisting in building democratic civil societies based on the rule of law, preventing local conflicts and promoting a cooperative system of security. In furtherance of these aims, the OSCE has developed a system of field activities and a variety of field missions. OSCE missions have been centred in the territories of the former Soviet Union and former Yugoslavia and include missions in Bosnia and Herzegovina, Georgia, Moldova, and Tajikstan; offices in Yerevan, Baku, and Central Asia; a presence in Albania; monitoring groups in Belarus; and activities in Estonia and Latvia. Kosovo is home to one of its most comprehensive operations to date with the OSCE working in concert with the United Nations and a host of other organizations and bodies.

As ethnic conflict is the main source of large-scale violence in contemporary Europe, there has been renewed interest in human rights in the region. Concern with the Human Dimension of the work of the OSCE has expanded considerably in recent years with the establishment of the Office for Democratic Institutions and Human Rights, the High Commissioner on National Minorities (both established by 1992), and, more recently the creation of a Representative on Freedom of the Media and a Special Representative and Coordinator for Combating Trafficking in Human Beings.

At heart, the OSCE aims to utilize human rights in an attempt to secure and maintain peace in the region. This correlates to the early approach advocated by the United Nations. The protection of human rights per se is not an enforceable goal—rather, the development of a culture of respect for human rights and, *ergo*, the evolution of democratic and peaceful societies is. In this respect, links can be made to the pioneering work of the Organization of American States Commission in developing and strengthening emergent democracies in a precariously unstable region.

7.6.1 **The Office for Democratic Institutions and Human Rights**

The Office for Democratic Institutions and Human Rights evolved from the Office for Free Elections. It was the first institution established in fulfilment of the Human Dimension of the OSCE's objectives and reflects the approach of the organization to human rights: democracy is viewed almost as a prerequisite to the facilitation of the realization of human rights in a State. Consequently there is considerable emphasis on the establishment of systems of free elections and democratic institutions within States. The OSCE has observed around a hundred elections and referenda in many emerging democracies (at the request of the States concerned). It also operates a comprehensive training programme to assist States in developing appropriate election processes. The Democratization Section is involved in projects aimed at strengthening the rule of law. To this end, the OSCE will endeavour to encourage the dissemination of human rights information, provide training and technical assistance to national human rights institutions, strengthen NGOs, and actively encourage work in certain areas of human rights including gender equality, combating torture, religious freedom, and combating trafficking in human beings. It will also monitor human rights and the progress in achieving the human dimension agenda. Roma and Sinti Communities are singled out for particular attention given the transnational scope of problems affecting such groups. Through the work of the Office for Democratic Institutions and Human Rights, the OSCE hopes to support States progressing towards free elections and democratic systems of government within which human rights and freedoms can prosper.

7.6.2 **The High Commissioner on National Minorities**

The High Commissioner on National Minorities is the principal response of the OSCE to the threat of further ethnic conflict within the region. By 1992 when the post was created, problems arising from the dissolution of the Eastern bloc and the former Yugoslavia were already apparent. The High Commissioner's role is to identify ethnic tensions which may endanger peace and stability within the OSCE. He will then strive to diffuse the conflict in furtherance of his mandate as 'an instrument of conflict prevention at the earliest possible stage'. As well as preventative diplomacy, the High Commissioner will also conduct on-site missions. Under the auspices of the High Commissioner, a detailed examination of the Sinti and Roma peoples has already been undertaken as well as national studies in States as diverse as Albania, Ukraine, Kazakhstan, and Hungary. There is no jurisdiction for individual complaints to be received or considered by the Commission. Silent diplomacy is the key. Integration of national minorities within a State (NB: not necessarily assimilation) is seen as essential to prevent conflict and division within a given territory thus the High Commissioner is charged with ameliorating the position of national minorities. However, the High Commissioner is not, per se, a champion of minorities.

Moves are made towards preserving the identity of minority groups and encouraging their participation in the public affairs of States. Among the examples of recommendations adopted to this end are the 1995 Hague Recommendations Regarding the Education Rights of National Minorities, the 1998 Oslo Recommendations on the Linguistic Rights of National Minorities, and the 1999 Lund Recommendations on the Effective Participation of National Minorities in Public Life. Preservation and promotion of the identity of minority groups was prominent during the era of the League of Nations and is slowly returning to prominence through the United Nations. Undoubtedly it is an issue of more immediate concern within Europe and the OSCE has proven itself competent to respond.

7.6.3 The Representative on Freedom of the Media

The newest institution, the Representative on Freedom of the Media, is tasked with furthering a free, independent, and pluralistic media (OSCE, p 112) within the territories of participating States. The Representative carries out early warning and early action functions. He may also receive complaints on censorship which are then investigated and attempts are made to assist the State in resolving the situation. The Representative is not a judicial body; the post is a conduit for political and diplomatic guidance aimed at resolving conflicts in an unobtrusive and mutually beneficial way. Efforts towards securing a free media are undertaken in concert with the United Nations and the Council of Europe.

7.7 European Union

The European Union came into being with the entry into force of the Treaty on European Union (the Maastricht Treaty). Prior to this, there were three distinct European Communities: the European Economic Community (now the European Community), the European Coal and Steel Community, and the European Atomic Energy Community. In the years since inception, these organizations (particularly the European Economic Community) have developed the application of human rights within their jurisdiction. The three initial communities now comprise the first pillar of the new European Union. European Community Law per se only applies to this pillar of the Union. (The other two pillars concern the Common Foreign and Security Policy and Cooperation in the Fields of Justice and Home Affairs.) The 1997 Treaty of Amsterdam further altered these divisions as well as prompting greater awareness of the importance of human rights within the European Union. Should the Treaty of Lisbon be ratified by Ireland, and enter into force (a decision will emerge in late 2009), the constitutional arrangements for the Union will be further refined. All Member States of the European Union are members of the Council of Europe and bound by the terms of the European Convention on Human Rights.

The original focus of the European Communities was the economic restoration of Europe in the post-war period, hence human rights were not mentioned in the constituent documents. The founders of the Communities considered that economic integration would not impact negatively on human rights and, moreover, the pre-existing Council of Europe would have human rights at the heart of its agenda thereby obviating the need for the Communities to address the area. It is interesting to note that many States in the eastern areas of Europe have joined the Council of Europe viewing that as a step towards satisfying the criteria for membership of the European Union. The logic proved unassailable. In May 2004, membership of the European Union increased from fifteen to twenty-five States. Bulgaria and Romania joined in 2007 to create a Union of twenty-seven States.

7.7.1 The European Court of Justice and human rights

The then new European Court of Justice found that it was asked to reconcile pro-visions of Community law with the rights of nationals of Member States. Conse-quently, a body of jurisprudence on human rights developed. Initially the European Court was reluctant to address issues of human rights as can be deduced from the early Case 1/58 *Stork*. The evolution of the doctrine of supremacy, by which Com-munity law took precedence over national law in concert with the principle of direct effect, forced a change in approach by the European Court of Justice. Case 29/69 *Stauder v Ulm* afforded the Court the opportunity to acknowledge the impact of human rights within Community law. Stauder claimed that his fundamental rights entrenched in the German Constitution (by the peace treaties) were violated by a requirement to prove his identity and thus entitlement to reduced price butter under a European initiative. In a preliminary ruling (now Art 234, Consolidated Version of the Treaty Establishing the European Community, as amended), the European Court opined that the disputed provision did not prejudice the 'funda-mental rights enshrined in the general principles of Community law and protected by the Court' (para 7). Respect for fundamental human rights was thus regarded as an integral aspect of the general principles of law which the Court is pledged to uphold. The Court elaborated on this in a series of cases: in Case 11/70 *Internation-ale Handelsgesellschaft mbH v Einfuhr- und Vorratsstelle für Getreide und Futtermittel*, the European Court rejected a reference from the German Constitutional Court that European Community law was contrary to the fundamental rights provisions of its constitution (the German Constitutional Court indicated it did not accept this—a similar clash occurred between the German Constitutional Court and the European Court of Human Rights); in Case 36/75 *Rutili v Minister for the Interior*, the European Court directly cited salient provisions of the European Convention; in Case C-13/94 *P v S and Cornwall County Council*, the European Court of Justice referred to earlier decisions of the European Court of Human Rights when ruling on the potential for discrimination against transsexuals.

7.7.1.1 *The overlap between the two courts*

As a result of this parallel system of two European Courts with potentially con-current jurisdiction over States, there has been the occasional conflict. The prime example is the different views adopted by the two courts on the issue of restricting information on abortion services overseas being distributed in the Republic of Ire-land where abortion is prohibited save in a few medically necessary situations: in Case C-159/90 *Society for the Protection of the Unborn Child v Grogan*, the prohibition was considered to fall outwith Community law although medical operations could be a 'service' under EC law though when the same circumstances were brought to the European Court of Human Rights the following year in *Open Door Counselling and Dublin Well Woman v Ireland*, it was held that Ireland had violated the European Convention.

The possibility of the European Union acceding to the European Convention has been mooted but initially appeared unlikely as only States can be parties to the Convention and, in any event, the European Court of Justice opined that 'as Community law now stands, the Community has no competence to accede to the Convention' (Opinion 2/94 *Accession by the Community to the Convention for the*

Protection of Human Rights and Fundamental Freedoms, para 36). However, Art 17 of Protocol 14 to the European Convention on Human Rights and the Treaty of Lisbon (EU) suggest accession of the Union to the Council of Europe is likely in the future.

7.7.2 Constitutional recognition of human rights in the European Union

Article F(2) of the Treaty on European Union provides the first explicit acknowledgement of human rights in EU constitutional law: 'The Union shall respect fundamental rights, as guaranteed by the European Convention for the Protection of Human Rights and Fundamental Freedoms.' With respect to the development of the Common Foreign and Security Policy, Article J(1)(2) refers to the need to develop and consolidate democracy and the rule of law with respect for human rights and fundamental freedoms. The Treaty of Amsterdam further extends the role of the European Court of Justice with respect to human rights in the Community by bringing more provisions of the Maastricht Treaty on European Union within Pillar One (over which the ECJ has jurisdiction). Interestingly enough, the seemingly bizarre step was taken at the signing of the Treaty of Amsterdam of attaching a Declaration noting the abolition of the death penalty in all Member States. This is a direct reference to Protocol 6 to the European Convention. Finally, the Treaty of Lisbon makes clear the centrality of respect for human rights in the Union.

7.7.3 The Charter of Fundamental Rights of the European Union

At the Nice Summit in December 2000, the text of the Charter of Fundamental Rights of the European Union was adopted (OJ C 364/1, 18/12/2000). It is incorporated into the Treaty of Lisbon (not yet in force), raising and consolidating the importance of fundamental rights within the Union. The Preamble reaffirms the goal of strengthening the protection of fundamental rights in the light of changes in society, societal progress, and scientific and technological developments by making the rights more visible in a Charter. Therefore, the Charter is viewed as codifying existing rights enjoyed by European Citizens (European Citizen is a term introduced by the Treaty on European Union which covers every person holding the nationality of a member State of the European Union—Art 17 Consolidated Version of the Treaty Establishing the European Community). The Union is claimed to be founded on 'the indivisible, universal values of human dignity, freedom, equality and solidarity', the principles of democracy, and the rule of law (Preamble). Cognizance is given to the work of the Council of Europe and the European Court of Human Rights in defining and interpreting human rights.

The rights enshrined in the Charter are to be recognized and applied by the institutions of the Community and by the Member States when implementing Community law (Art 51). It thus aims to make the institutions more accountable in terms of human rights. The rights enshrined in the Charter are somewhat vague but, in essence, are not new. They are invariably based on a precursor text, either various instruments of the European Community or jurisprudence of the European Court of Justice. The Charter espouses a holistic approach to fundamental right, embracing the indivisibility of human rights whilst reaffirming that human dignity is inviolable (Art 1). A wide range of rights are included, from civil and political rights reminiscent of the Council of Europe's Convention through to a comprehensive section on equality rights and a chapter on 'solidarity' rights (ie, social rights drawn from the principles of employment protection advanced by the Community) to a tabulation of citizen's rights vis-à-vis the operation of the Union. The latter rights include election rights, access to documents, and rights in remedy of maladministration. The Charter is most likely to be used by institutions of the Union, in particular the Court of Justice, when determining if their practice is in conformity with the general principles of law recognized and applied throughout the Union. In March 2007, the European Union Agency for Fundamental Rights (Regulation 168/2007/EC) was established. The Agency (FRA) collects information on fundamental rights within the Union and offers expert advice and assistance to both the EU Member States and to EU institutions and other bodies on fulfilling EU law and policy while protecting and promoting fundamental rights. The Agency is also furthering relations between the EU and the Council of Europe in furtherance of strengthening the protection of human rights in the region.

7.7.4 Social policy

It is with respect to social policy that the European Union has enjoyed most success in articulating rights. Taking a lead from the pioneering work of the International Labour Office, the European Union has adopted a number of instruments. These are discussed in more detail in the chapter on the right to work (Chapter 19).

7.7.4.1 *Non-discrimination*

A final mention has to be made of the new provisions of Community law regarding non-discrimination. From a gender basis, the European Community has now extended the effect of non-discrimination provisions in the workplace to a plethora of different grounds, including sexual orientation and age (Art 13; see also Flynn, L). On the basis of this provision, the Community has now passed Directives (legislative measures) which aim to ensure equal treatment in employment and occupation (Directive 2000/78 Establishing a General Framework for Equal Treatment in Employment and Occupation, covers discrimination on sexual orientation, age, disability, and religion, for example). These developments will be considered in context in the chapter on the right to work (Chapter 19).

7.8 Conclusions

Few would argue that the human rights aspects of the work of the Council of Europe have not been a success. Unlike its United Nations contemporaries, the Council of Europe has developed a system which ensures the protection of basic human rights through a judicial mechanism. The European Convention on Human Rights has certainly matured into the most sophisticated and effective human rights treaty in the world (Tarschys, D). It is the largest established human rights body and through its consistent case law has developed the most comprehensive jurisprudence on human rights. Organs of the Organization of American States and even the Human

Key case

Case 43/75 *Defrenne v SABENA* [1976] ECR 455

Defrenne was employed by SABENA (a Belgian airline). She was the subject of a number of references to the European Court of Justice concerning equality. In this instance (known as *Defrenne II*), as a female air hostess she was paid less than a male cabin steward, despite the fact both were doing the same job. These facts were not disputed. Article 119 (now 141) of the EC Treaty provides that States should ensure 'equal pay for male and female workers for equal work or work of equal value'. On its application in Belgium, reference was made to the Court by the national courts (for an opinion under Art 177, now 234):

The principle that men and women should receive equal pay, which is laid down by Article 119, is one of the foundations of the Community. It may be relied on before the national courts. These courts have a duty to ensure the protection of the rights which that provision vests in individuals, in particular in the case of those forms of discrimination which have their origin directly in legislative provisions or collective labour agreements, as well as where men and women receive unequal pay for equal work which is carried out in the same establishment or service, whether private or public ... [Article 119] forms part of the social objectives of the Community, which is not merely an economic union, but is at the same time intended, by common action, to ensure social progress and seek the constant improvement of the living and working conditions of their peoples, as is emphasized by the Preamble to the Treaty.

This case remains a cornerstone of the significant body of European social law, and has been referred to when considering comparators for equality between men and women in a number of work-related situations.

Rights Committee have considered its jurisprudence in subsequent cases as have many national courts worldwide: today the European Court acts almost as a constitutional tribunal. Its judgments are considered authoritative and tend to have *erga omnes* effect as the Court interprets and develops the Convention rather than merely applying it to the case in point. However, befitting its status as an international court, the European Court has developed the margin of appreciation doctrine which recognizes national sovereignty and permits States (sometimes considerable) discretion in applying human rights. Due to this evolved flexibility, State compliance is high. The fact that the Court cross-refers to its own judgments adds further weight to case specific opinions, creating what borders on a system of judicial precedent. However, the Council of Europe has its failings; not addressing economic, social, and cultural rights is a major one. The Framework Convention on National Minorities and the European Charter on Regional and Minority Languages goes some way to addressing minority issues, the Social Charter, and economic and social issues, though without the strong implementation mechanisms which characterize the European Convention.

The Organization of Security and Cooperation in Europe has successfully focused on minority issues and codified guides to good practice for States wishing to protect and promote their minority groups. True to its original political origin, the OSCE does not operate an enforceable system of rights per se. However, its contribution to the development of rights within the region cannot be underestimated, especially given its vast geographical spread. Encouraging fledgling democracies in newly independent States has enabled the Organization to lay the foundations for the protection of universally recognized human rights and fundamental freedoms. The work of the OSCE has also paved the way for the increase in membership of the Council of Europe with ever more States expressing their willingness to abide by the tenets of the European Convention on Human Rights. Finally, in respect of economic and social rights, the pioneering work of the European Community must not be forgotten.

The European Community/Union has a strong enforceable system of securing social rights and regulating the rights of workers in the labour market. Despite its economic origins, the Community has developed into the regional authority on social rights, overtaking the earlier work of the Council of Europe in importance as the Community's rights are enforceable. Human rights have achieved ever greater prominence in the Community as the adoption of the Charter demonstrates. As the Community expands eastwards with future enlargements, so the rule of law it advocates will be more widely applied.

CASES

Denmark v Greece (Applicn 3321/67), CM Res DH (70) 1.

Handyside v UK Ser A, No 24 (1976).

Internationale Handelsgesellschaft mbH v Einfuhr- und Vorratsstelle für Getreide und Futtermittel, Case 11/70, [1970] ECR 1125.

Ireland v United Kingdom Ser A, No 25 (1978).

Norway v Greece (Applicn 3322/67), CM Res DH (70) 1.

Open Door Counselling and Dublin Well Woman v Ireland Ser A, No 246 (1992).

Opinion 2/94 Accession by the Community to the Convention for the Protection of Human Rights and Fundamental Freedoms [1996] ECR I-1759.

P v S and Cornwall County Council, Case C-13/94, [1996] ECR I-2143.

Rutili v Minister for the Interior, Case 36/75, [1975] ECR 1219.

Society for the Protection of the Unborn Child v Grogan, Case C-159/90, [1991] ECR I-4685.

Stauder v Ulm, Case 29/69, [1969] ECR 419.

Stork, Case 1/58, [1959] ECR 423.

Sweden v Greece (Applicn 3323/67), CM Res DH (70) 1.

READING

Alston, P, Bustelo, M, and Heenan, J (eds), *The EU and Human Rights* (Oxford: Oxford University Press, 1999).

Alston, P, and de Schutter, O (eds), *Monitoring Fundamental Rights in the EU: The contribution of the Fundamental Rights Agency* (Oxford: Hart, 2005).

Betten, L, and Grief, N, *EU Law and Human Rights* (London: Longman, 1998).

van Bloed, A, and van Dijk, P (eds), *International Studies in Human Rights, xx: The human dimension of the Helsinki Process* (Leiden: Kluwer, 1991).

Bloed, A, et al (eds), *Monitoring Human Rights in Europe* (Dordecht: Martinus Nijhoff, 1993).

Brett, R, 'Human rights and the OSCE' (1996) 18 Human Rights Quarterly 668–93.

Clapham, A, 'On complementarity: Human rights in the European legal order' (2000) 21(8) Human Rights Law Journal 313–23.

Van Dijk, P, and van Hoof, G, *Theory and Practice of the European Convention on Human Rights*, 3rd edn (Leiden: Kluwer, 1998).

Feus, K (ed), *The EU Charter of Fundamental Rights: Text and commentaries* (London: Federal Trust, 2000).

Flynn, L, 'The implications of Article 13 EC: After Amsterdam, will some forms of discrimination be more equal than others?' (1999) 36 CMLR 1127–52.

Gomien, D, *Short Guide to the European Convention on Human Rights* (Strasbourg: Council of Europe, 1998).

Harris, DJ, O'Boyle, M, and Warbrick, C, *Law of the European Convention on Human Rights*, 2nd edn (Butterworths: London, 1999).

Heintze, H, 'Minority issues in West Europe and the OSCE High Commissioner on National Minorities' (2000) 7(4) International Journal of Minority and Group Rights 381.

Janis, M, Kay, R, and Bradley, A, *European Human Rights Law: Text and materials*, 2nd edn (Oxford: Oxford University Press, 2000).

Krüger, H, and Polakiewicz, J, 'Proposals for a coherent human rights system in Europe: The European Convention on Human Rights and the EU Charter of Fundamental Rights' (2001) 22 Human Rights Law Journal 1–13.

Letsas, G, 'Two concepts of the margin of appreciation' (2006) 26(4) Oxford Journal of Legal Studies 705–32.

Neuwahl, N, and Rosas, A (eds), *The EU and Human Rights* (The Hague: Martinus Nijhoff, 1995).

Tarschys, D, Preface to D Gomien, *Short Guide to the European Convention on Human Rights*, 2nd edn (Strasbourg: Council of Europe, 1988).

Wadham, J, and Said, T, 'What price the right of individual petition: Report of the Evaluation Group to the Committee of Ministers on the European Court of Human Rights' (2002) European Human Rights Law Review 169–74.

OSCE, *OSCE Handbook* (Vienna: OSCE, 2000).

Wildhaber, L, 'The European Convention on Human Rights and International Law' (2007) 56 International and Comparative Law Quarterly 217–32.

WEBSITES

www.coe.int—the Council of Europe.

www.coe.intt/conventions—texts of Council of Europe instruments.

www.echr.coe.int—the European Court of Human Rights.

www.coe.int/t/commissioner—the Commissioner for Human Rights.

europa.eu/index_en.htm—the European Union online (English).

curia.europa.eu/en—the European Court of Justice.

europa.eu/abc/rights_en.htm—Citizen's rights (European Union).

europa.eu/pol/socio/index_en.htm—index for European Union Social Affairs.

www.osce.org—Organization for Security and Cooperation in Europe.

www.osce.org/odihr—OSCE Office for Democratic Institutions and Human Rights.

www.osce.org/hcnm—OSCE High Commissioner on National Minorities.

8

The Organization of American States

In contrast to Europe, the Americas host only one major regional organization with a significant impact on human rights—the Organization of American States. This chapter will consider the monitoring and implementation of human rights through the organs of this organization.

The Organization of American States (OAS) was established in 1948 at the ninth Inter-American Conference (Bogotá, Colombia). Pan-American organizations began with the 1890 International Union of American Republics. Membership of the OAS is open to any State in the Americas. There are presently thirty-five Member States, twenty-five of which have ratified the American Convention on Human Rights (NB Trinidad and Tobago controversially denounced their ratification in 1998 thus there are now only twenty-four ratifications). Cuba is a member but, for political reasons, had its active participation suspended from 1962–2009. The United States of America, on the other hand, is a member which has signed, but not yet ratified, the Convention. Canada is not a party to the Convention either.

The Bogotá Conference also adopted the American Declaration on the Rights and Duties of Man, a notable achievement as it predates the Universal Declaration by some seven months and the European Convention by more than two years. However, the Declaration was not supported by any enforcement machinery. Monitoring of human rights was formalized later with the work of the Inter-American Commission on Human Rights and later still the American Convention on Human Rights 1969 which established the Inter-American Court of Human Rights. In spite of adopting one of the earliest transnational declarations on human rights, human rights were not the priority of the Organization. The OAS now has a very complex system of protecting rights through diplomatic, quasi-judicial, and judicial processes although the scale of activities of the Organization remains barely comparable to the successes of the Council of Europe.

8.1 The development of American human rights

The development of American human rights was not without difficulties. For many years, a number of Latin American States were in the grip of military rule and/or the turmoil of revolution. Democracy, as it is understood today, was not a feature of many States in the region. As a consequence, many governments were not receptive to the notion of universal human rights, and far less to the idea of States being held accountable for their actions in respect of individuals. Judiciaries in many States were not truly independent of the junta in power and thus could not be relied upon to uphold human rights. Powers of detention and arrest appeared often quite arbitrary, thousands of people disappeared without trace, and evidence of systematic torture and oppression of freedom of expression was widespread. Governments sometimes changed quickly with the all-too-often violent overthrow of the regime in power. Coups d'état were commonplace. It is against this background that the OAS attempted to create a standard of human rights. Although there was considerable need for this due to the instances of systematic gross violations of fundamental rights, the problem was developing a system that could be effective in all Member States.

8.2 **The Declaration and the Conventions**

The constituent document of the Organization of American States refers to the fundamental rights of man in its preamble and various Articles thereafter. However, these rights are neither defined nor listed. Further elaboration was required.

8.2.1 **The American Declaration**

The American Declaration on the Rights and Duties of Man is, in content, broadly similar to the Universal Declaration on Human Rights. The rights included encompass civil and political (life, liberty, religious freedom, inviolability of home and correspondence, fair trial), as well as economic, social, and cultural, rights (benefit of culture, leisure time, work, social security). However, it also sets out a number of duties incumbent upon the American citizen. The duties are varied ranging from civil and military service through the support, education, and protection of minor children to a duty to pay taxes. Many of the duties correlate to specific rights, for example, the citizen has a duty 'to acquire at least an elementary education' (Art XXXI) which links in to the right to an education. Similarly, the right to vote and participate in government is related to the duty to vote and the duty to work 'as far as … capacity and possibilities permit' (Art XXXVII) is subject to the right to work under proper conditions. Although the Declaration is not a treaty, the Inter-American Court has indicated that it may have binding status:

to determine the legal status of the American Declaration it is appropriate to look to the inter-American system of today in light of the evolution it has undergone since the adoption of the Declaration, rather than to examine the normative value and significance which that instrument was believed to have had in 1948. [*Advisory Opinion* OC-10/89, para 37]

Given that the Inter-American Commission is under an obligation to protect the norms enunciated in the Declaration, and the Declaration is frequently referred to by the General Assembly, the Court concluded that the Declaration was a source of international obligations related to the Charter of the Organization (para 45). Accordingly the Court concluded that the Declaration had some legal effect and that the Court had the power to interpret it in certain circumstances (para 47). Not all Member States of the OAS have ratified the Convention, therefore the Declaration will continue to have a significant role in shaping the human rights' obligations of certain States. This is evidenced by the work of the Inter-American Commission (*infra*).

8.2.2 **The American Convention**

In 1959, the Fifth Meeting of Consultation of Ministers of Foreign Affairs (Santiago, Chile) resolved that given the progress made since the Declaration was adopted and the parallel progressive development of human rights both in Europe and under the auspices of the United Nations, 'the climate in this hemisphere is favorable to the conclusion of a convention' (OEA/Ser.C/II.5, p 10—the same resolution established the Inter-American Commission on Human Rights). The American Convention of Human Rights was signed in 1969 in San José, Costa Rica; hence it is sometimes referred to as the Pact of San José. However, it was not until July 1978, following the deposit of the eleventh instrument of ratification, that the Convention entered into force. The purpose of the Convention is articulated in the preambular paragraphs as being to further the intention of the States 'to consolidate in this hemisphere, within the framework of democratic institutions, a system of personal liberty and social justice based on respect for the essential rights of man'.

The Convention restricts itself to a detailed tabulation of civil and political rights. Economic, social, and cultural rights are covered in a single Article (Art 26) which cross refers to the Charter of the OAS as amended by the Protocol of Buenos Aires. On this matter, it should be noted that in 1988, the OAS adopted an Additional Protocol in the Area of Economic, Social and Cultural Rights (the Protocol of San Salvador—discussed later). The Convention itself establishes the machinery to be employed in protecting the rights of all Americans. The Inter-American Commission is given various functions and powers with a detailed system for lodging individual petitions. However, this procedure is complementary to the pre-existing competence of the Commission to receive communications on human rights.

8.2.3 **Additional Protocols**

8.2.3.1 *Additional Protocol to the American Convention on Human Rights in the Area of Economic, Social and Cultural Rights (Protocol of San Salvador) 1988*

The Preamble to the Protocol emphasizes the indivisibility of the two sets of rights. However, most States were reluctant to follow their political rhetoric with ratification and the Protocol did not enter into force until 1999. It still has considerably fewer contracting parties than the Convention. The rights in the Protocol in the main reflect those of the International Covenant on Economic, Social and Cultural Rights. The connection is also apparent in the incumbent obligation on States:

to adopt the necessary measures, both domestically and through international cooperation, especially economic and technical, to the extent allowed by their available resources, and taking into account their degree of development, for the purpose of achieving progressively and pursuant to their internal legislations, the full observance of the rights recognized in this Protocol. [Art 1]

States are further obliged to adopt the necessary legislation to realize the rights within their jurisdiction (Art 2). The rights covered by the Protocol are essentially rights to work, social security, health, a healthy environment, food, education, culture, family protection, and trade union rights. Vulnerable groups in society, namely children, the elderly, and the handicapped, are singled out for particular protection.

8.2.3.2 *Protocol to the American Convention on Human Rights to Abolish the Death Penalty 1990*

Given the tendency among States to abolish the death penalty within their territory, partly in light of the 'irrevocable consequences' thereof, the Protocol seeks to abolish the death penalty in the region. Like the Council of Europe's Thirteenth Protocol, no exception is permitted in time of war or imminent threat of war.

8.2.4 Other conventions and instruments

The OAS has expanded the scope of its human rights protection with a number of further conventions.

8.2.4.1 *Inter-American Convention to Prevent and Punish Torture 1985*

The Convention was opened for signature in 1985 at the regular session of the General Assembly. It defines torture and specifies the liability of individuals for it. It required only two ratifications (achieved within two years) to enter force. The Convention provides for the training of police officers and those public officials responsible for detainees in order to eliminate torture during interrogation, detention, or arrest. The treatment of detainees was a notable problem in many States of the Americas, particularly during periods of military rule. The United Nations has also acted to prescribe standards of treatment for detainees and guidelines to be followed by law enforcement officers and the judiciary. The Convention also guarantees impartial reviews of torture allegations and addresses various jurisdictional issues regarding the trial and extradition of those implicated in the crime of torture.

8.2.4.2 *Inter-American Convention on the Forced Disappearance of Persons 1994*

In Belém do Pará, Brazil, the General Assembly laid open the Convention on Forced Disappearance of Persons which entered into force in 1996. Thousands of people disappeared without trace in the Americas during periods of military rule—an affront to the conscience of the hemisphere, according to the Preamble. Member States of the OAS reaffirmed in the Preamble that the systematic practice of forced disappearances of persons constitutes a crime against humanity. This is corroborated by Article 7(i) of the Statute of the International Criminal Court which includes enforced disappearances of persons within the ambit of crimes against humanity. Forced disappearances are defined in Art II of the Convention as:

the act of depriving a person or persons of his or their freedom, in whatever way, perpetrated by agents of the State or by persons or groups of persons acting with the authorization, support, or acquiescence of the State, followed by an absence of information or a refusal to acknowledge that deprivation of freedom or to give information on the whereabout of that person, thereby impeding his or her recourse to the applicable legal remedies and procedural guarantees.

Contracting parties agree not to practice, permit, or tolerate forced disappearances and to adopt legislation aimed at punishing those implicated in such a grave crime. Various jurisdictional issues are addressed, including extradition agreements. In keeping with the designation of forced disappearances as a crime against humanity, Art VIII renders the defence of due obedience to superior orders or instructions inapplicable.

8.2.4.3 *Inter-American Convention on the Prevention, Punishment and Eradication of Violence against Women (Convention of Belém do Pará) 1994*

This Convention was adopted at the same time as that on Forced Disappearances but proved more popular insofar as it entered into force in 1995. In some ways this may be surprising as forced disappearances were a comparatively new phenomenon in Latin America compared to the long and tortuous process of promoting the status of women in Latino culture. The Convention represents an amalgamation of the preceding Declaration on the Elimination of Violence against Women and various regional and international instruments. It is made clear that 'violence against women pervades every sector of society regardless of class, race or ethnic group, income, culture, level of education, age or religion and strikes at its very foundations' (Preamble). Physical, sexual, and psychological violence against women, which explicitly includes violence in the home, is prohibited (Art 2). However, the Convention goes on to articulate a number of rights enjoyed by women including the right to life, liberty, integrity, fair trial, association, religion, legal protection, and freedom from torture (Art 4). The duties States undertake when ratifying the Convention are spelt out in detail in Arts 7–9. States agree to do more than merely investigate, prosecute, and punish violence against women. For example, States agree to take measures to modify social and cultural patterns of conduct of men and women to counteract prejudices and customs based on inferiority of women and stereotyping of roles (Art 8). The duties imposed on the State are reasonably comprehensive and, as this example illustrates, go to the heart of the matter. Without appropriate training and education, cultural traditions are difficult to eradicate. Education is the key, as recognized by the American States. Parallels can be drawn with government-sponsored campaigns against domestic violence in many other States. The mechanisms of protection contained in the Convention include individual and NGO communications to the Inter-American Commission as well as periodic reports from Contracting States.

8.2.4.4 *Inter-American Convention on the Elimination of all Forms of Discrimination against Persons with Disabilities 1999*

The most recent initiative of the Organization of American States is an Inter-American Convention on the Elimination of all forms of Discrimination against Person with Disabilities. In terms of this instrument, a Committee for the Elimination of All Forms of Discrimination against Persons with Disabilities is established. Undoubtedly this Convention is progressive and represents a considerable advancement on the other systems. The United Nations is currently examining the rights of disabled person while in Europe, the treatment of people with disabilities has been left at the national level. It should be noted that the position in Europe is changing partly as a result of various non-discrimination initiatives adopted by the European Community.

8.3 The institutional framework

8.3.1 The Inter-American Commission on Human Rights

The Inter-American Commission on Human Rights (based in Washington DC) has an unusual duality of roles. It is an autonomous organ of the Organization of

American States and exercises functions in accordance therewith. More recently, the American Convention on Human Rights further empowered the Commission and imbued it with added responsibilities and functions.

8.3.1.1 *Historical development of the Commission*

The Inter-American Commission was established in 1959, coincidentally the same year as the European Court of Human Rights (Council of Europe), by resolution of the Fifth Meeting of Consultation of Ministers of Foreign Affairs (OEA/Ser.C/II.5). The Council of the OAS approved the Statute of the Commission in 1960 with the first elections occurring later that year. Ostensibly, the role of the Commission was to undertake investigations on various topics of general interest, furthering respect for human rights. However, it soon was inundated with complaints about violations of human rights. With no power to investigate them, the Commission confined itself to compiling records of these complaints, establishing the existence of gross, systematic violations of human rights upon which action could be taken. Publicizing these reports and raising them for discussion in the General Assembly would, it was hoped, exert political and moral pressure on the State in question. Sadly, this was not always the case. The year 1962 brought the first formal calls for the broadening of the Commission's Statute (the Eighth Meeting of Consultation of Ministers of Foreign Affairs in Punta del Este, Uruguay) though nothing happened until 1965. With the Buenos Aires Protocol of 1967, the Inter-American Commission on Human Rights was elevated to the status of a principal organ of the OAS.

8.3.1.2 *Structure of the Commission*

In accordance with the Convention, there are seven members of the Commission who are 'persons of high moral character and recognized competence in the field of human rights' (Art 34). They are appointed by the General Assembly of the OAS to serve in their personal capacity for a single, four-year, renewable term of office (Arts 36–7). No two members can be from the same Member State and, as with similar bodies elsewhere, the elections are staggered to take place every two years.

The General Secretariat of the OAS provides secretariat services for the Commission.

8.3.1.3 *Function of the Commission*

The Commission functions in accordance with its Statute and its own Regulations (Art 39). Its primary role is to keep vigilance over the observance of human rights (Art 150, as amended, Charter of the OAS). It has two sets of functions: those accruing under the Convention in respect of Contracting States and those pertaining to the entire membership of the OAS irrespective of ratification of the Convention. These latter functions are the pre-existing functions of the Commission derived both from practice and from the OAS Charter itself. The Rules of Procedure clearly differentiates between the two sets of procedure which the Commission can follow. Indeed, Art 1 of the Commission's Statute defines human rights as being: 'a) The rights set forth in the American Convention on Human Rights, in relation to the State Parties thereto; b) The rights set forth in the American Declaration of the Rights and Duties of Man, in relation to other Member States'.

In carrying out its mandate, the Commission receives, analyses, and investigates individual petitions alleging violations of human rights. This is considered in more detail below. Despite these developments, the examination of individual complaints took a back seat compared to the role of the Commission in undertaking more detailed country reports on systematic violations of human rights. Until the entry into force of the Convention, the Commission was the sole body with any kind of mandate to investigate and report on violations of human rights within the region (although obviously the United Nations could address certain aspects).

The Commission also stimulates public consciousness regarding human rights in the Americas; organizes conferences, seminars, and meetings on relevant issues; disseminates information on human rights; advises States on human rights obligation; and it can request 'precautionary measures' for a State to take while human rights abuses are being investigated. In terms of the American Convention, the Commission submits cases to the Inter-American Court and requests advisory opinion for the Court on the interpretation of the Convention. Oral hearings can be held by the Commission. In general, the Commission is highly accessible to NGOs and other non-State actors.

Its main function is to 'promote respect for and defense of human rights' (Art 41). To this end it is mandated to develop awareness of human rights, to prepare reports and studies, to provide information and advisory services to States, and to take action on petitions and other communications. Fact-finding, *in loco* investigations, and compilation of reports on the human rights situation in particular Member States remain an important aspect of the work of the Commission. The Commission submits an annual report to the General Assembly of the OAS.

8.3.2 The Inter-American Court of Human Rights

The Inter-American Court of Human Rights was established by the American Convention on Human Rights. However, the idea of a judicial organ to protect the 'rights of man' was first mooted in 1948 at the Bogotá International Conference of American States (OAS/Ser.L/V/II.14). Despite divided opinions, provision for a competent court was made in the Convention. The Court is 'an autonomous judicial institution whose purpose is the application and interpretation of the American Convention on Human Rights' (Art 1, Statute of the Court).

8.3.2.1 *Composition of the Court*
The Court consists of seven judges elected in their individual capacity from among 'jurists of the highest moral authority and of recognized competence in the field of human rights, who possess the qualifications required for the exercise of the highest judicial function' (Art 52). Judges are elected by the General Assembly for a single renewable term of six years with a staggered system of re-election every three years (Art 54). In the interests of fairness, the State Parties involved in any case being heard by the Court have the right to appoint an ad hoc judge to serve on the panel for the duration of the case (Art 55). The Court has its permanent seat is San José, Costa Rica, although it may convene elsewhere in the Americas.

8.3.2.2 *Functions of the Court*
The Court has its own Statute and Rules of Procedure under which it operates. Its initial Rules of Procedure were modelled closely on those of its Strasbourg sibling though over the years the procedure was streamlined and altered. The most recent

Rules of Procedure were approved December 2003. The principal change is that once the Court is seized of a case involving a violation of the Convention, the alleged victim/s, the next of kin, and/or appointed representatives will enjoy *locus standi in judico* (direct participation) at all stages of proceedings before the Court. However, in a situation akin to that of the original Council of Europe system (prior to Protocol 11), only the Commission and State Parties have *locus standi* to bring a case before the Court (Art 61).

The Inter-American Court has both advisory and adjudicatory jurisdiction. States elect whether they will accept the jurisdiction of the Court upon ratification of the Convention or at any time thereafter. When adjudicating on cases involving potential violations of the Convention, provisional measures may be ordered, even at the stage of the case being lodged with the Commission. Naturally this only occurs in situations of extreme gravity or urgency threatening 'irreparable damage' to persons (Art 63). This right to impose interim measures is similar to that enjoyed by the Committee against Torture or the Human Rights Committee. Provisional measures have been granted in a number of cases, including *Alemán Lacayo* and the *Case of Haitians and Dominicans of Haitian Origin in the Dominican Republic*.

Cases are brought to the Court by the Commission or Contracting States after a compulsory procedure has been carried out. Should the Court find that a State has violated a right or freedom protected under the Convention, then the Court has the power to request remediation and reparation, including awards of compensation to the individual concerned

Key case

Case of the Plan de Sánchez Massacre v Guatemala, Series C, No 105 (2004)

Some 268 people (mostly Maya Achí peoples) died in the government forces' attack on the village of Plan de Sánchez on 18 July 1982. Guatemala was gripped by a violent civil war at the time. The Mayan culture was not respected with regard to, inter alia, burial. Property sustained significant damage and, in general, the village and its population was decimated. National proceedings were instituted against the State but proved protracted. A complaint was filed with the Inter-American Commission which in turn referred the case to the Court. In 2004, the government conceded the facts and the Inter-American Court thus found violations of a range of Articles of the Convention, including the right to humane treatment; right to a fair trial; and freedom of conscience and religion, of thought and expression, and of association.

In the subsequent Reparations case, the Court ordered Guatemala to investigate the facts, identify, prosecute and punish the perpetrators, undertake a public act of acknowledgement in the village, repair the village chapel, provide free healthcare for victims etc, and pay costs and expenses. In addition, almost USD 8 million was awarded in pecuniary (USD 5,000 per victim) and non-pecuniary (USD 20,000 per victim) damages, one of the largest awards in human rights.

The first contentious cases referred to the Court by the Commission were the *Velásquez Rodríguez* (Honduran Disappearances) cases. As Honduras had not complied with requests for information made by the Commission in the initial stages of the process, the Court decided to conduct a trial *de novo*, obtaining evidence and attempting to ascertain the facts before adjudicating on the merits of the case.

The advisory jurisdiction of the Court allows the Court to provide interpretation of the Convention (or any other of the OAS Conventions). Since its inception, the Court has given a number of advisory opinions on a diverse range of issues including exceptions to the exhaustion of domestic remedies, habeus corpus in emergency situations, and, more recently, the right to information on consular assistance in the framework of the guarantees of the due process of law.

8.3.3 The Inter-American Council for Integral Development

The 1993 Protocol of Managua replaced the Inter-American Economic and Social Council and the Inter-American Council for Education, Science and Culture with this new body in 1996. The purpose of this body is to promote cooperation among Member States with the objective of achieving their integral development. In order to achieve this, the Council reflects the new approach to development which has also characterised the recent work of the United Nations. Rather than cooperation being of a donor–recipient relationship, essentially donor led, the OAS is embracing the new definition of cooperation as a participation partnership with joint ownership throughout the development cycle. This would be demand driven rather than donor driven, thus securing internal development of States.

Partnership for development in the OAS emphasizes 'multi-country activities' carried out within a framework of priority areas—cultural development, productive employment generation, economic diversification, integration and trade liberalization, strengthening of democratic institution, science, technological exchange and telecommunication, tourism development, and sustainable development and the environment (IACID, pp 2–4). The Council sees itself as playing a pivotal role in creating a shared agenda for development throughout the Hemisphere, thereby encouraging the creation of an integrated community of nations (IACID, p 2).

The Council reports directly to the General Assembly of the OAS. Its status as a pan-American initiative means that the Council can seek co-sponsorship, support, and technical assistance not only from other Member States but also from other inter-American organizations, sub-regional organizations and various international institutions such as the World Bank and United Nations' agencies such as UNDP, UNICEF, etc.

The elimination of extreme poverty is a key objective. Clearly, the work of this Council links in to the emerging right to development and the ongoing work of the United Nations in this respect (see Chapter 23).

8.3.4 The General Assembly

The General Assembly is the supreme organ of the OAS. All Member States have the right to be represented and vote in it. At its 2003 meeting, it approved the Santiago Declaration on Democracy and Public Trust, which it heralded as 'the principal hemispheric benchmark for the promotion and defence of shared democratic principles and values in the Americas'. This was developed further in 2004 at Quito, Ecuador.

8.3.5 **The Inter-American Commission of Women**

The Inter-American Commission of Women is a specialized organization of the OAS, dating to the 1928 Sixth International Conference of American States (Havana). Every member State contributes one delegate to the Commission and this Assembly of thirty-four delegates meets every two years. The mission of the Commission is to 'promote and protect women's rights', advancing equality of participation by men and women in all aspects of society.

Associated functions are carried out by the Permanent Secretariat and delegates throughout the hemisphere. Support and recognition of national women's movement occurs at all levels, from grass roots to governmental.

8.4 **Implementing human rights**

Compliance by Contracting States with the provisions of the American Convention is ensured through a combination of approaches: reports, inter-State, and individual complaints. Both the Inter-American Commission on Human Rights and the Inter-American Court of Human Rights have competency with respect to the fulfilment of commitments made by States under the Convention (Art 33). However, in the initial stages of the operation of the system, events should be placed in their historical context. The machinery established under the Convention could not operate in the same manner as its European counterpart as, on the whole, it was dealing with gross violations of fundamental rights on a scale not widely witnessed in Europe since the conclusion of the Second World War. Second, the regimes in power were often dismissive or even hostile towards attempts at external regulation. States of Emergency and, *ergo*, the suspension of legislation involving rights, were regular occurrences especially when military action and coups were imminent or in the aftermath thereof. Article 42 of the Regulations of the Inter-American Commission provides that when investigating individual complaints, the failure of a State to respond to the facts shall render the facts as true, unless there is evidence to the contrary. Such default judgments were commonplace until the end of the twentieth century.

As discussed, the American system is unusual in that all Member States of the OAS may find themselves subjected to investigation and report by the Inter-American Commission on Human Rights (Arts 19–20 of the Statute of the Inter-American Commission on Human Rights). Ratification, even signature of the American Convention is immaterial. There are thus three mechanisms by which human rights are protected within the OAS: the Commission monitoring compliance of non-State Parties to the Convention through its residual powers; the Commission monitoring compliance with the Convention of Contracting States; and the Court considering cases brought before it from those States which accept its compulsory jurisdiction. As a consequence, different States are subject to different enforcement mechanisms. In general, the English-speaking areas (North America and the Caribbean) remain outwith the Convention mechanisms though they may still be subject to investigation by the Commission under its residual powers.

8.4.1 **Monitoring human rights outwith the Convention**

Member States of the OAS who have not yet ratified the Convention on Human Rights remain accountable to the Inter-American Commission on Human Rights. At the second Special Inter-American Conference held in Rio de Janeiro (1965), it was resolved that the Statute of the Commission should be amended to authorize the examination of communications received and make recommendations thereon (OEA/Ser.C/I.13, pp 32–4). In 1966, the Commission formalized its procedure for handling individual complaints, enabling it to examine, then deliver an opinion on, violations of human rights in the territory of any member State of the OAS. It should be noted that these investigative functions still operate in respect of all Member States of the OAS, irrespective of whether they have ratified the Convention. According to its 2008 Report, the Commission has dealt with a total of 14,000 cases and petitions over the years. It received 1,323 complaints in 2008 and is currently processing 1,376 individual cases and petitions.

Key case

Goodman v Commonwealth of the Bahamas **Report no 78/07 Case 12.265, October 2007**

This case is an example of a violation of human rights which could have avoided scrutiny as the Bahamas has not ratified the Inter-American Convention, the case being brought to the Inter-American Commission on the alleged violations of the Declaration alone. Note that the Bahamas failed to respond to requests for information from the Commission.

Goodman was convicted of murder, kidnapping and armed robbery and sentenced to a mandatory death sentence for the murder, concurrent terms of ten years' imprisonment for kidnapping and fifteen years' imprisonment for armed robbery. He alleged violations of, inter alia, the right to a fair trial, right to life, and right to equality before the law. With the exception of the impartial hearing, violations were found. As the Commission noted, it is:

empowered under Article 20 of its Statute and Articles 49 and 50 of its Rules of Procedure to receive and examine any petition that contains a denunciation of alleged violations of the human rights set forth in the American Declaration in relation to OAS Member States that are not parties to the American Convention. [Para 41]

With regard to the fact:

the imposition of a mandatory death sentence precludes any effective review by a higher court as to the propriety of a sentence of death in the circumstances of a particular case ... There is no opportunity for a reviewing tribunal to consider whether the death penalty was an appropriate punishment in the circumstances of the particular offense or offender. This consequence cannot be reconciled with the fundamental principles of due process provisions. [Para 53]</ext>

The Commission recommended that the Bahamas amends its legislation and grants the applicant an effective remedy including commutation of sentence and compensation for the violations of the Declaration.

The main constraint on the work of the Commission is financial. The political constraints were addressed through very narrow fields of investigation in response to complaints. Moreover, the Commission is heavily reliant on the acquiescence of the State concerned and its active participation in the ensuing investigation. For obvious reasons, this was not always forthcoming. The Commission would produce a final opinion on a case but thereafter had no means of ensuring a change in State practice.

The Commission reports to the General Assembly on the general human rights situation in specific Member States. To facilitate the compilation of more detailed information on the human rights situation in any given Member State, the Commission carries out on-site visits. The first on-site visits were to the Dominican Republic, to Miami, Florida, USA (the Cuban refugees), El Salvador, and Honduras. In the case of the latter two States, a special delegation from the Commission remained *in situ* for several months in 1969. Recent on-site visits have included Guatemala (July 2005), Bolivia (June 2008), Chile (August 2008), and Jamaica (December 2008). Many such visits are undertaken by rapporteurs working with and for the Commission. In its first fifty years, the Commission undertook more than a hundred site visits and published seventy-five country reports and special subject reports. Through these visits, the Commission seeks to document and investigate the human rights situation. The rationale was initially the investigation of gross and systematic violations of human rights. Today, it has evolved into a system whereby human rights are monitored through visits and reports in all Member States. The Commission has a strong mandate and follows on-site visits with detailed reports and further monitoring of any situations deemed to be of concern. The process is considerably more successful than the on-site State visits currently employed by the African Commission on Human and Peoples' Rights which lack the public and formal structure which characterizes the American system.

As these procedures can apply to all Member States of the OAS, the Inter-American system is arguably stricter than either the United Nations or the other regional organizations in respect of human rights. The general powers of the United Nations' bodies in respect of human rights (Resolution 1253 and 1503 of ECOSOC, see Chapter 5) are less readily invoked. In Europe, all members of the Council of Europe have ratified the Convention thus there is no need for an extra-Conventional mechanism. However, arguably, the region could benefit from on-site visits by human rights monitors outwith the confines of the European Convention for the Prevention of Torture and Inhuman or Degrading Treatment or Punishment, and the diplomatic efforts of those involved in the OSCE.

8.4.2 Convention—reports

Unlike many other international human rights instruments, the American Convention contains no general duty relating to the submission of periodic reports by Contracting States. State Parties submit annual reports to the Executive Committees of the Inter-American Council for Integral Development with copies filed also with the Commission (Art 42). To date, States have not viewed this provision as a mandatory requirement. When reports are submitted, they can be used by the Commission to elicit responses from States as to specific human rights situations.

8.4.3 **Convention—inter-State complaints**

Article 45 provides that any State may recognize the competency of the Commission to receive and examine inter-State complaints. State declarations may be indefinite or for set periods of time or even for the benefit of any instant case. The inter-State procedure is thus optional.

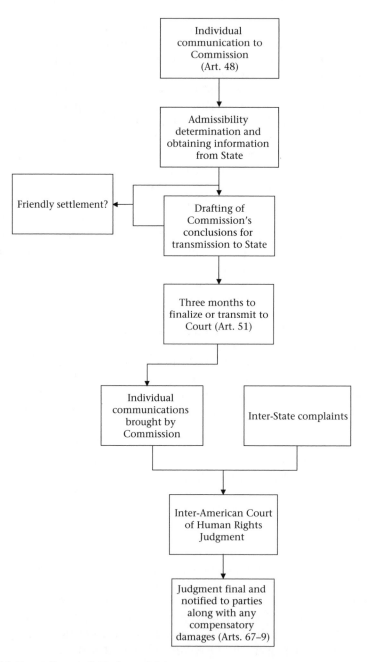

Figure 8.1 Convention—individual complaints.

Complaints will only be deemed admissible if all domestic remedies have been exhausted, the petition is lodged within six months of the final domestic decision, and the matter is not pending before any other international body (Art 46). In reflection of the historical reality of the 1960s in Latin America, provision is made for the voiding of the requirement of exhausting domestic remedies if 'the domestic legislation of the State concerned does not afford due process of law for the protection of the right or rights that have allegedly been violated' or the party has been denied access to domestic remedies or otherwise prevented from exhausting them (Art 46(2)).

8.4.4 Convention—individual complaints

Note that, as discussed above, individuals may also submit complaints to the Commission for consideration under the general OAS regulations. The American system is unique insofar as the individual complaints' mechanism has been used with some success to facilitate public examination and condemnation of systematic flagrant violations of human rights. Any person or group may lodge petitions with the Commission containing denunciations or complaints of violations of the Convention by any State Party (Art 44). The same right is accorded to nongovernmental entities legally recognized in at least one OAS State. In addition to the admissibility criteria mentioned above, individual complaints may not be anonymous and must contain specified details of the complainant (Art 46(d)). On the exhaustion of domestic remedies, the State must demonstrate domestic remedies exist and have not been exhausted (*Velásquez Rodríguez, Preliminary objections*, para 88), the burden of proof then shifts to the complainant who must demonstrate the applicability of the exceptions on ground of indigency or a generalized fear (*Exceptions to the Exhaustion of Domestic Remedies, Advisory Opinion*, para 41).

The Commission is currently processing over a thousand individual complaints. When receiving individual complaints concerning violations of the American Convention on Human Rights, the Commission is under an obligation to seek resolution of the matter before proceeding to Court. The procedure is prescribed in Arts 48–51 of the Convention. Once a communication is deemed admissible, the Commission will request the government of the State against whom the complaint is made to respond to the allegations within a specified period. Following the expiry of the period (and, hopefully but not necessarily, the receipt of the State response), the Commission will determine whether to proceed with the petition. The Commission will then investigate the complaint in full, possibly also soliciting oral statements or written submission from the parties concerned. Until the mid 1990s, States had responded overall to less than half of the requests for information and requests to participate in the process before the Commission. In such circumstances, a default judgment would be given, the Commission presuming the submitted facts to be true in the absence of refuting evidence by the State. This lack of interest in the process corroborates the assumption that human rights were not high on the agenda of States at that time. Partly through changes in government regimes, this situation altered in the closing stages of the twentieth century and now the participation rate is virtually 100 per cent (though the reliability of some submissions remains questionable).

Following receipt of the salient information, attempts will be made to secure a friendly settlement underpinned by respect for the human rights articulated in the Convention. If an appropriate friendly settlement is reached then the Commission will draw up a report summarizing the facts and the solution reached. This report will be transmitted to the parties concerned and, for publication, to the Secretary-General of the OAS. It should be noted that in serious and urgent cases, a shortened version of the process applies in order to facilitate a prompt examination of the facts.

Should the attempts to secure a friendly settlement fail, then the Commission draws up a comprehensive report of the case within a set period. This report will outline the facts as found and provide an opinion, proposals, and recommendations. The written and oral statements made by the parties and any dissenting opinions will be attached to the report. This report is transmitted to the State concerned and a period of three months then elapses to facilitate settlement by the State or the transmission of the matter to the Court either by the Commission or by the State. If the Court is not seized of the issue, then the Commission may make 'pertinent recommendations' and prescribe a period of time within which the State should institute measures to remedy the situation which gave rise to the complaint. After the period has elapsed, the Committee may decide to publish the report. Nine new cases were presented to the Court in 2008, though seventeen cases are in process.

Petitions are received and processed in any of the four working languages of the OAS—Spanish, Portuguese, English, and French.

8.5 Conclusions

The 2008 Annual Report of the Commission reflected on sixty years of the American Declaration and the Universal Declaration of Human Rights:

[e]ven though over the course of these six decades, progress has clearly been made toward strengthening and protecting human rights worldwide, and serious violations of human rights have been exposed and disavowed by the majority of states through their ratification of international instruments and their adoption, at the domestic level, of measures of protection, the ideals of 1948 are far from being fulfilled. Poverty, hunger, the continued failure to treat easily curable diseases, discrimination, illiteracy, torture, forced disappearance and injustice are still part of our contemporary reality and plague our region and other parts of the globe. Accordingly, the 60th anniversary of the American Declaration and Universal Declaration gives us cause to reflect more than to celebrate. It is an opportunity to renew the spirit that drove the authors of these important international instruments, to reflect upon the errors of the past and the progress achieved, and to rededicate to making human dignity, freedom, equality, justice and solidarity the main objective of States, and to cultivate the conditions that will enable every individual to realize his or her full potential and achieve happiness. [OEA/Ser.L/V/II.134, Doc. 5, rev. 1, para 2]

The Summit of the Americas in Miami (1994) called for preventative capacity in the Inter-American human rights system. To this end, studies are currently being carried out to ascertain what steps must be taken to achieve this. It is anticipated that the Court will be given power to adopt provisional measures for human rights protection in those situations where the national system does not so provide. The Plan of Action adopted in the Miami Declaration highlights three areas of action. The first is securing 'universal access to justice and effective means to enforce basic rights'. The leaders of the American States intended this to produce a climate of respect for human rights. Technical support is provided for States wishing to strive towards this goal. International experts and the Unit for the Promotion of Democracy can provide technical assistance and advise States on the measures required. The second aspect of the Miami Declaration is a pledge by governments to develop programmes for the promotion and observance of human rights. This is to include educational programmes which will inform people of their rights. This development alone is one of the first of its kind and represents a real attempt by States to fulfil their obligations under the various instruments to which they subscribe. The Inter-American Institute of Human Rights and NGOs are charged with assisting in this. Third, the Summit of the Americas pledged to review training curricula for law enforcement agents which should contribute to the defence of human rights. A comparative study of practices in Member States will contribute toward developing appropriate training courses, expert assistance being provided to those States which wish to redesign their existing programmes.

The Organization is now placing a special emphasis on indigenous peoples with the declared aim of producing a hemispheric declaration on indigenous rights. It is possible that this may prove a more successful process than the ongoing struggle to agree a text on indigenous rights under the auspices of the United Nations.

Technologically, the American system surpasses the other regional arrangements—there is provision for online submission of communications. As information technology extends its grip, there will be fewer places without internet access and thus this initiative is to be welcomed albeit the theory may at the moment be better than the practice. Indeed, the result has not been a dramatic increase in the number of applications filed.

Without doubt, the Inter-American system has succeeded in developing and flourishing over a period of instability in the region. It has played a key role in maintaining a profile for human rights. In many respects, the American system is in a similar position to the European system almost thirty years ago: a low number of individual complaints reach the Court and Commission; not all States participate in the various processes; few contentious cases have been heard. However, in the context of a region emerging from the shadow of systematic and gross violations of human rights, these differences are not as surprising.

Inevitably, the complexity of a system arising from the multiplicity of obligations undertaken by States can render the OAS system confusing. The anglophone 'opt-out' of the formal Convention mechanism unbalances the regional impact. Given that these States have, in the main, acceded to the United Nations Covenants, their reluctance to ascribe to the American system is unfortunate. This also contributes to the problem of States often omitting reference to the regional organization, preferring instead to work with the United Nations. However, this problem pervades the practice of some Contracting States, eg Brazil. The OAS thus has to be continually proactive in developing support for regional rights, striving to create a system which is recognized by the States concerned as a valid and effective method of monitoring and enforcing rights. The OAS has considerable potential, though at present that potential has not been fully realized.

CASES

Alemán Lacayo, Ser E, No 2, Order of 6 February 1997.

Case of Haitians and Dominicans of Haitian Origin in the Dominican Republic, Ser E, No 3, Order of 18 August 2000.

Exceptions to the Exhaustion of Domestic Remedies (Arts 46(1), 46(2)(a) and 46(2)(b) of the American Convention on Human Rights), Advisory Opinion OC 11/90, Ser A, No 11 (1990).

Habeus Corpus in Emergency Situations, Advisory Opinion OC-8/87, Ser A, No 8 (1987).

Interpretation of the American Declaration of the Rights and Duties of Man Within the Framework of Article 64 of the American Convention on Human Rights, Advisory Opinion OC-10/89, Ser A, No 10 (1989).

The Right to Information on Consular Assistance in the Framework of the Guarantees of the Due Process of Law, Advisory Opinion OC-19/99, Ser A, No 16 (1999).

Velásquez Rodríguez (Honduran Disappearances) cases, Ser C, No 4 (1988)

READING

It should be noted that the wealth of material, including books and articles, available in Spanish is excluded from the following list.

Buergenthal, T, and Shelton, D, *Protecting Human Rights in the Americas: Cases and materials*, 4th edn (Arlington: Engel, 1995).

Cavallan, J, and Brewer, S, 'Reevaluating regional human rights litigation in the twenty-first century: The case of the Inter-American Court' (2008) 102(4) American Journal of International Law 768-827.

Davidson, S, *The Inter-American Court of Human Rights*, 2nd edn (Aldershot: Dartmouth, 1992).

——, *The Inter-American Human Rights System* (Aldershot: Ashgate, 1997).

——, 'Remedies for violations of the American Convention on Human Rights' (1995) 44 International and Comparative Law Quarterly 405–14.

Deodhar, NS, 'First contentious cases before the Inter-American Court of Human Rights' (1988) 3 American University International Law Review 283.

Farer, T, *The Future of the Inter-American System* (Westport, Conn: Praeger, 1979).

——, 'The rise of the Inter-American HR regime: No longer a unicorn, not yet an ox' (1997) 19 Human Rights Quarterly 510–46.

Harris, D, and Livingstone, S (eds), *The Inter-American System for Human Rights* (Oxford: Clarendon Press, 1998).

IACID, *Building Bridges towards the Future of Partnership for Development, Background Information* (IACID, 1997).

Inter-American Commission on Human Rights, *Basic Documents Pertaining to Human Rights in the Inter-American System* (Washington DC: General Sec OAS, 2001).

Macklem, P, and Morgan, E, 'Indigenous rights in the Inter-American system: The amicus brief of the Assembly of First Nations in *Awas Tigni v Republic of Nicaragua*' (2000) 22(2) Human Rights Quarterly 569–71.

Medina, C, *The Battle of Human Rights: Gross, systematic violations and the Inter-American System* (Dordecht/Boston: Martinus Nijhoff, 1988).

Murray, R, 'On-site visits by the African Commission on Human and Peoples' Rights: A case study and comparison with the Inter-American Commission on Human Rights' (1999) 11 African Journal of International and Comparative Law 460–73.

OAS, *The Organization of American States: Advancing democracy, human rights and the rule of law in the Americas/A report of the Inter-American Dialogue Commission on the OAS* (Washington DC: Inter-American Dialogue, 1994).

Padilla, DJ, 'The Inter-American Commission on Human Rights of the Organization of American States: A CASE STUDY' (1993) 9 American University International Law Review 95.

Shelton, D, 'Improving human rights protections: Recommendations for enhancing the effectiveness of the Inter-American Commission and Inter-American Court of Human Rights' (1988) 3 American University International Law Review 323.

——, 'The jurisprudence of the Inter-American Commission on Human Rights' (1994) 10 American University International Law Review 333.

——, 'New rules of procedure for the Inter-American Commission on Human Rights' (2001) 22(5)–(8) Human Rights Law Journal 169–71.

Wilson, RJ, 'Inter-American Commission on Human Rights: Individual case resolutions' (1994) 10 American University International Law Review 19.

WEBSITES

www.oas.org—the Organization for American States.

www.corteidh.or.cr—Inter-American Court of Human Rights (partly in Spanish).

www.cidh.oas.org/DefaultE.htm—Inter-American Commission on Human Rights.

www.iacd.oas.org—Inter-American Council for Integral Development.

www.oas.org/cim/default.htm—the Inter-American Commission of Women.

www.padf.org—the Pan-American Development Foundation.

9

....

The African Union

In Africa, the African Union, formerly the Organization of African Unity, has played the prominent role in developing an African jurisprudence on human rights. The contribution of this to regional human rights will now be examined. The African system is in some ways considerably less developed than its American and European counterparts yet perhaps its greatest success lies in its very existence. It is the youngest system of the fully fledged (ie, monitored and implemented) regional systems for the protection and promotion of human rights. The Organization of African Unity (OAU) was created in 1963 in the wake of rapid and widespread decolonization. It was established to facilitate intra-African relations for the newly emergent States and to provide a forum for African policy vis-à-vis third States to be formulated and discussed. Human Rights were not the sole priority when the Charter was drafted although the OAU Charter provides that the constituent States will 'coordinate and intensify their collaboration and efforts to achieve a better life for the peoples of Africa'. The OAU Charter also stipulates that 'freedom, equality, justice and dignity are essential objectives for the achievement of the legitimate aspirations of the African peoples', acknowledging both the United Nations Charter and the Universal Declaration of Human Rights in passing (Art II(1)(e)).

The OAU has served as a talking shop for African States but has displayed considerable reluctance in intervening in systematic human rights abuses by various military regimes in the region. In the closing decade of the twentieth century there have been several instances of Member States intervening solely or jointly with peacekeeping missions to States with systematic and gross violations of human rights. However, the motives and methods of some of these missions could be questioned as some have unfortunately added more fuel than water to the fire of civil war.

The decision to establish an African Union was taken at the Sirte Extraordinary Session of the OAU in 1999. The Lome summit in Togo the following year adopted the Constitutive Act of the Union. With the entry into force of the Treaty on the Foundation of an African Union, the OAU ceased to exist, the Durban Summit in 2002 launched the new organization and convened the first Assembly of the Heads of State of the African Union. The primary function of the African Union is to promote the accelerated integration of the continent, promoting greater unity and solidarity between African countries. Peace, security, and stability are prerequisites for the realization of the Union's vision (AU Charter).

At present, there is little alteration to the existing mechanism for monitoring and implementing human rights formerly employed under the auspices of the OAU. The African Union is based on the principle of respect for human rights. The constituent documents emphasize the role of human rights within the region and within the Organization, claiming the promotion of rights as one of its aims (Art 3(f)).

9.1 Development of human rights protection

Given the prevalence of military dictators such as Amin, Kenyatta, and Nkrumah, achieving consensus on the desirability of a regional human rights system was a lengthy process, though consensus on the promotion of 'liberation' from colonialism was more forthcoming. In 1981, the OAU adopted the African Charter on Human and Peoples' Rights. It was designed to reflect African concepts of rights and thus is distinctive in its phraseology and underlying rationale. In 1998, a Protocol to the Charter was agreed—the Protocol on the Establishment of an African Court on Human and Peoples' Rights—which has yet to enter into force. Africa encompasses a number of different legal and linguistic traditions (Arabic, English, French, Portuguese, and Spanish) due to its colonial history. It also has a rich system of traditional and customary laws and rules that are still invoked by the indigenous peoples in some areas. In some respects, the region thus appears less homogenous than either Europe or America. However, there is a common historical tradition of rights in Africa, albeit without a coherent infrastructure, and there is a transnational recognition of the importance of the community and society to the individual. This is reflected in the Charter by the inclusion of distinct, 'peoples'' rights.

9.2 The African Charter and other instruments

9.2.1 The African Charter on Human and Peoples' Rights

The Charter (often referred to as the Banjul Charter) entered into force in 1986. It enshrines the African concept of rights and aims to be accessible to African philosophy: it is striking among international and regional instruments in its emphasis on human and peoples' rights and its cataloguing of the duties of the individual/ group to the State. A further notable feature is that, unlike other international and regional instruments, States are not permitted to derogate from the articles of the Charter. The rights and duties thus remain applicable during times of public emergency.

9.2.1.1 *The approach of the Charter*
Unlike the other regional organizations, the OAU adopted an integrated approach to human rights. The Preamble states that the parties are convinced that it is essential to pay particular attention to the right to development. Interestingly, the Preamble also notes that civil and political rights cannot be dissociated from economic, social, and cultural rights in their conception as well as their universality. Recognition of the indivisibility of human rights has progressively characterized

modern international and regional human rights instruments. However, the African Charter was one of the first instruments to combine all types of rights in one instrument. Inclusion of the right to development (Art 22) and the right to a 'generally satisfactory environment favourable to ... development' (Art 24) evidences a progressive system, ahead of then contemporary legal thought. The Charter goes further, emphasizing that 'the satisfaction of economic, social and cultural rights is a guarantee for the enjoyment of civil and political rights' (Preamble). This approach also challenged the then conventional approach which was to secure civil and political rights, while progressively working towards securing economic, social, and cultural rights (the International Bill of Rights, see Chapter 4).

Many of the rights in the Charter differ from their equivalents in other instruments—for example, condemnation of colonization is a theme—see Arts 19 and 20(2)–(3). Article 21(5) seeks to eliminate new forms of colonization: the economic exploitation of natural resources by international monopolies and foreign powers. The recent history of Africa is also recalled in Art 12(5) which prohibits mass expulsions of national, racial, ethnic, or religious groups.

There are several peoples' rights included in the Charter (Arts 19–24). These are exercisable collectively and include the right to an existence; the right to freely dispose of wealth and natural resources; the right to economic, social, and cultural development; the right to international peace and security; and the right to a general satisfactory environment favourable to the development of the people in point. In a pioneering decision, the African Commission has upheld violations of peoples' environmental rights and rights to natural resources (*Morka Social and Economic Action Centre et al v Nigeria*).

9.2.1.2 *Duties in the Charter*

Chapter II of the Charter focuses on duties. The duties prescribed in the Charter go beyond the mere corollary to the rights enjoyed by individuals (though Art 27(2) contains the more widespread duty on individuals to exercise their rights and duties with due regard to the right of others, collective security, morality, and the common interest). Rather, the individual is required to perform certain duties which go to the heart of African society. Article 27 declares a duty on every individual towards his family and society, the State and other legally recognized communities and the international community. Interestingly, non-discrimination and tolerance of others is also a duty. This is reflective of the 'right to be different' which is promulgated by some international commentators. Finally, individuals are under an obligation to preserve the harmonious development of the family, serve the community, preserve and strengthen national independence and territorial integrity, and preserve and strengthen positive African cultural values (Art 29). The lack of definition for some of these concepts and the problems which would arise in enforcing them are myriad. However, in many respects, the operation of the Charter itself is dependent on these duties with many of the rights being read in light thereof.

9.2.2 **The OAU Convention Governing the Specific Aspects of Refugee Problems in Africa 1969**

With civil unrest, authoritarian rule, inter-faction fighting, and natural disasters commonplace in African society, there is a frequent displacement of peoples,

Key case

Social and Economic Rights Action Centre (SERAC) and the Center for Economic and Social Rights (CESR) v Nigeria, **African Commission on Human and Peoples' Rights, Comm 155/96**

A novel feature of the African Commission is that it can consider violations of economic, social and group rights.

The Communication alleged that the government of Nigeria had been directly involved in oil production which caused 'environmental degradation and health problems resulting from the contamination of the environment among the Ogoni People' (para 1) and that:

oil reserves in Ogoniland [were exploited] with no regard for the health or environment of the local communities, disposing toxic wastes into the environment and local waterways in violation of applicable international environmental standards. The [oil] consortium also neglected and/or failed to maintain its facilities causing numerous avoidable spills in the proximity of villages. The resulting contamination of water, soil and air has had serious short and long-term health impacts, including skin infections, gastrointestinal and respiratory ailments, and increased risk of cancers, and neurological and reproductive problems. [Para 2]

Nigeria did not engage with the Commission thus their decision was made without a full exposition of Nigeria's defence (if any). Violations of a range of rights were alleged.

The Commission noted (para 44) that 'all rights - both civil and political rights and social and economic - generate at least four levels of duties for a State that undertakes to adhere to a rights regime, namely the duty to respect, protect, promote, and fulfil these rights'. The rights to a generally satisfactory environment favourable to development (Art 24) was stated as requiring the State 'to take reasonable and other measures to prevent pollution and ecological degradation, to promote conservation, and to secure an ecologically sustainable development and use of natural resources' (para 52). By their complicity in the destruction of Ogoniland, Nigeria was also in violation of Art 21, the right of peoples to dispose of their wealth and natural resources. Articles 14, 16, and 18(1) were combined to read a right to adequate housing into the African Charter (para 62).

Nigeria was found to be in violation of a range of rights in the Charter and ordered to make amends. (No Shell Petroleum settled a related case in US (2009))

whether to avoid hostilities or escape famine. Refugees are a major problem in some areas. It is thus perhaps inevitable that Africa should lead the way in drafting an instrument aimed solely at regulating refugees. Many of the provisions in the Convention reflect those of the United Nations Convention Relating to the Status of Refugees 1951 (Art VIII (2) describes the instrument as the 'effective regional complement in Africa' of the United Nations Convention). The granting of asylum is addressed, as is voluntary repatriation. The Convention also provides for cooperation between the OAU and the office of the United Nations High Commissioner for Refugees.

9.2.3 **The African Charter on the Rights and Welfare of the Child 1990**

The African Charter on the Rights and Welfare of the Child entered into force in 1999. In many respects it reflects the scope and popularity of the United Nations Convention on the Rights of the Child (to which all African States, bar Somalia, are party). It recognizes that children in Africa need special support and assistance— 'the situation of most African children remains critical due to the unique factors of their socio-economic, cultural, traditional and developmental circumstances, natural disasters, armed conflicts, exploitation and hunger' (Preamble). The rights of children are considered to impose duties on everyone. Many of the provisions are similar to those included in the United Nations Convention, though in Africa the rights extend to all those below the age of eighteen without exception. The best interests of the child will always be the primary consideration (Art 4). In keeping with the tone of the African Charter itself, children are instilled with responsibilities towards the family, society, the State, and the international community. These duties include respecting and caring for parents, superiors, and elders; serving the community; preserving and strengthening national solidarity and African cultural values; and contributing to the promotion and achievement of African unity (Art 31).

A Committee of Experts (Art 32) monitor the Charter on the Rights and Welfare of the Child. The first meeting of the Committee was held in 2002. It has a broad mandate to promote and protect the rights and welfare of the child (Art 42). Unlike the United Nations Committee, the Committee of Experts has competence to receive individual complaints which are to be dealt with confidentially (Art 44) though in line with the approach of the United Nations, reports of the Committee are to be widely disseminated.

9.2.4 **Protocol on Women's Rights**

A draft Protocol on Women's Rights was adopted by the Commission on Human Rights and forwarded to the OAU for discussion. It was adopted by the African Union in July 2003 and entered into force in November 2005, having secured the necessary ratifications. The Protocol seeks to respond to the Beijing principles (UN) and plan of action on combating discrimination against women and strengthening women's rights. The Protocol is part of the existing human rights machinery. The rights enshrined in the Protocol considerably advance women's rights, addressing issues related to abortion, female genital mutilation, and vulnerable groups such as the elderly and widowed.

9.3 **Institutional framework**

Following the establishment of the African Union, a distinct set of organs were created for the new organization. The assembly of Heads of State and Government is the supreme organ of the Union. An Executive Council (Ministers of Governments) is responsible to the Assembly. A Commission with eight Commissioners cover discrete policy areas: the Political Affairs Commissioner's portfolio includes, inter alia, rights, democracy, and refugees. The Lusaka Summit of 2001 also decided

Discussion topic

Ratification v Enforcement

The African Human Rights system covers the broadest range of human rights (civil, collective, economic, political, and social rights) and offers monitoring and individual complaints through its Commission. Yet Africa remains steeped in poverty, decimated by HIV/AIDS, and regularly blighted by coups d'état. Statistics on human development and human rights violations suggest that African States regularly fail to reach the human rights standards they have agreed upon. This raises the topical issue of why states ratify human rights treaties when they cannot or will not fully enforce the rights therein. A number of commentators are investigating this phenomenon. Ratification does not always mean enforcement. There is all too often (and not just in Africa) a huge gulf between the rhetoric of human rights treaties and the reality experienced by nationals of a state. Moreover, enforcement of opinions of the African Commission can be especially problematic for some African countries.

Is it better for all states to ratify human rights treaties and work towards the goals specified therein or should states wait until they are in a position to enforce all the rights before ratifying the treaty?

on the establishment of a Peace and Security Council, the constitutive Protocol for which is now in force, with members elected in 2006. Echoing other regional integrationist organizations, a Pan-African Parliament was inaugurated in March 2004 to provide a voice for all African peoples within the new organization, an Economic Social and Cultural Council will advise the Union's organs on areas within its competence and a Court of Justice was to be established. Finally, an African Central Bank, Monetary Fund, and Investment Bank complete the institutional framework of the new organization. Interim arrangements are in place for the transition period. In 2005, the African Union requested that a document on merging the Court of Justice with the Court on Human and Peoples' Rights be drafted. Nevertheless, in January 2006 it proceeded with creating the Court on Human and Peoples' Rights. This has yet to hear a contentious case and is now being replaced by a new court combining the human rights court and the planned court of justice.

9.3.1 The African Commission on Human and Peoples' Rights

9.3.1.1 *Composition and functions*

The African Commission, a body of eleven independent experts, was created in 1987. Members serve in their personal capacity and should be known for their high reputation, morality, integrity, impartiality, and competence in relevant matters (Art 31). In contrast to previous compositions, members of the Commission today satisfy most of these criteria as well as representing a broad geographical balance. The Commission is tasked with the promotion and protection of human and peoples' rights within the region (Art 30). To this end, the functions of the Commission include the promotion of human rights through collecting documents; undertaking studies on African problems in the field of human and peoples' rights; dissemination of information; organization of symposia; formulation of principles and rules aimed at solving legal problems relating to rights and freedoms; and cooperating with other African and international institutions concerned with the promotion and protection of human and peoples' rights, the protection of human rights in accordance with the Charter, and the interpretation of the Charter (Art 45).

The Commission is to 'draw inspiration' from salient international law including the various African instruments, the United Nations Charter, and the Universal Declaration on Human Rights (Art 60). African laws, traditions, and practices may also be relied upon insofar as they are consistent with the international norms on human and peoples' rights (Art 61).

9.3.1.2 *Meetings of the Commission*

The Commission meets twice a year for two week sessions, usually with each meeting being held in a different State. This facilitates access to the Commission by both the public (one week of each session is open to the public) and by States and NGOs. Despite the benefits of rotating sessions of the Commission, costs of transport and communications can be increased. As previously noted, the United Nations' Human Rights Committee tends to split its meetings between New York and Geneva although other monitoring bodies tend to be located in one city or country.

The Commission receives reports from Contracting States every two years. It is also competent to receive inter-State complaints and individual communications. A primary role of the Commission is the promotion of human rights. Generating an awareness of rights in a region often torn by strife and still characterized by oppressive regimes is the first step towards ensuring the promotion of fundamental rights and freedoms.

9.3.2 **The African Court of Justice and Human Rights**

The Protocol to the African Charter on the Establishment of the African Court on Human and Peoples' Rights 1998 sought to create a Court which complemented and reinforced the work of the Commission in furtherance of the protection of human and peoples' rights as enshrined in the Charter (Preamble). The Union of Comoros became the fifteenth state to ratify the Protocol which then entered into force in January 2004. The Assembly appointed the first judges in January 2006 (DOC. EX.CL/241(VIII)) and subsequent judges have been approved on a rotational basis. The Court has not sat on a case as yet. Moreover, the AU has since decided to establish a joint human rights and justice court. The Protocol on the Statute of the African Court of Justice and Human Rights was adopted in July 2008 in Sharm el Sheikh, Egypt (Doc ASSEMBLY/AU/13(XI)). It repeals the protocol on the African Court of Human and Peoples' Rights and the treaty on the African Court of Justice, providing instead for a merged African Court of Justice and Human Rights. At present, it appears that the new Court will sit in Tanzania, which is the opposite side of the continent from the Commission on Human and Peoples' Rights. It will take over the premises currently used for the ad hoc International Criminal Tribunal on Rwanda, a body which is currently winding up its work in furtherance of its mandate.

The Protocol has yet to attract sufficient ratifications to enter into force. Until it does, and the new judges are elected, the 2008 Protocol provides that the existing

Courts remain in operation. According to the transitional provisions, any cases pending before the Court on Human and Peoples' Rights will be transferred to the Human Rights Section of the African Court of Justice and Human Rights, but considered and concluded in accordance with the 'old' system as provided for by the 1998 Protocol (Art 5, 2008 Protocol).

9.3.2.1 *Proposed composition of new Court*

The 1998 Protocol Court of Human and Peoples' Rights consists of eleven judges elected to serve in an individual capacity from amongst 'jurists of high moral character and of recognized practical judicial or academic competence and experience in the field of human and people's rights' (1998 Protocol, Art 10). All judges of the African Court must be nationals of Member States. Judges will serve for terms of six years with the possibility of one period of re-election. In keeping with practices elsewhere, a staggered system of re-election (essentially four judges every two years) is prescribed (1998 Protocol, Art 14). Unlike other instruments, the Protocol makes explicit and detailed provision for the independence of the judiciary: judges cannot hear cases in which they have previously been involved in any capacity; judges will enjoy the immunities extended to diplomatic agents under international law throughout their term of office; and judges cannot be held liable for any decisions or opinions taken in the exercise of their functions (1998 Protocol, Art 15).

According to Art 2 of the Statute of the African Court of Justice and Human Rights (attached to the 2008 Protocol), the new Court will be the principal judicial organ of the African Union. It will have sixteen judges, three from each of the main geographical regions, though four from the west (Art 3, Statute). Interestingly, Art 6 provides that half the judges will be elected from a list of those with general international law expertise and the other half from a second list of those with recognized competence and experience in human rights. Judges will be eligible for a single re-election after their prescribed term of office of six years (Art 8). Appointees serve on a part-time basis, although the President and Vice-President are full-time appointments. This perhaps indicates that the Union does not expect a deluge of cases and thus will avoid the backlog issues of the European systems, both of which have full-time courts. Article 16 of the Statute provides that the Court has two sections: one a General Affairs Section; the other a Human Rights Section, each comprising of eight judges. Each section can sit in chambers and, of the course, the entire court can sit in plenary if seized of a relevant case.

9.3.2.2 *Proposed jurisdiction of the new Court*

The existing African Court of Human and Peoples' Rights has jurisdiction over all disputes and cases submitted to it concerning the interpretation and application of the Charter, Protocol, and any other African human rights Conventions (1998 Protocol, Art 3). It has advisory (issuing advisory opinions on any related legal matter) and declaratory (deciding cases) jurisdiction. Should the Court find a violation of a human or peoples' right, it can order appropriate measures to remedy the situation—this can include orders of compensation or other reparation and, in appropriate situations, the adoption of provisional measures (1998 Protocol, Art 24). Judgments of the Court are binding and final and are by majority (although separate and dissenting opinions may also be attached). The execution of any judgment of the Court is to be overseen by the Council of Ministers of the OAU (or similar body of the AU) on behalf of the Assembly (1998 Protocol, Art 27). To date, no cases have been concluded by the Court.

The new merged African Court of Justice and Human Rights enjoys a wide base of jurisdiction in terms of Art 28 of its Statute: general international law, all human rights instruments ratified by the parties, acts and decisions of the organs of the Union, interpretation of all Union constitutive documents and treaties. There is clear concurrent jurisdiction with the International Court of Justice and the UN treaty-monitoring bodies; however this is not necessarily a problem as the States Parties will elect the forum to raise any particular dispute.

9.3.2.3 *Locus standi*

The Commission and States have automatic *locus standi* before the existing Court of Human and Peoples' Rights. It is anticipated that cases brought by private parties will be initially brought before the Commission in terms of Art 55 of the Charter on Human and Peoples' Rights (discussed above). However, the 1998 Protocol on the Court does provide the possibility of exceptional jurisdiction being exercised over cases brought by individuals, non-governmental organizations, and groups of individuals (1998 Protocol, Art 6). Given that in normal individual applications, it is expected that the Court will only be seized of a matter once the Commission has prepared a report or taken a decision thereon, the operation of the new system appears similar to that practised by the Council of Europe prior to the entry into force of the Eleventh Protocol to the European Convention on the Protection of Human Rights and Fundamental Freedoms (see Chapter 7).

Given the broad jurisdiction of the merged Court, it is unsurprising that States, organs of the Union, and staff (the latter only for staff disputes) have *locus standi* (Art 29, Statute). For complaints over violations of human rights, *locus standi* is extended to States Parties, the African Commission on Human and Peoples' Rights, the African Committee of Experts on the Rights and Welfare of the Child, accredited African intergovernmental organizations, African national human rights institutions, and individuals or relevant accredited NGOs (Art 30, Statute). The Court can have reference to any applicable law accepted as such by the parties, including international treaties. Provisional measure (Art 35 can also be ordered), a useful mechanism in some human and peoples' rights cases.

9.3.2.4 *Towards the future*

Obviously, the operation of the merged Court will be determinant on the Rules of Procedure adopted by it when it is finally established. However, it is clear that it is envisaged that the new Court, as the existing Court, will work alongside the Commission in protecting human and peoples' rights within Africa despite their geographical locations. The new merged Court is innovative, combining functions discharged separately in other international and regional systems. Nevertheless it has the potential to be a major contributor towards human rights in Africa. Given the scarcity of work for the existing African Court of Human and Peoples' Rights, the biggest challenge for the proposed merged Court may be its first case. Thereafter, it is to be hoped that more cases will follow. However, as a body primarily destined to consider inter-State and internal (ie, between the organs of the AU and/ or their staff), complaints, there may be reluctance on the part of individuals to raise human and peoples' complaints in that forum. However, as Africa has a strong network of NGO human rights' advocates and defenders, this may be an unfounded fear. Obviously the first stage is to secure ratifications for the Protocol and then elect the judges. This could take some time. In February 2009, the Assembly of the Heads of State and Government requested the Commission to report on the possibility of the Court hearing cases on international criminal law (genocide, crimes against humanity, and crimes of aggression) as a response to the arrest warrants issued in Europe for the Chief of Protocol to the President of Rwanda (Decision Assembly/AU/Dec.213 (XII) (2009)).

9.3.3 **The Assembly of Heads of State and Government**

The Assembly of Heads of State and Government is the political organ of the Union. Its composition and functions are determined in accordance with the OAU Treaty and AU Treaty—it is the supreme organ of the Union. Ultimately enforcement of human rights lies with the Assembly. To this end, it receives annual reports from the African Commission on its work. As with other systems of human rights, enforcement remains in the domain of political actors. Naturally, enforcement is thus dependent on the collective political will of the Member States. To date, a 'softly, softly' diplomatic approach has been favoured, although there are a number of instances of more violent interventions in States. The latter have not necessarily been sanctioned by the then OAU (or indeed the United Nations). The Assembly also makes political and diplomatic statements on human rights issues, for example ASSEMBLY/AU/Dec.221 (XII) 2009 in which concern was expressed at the International Criminal Court approving the indictment of the president of the Republic of Sudan. This is a serious matter as initially African countries were amongst the staunchest supporters of the embryonic Criminal Court.

9.3.4 **The role of non-governmental organizations (NGOs)**

Although not a legal part of the institutional framework established by the African Charter, or even the OAU, NGOs play a prominent role in the system. Their inclusion is thus justified. The involvement of NGOs in the African system is quite unprecedented in international human rights. The African Commission has forged close relations with a number of NGOs, granting Observer Status to many. The Commission has even formalized the criteria NGOs must meet to be granted, or to maintain, observer status. The recognized NGOs may be transnational or national. NGOs provide the Commission with detailed information and statistics obtained 'on the ground' and, unlike elsewhere, NGOs may, and frequently do, bring cases before the Commission.

As the 1993 World Conference on Human Rights marked the watershed of NGO involvement in international human rights, the African system appears once more to be more forward thinking than its sibling systems (though it is acknowledged that many of the pre-existing United Nations' instruments had some NGO involvement at the drafting stage). There are many practical reasons for encouraging NGO involvement in the African system, not least the fact that NGOs may have the resources and dedication to bring cases forward. The individual may not be in such a fortunate position (though, as noted, individuals can be called to testify).

As Rachel Murray acknowledges, 'it could be argued that the need for NGOs in the African system is largely due to the weaknesses and ineffectiveness of the African Commission'. She concludes that NGO involvement is a necessary and integral part of the 'holistic and community responsibility' advocated by the Commission (Murray, R, p 102).

The participation of NGOs in the African system is a two-way process: whilst they enjoy access to the Commission and even some rights of participation in public meetings, NGOs also have responsibilities to promote human rights. They discharge these responsibilities through national training programmes, dissemination of materials, raising of the profile of the Charter at the national level, especially in rural districts, and promoting and facilitating Commission visits to States. On occasions, the Commission will explicitly utilize NGO information when the information cannot be obtained directly from the State.

9.4 **Enforcing human rights**

Like many human rights systems, the African organization operates a system of reports to monitor State compliance. Inter-State and individual reports to the African Commission enable more detailed discussion of situations of concern.

9.4.1 **Reports**

Article 62 of the Charter requires States to submit reports every two years on the legislative or other measures taken with a view to giving effect to the rights and freedoms recognized in the Charter. The two-year reporting period is considerably shorter than other human rights instruments. In many respects, a two-year process is a positive move for a young organization as it may serve to prompt States to continually strive to improve conditions within their jurisdiction. However, as with other international and regional bodies, the Commission has experienced considerable problems in securing prompt reports from States. Given the backlog of reports and the speed of change in some areas of Africa, reports may be outdated before they are even considered.

States send a representative to the Commission meeting at which the report is considered. The representative presents the report, responds to questions and discusses any issues raised.

9.4.2 **Inter-State complaints**

Inter-State complaints can be raised before the Commission in accordance with Art 47 of the Charter. In such instances, there is an emphasis on the peaceful resolution of the dispute between the parties with reference, as necessary, to the Commission. Before the Commission can be seized of an inter-State matter, it must ensure that all existing local remedies have been exhausted. This in itself can be somewhat problematic—while there may be sub-regional organizations which can be involved, it is less likely that an inter-State dispute will be settled (or even competent) in a national court. States must submit all relevant material to the Commission and may appear before it to give oral submissions. The Commission may also refer to 'other sources' (Art 52) in order to gain as clear as possible a picture of the contested event(s). Should no amicable solution be forthcoming, the Commission will prepare a report on its facts and findings for transmission to the States concerned, and the Assembly of Heads of State and Government.

As with other regional and indeed international bodies, States have been reluctant to file complaints, despite the frequency of gross violations of rights in certain African States. To date, the case brought by the *Democratic Republic of the Congo v Rwanda, Burundi and Uganda* is the only inter-State complaint to reach the Commission. A contemporaneous complaint was filed in the International Court of Justice, but deemed inadmissible (February 2006, judgement available online).

9.4.3 Individual complaints

The Commission has competence to receive individual communications, 'communications other than those of States parties to the present Charter' (Art 55). This is a broad mandate with *locus standi* for individuals, peoples, groups, and non-governmental organizations to submit complaints. Most complaints received under this Article have been brought by NGOs. The African NGO system is active and is becoming highly developed in a transnational dimension. Decisions on admissibility are taken by a simple majority of the Commission: domestic remedies should be exhausted and the complaint submitted within a reasonable time thereafter. Complaints may be dealt with on the basis on anonymity although the communication must indicate the identity of the author (Art 56(1)). The Chairman of the Commission brings the complaint to the notice of the State concerned prior to the consideration of it. In discussing a case, the Commission may have regard to 'any appropriate method of investigation' (Art 46). This can include information from NGOs and other interested bodies. The Commission will normally prepare a report on the communication.

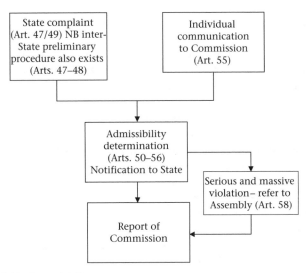

Figure 9.1 Individual complaints.

The objective of the individual complaint procedure is, in the words of the Commission, 'to initiate a positive dialogue, resulting in an amicable resolution between the complainant and the State concerned, which remedies the prejudice complained of' (*Free Legal Assistance Group et al v Zaire*). The emphasis is thus on securing a friendly settlement in what is clearly not meant to be a judicial process. Where there is no resolution of the matter, then the Commission is forced to reach a decision on the merits of the case (for example, *Mkongo Louis v Cameroon*). Unlike its Inter-American equivalent, the African Commission demonstrated a reluctance to adopt views in the absence of a State response to the allegations. However, in 1993, following receipt of a series of complaints about gross violations of human rights in Malawi, and in the face of no State response and the refusal of the Malawian authorities to allow an OAU Commissioner to undertake a mission to the State, the Commission adopted a resolution condemning the attitude of the Malawian authorities and declaring as found massive and serious violations of human rights. In 1994, the Commission decided it could uphold the existence of a violation when the allegation remains uncontested by the State concerned. Thus the position is now similar to that adopted by the Inter-American Commission almost from inception.

Should individual communications reveal the existence of 'a series of serious or massive violations of human and peoples' rights', the Commission must draw the situation to the attention of the Assembly of Heads of State and Government (Art 58). Thereafter, the Commission may be asked to complete an investigation into the cases and submit a report with associated findings and recommendations thereon. Similar in-depth studies may be carried out should the Commission notice a case of emergency in any State (Art 58(3)). In the short course of its history, many States in Africa could have been examined under this provision as the continent is frequently the scene of gross and systematic violations of rights.

9.5 Conclusions

In a relatively short period of time, the African Commission on Human and Peoples' Rights has made a substantial impact on human rights in Africa. States may now be held to account at a regional level for infringements of rights and freedoms. However, in comparison to the other regional bodies, the African system appears weak and ineffective. Like all monitoring bodies, the Commission experiences problems with the submission of reports (late or missing). The two-yearly cycles of reports and the speed of change in Africa renders most reports out of date on receipt. Progress, albeit slow, is being made towards securing prompt and regular State reports. The Commission will accept copies of reports filed to United Nations' bodies, for example, and non-submitting States will be named. Severely hampered by its reliance on diplomatic channels of action, the Commission is often regarded as impotent in the face of serious and systematic abuses of rights. Certainly, it has had a limited practical effect on abuses in the region. However, like all human rights systems, the Commission can act as a deterrent, albeit one which many regimes ignore. Publicity seems to be a key weapon in the development of the African system—publicity and promotion of rights and public condemnation of violations thereof.

Analysis of the statistics relating to the function and operation of the Commission reveals the dramatic upward curve in its activities. Ever-more cases are pending before the Commission, more fact-finding missions are undertaken, and the Commission tweaks the provisions of the Charter to imply a greater degree of protection for the African citizen. The creation of the African Court may deflect some of the criticisms levied at the Commission though its level of success and impact in reality remains to be seen. Africa itself is changing and is achieving a greater degree of democratization. In 1999, the OAU First Ministerial Conference on Human Rights in Africa was convened at Grand Baie, Mauritius, adopting a Declaration and Plan of Action for the promotion and securement of human rights in the region. Much has happened since then.

The African system is young and has undergone a steep learning curve. It has made remarkable progress in difficult conditions. Throughout, it has retained its distinctive African characteristics. Although the African system appears more holistic, the reality is less so; thus it is to be hoped that the Commission 'acquires the confidence to carry out its statements in practice' (Murray, R, 2000, p 201).

CASES

Democratic Republic of the Congo v Rwanda, Burundi and Uganda [2001] ICJ 2.

Free Legal Assistance Group and ors v Zaire, Cases 25/89, 47/90, 56/91, 100/93 9th AAR, Annex.

Mkongo Louis v Cameroon, Case 59/91, 8th AAR, Annex.

Morka, Social and Economic Action Rights Centre v Nigeria, Case 155/96, ACHPR/ COMM/A044/1 (2002).

READING

Agbakwa, SC, 'Reclaiming humanity: Economic, social and cultural rights as the cornerstone of African human rights' (2000) 5(5) Yale Human Rights and Development Journal (accessible from www.yale.edu/yhrdlj)

Ankumah, E, *The African Commission on Human and Peoples' Rights: Practices and procedures* (The Hague: Martinus Nijhoff, 1996).

Anyangwe, C, 'Obligations of State Parties to the African Charter on Human and Peoples' Rights' (1998) 10(2) African Journal of International and Comparative Law 625–59.

Benedek, W, 'The African Charter and Commission of Human and Peoples' Rights: How to make it more effective' (1995) 11 Netherlands Quarterly of Human Rights 25–40.

Danwood, C, 'Reclaiming (wo)manity: The merits and demerits of the African Protocol on Women's Rights' (2006) Netherlands International Law Review 63–93.

Killander, M, 'The African peer review mechanism and human rights: The first reviews and the way forward' (2008) 30(1) Human Rights Quarterly 41–75.

Kodjo, E, 'The African Charter on Human and Peoples' Rights' (1990) 11 Human Rights Law Journal 271.

Van der Mei, AP, 'The new African Court on Human and Peoples' Rights: Towards an effective human rights protection mechanism for Africa' (2005) 18 Leiden Journal of International Law 113–29.

Murray, R, *The African Commission on Human and Peoples' Rights and International Law* (Oxford: Hart, 2000).

——, 'On-site visits by the African Commission on Human and Peoples' Rights: A case study and comparison with the Inter-American Commission on Human Rights' (1999) 11 African Journal of International and Comparative Law 460–73.

——, 'Serious or massive violations under the African Charter on Human and Peoples' Rights: A comparison with the Inter-American and European Mechanisms' (1999) 17(2) Netherlands Quarterly of Human Rights 109–33.

Mutua, M, 'The African Human Rights' Court: A two-legged stool?' (1999) 21 Human Rights Quarterly 342–63.

Naldi, GJ, and Magliveras, K, 'Reinforcing the African System of Human Rights: The Protocol on the Establishment of a Regional Court of Human and Peoples' Rights' (1998) 16(4) Netherlands Quarterly of Human Rights 431–56.

Nmehielle, VOO, *The African Human Rights System: Its laws, practice and institutions* (The Hague: Martinus Nijhoff, 2001).

Odinkalu, C, and Christensen, C, 'The African Commission on Human and Peoples' Rights: The development of its non-state communication procedures' (1998) 20 Human Rights Quarterly 235–80.

Odinkalu, AC, 'Analysis of paralysis or paralysis by analysis? Implementing economic, social and cultural rights under the African Charter on Human and Peoples' Rights' (2001) 23(2) Human Rights Quarterly 327.

Umozurike, UO, *The African Charter on Human and Peoples' Rights* (The Hague: Kluwer, 1996).

Weissbrodt, D, 'The contribution of international non-governmental organizations to the protection of human rights' in T Meron (ed), *Human Rights in International Law* (Oxford: Clarendon Press, 1985).

WEBSITES

www.africa-union.org—the African Union.

www.achpr.org—the African Commission on Human and Peoples' Rights.

10

Monitoring, implementing, and enforcing human rights

This chapter continues the examination of international human rights with an analysis of structures and monitoring/implementation mechanisms. To quote the Secretary-General of the United Nations, '[t]he increasing demands on the United Nations human rights programme and the need to undertake responsibilities for which it had no experience revealed a number of shortcomings that reduced its impact at a time of increasing demands' (UN Doc A/51/950, 1997, para 197). This chapter will start with a review of the existing implementation methods before addressing some of the perceived problems therewith. The reports system, the inter-State complaints provisions and the mechanisms for receiving individual complaints will be considered in turn. Other methods of implementing human rights will also be considered. To facilitate a broader discussion and appropriate comparisons, this chapter will address not only the United Nations system but also those of the various regional organizations outlined in the preceding chapters. Some of the perceived faults of the system will be analysed before some general conclusions will be drawn on the success of the international community in preserving and promoting international human rights.

To date, there is no international tribunal on human rights, though some of the United Nations Committees appear to operate in a quasi-judicial manner: an impartial panel which functions under its own rules of procedure and which can hear expert testimony from selected parties before issuing an opinion, albeit not a legally binding one. The process, especially with bodies such as the Human Rights Committee and the Committee on the Elimination of All Forms of Racial Discrimination which can receive individual petitions, is judicialized though not to the extent of the European Court of Human Rights or the Inter-American Court of Human Rights. The Statute of Rome, which establishes a permanent international criminal court, offers hope for the realization of a truly judicial body, albeit only for serious 'crimes against humanity' while the success of the ad hoc Criminal Tribunals for Rwanda and the former Yugoslavia in raising the profile of some aspects of human rights should not be underestimated.

Inevitably, the problem of implementation goes to the very nature of international law. As a consensual arrangement based on agreement between States, reciprocity, and respect for national sovereignty/territorial integrity, the type of enforcement mechanisms employed at national levels are unlikely to be successful. The lawyers have drafted the standards of international human rights, cooperation from politicians is necessary to secure realization. In this respect, the role of the International Criminal Court is somewhat distinct from human rights monitoring bodies—the crimes have been defined and the International Criminal Court will decide whether or not any indicted individual is guilty of those crimes. This process reflects the traditional concept of trial by, and in accordance with, law unlike the process by which States would be found liable for infringing international human rights provisions.

10.1 The reports system

The reports system is the most prevalent system for overseeing the realization of human rights in Contracting States. For many, this is cited as a reason why human rights, indeed even international law, lacks teeth. However, the benefit of the system lies in publicity: many States are reluctant to be identified as an example of bad practice on the international arena. The publication of State reports and occasionally the international response thereto, on the World Wide Web, can assist this by disseminating the relevant material through the public domain.

The principal purpose of the reports system is to promote State compliance with their international human rights obligations. The drafting process itself should be almost a cathartic experience for States with an honest appraisal of their conformity to the treaty obligations. Public and government consultations may form part of this process. The process is not, of necessity, entirely negative—the State may highlight in its report examples of good practice and steps that have been taken to rectify problems identified in the previous periodic report or since ratification. Moreover, the reports are used as a basis for an active, supportive dialogue between the Committee and the State rather than as a submission to an adversarial proceeding. With some instruments requiring more positive action than others, reports can also be used to identify technical or vocational assistance the State may require in fulfilling its obligations. This approach characterizes many aspects of the work of the United Nations. The ongoing examination of reports submitted by States and the Concluding Observations thereon clarify the scope of the human rights instruments in a way that would not be possible otherwise. Given that human rights law is an evolving system, this is advantageous as the law can develop and expand freely within the constraints of the terminology employed in the original instrument.

Reports are not used in Europe for the principal Convention though periodic reports are required under additional instruments such as the European Charter for Regional or Minority Languages, the Framework Convention for the Protection of National Minorities, and the European Social Charter. In contrast the African system has wholly embraced the reporting tradition. Indeed it is the main method of supervision under the African Charter. Reports are primarily a means of monitoring State compliance and thus non-invasive. However, the use of non-governmental organizations' reports balances the evidence produced by a State, enabling the receiving body to form a view on the actual position of human rights within the State. This may provide a focus for dialogue between the monitoring body and State when the report is discussed. As a mode of ensuring State compliance, implementation reports may be less successful—many reports are excessively late, others erroneous. The absence of any form of sanctions, albeit an anathema to international human rights law, precludes the reports system from operating as an enforcement measure.

At the regional level, the American initiative of State visits and country reports has proven more successful than merely State reports.

The reporting system is the most common (often the only) means employed by the United Nations of supervising the implementation of a convention. Its success has led to reports being adopted as the primary mechanism for the Human Rights Council undertaking its universal periodic review of compliance with human rights and humanitarian law. Nonetheless, the reports system is not the only mechanism available.

10.2 Inter-State complaints

The next step up from an essentially self-regulating system of reports is that of State complaints. This is not necessarily an adversarial system. For practical, diplomatic reasons States will often prove reluctant to involve themselves in inter-State disputes as the experience of the International Court of Justice illustrates. (Note that some would argue the lack of adversarial judicial process demonstrates that non-contentious means of dispute resolution have proven successful.) Even in well-defined court systems, like that of the European Union and the Council of Europe, there have been very few inter-State complaints.

Some human rights systems allow for complaints to be levied by States, against other States. In instances such as *Ireland v United Kingdom* or *Cyprus v Turkey*, there were political reasons why the applicant State would want to be involved in a public case. In other applications to the Council of Europe, multiple infringements of the Convention prompted the complaint—for example the 1968 complaints against Greece by Denmark, Norway, and Sweden. See the inserted box in Chapter 6 for the inter-State complaints decided by the regional bodies.

Resolution of disputes concerning interpretation and application of treaties remain subject to international practice. Article 22 of the International Convention on the Elimination of All Forms of Racial Discrimination envisages the International Court of Justice exercising jurisdiction in such circumstances. This procedure has now been invoked by Georgia against the Russian Federation and preliminary proceedings are timetabled before the International Court of Justice.

Inter-State complaints offer little scope as a means of implementing or realizing human rights. Despite this, the potential for inter-State complaints will inevitably remain in deference to the traditional nature of international law (ie, primarily inter-State) and as a benign deterrent.

Should a State consider instituting proceedings, attempts will be first made to establish common ground, to reach a non-contentious compromise. A form of Creative Problem Solving, such a solution would require to be in conformity with the law yet allow both States to save face and retreat with dignity from a potentially explosive, destructive (from a diplomatic viewpoint) confrontation. The good offices of the international body concerned may be offered as a neutral venue for diplomatic negotiations in an attempt to secure conciliation. The maintenance of international peace and security remains a paramount consideration. Should peace and security be threatened, the United Nations Security Council may intervene irrespective of where the initial complaint was filed.

Key case

Georgia v Russian Federation **(2008–ongoing) ICJ online**

Georgia is alleging the Russian Federation has violated the International Convention on the Elimination of All Forms of Racial Discrimination in the Georgian territory of South Ossetia and Abkhazia. The complaint relates to three distinct periods between 1990 and August 2008. Provisional measures were ordered on 15 October 2008, by a majority of eight to seven votes. Both Parties are to refrain from any act of racial discrimination, sponsoring, defending or supporting racial discrimination, and to ensure, without distinction as to national or ethnic origin, security of persons, freedom of movement of persons and protection of property of displaced persons and refugees. When the full case is argued before the Court, a key issue will be whether the ICJ has jurisdiction: Georgia is likely to continue to claim jurisdiction under Art 22 of the CERD, while the Russian Federation is likely to argue that the facts at issue relate to the use of force and protection of territorial integrity as well as international humanitarian law rather than race discrimination (such arguments were posited during the hearings on provisional measures).

10.3 Individual complaints

Individual complaints are the third mechanism used to realize human rights. Complaints can be brought either through a court-like mechanism or through reports to an independent body. The complaint may or may not be made public. (Ombudspersons, often termed Human Rights Commissioners, are increasingly common at a national level. This is welcomed by the international and regional bodies: Part I, para 22 of the Vienna Declaration and Programme of Action requires that States should provide an effective framework of remedies to redress human rights grievances or violations.) The European Court of Human Rights, the Inter-American Court of Human Rights and the new African Court of Justice and Human Rights are all examples of adversarial systems established to ascertain facts and adjudicate on disputed rights. The United Nations Committees, on the other hand, are not as judicialized. They were termed committees for political expediency, ratification of any instrument by which a State agreed to cede sovereignty to an international court would have been excruciatingly slow. The Committee on the Elimination of All Forms of Racial Discrimination was one of the first treaty-monitoring bodies to be established with competency to receive individual communications. The Committee hears an account of the facts alleged and the relevant national law, the argument as to the violation and the response or justification of the State. If the individual is not legally represented, the Secretariat of the Committee will help to define the issues on which the Committee has to adjudicate.

There is now a general tendency towards accepting the jurisdiction of treaty-monitoring bodies vis-à-vis individual communications. In spite of this, most of the time of international committees is still spent examining State reports, not individual communications. It is principally a question of volume: few individual complaints reach the international committees while most States submit periodic reports.

An element of sanction can ascribe to a State found in violation of its treaty obligations. Consequently, individual communications contribute in part to the enforcement of human rights obligations—a State may comply rather than risk punitive sanctions being imposed. The nature of the body examining the complaint is related to the remedies at its disposal. As all such bodies are created in accordance with international law, the remedies are primarily political. However, both the European and American Courts can and do award financial compensation to victims of breaches of the regional convention. The African Commission requests compensation is addressed by the violating State but does not specify amounts. Frequently, the effect of a negative finding provides sufficient impetus for the State to change its infringing law or practice. Compensation may also be available through other avenues such as the Victim Compensation Funds operated at international and regional levels for victims of torture.

Greater success employing individual complaints as a method of enforcement occurs when individuals have a domestic remedy available to them. Whether through courts, ombudsperson, or State-appointed human rights defenders, the limitations on enforcing human rights at the international level disappear. Article 9 of the General Assembly Declaration on Rights and Responsibilities proclaims the right of everyone to complain about violations at both national and international level. National Human Rights Institutions, although not established in every State, are intended to facilitate some national-level complaints, deflecting complaints from the regional and international machinery but offering an effective and comparatively fast national remedy.

Individual complaints can also be directed to some of the special mechanisms operating under the auspices of the Human Rights Council.

10.4 Rapporteurs and special investigators

Rapporteurs are frequently used by international human rights monitoring bodies. The activities of country and thematic rapporteurs under the United Nations are extra-Conventional mechanisms, as they have no formal treaty basis. They may receive complaints from NGOs and individuals. However, this is not a formal complaint procedure. Country and thematic rapporteurs work in partial response to information received from various sources including individuals and groups. In principle, the special investigators and rapporteurs will consider only communications not previously submitted elsewhere in the United Nations. However, some special mechanisms have developed systems for considering violations of human rights. In some instances, rapporteurs draft and circulate questionnaires for the purpose of gathering information on selected salient issues across a wide range of States. Information on these can be obtained directly from the United Nations or from the rapporteurs and associated NGOs.

Country mandates within the United Nations at present include Afghanistan, Democratic Republic of the Congo, Haiti, Iraq, and the Palestinian territories occupied since 1967. Thematic mandates at present include a Working Group on Enforced or Involuntary Disappearances and a Working Group on Arbitrary Detention.

In situ investigations of human rights situations have been carried out under the auspices of all the regional organizations. The African Commission will undertake country visits with the consent of the State concerned while the Inter-American Commission has carried out a number of State visits. The Inter-American system has proven the worth of this mechanism, investigating and reporting on a number of States with systematic and gross violations of human rights. Although the European Convention on Human Rights makes no provision for State visits, the European Convention for the Prevention of Torture is based on a formal system of Committee visits to detention centres in States, a model copied by the UN's Torture Committee. Such impartial visits to detention centres by international and regional bodies are common and an important aspect of monitoring human rights. The detention facilities of the new International Criminal Court will be reviewed in a manner similar to that employed at The Hague and Arusha for those detained on indictment before the International Criminal Tribunals.

Without doubt, the work of the rapporteurs on selected rights and freedoms has raised the profile of human rights. Moreover, surveys and other statistical data collected by rapporteurs may be used to assist the international and regional bodies in developing standards. This is evident from the work of the special rapporteurs on education, discussed in Chapter 20, or the working group on forced disappearances. Similar advances have been made by the Inter-American Commission. Its rapporteurs have worked on a variety of issues. The African Union is increasingly establishing working groups to study specific topics with a view to identifying common ground and potential solutions. This model also appears to be embraced by ASEAN, though it is still at an early stage of evolution as regards human rights.

10.5 Ancillary bodies

A number of other bodies and organizations contribute to the enforcement of human rights and the development of international and regional human rights.

10.5.1 United Nations bodies

A number of United Nations bodies work towards the realization of universal human rights.

10.5.1.1 *United Nations High Commissioner for Refugees (UNHCR)*

The United Nations High Commissioner for Refugees was established by the General Assembly on 14 December 1950, commencing operations on 1 January 1951. According to its mission statement, the UNHCR leads and coordinates international action for the worldwide protection of refugees and the resolution of refugee problems. Its primary purpose is to safeguard the rights and well-being of refugees, assisting with asylum or repatriation, as appropriate. Of course, one of the main human rights' instruments that guides the High Commissioner's work is the 1951 United Nations Convention relating to the Status of Refugees 1951 (and Protocol). To achieve its aims, the organization works with States to reduce situations of forced displacement, thereby furthering the purposes and principles of the United Nations (international peace and security, respect for human rights, etc). The present incumbent is António Guterres.

10.5.1.2 *United Nations International Children's Emergency Fund (UNICEF)*

UNICEF was created by the General Assembly in 1946 to help children in Europe after the Second World War. Since 1953, it has exercised a permanent role in the United Nations, helping children worldwide. It is now known as the United Nations Children's Fund (though retains the UNICEF acronym). Inevitably, UNICEF strives to help children receive the care they need in early years, protecting them from death and illness, and during natural disasters. It actively promotes the rights of children, working closely with the United Nations Committee on the Rights of the Child to promote dissemination of materials on children's rights to children. According to UNICEF's mission statement, it advocates the protection of children's rights, helps meet their basic needs, and expands their opportunities to reach their full potential. Through multimedia packages and the World Wide Web the organization strives to inform all children of their human rights. Other UNICEF initiatives aim at improving the welfare of children, with, for example, partnership programmes on healthcare. Ann Veneman is the present executive director. The United Nations Special Session on Children (scheduled for 19–21 September 2001) was postponed until May 2002. This session aimed at reviewing progress made since the 1990 World Summit for Children and examining the State of the World's Children 2002. The final document, 'A World Fit for Children' seeks to secure the completion of the agenda set by the 1990 World Summit for Children. Every year, UNICEF publishes its State of the World's Children review, highlighting the plight of children globally and focussing on a selected issue.

10.5.1.3 *United Nations Educational, Scientific and Cultural Organization (UNESCO)*

UNESCO has a multifaceted role. Its constitution was adopted in November 1945, with entry into force the following year. As of May 2009, it has 193 Member States. The main objective of UNESCO is to contribute to peace and security by promoting collaboration among nations through education, science, culture, and communication in furtherance of, inter alia, the rule of law, human rights, and fundamental freedoms. It performs five main functions—prospective studies, the advancement, transfer and sharing of knowledge, standard-setting action, providing expertise (technical cooperation), and exchange of specialized information. In terms of standard-setting, various international instruments have been adopted which provide for rights of individuals: the 1960 Convention against Discrimination in Education; 1952 Universal Copyright Convention; 1954 Convention for the Protection of Cultural Property in the Event of an Armed Conflict; and the 1972 Convention relating to the Protection of the World Cultural and Natural Heritage.

UNESCO also operates a non-judicial individual communications procedure for violations of education, science, and culture rights. The system is non-contentious in nature and has enjoyed modest success (UNESCO Doc 104 Ex/Decision 3.3 (1978)).

10.5.2 **International Committee of the Red Cross**

The International Committee of the Red Cross (CIRC) has already been mentioned with respect to humanitarian law. However, it also has a significant role to play in modern human rights. Given its fiercely defended neutrality, the humanitarian impact of the organization cannot be underestimated. Although it will not stand witness against human rights violations by a State on grounds of its neutrality, the organization will provide emergency humanitarian aid to those in direst need. Given its neutrality in conflict, the CIRC can often negotiate rights for prisoners and captors alike, creating a human rights culture and ensuring compliance with fundamental rights and freedoms. The Geneva Conventions are to the forefront of the work of the Red Cross in conflict situations but other rights such as food, shelter, and water also characterize their operations.

10.5.3 **Non-governmental organizations (NGOs)**

In addition to the foregoing, there are a number of non-governmental organizations (NGOs) which play a role in the process. Many of these organizations send representatives as observers to the United Nations' discussions on human rights. The World Conference on Human Rights in Vienna 1993 was characterized by the presence of hundreds of NGO representatives. In its concluding Declaration (para 38), the World Conference noted the importance of NGOs in the protection of all human rights and in humanitarian activities. Their particular contribution to education, training, and research was highlighted with dialogue and cooperation between NGOs and States encouraged.

NGOs regularly participate in United Nations' working groups. The Committee on Economic, Social and Cultural Rights sets aside an afternoon in each of its sessions to receive views on the implementation of the Covenant by non-governmental and community organizations. NGOs also participate in the process by sending in reports on States. This can present quite a different view from that of the State report, not least as NGOs frequently consult more widely across the community in question without State 'bureaucratic' constraints. (Of course, the constraints on NGO activities can be severe with some NGOs operating covertly.)

The Committee on Economic, Social and Cultural Rights, for example, asked the United Nations Secretariat to compile a list of NGOs active in the territories of Contracting States in order that submissions can be obtained prior to consideration of State reports. NGO reports may also form part of the body of materials collated for consideration by the Human Rights Council during Universal Periodic Review of a State. Finally, publicity gained by an NGO on a particular human rights issue may bring that issue to global attention and prompt an international investigation or report. Both the African and American systems have strong NGO involvement and participation. This is partly due to the flagrant violations of rights and the fact that NGOs are willing to take action thereon: they often have the knowledge and the resources to take forward individual complaints, the individual may not.

The importance of NGOs in the system should not be forgotten. Although they have no formal role or *locus standi* before most Committees, there are many ways in which an NGO can bring matters to the attention of a Committee and convey their views to Committee members. When the report of a State is scheduled for consideration by a Committee, NGOs and other non-State actors may indicate their interest to the secretariat then prepare and submit their submission for the perusal of the Committee when considering the State report. NGOs will often widely disseminate their report on a State within that State and, in some instances, this might prompt a State to publicize more widely its own submission and even, occasionally, it will assist in raising popular awareness of the international instrument concerned and human rights in general. Greater circulation of reports has been one of the commended successes of the Committee on the Rights of the Child. It may be possible for non-formal meetings between NGOs and committee members prior to the Working group meeting and NGOs may usually be represented at the actual Committee meeting. A presence at the meetings themselves permits the NGO to take its own record of proceedings (though they may not address the Committee) and facilitates the dissemination of information back to the State concerned. Naturally dissemination by an NGO may be wider and more user friendly than that of the State. This can have a positive impact on human rights awareness in a State albeit achieved solely through the dedication of the NGO.

10.5.4 Individuals

The General Assembly, by Resolution 53/144 (1999), adopted a Declaration on the Right and Responsibilities of Individuals, Groups and Organs of Society to Promote and Protect Universally Recognized Human Rights and Fundamental Freedoms. 'Everyone has the right ... to promote and to strive for the protection and realization of human rights and fundamental freedoms at the national and international level' (Art 1). To this end, everyone has the right to assemble and to form, join and participate in NGOs or communicate therewith (Art 5). Although couched in terms of 'rights'—right of participation, knowledge (Art 6), access to information, and so on, some duties are included. Notably, Art 10 prohibits anyone from participating in violations of human rights and protects individuals from punishment should they refuse to violate human rights, while Art 11 imposes a duty on those in relevant professions to respect rights and comply with national and international standards. Individuals, groups, institutions, and NGOs are recognized as having 'an important role and a responsibility in ... promoting human rights and fundamental freedoms' and in contributing 'to the promotion of the right of everyone to a society and international order in which the rights and freedoms set forth in the Universal Declaration of Human Rights and other human rights instruments can be fully realized' (Arts 18(2)–(3)). Clearly, the duties incumbent on individuals pre-suppose knowledge of the salient standards. Realization of the right to human rights education, in which non-State actors have a significant role, is key in this respect (see also Chapter 20).

10.6 Overview of problems with the system

International human rights is a relatively new system of law. It has little more than fifty years of history in its present universal form and, as a consequence, is still evolving. When the systems were adopted, compromises had to be reached which allowed international human rights to coexist with respect for the territorial integrity and sovereign independence of the Contracting States. In the last fifty-five years, there has been a dramatic change in approach of States to human rights, even arguably to international law. Today, human rights are an accepted fact of international life. All States acknowledge being bound by human rights, the salient question is to what degree? States often sign up to instruments in order that they are seen to conform to the normative rights enshrined therein. However, due to the vagaries of the relationships between international and domestic law, this does not by necessity mean that the individuals of a State enjoy each and every one of those rights. The unfettered enjoyment of universal rights is not a reality in any State.

In some respects, international human rights is a victim of its own success. The proliferation of international and regional systems has already been discussed. The increase in membership of the United Nations and regional organizations has prompted a corresponding increase in States acceding to human rights instruments. However, this has not coincided with an increase in resources and facilities for the monitoring/implementing bodies.

There have been a number of expert reviews of the state of the international human rights system. For ease of reference, two main reports will be used in the section: Professor Philip Alston's report to the United Nations (hereinafter 'Alston') and Professor Ann Bayefsky's report to the International Law Association (hereinafter 'Bayefsky')—citations in the Reading section at the end of the chapter.

The following issues will be examined in turn: ratifications, declarations, and reservations; State reports—quantity and quality; the Committees—composition, role, and functions; resources; implementation and sanctions; individual petition.

10.6.1 Ratifications, declarations, and reservations

The goal of the United Nations was the universal ratification of the major instruments on human rights before now. As Alston states, '[u]niversal ratification of the six core United Nations human rights treaties would establish the best possible foundations for international endeavours to promote respect for human rights' (para 14). The World Conference on Human Rights in the Vienna Declaration and Programme of Action, following receipt of Alston's interim report (UN Doc A/CONF.157/PC/62/Add.11/Rev.1), set guidelines for universal ratification of the principal instruments, guidelines which time has proven to have been overly optimistic. However, the Conference did anticipate the economic and political factors which may preclude ratification. It recommended that the Secretary General and the treaty bodies should 'consider opening a dialogue with States not having acceded to these human rights treaties, in order to identify obstacles and to seek ways of overcoming them' (Part II, para 4). The Secretary-General and the High Commissioner for Human Rights periodically appeal to States to ratify those treaties to which they are not already party (UN Doc E/CN.4/2000/98, para 57). The United Nations Millennium Declaration (UN Doc A/55/L.2) promotes respect for all internationally recognized human rights and fundamental freedoms (para 24). Steps have been taken to remove obstacles preventing ratification—for example, the Human Rights Strengthening Programme developed by the Office of the High Commissioner for Human Rights and the United Nations Development Programme aims at providing practical assistance to States wishing to accede to the various instruments (para 58).

10.6.1.1 *The influence of global opinion*

There are some inconsistencies in State practice, most notably arising out of the Convention on the Rights of the Child. With its almost universal ratification, perhaps questions should be asked as to why States are willing to provide a full range of civil, political, economic, social, and cultural rights to children but not to adults. After all, few of the rights in the Convention on the Rights of the Child are not drawn from the International Covenants. The success of the Convention on the Rights of the Child arguably vindicates States of their reluctance to ascribe to international supervisory control. Perhaps the rationale is that States will follow global political will, and the wave of popular support for children's rights enables this extraordinary success story. The Migrant Workers Convention, however, took thirteen years from adoption to entry into force.

The profile of human rights instruments may, it would appear, contribute towards their success. However, international human rights should not be a popularity contest with the 'trendiest' convention attracting most ratifications. Not many States have ratified all seven core instruments with only around thirty-three (including Azerbaijan, Costa Rica, Denmark, Ecuador, Finland, Hungary, France, Italy, Iceland, Poland, Russian Federation, South Africa, Senegal, and Slovakia) accepting all the optional reporting obligations rights to individual petition. Alston recommends that the High Commission on Human Rights should consult with the various international agencies (UNESCO, World Bank, WHO, UNDP, etc) to ascertain what initiatives, if any, they may take to encourage universal ratification (para 32). Further suggestions relate to the streamlining of the process to eliminate some of the financial onus presently incumbent on States.

Given its role in promoting human rights globally, the reluctance of the United States of America to ratify the principal Human Rights' treaties may seem surprising. The Convention on the Prevention and Punishment of the Crime of Genocide was the first international standard instrument ratified by the United States. This was only in 1988. Those instruments which have been ratified since have been made non-self-executing. As one commentator notes,

[t]hose states which seek to strengthen the treaty system must find a way to prevent United States' attitudes, as reflected in its reservations, from being used as an example and justification by countries which lack the right provided by the United States Constitution. It will not be easy. [Grant, S, p 329]

10.6.1.2 *Reservations and declarations*

Signing instruments does not necessarily mean that a State accepts the entire convention without exception. Many States make declarations or make ratification subject to reservations to some or all Articles of the convention. These reservations sometimes reflect the different cultural and religious traditions of the States in question. However, undoubtedly they can undermine the universality of the rights. Reservations are generally opt-outs whereby a State specifies which Articles or parts thereof it will not accede to. Declarations, on the other hand, are clarifications of meaning and scope of the instrument. For example, when France acceded to the International Covenant on Civil and Political Rights, it declared that it had no minorities and thus Art 27 was inapplicable. The subsequent case of *Guedson v France* was thus inadmissible. Many States make ratification subject to the compliance of the obligations with Islamic law while others make a reservation that nothing in the convention should be read as contrary to the constitution of the State itself. Clearly, in some such instances, the actual obligation assumed by the State is positively minimal.

The various Committees of the United Nations frequently query the continuation of reservations in their concluding observations on State reports. The General Assembly too has frequently called upon States to reconsider the continuation of reservations and declarations in respect of obligations assumed under the international conventions. As has been seen, instruments such as the Convention on the Elimination of all Forms of Discrimination against Women are beset by problems due to the extraordinarily high number of reservations thereto. In the initial stages of achieving universal ratification, reservations should perhaps be viewed as a necessary evil. As States ratify the seven core instruments, the process of eliminating reservations and declarations must be the next goal.

Some States do not sign up to obligations to which they do not wish to conform. Other States sign up then fail to submit periodic reports, refuse to accept the jurisdiction of the implementing bodies, or simply ignore the content of the instrument. The Vienna World Conference on Human Rights in 1993 urged the universal ratification of human rights treaties, with all States being encouraged to accede to the international instruments, avoiding, as far as possible, resort to reservations (para 26).

Bayefsky considers that the implementation 'crisis' and the quest for universal ratification of the core instruments is inherently related: 'ratification by human rights adversaries is purchased at a price, diminished obligations, lax supervision, and few adverse consequences from non-compliance. The cost of membership has been deliberately minimized' (pp 689–90).

The need for human rights is undiminished: 'Humanity will not enjoy security without development, it will not enjoy development without security, and it will not enjoy either without respect for human rights' (Kofi Annan, *In Larger Freedom*, executive summary, para 2).

Discussion topic

UN Treaty bodies

In human rights terms the twentieth century yielded a valuable legacy of internationally agreed standards and the creation of a set of institutional arrangements designed to monitor compliance with those standards. But the overriding challenge for the future is to develop the effectiveness of those monitoring systems. [Professors J Crawford and P Alston, from *The Future of UN Human Rights Treaty Monitoring* Cambridge: Cambridge University Press, 2000), p xv]

The United Nations and a plethora of experts have devoted great efforts to trying to render the current system more effective. While this is laudable, there are some critics who maintain that human rights remain almost an anathema to international law and any system which seeks to regulate the manner in which a State treats its nationals is doomed to failure.

10.6.2 **State reports—quantity and quality**

The reports system is often regarded as weak because it is dependent upon the will of States to comply. In many instances reports, if and when submitted by States, are formal and prosaic—repetition of national laws which conform to the specified norm. They may have a tendency to be biased towards the State. Reports of States are rarely critical evaluations of performance with honest appraisals of problems encountered. Self-appraisal may be entering mainstream management practice in the developed world, it has yet to reach mainstream international law. Some bodies, including the OAS Inter-American Commission and more recently the Committee on the Elimination of all Forms of Racial Discrimination and the Committee on Economic, Social and Cultural Rights have, in the face of non-submission of reports, issued comments based on additional information submitted by NGOs and various specialized United Nations agencies. These, too, may be biased, this time against the State. The answer may lie in a more open approach with both 'sides' being encouraged to submit observations. States may be more honest and open about problems encountered in the knowledge that the monitoring body will also be receiving full reports from NGOs. In the Americas, not all NGOs are entitled to submit detailed reports—in general the NGO must be recognized in two or more States.

10.6.2.1 *Addressing the issues*

Some attempts have been made to address these issues. For example, the World Conference on Human Rights in its Vienna Declaration and Programme of Action, Part II, para 7, recommends that human rights officers be assigned to regional United Nations offices for the purpose of disseminating information and offering training and other technical assistance in human rights to requesting States. Human rights training for international civil servants working in the field should also be organized. Alston identifies two reasons why States do not report: administrative incapacity due to a lack of specialist expertise or the lack of political will. Sometimes it is a combination of both (para 43). Specialist expertise is now being provided, thus that reason will recede. Political will cannot be changed by international rhetoric and law alone.

10.6.2.2 *Changing the reporting conditions*

There has been considerable discussion over the possibilities of limiting the length of State reports. It has been argued that limiting the length will improve the quality as it will prevent irrelevant material being duplicated and may focus State attention on the subject matter. However, on the contrary, most of the human rights bodies have issued detailed guidance to States on what should be included in their report. In some instances, the Committees appear keen to receive quite detailed reports (the Committee on the Rights of the Child is a case in point). Perhaps what should be considered is a better system for cross-referring reports, precluding duplication. The general idea at present is that a State's initial report should be detailed and comprehensive, and thereafter the basic information need not be repeated unless significant changes have occurred. A single implementing body could be established through which all reports are channelled. The issue of duplication is important as some commentators suggest that smaller States are perhaps more reluctant to accede to international instruments due to what is perceived as the onerous reporting requirements. Alston suggests that support should be given to newly ratifying States, especially developing countries, to support the preparation of the initial reports (para 34). Compounding this is the frequency with which some periodic reports are to be submitted. As is discussed *infra*, the frequency of reports, in conjunction with the backlog of reports before monitoring bodies, renders the report system less of a dialogue than a disjointed discourse.

10.6.2.3 *Overlapping obligations*

When one considers the overlap between some of the provisions of the treaties—for example, the prohibition on torture in Art 7 of the International Covenant on Civil and Political Rights, Art 37 of the Convention on the Rights of the Child, and as elaborated in the Convention Against Torture or the duplication of provisions on the enjoyment of rights and freedoms without discrimination on grounds of gender or racial origin—the benefit of some consolidation is obvious, especially for those States who have ratified several of the treaties. However, it should be noted that there may be implicit or explicit discrepancies in the provisions of the different instruments. Eric Tistounet identifies and discusses some of the practical problems that have arisen as a result of overlap. There is clear potential for a divergence of views with teleological interpretation contributing to these differences. This can result in States receiving slightly conflicting messages. The advent of Inter-Committee meetings of the UN treaty-monitoring bodies (2005) should ameliorate this.

Alston suggested preparing consolidated reports and even proposed consolidating the existing treaty bodies in his first report (UN Doc A/44/668, paras 179–82). There is considerable logic in this—if a State has ratified all the treaties, then six reports are required, possibly many at almost the same time, six lots of representation in Geneva or New York are required and six different sets of concluding observations require to be implemented. Progress is being made towards a system entailing a single core document supported by appropriate treaty-specific information. Draft guidelines for such a core document were prepared in 2004 (UN Doc HRI/GEN.2/Rev.2 (2004)) and revised thereafter (UN Doc HRI/MC/2006/3). A number of Core Documents have been received by the United Nations to date. The African Commission has indicated that it is willing to accept State reports based on a report the State has previously submitted to another United Nations' body. Only minor adjustments or an annex may be necessary to situate the report in the regional context. This initiative is intended to encourage States to submit reports—naturally submission of any report is better than non-submission. A similar approach at the international level, although possibly used in practice by some States, is neither encouraged nor condoned.

As an interim measure, pending the long-term establishment of a single international monitoring body, Elizabeth Evatt suggests that a member of one treaty-monitoring body could sit as an observer on other treaty-monitoring bodies. This could prevent some of the repetition in both the examination, clarification and observations (p 466). Note that a former High Commissioner submitted a concept paper on a unified standing treaty body (2006, UN Doc HRI/MC/2006/2). Although supported in some quarters, the current system of individual treaty bodies looks set to continue. Nevertheless, there is growing evidence of the committees drawing on each others work, not least through consideration of relevant concluding observations from bodies with overlapping treaty obligations. Moreover, greater interaction between the Committees and the better availability of reports and concluding observations have combined to render the existing system more coherent than disjointed.

10.6.2.4 *Work of the committees*

Greater consistency in the format of the concluding observations and a consolidated approach to public relations may further enhance the functioning of the committees. The use of online media greatly facilitates dissemination of materials but is not necessarily a huge factor in every State. Part D of the Vienna Declaration and Programme of Action II (Human Rights Education) emphasizes the need for dissemination of public information on human rights. A system of online submission of reports with online publication thereof would go a long towards remedying some of the perceived deficiencies of the present system but may not prove popular with States.

The Committees have shown willingness to consider exceptionally alternatives to full written reports. The Committee on the Elimination of Discrimination against Women and the Human Rights Committee have both indicated a willingness to entertain oral reports and abridged reports in certain situations. This is not viewed as an alternative to a full periodic report, merely as a one-off, the lesser evil to defaulting on reporting obligations. The same has been used in Africa at the regional level.

10.6.2.5 *Backlog*

The backlog is another issue of considerable concern. Given that it can take an average of three years for a State report to be considered and the obligation to submit periodic reports may be every two years (CERD), the problem is obvious. If the committees were criminal courts, such a time delay would potentially infringe provisions on expeditious trials. Moreover, States with a rigorous policy of submitting on time (not many, admittedly) will find their report being considered almost as their next report should be ready for submission. The need for updating material in the reports is another problem. Perhaps the Committees could break into smaller groups with only one or maybe two members examining a report. Clearly, this may give rise to further problems and allegations on independence. However, it is a potential solution to the backlog. The other alternative would be to increase the number of members on the Committee. However, care must be taken not to increase membership to an unwieldy number. The experience of the European Court of Human Rights is a salutory lesson. Despite the Court increasing in numbers, and working in smaller Committees and Chambers on a full-time basis, a significant backlog remains (not helped by the continued increase in individual applications submitted to it). Protocol Fourteen's reforms are the latest attempt to reduce the backlog in Europe, restricting justiciable issues to focus the work of the Court.

10.6.3 **The Committees—composition, role, and functions**

In the Vienna Declaration and Programme of Action, the World Conference on Human Rights recognized that the activities of the United Nations in the field of human rights should be rationalized and enhanced in order to strengthen the United Nations machinery thereby furthering the objectives of universal respect for the observance of international human rights standards (Preamble).

Attendance of State Parties at all meetings in which their reports are being considered is clearly advantageous. However, the cost implications make this impractical. Perhaps consideration should be given to means of using General Assembly or Swiss permanent representatives (ie, those international diplomats based in Switzerland, perhaps the permanent representatives to the United Nations Office in Geneva), or even video conferencing. Naturally, video conferencing and web conferencing have implications for States without the resources and, potentially, there are also security implications which must be addressed.

Increasing the number of sessions is one way of securing an expeditious process. However, this has considerable resource implications. Committee members are paid allowances and in some instances a small honorarium. Increasing the number of sessions will have an adverse effect on this significant goodwill gesture on the part of many individuals. Clearly, making States responsibility for the funding of individuals can have some repercussions for the question of independence and the geographical spread. Once again, increasing the number of members is a possible alternative—on any committee, around ten per cent of the United Nations' membership is represented at any given time. An increase in numbers (as occurred with the CEDAW) could increase efficiency without altering the nature of the committees themselves. The Committees could run consecutive sessions. However, as much of the background work is carried out between sessions by the secretariat, this would not necessarily prove helpful.

10.6.4 **Resources**

'Maintaining the supervisory procedures of the human rights treaty bodies calls for a certain sleight of hand—to turn less into more' (Evatt, p 461). The dire financial straits of the United Nations' monitoring bodies was highlighted at the Vienna Declaration and Programme of Action, the World Conference on Human Rights expressing concern over the 'growing disparity between the activities of the Centre for Human Rights [now subsumed by the Office of the High Commissioner for Human Rights] and the human, financial and other resources available to carry them out' (Part II, para 9). The World Conference called for an increase in resources and, suggested the possibility of readjusting the budget to achieve resources commensurate with the increased mandates of the treaty bodies. Even after the major UN changes in 2006, finance remains an ongoing problem. Many of the members of the UN treaty-monitoring bodies are dependent on independent funding (for example by their employer if a university) to support their attendance at Committee meetings.

Financial problems beset the treaty-monitoring bodies. At present most of them meet on a regular but infrequent basis, often as little as twice a year for two- or three-week periods. At such levels, it is almost impossible to process the reports and complaints they receive. In some ways, this is a natural problem. When many of these treaties were drafted the number of potential Contracting States was less than half the current membership of the United Nations. The increase in workload is inevitable with the increase in the number of independent States.

10.6.4.1 *Translation costs*

A further problem occasioned by the increase in participation is the associated increase in translation costs. In Europe, documents are lodged in the original languages yet judgments are published in all State languages. The Americas and Africa have fewer official languages (although no less linguistic diversity) than Europe; thus, the problem is not so marked. In the United Nations, reports must be translated into the official languages of the United Nations (Chinese, English, French, Russian, Spanish, and sometimes Arabic) and possibly into other languages—the broad base of membership of the Committees means greater linguistic diversity. In Europe, English, and French are spoken by most judges, though the recent expansion of the Council of Europe into Eastern Europe has altered this. In the Americas, Spanish is widely spoken.

Professor Alston, in his report to the United Nations on enhancing the long-term effectiveness of the United Nations human rights treaty system, refers to the 'unmentionable language question'. English, French, and Spanish are stated as the three main languages in use with simultaneous translation only usually provided into Spanish. Professor Alston notes that although the General Assembly has reaffirmed its strong commitment to linguistic diversity, the reality of national trends and United Nations practice is that English is predominating: English-language materials are dominating the *travaux préparatoires* of State reports and the treaty bodies themselves are gravitating towards the adoption of English as the lingua franca. Moreover, perusal of the World Wide Web reveals that the majority of material available on human rights is in the English language. Although the commitment to linguistic diversity is clearly advantageous and in line with contemporary thinking on cultural rights and even some of the provisions of aspects of international instruments, the reality is 'a situation of dire financial stringency the resulting inflexibility [of which] will, on the one hand, wreak havoc and on the other, provoke resort to ever more creative and devious strategies to circumvent unworkable rules' (Alston, P, para 105). In the absence of the necessary increase in funds to facilitate appropriate translation, Professor Alston recommends that the principal committee members should be able to communicate in at least one of English, French, and Spanish. Moreover, working groups should be arranged in such a way as to minimize, preferably obviate translation costs (para 106). This proposal was met with some dismay by NGOs such as the North–South XXI which expressed regret at the linguistic domination of English (UN Doc E/CN.4/1998/85, p 20). Summary record reports are now prepared in English and French only to minimize delay. However, the United Nations still prefers translation into all official languages before publication occurs. In reality, material is uploaded online when available.

10.6.4.2 *Problems caused by lack of funds*

In some instances, committees have been forced to cancel meetings due to lack of funds. The Committee on the Elimination of all Forms of Racial Discrimination has suffered from this in recent years. The General Assembly has expressed its 'profound concern' that many States have not fulfilled their financial commitments to CERD and calls on States to fulfil their outstanding financial commitments (GA Res A/RES/53/131, 9/12/98). The Secretary-General was requested to ensure that adequate financial arrangements were made to enable the Committee to continue its work. *In situ* investigations and the work of rapporteurs is also often curtailed due to lack of funds.

10.6.4.3 *Redeploying resources?*

Given global economics, it is unlikely that the financial situation of the United Nations will undergo any dramatic upturn. The best that can be hoped for is therefore improved utilization of the available funds. There are various ways in which the available resources could be better utilized—a consolidation of secretarial support, use of automated translation facilities, etc. The resources currently available to the Committees are insufficient to complete their business. The European Court of Human Rights was forced to go full time in order to cope with its increased workload yet the United Nations Committees have in effect been downsized. It is all too easy to sit back and promulgate an increase in meeting times and terms and radical action to call in overdue reports. However, the reality is that the money is not available to assist with this.

The realistic options are, therefore, to consolidate reporting requirements thus reducing the amount of material that has to be discussed and translated. In 1997, the Secretary-General in his report Renewing the United Nations: A Programme for Reform (UN Doc A/51/950 (1997)), agreed to ask the High Commissioner for Human Rights to review the human rights machinery and recommend further ways of streamlining and rationalising it (Action 16). In his 2000 report (UN Doc E/CN.4/2000/98, para 61) the Secretary-General noted that no clear consensus on the desirability of consolidating reports has been reached though note the work of the Committee of Chairpersons (discussed *supra*). However, attempts have already been made to biennialize items under consideration and to institute more directed examinations of State reports—seeking specific clarifications, for example. Perhaps one solution is to increase the time between the submission of periodic reports, invoking the special report system if there is a problem with a particular State which has been identified or there is a radical change of government. Should more work be passed on to the various regional bodies? This would certainly be feasible in Europe and possibly in the Americas. This would obviously assist in reducing the workload but at the cost of imposing another hierarchical layer of human rights legislation. The regional bodies would be seen as acting on behalf of the United Nations and thus could not pursue more radical regional agendas. This would also place an undue burden on already over stretched regional systems.

10.6.4.4 *Streamlining the system*

The Secretary-General has noted the need to streamline the work of the treaty-monitoring bodies. However, this is partly aimed at reducing the reporting burden on States rather than easing the financial situation of the United Nations (UN Doc E/CN.4/2000/98). Greater cooperation between the treaty-monitoring bodies and the streamlining of reporting guidelines is in progress (UN Doc A/58/351, para 7). A further criticism which may be levied at the present system is that it is too unwieldy given the current resources available to it. The European system was reformed with increased use of Chambers and a pre-vetting of complaints with Protocol Fourteen empowering a single judge to determine admissibility. There are some academics who see merit in the idea of a single Universal Court of Human

Rights instead of the variety of committees which concurrently enjoy jurisdiction over Member States. Such a move would allow the combination of resources: financial resources, personnel, secretariat, and translation. Thomas Buergenthal, for example, suggests that the six existing treaty bodies could be replaced by two consolidated committees, one assuming the function of reviewing State reports, the other focusing on individual and inter-State complaints (p 299). This would obviously lighten the administrative burden both on States (one report rather than up to six) and the committees themselves (though it is expected that interim updates would be required). Buergenthal advocates that the new bodies would sit in panels, facilitating an increased efficiency in workload. This could alleviate any backlog that builds up. Perhaps more controversially, Buergenthal also recommends the creation of a United Nations Court for Human Rights (p 301). In the first instance, he proposes that such a court only enjoy advisory jurisdiction; thus, the proposal stands a greater chance of being accepted by States and thus becoming a reality. This idea is perhaps partially reinvigorated by the universal periodic human rights review power of the Human Rights Council. The success (or otherwise) of this function of the Human Rights Council remains to be seen, the first full cycle has not yet been completed.

A more judicialized system would be a hard pill to swallow for many States but would allow binding judgments to be issued and would be more conducive to political back up—the General Assembly could function as an enforcement agency in much the way that was envisaged for the Committee of Ministers in the Council of Europe.

10.6.5 Implementation and sanctions

Inevitably, there are States which will not adhere to the prescribed norms, even when they have ratified them. A frequent allegation against the United Nations is that it is powerless to force States to comply with its rules. There are limited possibilities for the applications of sanctions and clearly a State cannot be incarcerated. However, the remedies available to the United Nations are not inconsiderable. For a detailed discussion of this topic, reference should be had to any standard textbook on the United Nations and international law. In terms of the Charter, options available to the United Nations include sanctions, the use of force and, ultimately expulsion. Under the Charter, any State not complying with the requirements of the organization could be asked to leave. However, as the actions of the United Nations frequently prove, it is often preferable to have a State within the fold and thus subject to review by the organization than to expel it and have no control whatsoever.

10.6.5.1 Denouncing treaties

The international bodies have been reluctant to allow States to pick and choose when human rights provisions bind them. For example, when North Korea sought to withdraw from the International Covenant on Civil and Political Rights in 1997, the Secretary-General of the United Nations held that such an action would only be possible if consensus was reached. This represents a strict application of the Vienna Convention on the Law of Treaties: the ICCPR is a multilateral instrument; thus, technically all other States must agree. (The Optional Protocol to the ICCPR is, as the name suggests, optional. Thus, as noted elsewhere, several Caribbean States withdrew the right of individual petition following an increase in communications forwarded to the Human Rights Committee.)

10.6.5.2 *Political enforcement*

Frequent complaints have been made against many Member States, including permanent members of the Security Council. Although in some instances human rights are infringed due to economic factors, all too often the reasons are political. The perpetrators are well aware that their actions violate norms of human rights. Why else would they attempt to justify their actions or hide the evidence? The tragic examples of genocide in Rwanda and the Balkans were evidenced by the discovery of mass graves.

Given the comparative success of the United Nations system, its lack of follow-up and enforcement mechanisms is perhaps surprising. In Europe, follow-up is provided for by the Convention—Article 46 provides that the Committee of Ministers (a political body) has responsibility for supervising execution of the final judgment of the Court. The United Nations system, by comparison, has almost no follow-up or enforcement mechanism. Some attempts have been made. For example, the conventional mechanisms (committees) have begun to establish special rapporteurs to follow up decisions. What is needed, however, is political follow-up—the active involvement of the United Nations Commission on Human Rights, ECOSOSC, and even the General Assembly and Security Council. Obviously, in extreme situations, only the Security Council has the power to enforce international law and, *ergo*, international human rights. The only problem is the need for classification of the situation as a threat to international peace and security and, by definition, many of the individual complaints received by the Committees are not. In principle, however, this power gives the United Nations a stronger hand to play than, for example, the Council of Europe. Despite this, the decisions of the European Court are more readily implemented by States than those of the United Nations treaty-monitoring bodies.

10.6.5.3 *The success of the United Nations*

In the circumstances, it may be contended that the United Nations is remarkably successful. The publicizing of reports frequently highlights problem States thereby prompting compliance. At the end of the day, States wishing to pursue a different agenda from that prescribed by the international organization will do so. There is little that can be done to prevent States that choose to disregard the international standards from so doing. Yes, there are deterrents, but no, they cannot deter everyone. The same is true of any domestic system of law; there will always be people who choose to break the law irrespective of any penalties ensuing. What is of paramount importance is that the United Nations continues to provide an international standard for all peoples, a set of fundamental rights and freedoms which should form the basis of human dignity.

International law has moved from mere passive promotion of human rights to the more active protection of the articulated rights. However, the next stage of implementation essential for full realization of the rights, is a little way off. In international law, enforcement will always, by definition, be achieved through political means. International law is essentially consensual in nature; a concerted political response to infringing States is thus required.

10.6.5.4 *Problems of reports and backlogs*

The reluctance of Member States to adhere to their reporting obligations poses another problem. Hundreds, if not thousands, of State reports are overdue. As the Secretary-General notes, this 'detracts significantly' from the purpose of the treaty-monitoring system (UN Doc E/CN.4/2000/98, para 60). The resource implications of the backlog render pursuit impractical. Even if every overdue report were to be submitted, it would take years to clear the backlog and further reports would be accrued. It is clear that some kind of reform is necessary. Even the Council of Europe's permanent court has failed to reduce substantially the backlog of individual complaints, hence the new Protocol Fourteen which will once more attempt to reform the system and improve efficiency.

The obvious solution to criticisms of non-implementation is to involve the other United Nations bodies. More vocal political support from, perhaps, the General Assembly, would lend greater weight to the reports produced by the treaty bodies. Some method of stimulating media interest would also be beneficial. To achieve greater effect, there should be more of an onus upon States to publicize and circulate their periodic reports and the views of the salient committee thereon. It would also be helpful, though perhaps not financially viable, if the Committees themselves more widely disseminated their reports. The Office of the United Nations High Commissioner for Human Rights has established a website which goes some way towards achieving this goal in a relatively easy, inexpensive way. Moreover, the treaty-monitoring bodies have agreed annually to compile a report on the status of all States vis-à-vis their reporting obligations (Secretary-General, para 62).

10.6.6 **Individual petition**

The principal criticism which may be levied against the present individual petition system is its under utilization. Comparatively few individual petitions have reached the treaty bodies when one considers the millions of people eligible to submit communications to the various international and regional bodies. There are many reasons for this. The inaccessibility of any given system is one. In the Americas, the regional network is much more accessible and even more user friendly, as well as geographically and linguistically preferable, for the wronged individual. The United Nations is often perceived as distant and having little interest in individuals. In spite of this, the regional systems are also, arguably, under utilized—a comparison of the figures of individual complaints to the Inter-American and European systems demonstrates this.

10.6.6.1 *Compulsory individual petition*

One partial solution would be to make ratification of the individual petition provisions compulsory upon ratification of the treaty. Ideally, States should not be permitted to accede and denounce at will. A much higher profile is needed worldwide of the right to submit individual petitions. This should facilitate an increase in petitions which in turn will cause more resource problems. At present individual petitions are not competent under all of the core conventions. Permitting individual communications in respect of rights which are being achieved progressively (economic, social, and cultural rights) is an interesting development, with any resultant opinions sure to make interesting reading.

At a regional level, steps are being taken to remedy this. The entry into force of Protocol 11 to the European Convention on Human Rights removed the pre-existing option regarding individual petitions. The European regional system is now the first system with an automatic right of individual petition. Naturally, this cannot be emulated elsewhere without the necessary political will. In reality, European States had more readily accepted the optional individual petition system before the entry into force of Protocol 11. However, the resultant rise in petitions and the seemingly insurmountable backlog with the European court has accrued, has prompted a rethink on realizing effective individual petitions.

10.6.6.2 *A more efficient process*

The process of examining individual complaints should be faster, more public, more fully reasoned, and should be supported by a comprehensive follow up (Bayefsky, A, pp 697–8). Bayefsky also suggests some reforms which are untenable in the current financial situation though admirable in sentiment: holding public hearings for individual communications in the State concerned; regional briefing meetings with lawyers; and follow-ups to State reports for example (ibid). All treaty-monitoring bodies have been urged to adopt specific 'follow-up procedures' and 'take measures that would encourage the timely submission of reports' (UN Doc A/58/351, para 7). When compared to the regional systems, there is perhaps some room for improvement at the international level. Again, there is a potential role for the new Human Rights Council. The Inter-American and European Courts of Human Rights both hold public sessions when considering individual petitions. Decisions are also delivered in public session and published quickly. In both cases, reasoned opinions and dissenting opinions are given. This further contributes to the transparency of process and helps to encourage participation.

10.7 **Pluralism and homogeneity**

It is perhaps inevitable that the United Nations will run into trouble when trying to enforce a set of prescribed human rights in the present global environment. Allegations that human rights are prescribed by the privileged few for the world at large still appear. Whilst the argument is partially justified, the alternative to the present system is unthinkable. Without some prescribed set of rights, delineating the parameters within which States should act, many more atrocities would go unchallenged in the world. In an increasingly pluralistic global village, greater interaction between peoples and cultures inevitably leads to a greater awareness of rights and privileges. The optimistic, perhaps idealistic, aim of the United Nations is even more relevant to society at the dawn of the twenty-first century.

The United Nations system may be claimed by some to be predominantly 'Western' in origins and drawn from a Christian ethos. However, as society becomes increasingly pluralistic, differences have to be tolerated. Multicultural societies are a fact that must be dealt with by States. Different racial, religious, linguistic, and ethnic groups must live together as co-nationals in a variety of States. Adhering to a basic tenet of rights is one facet of this. It provides a ground for States to adhere to which aids coexistence. No group of peoples steadfastly denounces any of the basic rights enumerated in the Universal Declaration. This reinforces the true universality of rights therein. The world is not homogenous; thus, what the experience with human rights demonstrates is a common sense approach with the common denominator being the threshold of protection for all. As has been seen when regional instruments were examined, it is much easier to prescribe a system of rights for smaller, relatively homogenous groups of people and States than for the entire global community. In spite of this, the regional systems have still encountered problems in this respect. Both the African and Arab Charters claim to enshrine systems of rights specifically tailored to, respectively, the African continent and the Arab world. The ASEAN countries, in contrast, are pursuing a 'lighter' touch, aiming at reinforcing respect for general human rights and strengthening the national mechanisms (especially national human rights institutions).

10.8 **Reform? Some observations**

No system for the international protection of human rights can be completely watertight. The international community must strive to hit the balance between protecting vulnerable individuals from abuses of power by States and respecting the sovereignty and territorial integrity of each State. As Bayefsky acknowledges, '[t]he international lawyer does not operate in a vacuum. Norms are not intended to be drafted for their own sake. Ratification of human rights treaties was not meant to be an end in itself … the record reveals a serious rift between standard-setting and implementation' (p 682). The international standards are set and, in a relatively short period of time, some have achieved universal acceptance. The attention of the international community is now turning to securing means for enforcement of those standards. However, just as political will was required to enable the formation of the pertinent legal instruments, it will be needed to progress through to the enforcement of those norms. Follow-ups to State reports by the treaty-monitoring bodies are limited in effect without political support. This lack of political will to confirm the recommendations and decisions of the treaty-monitoring bodies is regarded by Manfred Nowak as revealing 'a certain hypocritical attitude of governments towards the international protection of human rights' (p 254). He concludes that enforcement is the responsibility of those establishing the treaty-monitoring bodies in the first place. Indeed, the United Nations views national human rights institutions as being able to play a stronger role (UN Doc A /58/351, para 6). The Paris Principles relating to the status and functioning of national institutions for protection and promotion of human rights (GA Res A/RES/48/134 on 20 December 1993) have been embraced by many treaty-monitoring bodies in concluding observations on State reports and General Comments. General Comment 10 of the Committee on Economic, Social and Cultural Rights (1998) and General Comment 2 (2002) of the Committee on the Rights of the Child are examples that elaborate on this.

The international community has clearly articulated the fundamental rights and freedoms which should be guaranteed to all. It is up to the States to give effect to them at the national level and it is up to individuals to use those rights. What is essential, as is recognized by the United Nations itself, is the necessity for education. Every citizen should be aware of the rights he or she enjoys. International human rights are available to all, the rhetoric is slowly becoming a reality. Computer technology provides a partial solution for those with access thereto—for example, the Universal Declaration on Human Rights is available on the Internet in over three hundred language versions.

Now, over a billion people have the right to petition some of the United Nations bodies while millions can apply to the Inter-American Court and the European Court. Educators have responsibility for galvanizing progress. Throughout the world, people have a better understanding of the rights they should enjoy. Better dissemination of information, a higher media profile of decisions, and action by NGOs has raised awareness of human rights to new levels. In the Americas, individual complaints can be submitted to the Inter-American Commission online, in Europe, the Strasbourg machinery receives a great deal of media coverage. By comparison, the United Nations sometimes seems like a poor relation. Only an élite inner circle of academics, activists, and politicians tends to be aware of the content of State reports and the concluding observation of a United Nations Committee in respect of the State.

The General Assembly has resolved that the United Nations information centre in each country should make available copies of recent reports to the treaty bodies by the State, the summary records, and concluding observations adopted by the treaty bodies. The availability of these documents varies considerably from State to State.

In general, governmental authorities are only too well aware of their obligations under international law and the associated human rights instruments they have ratified. The problem lies with dissemination—many law enforcement officers, judges, etc, in Member States may not be so familiar with the terms of international instruments. Moreover, there is sometimes reluctance on the part of judges to apply what is regarded as 'foreign' law, especially given the problem in obtaining detailed jurisprudence thereon. The heart of the matter lies with domestic implementation. If an instrument is incorporated into national law, then it stands a much greater chance of being enforced in that State, as the State will explicitly have endorsed its content. A detailed discussion of monism and dualism is outwith the scope of this text. Once an international or regional instrument has been formally incorporated then the judges will apply it and the rights enshrined therein become a reality. The Committee on the Elimination of Racial Discrimination, for example, provides model laws for States wishing to incorporate the Convention effectively into domestic law. If one peruses a cross section of national case law in any given State, it would be unusual to find copious references to the United Nations' human rights instruments. Rather, the only reference one is likely to encounter is a State justifying actions as being not against the Constitution, the European Convention on Human Rights, the International Covenant on Civil and Political Rights, or whatever. The same is true for other aspects of international law. Perhaps there is merit in considering the status quo as 'a world rich in human rights norms and ideals but wanting in political will and enforcement' (Steiner, H, p 53).

CASES

Cyprus v Turkey, 2 DR 125 (1975).

Denmark v Greece (Applicn 3321/67), CM Res DH (70) 1.

Georgia v Russian Federation, ongoing International Court of Justice.

Guedson v France, HRC 1990, UN Doc CCPR/C/39/D/219/1986.

Ireland v United Kingdom, Ser A, No 25 (1978).

Norway v Greece (Applicn 3322/67), CM Res DH (70) 1.

Sweden v Greece (Applicn 3323/67), CM Res DH (70) 1.

READING

Adham, J, and Said, T, 'What price the right of individual petition: Report of the Evaluation Group to the Committee of Ministers on the European Court of Human Rights' (2000) European Human Rights Law Review 169–74.

Alston, P, *Effective Functioning of Bodies Established Pursuant to United Nations Human Rights Instruments: Final report on enhancing the long-term effectiveness of the United Nations human rights treaty system* UN Doc E/CN.4/1997/74, 27/3/97.

Alston, P, and Crawford, J, *The Future of UN Human Rights Treaty Monitoring* (Cambridge: Cambridge University Press, 2000).

Annan, K, *Effective Functioning of Human Rights Mechanisms: Treaty bodies: Report of the Secretary-General on the consultations conducted in respect of the report of the independent expert on enhancing the long-term effectiveness of the United Nations human rights treaty system*, UN Doc E/CN.4/2000/98.

——, *In Larger Freedom: Towards development, security and human rights for all*, UN Doc A/59/2005.

Arambulo, K, *Strengthening the Supervision of the International Covenant on Economic, Social and Cultural Rights: Theoretical and procedural aspects* (Antwerp: Intersentia, 1999).

Bailey, P, 'Implementing human rights: The way forward' (1999) 5(2) Australian Journal of Human Rights (www.austlii.edu.au/au/journals/AJHR/1999).

Bayefsky, A, *Report on the UN Human Rights Treaties: Facing the implementation crisis*, first report of the Committee on International Human Rights Law and Practice, International Law Association, Helsinki Conference 1996, reproduced in A Bayefsky (ed), *The UN Human Rights Treaty System in the 21st Century* (The Hague: Kluwer, 2000), pp 681–99.

—— (ed), *The UN Human Rights Treaty System in the 21st Century* (The Hague: Kluwer, 2000).

——, *How to Complain to the UN Human Rights Treaty System* (Hague: Kluwer, 2003).

Boerefijn, I, 'Towards a strong system of supervision: The Human Rights Committee's role in reforming the reporting procedure under Article 40 of the Covenant on Civil and Political Rights' (1999) 17(4) Human Rights Quarterly 766–93.

——, *The Reporting Procedure Under the Covenant on Civil and Political Rights* (Antwerp: Intersentia, 1999).

Boniface, DJ, 'More changes proposed in addition to the changes already proposed: The Human Rights and Responsibility Commission—a friend in need?' (1999) 5(1) Australian Journal of Human Rights (www.austlii.edu.au/au/journals/AJHR/1999).

Bruderlein, C, and Gassman, P, 'Managing security risks in hazardous Missions: The challenges of securing United Nations access to vulnerable groups' (2006) Harvard Human Rights Journal 235–56.

Buergenthal, T, 'A court and two consolidated treaty bodies' in A Bayefsky (ed), *The UN Human Rights Treaty System in the 21st Century* (The Hague: Kluwer, 2000), pp 299–302.

Butler, A, 'Legal Aid before Human Rights Treaty monitoring bodies' (2000) 49 International and Comparative Law Quarterly 360–89.

Butler, F (ed), *HR Protection: Methods and Effectiveness* (The Hague: Kluwer, 2001).

Conforti, B, and Francioni, F, *Enforcing International Human Rights in Domestic Courts* (The Hague: Martinus Nijhoff, 1997).

Connors, J, 'An Analysis and Evaluation of the System of State Reporting' in A Bayefsky (ed), *The UN Human Rights Treaty System in the 21st Century* (The Hague: Kluwer, 2000), pp 3–21.

Craven, M, 'Humanitarianism and the quest for smarter sanctions' (2002) 13(1), European Journal of International Law 43–61.

Douzinas, C, *The End of Human Rights* (Oxford: Hart, 2000).

Evatt, E, 'Reflecting on the role of international communications in implementing human rights' (1999) 5(2) Australian Journal of Human Rights (www.austlii.edu.au/au/journals/AJHR/1999).

——, 'Ensuring effective supervisory procedures: The need for resources' in P Alston and J Crawford (eds), *The Future of UN Human Rights Treaty Monitoring* (Cambridge: Cambridge University Press, 2000), pp 461–79.

Fitzpatrick, J, 'Human rights fact-finding' in A Bayefsky (ed), *The UN Human Rights Treaty System in the 21st Century* (The Hague: Kluwer, 2000), pp 65–95.

Van Genugten, WJM, and de Groot, GA, *United Nations Sanctions* (Antwerp: Intersentia, 1999).

Gordon, J, 'When intent makes all the difference in the world: Economic sanctions on Iraq and the accusation of genocide' (2002) 5 Yale Human Rights and Development Journal (www.islandia.law.yale.edu/yhrdlj/).

Grant, S, 'The United States and the international human rights treaty system: For export only?' in P Alston and J Crawford (eds), *UN Human Rights Treaty Monitoring* (Cambridge: Cambridge University Press, 2000).

Hossain, K, et al (eds), *HR Commissioners and Ombudsman Offices: National experiences through-out the world* (The Hague: Kluwer, 2001).

McGoldrick, D, *The Human Rights Committee* (Oxford: Oxford University Press, 1991).

Nowak, M, 'The UN High Commissioner for Human Rights: A link between decisions of expert monitoring bodies and enforcement by political bodies' in A Bayefsky (ed), *The UN Human Rights Treaty System in the 21st Century* (The Hague: Kluwer, 2000), pp 251–4.

O'Connell, M, 'Debating the law of sanctions' (2002) 13(1) European Journal of International Law 63–79.

Pentassuglia, G, 'Monitoring minority rights in Europe: The implementation of the Frame-work Convention for the Protection of National Minorities with special reference to the role of the Advisory Committee' (1999) 6(4) International Journal of Minority and Group Rights 417–62.

Ratner, SR, and Abrams, JS, *Accountability for Human Rights Atrocities in International Law: Beyond the Nuremberg legacy*, 2nd edn (Oxford: Oxford University Press, 2001).

Risse, T, Ropp, SC, and Sikkik, K (eds), *The Power of Human Rights: International norms and domestic change* (Cambridge: Cambridge University Press, 1999).

Schmidt, M, 'Servicing and financing human rights supervision' in P Alston and J Crawford (eds), *The Future of UN Human Rights Treaty Monitoring* (Cambridge: Cambridge University Press, 2000), pp 481–98.

Shelton, D *Remedies in International Human Rights Law* (Oxford: Oxford University Press, 1999).

Smith, A, 'The unique position of national human rights institutions: A mixed blessing' (2006) 28(4) Human Rights Quarterly 904–46.

Steiner, H, 'Individual claims in a world of massive violations: What role for the Human Rights Committee?' in P Alston and J Crawford (eds), *The Future of UN Human Rights Monitoring* (Cambridge: Cambridge University Press, 2000), pp 15–53.

Symonides, J, *Human Rights: International protection, monitoring and enforcement* (Aldershot: Ashgate 2003).

Tistounet, E, 'The problem of overlapping among different treaty bodies' in P Alston and J Crawford (eds), *The Future of UN Human Rights Treaty Monitoring* (Cambridge: Cambridge University Press, 2000), pp 383–401.

Williams, D, 'Reforming human rights treaty bodies' (1999) 5(2) Australian Journal of Human Rights (www.austlii.edu.au/au/journals/AJHR/1999).

WEBSITES

www.ohchr.org—contains links to the treaties, the Committees and other related materials.

www2.ohchr.org/english/bodies/petitions/index.htm—United Nations' individual communications.

www2.ohchr.org/english/bodies/chr/complaints.htm—UN Communications under extra-conventional mechanisms.

www.coe.int—the Council of Europe.

www.oas.org—the Organization of American States.

www.africa-union.org—the African Union.

11

....

Substantive rights—general comments

To this point, the text has focused on the institutional framework within which rights and freedoms are protected. The main human rights instruments which enshrine those rights have also been discussed. Having thus established the parameters within which State interference with human rights and freedoms should be controlled, attention will now turn to the substantive content of international human rights law. As a comparatively young system of law, operating as part of international law and with deep philosophical roots, norms of human rights are still growing and developing. Some aspects are fairly well developed—the prohibitions on torture and slavery, for example—others, such as the right to work, are less clearly defined in scope or effect. 'New' human rights appear regularly, further expanding the written codification of the concept.

Before discussing the content of selected rights in the following chapters, it is essential to first characterize the limitations on the various rights and the extent to which States can derogate from responsibility in terms of international human rights law.

11.1 **Content of rights**

By their very nature, universal human rights are to be enjoyed by all people irrespective of race, language, religion, or ethnic origin. This presented the drafters with a major problem—reconciling all beliefs, traditions, and cultures to a common denominator of international human rights law, an international minimum standard of treatment. Declaring such a standard was in itself problematic as the set of rights could not be so minimal as to negate their very existence. In scope (as was seen in Chapter 4) many of the rights contained in the Universal Declaration are aspirational, goals States agree to strive for. This form of standard-setting is inherently problematic. It is difficult to ascertain a State's exact obligations at any given time when rights are to be progressively achieved.

A related allegation often levied against human rights provisions is the lack of specificity. The breadth of Articles inevitably is conducive to teleological interpretation in keeping with the progressive evolution of the rights. As society advances, more rights are realized and moral and global standards change. Human rights are not static: they are inherently flexible, the precise meaning of rights may change over the years. This is inevitable given that the human rights instruments to which States subscribe represent the legal embodiment of a philosophical theory. The written text enshrines what was agreed at the preparatory stage, not necessarily the entire scope of the philosophy underpinning it. Reliance on the general underlying principle enables supervisory bodies to apply any provision in a teleological manner with reference to the overall spirit of the instrument. General comments and recommendations of the UN treaty bodies, for example, intimate the approach likely to be taken by the Committee when monitoring state compliance with certain rights and freedoms.

Whilst some regard this lack of specificity as a weakness of the present system, others regard it as a strength. The international instruments are very much living laws, a framework which grows and develops as the years go by. The only limitation on the development of the laws is consensus—any international or regional body can only act in accordance with the general will of participating States. The European Convention on Human Rights and the Convention on the Rights of the Child have been leading examples of teleological interpretation in recent years.

11.2 **State discretion and other limitations**

The nature of international law demands the goodwill of States to secure implementation of standards of human rights. Consequently, it is open to States to pick and choose which parts, if any, of a particular instrument they accept. Changes in government and stability may prompt States to derogate from an instrument or even to denounce it completely. Moreover, there may be a degree of State discretion inherent in the operation of human rights instruments—a recognition that the rights are not absolute and may be limited to an extent depending on situations of national security, politics, morality, or health.

11.2.1 **State discretion**

Inevitably, States enjoy a degree of flexibility in implementing human rights. The instruments are, in general, not phrased in absolute terms. All rights are subject to limitations imposed by international law. Many national and regional instruments state that they should not be interpreted to restrict international rights and thus there is a partial recognition of the superiority of the international system. However, in many instances the international systems lack specificity and are relatively unenforceable. Moreover, international instruments usually indicate that nothing in them should be taken as restricting more beneficial rights prescribed by national law—Art 41 of the United Nations Convention on the Rights of the Child is an example of this. Phrases such as 'as far as possible', 'in accordance with national law', and 'as necessary' indicate a degree of flexibility. This is essential to ensure State support for the instrument. Moreover, it is an important, though subtle, reminder of the limits of human rights and international law. States retain paramount power as the primary subjects of international law and thus reserve the right to limit the application of human rights when deemed appropriate and necessary. Furthermore, there will always be aspects of, for example, terminology, which depend on national law—the scope of 'national' is an example. Should national security be threatened or a public emergency arise, the State should, at all times, respond proportionately to the situation to minimize the risk of violating human rights obligations.

Inevitably the regional systems have also had to contend with attempts to limit rights. State discretion, the 'margin of appreciation' accorded to States, is most developed in Europe through the pioneering work of the European Court of Human Rights. The margin of appreciation is the degree of flexibility accorded to States in determining whether certain measures are necessary. Its invocation is most easily evidenced by reference to the jurisprudence of the Court. Thus, in the case of *Handyside v United Kingdom* concerning the prohibition of a book in the United Kingdom under the obscene publications legislation, the European Court recognized that by virtue of their direct and continuous contact with the vital forces of their countries, State authorities are in a better position to elucidate the exact content of public morals and such like. The overall responsibility for the protection of human rights thus lies with the States, the regional and international bodies merely exercising a supervisory role. None of the international bodies act as appellate courts, adjudicating on decisions of national courts. The creation of a margin of appreciation allows States to participate in the European Convention because State sovereignty is clearly respected and national standards of morals and security can be adhered to. Consequently, prohibitions on divorce in Roman Catholic States can be upheld while divorce and remarriage is permitted in many other States. Perhaps the most obvious example of the margin of appreciation lies with newer challenges to rights and discrimination—the laws relating to homosexuals and transsexuals. Within Europe, prohibitions on homosexual relations appear no longer to be acceptable (see the cases from *Dudgeon v United Kingdom* through to *ADT v United Kingdom*), while the situation on recognition of transsexuals has evolved considerably (*Rees v United Kingdom, Cossey v United Kingdom, Sheffield and Horsham v United Kingdom, Goodwin and I v United Kingdom*). The margin of appreciation States enjoy varies depending on the right in question; thus there is little discretion permitted in interfering with the private life of an individual but a greater margin of appreciation regarding, for example, the right to marry (each State may specify the legal capacity requirements). With respect to national security, the situation may be compared with the invocation of derogations—discussed later. Since a perceived threat from terrorism is most easily identified by the State concerned, international bodies are unlikely to interfere. States thus enjoy considerable discretion in such circumstances.

Even in the United Nations there is growing evidence of recognition of a margin of discretion for States (see eg, *Hertzberg et al v Finland*, para 10.3). Such a device is perhaps an inevitable consequence of enforceable universal rights.

11.2.2 Clash of rights

Rights such as freedom of expression and association are frequently only exercisable to the extent such exercise does not impinge upon the rights of others. There may thus be a balancing act between two conflicting exercises of rights: an individual suffering from a dangerous contagious disease may be detained in order to preserve the right to health of others; or a newspaper may be prevented from publishing material in exercise of freedom of expression when such material violates the right to privacy or family life of another or prejudices the continuance of a fair trial. In such situations, a decision will have to be made on which right is accorded priority. Given the indivisibility of all human rights, such cases tend to be decided on an individual basis, taking into consideration all the facts and circumstances of the case. Arguably, such a determination entails inferring some sort of hierarchy into human rights instruments. On the other hand, it is a practical necessity that some rights may conflict, and just as with conflict of laws (private international law), it is for the courts to determine which right/law should be prioritized. Non-derogable rights will usually be favoured against rights containing considerable scope for State discretion. In accordance with the approach adopted in determining the legitimacy of restrictions on rights, the test will be one of proportionality.

11.2.3 **Derogations**

In time of public emergency threatening the life of the nation and the existence of which is officially proclaimed, the State Parties to the present Covenant may take measures derogating from their obligations under the present Covenant to the extent strictly required by the exigencies of the situation (Art 4(1), International Covenant on Civil and Political Rights: see also, Art 17 European Convention on the Protection of Human Rights and Fundamental Freedoms; Art 27 American Convention on Human Rights).

11.2.3.1 *Introduction*

The Human Rights Committee deems Art 4 of 'paramount importance' for the system of protection of human rights (General Comment 29, para 1). Many international and regional instruments permit derogation in times of armed conflict or other public emergencies. The relevant situation would have to be of a serious nature and frequently will be an event which is of concern to the international community in terms of the maintenance of peace and security—not every national emergency qualifies. Any derogation is limited to the 'exigencies' of the situation, that is only to the extent absolutely necessary to achieve the goal: this covers 'duration, geographical coverage and material scope' (General Comment 29, para 4). The exercise of the derogation is thus subject to the restrictions laid down in the instrument itself.

11.2.3.2 *Non-derogable rights*

Derogations are not permitted from all aspects of the instruments: for example, there is usually no derogation from the right to life, freedom from torture, freedom from slavery, discrimination, thought, conscience and religion, or the prohibition on retroactive penal legislation. Naturally should hostilities occur, the Geneva and Hague Conventions governing the conduct thereof will be operational extending rights to combatants and civilians alike under norms of humanitarian law (discussed briefly in Chapter 2). The creation of a body of non-derogable rights within human rights law has sometimes been taken to add weight to the notion of a hierarchy of rights with the non-derogable rights being somehow higher than the others. In General Comment 29, the Human Rights Committee extends the list of non-derogable rights from those prescribed in Art 4. The Committee opines that the right of all persons deprived of their liberty to be treated with humanity and respect; the prohibition on taking hostages, abductions or unacknowledged detention; elements of minority rights (especially genocide and non-discrimination); deportation or forcible transfers of population outwith specified grounds; or incitement to or advocacy of national, racial, or religious hatred are essentially non-derogable due to their grounding in non-derogable principles of international law (para 13). There are practical reasons for deeming certain rights non-derogable. For example, the rule of law must be maintained thus derogations cannot compromise it, irrespective of any public emergency. Moreover, there are certain rights it is virtually impossible to restrict—for example there can be no derogation from freedom of thought. In other instances, the continued operation of a right is not dependant on the maintenance of legitimate State control thus there is no justification for derogation in event of a threat to, or breakdown in, State control.

It is interesting to note that the African Charter on Human and Peoples' Rights has no derogation clause. This is perhaps all the more surprising given that the recent history of many African States evidences numerous situations in which derogation under other international instruments would be applicable. The indivisibility of all human rights is enforced in Africa, the onus on States heightened. With the establishment of the African Court, it is possible that attention will turn to the potential for implying some flexibility in the event of public emergencies, though this remains to be seen.

11.2.3.3 *Procedural requirements*

In its General Comment No 5, the Human Rights Committee acknowledged that Art 4 of the International Covenant had caused a number of problems. The need for informing the Secretary-General and therefore other State Parties was emphasized thereby stressing the importance of States being open about the circumstances in which they choose to derogate. According to the Human Rights Committee, all such derogations should also be explained in subsequent periodic reports submitted by the State to allow the Committee to determine the efficacy thereof. Note that the invocation of Art 4 does not absolve a State from its responsibility to submit periodic reports.

Derogations should not last ad infinitum. Rather, States should regularly review any derogations and assess the continued need for the derogation. Some States have provisions under constitutional law which allow such review. Derogations may be lodged with respect to particular situations affecting a part, or all of a State and may affect all or only some rights. For example, in response to perceived threats of terrorist activity, many States seek to derogate from those aspects of liberty which govern detention of suspects. However, in such circumstances, individuals must not be arbitrarily deprived of their liberty, some checks must be retained to ensure the legitimacy of detention.

As has been discussed, any exercise of any derogation is subject to monitoring by the salient international or regional body and not all instruments permit such derogations.

11.2.4 **Reservations**

Reservations are a plague of international human rights law. Many States ratify instruments subject to a number of reservations and declarations. Reservations are legally binding statements of limitation on the application of specified rights which exonerate States from liability under a particular part of a treaty.

States view reservations as an essential facet of State sovereignty and a means of being seen to comply with international law (by ratifying) yet not dramatically altering national law to conform thereto (through the application of reservations). For international and regional organizations, reservations erode the effectiveness of the instrument in question, undermining the benefits of the right and the universality of human rights in general. For the individual, the potential victim of a violation, obviously reservations can ultimately remove a right which the Convention purports to protect.

11.2.4.1 *Definition and scope of reservations*

A reservation is defined in Art 2 of the Vienna Convention on the Law of Treaties 1969 as 'a unilateral statement, however phrased or named, made by a State, when signing, ratifying, accepting, approving, or acceding to a treaty, whereby it purports to exclude, or to modify the legal effect of certain provisions of the treaty in their application to that State'. Reservations may thus be termed declarations—it is the content not the form of the statement which is important. Not all instruments permit reservations. However, there is a presumption in favour of the right of States to enter reservations unless the instrument expressly states to the contrary. The Human Rights Committee (writing with respect to the International Covenant on Civil and Political Rights) suggests that no reservations which 'offend peremptory norms' are compatible with human rights instruments. In light of this finding, States cannot enter reservations which significantly affect the application of elements of customary international law which are codified in the Covenant—the presumption of innocence, freedom from torture and slavery, freedom from arbitrary detention, and freedom from advocacy of religious, national, or racial hatred are deemed non-reservable as are the rights of minorities (Art 27, ICCPR), the prohibition on execution of pregnant women and children and the right of persons free from legal impediment to marry. General Comment 24 further notes that certain reservations to the right to a fair trial may be legitimate (para 8). As general international law prohibits reservations being made which are not compatible with the object and purpose of the instrument, any reservations to non-derogable rights must be justified by the State concerned. According to the Human Rights Committee, there have been reservations to both Arts 6 and 7 of the International Covenant (right to life and prohibition on torture) but their terms have not reserved the right to torture or the right to arbitrarily deprive persons of their right to life (para 10).

The test to be applied in determining whether a reservation is compatible with the object and purpose of an instrument is generally an objective one, with the adjudicating body (usually the salient Court, Commission or Committee) having regard to legal principles. To facilitate this, States should carefully formulate their reservations, rendering transparent, clearly defined statements, the compatibility of which can easily be ascertained. General reservations on the content of rights should be avoided.

11.2.4.2 *Other reservations*

Reservations to human rights instruments may relate to more general matters. For example, many States note on ratification of any multilateral instrument that the act of ratification does not signify recognition of certain other State Parties (most commonly Taiwan or Israel). Similarly, reservation may affect the territorial application of an instrument to dependent territories and/or colonies of the ratifying State. Finally, general reservations may affect the operation or implementation of an instrument. These may be valid so long as the reservation does not negate the object and purpose of the instrument itself.

11.2.4.3 *Can States object to reservations?*

Traditionally, all States had to agree to any reservation made by any other State. Given that most international human rights instruments are now large multilateral affairs, the need for consensus on the content of reservations is precluded in accordance with practice and underlying principles invoked by the International Court of Justice in its advisory opinion on the *Reservations to the Genocide Convention Case*. Although this case was concerned primarily with the Genocide Convention, much of the opinion is regarded as reflective of customary international law. However, some instruments specify a system for evaluating objections to reservations—Art 20(2) of the International Convention on the Elimination of All Forms of Racial Discrimination states that a reservation will be deemed incompatible if at least two-thirds of the State Parties object thereto. Although no similar provision appears in the International Covenants, the Human Rights Committee at para 17 of its General Comment suggests that the role of State objections to reservations is not relevant. Experience has shown that State objections to reservations is sporadic and the Committee deemed it unsafe to assume that failure to object meant acceptance.

11.2.4.4 *Removing and reviewing reservations*

In Part IIA of the Vienna Declaration and Programme of Action adopted in 1993, the World Conference on Human Rights calls on States to consider limiting the extent of any reservations they lodge to international human rights instruments and to narrowly and precisely formulate all reservations. Moreover, States are urged to regularly review reservations with a view to progressively withdrawing them. Periodic review is inevitable given that States are encouraged to enforce all international human rights instruments in the spirit of the universality and indivisibility of all rights. However, the calls by the World Conference for all States to ratify international human rights instruments (Part II, para 4) are unlikely to be answered in the affirmative unless reservations are permitted.

11.2.4.5 *Conclusions*

Reservations are undoubtedly a 'necessary evil' of any emerging system of international human rights: their existence facilitates the goal of universal acceptance of human rights while enabling States to 'opt out' as necessary. As with international law in general, it is deemed better to have at least token conformity than none at all (at least a wolf within a flock can be 'controlled'). Reservations are normally subject to scrutiny during review of initial and periodic reports with treaty-monitoring bodies urging States to consider withdrawing reservations. Naturally a State cannot be held in violation of any provision of an instrument in respect of which a valid reservation has been entered. Similarly, in terms of the Vienna Convention on the Law of Treaties, a reservation to a multilateral instrument operates on a basis of reciprocity: if State R enters a reservation to the effect that Article L of an instrument is inapplicable to R then neither State S can bring an action against R for failure to implement Article L nor can State R bring an action against S in respect of its failure to implement Article L, even where State S has entered no such reservation. In effect, reservations operate to fragment a multilateral agreement into a myriad of bilateral agreements under the umbrella of a single multilateral framework. In this respect, the views of the Human Rights Committee in General Comment 24 should be noted. The Committee stated that in the light of the special characteristics of the International Covenant on Civil and Political Rights as a human rights instrument, 'it is open to question what effect objections have between States inter se'. Given the lack of inter-State complaints, this is perhaps a moot point. Maybe this comment is best viewed in the general context of the Committee delineating its role under the Covenant.

11.2.5 Declarations

Declarations are distinct from reservations. They are essentially interpretative in nature, statements as to the understanding of a State as to the scope, meaning, or application of a particular right. International bodies are rarely swayed by declarations that all human rights' obligations accepted within an instrument are deemed to be identical in content and effect to similar provisions of national law. Such declarations undermine the effectiveness of the instrument in question, removing the power of interpretation from the Court, Commission, or Committee. Frequently, regional or international autonomous meanings develop over time which inevitably may be distinct from national law. The scope of 'family' and the differentiation between torture, inhuman treatment, cruel punishment, and degrading treatment or punishment are two examples. Declarations can inevitably be more problematic than reservations as the effect of a declaration is less clear. There may be further confusion as many States make little distinction between reservations and declarations thus the relevant bodies must look at the context and nature of the statement to determine its intended classification.

11.2.6 Denunciations

As treaties are essentially consensual in nature, States may accept or denounce the obligations thereunder at will. As has been noted, certain Caribbean States have denounced the right of individual petition under the Optional Protocol to the International Covenant on Civil and Political Rights. Similarly, Greece opted to withdraw from the European Convention on Human Rights as a temporary measure in the wake of a number of inter-State complaints, though it has since rejoined the Convention mechanisms.

However, not all treaties enshrine rights of denunciation. The variations are illustrated by examination of the principal treaties which are subject to international supervision by a dedicated body. Neither the International Covenant on Civil and Political Rights, the International Covenant on Economic, Social and Cultural Rights, nor the Convention on the Elimination of All Forms of Discrimination Against Women provide for denunciation. On the other hand, Art 21 of the International Convention on the Elimination of All Forms of Racial Discrimination, Art 31 of the Convention against Torture and Other Cruel Inhuman or Degrading Treatment or Punishment, and Art 52 of the United Nations Convention on the Rights of the Child permit States to denounce the instrument upon receipt of one year's written notice. States may also withdraw from the Statute of the International Criminal Court (Art 127).

At the regional level, Art 58 allows States to withdraw following six months' notice from the European Convention on Human Rights, while one year's notice is required under Art 78 of the American Convention on Human Rights. The African Charter, in contrast, has no provision for denunciation.

General Comment 26 of the Human Rights Committee reiterates the international legal position for instruments with no denunciation provisions. In order to permit termination, withdrawal, or denunciation in the absence of express provisions, State Parties must demonstrate that the Parties intended to permit such action, or that it can be inferred from the nature of the instrument itself (Art 56 Vienna Convention on the Law of Treaties 1969). With respect to the International Covenant on Civil and Political Rights, the Human Rights Committee notes that State Parties did not permit the possibility of denunciation. This finding is based on the fact that in direct contrast, withdrawal from the Optional Protocol is expressly provided for (Art 12 of the First Optional Protocol). The Committee states that the International Covenant is 'not the type of treaty which, by its nature, implies a right of denunciation' (para 3). An International Bill of Rights is deemed not to have a 'temporal character' typical of those instruments permitting denunciation. Therefore the application of the Covenant continues irrespective of changes in government or territory. The Committee concludes that 'international law does not permit a State which has ratified or acceded or succeeded to the Covenant [on Civil and Political Rights] to denounce it or withdraw from it' (para 5).

11.3 Interpretation and application

In many respects, the meaning of all human rights is dependent on the interpretation and application thereof. Consequently, responsibility lies with the treaty-monitoring bodies to clarify the scope of the rights and freedoms. This tends to be achieved in the United Nations with the adoption of General Comments by the various Committees established to supervise implementation. At a regional level, the decisions and expressed views of the Commissions and Courts perform a similar role. An analysis of the associated jurisprudence can considerably illuminate the definition of any right.

The monitoring bodies tend to adopt a teleological approach to the interpretation of human rights, allowing the rights to be applied in a manner which is consistent with the spirit and goal of the instrument. Examples of interpretative illumination of rights includes the implication of a right of access to a court in the right to a fair trial within Europe (ECHR—*Golder v United Kingdom*) and the extension of rights to life, humane treatment, and liberty to include unexplained disappearances in Honduras (ACHR—*Velásquez Rodríguez*). Teleological interpretation also enables the monitoring and supervisory bodies to develop rights over time—the world in 2009 is quite different to that last century when many of the international and regional instruments were drafted. Notions of public morality have changed in many States as have notions of privacy. At the same time, threats to the life of a State are no longer the preserve of imminent acts of war, the use of force by States and terrorist bodies having changed dramatically from the twilight of the Second World War through the Cold War era to the present day under the pacifist leadership of the United Nations. In its supervisory role, a monitoring body can respond to these changes, guiding States and shaping legal norms.

11.4 Examining human rights

In many respects, the scope of human rights is open-ended. In a text of this size, it is impossible to comprehensively analyse all the rights and freedoms covered by the various instruments discussed. However, it is necessary to overview some of the rights in order to provide an understanding of the nature of international human rights law. The rights selected are reflective of the breadth of the subject and also are indicative of the main concerns of the international and regional bodies. In general, the salient provisions of the Universal Declaration will be given at the start with reference made to similar Articles appearing in other international and regional texts. The content of the rights will then be discussed, illustrated by brief references to some of the jurisprudence emanating from the United Nations and regional bodies.

Rights are selected from across the spectrum of human rights and fundamental freedoms. The survey will start with a discussion of equality and non-discrimination (Chapter 12), principles which underpin the application of all rights and freedoms. Entitlement to rights and freedoms for all without distinction is a feature of the United Nations' approach to human rights. The discussion of rights and freedoms thereafter concludes with a review of the right to education and human rights education (Chapter 20). Education is viewed by the United Nations as a key to the universal securement of all rights and freedoms.

Individual rights addressed include the right to life (Chapter 13), freedom from torture (Chapter 14), liberty of person (Chapter 15), fair trial (Chapter 16), and freedom of expression (Chapter 18). The foregoing are essentially civil and political rights. The right to work (Chapter 19) is an example of an individual economic, social, and cultural right. The scope of collective rights is illustrated by reference to self-determination (Chapter 17), minority rights (Chapter 21), and group rights (Chapter 22). In general, these rights have been reviewed by reference to the regional and international bodies, thus they can be discussed in terms of the salient jurisprudence.

The right to life is the most fundamental of all rights hence it is examined first. All other rights add quality to life: freedom from torture and liberty of person clearly correlate to the maintenance of human dignity while the right to equality before the law and a fair trial is drawn from the rules of natural justice and the rule of law. Self-determination is unusual in that it appears in both International Covenants. Although originally tied to the United Nations' decolonization policy, its application in the aftermath thereof is less clear. Following self-determination, former colonies strove to achieve democracy—freedom of expression is an important indicator of democracies, both existing and emergent. The right to work encompasses a variety of rights and freedoms, only a flavour of it can be given in the present text. Reference will be made to the work of regional bodies (especially in Europe) and the standard-setting of the International Labour Organization. Chapter 2 reviewed the development of minority rights in Europe and under the League of Nations. It is logical thus to return to minority rights which, though omitted from the Universal Declaration, are currently re-emerging on the international stage.

Chapter 22 focuses on group rights. Unlike elements of collective rights, and minority rights, group rights can ascribe to and be enforced by individuals. In effect, the instruments discussed in this chapter represent the emerging sectoral approach to international rights and freedoms characterizing international law.

First, the laws relating to non-discrimination, as they evolved through the international regime, will be considered. Non-discrimination provisions are common to all international and regional instruments as the principle of non-discrimination strikes at the heart of the concept of human rights and the equal enjoyment of rights by all peoples.

CASES

ADT v United Kingdom, No 35765/97, ECHR 2000-IX.

Cossey v United Kingdom, Ser A, No 184 (1990).

Dudgeon v United Kingdom, Ser A, No 45 (1981)

Golder v United Kingdom, Ser A, No 12 (1975).

Goodwin v United Kingdom, ECHR No 28957/95, ECHR 2002.

Handyside v United Kingdom, Ser A, No 24 (1976).

Hertzberg and ors v Finland, UN Doc CCPR/C/15/61/1979.

I v United Kingdom, ECHR No 25680/94, ECHR 2002.

Rees v United Kingdom, Ser A, No 106 (1986).

Reservations to the Genocide Convention Case [1951] ICJ Reps 15.

Sheffield and Horsham v United Kingdom, ECHR 1998-V, part 84.

Velásquez Rodríguez, Ser C, No 4 (1998).

READING

Arai-Takahashi, Y, *The Margin of Appreciation Doctrine and the Principle of Proportionality in the Jurisprudence of the ECHR* (Antwerp: Intersentia, 2002).

Arai, Y, 'The margin of appreciation doctrine in the jurisprudence of Article 8 of the European Convention on Human Rights' (1998) 16 Netherlands Quarterly of Human Rights 41–61.

Van Dijk, P, 'A common standard of achievement: About universal validity and uniform interpretation of International Human Rights Norms' (1995) 13 Netherlands Quarterly of Human Rights 105–21.

Human Rights Committee General Comment 29 (2001) UN Doc CCPR/C/21/Rev.1/Add.11, General Comment 5 (1981) reprinted in UN Doc HRI/GEN/1/Rev.9 (Vol I), at 5, General Comment 26 (1997) UN Doc A/53/40, annex VII.

Lijnzaad, L, *Reservations to UN Human Rights Treaties: Ratify and ruin* (Dordecht: Martinus Nijhoff, 1994).

Lillich, R (ed), *U.S. Ratification of the Human Rights Treaties: With or without reservations?* (University of Virginia Press, 1988).

Stewart, D, 'U.S. ratification of the Covenant on Civil and Political Rights: The significance of the reservations, understandings and declarations' (1993) 14 Human Rights Law Journal 77.

Ziemele, I (ed), *Reservations to Human Rights Treaties and the Vienna Convention Regime* (Leiden, Martinus Nijhoff, 2004).

READING—SPECIFIC RIGHTS

There are a growing number of books on aspects of international human rights and detailed texts on regional systems, particularly the European Convention on Human Rights. The following is merely illustrative of texts addressing a variety of rights and freedoms and the problems associated with international human rights.

Alfredsson, G, and Eide, A (eds), *The Universal Declaration of Human Rights: A common standard of achievement* (The Hague: Martinus Nijhoff, 1999).

An-Na'im, A, and Deng, F (eds), *Human Rights in Africa: Cross-cultural perspectives* (Washington DC: Brookings Institute, 1990).

Buergenthal, T, Skelton, D, and Stewart, D, *International Human Rights in a Nutshell*, 3rd edn (St Paul, Minn: West Group, 2002).

Craven, M, The International Covenant on Economic, Social and Cultural Rights: A perspective on its development (Oxford: Clarendon Press, 1995).

Davidson, S, *The Inter-American Human Rights* System (Aldershot: Ashgate, 1997).

Van Dijk, P, and Van Hoof, G, *Theory and Practice of the European Convention on Human Rights*, 3rd edn. (Leiden: Kluwer, 1998).

Eide, A, et al, *The Universal Declaration of Human Rights: A commentary* (Oslo: SUP, 1992).

Eide, A, Krause, C, and Rosas, A, *Economic, Social and Cultural Rights: A textbook*, 2nd edn (The Hague: Kluwer, 2001).

Joseph, S, et al, *The International Covenant on Civil and Political Rights: Cases, materials and commentary*, 2nd edn (Oxford: Oxford University Press, 2005).

Merrills, J, and Robertson, A, *Human Rights in Europe: A study of the European Convention on Human Rights*, 4th edn (Manchester: Juris, Manchester University Press, 2001).

Nowak, M, *UN Covenant on Civil and Political Rights, CCPR Commentary*, 2nd edn (Kehl: Engel, 2005).

——, *Introduction to the International Human Rights Regime* (Leiden: Martinus Nijhoff, 2003).

O'Byrne, D, *Human Rights: An introduction* (Harlow: Longman 2003).

Smith, RKM, and van den Anker, C (eds), *The Essentials of Human Rights* (London: Hodder Arnold, 2005).

Starmer, K, and Kilroy, C, *European Human Rights Law*, 2nd edn (London: Legal Action Group, 2009).

Steiner, H, Alston, P, and Goodman, R, *International Human Rights in Context: Law* Politics Morals, 3rd edn (Oxford: Oxford University Press, 2007).

WEBSITES

The following websites contain links to the texts applied by the monitoring bodies and their jurisprudence.

www.ohchr.org—the Office of the United Nations High Commissioner for Human Rights

http://www2.ohchr.org/english/bodies/treaty/index.htm—United Nations Conventional Mechanisms links www.echr.coe.int—the European Court of Human Rights

www.corteidh.or.cr—Inter-American Court of Human Rights (partly in Spanish)

www1.umn.edu/humanrts—University of Minnesota Human Rights Library

sim.law.uu.nl/SIM/Dochome.nsf?Open—Netherlands Institute of Human Rights (SIM)-Documentation site

12

Equality and non-discrimination

Everyone is entitled to all the rights and freedoms set forth in this Declaration, without distinction of any kind, such as race, colour, sex, language, religion, political or other opinion, national or social origin, property, birth or other status. [Art 2, Universal Declaration (hereinafter UDHR): see also Art 2(1), International Covenant on Civil and Political Rights (hereinafter ICCPR); Art 2(2), International Covenant on Economic, Social and Cultural Rights (ICESCR); Art 14, European Convention for the Protection of Human Rights and Fundamental Freedoms (ECHR); Art 1, American Convention on Human Rights (ACHR); Art 2, African Charter on Human and Peoples' Rights (ACHPR); Art 20(2), Commonwealth of Independent States Convention on Human Rights and Fundamental Freedoms (CIS); Art 3, Arab Charter on Human Rights (AL)]

Virtually every human rights instrument includes a non-discrimination clause. Given that the very universality of human rights is based on the premise that all people are born 'free and equal in dignity and rights' (Art 1, Universal Declaration), a prohibition on discrimination in the enjoyment of those rights is inevitable. While some instruments enshrine a general prohibition on discrimination, others restrict the prohibition on discrimination to the extent necessary to ensure equal enjoyment of the rights and freedoms. This chapter will focus on the principal grounds of discrimination which are common to the various instruments—sex, race, religion, and, to an extent, language. An overview of the expansion of non-discrimination to other grounds will also be provided. As will become apparent, there is a clear link between the concept of equality and that of non-discrimination. Indeed, the rule of non-discrimination is basically the negative restatement of the principle of equality (Lerner, N, p 25).

12.1 The concept of equality

The concept of equality is rooted in philosophical debate, a detailed analysis of which is outwith the scope of the present text. However, international law has long concerned itself with inequalities—for example, the law of aliens prohibited States from treating foreigners less well than a national of the State. Equality is the cornerstone of all democratic States—equality of persons before the law, equality of opportunity, equality of access to education, and so on and so forth. Rights to education, work, and a fair trial further expand this. Discrimination, by comparison, focuses on the negative aspects of this, or inequality of opportunity, inequality of treatment. 'Equality between members of the majority and minority must be an effective and genuine equality' opined the Permanent Court of International Justice in its *Advisory Opinion on the Minority Schools in Albania*.

With issues of equality and discrimination, the usual rule applies: a situation is discriminatory or unequal if like situations are treated differently or different situations are treated similarly. Unlike other aspects of human rights, practising equality, *de jure* equality, will not necessarily result in de facto equality. If two people start off in incomparable situations, treating them similarly will merely perpetuate this, further accentuating the differences. For this reason, realization of de facto equality may be dependent on affirmative action/positive discrimination policies whereby discrimination in favour of the person or group in the poorer position is allowed. Examples of this in practice can be seen in certain Scandinavian employment practices favouring women or the former access to higher education scheme in Australia which promoted higher education for the previously under-represented indigenous peoples. A United Nations special rapporteur, Mr Marc Bossuyt, completed his report on the concept and practice of affirmative action in 2002, noting that the issue is complex and there is not yet a common ground of understanding of its limits (UN Doc E/CN.4/Sub.2/2002/21). The Human Rights Committee has confirmed that affirmative action policies are compatible with international human rights (eg, *Stalla Costa v Uruguay*) albeit they remain controversial.

Although the concepts of equality and discrimination can be differentiated, perusal of international instruments reveals that the goal of equality is usually achieved in the first instance through a prohibition on discrimination.

12.2 The prohibition on discrimination

Discrimination on a variety of specified grounds is prohibited by diverse international instruments. Tracing the various clauses adopted over the years reveals much about the evolution of global society. The United Nations Charter, with its progressive goal of equality, mentions only race, sex, language, and religion (Arts 1 and 55). Contrast this with the most recent international instruments impinging on non-discrimination: those adopted under the auspices of the European Community—discrimination is prohibited on grounds of sex, racial or ethnic origin, religion or belief, disability, age, or sexual orientation (Art 13 of the Consolidated Version of the Treaty establishing the European Community, as amended. This clause was added by the 1997 Treaty of Amsterdam). The Charter of Fundamental Rights of the European Union which followed contains one of the more far-reaching provisions on non-discrimination. Article 21 prohibits 'discrimination based on any ground such as sex, race, colour, ethnic or social origin, genetic features, language, religion or belief, political or any other opinion, membership of a national minority, property, birth, disability, age or sexual orientation' (OJ C 364/1, 18/12/2000).

By definition, universal rights should be applied to all without distinction. In the words of the Vienna Declaration and Programme of Action, '[r]espect for human rights and for fundamental freedoms without distinction of any kind is a fundamental rule of international human rights law' (1993, para 15). Considering the Universal Declaration of Human Rights was drafted in the 1940s, its phraseology is remarkable—non-gender specific language was used throughout despite earlier drafts proclaiming that 'all men are brothers'. In spite of this, the United Nations has frequently had cause to reiterate the universal nature of human rights whilst simultaneously reproducing those rights in instruments dedicated to specific groups. For example, although children are people too they have been offered additional protection via the Convention on the Rights of the Child. Clearly, the child is particularly vulnerable due to age and the dependence of the child on adults in the formative years. Children tend to have limited rights in all Member States in comparison to adults. Other specific groups of peoples accorded rights are discussed in Chapter 22.

Non-discrimination, as a concept, is normally ascertainable only with regard to legal and political considerations. The need for equality and an absence of discrimination in reality, as well as in law, was originally advocated by the Permanent Court of International Justice (*Advisory Opinion on Minority Schools in Albania*). Today, discrimination is used in the 'pejorative sense of an unfair, unreasonable, unjustifiable or arbitrary distinction' which applies to 'any act or conduct which denies to individuals equality of treatment with other individuals because they belong to particular groups in society' (McKean, W, pp 10–11).

12.3 **Sex discrimination**

Equality between men and women is one of the building blocks of the United Nations—in the Preamble to the Charter of the United Nations, the peoples of the United Nations reaffirm their faith 'in the equal rights of men and women'. Rapid progress has been made in the years since the United Nations was established. Political rights of women, for example, have been established from the point in 1945 when they were the exception rather than the rule. The inferior position of women in many cultures has long occupied the concerns of the international community. United Nations' statistics reveal that women are the majority of the world's poor and illiterate, they tend to earn significantly less money than men and often work unpaid. Health is another area of concern with the health of women being inextricably linked to the health of their infants. A number of international initiatives aim at remedying this inequality with projects aimed at educating young women and encouraging self-sufficiency. Promotion of female financial management is popular within cottage industries in India whilst health education, including reproductive health, is a feature of many projects in sub-Saharan Africa.

Arguably, international law has contributed towards discrimination by its early protectionist approach. The International Labour Organization, for all that it recognized that women need special protection, implicitly discriminated against women by initially protecting their rights as mothers at the expense of their equal right to work. However, perhaps more than other aspects of discrimination, there have been almost insurmountable cultural barriers to cross in reversing sex discrimination. Initially, concern for women manifested itself in the form of additional protection. Women were treated as a vulnerable group (see also Chapter 22). In 1993, the Vienna Declaration and Programme of Action clarifies that '[t]he human rights of women and of the girl-child are an inalienable, integral and indivisible part of universal human rights' (1993, para 18). This represented a culmination in the progression from protective discrimination (albeit well intended) to recognition of full equality.

Key case

Case C-409/95 *Marschall v Land Norhein-Westfalen* [1997] ECR I-6363

Mr Marschall was a teacher in Germany who applied for a promoted post. He was informed that the preference would be to appoint a female candidate as there were fewer females than males appointed at that level. Mr Marschall argued that this was contrary to the EU laws on equality of opportunity between men and women. The German authorities, however, argued that the measure was necessary to redress the gender imbalance in employment at senior levels. Compatibility of the German law with EU law on equality was queried before the European Court of Justice.

The court noted that:

it appears that even where male and female candidates are equally qualified, male candidates tend to be promoted in preference to female candidates particularly because of prejudices and stereotypes concerning the role and capacities of women in working life and the fear, for example, that women will interrupt their careers more frequently, that owing to household and family duties they will be less flexible in their working hours, or that they will be absent from work more frequently because of pregnancy, childbirth and breastfeeding. [Para 29]

Accordingly a male and female candidate with equal qualifications and experiences do not have equal chances of being appointed. In response to the question referred by the national court under the ECJ preliminary ruling procedure:

a national rule which, in a case where there are fewer women than men at the level of the relevant post in a sector of the public service, and both female and male candidates for the post are equally qualified in terms of their suitability, competence and professional performance, requires that priority be given to the promotion of female candidates unless reasons specific to an individual male candidate tilt the balance in his favour is not precluded by Article 2(1) and (4) of the Directive, provided that: in each individual case the rule provides for male candidates who are equally as qualified as the female candidates a guarantee that the candidatures will be the subject of an objective assessment which will take account of all criteria specific to the individual candidates and will override the priority accorded to female candidates where one or more of those criteria tilts the balance in favour of the male candidate, and such criteria are not such as to discriminate against the female candidates. [Para 35]

(See also *Guido Jacobs v Belgium*, UN Doc CCPR/C/81/D/943/2000 (2004) in which the Human Rights Committee concluded no violations of the ICCPR in respect of a quota system introduced to secure more female appointments to the High Council of Justice.)

12.3.1 The Declaration on the Elimination of Discrimination against Women

In 1967, the General Assembly adopted a Declaration on the Elimination of Discrimination against Women. The Declaration is unequivocal in its condemnation of such discrimination. Article 1 states that discrimination against women, denying or limiting as it does their equality of rights with men, is fundamentally unjust and constitutes an offence against human dignity. This reinforces the Preamble which acknowledges the great contribution made by women to social, economic, political, and cultural life and reiterates that the full and complete development of a country and the welfare of the world, as well as the cause of peace, requires the maximum participation of women as well as men. Cognisance is given to the need to educate public opinion in favour of eradicating prejudice and all practices based on the idea of inferiority of women (Art 3). In spite of the passage of forty years, the need for such education remains acute in many States.

Civil and political rights are prescribed in the Declaration as well as economic and social rights. Interestingly, Art 10(3) permits prima facie discriminatory measures to be taken to protect women in certain types of occupation due to the physical nature of the work. This echoes slightly the ILO approach which has already been mentioned. Pregnancy is not to be a ground for dismissal and women should be entitled to return to work after paid maternity leave with the provision of childcare facilities enabling this. Other provisions relate to traditional sources of sex discrimination— nationality after marriage, property rights, trafficking and exploitation, and such like. Given the clear link between the concept of equality and the Charter of the United Nations, all States were urged to promote the implementation of the principles enshrined in the Declaration. Even with a source such as the Charter itself cited, this proved unduly optimistic.

12.3.2 Developing the law

Five years after the Declaration's adoption, the Secretary-General of the United Nations asked the Commission on the Status of Women to consult with States regarding the form and content of a possible international instrument on the human rights of women. ECOSOC established a working group to this end and in 1974, the drafting process began. 1975 was observed as International Women's Year with the first United Nations World Conference on Women held in Mexico City. It served as the catalyst for the declaration of a United Nations Decade for Women (1976–85). In turn this prompted a greater global focus on the plight of women. The Commission pressed ahead with the drafting process. Duly encouraged, and using the Declaration as a building block, the General Assembly adopted the 1979 Convention on the Elimination of all forms of Discrimination against Women (CEDAW).

Even without the invocation of the Convention, the general Human Rights committees and courts have considered discrimination against women. International bodies have considered a number of claims of discrimination brought by women. Most examples which have reached the international bodies are clearly discriminatory: *Lovelace v Canada* for example. The author of the communication, Sandra Lovelace, was born and registered as a Maliseet Indian, but lost her rights and status as an Indian (in accordance with domestic law) when she married a non-Indian. This presented problems when Ms Lovelace subsequently split from her husband and was unable to return to her native band. An Indian man who marries a non-Indian woman does not lose his Indian status, hence the sex discrimination issue. The Human Rights Committee contended that Art 27 (minority rights) had been breached by Canada as Ms Lovelace was not permitted to realize her natural cultural attachment to the Tobique band following the break up of her marriage. The element of discrimination was a key factor in the decision. Similarly, in *Ato del*

Avellanal v Peru a Peruvian woman submitted a communication to the Human Rights Committee claiming she was denied access to justice because of her gender. Under Peruvian law, only the husband may appear in court if matters concerning matrimonial property are at issue. The Human Rights Committee considered that as a consequence of this, women in Peru were denied equality before the courts—there was thus discrimination.

Within the Council of Europe's mechanisms, Art 14, the non-discrimination clause, may not be raised on its own, therefore there is no freedom from discrimination per se in Europe. Article 14 must be raised in conjunction with the violation of another right. (Optional Protocol 12; a stand-alone non-discrimination clause, is ratified by few states.) For example, the United Kingdom did not violate the right to family life when immigration law made it easier for male immigrants to be joined by female spouses than vice versa. However, it was a violation of Art 14 taken in conjunction with the right to family life in Art 8 (*Abdulaziz, Cabales and Balkandali v United Kingdom*). This can be compared to the approach of the Human Rights Committee: Mauritian law which rendered men married to Mauritian women, but not vice versa, subject to possible deportation was deemed contrary to the International Covenant, according to the Human Rights Committee (*Aumeeruddy-Cziffra v Mauritius*). Differentiation in treatment between husbands and wives in the choice of the family surname occasioned a violation of the European Convention against Switzerland in *Burghartz v Switzerland*, the European Court stating that 'very weighty reasons would have to put forward before a difference of treatment on the sole ground of sex could be regarded as compatible with the Convention' (para 27). The invocation of State discretion thus appears to be limited given the importance of the prohibition on discrimination on grounds of sex under international law. Other human rights bodies appear to take a similar restrictive view though, obviously, States could make reservations or declarations to a contrary effect on ratification despite this undermining the principle.

12.3.3 The Convention on the Elimination of all Forms of Discrimination against Women

Echoing the Declaration, the Preamble to the Convention recalls that discrimination against women violates the principle of equality of rights and respect for human dignity. Unlike the Declaration, the Convention seeks to be an international bill of rights for women. Certainly the range of rights included in its ambit is reflective of this goal. It requires States to eliminate discrimination against women in the enjoyment of all civil and political, economic, social, and cultural rights. The Convention is implemented through a system of State periodic reports although the 1999 Optional Protocol thereto seeks to provide a mechanism for the consideration of individual communications. As discussed in Chapter 5, a Committee on the Elimination of Discrimination against Women was established by the Convention to consider State progress (Art 17).

Discrimination is defined in the Convention as 'any distinction, exclusion or restriction made on the basis of sex which has the effect or purpose of impairing or nullifying the recognition, enjoyment or exercise by women, irrespective of their marital status, on a basis of equality of men and women, of human rights and fundamental freedoms in the political, economic, social, cultural, civil or any other field' (Art 1). State Parties condemn discrimination against women and agree to pursue a policy of eliminating it. To this end they agree to embody the principle of equality in their constitution or equivalent; adopt legislation (with sanctions) prohibiting discrimination against women; establish a legal system for securing equal rights; eliminate all discriminatory practices; and repeal and abolish all discriminatory legislation still applicable (Art 2).

States also accept a positive obligation to ensure the development and advancement of women towards a situation of equality of rights. As proposed in the Declaration, the parties to the Convention agree to modify the social and cultural patterns of conduct of men and women 'with a view to achieving the elimination of prejudices and customary ... practices' based on the inferiority of women. Family education is required to recognize 'maternity as a social function' (Art 5). Trafficking and exploitation or prostitution of women is prohibited.

Reiterating the Convention on the Political Rights of Women, Arts 7–8 address the elimination of discrimination against women in the political and public life of their country as well as at the international level. Nationality rights and marriage are addressed as are the rights of women to freedom from discrimination in education, employment, and health rights. Equality before the law and equality in marital matters are elaborated in Arts 15–16.

Reflecting the reality of the concerns of the international community, particular attention is focused on the rights of 'rural women', given the significant role they play in the economic survival of their family. Accordingly, women are entitled to access and participate equally in the creation of development strategies for the region, to participate in all community activities, and to enjoy adequate living conditions, 'particularly in relation to housing, sanitation, electricity and water supply, transport and communications' (Art 14). In furtherance of the promotion of rural women, provision is also made for health and family planning facilities and services, access to education and training and, as previously mentioned, access to and participation in self-help groups and cooperatives, agricultural credit and loans, and participation in land resettlement schemes.

Affirmative action (positive discrimination as it is sometimes referred to) is permissible:

[a]doption by State Parties of temporal special measures aimed at accelerating de facto equality between men and women shall not be considered discrimination as defined in the present Convention, ... These measures shall be discontinued when the objectives of equality of opportunity and treatment have been achieved. [Art 4(1)]

Ratification of the Convention was rapid with it entering into force in 1981. However, the swiftness of this perhaps presents an overly optimistic view. States have lodged a number of reservations and declarations when ratifying. Many commentators regard the number of reservations and declarations not only as undermining the effectiveness of the Convention as a legal instrument but also as evidence of the inherent weakness in the consensual United Nations Human Rights system. Encouragingly, the number of reservations is being slowly but steadily reduced.

12.3.4 Strengthening women's rights

A second World Conference on Women was held in Copenhagen in 1980. At this time, an action programme was adopted to address issues of education, employment, and health of women during the latter half of the international decade. Progress was slow and ongoing, many of the goals were thus incorporated into an overarching framework of strategies for the realization of equality of women. Forward-looking Strategies for the Advancement of Women to the Year 2000 were adopted at the third international conference in Nairobi in 1985.

The Fourth World Conference on Women was held in Beijing in 1995. This conference represented the most comprehensive review of women's rights, and progress in achieving them, to date. It was also the largest international meeting ever convened under the auspices of the United Nations. The Beijing Platform for Action adopted at the Conference remains the blueprint for international efforts aimed at securing gender equality. Commitments made by States at the Beijing Conference were far reaching, though again often accompanied by reservations. The United Nations Commission on the Status of Women was tasked with providing advice to States on the implementation of the Platform for Action.

A special session of the United Nations General Assembly built upon the Beijing Conference, facilitating a review on the progress made towards achieving equality for men and women. At the Beijing +5 International Conference held in June 2000, assistance to women and girls currently subject to discrimination and disadvantage was one of the critical areas of concern. This was reiterated during Beijing +10 discussions in 2005.

Other aspects of gender equality are covered by more specific conventions—the 1960 UNESCO Convention against Discrimination in Education provides for equal educational opportunities for men and women and the 1952 Convention on the Political Rights of Women commits Member States to involving women equally in political participation.

Finally, 8 March is International Women's Day. This day is commemorated by the United Nations though its roots go back to before the First World War. The honouring of women's contribution to rights and the development of universal suffrage began in the United States of America in 1909 and spread throughout Europe by 1914. It provides an annual focus for evaluation by the international community and States of the progress made towards securing non-discrimination against women and true equality of enjoyment of rights and freedoms.

12.4 Race discrimination

All peoples demand, and deserve, to be treated as the equal(s) of the other inhabitants of the State in which they live. Such equality is, as has been noted, dependent on the abolition of all forms of discrimination. Racial discrimination is deemed particularly acute as individuals are discriminated against solely on account of the colour of their skin or their ethnic origin, factors over which they clearly have no control (Santa Cruz, H). In this respect, racial discrimination is comparable to sex discrimination (discussed *supra*).

The atrocities committed during the Second World War heightened public awareness of the problems of racism and the catastrophic results of its going unchallenged in the world. Peoples are often discriminated against solely because of their racial origin; apartheid is an extreme example. This section will consider the international response to the omnipresent threat and practice of racial discrimination through-out the world and examine the international instruments which purport to counter it. Eliminating all aspects of racial discrimination has long occupied the work of the United Nations. In 2001, the international community met in Durban, South Africa for the World Conference with a review in Geneva, 2009. The prohibition on race discrimination is entrenched in international law, indeed it is already considered by many scholars to be an example of *ius cogens* (eg, Lerner, N, p 24).

12.4.1 Development of international law

A corpus of law has developed under the auspices of the United Nations concern-ing racial discrimination. These laws were essentially a product of the international community's horror at the racial discrimination and incitement to racial hatred atrocities perpetrated during the Second World War. Although religious discrimina-tion was also a relevant factor, the international provisions thereon are compara-tively weaker, as will become clear.

Various specialized international texts have addressed the problem of racial discrimination in definable fields: the Convention concerning Discrimination in respect of Employment and Occupation adopted by the International Labour Organization in 1958 and the Convention against Discrimination in Education 1960, which was concluded under the auspices of the United Nations Educational, Scientific and Cultural Organization, are two of the most notable of these texts. As early as 1949, the Draft Declaration on the Rights and Duties of States provided that '[e]very State has the duty to treat all persons under its jurisdiction with respect for human rights and fundamental freedoms without distinction as to race, sex, language or religion'. However, the need for an instrument on a global scale which dealt with the issue as a whole, across the whole spectrum of the global society, became increasingly pressing.

12.4.2 The Declaration and the Convention

Growing international concern prompted the General Assembly to adopt a Declaration on the Elimination of All Forms of Racial Discrimination in 1963. This Declaration condemns all forms of racial differentiation, decrees government policies based on racial superiority an endangerment to international peace and security, and proclaims the goal of the United Nations as being a global society free from racial segregation and discrimination. Two years later, the General Assembly adopted an international convention which sought to embody these principles in a legally binding format—the International Convention on the Elimination of All Forms of Racial Discrimination 1966 which was adopted pursuant to the United Nations General Assembly Declaration on the Elimination of All Forms of Racial Discrimination of 1963 (GA Resn 1904, GA Doc A/RES/1904 (XVIII), 21/11/63). The Preamble to the Declaration specifically mentions the anti-colonial policies of the United Nations and condemns all doctrines of racial differentiation or superiority as morally and socially unjust and dangerous. The practice of apartheid was also at the forefront of international concern at the time. Many of the Declaration's Articles find legal force in the terms of the subsequent Convention. Underpinning both of these documents is the principle of respect for human dignity as enshrined in the Charter of the United Nations and the general principles concerning human rights and fundamental freedoms which are expressed in the Universal Declaration of Human Rights.

The General Assembly adopted the text of the Convention on 19 January 1966, declaring that racial discrimination was a subject which was appropriate to consider under the auspices of the United Nations. What must be remembered is that the Convention is true to its origins in the particular political situation of the 1960s: it represented a consensual view against racial discrimination caused by doctrines of racial superiority (apartheid) and by colonialism. Given that this was an active period of decolonization, few signatory States felt that racial discrimination was a problem in their jurisdiction although as the Committee's work evolved, so too has the de facto definition of racial discrimination to include hitherto ignored instances of racial discrimination within almost every State. Combating 'ethnic cleansing' is one of the new challenges being faced by those applying the Convention.

The preambular paragraphs of the Convention are similar to those of the Declaration, reiterating the repugnance of racial barriers, condemning the practice of apartheid, and reaffirming the commitment of the United Nations to the speedy elimination of racial discrimination. The Convention comprises three parts: the first details the scope of the Convention and the incumbent obligations on contracting parties; the second is devoted to the implementation/enforcement machinery; and the third contains the final clauses of the instrument. It has received a favourable response from the international community and boasts a high number of ratifications—173 State Parties as of July 2009.

12.4.3 Definition of 'racial discrimination'

Article 1(1) of the Convention provides the working definition of 'racial discrimination':

any distinction, exclusion, restriction or preference based on race, colour, descent, or national or ethnic origin which has the purpose or effect of nullifying or impairing the recognition, enjoyment or exercise, on an equal footing, of human rights and fundamental freedoms in the political, economic, social, cultural or any other field of public life.

Natan Lerner considers this definition broad enough to include 'all discriminatory acts, whether intentional or not, and whether successful or not, provided the purpose or effect exists' (p 26). The four specified actions (distinction, exclusion, restriction, and preference) were intended to cover all aspects of discrimination. Lerner states that in order for any of these four acts to be considered discriminatory, there are two conditions to be fulfilled. The distinction, exclusion, restriction or preference must '(1) have the purpose of nullifying or impairing the recognition, enjoyment or exercise, on an equal footing, of human rights and fundamental freedoms, or (2) have such an effect' (Lerner, N, p 49).

It is perhaps interesting to note that, in certain circumstances, what may be positive discrimination/affirmative action is, in effect, permitted. Article 1(4) states:

[s]pecial measures taken for the sole purpose of securing adequate advancement of certain racial or ethnic groups or individuals requiring such protection as may be necessary in order to ensure such groups or individuals equal enjoyment or exercise of human rights and

fundamental freedoms shall not be deemed racial discrimination, provided, however, that such measures do not, as a consequence, lead to the maintenance of separate rights for different racial groups and that they shall not be continued after the objectives for which they were taken have been achieved.

Consequently, it would be acceptable for a State to accord indigenous persons favoured treatment for the time necessary to elevate their standing to that of the rest of the community in which they live.

Contracting States undertake to amend national laws in order to render the practice and/or encouragement of racial discrimination a criminal offence (Art 4). In essence, all nationals of a State, irrespective of their racial origin (Art 5) must ultimately enjoy full equality (before the law). Thus the denial of freedom of movement and the non-issue of passports to various indigenous groups in border areas could, if legally enforced by the relevant government, violate the Convention. Many States have proven unwilling to admit problems in this area. The comments of States to the Committee provide evidence of this disturbing trend. Many States claim that they have no ethnic groups who may be subject to discrimination in their territories, while others claim that racial tensions are unknown. Some of these problems are self-perpetuating. For example, the definition of racial discrimination laid down by the United Nations facilitated South Africa's early claims that apartheid did not constitute racial discrimination as it provided the same racial opportunities for each racial group with the aim of separate development. Nevertheless apartheid was outlawed by the subsequent 1973 International Convention on the Suppression and Punishment of the Crime of Apartheid (the operation of this instrument has now been suspended).

12.4.4 Conclusions

The Racial Discrimination Convention aims at protecting a group from discrimination on grounds of race. States have maintained that religion, language, and culture may be distinguished from race, but perhaps an extension of the approach of the international community in viewing apartheid as racial discrimination may be indicative of a wider approach which could equally prohibit discrimination on such grounds. The provisions of the Convention expand upon but a small part of the wider and more general international prohibition on discrimination. However, in the words of the Secretary-General, the Convention has 'the strong moral force of virtual universality rooted in the overriding principle (*ius cogens*) that racial discrimination must be eliminated everywhere.' (UN Doc A/42/493, p 10). Thus, the effect of the Convention cannot be underestimated.

Adding further weight is the fact that in many instances a prohibition on discrimination forms a cornerstone of national constitutions. Germany and South Africa, for example, now have unequivocal prohibitions on racial discrimination enshrined in their constitutions.

The period 1993–2003 was the third decade to Combat Racism and Racial Discrimination. As part of this initiative, the United Nations has produced Model National Legislation for the Guidance of Governments in the Enactment of Further Legislation against Racial Discrimination. A special rapporteur (Mr Maurice Glele-Ahanhanzo) was appointed with a mandate relating to contemporary forms of racism, racial discrimination, xenophobia, and related intolerance. International attention was further focused on the subject through the World Conference against

Racism, Racial Discrimination, Xenophobia and Related Intolerance (Durban, South Africa, 2001) which sought to create a new world vision for the fight against racism in the twenty-first century. Progress was celebrated at the April 2009 Durban Review Conference in Geneva. Whilst this event certainly added weight to the cried for universal eradication of racial discrimination and indeed other (related) forms of discrimination, the surrounding controversy caused by State withdrawals and delegation walk outs dulled the positive effect.

12.5 **Religious discrimination**

Religious discrimination and intolerance is one of the oldest causes of international conflict and, as the Israel/Palestine clashes so clearly demonstrate, it remains a cause of conflict today. Religion, particularly religious discrimination, persecution, etc played a significant role in history, with a number of international disputes and wars being caused by ideological differences between State majorities. More recently, religious and ideological differences between major groups within States have been the cause of civil unrest and threats to international peace and security. The Balkans is a prominent example.

Religion is a more problematic ground in non-discrimination law. When the Universal Declaration was drafted, the fact that much of the world had State religions and thus the laws of the countries were governed by religious not secular laws was not considered. There are therefore a number of anomalies in the practice of States. The Cairo Declaration on Human Rights in Islam 1990 adopted by the Islamic States refers throughout to the Shari'a law and thus an inherent degree of superiority before the law in public and private of males. This can be contrasted with the gender neutral Arab Charter on Human Rights 1994, which restricts references to the Islamic Shari'a to the preambular paragraphs. There have inevitably been many allegations of bias in the present human rights system as it is felt to have a 'Western' basis although as jurisprudence demonstrates, this is not always the case. As far as possible, international human rights should be non-denominational. For example, in the case of *Hoffman v Austria*, the European Court of Human Rights concluded that Austria had violated the European Convention by basing its refusal to confer parental rights on a mother essentially on the basis of her being a Jehovah's Witness.

12.5.1 **Developing the international prohibition**

Freedom of religion in a State is facilitated when there are corresponding provisions prohibiting discrimination on religious grounds. The prohibition on discrimination on grounds of, inter alia, religious belief is entrenched in international human rights law. Individuals must be free in exercise of this, one of the most fundamental human rights available, to determine his or her own theological or philosophical convictions and to manifest such beliefs free from State interference, at least insofar as the religious practice does not infringe or impede the exercise of the fundamental rights of others. The United Nations special rapporteur (Ribiero) acknowledged this, stating:

[a] broadly based school of legal thought maintains that the individual should be free not only to choose among different theistic creeds and to practise the one of his choice freely, but also

to have the right to view life from a non-theistic perspective without facing disadvantages vis-à-vis believers. The Special Rapporteur reflects that in the same way as believers must enjoy their right to practise their religion unhindered, non-believers (free thinkers, agnostics and atheists) should not be discriminated against. (UN Doc E/CN.4/1990/46, para 113]

The rule of non-discrimination on grounds of belief thus must encompass all kinds of belief. It is the lack of tolerance on the part of some States which is responsible for tension between religious groups. As with language, religion has, historically, been used as a weapon by battling factions. Religion was the dominant theme during the Reformation and the wars in Germany in the sixteenth century. At that time, it was accepted that the ruling authority would proclaim a State religion and proscribe all others. Intolerance was, effectively, State policy. As a rapporteur of the United Nations noted in a study on religious discrimination:

Tolerance was accorded, in the beginning, to one or a few specified religions or beliefs; and only later was it extended to all such groups. Moreover, the measure of tolerance extended to various groups was often very narrow at first; and only by a gradual expansion was full equality achieved. [Arcot Krishnaswami, UN Doc E/CN.4/Sub.2/200/Rev. 1, p 4]

In exercising tolerance in respect of different religious groups, a State imposes a prohibition on discrimination on grounds of adherence or non-adherence to that religion. Indeed, Natan Lerner states that '[i]nternational protection of human rights started in areas related to religion' (p 75).

   The insertion of religion into non-discrimination clauses characterizes religion as a personal attribute analogous to race, sex, and language. 'It [religion] is viewed as a "natural" phenomenon, on the basis of which it would be unjust to discriminate when recognizing rights and freedoms' (Dickson, B, p 332). These criteria for non-discrimination are reiterated in all succeeding human rights instruments, so

Discussion topic

Cases: Freedom of religion

State policies on secularity ripen the opportunities for clashes between religion and education. France prohibited religious clothing and jewellery in public schools (Law No 2004-228 of 15 March 2004). More specific laws on female head-coverings have ignited debate across the globe—Iran now requires more modest head-coverings, while Turkey has prohibited headscarves in, for example, universities. Courts and committees have reached various conclusions on the compatibility of such moves with international human rights (*Dahlab v Switzerland*, Application 42393/98, European Court of Human Rights; *Sahin v Turkey*, Application 44774/98, European Court of Human Rights, judgment 29 June 2004, Grand Chamber judgment 10 November 2005; *Hudoyberganova v Uzbekistan*, Application 931/2000, Human Rights Committee, UN Doc CCPR/C/82/D/931/2000).

   The fundamental question is whether a headscarf, bangle, crucifix, yarmulke, etc is an expression of faith or an essential tenet of faith. It appears that international human rights will only actively protect the essential tenets of faith, other overt manifestations of faith being regarded as a private matter and thus subject to State Control.

discrimination on grounds of religious beliefs is clearly prohibited by international law. It has even been suggested that religious discrimination is an example of *ius cogens* (Brownlie, I, p 513). The notion of equality of all peoples, irrespective of race, religion, sex, or language is now so firmly entrenched in international law as to arguably embody a general principle of international law, applicable by all nations. By its very nature, the universal acceptability of this norm is borne out by the examination of the regional and domestic documents on human rights.

The desirability of international provisions against discrimination on grounds of religion and belief was emphasized in the report of a special rapporteur and subsequently realized in a Declaration of the United Nations General Assembly.

12.5.2 **Developing the Declaration**

Arcot Krishnaswami, special rapporteur of the former Sub-Commission on Prevention of Discrimination and Protection of Minorities, was appointed in 1956 to research and present a study of discrimination in the matter of religious rights and practices. His final report was characterized as 'a landmark in the efforts of the United Nations to eradicate prejudice and discrimination based on religion or belief' (Benito, O, UN Doc E/CN.4/Sub.2/1987/26, p 1). The report was lodged at a time when there was a considerable rise in the number of instances of religious intolerance in Europe. On the recommendation of the Sub-Commission on Prevention of Discrimination and Protection of Minorities, the General Assembly then adopted Resolution 1779 on 7 December 1962 which demanded the rescission of discriminatory laws that had the effect of perpetuating, inter alia, religious intolerance, and adopting any necessary legislation to prohibit such. Preparation of a draft convention on the elimination of all forms of religious intolerance was also initiated at this time (GA Resn 1781, 1962) though no draft has yet been adopted. Given the slow progress on articulating a convention, the General Assembly eventually decided to accord precedence to completion of a draft declaration.

Following protracted negotiations and debate, the United Nations' General Assembly, on 25 November 1981, adopted, without a vote, a Declaration on the Elimination of All Forms of Intolerance and of Discrimination Based on Religion or Belief (GA Resn 36/55). Within the ambit of the Declaration, the General Assembly states its consideration that 'religion or belief, for anyone who professes either, is one of the fundamental elements in his conception of life and that freedom of religion or belief should be fully respected and guaranteed' (proclamation preceding the Declaration). The use of religion and religious beliefs as a tool for justifying foreign interference in the internal affairs of States and for kindling hatred between people and nations is also mentioned. It is acknowledged that true freedom of religion and belief will contribute towards attainment of the United Nations' goals of world peace, social justice, and friendship among all peoples.

12.5.3 **Content of the Declaration**

For the purposes of the Declaration, 'intolerance and discrimination based on religion or belief' is defined as encompassing any distinction, exclusion, restriction, or preference based on religion or belief, which has as its purpose or effect the nullification or impairment of the recognition, enjoyment, or exercise of human rights and fundamental freedoms on a truly equal basis (Art 2). Any such discrimination is denounced as violating the United Nations Charter and associated documents and condemned accordingly as 'an affront to human dignity and a disavowal of the principles of the Charter of the United Nations' as well as 'an obstacle to friendly and peaceful relations between nations' (Art 3).

All of the rights and freedoms articulated in the Declaration should be applicable to all without discrimination. Article 6 of the Declaration enshrines a non-exhaustive list of the freedoms included in the right to freedom of thought, conscience, religion, or belief:

(a) To worship or assemble in connection with a religion or belief, and to establish and maintain places for these purposes;

(b) To establish and maintain appropriate charitable or humanitarian institutions;

(c) To make, acquire and use to an adequate extent the necessary articles and materials related to the rites or customs of a religion or belief;

(d) To write, issue and disseminate relevant publications in these areas;

(e) To teach a religion or belief in places suitable for these purposes;

(f) To solicit and receive voluntary financial and other contributions from individuals and institutions;

(g) To train, appoint, elect or designate by succession appropriate leaders called for by the requirements and standards of any religion or belief;

(h) To observe days of rest and to celebrate holidays and ceremonies in accordance with the precepts of one's religion or belief;

(i) To establish and maintain communications with individuals and communities in matters of religion and belief at the national and international levels.

Consequently, all self-identified followers and believers should be treated in a like manner by the State concerned. Groups and individuals are similarly charged with demonstrating religious tolerance and peaceful coexistence (Art 2).

Non-discrimination and mutual tolerance, although the cornerstones of the Declaration, are in no way monochrome. Inevitably the full exercise of religious freedom can infringe on other human rights with clashes of cultures almost inevitable. The Human Rights Committee had cause to examine this in the case of *Singh Bhinder v Canada*. The author of the communication lost his job as a maintenance electrician with the Canadian Railway Company because of his refusal to wear the mandatory hard hat. As he was a Sikh, he argued that he should be allowed to wear his turban. However, in this case, common sense prevailed and the need for protection of the health and safety of the author overrode respect for his religious beliefs.

Many of the rights contained in the Declaration are group rights, exercisable only by an individual in concert with fellow believers: the right to assemble in connection with a religion or belief and maintain a place for that purpose (Art 6(a)), for example.

Although not legally binding, Natan Lerner states that the Declaration 'does have certain legal effects and exerts a high degree of expectation of obedience by members of the international community to the extent that it may be eventually considered as stating rules of customary international law' (p 89). The Declaration is the only international document concerned solely with the practise of a religion or belief and, as such, is both informative and of persuasive authority. The Declaration is a breakthrough insofar as it achieves for religious groups at least some of the protection granted to racial and ethnic groups. The rights enshrined in the Declaration may be viewed as general international guidelines, the realization of which not only prohibits discrimination and intolerance based on religious beliefs, but goes some way towards ensuring freedom of religion within the State.

12.5.4 Developing the concept

Using the Declaration as terms of reference, the Commission on Human Rights requested the Sub-Commission on Prevention of Discrimination and Protection of Minorities to undertake a comprehensive and thorough study of the current dimensions of the problems of intolerance and of discrimination on grounds of religion or belief. Mrs Elizabeth Odio Benito was subsequently appointed special rapporteur and requested to report on the various manifestations of intolerance and discrimination on the grounds of religion or belief in the world and the root causes thereof, as well as being requested to make recommendations as to specific measures that could be adopted to combat intolerance and discrimination on the grounds of religion or belief, with special emphasis on action that could be taken in the field of education.

Mrs Benito isolated two stages to every manifestation of religious intolerance: an unfavourable attitude of mind towards persons or groups of a different religion or belief and the manifestations of such an attitude in practice (United Nations Study on the current dimensions of the problems of intolerance and of discrimination on grounds of religion or belief, para 15). The one common denominator of intolerance (that of the inequality of material benefits accruing, respectively, to the author of the communication and to the victim) was identified (para 16). Not surprisingly, one of the primary recommendations of the Special Rapporteur was the elaboration of an international convention for the elimination of all forms of intolerance and discrimination based on religion or belief embodying the terms of the 1981 Declaration.

12.5.5 Special thematic rapporteurs on religious intolerance and discrimination

Before receiving Benito's report in 1987, in response to the number of violations of the Declaration and the increasing number of instances of actions inconsistent with the principles of the Declaration, the Human Rights Commission appointed another special rapporteur (Angelo Vidal d'Almeida Ribeiro, replaced by Abdelfattah Amor) to conduct a detailed examination of such incidences and to recommend remedial action. Ribeiro's reports spanned (in time) the improving relations between the former communist-bloc countries and the churches, the death threat (fatwah) on author Salman Rushdie, and a number of incidences of religious discrimination worldwide. The new special thematic rapporteur broadened his remit to include more visits to countries and more lengthy and detailed consultations with governments and non-governmental organizations, a policy embraced by Asma Jahangir, the current rapporteur. However, such a special rapporteur has no power to enforce his recommendations, functioning more as an information-gathering service:

[t]he dialogue established with Governments by the Special Rapporteur and the transmittal of allegations concerning their countries in no way implies any kind of accusation or value

judgement on the part of the Special Rapporteur, but rather a request for clarification with a view to finding, along with the Government concerned, a solution to a problem which goes to the very heart of fundamental rights and freedoms. [UN Doc E/CN.4/1994/79, para 17]

The role of the special rapporteur is thus not to make value judgments or level accusations, but rather to seek to isolate the underlying causes of any instances of intolerance or discrimination within a State (para 101). Concern over a rise in religious intolerance prompted the adoption of General Assembly Resolution 60/166 (2005) which condemns Islamophobia, anti-Semitism, and Christianophobia (para 5).

As with racial discrimination, the realization of the principle of non-discrimination in respect of religious and other beliefs is only attained through the application of laws across all spheres of life and society.

12.5.6 Conclusions

Equality for all, irrespective of religious beliefs, is an essential requirement in any fair, pluralistic society. The multicultural character of societies today renders the mutual toleration of differences important. Religious (or other) beliefs underpin the conduct of the life of an individual. Moreover, religious/moral precepts designate legal from illegal, right from wrong, in society. Courts, in adjudicating disputes before them, apply the stated beliefs of the society in which they operate. It is thus probable that, in a pluralistic society with a multitude of religious and other beliefs, some groups will not have their principles applied in full by the courts and thus are arguably discriminated against. Similarly, work schedules—the allocation of holidays/weekends—and even the selection of menus in the majority of restaurants and hotels reflect the predominant beliefs of the society. Some groups will inevitably feel discriminated against. However, what is important to note is that freedom from discrimination does not demand full equality in the first instance. What would be required in these examples is the acceptance by all of the inherent divergence of views on these matters and the provision of alternative holidays and menus, where appropriate.

Non-discrimination requires religious or other convictions not to be a pertinent issue in assessing the suitability of a candidate for employment, education, or training opportunities. The beliefs of an individual may not be cited to the detriment of him or her in any situation. A policy of non-discrimination does not necessarily guarantee freedom of religion, but can improve the legal and social position of followers of non-State religions.

12.6 Other grounds of discrimination

12.6.1 Language

The other ground of discrimination covered by the Universal Declaration is language. However, this is by far the poorer relation of sex, race, and religion. Linguistic rights have attracted comparatively little attention on the world scene, though inevitably there may be an overlap with other grounds of discrimination. For example, a person who speaks a different language from the majority of the State may also be of a different race or hold different beliefs. It may thus be difficult to single out the cause of discrimination. Most national systems make more substantial provisions for racial and sex discrimination than for linguistic discrimination. There are many reasons for this, not least the fact that it is deemed quite acceptable for a State to have a single official language and thus, by definition, to discriminate against other languages. However, in an increasingly pluralistic global society there are few, if any, monolingual States; thus, linguistic discrimination is a reality for many thousands of languages spoken throughout the world. This would appear to have reduced the urgency with which the international community addresses it. In spite of this, linguistic discrimination can be as distressing as any other of the grounds discussed. Language goes to the root of education and thus linguistic discrimination may limit the access to education of linguistic minorities in a State (see the submissions to the European Court of Human Rights in the *Belgian Linguistics Case*). Clearly this can be very prejudicial to children. Access to employment is also potentially problematic for those speaking a different language, as is access to vocational training programmes. Sometimes linguistic discrimination is deemed more justifiable than other grounds of discrimination—there is a greater degree of discretion accorded to States. This is so despite language being inextricably linked to culture and growing international concern over the need to actively preserve and promote cultural pluralism. For example, the European Court of Justice upheld a requirement in Ireland for a teacher to speak the Irish Gaelic language despite the language of instruction in the college being English. The justification for this was cultural protection and the promotion of the indigenous Irish culture (*Groener v Minister for Education*). The link with culture is obvious given that Art 27 of the International Covenant on Civil and Political Rights (minority rights) is the principal provision affecting linguistic groups (minority rights are considered in more detail in Chapter 21). Cases considered include *Guedson v France* and *Ballantyne, Davidson and MacIntyre v Canada*.

The United Nations adopted a Declaration on the Rights of Persons Belonging to National or Ethnic, Religious and Linguistic Minorities in 1992, which provided minority language users with the right to use their language 'in private and in public, freely and without interference or any form of discrimination' (Art 2(1)). This is the main instrument relating to linguistic discrimination adopted by the United Nations. There have been more significant developments in Europe—the European Charter for Regional or Minority Languages 1992 and the Framework Convention for National Minorities 1995 (Council of Europe) and the series of recommendations adopted under the auspices of the Organization for Security and Cooperation in Europe (the Lund Recommendations, for example).

Linguistic discrimination is potentially damaging to individuals and even, arguably, threatens human dignity given the negative effect it has on cultural identity of individuals. Despite this, it appears not yet to have given rise to much concern at State or international level.

12.6.2 **Ability/disability**

The UN followed its Declaration on the Rights of Persons with Disabilities with a Convention on the same topic. Although regarded by some commentators as addressing a 'minority' group, others regard it as a discrimination treaty. Certainly many of the key provisions in the treaty emphasise that there should be no discrimination on grounds of disability as regards enjoyment of specified rights.

12.6.3 **Others**

Many instruments list additional grounds of discrimination while others embody a general 'or other status' ground of discrimination in their non-exhaustive list. The plethora of other grounds which have sprung up over the years have had more limited effect, occasioning fewer violations than sex, race, and religion before the enforcing bodies.

Discrimination on grounds of nationality was upheld in *Gueye and ors v France*. The Human Rights Committee deemed nationality a ground of 'other status' in terms of the International Covenant and upheld claims by several hundred Senegalese soldiers who, on retiral from the French army, found their pensions were less than those offered to French nationals with similar service records in the French army (note that the salient military service was, of course, prior to the independence of Senegal in 1960). Regionally, the European Court missed an opportunity to pronounce on the scope of 'other status' within the Council of Europe, discounting a claim of discrimination on royal status in the case of *The Former King of Greece v Greece* as a violation of another part of the Convention had been found. Birth was considered as a ground of discrimination in the European case of *Marckx v Belgium* as illegitimate children were disadvantaged vis-à-vis inheritance rights under Belgian law.

Many other grounds of discrimination are essentially evolutionary in nature, responding to developments in society and the expansion of political will. For example, in Europe, the potential for discrimination on grounds of sexual orientation (homosexuality) has progressively been eroded. This is now being echoed in the United Nations with calls for the abolition on discrimination on grounds of sexual orientation. To date, the position on transsexuals has not developed to the same extent; thus States appear still to enjoy a reasonable margin of appreciation in many instances. Following the Durban Review Conference in 2009, discrimination against those with HIV/AIDS was highlighted as a growing problem. It seems that new grounds for discrimination are sadly always emerging.

12.7 **Conclusions**

Human rights norms do not treat people as if they were equal because they are not. They demand that people be recognized as having equal rights ... The main aim of human rights is to accord everyone equal opportunities for free and full development; hence methods of eliminating discrimination include redressing factual inequalities in the enjoyment of human rights. [Tomaševski, K, p 242]

Universal recognition of human rights is not yet a reality. Neither then is the realization of the equality of the rights all peoples enjoy. For sure, progress has been made. States today are more acutely aware of their legal obligations to guarantee universal rights to all and advancement has been made for those discriminated against on grounds of sex and race. United Nations Declarations demonstrate a willingness to address other forms of discrimination. In the meantime, discrimination will continue to be viewed as an aggravated form of violation of rights or, at best, as a contributing factor to a violation.

Elizabeth Odio Benito, special rapporteur of the United Nations Sub-Commission on Human Rights, concludes perfectly on the crucial aspect of norms of equality and indeed non-discrimination, which underpins the entire United Nations' system:

Equality, however, is not unfortunately uniformity. A regime of absolute respect for human rights must reconcile unity with diversity, interdependence with liberty. The equal dignity owed to all seeks respect for the differences in the identity of each person. It is in absolute respect for the right to be different that we find authentic equality and the only possibility of the full enjoyment of human rights without racial, sexual or religious discrimination. [Study of the Current Dimension of the Problems of Intolerance and of Discrimination on Grounds of Religion or Belief, UN Doc E/CN.4/Sub.2/1987/27, para 17]

CASES

Abdulaziz, Cabales and Balkandali v United Kingdom, Ser A, No 94 (1985).

Advisory Opinion on Minority Schools in Albania, PCIJ Reps. Ser. A/B, No 64, p 19 (1935).

Ato del Avellanal v Peru, UN Doc CCPR/C/34/D/202/1986 (1988).

Aumeeruddy-Cziffra v Mauritius, UN Doc CCPR/C/12/D/35/1978 (1981).

Ballantyne, Davidson and MacIntyre v Canada, UN Doc CCPR/C/47/D/359 and 385/1989 (1993).

Belgian Linguistics Case, Ser A, No 34 (1968).

Burghartz v Switzerland, Ser A, No 280-B (1994).

Groener v Minister for Education, Case 379/87, [1989] ECR 3967.

Guedson v France (Comm 219/1986 (1990)), UN Doc CCPR/C/39/D/219/1986.

Gueye and ors v France, UN Doc CCPR/C/35/D/196/1985 (1989).

Hoffman v Austria, Ser A, No 255-C (1993).

Lovelace v Canada, UN Doc CCPR/C/13/D/24/1977 (1981).

Marckx v Belgium, Ser A, No 31 (1979).

Singh Bhinder v Canada, UN Doc CCPR/C/37/D/208/1986 (1989).

Stalla Costa v Uruguay, UN Doc CCPR/C/30/D/198/1985 (1987).

The Former King of Greece v Greece ECHR, 2000, No 25701/94 (2000).

READING

Bell, M, *Anti-Discrimination Law and the European Union* (Oxford: Oxford University Press, 2002).

Brownlie, I, *Principles of International Law* 6th edn (Oxford: Oxford University Press, 2003).

Van Boven, T, 'Combating racial discrimination in the world and Europe' (1993) 11 Netherlands Quarterly of Human Rights 163–72.

Charlesworth, H, 'Not waving but drowning: Gender mainstreaming and human rights in the UN' (2005) 18 Harvard Human Rights Journal 1–18.

Dickson, B, 'The United Nations and freedom of religion' (1995) 44 International and Comparative Law Quarterly 327.

Flynn, L, 'The implications of Article 13 EC: After Amsterdam, will some forms of discrimination be more equal than others?' (1999) 36 Common Market Law Review 1127–52.

Fredman, S, *Discrimination and Human Rights: The case of racism* (Oxford: Oxford University Press, 2001).

Lerner, N, *Group Rights and Discrimination in International Law* (The Hague: Martinus Nijhoff, 1991).

Loenen, T, and Rodrigues, P (eds), *Non-discrimination Law* (The Hague: Kluwer, 1999).

McKean, W, *Equality and Discrimination under International Law* (Oxford: Clarendon Press, 1993).

Mégret, F, 'The Disabilities Convention: Human rights of persons with disabilities or dibaility rights?' (2008) 30(2) Human Rights Quarterly 494–516.

Meron, T, 'Enhancing the effectiveness of the Prohibition on Discrimination against Women' (1990) 84 American Journal of International Law 215.

Santa Cruz, H, *Racial Discrimination* (New York: United Nations, 1971).

Taylor, P, *Freedom of Religion* (Cambridge: Cambridge University Press, 2005).

Tomaševski, K, 'Women's rights' in J Symonides (ed), *Human Rights: Concept and Standards* (Paris: UNESCO, Ashgate and Dartmouth, 2000), pp. 231–58.

United Nations Human Rights Committee, General Comment 18 (1989) reprinted in UN Doc HRI/GEN/1/Rev.9 (Vol I), at 146.

Wang, L, 'Weight discrimination: One size fits all remedy?' (2008) 117 The Yale Law Journal 1900–45.

WEBSITES

www.un.org/womenwatch—the United Nations' Gateway on the Advancement and Empowerment of Women.

www.un.org/womenwatch/daw/cedaw—United Nations' Committee on the Elimination of Discrimination against Women.

www2.ohchr.org/english/bodies/cerd/index.htm—United Nations' Committee on the Elimination of Racial Discrimination.

www2.ohchr.org/english/issues/indigenous/index.htm—Office of the United Nations High Commissioner for Human Rights—indigenous peoples.

http://www2.ohchr.org/english/issues/religion/index.htm—United Nations High Commissioner for Human Rights—links page on religious intolerance.

http://www2.ohchr.org/english/issues/hiv/index.htm—United Nations High Commissioner for Human Rights—links page on other forms of discrimination (includes discrimination on disability and on HIV/AIDS status).

www.ilo.org—the International Labour Organization.

www.europarl.europa.eu/charter/default_en.htm—European Union Charter of Fundamental Rights.

www.coe.int/T/e/human_rights/equality—Council of Europe's equality site.

13

··

The right to life

Everyone has the right to life, liberty and the security of person. [Art 3, UDHR: see also Art 6, ICCPR; Art 2, ECHR; Art 4, ACHR; Art 4, ACHPR; Art 2, CIS; Art 5, AL]

This chapter will examine the right to life as interpreted and applied by the various international regional bodies. A broad approach will be taken—thus, genocide, a designated international crime, is also considered.

13.1 Right to life

The right to life is undoubtedly the most fundamental of all rights. All other rights add quality to the life in question and depend on the pre-existence of life itself for their operation. The Human Rights Committee refers to it as 'the supreme right from which no derogation is permitted even in time of public emergency' (General Comment 6). To those commentators arguing in favour of a hierarchy of rights, the right to life is undoubtedly at the apex of that hierarchy; to those submitting arguments for universal fundamentality and thus no hierarchy, the right to life is still recognized as pre-eminent given violations can never be remedied.

In spite of this, the right to life is one of the more controversial rights, due to the inherent problems in defining its scope at the peripheries—the beginning and end of life. Furthermore, the right to life is not absolute as is illustrated by the application of the salient laws in time of armed conflict. However, note that the use of armed force is technically prohibited by the United Nations unless within narrow, specifically authorized, limits (Art 2(4) UN Charter). International humanitarian law includes safeguards respecting life during hostilities. However, particularly in internal conflicts, persecution of minorities is not uncommon—the crime of genocide is inevitably linked to the right to life as it involves the systematic elimination of a group of people in flagrant violation of the right to life. An overview of the contemporary provisions on genocide is thus provided *infra*.

Article 3 of the Universal Declaration links the right to life, liberty, and security of person. However, subsequent instruments separate these out. The International Covenant on Civil and Political Rights, for example, provides for the right to life in Art 6, elaborating the right to liberty and security of person in Art 9. This chapter will focus on the right to life, aspects of the right to liberty and security of person are addressed in Chapter 15.

13.1.1 **A positive obligation to protect life**

The International Covenant and many of the other international and regional instruments clearly enshrine a positive obligation incumbent on States to protect life. States must thus take certain steps to demonstrate they are actively protecting the right to life of those within their territory.

13.1.1.1 *Obligations to legally protect life*

States must take all reasonable steps to ensure the right to life is protected within their jurisdiction. An African State was found to have provided insufficient protection against non-State actors in *Ouédraogo v Burkino Faso*. States clearly cannot

 Key case

Yildirim v Austria, **UN Doc CEDAW/C/39/D/6/2005**

Fatima Yildirim, an Austrian national died after being stabbed by her husband. The husband was convicted of murder and sentenced to life imprisonment. Two organizations previously involved in the national case and who seek to protect women from domestic violence, the Vienna Intervention Centre against Domestic Violence and the Association for Women's Access to Justice, instituted the communication to the Committee on the Elimination of All Forms of Discrimination Against Women, claiming that Yildirim was a victim of a violation by the State party of Art 1–3 and 5 of the Convention on the Elimination of All Forms of Discrimination against Women. Yildirim had been threatened by her husband on several occasions over the three months leading to her death. These had been reported to the appropriate authorities and action (albeit limited) had been taken to prevent the husband approaching her apartment and workplace. Nevertheless the husband had regularly threatened her (in person and by phone) and the police intervened on various occasions.

'The Committee considers that the facts disclose a situation that was extremely dangerous to Fatma Yildirim of which the Austrian authorities knew or should have known' (at 12.1.4). Austria was thus under a positive obligation to protect Yildirim, using appropriate channels and methods. Austrian authorities indicated their view that arresting and detaining the husband would have been unduly intrusive, however, the committee note that 'the perpetrator's rights cannot supersede women's human rights to life and to physical and mental integrity' (at 12.1.5). Clearly the right to life must be protected and accorded some priority over other rights of other parties. Consequently, the Committee found that 'the facts before it reveal a violation of the rights of the deceased Fatma Yildirim to life and to physical and mental integrity under article 2 (a) and (c) through (f) and article 3 of the Convention read in conjunction with article 1 and general recommendation 19 of the Committee' (at 12.3).

Austria was advised to strengthen its criminal laws pertaining to domestic violence; ensure criminal and civil remedies were implemented to protect women with all appropriate coordination between legal, judicial, and civil society entities; strengthen training and education for law enforcement officers and judges; and ensure the prompt prosecution of perpetrators.

be passive. They must protect life by enacting criminal legislation which aims to punish individuals who deprive others of their right to life—ie, murder, manslaughter, culpable homicide, etc. Such laws seek to deter potential offenders and prosecute those responsible for unlawful deprivation of life. The provision of police and similar authorities empowered to maintain law and order and investigate criminal loss of life further discharges the State's obligation in this respect. A potential grey area is the extent to which a State can protect an individual against criminal behaviour. For example, in the case of *Akkoc v Turkey*, the European Court of Human Rights held that the right to life had been violated by the respondent State as it had not taken sufficient steps to protect the applicant's husband from being murdered. The man was of Kurdish origin and a member of a trade union deemed illegal by the Turkish authorities. Death threats had been made against him and his wife. The European Court considered there to be a real and immediate threat to the life of the man, a threat which the authorities should have been aware of (the couple had made complaints to the authorities on the matter before the fatal shooting). The State thus infringed the right to life of the man by not adequately taking steps to protect his life in these circumstances. (There were suggestions that the State was implicated in the shooting but the European Court dismissed these on grounds of insufficient evidence.) This case is similar to that of *Commission Nationale des Droits de l'Homme et des Libertes v Chad* brought before the African Commission.

13.1.1.2 *Obligation to investigate deaths*

States should also take steps to ensure that any deprivation of life is fully investigated in an open and transparent way. Consequently, States may set up bodies with powers of investigation for specific deaths (for example, the Australian Royal Commission which investigated aboriginal deaths in custody, 1991), or bodies to investigate the cause of death in certain circumstances in order to determine whether and to whom blame should be attached (the coroners' system is an example of this). A number of violations of the right to life have been occasioned by procedural errors on the part of States following the deprivation of life of an individual. In *Akkoc v Turkey*, a twelve-day investigation, with little testimony, was found to be wholly inadequate and ineffective thereby violating the right to life of the deceased.

13.1.1.3 *Link to healthcare*

The need for positive protection clearly does not apply literally to all lives. A State cannot prevent individuals from dying should their injuries or illnesses not be treatable or curable by the available healthcare. Following this line of argument, nonetheless one could argue that a State has a positive obligation to provide appropriate healthcare to facilitate the right to life. The right to healthcare is provided for in Art 25 of the Universal Declaration, as part of the right to an adequate standard of living, and in Art 12 of the International Covenant on Economic, Social and Cultural Rights. Article 12 urges States to take steps to reduce the stillbirth rate and to prevent, treat, and control epidemic and endemic diseases. In General Comment 6, the Human Rights Committee notes, at para 5, that the right to life should be interpreted broadly, requiring States to 'take all possible measures to reduce infant mortality and to increase life expectancy, especially in adopting measures to eliminate malnutrition and epidemics'.

13.1.2 **Parameters of life**

At the drafting stage of the Universal Declaration, some consideration was given to proposals to specify the point at which the right to protect life began. Nevertheless, the final text left open the question of the application of the instrument to abortion and euthanasia. The principal problem with the right to life lies in the moral and religious controversy over the beginning of life, including the rights of the unborn child. However, there is also increasing debate over scope for the application of the right to the end of life and the potential existence of a right to die, euthanasia.

13.1.2.1 *The start of life*

With respect to the inception of the right to life, this is generally taken as being the time of birth. Attempts to extend it to the unborn child have not proven successful. Medical advancements consistently pushed back the point of viability of the unborn child over the last fifty years. However, perhaps overly cautiously, human rights bodies have always opted to extend the right to life only to liveborn infants. At this stage, the right to life does not necessarily entail a right to the necessary healthcare to allow life to continue, although, as mentioned, the Human Rights Committee desires the lowering of stillbirth rates. The International Covenant on Civil and Political Rights makes an oblique reference to the right of the unborn child insofar as Art 6(5) provides that sentence of death shall not be carried out on pregnant women. Clearly there is a humanitarian justification (other international instruments testify to the special consideration which should be given to pregnant women). However, it also may be construed as preventing the death of the unborn child. Only the American Convention explicitly provides for the right to life 'in general, from the moment of conception' (Art 4). This may perhaps be viewed as an inevitable result for an instrument drafted and adopted by a regional organization, the majority of whose Member States adhere primarily to the teachings of the Church of Rome.

In a region of multi-Christian denominations (Europe), both the European Court and Commission have been reluctant to become embroiled in the moral mire of the right to life at its parameters. According to the European Commission on Human Rights, there is no absolute right to life from conception. In the case of *Paton v United Kingdom*, the complaint of a man seeking to prevent his estranged wife from having an abortion was deemed inadmissible, the Commission commenting that 'everyone' applied postnatally and the life of the foetus (in the instant case, the foetus was not yet medically viable) was linked to the life of the mother. Abortions, in certain circumstances, are deemed to be in conformity with the European Convention. Interestingly, there is some provision elsewhere in the Council of Europe's documentation for embryo protection. The Convention for the Protection of Human Rights and Dignity of the Human Being with Regard to the Application of Biology and Medicine 1997—Art 18—demands adequate protection for the embryo where the law allows research on embryos *in vitro*. The Article also prohibits the creation of human embryos for research purposes with interesting implications for current discussions on, for example, cloning. Note that the European Court has proven equally reluctant to support euthanasia (*Pretty v United Kingdom*).

Key case

Vo v France **(2004) 40 EHRR 12**
Evans v UK **(2007) 43 EHRR 21**

In *Vo v France*, a woman had to undergo a therapeutic abortion at five months gestation following an erroneous medical procedure in a hospital. The doctor was prosecuted in accordance with French law though ultimately acquitted. The complaint brought before the European Court concerned whether the right to life of the (aborted) foetus was infringed. Controversially, the Court held that French administrative law offered sufficient remedies to discharge any possible issue with the right to life and that there was no European consensus as to whether a foetus was a person and entitled to respect for life thus it was not desirable to pronounce on whether a foetus had a right to life.

In *Evans v United Kingdom,* the applicant was claiming the right to have her embryos, which were removed prior to successful treatment for ovarian cancer, implanted. However, her former fiancé, whose sperm had fertilized the embryos, had withdrawn consent and thus the embryos should have been destroyed. A Grand Chamber of the European Court of Human Rights ruled unanimously that there was no infringement of the right to life should the embryos be destroyed.

13.2 Permissible deprivation of life

The right to life is, as has been noted, not absolute in the literal sense. Although a non-derogable right, there are recognized circumstances in which deprivation of life may be legitimate. This section will consider the use of the death penalty, death caused by national security forces, and death during armed conflict.

13.2.1 Death penalty

Traditionally, international human rights has recognized the right of States to apply the death penalty as the ultimate punishment for the severest crimes, following lawful conviction by a competent court. Today, however, international law appears unequivocal in its condemnation of the death penalty. As the twentieth century drew to a close, the political climate was such that most international bodies adopted protocols and conventions abolishing the death penalty. As yet, such moves have not been endorsed by all States. For example, the death penalty is still a legitimate form of punishment in some parts of the United States of America, Saudi Arabia, and China. The International Covenant on Civil and Political Rights itself was indicative of the international view against the death penalty—Art 6 implores those States which have not abolished the death penalty to exercise caution in carrying out this penalty. Article 6(6) makes it clear that nothing in the Article should be invoked 'to delay or to prevent the abolition of capital punishment by any State Party to the present Covenant'. In General Comment 6, the Human Rights Committee noted from State reports that progress being made towards abolition was quite inadequate (para 6). The Committee also opined that although States are not obliged to abolish the death penalty totally, they are obliged to limit its use to only the most serious crimes (para 6). The use of the death penalty should be 'a quite exceptional measure' with appropriate safeguards observed for the trial itself, a right to review and the possibility of the condemned person seeking pardon or commutation of sentence (para 7). Naturally, as complaints before the African Commission have evidenced, the right to life will be violated when an individual is executed pursuant to a conviction delivered in circumstances which infringe the right to a fair trial.

13.2.1.1 *Abolishing the death penalty*

International opinion was such that a Second Optional Protocol to the International Covenant on Civil and Political Rights, which aims at the abolition of the death penalty, was adopted in 1990 and is in force. State Parties to the Protocol believe that abolition of the death penalty 'contributes to enhancement of human dignity and progressive development of human rights' (Preamble). This Optional Protocol requires States to cease executions and take all necessary measures to abolish the death penalty (Art 1). No reservations are permitted to the Protocol although States may reserve the right to use the death penalty in time of war 'pursuant to conviction for a most serious crime of a military nature committed during wartime' (Art 2). Any State entering such a reservation must notify the United Nations' Secretary-General of the beginning and ending of any salient state of war.

13.2.1.2 *Regional developments*

Within the Council of Europe, the 1983 Sixth Protocol to the European Convention concerns the abolition of the death penalty. The Protocol reflects 'the evolution that has occurred in several Member States ... [expressing] a general tendency in favour of abolition of the death penalty' (Preamble). This Protocol is very similar in scope, application and content to that subsequently adopted by the United Nations. More progress has been made in Europe. Protocol 13 seeks to render the abolition absolute—removing all permissible exceptions.

The evolving tendency of American States to abolish the death penalty prompted the OAS to adopt, in 1990, a Protocol to the Inter-American Convention on Human Rights to Abolish the Death Penalty. The Protocol is similar to those of the United Nations and Council of Europe, prohibiting the application of the death penalty in the territory of Contracting States. However, potentially the death penalty could thus remain a theoretical punishment as long as it is not applied. As with the comparable protocols, no reservations to its provisions are permitted.

The death penalty is still a valid form of punishment in many Arab States, and is in accordance with the Shari'a law. However, the region's leaders recognized the gravity of compromising the sanctity of life; thus, Arts 6–7 of the revised Arab Charter on Human Rights prescribe limits outwith which the imposition of the death penalty is prohibited. The death penalty may only be imposed for the 'most serious crimes' with sentenced persons enjoying the right to seek a pardon or other commutation of the sentence. Under 18s, pregnant women, and women who have given birth within less than two years are immune from application of the death penalty. The Convention of the Commonwealth of Independent States makes similar provisions in Art 2(2–3).

13.2.2 **Death by actions of State security forces**

The deprivation of life by the authorities of a State is viewed particularly seriously by all international bodies. In spite of this, the right of States to kill individuals in certain narrowly defined circumstances is recognized. States may authorize the use of lethal force, for example, to prevent a greater loss of life or to quell a riot or insurrection. Art 2(2) of the European Convention on Human Rights articulates the circumstances in which such loss of life is deemed acceptable: in defence of any person from unlawful violence; in order to effect a lawful arrest or to prevent the escape of a person lawfully detained; and in action lawfully taken for the purpose of quelling a riot or insurrection. On the other hand, the Commonwealth of Independent States' Convention in Art 2(4) legitimizes the deprivation of life 'when it results from the use of force solely in such cases of extreme necessity and necessary defence as are provided for in national legislation'—apparently considerably broader grounds than those authorized by the Council of Europe.

13.2.2.1 *Application by the Human Rights Committee*

In *Baboeram, Kamperveen, Riedewald, Leckie, Oemrawsingh, Solansingh, Raham and Hoost v Suriname*, the Human Rights Committee found a violation of Art 6(1) of the International Covenant on Civil and Political Rights. These joined cases were brought by a combination of widows, sons, and brothers of the deceased, then all resident in the Netherlands. The deceased were formerly professionals resident in Suriname (lawyers, businessmen, trade union representatives, journalists, and academics) who were arrested at their respective homes on 8 December 1982, following a declaration by Surinamese authorities that a coup attempt had been foiled. The following day it was announced that a number of arrested persons (fifteen) had been killed while attempting to escape. The victims' bodies showed numerous wounds, particularly on the front and sides as well as fatal bullet wounds. Injuries included broken teeth and jaws as well as contusions and lesions on face and body. No autopsies or official investigations of the deaths occurred. At the time of the review by the Human Rights Committee, Suriname was being investigated by the Inter-American Human Rights Commission of the Organization of American States, the International Committee of the Red Cross, the International Labour Organization, and even the United Nations rapporteur on summary or arbitrary executions. When Suriname eventually produced the requested death certificates, they were dated almost two years after the killings occurred and only stated that the deaths were 'probably' caused by gunshot wounds. The Human Rights Committee concluded that Art 6(1) of the International Covenant on Civil and Political Rights enshrines the 'supreme right of the human being'. Given that the State had been unable to substantiate the alleged escape, the Committee concluded that '15 prominent persons lost their lives as a result of the deliberate action of the military police' and that the deprivation of life was intentional (para 14). Accordingly, Suriname was in violation of Art 6 and was urged to investigate the killings, bring to justice those responsible, compensate the relatives of the victims, and ensure that the right to life is properly protected within Suriname.

Similar cases have been judicially considered by the European Court of Human Rights. Article 2 on the right to life was held to have been violated by Turkey in a number of cases involving deaths in suspicious circumstances. The African Commission has also had cause to address the issue of extrajudicial killings in a number of complaints brought before it.

13.2.2.2 *Application to actions of security forces*

The perceived terrorist threat to a number of States has prompted the institution of 'shoot to kill' policies in certain situations. Such policies are viewed with gravity by the treaty-monitoring bodies which have considered a number of cases. In all cases, the test of proportionality appears to be employed—ie, was the use of force absolutely necessary in light of all the facts and circumstances of the case, or could a neutralization of the threat have been achieved by other means? At all times, the State must demonstrate it has taken reasonable steps to preserve life.

Thus, in the case of *McCann, Farrell and Savage v United Kingdom*, the applicants were bringing the action on behalf of kin who had been shot dead by members of the British special armed forces. The victims were Irish Republican Army members who had been suspected of planning a terrorist bomb attack in Gibraltar (part of the United Kingdom). The armed forces shot and killed the suspects in Gibraltar. While the European Commission of Human Rights considered that the lethal use of force was proportionate to the perceived terrorist attack, the European Court disagreed. The United Kingdom was held to have violated the right to life of the victims, not by the act of killing the victims, but rather by not exploring alternatives to prevent them setting off the device in Gibraltar, for example preventing them from entering the territory in the first place. On the other hand, in the case of *Ogur v Turkey*, when the applicant's son was shot dead by the Turkish security forces, there was found to be insufficient evidence to establish that the security forces were under attack and thus acted in defence. Employing lethal force was thus held to be gross negligence and definitely not absolutely necessary. Similarly, the 'arbitrary' shooting of peaceful protesters who were on strike in Malawi clearly violated the African Charter on the right to life—*Acutan and Amnesty International v Malawi*.

13.2.2.3 *Application to 'forced disappearances'*

The right to life has also been found to have been violated by States engaging in the forced disappearance of persons. In the words of the Inter-American Court of Human Rights in the landmark *Velásquez Rodríguez Case*, the systematic and repeated nature of disappearances, either permanently or briefly, to create a general state of anguish, insecurity, and fear is a recent phenomenon though disappearances themselves are not new in the history of human rights (para 149). Multiple violations of rights are possible in these circumstances. However, focusing on the right to life, the Court reasoned that a disappearance followed by a lack of information after a period of years could create a reasonable presumption that the individual was killed. In terms of para 188, even a minimal margin of doubt is discounted in favour of a presumption that the authorities decided the fate of the individual concerned and systematically executed detainees without proper trial, concealing the bodies to avoid punishment. When considered in combination with the failure to investigate, the Court found Honduras in violation of Art 4(1) of the American Convention. More recently, the Inter-American Court upheld a violation of Art 4 for an individual who disappeared in Bolivia around 1972. Bolivia did start an investigation in 1999 and, in the *Trujillo Oroza Case*, acquiesced with the facts as presented. Similarly in *Tas v Turkey*, the applicant's son had disappeared follow-ing detention by the security forces. He was subsequently presumed dead. Turkey was found in violation of Art 2 of the European Convention on that count and due to its failure to investigate the death. Article 2 was also infringed in *Cyprus v Turkey* in respect of peoples whose disappearances in North Cyprus had not been investigated.

One of the first acts of Human Rights Council was to adopt an International Convention for the Protection of All Persons from Enforced Disappearances (Resn 1/1, 2006). The Convention is awaiting the required number of ratification to enter into force.

13.2.3 Death during armed conflict

Naturally any armed conflict situation raises the potential for loss of life. Indeed some of the earliest examples of international human rights are traceable to conflict situations.

13.2.3.1 *Civil unrest*

Civil as well as transnational conflicts characterize contemporary internation-al relations. The death of a non-combatant within civil war situations may also violate the right to life under the African Charter—*Commission Nationale des Droits de l'Homme et des Libertés v Chad*. Non-combatants are not party to the civil unrest and thus there can be no defence of killing to prevent insurgency.

13.2.3.2 *International conflicts*

International conflicts, on the other hand, bring an added dimension—loss of life is not necessarily directly attributable to the State. Reference may be had to the law on armed conflict and international humanitarian law which seeks to preserve the right to life, where possible, in conflict situations. A detailed analysis of this area of law is outwith the scope of the current text although the salient provisions were outlined in Chapter 2. Essentially non-combatants and wounded members of the armed services should be protected. The neutrality of hospitals and Red Cross/Red Crescent/Red Crystal workers should be protected. As regards the actual combatants, international law clearly prescribes certain limits which should be adhered to: for example, the use of chemical and biological weapons and landmines is proscribed.

Ultimately, in both civil and international conflicts, mass exterminations of sections of the population may occur. Of the regional systems, Africa alone has had to address such gross violations of the right to life. Such situations may constitute the international crime of genocide—one of the most serious infringements of the right to life.

13.3 Genocide

In an historical context, it should be remembered that the Universal Declaration of Human Rights was adopted by the General Assembly the day after the Genocide Convention. There is thus a temporal link and, perhaps, an understanding that the two documents may be read together. Indeed, when adopting the International Covenant on Civil and Political Rights, the international community made explicit the primacy of the prohibition on genocide (Art 6(3)).

As Natan Lerner states, '[t]he right to the life of the group is an essential condition for the enjoyment of all other rights and its preservation should be kept permanently on the international agenda' (p 145). History provides countless examples of attacks on groups of people—in Australia, the aboriginal population were shot for sport in the early years of colonialization; in Europe fifty years ago, the Jewish and Romany populations were the victims of a mass extermination policy by the Nazi regime; and, more recently, 'ethnic cleansing' along religious divides in the former Yugoslavia and the decimation of the Tutsi people by the Hutu in Rwanda have shocked the international community. The simplest solution to a perceived problem of ethnic groups in a State is to remove them—either by transfers of population or by complete elimination. The latter is the practice of genocide.

Genocide encompasses both the physical and the cultural extermination of a group. The word 'genocide' is a modern term for an ancient crime, a term created in the aftermath of the Jewish Holocaust of the Second World War. Indeed the Genocide Convention has been characterized as:

the product of an international bad conscience over the failure to take action to frustrate the genocidal projects of the Nazi Government, and of a determination to support the somewhat shaky foundations of the law of the International Military Tribunal at Nuremberg and to expand the scope of that law to cover peace-time crimes against humanity. [Claude, I, p 156]

13.3.1 Definition of genocide

'Genocide' was not an internationally acceptable term until the Convention's adoption after the Minorities Protection Guarantees and Guidelines of the League of Nations had proven ineffective when tested against totalitarian threats. The Charter establishing the Military Tribunal at Nuremberg condemned practices of 'extermination' (Nuremberg Charter, Art 6(c)), not 'genocide'. However, among the indictments of the alleged German war criminals on trial at Nuremberg, the first recorded use of the term 'genocide' may be found. On 8 October 1945, the indictment of some of Germany's major war criminals referred to their participation in acts of 'deliberate and systematic genocide'. Perhaps surprisingly, the judgment of the Tribunal does not mention 'genocide' despite considering at length the reality of it.

One of the original proponents of this newly deemed crime of genocide, Raphael Lemkin, defined genocide as:

a coordinated plan of different actions aimed at the destruction of essential foundations of the life of national groups ... The objective of such a plan would be disintegration of the political and social institutions of culture, language, national feelings, religion, and the economic existence of national groups and the destruction of the personal security, liberty, health, dignity and even the lives of the individuals. Genocide is directed against the national group as an entity, and the actions involved are directed against individuals, not in their individual capacity, but as members of the national group. [Lemkin, R, 1944, p 79]

Lemkin reiterated and expanded on this definition in a subsequent article, defining genocide as, essentially, the intent to 'destroy or partly cripple a human group' (1947, p 147). The pre-existence of a definable 'group' clearly is a pivotal concept in this definition.

International legal recognition of genocide first appears in General Assembly Resolution 96I: 'Genocide is the denial of the right of existence of entire human groups'. These groups may be racial, religious, political or other groups, however there must be a discernible 'group'. The General Assembly Resolution requested the Economic and Social Council of the United Nations to prepare a draft convention for the prevention and punishment of the crime of genocide. The resulting convention, The Convention on the Prevention and Punishment of the Crime of Genocide, was adopted in General Assembly Resolution 260II on 9 December 1948 with no dissenting votes. 'Genocide', within the context of the Convention, however, embraces little more than mere physical genocide.

13.3.2 The Genocide Convention

Article II of the Convention states:

[I]n the present Convention, genocide means any of the following acts committed with intent to destroy, in whole or in part, a national, ethnical, racial or religious group, as such:

(a) killing members of the group;

(b) causing serious bodily or mental harm to members of the group;

(c) deliberately inflicting on the group conditions of life calculated to bring about its physical destruction in whole or in part;

(d) imposing measures intended to prevent births within the group;

(e) forcibly transferring children of the group to another group.

The Convention clearly reinforces the group criteria first expounded by Lemkin, but extends the crime to cover acts in times of peace and war (Art I). Consequently, the State is not sacrosanct; genocide may be committed behind the closed doors of statehood. Genocide is now accepted as an international war crime—one of the new generation of crimes against humanity decried at Nuremberg.

The importance of the Convention lies primarily with its definitive recognition of genocide as an international crime, an 'odious scourge' which mankind should be liberated from and which is 'contrary to the spirit and aims of the United Nations and condemned by the civilised world' (Preamble). The International Court of Justice, when called upon to consider the Convention, stated 'the Convention was manifestly adopted for a purely humanitarian and civilizing purpose' with the declared purpose of condemning and punishing genocide as an international crime involving 'a denial of the right of existence of entire human rights groups, a denial which shocks the conscience of mankind and results in great losses to humanity' (*Reservations to the Convention on Genocide Case*, p 23).

Condemned policies adopted by Nazi Germany document the full spectrum of genocide: political genocide erodes the whole governmental structure; cultural genocide entails prohibitions on regional languages and the destruction of cultural relics and books; while biological genocide signifies an unnatural interference with birth policies to manipulate the demographic definition of groups within the State. At the time of the drafting of the Genocide Convention, the world was in political turmoil. The Soviet delegation supported the removal of 'political groups' from the draft because of the perceived link with Nazi-fascism. France, on the contrary, considered political genocide to be, as time has sadly corroborated, one of the most likely forms of genocide in the future. The provisions on the forcible removal of children from their parents, however, imply recognition of cultural genocide—the removal of children clearly precludes continuation of the group's identity.

13.3.3 Genocide as an international crime

Article 6 of the 1998 Rome Statute of the International Criminal Court provides:

For the purpose of this Statute, 'genocide' means any of the following acts committed with intent to destroy, in whole or in part, a national, ethnical, racial or religious group, such as:

(a) Killing members of the group;

(b) Causing serious bodily or mental harm to members of the group;

(c) Deliberately inflicting on the group conditions of life calculated to bring about its physical destruction in whole or in part;

(d) Imposing measures intended to prevent births within the group;

(e) Forcibly transferring children of the group to another group.

Article 7 provides for other crimes against humanity including cultural persecution. Combining such 'crimes against humanity' with crimes of genocide (as articulated in the Convention) would result in an almost full articulation of Lemkin's original categorization of forms of genocide.

Genocide is now widely accepted as an international crime, at least insofar as its perpetration may be regarded as a crime against humanity. The International Court of Justice was afforded an early opportunity of pronouncing on the status of genocide as an international crime in the case *Reservations to the Convention on Genocide*:

The origins of the Convention show that it was the intention of the United Nations to condemn and punish genocide as 'a crime under international law' ... The first consequence arising from this conception is that principles underlying the Convention are principles which are recognized by civilised Nations as binding on States, even without any conventional obligation. [p 23]

The instruments establishing the International Criminal Tribunals for crimes committed in the former Yugoslavia and in Rwanda corroborate this—genocide was intended to be an international crime. Ian Brownlie cites genocide as an example of *ius cogens* while Patrick Thornberry concludes that:

The post-war world, the new ordo rerum, began with documents and institutions enshrining human rights and freedoms and criminalizing their gross violation—the United Nations Charter, the Law of Nuremberg, the twin pillars of the new world order as the protection of human rights and the promotion of international peace. The criminalization of the deliberate destruction of races, genocide, is part of the self-perception of the age; the crime is the most fundamental denial of human dignity and equality, and its prohibition is fittingly jus cogens. [p 100]

The Convention has exceeded expectations—it is now universally accepted as the embodiment of international law in respect of this most serious war crime. Indeed, it may be submitted that the prohibition on genocide is so well entrenched in the international norms that it has crystallized into customary international law.

13.3.4 **The work of the International Criminal Tribunals**

13.3.4.1 *Rwanda*

Much of the work of the International Criminal Tribunal for Rwanda has been on genocide. To date, forty-four cases have been completed and three individuals have already completed their sentences. Charges have included genocide and crimes against humanity. Jean-Paul Akayesu was the first-ever individual convicted of genocide by an international tribunal. He was found guilty of nine counts of his indictment and sentenced to life imprisonment (his sentences, ranging from ten years to life run concurrently). This case was the first international interpretation and application of the Genocide Convention—the Trial Chamber concluded that rape and sexual violence were capable of constituting genocide if committed with intent to destroy the targeted group. Later, the Tribunal convicted Jean Kambanda, the former Rwandan prime minister, of genocide and crimes against humanity. He pleaded guilty at first instance and was convicted in 1998; his appeal (at The Hague) was unsuccessful; with the convictions and sentence of life imprisonment standing. He is the first head of government to be convicted of genocide. To date judgments have involved one prime minister, some six ministers, a prefect, and bourgmastres among those in authority as well as various religious leaders. The role of the media has also been examined with three persons convicted at first instance on counts relating to genocide despite not being physically involved (*Nahimana and ors*). A completion strategy has been prepared to indicate progress as, by definition, the Tribunal's role in Rwanda is finite (UN DOC. S/2008/726 contains the 2008 report on progress under the completion strategy). Most first instance cases are concluding although appeals are continuing in The Hague.

13.3.4.2 *Former Yugoslavia*

The Tribunal was established by the Security Council by Resolution 827 (1993) for the prosecution of those responsible for the serious violations of international humanitarian law in the former Yugoslavia from 1991 onwards. It has indicted over 160 people and convicted more than 60. In the first full case to go through the Tribunal, Duško Tadic´ was convicted of various war crimes including murder but not of genocide. The doctrine of command responsibility was explored in more detail in the Čelebic´i Judgment which had repercussions for those implicated in genocide. The high-profile trial of former president of the Federal Republic of Yugoslavia, Slobodan Miloševic´, was terminated by his death in 2006. He was indicted on a number of counts related to the right to life, including extermination, genocide, murder, and wilful killing arising, inter alia, from actions attributed to him as president and supreme military commander in Kosovo, Croatia, and Bosnia and Herzegovina. Radovan Karadžic´ was 'found' in Serbia and remitted to The Hague for trial in July 2008. The Appeals Chamber of the Tribunal unanimously found that genocide was committed in Srebenica in 1995 (*Prosecutor v Radislav Krstic*). Of importance in this case is the *dicta* on the scope of the group, or part thereof, which is exterminated. The Bosnian Muslims of Srebrenica or Eastern Bosnia, while a small fraction of the total population in the new State, was sufficient in the instant case. Moreover, the massacre of all men of military age in the community was sufficient to evidence 'intent to destroy'. Many non-combatants (by virtual of physical capacity, age, etc) were also killed and the elimination of more than 7,000 men clearly had a significant effect on the survival of the community. Galić, a Bosnian-Serb Army Commander, was sentenced to life imprisonment for 'acts or threats of violence' spreading terror among the civilian population of Sarajevo (September 1992–August 1994). The trial chamber had originally only sentenced him to twenty years.

As with Rwanda, this tribunal is also winding up proceedings, with declared plans for concluding all first instance trials in 2010 and appeals within a year thereafter.

13.3.5 **Conclusions on the prohibition on genocide**

In its present form, the Genocide Convention is only effective against an overt and manifest act of genocide perpetrated against a distinct ethnic group within a State. Although it may therefore benefit some ethnic groups, it is unlikely that, desirable though it may be, religious or linguistic minority groups will be able to rely on the defence of the Convention. The willingness of the international community to expand the realms of genocide into crimes against humanity heralds hope for such groups although the inherent qualification of proving the 'grossness' required— the acts committed must be atrocious—is hardly possible for the loss of cultural identity.

The recognition of genocide as an international crime in the last century or so would, if enforcement had been possible, undoubtedly have resulted in the demographic definition of the world being completely different to that of today. More realistically, it is to be hoped that the Genocide Convention will be invoked to prevent further genocidal actions by punishing and deterring potential perpetrators. As the Secretary-General commented, the international community failed the peoples of Rwanda. April 2009 marked the fifteenth anniversary of the Rwandan genocide. The international community again took the opportunity to reflect on steps necessary to ensure no repeat. The International Criminal Court is now constituted in The Hague; a permanent forum for trying those indicted for genocide and other crimes against humanity has thus been established. The Court can follow the jurisprudence of the Tribunals and may, in time, further develop the concept of genocide.

13.4 **Conclusions**

The right to life is clearly of paramount importance in international human rights law. International law comprehensively covers not only the straightforward human rights aspects (preventing arbitrary killings in a State) but also extends to the prevention and punishment of the crime of genocide. In those situations when international human rights are not applied, or a State has not ratified the relevant instruments, the laws on genocide are still applicable. Moreover, when society is challenged by the use of armed force, the laws of war and international humanitarian law provide ultimate protection of the right to life.

CASES

Ouédraogo v Burkino Faso, Communication 204/97, ACHPR 29th Sess (2001).

Akkoc v Turkey, 2000, Nos 22947 and 8/93, ECHR 2000-X.

Commission Nationale des Droits de l'Homme et des Libertes v Chad, Communication 74/92, 9th AAR, Annex (1995).

Paton v United Kingdom (1980) 19 DR 244.

Pretty v United Kingdom [2002] ECHR 427.

Baboeram, Kamperveen, Riedewald, Leckie, Oemrawsingh, Solansingh, Raham and Hoost v Suriname, UN Docs CCPR/C/24/D/146 and 148 and 154/1983; UN Doc Supp. No 40 (A140/40) at 187.

McCann, Farrell and Savage v United Kingdom, Ser A, No 324 (1995).

Ogur v Turkey, No 21594/93, ECHR 1999-III.

Acutan and Amnesty International v Malawi, Communications 64/92, 68/92, 78/92, 7th AAR, Annex.

Velásquez Rodríguez Case, Ser C, No 4 (1988).

Trujillo Oroza Case Ser C, No 64 (2000).

Tas v Turkey, No 24596/94, ECHR 2000.

Reservations to the Convention on Genocide Case (1951) ICJ Reps 15.

Prosecutor v Akayesu, Case No ICTR 96–4-A, Judgment 2 September 1998, Appeal Chamber, 1 June 2001.

Prosecutor v Galic´, Case No IT-98–29-T, Appeals Chamber, 30 November 2006.

Prosecutor v Kambanda, Case No ICTR 97–23-A, Judgment 4 September 1998, Appeal, 19 October 2000.

Prosecutor v Nahimana, Barayagwiza and Ngeze, Case No ICTR 99–52-T, Judgment 3 December 2003.

Prosecutor v Zejnil Delalic, Zdravko Mucic, Hazim Delić and Esad Landzo (the Čelebići Judgment), Case IT 96–21-T, 16 November 1998.

Prosecutor v Duško Tadić, Case IT 94–1, Judgment 7 May 1997, Appeal Chamber 15 July 1999.

Prosecutor v Slobodan Milošević, Case IT 02–54, terminated.

Prosecutor v Radislav Krstić, Case IT 98–33-A, Judgment 2 August 2001, Appeal, 19 April 2004.

READING

Claude, I, *National Minorities: An international problem* (New York: Greenwood, 1969).

Destexhe, A, *Rwanda and Genocide in the Twentieth Century* (New York: New York University Press, 1995).

De Than, C, and Shorts, E, *International Criminal Law and Human Rights* (London: Sweet and Maxwell, 2003).

Hood, R, *The Death Penalty: A worldwide perspective*, 3rd edn (Oxford: Oxford University Press, 2002).

Lemkin, R, 'Genocide as a crime under international law' (1947) 41 American Journal of International Law 147.

——, *Axis Rule in Occupied Europe: Laws of occupation, analysis of government, proportionality for redress* (Germany: Fertig, 1973 reprint).

Lerner, N, *Group Rights and Discrimination in International Law* (Leiden: Kluwer, 1991).

Ramcharan, BG (ed), *The Right to Life in International Law* (Dordecht: Martinus Nijhoff, 1985).

Schabas, W, *Genocide in International Law: The crime of crimes* (Cambridge: Cambridge University Press, 2000).

Spjut, RJ, 'The "official" use of deadly force by the security forces against suspected terrorists' (1986) Public Law 38.

Thornberry, P, *International Law and the Rights of Minorities* (Oxford: Clarendon Press, 1991).

United Nations Human Rights Committee General Comment No 6, HRI/GEN/1/Rev.9 (Vol I).

WEBSITES

www.ohchr.org—the Office of the High Commissioner for Human Rights.

www.ictr.org—the International Criminal Tribunal for Rwanda.

www.un.org/icty/index.html—the International Criminal Tribunal for the former Yugoslavia.

www.un.org/law/icc/index.html—the International Criminal Court.

14

Freedom from torture; cruel, inhuman, and degrading treatment; or punishment

No one shall be subjected to torture or to cruel, inhuman or degrading treatment or punishment. (Art 5, UDHR: see also Art 7, ICCPR; Art 3, ECHR; Art 5(2) ACHR; Art 5, ACHPR; Art 3, CIS; Art 8, AL]

In addition to the basic provisions enshrined in the initial instruments, there have been several additional treaties aimed solely at prohibiting torture. In 1984, the United Nations adopted the Convention against Torture and other Cruel, Inhuman or Degrading Treatment or Punishment, while at a regional level, both Europe and the Americas have separate instruments furthering the prevention of torture: respectively the 1987 European Convention for the Prevention or Torture and Inhuman or Degrading Treatment or Punishment and the 1985 Inter-American Convention to Prevent and Punish Torture.

The Universal Declaration of Human Rights represents the first step towards the abolition of torture in modern times. Given the historical background, there was never any dispute over the inclusion of torture in the Declaration. Torture was originally prohibited from involvement in criminal procedure during the Age of Enlightenment though is currently undergoing a most unfortunate revival in many different countries. In this chapter, a holistic approach will be taken, overviewing the parameters of infringing treatment in light of decisions taken by the various international bodies. The specialist conventional mechanisms against torture are included.

14.1 A hierarchy of treatment?

Torture is a serious violation of the physical and mental integrity of the person. It is an ancient crime, still prevalent today. In light of this, the scope of the prohibitions on torture is perhaps surprisingly broad. Over the years, a variety of physical and mental maltreatment has been brought within its ambit as have a number of instances of lesser seriousness and even the threat of violating acts. The various Articles cover an inherent hierarchy of treatment, with torture at the apex, the gravest form of treatment. In many respects it is an aggravated form of inhuman treatment that in itself is classified as a more serious form of treatment or punishment than those degrading situations. All three are prohibited by each instrument. The European Convention excludes the word 'cruel' though this is of little significance since any form of cruel treatment will almost inevitably be brought within the ambit of inhuman or degrading in terms of the European Convention. For example, in the case of *Ireland v United Kingdom*, the European Court concluded that it was the intention of the Convention that the term 'torture' attached to deliberate inhuman treatment causing very serious and cruel suffering (para 167).

14.1.1 The extension to mental suffering

Only Art 13 of the Arab Charter and, of course, Art 1 of the Convention Against Torture, highlight the fact that torture and other infringing acts can be physical or mental. In spite of this, mental suffering has been found to infringe or contribute towards infringement of the other instruments. According to the Human Rights Committee, solitary confinement, especially when the person is kept incommunicado, may be contrary to Art 7 of the International Covenant on Civil and Political Rights (General Comment 7, para 2). The European Court of Human Rights decided that sufficiently severe mental suffering may occasion a violation of Art 3 of the European Convention in the case of *Selçuk and Asker v Turkey*. In that case, the applicants (both over fifty years old) had to stand by and watch their homes, personal property, and indeed village, being burned by the security forces. As they had spent almost their entire lives in the village and the burning destroyed their entire livelihoods, the action of the forces was categorized as inhuman treatment. This principle has been extended to forced disappearances—the European Court upheld a claim of violation of inhuman and degrading treatment brought by a woman who had witnessed the detention and non-reappearance of her son. The prolonging of the anguish contributed to it (*Kurt v Turkey*), though note that a similar complaint brought by the brother of a disappeared person was not upheld in *Çakici v Turkey*—the brother did not witness the detention. The cases before the American Commission and Court on disappeared persons have focused on the ill treatment suffered by the detainee rather than relatives though, of course, the relatives have received compensation.

It is apparent from the foregoing that treatment, involving little or possibly no physical injury, may infringe the provisions on maltreatment and human dignity. This may be viewed as a logical development from the evolving jurisprudence of violations arising from threats of infringing treatment.

14.2 Torture

Although the Human Rights Committee has indicated that 'it may not be necessary to draw sharp distinctions between the various prohibited forms of treatment or punishment' (General Comment No 7, para 2), the term 'torture' tends to be reserved solely for the most serious offences against human dignity and personal integrity.

14.2.1 The international position

Neither the Universal Declaration nor the International Covenant on Civil and Political Rights defines torture. However, the more specific torture instruments provide elucidation. The term 'torture' means:

any act by which severe pain or suffering, whether physical or mental, is intentionally inflicted on a person for such purposes as obtaining from him or a third person information or a confession, punishing him for an act he or a third person has committed or is suspected of having committed, or intimidating or coercing him or a third person, or for any reason based on discrimination of any kind, when pain or suffering is inflicted by or at the instigation of or with the consent or acquiescence of a public official or other person acting in an official capacity. [Art 1, United Nations Convention against Torture 1984].

Torture generally occurs in a limited range of circumstances, for example, it is used during a period of detention (legal or otherwise) to extract information or confessions or issued as a punishment. The General Assembly stated that torture is 'an aggravated and deliberate form of cruel, inhuman and degrading treatment or punishment' (GA Resn 3452(XXX), 9/12/75).

On the occasion of the twenty-fifth anniversary of the United Nations Charter, the General Assembly was called upon to revisit the prohibition on torture. At that time, instances of torture in Chile by the military government were receiving a high profile. The United Nations Declaration on the Protection of all Persons from being subject to Torture and Other Cruel, Inhuman or Degrading Treatment or Punishment 1975 followed. Events culminated in the adoption of the United Nations Convention against Torture and Other Cruel, Inhuman or Degrading Treatment or Punishment 1984. An Optional Protocol provides for a United Nations' body which visits places of detention. It was inspired by the ongoing work of the International Committee of the Red Cross. The visits have a strong preventative role—States should be dissuaded from violating conduct due to the possibility of on-site visits. As the key to eradicating torture was identified by the 1993 Vienna Conference as prevention, States were urged to ratify the Optional Protocol to the Torture Convention at the earliest opportunity in order to ensure all States were subject to site visits. The Committee will also enter into periods of dialogue with States in an attempt to try and assist them in improving detention centres. This initiative is reminiscent of the regional models but not yet universal.

A large number of cases involving torture have concerned States in Latin America. From the Human Rights Committee and numerous condemnations of Uruguay in the 1980s and also violations elsewhere in South America and in Zaire, to the deliberations and reports of the OAS Inter-American Commission and Court of Human Rights with actions of the military regimes in Bolivia, El Salvador, Chile, Haiti, and Guatemala, torture has rarely been off the international agenda. Due to the time taken to process individual petitions, some communications have been considered long after the military regime has ended. However, as the Human Rights Committee acknowledged in *Acosta v Uruguay*, this does not exonerate the new government from remedial responsibility. Accordingly, Uruguay was still obliged to provide compensation in remedy of the violations of rights suffered by Acosta, and indeed many others.

In recognition of the seriousness of torture, the United Nations has designated 26 June as its International Day in Support of Victims of Torture. The 1993 World Conference on Human Rights (Vienna) is unequivocal in its condemnation of the 'evil' of torture, and in its final Declaration and Programme of Action, calls were made for the establishment of appropriate assistance and remedies aiming at the rehabilitation of victims of torture. The establishment and maintenance of such funds is an ongoing process.

> ### Discussion topic
>
> **Can torture ever be justified?**
>
> The philosophical arguments surrounding the 'ticking bomb' theory were raised by Professor Dershowitz and revisited regularly with the political and security arguments over the 'enhanced interrogation' techniques deployed by the United States of America during the so-called 'war on terror'. The Republican executive approved a number of interrogation techniques, which were subsequently banned by the incoming Democratic executive.
>
> In strict legal terms, torture is prohibited outright, with no possibility of derogations. The classification of any particular treatment or punishment as 'torture' is crucial from a legal perspective, and indeed political perspective, as no government would willingly concede to official practice of torture. Yet torture continues unabated around the world.
>
> Discussions continue on whether an absolute prohibition on torture is realistic and/or helpful in the twenty-first century.
>
> See, eg, Dershowitz, D, 'Tortured reasoning' in S Levinson (ed), *Torture: A collection* (Oxford: OUP, 2004), Chapter 14 and response by Scarry, E, Chapter 15 in Twiss, S. 'Torture, justification, and human rights: Towards an absolute proscription' (2007) 29(7) Human Rights Quarterly 346–67.

14.2.2 The Inter-American system

The Inter-American Convention to Prevent and Punish Torture 1985 defines torture in Art 2 as being:

any act intentionally performed whereby physical or mental pain or suffering is inflicted on a person for purposes of criminal investigation, as a means of intimidation, as personal punishment, as a preventative measure, as a penalty, or for any other purpose. Torture shall also be understood to be the use of methods upon a person intended to obliterate the personality of the victim or to diminish his physical or mental capacities, even if they do not cause physical pain or mental anguish.

Individual liability for torture is established under Art 3, liability not only arising if the public servant or employee commits torture but also if such a person orders someone else to inflict torture or even fails to prevent torture. Acting on superiors' orders is not a defence (Art 4). The Convention provides that the prohibition on torture is a non-derogable right, even in times of war or other public emergency. Considerable effort has been made in the Inter-American Convention to guarantee the rights of victims of torture, including the right of compensation. Various jurisdictional issues, including extradition, are addressed by the Convention. Many of these issues are indicative of the political and factual situation in which many Latin-Americans found themselves in the 1970s and 80s.

14.2.3 The European system

The European Convention for the Prevention of Torture and Inhuman or Degrading Treatment or Punishment 1987 is a comprehensive instrument. Serious violations of the right to torture are not particularly common in Europe. The principal cases alleging torture tend to have arisen out of the Prevention of Terrorism measures in the United Kingdom and Ireland and from events in parts of Turkey. Unsurprisingly, the European Torture Convention adopts a preventative approach to the issue. Under the Convention, a Committee is established to visit detention centres with a view to establishing if the conditions therein conform to the Convention. During 2009, visits were scheduled to Austria, Belgium, Greece, Hungary, Luxemburg, Poland, Slovak Republic, Sweden, Turkey, and Ukraine. Reflecting growing concern about, inter alia, the detention and non-trial of alleged terrorists in the UK, visits were made to detention centres for juveniles, terrorists and failed asylum seekers were undertaken in 2007 and 2008. In 2008, the Committee also visited French Guyana to assess the detention of aliens in that area of French territory.

14.2.4 **Threat of torture**

The gravity of torture is such that even the threat of it can suffice for an infringement of human rights. This is crucial when a State is faced with refugees, asylum seekers, and criminal (or occasionally civil) extradition orders. It is regarded as an infringement to return or extradite an individual to a State in the knowledge that the individual will be subjected to torture. Article 3 of the United Nations Convention against Torture and other Cruel, Inhuman or Degrading Treatment or Punishment provides: 'No State Party shall expel, return (refouler) or extradite a person to another State where there are substantial grounds for believing that he would be in danger of being subjected to torture.' States are thus required to ascertain whether torture will occur upon repatriation/extradition before expelling the individual concerned. To determine whether there are such grounds, a State should take into account all relevant considerations including any pattern of 'gross, flagrant or mass violations of human rights' (ibid, Art 3(2)).

   The United Nations Committee against Torture has considered a number of cases involving possible torture following extradition, etc. For example, it concluded that the Convention would be violated if Switzerland returned Mutombo to Zaire (*Mutombo v Switzerland*) and if Canada sent Khan to Pakistan (*Khan v Canada*). This extraterritorial liability emphasizes the gravity of violating the freedom from torture. A State may be liable even if the torture occurs outwith its jurisdiction and prima facie control if knowledge of the situation can be implied. This is particularly important in asylum law, creating a valid ground for claiming asylum. A full discussion of the right to asylum is outwith the scope of this text but humanitarian law and international human rights law both recognize the right to seek asylum. Similar cases (eg, *Vilvarajah v United Kingdom*) have reached the European Court of Human Rights.

   The United Nations Committee, however, will uphold a State's right to repatriate an individual if it is of the opinion that such an action would not pose a risk of torture. For example, in the September 2000 views adopted in the case of *TPS v Canada*, the author of the communication was an Indian national seeking asylum in Canada at the time the communication was lodged. He had been convicted in a Pakistani court of hijacking an Indian Airlines aeroplane and sentenced to life imprisonment. The purpose of the hijacking (during which there were no injuries) was to draw attention to the 'general maltreatment of Sikhs' by the Indian government. After eight years incarceration, he was released on condition he left Pakistan. TPS used false documentation to enter Canada but was subsequently arrested. Following due process in Canada, he was issued with a deportation order. The United Nations Committee requested maintenance of the status quo as a provisional measure pending a decision. However, this communication reached Canada just as the Canadian authorities had finished evaluating the risk of torture. He was deported shortly thereafter. The main influencing factor for the Committee was that nearly two and a half years had elapsed since TPS had been deported to India and, in the absence of any infringing treatment, 'it is unlikely that the author is still at risk of being subjected to acts of torture' (para 15.5). Accordingly, there was no breach of Art 3 of the Convention.

In February 2001, the Committee against Torture held that Switzerland was not violating the Convention by denying asylum to, and thus deporting, an individual to Bangladesh. The author of the communication was allegedly a member of the Bangladesh National Party (BNP) and argued that there was a real risk of torture on his return to Bangladesh. However, the Committee agreed with Switzerland that there was insufficient evidence to prove a 'real and foreseeable risk' of being tortured in Bangladesh (*MRP v Switzerland*, para 6.6).

14.2.5 Scientific and medical experimentation

Modern international instruments clearly proscribe medical and scientific experimentation on non-consenting individuals (second para, Art 7, ICCPR). The inclusion of such a provision was discussed by the drafters of the Universal Declaration (for obvious reasons, given the experimentation which occurred in war camps) but rejected. Interestingly, the Human Rights Committee has noted that State reports provide little information on this. The Committee requests that 'at least in countries where science and medicine are highly developed ... more attention should be given to the possible need and means to ensure the observance of this provision' (General Comment, at para 3). Of course, the boundaries of science are forever being extended through discovery, innovation, and experimentation. The extension of human rights to other medical forms of intervention such as the use of tissue has been addressed by the Council of Europe—the 1997 Convention for the Protection of Human Rights and Dignity of the Human Being with regard to the application of Biology and Medicine: Convention on Human Rights and Biomedicine being in point. A 1998 Protocol thereto explicitly prohibits the cloning of human beings. Medical Ethics have also been considered by the United Nations (GA Resn 37/194, 18/12/82) and UNESCO (1997 Universal Declaration on the Human Genome and Human Rights).

It would appear that denial of appropriate medical treatment may also infringe the provisions as inhuman treatment, if not torture. The European Court considered deportation of a terminally ill man in the advanced stages of AIDS to his homeland (St Kitts), which had poorer medical resources, was 'inhuman treatment' in the case of *D v United Kingdom*. This case has further potential repercussions for the policy makers addressing asylum and deportation issues in the future. However, humanitarian norms should influence State behaviour.

14.2.6 Compensation for victims

A number of initiatives aim at providing victims of torture with compensation. The United Nations has a Voluntary Fund for Victims of Torture, the proceeds of which are used through NGOs to provide legal, economic, medical, psychological, and other assistance to victims and their families worldwide. The Vienna World Conference on Human Rights encouraged States to increase contributions to the Voluntary Fund as a means of securing the necessary resources to achieve the objective of eradicating the practice (para 59). Parties to the United Nations Convention against Torture agree to providing an enforceable right to fair and adequate compensation for the victim (or in event of death caused by torture, relatives) (Art 14). Article 9 of the Inter-American Convention to Prevent and Punish Torture similarly makes provision for compensation to be given to victims of torture.

14.3 Inhuman or degrading treatment or punishment

There are no universal definitions of the scope of inhuman or degrading treatment/punishment outwith a general understanding that inhuman treatment entails a lesser degree of severity, intensity, and cruelty of treatment than torture. Often international bodies do not differentiate between the different categories of rights thus there is no universally accepted definition of inhuman treatment, degrading punishment or, indeed, any other combination of the terms. Nevertheless distinctions are often made.

14.3.1 Corporal punishment

Corporal punishment remains a feature of many legal systems. The various treaty-monitoring bodies have tended to condemn judicial corporal punishment. In contrast, they appear more disposed to accept limited (essentially parental) corporal punishment of children. Corporal punishment, involving behaviour which would otherwise constitute assault, is viewed as threatening the physical integrity of the individual and affronting the inherent dignity of the person concerned. The approach of the international and regional bodies is best understood by reference to cases and complaints.

14.3.1.1 *Judicial corporal punishment*

Many of the cases heard by the Human Rights Committee have involved corporal punishment. As previously mentioned, the plethora of cases emanating from the Caribbean States in this regard has resulted in, inter alia, Jamaica denouncing the right of individual petition under the Optional Protocol. The Human Rights Committee is processing all the communications lodged against Jamaica up to the date the denunciation took effect, hence views were issued on the following case in April 2000. The author of *Osbourne v Jamaica* was convicted of illegal possession of a firearm, robbery with aggravation, and wounding with intent in a Jamaican court. He was sentenced to fifteen years' imprisonment with hard labour and ten strokes of the tamarind birch. The communication alleged that the use of the birch was contrary to the International Covenant on Civil and Political Rights, Art 7. Although the use of the birch is protected from unconstitutionality by the Jamaican constitution, the fact that it is a legitimate punishment does not render it in accordance with the Covenant. Therefore, it was the 'firm opinion of the Committee that corporal punishment constitutes cruel, inhuman and degrading treatment or punishment'. Imposing a sentence of whipping is thus contrary to the Covenant.

Key case

Doebbler v Sudan, African Commission on Human and Peoples' Rights, Comm No 236/2000 (2003)

The complainant alleged that eight students were arrested and subsequently convicted for violating public order. They were students who had been picnicking (with permission) on the banks of the river in Khartoum. Offences included 'girls kissing, wearing trousers, dancing with men, crossing legs with men, sitting with boys and sitting and talking with boys' (para 3). Both parties agreed that the students were sentenced to fines and between twenty-five and forty lashes, carried out in public on the bare backs of the women using a wire and plastic whip that leaves permanent scars (para 30). Sudan submitted that this sentence permitted the students to continue normal life; a period of detention would not. The African Commission referred to the similar case of *Tyrer v UK* in the European Court of Human Rights (para 38). Sudan was found in violation of Art 5 of the African Charter on Human and Peoples Rights and ordered to amend their criminal law, repeal the penalty of lashes and ensure the victims were compensated.

In an earlier case, the European Court of Human Rights had cause to examine the European Convention and its application to judicial corporal punishment. Institutionalized corporal punishment—imposed by a court as a punishment for a juvenile offender—was held to violate the Convention (*Tyrer v United Kingdom*). The minor was sentenced to the birch as a court-imposed penalty.

It would appear that judicial corporal punishment is unlikely to be upheld by the international or regional bodies. Other forms of punishment, preferably aimed at rehabilitation and not retribution, should thus be found.

14.3.1.2 *Corporal punishment of children*

Corporal punishment of children occurs primarily during the education process or at the hands of parents or guardians. The United Nations Human Rights Committee noted in its General Comment that the prohibition in Art 7 of the ICCPR also includes corporal punishment and excessive chastisement as educative or punitive measures. Arguably a school dispensing corporal punishment is acting on delegated parental powers. The use of the tawse (belt), a then popular and widely accepted form of punishment in Scottish schools, did not infringe the European Convention (*Campbell and Cosans v United Kingdom*), the reason being that no evidence was led to show that the boy in question had been degraded in his own eyes or those of his peers when given the belt. The punishment was thus accepted as an integral part of the education process, neither reaching the required level of severity nor the required mental anguish to occasion a violation (note that a violation was found in respect of the right to education in accordance with parental philosophical convictions—Art 1(2), First Protocol).

As with the right to life (Chapter 13), States may be under a positive obligation to act when an individual's rights under the salient articles are infringed. For example, in *A v United Kingdom*, the European Court in Strasbourg opined that the United Kingdom had violated the Convention (Art 13) in not providing an adequate remedy for an individual subjected to treatment by a non-State actor. The treatment, severe beating (with an implement) of a child by a step-parent, was not within the direct responsibility of the State. However, failure of the State to punish the offender (due to the invocation of the defence of reasonable chastisement) opened the State to liability under the European Convention.

Parental chastisement of children has not received the same level of condemnation. As yet, no international body has found a State in breach of international human rights by not prohibiting physical parental chastisement of children (or conversely by prohibiting it). Of their own volition, and in accordance with popular support, many States have banned the practice (particularly in Europe). This has led to the United Nations Committee on the Rights of the Child urging States to consider their laws in this respect. Article 37 of the United Nations Convention on the Rights of the Child does not expressly address the issue. Nevertheless, the interpretation by the Committee, in light of State practice and evolving norms, is shaping the law in this area. General Comment 8 (2006) addresses the right of the child to protection from corporal punishment in considerable detail. The submission is that the spirit of the Convention demands that any physical assault on a child is treated seriously by the State.

14.3.2 Death-row phenomenon

Another interesting development in the law is its invocation in respect of what is known as 'death-row phenomenon'. There have been a number of situations in which individuals have successfully argued that a lengthy period of detention following the handing down of a lawful sentence of death by a competent court may give rise to inhuman treatment. As the death penalty is still lawful (and not *ipso facto* contrary to international law), there can be no claim for violation of the right to life. The invocation of the prohibition on inhuman treatment is an interesting development. This is especially so since the infringement occurs during the appeal process, a process which international human rights law demands as a safeguard prior to execution.

The European Court of Human Rights paved the way for this in the 1989 case of *Soering v United Kingdom*. Extradition of Soering was sought. The case represented his last attempt to challenge the extradition order. Soering was wanted for murder in the United States of America and, if convicted, would most probably have been sentenced to death. The death penalty was still legal in Virginia where the alleged offence occurred. It was submitted that his return to the United States would cause the United Kingdom to infringe his freedom from inhuman treatment. The key issue before the Court was the time the applicant would spend on death row following a conviction—potentially over six years. In the instant case, the European Court decided that exposure to the delay from the 'real risk' of conviction to the execution itself gave rise to a violation of Art 3 of the European Convention. At para 89, the European Court did note that care had to be taken not to create safe havens for fugitives and thus undermine the foundations of extradition. Consequently, a pragmatic solution was reached and the eventual extradition was on guarantee of no death penalty.

In applying Art 7 of the ICCPR, the Human Rights Committee came to a similar conclusion. In *Ng v Canada*, the author of the communication was a British subject born in Hong Kong and a resident of the United States of America. He was convicted in Canada for attempted theft and shooting. The United States then requested the author be extradited to stand trial in California on nineteen counts including kidnapping and twelve murders. Conviction could result in the death penalty. Canada effectively had abolished the death penalty but was not party to the Second Protocol of the International Covenant on Civil and Political Rights. The Canadian Supreme Court decided that extradition would not prejudice Canadian constitutional human rights or those protected under international law and ordered the extradition. The Human Rights Committee, on the other hand, decided that execution by gas asphyxiation constituted cruel and inhuman treatment (para 16.4) and thus Canada was in violation of Art 7 of the Covenant.

It is evident from these examples that States must exercise caution before agreeing to extradite individuals sought for trial in other jurisdictions. The international instruments appear to apply extraterritorially in such situations. Even though the actual breach of the instrument (the stay on death row) occurs outwith the geo-

Discussion topic

Electronic control devices

Deploying so-called 'less-lethal' weapons is proving increasingly popular for law enforcement officers yet the use of these devices continues to be controversial. There are competing human rights issues: a suspect is entitled to respect for his/her life and to be free from torture, inhuman or degrading treatment or punishments; while the police are similarly entitled to respect for their right to life, not least when undertaking arrests and maintaining or restoring public order. Deploying any force is potentially problematic and must be justifiable as proportionate. Any injury or death which ensues must be fully investigated. Nevertheless the position is confusing for States. On the one hand, the UN Basic Principles on the Use of Force and Firearms by Law Enforcement Officials states:

Governments and law enforcement agencies should develop a range of means as broad as possible and equip law enforcement officials with various types of weapons and ammunition that would allow for a differentiated use of force and firearms. These should include the development of non-lethal incapacitating weapons for use in appropriate situations, with a view to increasingly restraining the application of means capable to causing death or injury to persons. [UN Basic Principles on the Use of Force and Firearms by Law Enforcement Officials, text adopted by the Eight UN Congress on the Prevention of Crime and the Treatment of Offenders, Havana, Cuba, 1990, Principle 2]

On the other hand, the UN Committee against Torture has criticized the use of TASER and similar weapons in concluding observations on a number of states including Portugal (2007 UN Doc CAT/C/PRT/CO/4, para 14) and Switzerland (2005 UN Doc CAT/C/CR/34/CHE, para 4) and discussed the issue with various other States.

The use of electronic control devices are thus subject to scrutiny internationally and the question of whether their use is compliant with international human rights appears open to debate.

graphical control and territorial jurisdiction of the extraditing State, that State may still be liable. This would obviously be so even if the State which eventually carries out the death penalty is not party to any of the salient international or regional human rights instruments.

14.4 The treatment of detainees

As has been mentioned, a number of more specific instruments, aimed solely at preventing torture, have been adopted by the various human rights organizations. Some of these take preventative and punitive measures considerably further than the parent instrument. A feature of many of these instruments has been the focus on the treatment of detainees/prisoners. A series of committees now operate at international and regional levels with the power to conduct onsite visits, particularly of detention centres, to ensure conditions are compatible with the relevant provisions on the freedom from torture and other inhuman or degrading treatment or punishment.

14.4.1 The international position

The 1984 United Nations Convention against Torture (Art 20) provides for *in situ* investigations of allegations of systematic torture by any State Party. These investigations are confidential and require the consent of the State concerned. The Committee can only investigate and seek information on the State from external sources if consent for a visit is withheld. An additional Protocol to the Convention against Torture was adopted by the General Assembly in 2002. This Protocol establishes a mechanism of national and international protective and preventative monitoring of places of detention.

Turning to the standards of treatment of detainees, there are United Nations Standard Minimum Rules for the Treatment of Prisoners 1955 (approved by ECOSOC). These rules provide that corporal punishment, punishment by placing in a dark cell, and any cruel, inhuman, or degrading treatment or punishment shall be unacceptable (para 31). Such principles should be read as guidance for States in any situation when a person is deprived of his or her liberty. United Nations General Assembly Resolution 45/111, 14/12/90 contains the Basic Principles for the Treatment of Prisoners which, in some ways, updates the earlier Minimum Rules. Finally, in 1988, the Body of Principles for the Protection of All Persons under Any Form of Detention and Imprisonment was adopted by the General Assembly. This further clarifies the application of torture to detention situations. The General Assembly Code of Conduct for Law Enforcement Officials and Basic Principles on the Use of Force and Firearms by Law Enforcement Officials (GA Resn 34/169, 12/79) creates a system of rules within which law enforcement officers should operate. This can be linked to Art 10 of the United Nations Convention against Torture which requires States to ensure that law enforcement officers are sufficiently trained and educated as to the prohibition on torture.

14.4.2 **The regional position**

14.4.2.1 *The Americas*

In many respects, the Inter-American Convention to Prevent and Punish Torture represents the progress towards democracy in many American States. It was adopted in 1985, just as many American States were embarking on the long path to stable and democratic systems of government. Bear in mind that disappearances and summary executions were commonplace in many Latin American States until late in the twentieth century. The Convention provides for the training of police officers and other public officials responsible for the temporary or definitive custody of persons legitimately deprived of their freedom with particular emphasis on the prohibition of torture during interrogation (Art 7).

14.4.2.2 *Europe*

The European Convention for the Protection of Torture and Inhuman or Degrading Treatment of Punishment is less flexible. It establishes a Committee for the Prevention of Torture and Inhuman or Degrading Treatment or Punishment which, by means of visits, shall 'examine the treatment of persons deprived of their liberty with a view to strengthening, if necessary, the protection of such persons from torture and from inhuman or degrading treatment or punishment' (Art 1). On ratification, contracting States accept this role of the Committee and agree to grant the Committee access to all detention centres within their territory. Visits are undertaken by a minimum of two Committee members. They are granted the right to travel without restriction, full information on detention places, and unlimited access thereto. Private interviews with detainees may be held. Reports of visits are communicated to the State in question with recommendations for any necessary improvements of the protection of detainees.

14.4.2.3 *Africa*

No specific discrete instrument addresses the acceptable level of treatment for prisoners in Africa. Information on the standards can be gleaned from the jurisprudence of the African Commission. For example, in the case of *Acutan and Amnesty International v Malawi*, beating by prison warders, poor food, overcrowding, the use of shackles, and excessive use of solitary confinement gave rise to multiple violations of Art 5 of the African Charter on Human and Peoples' Rights.

14.5 **Emergency situations**

'No exceptional circumstances whatsoever, whether a state of war or a threat of war, internal political instability or any other public emergency, may be invoked as a justification for torture' (Art 2(2) UN Convention against Torture). No derogation from the provisions prohibiting torture is therefore acceptable. The Genocide Convention arguably prohibits some of the most extreme forms of torture though other aspects of international humanitarian law are also relevant. The Geneva Convention prescribes strict limits for the treatment of civilians and military personnel in times of conflict.

Article 3 of all four Geneva Conventions prohibits, inter alia, 'mutilation, cruel treatment and torture'. Torture is never acceptable. Indeed, as events in the Balkans and Rwanda have so tragically illustrated, crimes against humanity may also encompass systematic torture and elements of serial mental and sexual abuse. The latter also fall within the scope of torture and inhuman treatment. For this reason, the permanent International Criminal Court will consider torture a crime within its jurisdiction.

The Geneva Conventions provide for intervention by the International Committee of the Red Cross to verify that torture and other forms of prohibited treatment do not occur during conflict situations. To this end, the International Committee of the Red Cross and the International Red Crescent regularly visit places of detention for political prisoners and armed-conflict prisoners (formerly POWs) to verify that conditions fall within the terms of the Geneva Conventions. Obviously, this presupposes that the State in question has ratified the Conventions. However, even if not, States are often accepting of its neutrality, facilitating visits on request. Independent verification of conditions of hostages and guarantees that the individuals have not been subjected to torture, or other inhuman or degrading treatment or punishment during their captivity also forms part of the International Committee of the Red Cross/Red Crescent/Red Crystal's work.

14.6 **Conclusions**

Torture is clearly regarded as an affront to human dignity and thus proscribed by international human rights law. Reflecting the seriousness of this, systems of checks and in situ visits undertaken by international and regional bodies monitor situation in, for example, various detention units. However, the scope of the provisions on torture and cruel, inhuman, and degrading treatment or punishment is considerably wider, covering mental and physical suffering. Exhaustive definitions of the components of the prohibition on torture would not assist the abolition of the practice, rather there is a real risk such a list would encourage ever more innovative and horrific examples of inhumanity. The extension of the law to anticipated infringing treatment will be of continuing importance in a world of refugees and asylum seekers.

As society continues to evolve, the scope of these provisions will continue to expand beyond strict literal definitions: new forms of treatment may be brought within the ambit of the law deemed threats to the dignity and worth of the human person.

CASES

A v United Kingdom, ECHR Vol 1998-VI, No 90 (1998).
Acosta v Uruguay, UN Doc CCPR/C/34/D/162/1983 (1988).
Acutan and Amnesty International v Malawi, Nos 64/92, 68/92, and 78/92, 7th AAR, Annex.
Çakici v Turkey, [GC] No 23657/94, ECHR 1999-IV (1999).
Campbell and Cosans v United Kingdom, Ser A, No 48 (1982).
D v United Kingdom, ECHR Vol 1997-III, No 37 (1997).
Ireland v United Kingdom, Ser A, No 25 (1978).
Khan v Canada, UN Doc CAT/C/13/D/15/1994.

Kurt v Turkey, Vol 1998-III, No 74 (1998).

M.R.P. v Switzerland, CAT/C/25/D/122/1998.

Mutombo v Switzerland, UN Doc CAT/C/12/D/13/1993.

Ng v Canada, UN Doc CCPR/C/49/D/469/1991 (1994).

Osbourne v Jamaica, UN Doc CCPR/C/68/D/759/1997 (2000).

Selçuk and Asker v Turkey, Vol 1998-II, No 71 (1998).

Soering v United Kingdom, Ser A, No 161 (1989).

TPS v Canada, UN Doc CAT/C/24/D/99/1997.

Tyrer v United Kingdom, Ser A, No 26 (1978).

Vilvarajah v United Kingdom, Ser A, No 215 (1991).

READING

Burgers, J, and Danelius, H, *The United Nations Convention Against Torture: A handbook on the Convention against Torture and Other Cruel, Inhuman or Degrading Treatment or Punishment* (Dordecht: Martinus Nijhoff, 1988).

Duffy, P, 'Article 3 of the European Convention on Human Rights' (1983) 32 International and Comparative Law Quarterly 316.

ECOSOC Resolution 1984/50 of 25 May 1984 on safeguards of the rights of those facing the death penalty.

Evans, MD, *Preventing Torture: A study of the European Convention for the Prevention of Torture and Inhuman or Degrading Treatment or Punishment* (Oxford: Clarendon Press, 1998).

Evans, M, and Morgan, R, 'The European Convention for the Prevention of Torture: Operational practice' (1992) 41 International and Comparative Law Quarterly 590.

Nowak, M, 'What practices constitute torture? US and UN standards' (2006) 28(4) Human Rights Quarterly 809–41.

Pérez Solla, M, *Enforced Disappearances in International Human Rights* (Jefferson, NC: McFarland, 2006).

Rodley, N, *The Treatment of Prisoners under International Law*, 2nd edn (Oxford: Oxford University Press, 2000).

Roth, K, and Worden, M (eds), *Torture: A human rights perspective* (London: New Press, 2005).

Twiss, S, 'Torture, justification, and human rights: Towards an absolute proscription' (2007) 29(7) Human Rights Quarterly 346–67.

United Nations Human Rights Committee, General Comment Nos 9, 20, reprinted in UN Doc HRI/GEN/1/Rev.9 (Vol I).

United Nations Standard Minimum Rules for the Treatment of Prisoners, adopted by the First United Nations Congress on the Prevention of Crime and the Treatment of Offenders, held at Geneva in 1955, and approved by the Economic and Social Council by its resolutions 663 C (XXIV) of 31 July 1957 and 2076 (LXII) of 13 May 1977.

United Nations Basic Principles for the Treatment of Prisoners, UNGA 45/111, 14 December 1990.

United Nations Body of Principles for the Protection of All, adopted by General Assembly resolution 43/173 of 9 December 1988.

WEBSITES

www.ohchr.org—Office of the United Nations High Commissioner for Human Rights.

www2.ohchr.org/english/bodies/cat/index.htm—United Nations Committee against Torture.

www.coe.int—Council of Europe.

www.echr.coe.int—European Court of Human Rights.

www.cpt.coe.int/en—European Committee for the Prevention of Torture and Inhuman or Degrading Treatment or Punishment.

www.oas.org—Organization of American States.

www.africa-union.org—African Union.

www.osce.org/odihr/13480.html—OSCE Office for Democratic Institutions and Human Rights monitoring of places of detention.

www.apt.ch—Association for the Prevention of Torture—NGO.

www.amnesty.org—Amnesty International—NGO.

www.omct.org—World Organization against Torture—NGO collaboration.

www1.umn.edu/humanrts/links/torture.html—University of Minnesota Human Rights Library—entries on Torture.

www.consilium.europa.eu/uedocs/cmsUpload/TortureGuidelines.pdf—EU operational guidelines on torture.

15

··

The right to liberty of person

No one shall be held in slavery or servitude; slavery and the slave trade shall be prohibited in all their forms. [Art 4 UDHR: see also Art 8, ICCPR; Art 4, ECHR; Art 6, ACHR; Art 5, ACHPR; Art 4, CIS; Art 10, AL]

Everyone has the right to life, liberty and the security of person ... No one shall be subjected to arbitrary arrest, detention or exile. [Arts 3 and 9, UDHR: see also Arts 9(1) and 10, ICCPR; Art 5, ECHR; Art 7, ACHR; Art 6, ACHPR; Art 5, CIS; Art 14, AL]

Anyone who is arrested shall be informed, at the time of arrest, of the reasons for his arrest and shall be promptly informed of any charges against him.

Anyone arrested or detained on a criminal charge shall be brought promptly before a judge or other officer authorized by law to exercise judicial power and shall be entitled to trial within a reasonable time or to release. It shall not be the general rule that persons awaiting trial shall be detained in custody, but release may be subject to guarantees to appear for trial, at any other stage of the judicial proceedings, and, should occasion arise, for execution of the judgement.

Anyone who is deprived of his liberty by arrest or detention shall be entitled to take proceedings before a court, in order that that court may decide without delay on the lawfulness of his detention and order his release if the detention is not lawful.

Anyone who has been the victim of unlawful arrest or detention shall have an enforceable right to compensation. [Arts 9(2–5), ICCPR: see also Art 5, ECHR; Art 7, ACHR; Art 5, CIS Art 14, AL]

This chapter will examine the international human rights norms impacting on deprivation of liberty. The gravest threat to an individual's right to liberty will be considered first—slavery. Attention will then turn to the application of the general rights of liberty and security of person. The final area to be addressed is that of detention of individuals. Concepts of slavery and liberty have altered over the years but remain entrenched today in international human rights instruments and most national constitutions.

15.1 **Slavery and servitude**

Slavery was the first human rights' issue to awaken broad international concern. Despite global condemnation, the international community continues to be confronted with practices analogous to slavery. Sadly, it is still relevant to international human rights in the twenty-first century. Manfred Nowak describes slavery as 'the most extreme expression of the power human beings possess over their fellow human beings, representing the most direct attack on the essence of the human personality and dignity' (p 80). Any assault on the dignity and worth of the human being is prohibited by the United Nations Charter and human rights instruments. However, although traditional forms of chattel slavery have all but disappeared, there are many contemporary forms—debt bondage, trafficking of women and children, and exploitation—which are analogous to slavery and also condemned by the international community.

15.1.1 **Slavery**

Operation of the 1926 Slavery Convention was extended after the founding of the United Nations by a 1953 Protocol. According to Nowak, Mauritania was the last country in the world to officially abolish slavery—this was only achieved in 1983 (ibid). Global society has evolved and slave ships are less common than they once were. However, many people are still 'sold' by families into prostitution, paedophilia, and domestic labour while others undertake forced labour and compulsory marriages, with no respect for free choice.

Slavery is defined in the 1926 League of Nations Convention as 'the status or condition of a person over whom any or all of the powers attaching to the right of ownership are exercised' (Art 1(1)). Correlations can be drawn between the prohibition on slavery and the right of a person to respect for human dignity, to be recognized as a person before the law, and to enjoy equality before the law (considered in more detail in Chapter 16). Because slavery is the antithesis of respect for human dignity and the principle of equality of all, it can never be justified. Slavery per se is essentially a narrow concept entailing the total eradication of the legal personality of the individual concerned.

Much of the work of the League of Nations focused on eradicating slavery in the swathes of Africa which were under colonial rule, mandates, and trusts at the time. Without doubt, slavery entered into decline during this period. This history is nevertheless reflected in the regional instrumentation of the AU. The African Charter links slavery to the right to respect of the dignity inherent in a human being. To quote Art 5, '[a]ll forms of exploitation and degradation of man particularly slavery, slave trade, torture, cruel, inhuman or degrading treatment or punishment and treated shall be prohibited'. Being held in South Africa, inevitably the 2001 World Conference on Racism focused world attention on the legacy of the slave trade in Africa, though these issues were also raised in 2009.

As there are few documented instances of traditional slavery today, the focus has switched to people trafficking and servitude, practices which stop short of slavery.

15.1.2 **Slave trade and trafficking**

The 1926 Convention defined slave trade as including 'all acts involved in the capture, acquisition or disposal of a person with intent to reduce him to slavery; all acts involved in the acquisition of a slave with a view to selling or exchanging him; all acts of disposal by sale or exchange of a slave acquired with a view to being sold or exchanged, and, in general, every act of trade or transport in slaves' (Art 1(2)). Contemporaneous to the decline in slavery, the slave trade should also enter terminal decline. However, the related practice faced by international law is the trafficking of human persons for profit. The standard established in the 1926 Convention has therefore been elaborated on by the United Nations.

In 1949, the General Assembly of the United Nations adopted the Convention for the Suppression of the Traffic in Persons and of the Exploitation of the Prostitution of Others. This Convention deems prostitution and the 'accompanying evil' of the traffic of persons for the purpose of prostitution incompatible with the dignity and worth of the human person (Preamble). In many respects, this convention is not new law as it draws on and consolidates preceding international instruments—1904 International Agreement for the Suppression of the White Slave Trade; 1910 International Convention for the Suppression of the White Slave Trade; 1921 International Convention for the Suppression of the Traffic in Women and Children; 1933 International Convention for the Suppression of the Traffic in Women of Full Age—all which were extended in application to the present by amending Protocols adopted by the General Assembly in its inaugural meetings. The 1949 Convention requires contracting States to punish:

any person who, to gratify the passions of another:

(1) procures, entices or leads away, for the purposes of prostitution, another person, even with the consent of that person;

(2) exploits the prostitution of another person, even with the consent of that person. [Art. 1]

Punishment should also be instigated against any person who:

(1) keeps or manages, or knowingly finances or takes part in the financing of a brothel;

(2) knowingly lets or rents a building or other place or any part thereof for the purpose of the prostitution of others. [Art 2].

It is perhaps interesting to note that, where possible, the Convention requires that international participation in the foregoing activities should also be punishable under domestic law (Art 3) with involvement in any such activity (nationally or internationally) a ground for extradition (Art 8). Much of the Convention is concerned with jurisdictional issues and elements of procedures for punishing those involved in trafficking and prostitution though rehabilitation of victims is also covered. It is, in nature, a repressive instrument, indicative of the gravity with which the international community views these practices.

Although the Convention does not mention slavery per se, evolving international notions seem to categorize the activities covered by the Convention as slave-like practices. The General Assembly and ECOSOC have both condemned trafficking in women and girl children as akin to slavery and thus practices to be condemned by the international community. States are further urged to take all necessary steps to combat trafficking in women by the 1979 Convention on the Elimination of All Forms of Discrimination against Women, Art. 6. Other conduct included in the notion of 'trafficking' by the international community includes clandestine movements across borders of women and girl children into sexually or economically oppressive or exploitative situations which profit the traffickers/exploiters/recruiters or criminal syndicates as well as related activities such as forced domestic labour, false adoption (sometimes used to obviate allegations of forced labour of children) and false marriages (used to justify instances of forced domestic labour).

Discussion topic

Contemporary forms of slavery

Human trafficking is a worrying global phenomenon. The UN Office on Drugs and Crime (UNODC) conservatively estimates there are some 2.5 million victims of trafficking at any time. Trafficking reflects the basic tenets of the marketplace: there is a demand for people (the greatest number of trafficked people (79 per cent) are sexually exploited, the next-highest percentage are used for forced labour), there are people who are able to be trafficked and there is the middle group, the traffickers, who answer the demand they perceive with a supply of women, children and men. Europe is the destination for the widest range of trafficked persons (see generally, UNODC, Global Report on Trafficking in Persons (February 2009, available at http://www.unodc.org/documents/Global_Report_on_TIP.pdf). Although trafficking has no cross-border requirement, many trafficked persons have been coerced by promises of a 'new life' in a new country. They are often then smuggled into that new country illegally and thus are reluctant to seek assistance from the authorities when the reality of their situation becomes apparent. While many countries which have ratified the protocol are now criminalizing trafficking, it remains a lucrative trade.

To end trafficking supply of, demand for and trade in people must be eradicated. The UNODC is a major step towards this, analysing trends in trafficking and evaluating responses in 155 countries.

Article 10 of the International Covenant on Economic, Social and Cultural Rights demands that children are protected from economic and sexual exploitation. This call is endorsed by the Convention on the Rights of the Child which strives to protect children from economic exploitation, hazardous working conditions, sexual exploitation and abduction, sale, and traffic. Despite this, trafficking in people remains one of the most profitable activities of international organized crime, according to INTERPOL.

The OAS adopted the Inter-American Convention on International Traffic in Minors in 1994. Meanwhile, the Optional Protocol to the United Nations Convention on the Rights of the Child on the sale of children, child prostitution, and child pornography declares the sale of children illegal and subjects perpetrators to national penal law and possible extradition.

15.1.3 **Analogous practices**

The 1956 Supplementary Convention on the Abolition of Slavery, the Slave Trade, and Institutions and Practices Similar to Slavery commences by declaring that 'freedom is the birthright of every human being' (Preamble). The purpose of this convention was not only to strengthen the resolve of the international community to implement the 1926 Convention, but also to extend the operation of anti-slavery provisions to other practices similar to slavery. Consequently, debt bondage and serfdom are proscribed as are practices of forced marriages, situations when a wife may be transferred by her husband to another, and those whereby a widow is 'inherited' by another person. With respect to children, situations of false adoption and the transfer of children under the age of eighteen for exploitation and labour are condemned (Art 1). The element of reciprocity with an exchange of a person for money or other reward is also abandoned. Unfortunately many examples of these forms of treatment are documented every year, many more undoubtedly go unreported.

Racist aspects of colonialism and apartheid are included within the ambit of slavery-like practices by ECOSOC (Resn 1232 (XLII) of 1967, for example). This reflected the then pertaining situation in parts of Africa, practices which were attracting international condemnation. Naturally designation of such practices as slavery-like added further weight to the United Nations' campaign against apartheid and in favour of decolonization and self-determination.

The Sub-Commission on Prevention of Discrimination and Protection of Minorities appointed a Working Group on Contemporary Forms of Slavery in 1974. This Working Group continues to raise the profile of slavery, drawing global attention to slavery-like practices still perpetrated today. The United Nations Voluntary Trust Fund on Contemporary Forms of Slavery extends humanitarian, legal, and financial aid to individuals whose lives have been severely affected by slavery and slavery-like practices.

Due to the diverse nature of slavery-like practices, some commentators argue that a much more comprehensive approach by States, with combined efforts and coordination of information and best practice is needed to deal with the matter (see, for example, Lassen, N).

15.1.4 Forced or compulsory labour

Forced and compulsory labour is also prohibited by norms of human rights. Notwithstanding any similarity to slavery and analogous practices, it appears that there are circumstances in which forced labour may be accepted; in other words, occasions when derogations may be legal.

Perhaps reflecting regional history, the European and CIS texts prohibit forced or compulsory labour though military service and work carried out during lawful detention are explicitly excluded from the ambit of the provisions. With a history of military service and labour detention camps, these provisions are not surprising. The African Charter, on the contrary, makes no mention of servitude or forced labour. By way of contrast, in those Arab States ratifying their regional instrument, forced labour is prohibited in the same Article in which the right to choose work is protected—Art 31 of the Arab Charter on Human Rights—with the express exception of work imposed by a court as a penalty.

Forced and compulsory labour was considered initially by the International Labour Organization culminating in the adoption of Convention No 29 Concerning Forced Labour (1930). This instrument defines forced or compulsory labour as including 'all work or service which is exacted from any person under the menace of any penalty and for which the said person has not offered himself voluntarily' (Art 2(1)). Many categories of work are excluded expressly from this definition: purely military work undertaken in fulfilment of compulsory military service; work forming part of the normal civic obligations of a citizen; work carried out under the supervision and control of a public authority pursuant to conviction in a court of law; work or service exacted during an emergency or other calamitous situation endangering all or part of a State (earthquakes, fire, famine, insect invasion, epizootic diseases, etc); and minor communal civic obligations (Art 2(2)). Jury service, military service, and civil defence/national guard service are acceptable, as are calls for assistance in times of public emergency. Although in the latter category most citizens would feel morally obliged to assist, it is clear from the provisions of international human rights that reluctant volunteers may be coerced into providing whatever assistance they can. Naturally, such coercion must not infringe the non-derogable provisions on torture.

The Convention articulates a number of safeguards for an individual involved in forced or compulsory labour situations which do not infringe it. A related aim of the Convention was the progressive abolition of forced or compulsory labour exacted as a tax and/or for the execution of public works. Such practices still exist in some States, often as an extended aspect of military service. The use of these practices probably hit its zenith in the era of rebuilding and reinforcing Communist States with public service demanded as part of a citizen's tax. The parameters within which such service can operate is strictly confined by the Convention (Arts 10–13). Consideration of health and safety requirements are essential as are payments and working conditions of the forced labourer. At all times, there should be a parity of treatment between the forced and the voluntary labourer. Obviously, in many situations, it will be difficult to ascertain how this is realized—payment of a specified minimum wage and conformity with the maximum working hours and minimum working conditions elaborated on in additional Conventions by the International Labour Organization may suffice.

The principal problem with forced and compulsory labour lies with the vagueness of terminology employed. As a consequence, it is often difficult to categorize borderline work practices. This has, in turn, contributed to the relatively small number of individual complaints raising the issue before the international bodies.

Most cases have been raised in Europe before the Strasbourg authorities though few have been found to give rise to violations of Art 4 of the European Convention. In *Van der Mussele v Belgium*, the European Court had recourse to Convention No 29 of the International Labour Organization when deliberating a case raised by a Belgian pupil avocat who received no remuneration for representing a client through the Belgian Legal Advice and Defence Office. Given that the applicant had voluntarily sought to enter the legal profession and was aware of the system of providing free assistance at that point, the Court concluded that there was no unreasonable imbalance between the aim pursued and the obligations undertaken (para 40). Accordingly, there was no violation of the European Convention. Again, following the approach of the International Labour Organization, the European Court held that compulsory labour could be a legitimate form of punishment and even a legitimate part of the rehabilitation process in the case of *Van Droogenbroeck v Belgium*.

In Europe, civic duties can include compulsory fire service work (or payment in lieu) as was evidenced in *Schmidt v Germany* (as only men were liable for this service/compensatory payment, a violation of Art 14 (non-discrimination) of the European Convention in connection with Art 4 was found).

In conclusion, in accordance with the restrictive view taken by the treaty-monitoring bodies of any restriction on the liberty of a person, the circumstances in which compulsory labour is acceptable are narrowly defined and applied. No one should be held in slavery or subjected to trafficking—such activities deny fundamental rights of dignity as well as liberty. Elements of compulsory labour in strictly defined situations are, however, acceptable.

15.2 Liberty and security of person

There is nothing novel about rights to liberty. A right to personal liberty was enshrined in English law by Magna Carta in 1215, albeit only for a limited section of the population (feudal noblemen). Magna Carta dictates that no free man shall be taken, imprisoned, outlawed, or exiled except by lawful judgment by peers or other application of the law of the land. In England, this was followed by the Bill of Rights in 1688 and the Habeus Corpus Acts of 1640 and 1679. Mention of liberty also appears in the Declaration of Arbroath 1320 (Scotland) and the French Declaration of the Rights of Man 1789. In both cases, liberty refers to the freedom of person within comparatively narrow confines. Habeas corpus is an integral part of the right to liberty and security of person. In general, international instruments do not prohibit deprivation of liberty; rather, they restrict themselves to establishing procedural guarantees and minimum standards for those deprived of their liberty. The United Nations Declaration of Human Rights broadened many of the rights of persons. However, the final text represented a 'short and programmatic version' of the right to liberty (Niemi-Kiesiläinen, J, p 210). Elaboration of the concept in modern human rights was left to future instruments. In accordance with Art 9 of the International Covenant on Civil and Political Rights, it emerges that deprivation of liberty will only be valid on grounds and in accordance with procedures established by law.

Deprivation of liberty is only permissible if the grounds of detention are lawful and the procedure followed upon detention is also in accordance with the law. Accordingly, the remainder of this chapter will focus on the right to liberty and security of person. Discussion will be split into two sections: the circumstances in which a person can be deprived of liberty and secondly, the procedures which must be followed in order to legitimize detention.

15.2.1 Deprivation of liberty

Incidences of arbitrary arrest and detention have long been a matter of concern for the international community. Arbitrary arrest and detention was commonplace throughout much of Central and South America during the period of military rule and occurred regularly during the Communist era in the Soviet Union. More recently, it has been documented in certain regions of Africa and the Middle East. It tends to be a characteristic of oppressive military regimes. In many instances, the detention is justified on grounds of 'political crimes' or is a seemingly arbitrary arrest on grounds of political or religious beliefs. The United Nations commissioned a detailed study on the subject. In the report, an arrest is considered arbitrary if it is '(a) on grounds or in accordance with procedures other than those established by law, or (b) under the provisions of a law the purpose of which is incompatible with respect for the right to liberty and security of person' (UN Publication). It is therefore clear that States cannot legislate contrary to international human rights norms protecting liberty.

The right to liberty and security of person has featured frequently in the case law of the Human Rights Committee. From the resulting jurisprudence, it would appear that States have a right to protect citizens whose life or physical integrity is threatened by private persons. Clearly no such right can be absolute, States cannot be held responsible for all acts of private parties. As with the right to life, enforcement of criminal law is one safeguard which a State can offer the threatened party. In a number of cases, the Human Rights Committee has found violations of the right to security of person (for example, *Delgado Paéz v Columbia*, *Chiiko v Zambia*, *Oló Bahamonde v Equatorial Guinea*, *Mojica v Dominican Republic*, or *Dias v Angola*).

15.2.2 Grounds of detention

To define the grounds on which deprivation of liberty may be lawful, regard must be had not only to the various human rights instruments, but also to the jurisprudence of the various treaty-monitoring bodies. The case law in this area is complex, turning as it does on the peculiar facts of each complaint. The law is expanded through other instruments and through the work of special rapporteurs. However, there remains a definite lack of a precise legally binding definition of the scope of 'lawful detention'. There is a recognized need for a legal basis on which to detain (*Chaparro, Crespo, Arroyo and Torres v Colombia*, views of the United Nations Human Rights Committee). In many respects, interpretation is by reference to other, more specific, provisions. Article 11 of the International Covenant on Civil and Political Rights, Art 7(7) of the American Convention on Human Rights, and Art 1, Protocol 4 of the European Convention on Human Rights all decry detention for failure to fulfil a contractual obligation, 'for debt' to quote the American Convention. In other circumstances, it is a matter of analysing the facts and circumstances of the case. Discretion as to the grounds of legitimate detention tends to be left as a matter for national law, the international bodies merely exercising a supervisory role to ensure no other rights or freedoms are compromised.

The Council of Europe has elected to elaborate considerably on the grounds for legitimate detention:

(a) the lawful detention of a person after conviction by a competent court;

(b) the lawful arrest or detention of a person for non-compliance with the lawful order of a court or in order to secure the fulfilment of any obligation prescribed by law;

(c) the lawful arrest or detention of a person effected for the purpose of bringing him before the competent legal authority on reasonable suspicion of having committed an offence or when it is reasonably considered necessary to prevent his committing an offence or fleeing after having done so;

(d) the detention of a minor by lawful order for the purpose of educational supervision or his lawful detention for the purpose of bringing him before the competent legal authority;

(e) the lawful detention of persons for the prevention of the spreading of infectious diseases, of persons of unsound mind, alcoholics or drug addicts or vagrants;

(f) the lawful arrest or detention of a person to prevent his effecting an unauthorised entry into the country or of a person against whom action is being taken with a view to deportation or extradition. [Art 5(1) ECHR]

Key case

A and ors v United Kingdom, Application 3455/05, European Court of Human Rights Judgment 19 February 2009

On 11 November 2001, the UK government prepared a derogation from Art 5 of the European Convention on Human Rights upon passing a national law, the Anti-Terrorism Crime and Security Act 2001. The eleven applicants were detained under this national law as they were suspected of being terrorists and representing a threat to the UK. The UK claimed they could not deport these foreigners as deportation would infringe Art 3 of the European Convention (the detainees would be subjected to possible torture and illtreatment etc following deportation) thus they were detained.

'The Court is acutely conscious of the difficulties faced by States in protecting their populations from terrorist violence' (para 126). It found a violation of Art 5 (on deprivation of liberty) in respect of the indeterminate detention of several of the applicants. Although a derogation was acceptable as there was accepted as being a threat to the life of the nation, the measures taken were considered to be disproportionate to the threat posed (para 190). Violations of a number of aspects of Art 5 were found for a number of the applicants. Nevertheless, the Court concluded that the UK had acted in good faith in the face of a terrorist threat and thus awarded comparatively small sums of compensation (para 253).

Some of these grounds are comparatively obvious and relatively non-controversial. Few will dispute the potential for detention following conviction by a lawful court. However, violations may occur when the length of that detention is not made clear—for example, indeterminate detention without regular reviews of the continued legitimacy thereof will infringe human rights. Irrespective of the ground, certain minimum standards of monitoring and recording apply (GA Resn 43/173, Body of Principles for the Protection of all Persons under any form of Detention or Imprisonment, for example).

15.2.2.1 *Detention following conviction by a competent court*

A principal means of punishment imposed by courts of law throughout the world is incarceration. Detention following conviction is thus one of the most common means of depriving an individual of his or her liberty. The emphasis is on the legitimacy of the detention and the treatment of the prisoners thereafter. Detention can include the period after initial conviction pending appeal (*Monnell and Morris v United Kingdom*), such detention being legitimate even if the prisoner is subsequently released on appeal (*Benham v United Kingdom*).

15.2.2.2 *Extradition, expulsion, or deportation*

This ground of detention arises in many situations in an international community which increasingly relies on extradition treaties to facilitate trials and in a climate of increasing numbers of refugees and asylum seekers. Many States conclude extradition treaties with their allies. However, various international instruments impose an obligation on States to extradite suspects accused of certain crimes if requested. For example, torture is deemed an extraditable crime under Art 13 of the Inter-American Convention to Prevent and Punish Torture. Outwith the traditional human rights arena, various international instruments on terrorism, hijacking, and piracy contain obligations on contracting States to extradite alleged offenders for trial, unless the host State or State of nationality decides to try the individual concerned. The Statute of Rome establishing the International Criminal Court, on the other hand, requires States to arrest on request specified individuals before surrendering them to the International Court (Art 59). This represents an additional ground of legitimate detention—detention pending surrender to the International Criminal Court.

In many situations, national courts have condemned the actions taken by governments to detain asylum seekers pending decisions on deportation or to prevent access of would-be asylum seekers in the first place. The same principle applies whether the detention is for extradition or deportation—the State is seeking to detain the individual in question to prevent flight and thus to effect the deportation or the extradition. It is perhaps worth noting that the international law on refugees and asylum seekers is covered in detail by a number of specialist instruments including the 1951 Geneva Convention relating to the Status of Refugees, with 1967 Protocol, and the 1969 OAU Convention Governing the Specific Aspects of Refugee Problems in Africa. It is outwith the scope of this text to devote discussion to the considerable number of human rights issues raised by the increasing numbers of refugees in crisis today.

In *Amuur v France*, the European Court held that France's decision to restrict the applicants, who were fleeing from Somalia, to the international transit area of Orly airport for some twenty days pending the decision on their application for asylum infringed the European Convention. At that time, the international transit area was not regarded as French territory.

15.2.2.3 *Minors*

Article 37 of the United Nations Convention on the Rights of the Child provides that children may be deprived of their liberty if such detention is in accordance with the law. However, it states that deprivation of liberty should only be used 'as a measure of last resort' and for the shortest appropriate time. Children may obviously be deprived of their liberty on suspicion of committing a crime. On many occasions, detention of minors may involve the exercise of parental rights. In such situations, there is a clear onus on the State to ensure that parental rights are exercised in accordance with the law and in a manner which is not to the detriment of the child (*Nielsen v Denmark*).

15.2.2.4 *Compulsory residence orders*

The right to liberty entails a freedom of movement within a State. Confinement must only be used when absolutely necessary to achieve a goal. Italy was found to have infringed the European Convention when a Milanese court imposed a compulsory residence order on a suspected Mafia member. The applicant was confined to part of the island of Asinara for a set period of time, was subject to a curfew and was required to report daily to the police. The European Court of Human Rights considered that the difference between deprivation of liberty and restriction upon liberty is 'merely one of degree or intensity, and not one of nature or substance' (*Guzzardi v Italy*, para 93).

15.2.2.5 *Detention for medical reasons*

It is legitimate to detain an individual when it is in the best interests of that individual or of the rest of the population. Thus, it is often legitimate to detain a person who is suffering from a highly contagious disease to prevent the disease being spread and it may be legitimate to detain an individual under mental health legislation to prevent problems arising. It is essential that appropriate procedures are carried out before an individual is detained in such circumstances. In the case of *A v New Zealand*, the author's detention under the Mental Health Act from 1984–93 was not found to infringe the Covenant (Art 9) because the author had demonstrated aggressive and threatening behaviour. The committal order was issued according to law, on the recommendation of three psychiatrists, and was reviewed periodically (para 7.2); thus the detention was justified.

15.2.2.6 *Detention on suspicion of a criminal offence*

For the promotion and preservation of the rights of others, State authorities may elect to detain a suspect. This can be in order to prevent further offences occurring or in order to prevent flight, or interference with material facts or witnesses. There is a tendency under human rights law to require that such detention is only used when necessary, accused persons should normally be released on condition of appearance at a specified court of law and specified time. The provisions of the Statute of the International Criminal Court deal with this issue—Art 60 provides for the possibility of conditional release pending trial.

There is a clear need for substantial evidence to justify the detention in these circumstances. Failure to base the arrest on appropriate evidence renders the arrest arbitrary. In *Loukanov v Bulgaria*, the European Court found the detention of the former prime minster on suspicion of misappropriation of funds was not legitimate as no evidence was led to show the action of the applicant was criminal. Detention succeeding arbitrary arrests frequently lack the necessary procedural guarantees to render such detention in accordance with international human rights law. Arrests for suspected political activities infringed Art 4 of the African Charter on Human and Peoples' Rights in the case of *Achutan and Amnesty International v Malawi*.

15.2.3 **Procedural guarantees**

Detention of persons and, *ergo*, deprivation of liberty is, of course, in some cases legitimate. International human rights law seeks not only to delineate the circumstances in which individuals may be deprived of their liberty but also to enforce procedural guarantees which safeguard individuals from abuses of power by States. These procedural guarantees will now be considered.

15.2.3.1 *Prompt determination of legitimacy of detention*

Any detainee must be informed promptly of the reason for the detention. In some respects, this echoes the right of an accused to be informed promptly of the charge levied under the provisions on a fair trial. A detainee has the right to have the legitimacy of any period of detention confirmed by a competent legal authority within a reasonable time. Even during periods justifying the invocation of derogations from certain of the provisions relating to detention, the legitimacy of the detention must still be determined. A slightly longer period may be justifiable but indeterminate detention without judicial approval is not.

The requirement of judicial review of detention is provided for in Art 9(3) of the International Covenant on Civil and Political Rights, Art 5(3) of the European Convention on Human Rights, and Art 7(5) of the American Convention on Human

Key case

Fillastre v Bolivia (336/1988) UN Doc CCPR/C/43/D/336/1988

6.5 Under article 9, paragraph 3, anyone arrested or detained on a criminal charge 'shall be entitled to trial within a reasonable time … '. What constitutes 'reasonable time' is a matter of assessment for each particular case. The lack of adequate budgetary appropriations for the administration of criminal justice alluded to by the State party does not justify unreasonable delays in the adjudication of criminal cases. Nor does the fact that investigations into a criminal case are, in their essence, carried out by way of written proceedings, justify such delays. In the present case, the Committee has not been informed that a decision at first instance had been reached some four years after the victims' arrest. Considerations of evidence-gathering do not justify such prolonged detention. The Committee concludes that there has been, in this respect, a violation of article 9, paragraph 3.

Rights. Detainees are entitled to be brought promptly before a judicial organ and then to a trial within a reasonable time.

15.2.3.2 *Release pending trial*

There is a presumption that individuals may be released pending trial. Naturally, a court may approve continued detention pending trial, should the circumstances so demand. Conditions (bail) may be attached to any such release in order to guarantee the return of the accused person to face trial.

15.2.3.3 *Review of legitimacy of detention*

Detention is, of course, a legitimate form of punishment following conviction by a competent court. However, detention should be for a specified time. Indeterminate detention may be legitimate but the continued legitimacy of the detention must be subject to judicial review. This applies in all situations. It is particularly important when individuals are detained on mental health grounds—an appropriate authority must verify the continued existence of the circumstances justifying the detention.

15.2.3.4 *Compensation for non-justified detention*

Given the importance attached to liberty and security of person by international human rights law, it is perhaps not surprising that compensation is due to those victims of unlawful deprivation of liberty. The Human Rights Committee has frequently demanded that a State pay compensation to victims of unlawful detention. For example, in the case of *Chaplin v Jamaica*, a violation of Art 10(1) of the International Covenant was found and the State was ordered to provide an effective remedy, including compensation. In that case, the State was given three months to respond to the Human Rights Committee with information as to the measures it had taken. In a number of cases in the 1970s and 1980s, Uruguay was requested to provide appropriate remedies to those deprived of their liberty in an unlawful manner (see, for example, *Valcada v Uruguay* and *de Bazzano, Ambrosini, de Massera and Massera v Uruguay*).

15.2.3.5 *Link to conditions for treatment of prisoners*

The treatment of prisoners is a major area of application of these provisions. International human rights seeks to establish minimum conditions for the treatment of prisoners irrespective of the crime committed and the economic situation of the State concerned. The right to security of person allows international bodies to extend the application of the provisions on torture and other inhuman or degrading treatment or punishment (discussed in Chapter 14) to less life threatening treatments.

General Comment No 9 of the Human Rights Committee details the view of the Committee with respect to the right to humane treatment and respect for dignity of detainees. For example, juveniles should be separated from adults (see also Art 37(c) of the Convention on the Rights of the Child) and convicted persons should be segregated from non-convicted detainees (paras 6 and 8, respectively). The segregation of persons before and after trial is considered necessary to preserve the right to the presumption of innocence of the suspect.

At all times, detained people should be treated humanely. The detention of minors should be dedicated to their rehabilitation. Provisions on inhuman and degrading treatment or punishment should clearly not be infringed. In *Párkányi v Hungary*, the Human Rights Committee concluded that Art 10 of the International Covenant for Civil and Political Rights was violated by Hungary as the author, a prisoner, was allowed only five minutes per day for exercise and the same amount of time for personal ablutions. Obviously, all detainees are entitled to the protection of the full range of human rights. Therefore, they have rights of dignity, humane treatment, access to legal advice, and even correspondence. Many of these issues are addressed elsewhere in this text where the relevant aspects of human rights are studied. The *in situ* visits of international and regional bodies to detention centres seek to ensure that the rights to liberty and security of detainees are not compromised as well as verifying the treatment of detainees vis-à-vis guarantees against torture and other cruel, inhuman or degrading treatment or punishments.

15.2.3.6 *Link to forced disappearances*

One of the problems encountered with examples of detention has been the issue of forced disappearances—see generally Chapters 13–14. To combat this, the Inter-American Convention on the Forced Disappearance of Persons 1994, Art XI requires States to maintain a register of detainees. Such a formalization of status serves as a public record of detention and should prevent arbitrary disappearances. Many States document detention, often through court, police, and prison records. This practice is to be encouraged.

Similar provisions are found in the International Convention for the Protection of All Persons From Enforced Disappearances, Art 17 of which requires contracting parties to enact legislation establishing when liberty can be deprived, who can authorize a deprivation of liberty, hold people only in officially recognized and supervised (non-secret) places and maintain registers of those held in detention. Documentation must record the name of the detainee, the date, time and place of detention and release, details of the entity authorizing detention, ground of deprivation of liberty and state of health of detainee/the full circumstances surrounding the death of a detainee should s/he die while in custody.

15.2.4 **Derogations from the provisions**

States increasingly seek to derogate from the provisions on detention during civil strife or on suspicion of involvement in terrorist activity. Detention is viewed as preventing a potentially greater threat to the well-being of the State and its peoples. All such derogations require to be notified to the relevant authority in accordance with the provisions of the instrument in point.

15.3 **Conclusions**

Given the importance attached to the right of liberty and security of person, it is inevitable that slavery is proscribed in international law. Undoubtedly, slavery, servitude, and trafficking of people are acts so debasing that they are an anathema to the concept of human dignity. With such a background, it is inevitable that international human rights law takes a serious approach to any other deprivation of liberty.

For other deprivations of liberty to be in conformity with international law, the detention must be in accordance with a procedure prescribed by law, for a legitimate purpose, and subject to review on appeal. Continued detention must be reviewed on a regular basis. During any period of detention, the detainee must be treated with respect for security of person and regard for the rights of access to legal representatives and others as well as freedom from torture and inhuman or degrading treatment or punishment.

CASES

A v New Zealand, UN Doc CCPR/C/66/D/754/1997 (1999).

Acutan and Amnesty International v Malawi, Nos 64/92, 68/92 and 78/92, 7th AAR, Annex.

Amuur v France, ECHR 1996, Vol 1996-III, No 11.

Benham v United Kingdom, ECHR 1996, Vol 1996-III, No 10.

Chaparro, Crespo, Arroyo and Torres v Colombia, UN Doc CCPR/C/60/D/612/1995 (1997).

Chaplin v Jamaica, UN Doc CCPR/C/55/D/ 596/1994 (1995).

Chiiko v Zambia, UN Doc CCPR/C/48/D/314/1988 (1993).

de Bazzano, Ambrosini, de Massera and Massera v Uruguay, UN Doc. CCPR/C/7/D/5/1977 (1979).

Delgado Paéz v Columbia, UN Doc CCPR/C/39/D/195/1985 (1990).

Dias v Angola, UN Doc CCPR/C/39/D/ 711/1996 (2000).

Guzzardi v Italy, Ser. A, No 39 (1980).

Loukanov v Bulgaria, ECHR 1997, Vol 1997-II, No 34

Mojica v Dominican Republic, UN Doc. CCPR/C/51/D/449/1991 (1994).

Monnell and Morris v United Kingdom, Ser A, No 115 (1987).

Nielsen v Denmark, Ser. A, No 144 (1988).

Oló Bahamonde v Equatorial Guinea, UN Doc CCPR/C/49/D/468/1991 (1993).

Párkányi v Hungary, UN Doc CCPR/C/45/D/410/1990 (1992).

Schmidt v Germany, Ser A, No 291-B (1994).

Valcada v Uruguay, UN Doc CCPR/C/8/D/9/1977 (1979).
Van der Mussele v Belgium, Ser A, No 70 (1983).
Van Droogenbroeck v Belgium, Ser A, No 44 (1982).

READING

Clark, D, and McCoy, G, *The Most Fundamental Right: Habeus Corpus in the Commonwealth* (Oxford: Oxford University Press, 2000).

Farrior, S, 'The international law on trafficking in women and children for prostitution: Making it live up to its potential' (1997) 10 Harvard Human Rights Journal 213.

Gallagher, A, 'Human rights and the new UN Protocols on trafficking and migrant smuggling: A preliminary analysis' (2001) 23(4) Human Rights Quarterly 975–1004.

Kock, IE 'Social rights as components in the civil right to personal liberty: Another step forward in the integrated human rights approach' (2002) 20(1) Netherlands Quarterly of Human Rights 29–51.

Lassen, N, 'Article 4' in G Alfredsson and A Eide (eds), *The Universal Declaration of Human Rights: A common standard of achievement* (The Hague: Martinus Nijhoff, 1999) 103–19.

Morgan, R, and Evans, MD, *Protecting Prisoners: The standards of the European Committee for the Prevention of Torture in context* (Oxford: Oxford University Press, 1999).

Niemi-Kiesiläinen, J. 'Article 9' in G Alfredsson and A Eide (eds), *The Universal Declaration of Human Rights: A common standard of achievement* (The Hague: Martinus Nijhoff, 1999).

Nowak, M, 'Civil and political rights' in J Symonides (ed), *Human Rights: Concept and standards* (Aldershot: Dartmouth, 2000) 69–107.

Office of the High Commissioner for Human Rights, *Fact Sheet No 14: Contemporary forms of slavery* (Geneva: OHCHR, 1996).

Quirk, J, 'The anti-slavery project: Linking the historical and contemporary' (2006) 28(3) Human Rights Quarterly 565–98.

United Nations, *Study on the Right of Everyone to be Free from Arbitrary Arrest, Detention and Exile* (New York: UN Publication, 1965).

United Nations Human Rights Committee General Comments Nos 8, 9, and 21, reprinted in UN Doc HRI/GEN/1/Rev.9 (Vol I).

WEBSITES

www.ilo.org—The International Labour Organization.

www.ilo.org/public/english/standards/ipec/index.htm—The International Programme for the Elimination of Child Labour.

www.interpol.int/Public/THB/default.asp—INTERPOL Children and Human Trafficking.

www.unicef.org—UNICEF.

www2.ohchr.org/english/issues/children/rapporteur/index.htm—Special Rapporteur of the Commission on Human Rights on the sale of children, child prostitution and child pornography.

www.antislavery.org—NGO focusing on eliminating slavery and analogous practices.

www2.ohchr.org/english/issues/trafficking/index.htm—Special Rapporteur on trafficking in persons, especially in women and children.

16

Equality before the law—the right to a fair trial

Everyone has the right to recognition everywhere as a person before the law ... All are equal before the law ... Everyone is entitled in full equality to a fair and public hearing by an independent and impartial tribunal, in the determination of his rights and obligations and of any criminal charge against him ... Everyone charged with a penal offence has the right to be presumed innocent until proven guilty according to law in a public trial at which he has had all the guarantees necessary for his defence. None shall be held guilty of any penal offence on account of any act or omission which did not constitute a penal offence, under national or international law, at the same time when it was committed. Nor shall a heavier penalty be imposed than the one that was applicable at the time the penal offence was committed. [compiled from Arts 6, 7, 10, 11, UDHR: see also Arts 14–16, ICCPR; Arts 6–7, ECHR and Arts 2–4, Protocol 7; Arts 3, 8–10, ACHR; Arts 3 and 7, ACHPR; Arts 6–7, CIS; Arts. 12–13, 15–19, AL]

One of the cornerstones of the rule of law itself is the notion of a fair trial. The common philosophical origin and thus the interdependence of the rule of law and human rights is highly apparent in the right to a fair trial. Fair trials form an essential part of all legal systems which purport to be founded on the rule of law. Such fairness demands a fair judicial process administered by an impartial judiciary.

The right to equality before the law is distinct from the provisions on equality of persons and the freedom from discrimination although there is a degree of overlap. Equality before the law requires all individuals to have equal access to the courts and to be viewed in law in a non-discriminatory manner, especially with respect to the judicial determination of their rights and freedoms under international human rights law. International human rights demand that all persons can access and use the law in the determination of their rights and duties. A number of factors are incorporated: inter alia, the presumption of innocence, the right to a fair trial, the right to a public trial, a speedy determination of the law, the right to an adequate defence, the right to appeal, and compensation in the event of a mistrial.

The Universal Declaration of Human Rights was adopted from a newly established position of equality of all persons and non-discrimination. It is natural that these concepts should underpin the codified laws on equality before the law and fair trials. The Human Rights Committee in its thirteenth General Comment (1984) elaborated the related provisions of the International Covenant. Without a doubt, the provisions on the right to a fair trial have received most judicial consideration at the regional level, particularly within Europe where the equivalent provision (Art 6) has proven the most common ground of jurisdiction in cases brought before the European Court thereby giving rise to comprehensive jurisprudence.

For reasons of space, it is impossible to provide more than an overview of the associated rights and jurisprudence in the current text. As has been stated, the right to a fair trial is one of the most inventively elaborated and dynamically interpreted rights today, it is 'judge-made law' in the true sense of the word, constantly developing (Lehtimaja, L, and Pellonpää, M, p 225). Reference should be had to the more specialized texts on the various international and regional instruments for more detailed analysis. This chapter will overview the right to be recognized as a person before the law/equality and the prohibition on retroactive penal legislation before considering the position of courts under the law, the presumption of innocence, and those rights which accrue primarily to accused persons.

16.1 Recognition, equality, and access issues

Everyone has the right to recognition everywhere as a person before the law. [Art 6, UDHR: see also Arts 16 and 26, ICCPR; Art 3, ACHR; Art 5, ACHPR; Art 9, AL]

The first and certainly most crucial aspect of those rights associated with a fair trial is the right to be recognized as a person before the law. Clearly non-recognition presents severe challenges to the individual wishing to enforce rights before, or even appear before, a court or tribunal. One also has the right to be treated equally by the courts and, as has emerged through jurisprudence, every person has the right of access to courts.

16.1.1 Recognition as a person before the law

The right to recognition as a person before the law is embedded in the concept of the right to an existence. It enables the individual to enter into certain legal obligations including contracts and facilitates the exercise and enforcement of rights before the courts. Every person thus has the right to bear legal rights and obligations. It is not open to a State to subject a citizen to a 'civil death', that is to deprive an individual of legal personality. Any total or partial denial of legal personality will infringe these provisions.

The American Convention on Human Rights has the right to recognition as a person before the law tabled as the first civil and political right (Art 3). It is, moreover, a non-derogable right in terms of the International Covenant on Civil and Political Rights in reflection of its importance. After the right to life, it is arguably the pre-eminent right for individuals as non-recognition as a person before the law precludes the exercise of all other rights. In bygone years, slaves were denied recognition as legal persons, being regarded as the legal property of their owners. More recently, under South Africa's apartheid regime, racial criteria determined legal rights. In other regions, there are examples of indigenous peoples, minorities, and refugees/asylum seekers being denied legal status, and thus encountering problems when trying to engage with national laws.

Recognition as a person before the law facilitates enforcement of rights and freedoms derived from international human rights instruments. As human rights accrue to all persons, the recognition of personification is an essential prerequisite to the enjoyment of those rights. Fair trial procedures should be used in all court proceedings to ensure the rule of law is respected.

16.1.2 **Lack of capacity to enter legal obligations**

Recognition as a person before the law does not, *ipso facto*, require that the individual has full legal capacity. Minors and those lacking mental capacity, for example, though having no legal capacity to enter into contracts or conduct business, are still recognized as persons before the law. The law relating to children's rights that focus on the best interests of the child and many national laws relating to individuals with mental health problems corroborate this. Should the rights of such people be compromised, it is normal for their interests to be represented by another person or party. For example, if a person lacks the capacity to enter obligations, a legal guardian may be appointed to act on his or her behalf, always ensuring that the best interests of the individual concerned are pre-eminent. Such legal guardians may be appointed by the court or by those responsible for the individual concerned. However, note that in some parts of the world, lack of legal capacity does equal denial of legal recognition.

It should be noted that Art 12 of the Convention on the Rights of the Child envisages an evolving capacity of a minor, commensurate with individual development. Moreover, where criminal charges are concerned, international human rights law requires that very young children do not have full criminal responsibility. Article 40(3)(a) imposes an obligation on State Parties to promote the establishment of laws and procedures with the aim of establishing a minimum age below which a presumption of non-infringement of penal law applies. Very young children are thus deemed not to have the legal capacity to commit crimes.

16.1.3 **Problems with defining 'persons'**

In essence, the right to be a person before the law means that once national law recognizes you as a person (usually after birth—but see the discussion on the parameters of the right to life in Chapter 13), then you assume the rights and duties of all people. From thenceforth forward, you are entitled to exercise all ascribed rights. Given the disparities between different States on the start of the right to life and the time of legal death, recognition is not necessarily transnational. Adding in conflict of laws/private international law, there is the theoretical possibility of some

 Discussion topic

Age of criminal responsibility

The UN Committee on the Rights of the Child is working steadily towards raising the age of criminal responsibility to eighteen. This is controversial in many States. In 2009, Indonesia and Scotland, for example, are discussing raising the age of criminal responsibility from eight to twelve years. China, in contrast, has a tiered system of responsibility with limited responsibility for those from 14–16 years, and no responsibility below that age.

Debate continues among many sectors of society over whether children (under eighteen) should be held criminally responsible for their actions and, if so, what modifications to the adult criminal justice system are required to protect a child.

borderline cases in which individuals are deemed to be alive and thus a 'person' in one State, but not in another. Such cases are rare but have potential implications for national laws and, occasionally, international human rights.

16.1.4 Equality of persons before the law

A further extension of this right may be found when the notion of equality is added. The concept of equality before the courts can be traced to Art 7 of the 1789 French Declaration. Everyone has the right to equality before the courts and tribunals of law. Consequently, restricting capacity to sue in respect of matrimonial property to the male partner infringed the International Covenant on Civil and Political Rights (*Ato del Avellanal v Peru*) as did differing burdens of proof for male and female social security claimants in the Netherlands (*Broecks v Netherlands*). Equal protection of the law is also often demanded by international human rights, thus when Mauritian laws enabled foreign husbands of Mauritian women to be deported but not for-eign wives of Mauritian men, Mauritian law was held to run contrary to the notion of equal protection of the law. Families were not accorded equal protection, thus Arts 2(1), 3 and 26 of the International Covenant on Civil and Political Rights were found by the Human Rights Committee to have been violated (*Aumeeruddy-Cziffra v Mauritius*).

A General Comment issued by the Human Rights Committee provides further information on the prohibition of discrimination before the law (No 18 (1989)): although noting that the Covenant does not define 'discrimination', the Committee believes that the term should imply 'any distinction, exclusion, restriction or prefer-ence which is based on any ground such as race, colour, sex, language, religion or other opinion, national or social origin, property, birth or other status, and which has the effect of nullifying or impairing recognition, enjoyment or exercise by all persons, on an equal footing, of all rights and freedoms' (para 7). The need for affir-mative action is accepted (para 10) while the inherent non-equality principles are noted—eg, the prohibition on the death penalty being carried out on those below eighteen years (para 8). The Committee considers that Art 26 of the Covenant pro-vides an autonomous right, prohibiting discrimination in law or in fact (para 12).

16.1.5 A right of access to a court?

With the Council of Europe, elements of this have been extended to the articula-tion of a general right of access to a court. The landmark case is that of *Golder v United Kingdom*. The applicant had been convicted of robbery with violence and imprisoned in Parkhurst Prison. He was subsequently implicated in a disturbance within the prison and accused of assaulting a prison officer though was eventu-ally exonerated due to mistaken identity. Thereafter, Golder decided to bring a civil action (libel) against the prison officer to ensure his prison file did not reflect his alleged wrongdoing. However, the Home Office refused Golder access to a solicitor for this purpose. On the basis of this refusal, Golder took his complaint to the Euro-pean Commission on Human Rights. Both the Commission and, subsequently, the Court of Human Rights concluded that Golder's rights under the European Conven-tion had been violated. The Court stated that Art 6 'embodies a "right to a court", of which the right to access, that is the right to institute proceedings before courts in civil matters, constitutes one aspect only' (para 36). Subsequent cases in Europe have expanded this line of thinking—*Airey v Ireland* demonstrated that access must be effective access, hindrance was just as likely to violate the Convention as would a legal impediment to access. In that case, the applicant had been indirectly denied access to a court through the refusal of legal aid to seek a judicial separation. Mrs. Airey could go to the court and represent herself and thus technically could access a court. However, the European Court held that due to the complexity of such actions, the applicant could not reasonably be expected to bring the action herself. Accordingly, the denial of legal aid resulted in a violation of Art 6(1). More recently, the European Court decided that the need for multiple Ministerial certificates on security issues occasioned a violation of Art 6(1) when the applicant was trying to claim discrimination in Northern Ireland (*Tinnelly and McElduff v United Kingdom*).

It is clear from this line of cases that the right to recognition as a person before the law entails not only recognition of legal personality, but also equality of treatment and a right of effective access to courts for the judicial determination of disputes. This can impose a significant burden on a State, especially when financial support, such as legal aid, is required to facilitate the realization of the right. However, the importance of equal access to the courts to the concept of the rule of law, which underpins these human rights, is paramount. It is reasonable to expect similar lines of reasoning to be adopted by other regional and international bodies faced with questions of access to courts.

16.2 Prohibition on retroactive penal legislation

No one shall be held guilty for any penal offence on account of any act or omission which did not constitute a penal offence, under national or international law, at the time when it was committed. Nor shall a heavier penalty be imposed than the one that was applicable at the time the penal offence was committed. [Art 11(2), UDHR: see also Art 15, ICCPR; Art 7, ECHR; Art 9, ACHR; Art 7(2), ACHPR; Art 7, CIS; Art 6, AL]

Basic concepts of fairness and justice require that one cannot be punished for something which was not a crime at the time it was committed—*nullum crimen sine lege* and *nulla poena sine lege*. The Rome Statute of the International Criminal Court codifies these principles in Arts 22–3. Although 'ignorance of the law is no excuse', it is essential that individuals can ascertain the content of the laws which govern their behaviour should they so wish. The prohibition on retroactive penal legislation is linked to the right to a fair trial, as it is irrevocably an example of an unfair trial. Legal certainty demands that criminal offences are defined and prescribed in law. The prohibition on retroactivity of laws finds early expression in the Constitution of the United States 1787 and in the earlier Declarations of Rights adopted by various North American colonies.

16.2.1 National and international crimes

As the Universal Declaration makes clear, individuals can be held responsible for violations of international law, even if national law does not render the offence a crime. Thus an individual committing piracy, implicated in genocide, or even setting up a paedophile ring may be in violation of international law—the Geneva Convention on the High Seas 1958, the Genocide Convention, and the Convention on the Rights of the Child further elaborate these 'crimes'. The latter is not an international crime per se but it may be argued that the Convention on the Rights of the Child (and Protocol) provides a legal basis for criminalization of such activity. Crimes against humanity have long been condemned under international (sometimes customary) law. Additional criminal jurisdiction is provided with the establishment of the International Criminal Court. Naturally the International Criminal Court is also bound by these provisions thus there is a guarantee to individuals that they will not be held accountable at the international level for actions which were not deemed criminal at the time of commission or omission.

The inclusion of 'international law' provides the State with a wider scope for punishing crimes than mere reliance on national criminal law. Consequently many States have enacted legislation facilitating the prosecution of individuals found within their jurisdiction who have committed war crimes, crimes against humanity, specified acts of terrorism, piracy, and hijacking as defined and provided for under the salient international treaties. As the act was a 'crime' under international law at the time it was committed, there is no issue of retroactivity of criminal legislation. Article 5 of the Statute of the International Criminal Court limits the jurisdiction of the Court to the 'most serious crimes of concern to the international community as a whole': genocide, crimes against humanity, war crimes, and crimes of aggression. Further elaboration is provided within the Statute.

16.2.2 Defining crimes

In many States, there is a criminal code which tabulates criminal offences. In other States, a variety of individual laws provide the basis for action. The precise scope of the crime should be clear. Occasionally, laws provide that mere criminal intention is suffice to give rise to liability. In most legal systems, there is an inherent flexibility which allows judicial teleological interpretation to effect punishment of criminal activity which is not proscribed in national law. This is likely to be used in very restrictive situations—most likely in common-law traditions, and for the punishment of offences with clear evidence of criminal intent.

16.2.3 Examples of violations

Many States have been found lacking in respect of this right. In several cases against Uruguay, the Human Rights Committee found violations. In *Weinberger v Uruguay*, the author was convicted for membership of a political party which was subsequently banned, while in *Pietraroia v Uruguay*, the charge was one of subversive association with a trade union, the activities of which were lawful at the salient time (albeit subsequently outlawed). In *Ireland v United Kingdom*, the United Kingdom had enacted a provision for retroactive penal legislation. However, as the government gave an undertaking that no one had been or would be convicted under the legislation, this aspect of the complaint lodged against the United Kingdom was dropped. Most courts have recourse to these fundamental principles—for example the European Court of Justice in *Regina v Kent Kirk*.

Given the recent profile of the two International Tribunals for Rwanda and the former Yugoslavia, respectively, it should be noted that the United Nations authorities apply customary international and humanitarian law as well as codified laws such as that found in the Geneva and Hague Conventions on the conduct of war and genocide. The progressive criminalization of international humanitarian law is, apparently, acceptable (*International Prosecutor v Duško Tadi*). The enforcement of international humanitarian law through the international justice system will further strengthen the law in this area. In this respect, the work of the International Criminal Court is awaited; in the interim, the spate of national cases in the US and UK military tribunals, and the special court systems in, for example, Iraq, Cambodia and Sierra Leone is noted.

16.3 What are 'courts and tribunals'?

Before a more detailed examination of the right to a fair trial can begin, it is necessary to establish what bodies constitute courts and tribunals and thus are obligated to conduct proceedings fairly. Essentially, all courts and tribunals, whatever their form, are covered by the terms of the provisions. Accordingly, many entities not entitled 'court' may be covered. The key requirement is that the body functions as a court—adjudicating on disputes and ascertaining a solution with reference to the law.

Key case

Kavanagh v Ireland, UN Doc CCPR/C/71/D/819/1998

The author was tried by a special criminal tribunal. These were established temporarily in the 1970s, with the caveat that:

if at any time the Government or the Parliament is satisfied that the ordinary courts are again adequate to secure the effective administration of justice and the preservation of public peace and order, a rescinding proclamation or resolution, respectively, shall be made terminating the Special Criminal Court regime. [Para 2.1]

Special Criminal Courts operated with a panel of three judges, no jury, and a different set of procedures. Kavanagh challenged the use of the special court process. The Human Rights Committee found that Ireland had:

failed to demonstrate that the decision to try the author before the Special Criminal Court was based upon reasonable and objective grounds. Accordingly, the Committee concludes that the author's right under article 26 to equality before the law and to the equal protection of the law has been violated. [Para 10.3]

Countries establishing special tribunals to try alleged terrorists and war criminals are required to ensure that there are good reasons for electing to prosecute in such fora.

As with other aspects of human rights law, there is no solitary static definition which applies, no exhaustive list of entities which are covered. States may periodically create new bodies which have court-like functions and so these too may fall within the ambit of regional and international regulation. The Human Rights Committee has closely examined a plethora of ad hoc bodies which appear to dispense justice in States, including temporary bodies. Military and revolutionary courts and tribunals are generally covered but their existence occasions more detailed consideration by the Committee due to the potential for bias, etc. Special attention is also paid to the conduct of Shari'a courts and any 'special courts' noted in the initial or periodic reports of States.

Administrative bodies may be covered—in *Albert and Le Compte v Belgium*, the European Court of Human Rights considered a professional medical association which conducted disciplinary hearings to fall within the ambit of Art 6(1) of the European Convention, while in *Zumbotel v Austria*, the order made by a government office regarding expropriation complied as there was a viable appeal process to the Austrian Administrative Court.

It is clear from the foregoing that human rights monitoring bodies will adopt a broad view of what is meant by a court or tribunal. If the body concerned appears to be settling disputes and adjudicating in accordance with law, the interests of justice demand that it functions in accordance with the provisions tabulating the right to a fair trial.

16.3.1 The treaty-monitoring bodies?

Note that the various international human rights monitoring bodies are not regarded as courts. The role of these bodies is to supervise the implementation of the various human rights documents by member States. Even when reviewing individual communications, there is no judicial framework—the Committee merely delivers views on the extent to which the facts before it evidence compliance with the obligations assumed by the States under the instrument in question. In contrast, the International Criminal Court will be regarded as a court and will thus be bound by the principles relating to fair trials (as mentioned, these provisions are laid out in detail in the Statute of the Court).

16.4 An independent and impartial court

The interests of justice are best served by an independent judiciary adjudicating on the merits of a given case based on application of the salient law. To this end, there should be a separation of powers between the executive and judiciary in the State. Article 41(2) of the Statute of the International Criminal Court provides that '[a] judge shall not participate in any case in which his or impartiality might reasonably be doubted on any ground'. Among the issues considered here will be the rules and procedures governing appointment and dismissal of judges, the terms and conditions of service of judges, the qualifications and training required and undertaken by judges, and also the procedural, specific, and legal guarantees that seek to secure the impartiality of the judiciary. General Comments No 13+32 issued

> ### Key case
>
> **Human Rights Committee General Comment 32 (2007) UN Doc CCPR/C/GC/32**
>
> General Comment 32 replaces General Comment 13 (1984). On independence of the judiciary, the Committee notes: 'The requirement of competence, independence and impartiality of a tribunal in the sense of article 14, paragraph 1, is an absolute right that is not subject to any exception. The requirement of independence refers, in particular, to the procedure and qualifications for the appointment of judges, and guarantees relating to their security of tenure until a mandatory retirement age or the expiry of their term of office, where such exist, the conditions governing promotion, transfer, suspension and cessation of their functions, and the actual independence of the judiciary from political interference by the executive branch and legislature. States should take specific measures guaranteeing the independence of the judiciary, protecting judges from any form of political influence in their decision-making through the constitution or adoption of laws establishing clear procedures and objective criteria for the appointment, remuneration, tenure, promotion, suspension and dismissal of the members of the judiciary and disciplinary sanctions taken against them. A situation where the functions and competencies of the judiciary and the executive are not clearly distinguishable or where the latter is able to control or direct the former is incompatible with the notion of an independent tribunal. It is necessary to protect judges against conflicts of interest and intimidation. In order to safeguard their independence, the status of judges, including their term of office, their independence, security, adequate remuneration, conditions of service, pensions and the age of retirement shall be adequately secured by law.' (para 19).

by the Human Rights Committee states that impartiality and independence should be established with reference not only to the above criteria but also to the actual independence of the judiciary from the executive branch and legislature.

16.4.1 Jurisprudence

A considerable volume of jurisprudence on the subject has emanated from the European Court of Human Rights. The European Court indicates the factors to be addressed when considering if a body is independent: 'the manner of appointment of its members and the duration of their term of office, the existence of guarantees against outside pressures and the question whether the body presents an appearance of independence' (*Campbell and Fell v United Kingdom*, para 78). Judges who are closely connected in a personal capacity to the complaint being heard may not be regarded as impartial (see, for example, *Demicolo v Malta*). The same principles govern jury trials—any jury deciding a case should be independent and impartial—links between members of the jury and the defendants or prosecutors may also be found to contravene the provisions on fair trial (eg, *Holm v Sweden*). It appears from the jurisprudence that the entire process should be overviewed by an impartial and independent body. Hence in the case of *V v United Kingdom*, the European Court on Human Rights queried the practice of the United Kingdom

Home Secretary determining the minimum length of imprisonment for a convicted murderer sentenced to be detained 'during Her Majesty's pleasure' (para 114). The Home Secretary was clearly not independent of the executive. The United Kingdom responded swiftly with the Home Secretary referring the case to the Lord Chief Justice for determination of length of sentence. Given V was one of the juveniles convicted for murdering the toddler James Bulger, this decision attracted a lot of publicity in the United Kingdom.

The role of State prosecutors and the use of Advocates General has also been scrutinized (eg, UN Guidelines on the Role of Prosecutors). Care must be taken to ensure that such people are also subject to the stringent requirements of the judiciary as regards appointment and independence. In many States, such appointees serve as preliminary investigators. This can give rise to substantial queries over the independence and impartiality of the judiciary. To ensure impartiality is maintained, Art 41(2)(a) of the Statute of the International Criminal Court provides that a judge shall be disqualified from cases before the Court if he or she has previously been involved with that case at any level and in any capacity. Such a strict separation of function is lacking in some national systems. For example, in Belgium, judges can act as investigating judges before the trial—this may give rise to public doubt over impartiality (*DeCubber v Belgium*). A judge sitting on a case who had previously been head of the public prosecutor's department at the time the case was being investigated has been held to breach an objective test of impartiality (*Piersack v Belgium*). Thereafter, a judge taking over the role of prosecution during a trial gave rise to a legitimate doubt over impartiality in the case of *Thorgeirson v Iceland*. Judges should not preside over more than one stage of the process. Consequently, a judge who has sat on the initial trial should not sit on an appellate trial for the same case (*Oberschlick v Austria*).

It is a matter of degree and each decision of the international and regional bodies turns on the particular facts of the case. As a general rule of thumb, an appearance of bias may be sufficient to give rise to a complaint. Certainly in Europe, an objective test is applied and many violations have been found based on what appears to be injustice rather than any proven impartiality on the part of the judge in question. A high standard of independence is clearly required.

The operation of military courts and tribunals has been noted as a potential problem area by both international and regional organizations. General Comment 13 of the Human Rights Committee states that military courts or tribunals which try civilians can present 'serious problems as far as the equitable, impartial and independent administration of justice is concerned' (para 4). Accordingly, the Committee seeks detailed comments from States in their reports on the safeguards in place to protect civilians being tried in such courts.

16.5 Presumption of innocence

Everyone charged with a penal offence has the right to be presumed innocent until proven guilty according to law in a public trial at which he has had all the guarantees necessary for his defence. [Art 11(1), UDHR: see also Art. 14(2), ICCPR; Art 6(2), ECHR; Art 8(2), ACHR; Art 7(1) (b), ACHPR; Art 6(2), CIS; Art 7, AL; Art 66, Statute of the International Criminal Court]

The presumption of innocence is an essential principle of a fair trial and a cornerstone of democratic society, a universally accepted rule of natural justice. It can be found in early human rights documentation such as the 1789 Declaration on the Rights of Man. An accused is entitled to be regarded as innocent until guilt is established pursuant to the criminal legal process. This right does not mean that an individual cannot be incarcerated pending trial—detention following arrest is lawful under all human rights conventions, albeit subject to controls (Chapter 15). The presumption of innocence is essentially a procedural guarantee—the adjudicators must commence proceedings with an open mind and no preconceived notions of guilt. The burden of proof is on the State bringing the criminal action; it must prove the guilt of the accused. The finding of guilt must be based on the evidence, whether direct or indirect, which is led before the Court. However, statutory offences (strict or automatic liability) do not, prima facie, violate international human rights. Authority for this may be obtained from the European case of *Salabiaku v France*, in which the French courts had convicted the applicant of drug smuggling. He had been caught at an airport with a quantity of cannabis in his luggage. The presumption in French law that such possession was smuggling was held not to be a violation of the European Convention's presumption of innocence.

However, international law does recognize that the burden of proof may shift to the accused in certain situations. For example, an accused relying on a special defence may be required to justify its invocation—in the case of *Lingens v Austria*, the onus was on the applicant to prove veritas as a defence in a libel action. In general the mechanics for securing a rebuttal of the presumption of innocence is a matter for national law.

As a general principle, in criminal trials, proof must be beyond reasonable doubt. Attempts to incorporate this standard into the International Covenant on Civil and Political Rights failed although in General Comment No 13, para 7, the Human Rights Committee states that '[n]o guilt can be presumed until the charge has been proved beyond reasonable doubt'. Now, however, Art 66(3) of the Statute of the International Criminal Court applies this standard to trials conducted before the court. At the regional level, the European Court of Human Rights has endorsed the notion that any doubt should benefit the accused but has not elaborated further (*Barberà, Messegué and Jabardo v Spain*).

The presumption of innocence also extends to State protection against excessive or prejudicial media coverage. For example, in a high-profile criminal trial with a jury, the State must take reasonable steps to ensure that the jury will not be prejudiced in their deliberations by the publicity received. For this reason, many States impose embargoes on matters under investigation and trial. In the case of *Gridin v Russian Federation*, there had been a wide media profile of the case, including reports of public statements made by high ranking law enforcement official portraying the author of the communication as guilty. The author was eventually convicted of murder, attempted rape and various assaults. His death sentence was commuted to life imprisonment. Referring to General Comment No 13 on Art 14, the Human Rights Committee considered that the presumption of innocence had been violated as the public authorities had not exercised the required restraint in refraining from prejudicing the outcome of the trial.

Attempts have been made to extend this right to a more general freedom from self-incrimination. In articulating the minimum guarantees for accused persons in criminal trials, Art 14(3)(g) of the International Covenant on Civil and Political Rights provides that an individual should not be compelled to confess guilt or testify against himself. Article 55(1)(a) of the Statute of the International Criminal Court makes similar provision for the conduct of investigations thereunder. The main communications considered under this section by the Human Rights Committee have involved allegations of confessions extracted under duress. For example, in *Estrella v Uruguay*, the accused was a professional pianist who alleged that he had been threatened with dismemberment of his hands should he fail to admit subversive activities. This was held to be a violation of the Covenant though it should be noted that the opinion of the Committee was given in default—Uruguay refused to submit observations on the complaint.

The communication from *López v Spain* raised issues of self-incrimination. However, the complaint was found inadmissible as the penalty imposed on the author was for a failure to cooperate with the authorities (in the instant case by identifying who had been driving his vehicle when it was clocked speeding by a police radar) not for failure to incriminate himself by confessing to be the driver. This is an interesting decision when compared to similar decisions under the European Convention. In a series of cases (including *Funke v France*), the European Court of Human Rights has reiterated its view that the right to remain silent under police questioning and the privilege against self-incrimination are generally recognized international standards which lie at the notion of a fair procedure (*Murray v United Kingdom*, para 45). However, certain inferences may be drawn from the evidence led and the silence in the face thereof. Thus, in *Murray v United Kingdom*, there was no violation of the European Convention as the applicant had, through silence, failed to explain his presence at a property in Northern Ireland where a suspected IRA informer was also found. The suspected informer had been unlawfully detained, allegedly by Murray and others, interrogated and, it was claimed, plans were afoot to have him killed. In such a situation, inferences could be drawn about the presence of the accused in the property.

The Statute of the International Criminal Court details rights of silence and freedom from self-incrimination for the accused person in Art 55(1)(a) and (2)(b), and Art 67(g).

16.6 Minimum guarantees for criminal trials

International instruments on the rights of peoples to fair trials draw heavily on notions of *egalité des armes*, the need for both parties in a dispute to be on an equal footing. Magna Carta is often regarded as one of the first instruments which documented 'due process'. This concept underpins the notion of all fair criminal trials, providing a set of procedural and legal guarantees for the accused person. The rights most commonly accorded to accused persons may now be found in Art 67 of the Statute of the International Criminal Court. It would appear that the principle of equality before the law requires not only equality between accused persons (freedom from discrimination) but also equality between the accused and the State in relative terms. Hence, many States have extensive procedural and evidential requirements which seek to ensure that the parties have the opportunity to prepare and defend allegations and witness testimony. Inevitably, when the State is prosecuting an individual, an element of David and Goliath will be perceived. It is the role of human rights to ensure that the rights of the individual are not compromised and justice is thus fully served. International human rights also impose on national courts an obligation to investigate any claims of infringing behaviour during the trial. In accordance with the old adage, it is not enough that justice is done; it must also be seen to be done.

16.6.1 The language of the trial and charges

Defendants must be informed of the charge(s) against them in a language which they understand and must be given appropriate time to prepare a defence thereto.

The language requirement is of fundamental importance as an accused cannot be expected to respond to allegations without knowing the substance of them. Notification of charges should be prompt, preferably as soon as a competent authority first makes the charge. It may be necessary for a State to provide interpretation and translation facilities when charging those who do not speak the language of the State concerned. The onus is on the State to prove that all due steps were taken to ensure that the accused understood the charges levied. In the case of the International Covenant, the charge should be stated either orally or in writing, indicating both the law and the alleged facts on which it is based (General Comment No 13, para 8). The accused person has no right to select the language in which the charges are made. Thus, for example, a bilingual French/Spanish speaker arrested in Cameroon may not insist on being charged in Spanish if French is used. Similarly, individuals may not seek to use a regional language if they understand competently the official language of the court in question. This was illustrated in the case of *Barzhig v France*—the author of this communication to the United Nations Human Rights Committee claimed that France infringed the Covenant by refusing to provide an interpreter during his trial. The author was a French citizen, resident in Brittany, who wished to conduct the trial in Breton. However, the State conducted the trial in French as the accused and witnesses were francophone. Following a pronouncement that individuals may not expect to choose any language for a trial, the Human Rights Committee decided that there was no violation of the Covenant. Although perhaps not particularly supportive of minority languages, this decision and others like it are certainly in accordance with the notion of a fair trial. As this communication illustrates, the right is to be informed of charges made and to partake in a trial held in a language which is understood. There is no right to select the language of trial. In a case before the European Court of Human Rights, *Brozicek v Italy*, the accused was charged with tearing down political flags and injuring a police officer in Italy. The applicant was a Czechoslovakian-born German resident. In response to a communication from the Italian authorities, he wrote to the Italian authorities, claiming he would receive communications about his trial either in German or in any official language of the United Nations (French, English, Russian, Chinese, Spanish) but not in Italian which he did not understand. The Italian authorities continued to send materials to the accused in Italian thereby violating the European Convention.

As this case suggests, there is an onus on the accused person to notify the court in question of any linguistic issues. Although the onus is on the State to ensure that charges levied against a person are understood fully, the State is permitted to assume comprehension of the language of the court unless there are indications to the contrary.

An accused must thus indicate if the use of an interpreter is necessary and, indeed, whether any translation facilities which are provided are appropriate (see *Griffin v Spain*— the Canadian author had raised no objections during the trial to being tried in Spain with the assistance of an interpreter who spoke little English and who therefore translated into French, a language in which the author had only a basic understanding. The Human Rights Committee held there had been no violation even although the eventual conviction was allegedly based on a response to a mistranslated question).

The images of the trial at Camp Zeist in the Netherlands of the two people suspected of involvement in the bombing of Pan Am flight 103 were characterized by the presence of interpreters, both for the accused persons and for the judges. Although this was a domestic (Scots law) trial, its conformity to international standards is beyond question in this regard. The conduct of the International Criminal Tribunals is similar with comprehensive translation facilities provided, while the Statute of the International Criminal Court prescribes a right for the accused to have competent translation and interpretation facilities before (Art 55(1)(c)) and during (Art 67(f)) the trial.

It should also be noted that the interests of fairness demand that any essential translation and interpretation costs be borne by the State. Clearly, forcing the accused to pay in order to be tried runs contrary to the notion of equality before the law. The Human Rights Committee, for example in its General Comment No 13, concludes that free interpretation must be provided where necessary and the costs must be met by the State, irrespective of the outcome of the case. Translation costs cannot be a punitive measure.

16.6.2 Adequate time and facilities to prepare and conduct a defence

Clearly, international human rights law will not condone so-called 'kangaroo courts'. Accused persons have the right to prepare an appropriate defence to the charges which have been levied. Consequently, those charged must be allowed access to potential legal counsel and free communication with any such counsel, witnesses must be permitted to be called and examined in court, with appropriate cross-examination of any witnesses called by the prosecution. The Human Rights Committee has even had cause to point out that any court-appointed counsel should be legally trained (*Vasilskis v Uruguay*). In that case, the Military Court had appointed a non-lawyer as defence counsel for the applicant when charged (and convicted) of being a member of the Tupamaros National Liberation Movement. On appeal, her sentence had been increased to thirty years' rigorous imprisonment and from five to ten years' precautionary detention.

As a variety of cases prove, holding an accused person incommunicado with no access to counsel is a clear violation of human rights. The State is obligated to facilitate some kind of channel of communication between a detained suspect and any appointed legal counsel. For this reason, prisoners have visiting rights and communication rights with counsel. The specifics of each case is dependant on the circumstances of each case; communication may be written, oral, or in person. The period of political upheaval in Latin America provided many infringing cases with accused persons being denied access to counsel, time, or facilities to compile a proper defence. In many of these instances, there was no trial, or even indictment— the suspects were detained nevertheless.

Discussion topic

Reasonable length of time for a trial

The question of what is a reasonable length of time for a trial is fraught with potentially conflicting issues. Too short a length of time and there may be inadequate opportunities to present a defence, too protracted a process and human rights are also infringed. A number of factors influence the balance—the volume of essential evidence, availability of witnesses and courtroom, the complexity of the evidence etc. In *Muñoz v Peru*, UN Doc CCPR/C/34/D/203/1986, seven years was unreasonable; in *Kelly v Jamaica*, UN Doc CCPR/C/41/D/253/1987, one and a half years not unreasonable; in *Morael v France*, UN Doc CCPR/C/36/D/207/1986, as the bankruptcy proceedings were complicated, almost four years of proceedings not unreasonable; in *Bozize v Central African Republic*, UN Doc CCPR/C/50/D/428/1990, over four years' detention without first-instance trial was a violation of Art 14, ICCPR; in *Lubuto v Zambia*, UN Doc CCPR/C/55/D/390/1990, eight years from arrest to the Supreme Court dismissing the final appeal was also unreasonable, irrespective of the difficult economic situation of the State.

The question of reasonableness does indeed depend on all the facts and circumstances of the individual case. The same range of times and diverse findings is found in the jurisprudence of the European Court of Human Rights, the international body with the greatest number of cases on the right to a fair trial.

In *Setelich on behalf of Antonaccio v Uruguay*, one of the earlier cases on this point, various violations of the right to a fair trial were found by the Human Rights Committee. The fact that the author of the communication had not been able to communicate with his appointed counsel was considered to prevent the preparation of a proper defence while the failure of a military tribunal to permit Antonaccio to call witnesses in his defence was also held to be an infringement of Art 14 of the International Covenant on Civil and Political Rights. Any appointed counsel must consult with the accused and be actively involved in the preparation of the defence. This is particularly true in schemes operated in many States where public defence lawyers are assigned to cases. The assigned counsel must regularly meet with the accused and prepare the case with due diligence (see also *Oxandabarat on behalf of Scarrone v Uruguay*).

In spite of the emphasis on equality of the parties before the courts and full preparation of the defence, it should be noted that an accused person does not per se have the right of access to all documents accrued during the criminal investigation process. Corroboration for this can be obtained from the Human Rights Committee in *OF v Norway*, para 5.5 (ultimately inadmissible). In contrast, in *Äärelä & Näkkäläjärvi v Finland*, the Human Rights Committee held that it was 'a fundamental duty of the courts to ensure equality before the parties, including the ability to contest all the argument and evidence adduced by the other party' (para 7.4). In that particular case, the applicants in a dispute concerning logging were not permitted to comment on a brief containing the legal arguments submitted by the Forestry

Authority, despite the document being considered by the Finnish court (which decided in favour of the Forestry Authority).

16.6.3 Trial in absentia

Being present at the hearing of one's case is often of crucial importance to the accused. In general, one has the right to attend one's own trial although if disruptive, one may be required to monitor the trial through other means (Art 63(2), Statute of the International Criminal Court). Trial *in absentia* can be in violation of international human rights. In *Mbenge v Republic of Congo (Zaire)*, the author of the communication to the Human Rights Committee was twice tried and sentenced to death in Zaire while he was resident in Belgium. He discovered this fact through press reports. The Human Rights Committee concluded that the State had not taken all appropriate steps to contact the author and inform him of the charges thus he was not afforded the time to prepare his defence. Indeed, the summons to the second trial was issued by the authorities a mere three days before proceedings commenced in the court. The International Covenant was thus infringed. However, it would appear that should an accused wilfully fail to attend a trial, trial *in absentia* is not such an issue.

Although one has the right to attend, there is no right per se to full oral proceedings. In certain circumstances, it would appear that written submissions might suffice for due process. Discrepancies between international and regional systems have produced some anomalies. At one point, Finland's regional system of written submissions was deemed compatible with the International Covenant (*RM v Finland*), but, due to European Human Rights' jurisprudence, Finland had to enter a reservation in respect of Art 6 of the European Convention to prevent cases being brought to Strasbourg on the same issue.

16.6.4 Legal aid

In order to prevent persecution and victimization, accused individuals are entitled to legal assistance in the preparation of their defence. Such legal assistance should be provided by the court, if the accused cannot pay it (for example, Art 67(d) of the Statute of the International Criminal Court). The denial of legal aid can be viewed as a denial of justice (see *Airey v Ireland*). A feature of many States is the provision of State-funded defence litigators or, indeed, a system of legal aid by which those prevented by cost from funding legal representation can be assisted in this by the State. Obviously, any such lawyers appointed by the State have a duty to act in the best interests of the client even when the State is picking up the bill for the expenses. A non-independent system of legal assistance could be subject to challenge.

16.6.5 Trial within a reasonable time

Many instruments require that a trial be held within a reasonable time. This, depending on the instrument, may also apply to civil procedures. A slow and laborious judicial procedure may be viewed almost as a denial of justice if no reasons are forwarded in mitigation. The concept of what constitutes a reasonable time after the charges are levied is, of course, a matter of circumstance and degree. Naturally, the alacrity with which the trial is held assumes greater importance where the accused is detained pending trial. Thus, in *Sextus v Trinidad and Tobago*, detention from the date of the murder until trial twenty-two months later in a straightforward case was held to violate Arts 9(3) and 14(3)(c) of the International Covenant on Civil and Political Rights. At para 7.2, the Human Rights Committee stated that 'substantial reasons' must be shown to justify such a delay. General problems following an attempted coup did not count. This opinion followed *Barroso v Panama* which had a three and a half year period of detention between indictment and trial. Consequential to the presumption of innocence, detained persons should be brought swiftly to trial in order that their guilt or innocence can be ascertained. Thereafter, if innocent, the deprivation of liberty will end as extratemporal detention may result in a challenge under the provisions on deprivation of liberty. In general, the calendar starts running on the date the person is charged. The nature of the proceedings and the conduct of the parties are taken into consideration when ascertaining if the trial is held promptly. Inevitably, application of the notion of 'reasonable' time is subjective.

It is unfortunate that the Human Rights Committee has not produced more concrete guidelines on this area. In State reports, various issues are raised including political, evidentiary and even geographical reasons for delaying trials. For example, in rural areas, it may take longer to constitute a court for a trial—this issue has been raised in earlier Australian State reports but is equally applicable to many other countries with a widely dispersed population.

Swiftness of process is also required at the appeal stage of a hearing. Thus the Human Rights Committee considered that a delay of some thirty-four months from conviction to appellate procedure occasioned by delay in transcription of the trial contravened the International Covenant on Civil and Political Rights (*Pinkney v Canada*). In the case of *Sextus v Trinidad and Tobago*, a delay of four years and three months between conviction and appellate judgment was considered unreasonable. It should also be remembered that it has been held that the very lengthy appeal process which precedes the execution of a convict in, for example, the United States, can, while not violating the right of a fair trial (it is very much in the interests of the accused to exhaust every conceivable appeal avenue) violate the right of a person to humane treatment and respect for personal dignity (discussed in Chapter 14 on freedom from torture and other inhuman and degrading treatments or punishment).

16.6.6 Public hearing

Integral to the notion of a fair trial is the quality assurance mechanism of public scrutiny. As is previously noted, justice should be seen to be done thus the entire judicial process should be public. Naturally, demands of national security may necessitate closed courts and the interests of minors may demand the exclusion of the public and imposition of reporting restrictions. In such instances, there will be no violation of international human rights. However, in the case of national security, it may be necessary for there to exist some mechanism for reviewing the decision to shroud the case in privacy. A form of judicial review, for example, may enable the national security implications to be verified.

Closed trials which give rise to particular concern are those of a military or revolutionary nature when 'political' crimes are discussed. Although such trials were comparatively common in, for example, parts of Latin America, Africa, and Central Asia, the number would appear to be decreasing with the increase in publicly accountable democratic States.

16.6.7 Double jeopardy

The notion of *ne bis in idem* (double jeopardy) is expanded on in the 1791 Bill of Rights (Fifth Amendment) of the United States, while in England and Wales the law was amended recently to allow certain serious offences to be retried if new and compelling evidence emerges. The International Covenant on Civil and Political Rights (Art 14(7)) and the American Convention (Art 8(4)), both enshrine protection against double jeopardy. The International Covenant provides that no one should be tried or punished for a crime for which he has already been convicted or acquitted. The Inter-American provision provides protection following acquittal only.

National jurisprudence exists in many jurisdictions on this. It is an issue of particular concern when conflict of laws/private international law issues are raised. Thus for example, consider the hypothetical case of a Kenyan man who kills a Thai woman and an Australian man in Paraguay. He is convicted of murder in Paraguay and serves a prison sentence. On release, he returns to Kenya and is arrested on arrival. He cannot be retried and punished for the same murders. The same rule would apply should the murderer subsequently visit Thailand or Australia though both countries could exercise jurisdiction over the man. He has already served his sentence. In some situations, it may be possible for two courts to adjudicate in a matter but, in such circumstances, the second court must take account of the penalty imposed by the first court. An example can be seen in European competition law—in *Wilhelm v Bundeskarttellamt*, the company was on trial in Germany and being investigated by the European Commission (European Union). On a preliminary ruling (Art 234, Treaty of Rome, as amended) the European Court of Justice opined that the company could be tried twice as long as the second court took into account any penalty already imposed. This was permissible because two different angles of the case were being simultaneously investigated—the internal effects by Germany and the transnational effects by the European Commission. Note also the potentially concurrent jurisdiction in international criminal law, although precedence is normally given to the relevant international system (eg, the Yugoslav Tribunal).

16.6.8 Appeal hearing

Following conviction, an accused person must have the right to have the sentence and conviction reviewed by a higher tribunal or court, according to law. There is no general right of appeal ad infinitum. However, at least one court should review the decision of the lower court. The higher court should re-examine the facts and application of the law in order to challenge or verify the decision of the lower court. In some jurisdictions, a branch of the court of first instance undertakes the appellate function. This is most likely when a particularly heinous crime is involved and jurisdiction is reserved for a higher court. Appeals may be to a smaller committee or chamber of the same court. As long as the judges are different and they have the constitutional power to reverse the decision, this will be in conformity with international law.

16.7 Conclusions

The right to equality before the law clearly goes to the heart of human dignity. It is one of the major embodiments of the freedom from discrimination advocated by the United Nations in the Charter itself. As has been stated, human rights can be said to represent the modern codification of the traditional concept of the rule of law which underpins societies across the world and is entrenched into numerous constitutions. The right to a fair trial, the equality of arms of parties to a legal dispute (especially when the State is a party/criminal law is involved), is fundamental to the operation of the rule of law. The standards set by international law are comprehensive; States are accorded little flexibility. Should further elaboration on the application of the law to criminal trials be required, one only has to look at the Statute of the International Criminal Court.

CASES

Äärelä and Näkkäläjärvi v Finland, UN Doc CCPR/C/73/D/779/1997 (2001).

Airey v Ireland, Ser A, No 32 (1979).

Albert and Le Compte v Belgium, Ser A, No 58 (1983).

Ato del Avellanal v Peru, UN Doc CCPR/C/34/D/202/1986 (1988).

Aumeeruddy-Cziffra v Mauritius, UN Doc. CCPR/C/12/D/35/1978 (1981).

Barberà, Messegué and Jabardo v Spain, Ser A, No 146 (1988).

Barroso v Panama, UN Doc CCPR/C/54/D/473/1991 (1995).

Barzhig v France, UN Doc CCPR/C/41/D/327/1988 (1991).

Broecks v Netherlands, UN Doc CCPR/C/29/D/172/1984 (1987).

Brozicek v Italy, Ser A, No 167 (1989).

Campbell and Fell v United Kingdom, Ser A, No 80 (1984).

DeCubber v Belgium, Ser A, No 86 (1984).

Demicolo v Malta, Ser A, No 210 (1991).

Estrella v Uruguay, UN Doc CCPR/C/18/D/74/1980 (1983).

Funke v France, Ser A, No 256-A (1993).

Golder v United Kingdom, Ser A, No 18 (1975).

Gridin v Russian Federation, UN Doc CCPR/C/69/D/770/1997 (2000).

Griffin v Spain, UN Doc CCPR/C/53/D/493/1992 (1995).

Holm v Sweden, Ser A, No 279-A (1993).

Ireland v United Kingdom, Ser A, No 25 (1978).

Lingens v Austria, Ser A, No 103 (1986).

López v Spain, UN Doc CCPR/C/67/D/777/1997 (1999).

Mbenge v Republic of Congo (Zaire), UN Doc CCPR/C/18/D/16/1977 (1983).

Murray v United Kingdom, Ser A, No 300-A (1994).

Oberschlick v Austria, Ser A, No 204 (1991).

OF v Norway, UN Doc CCPR/C/23/D/158/1983 (1984).

Oxandabarat on behalf of Scarrone v Uruguay, UN Doc CCPR/C/20/D/103/1981 (1983).

Piersack v Belgium, Ser A, No 53 (1982).

Pietraroia v Uruguay, UN Doc CCPR/C/12/D/44/1979 (1981).

Pinkney v Canada, UN Doc CCPR/C/14/D/27/1977 (1981).

Prosecutor v Duško Tadi, ICTY, Case No IT941AR72 (1995).

Regina v Kent Kirk, Case 63/83 [1984] ECR 2689.

RM v Finland, UN Doc CCPR/C/35/D/301/1988 (1989).

Salabiaku v France, Ser A, No 141-A (1988).

Setelich on behalf of Antonaccio v Uruguay, UN Doc CCPR/C/14/63/1979 (1981).

Sextus v Trinidad & Tobago, UN Doc CCPR/C/72/D/818/1998 (2001).

Thorgeirson v Iceland, Ser A, No 239 (1992).

Tinnelly and McElduff v United Kingdom, ECHR 1998, Vol 1998-IV, No 79.

Vasilskis v Uruguay, UN Doc CCPR/C/18/D/80/1980 (1983).

V v United Kingdom [GC] No 24888/94, ECHR, 1999-IX.

Weinberger v Uruguay, UN Doc CCPR/C/11/D/28/1978 (1980).

Wilhelm v Bundeskarttellamt, Case 14/68 [1969] ECR 1.

Zumbotel v Austria, Ser A, No 268-A (1993).

READING

Cassesse, A, et al, *The Rome Statute for an International Criminal Court: A commentary* (Oxford: Oxford University Press, 2002).

Lehtimaja, L, and Pellonpää, M, 'Article 10' in G Alfredsson and A Eide (eds), *The Universal Declaration of Human Rights: A common standard of achievement* (The Hague: Martinus Nijhoff, 1999).

Stavros, S, *The Guarantees for Accused Person under Article 6 of the European Convention on Human Rights: An analysis of the application of the Convention and a comparison with other instruments* (The Hague: Kluwer, 1993).

Weissbrodt, D, *The Right to a Fair Trial under the Universal Declaration of Human Rights and the International Covenant on Civil and Political Rights: Background, development and interpretation* (The Hague: Kluwer, 2001).

Weissbrodt, D, and Hallendorf, M, 'Travaux préparatoires of the fair trial provisions: Articles 8–11 of the Universal Declaration of Human Rights' (1999) 21 Human Rights Quarterly 1061–96.

United Nations Human Rights Committee General Comments Nos 13 and 18 reproduced in UN Doc. HRI/GEN/1/Rev.9 (Vol. I).

WEBSITES

www.un.org/law/icc/index.html—International Criminal Court

www.un.org/icty/index.html—International Criminal Tribunal for the former Yugoslavia

www.ictr.org/—International Criminal Tribunal for Rwanda

www.echr.coe.int—European Court of Human Rights

www.corteidh.or.cr—Inter-American Court of Human Rights

17

....

The right to self-determination

1. All peoples have the right of self-determination. By virtue of the right they freely determine their political status and freely pursue their economic, social and cultural development.
2. All peoples may, for their own ends, freely dispose of their natural wealth and resources without prejudice to any obligations arising out of international economic co-operation, based on the principle of mutual benefit, and international law. In no case may a people be deprived of its own means of subsistence.
3. The State Parties to the present Covenant, including those having responsibility for the administration of Non-Self-Governing and Trust Territories, shall promote the realization of self-determination, and shall respect that right, in conformity with the provisions of the Charter of the United Nations. [Art 1, ICCPR/ ICESCR: see also Art 1(2), UN Charter; Art 20(1), ACHPR; Art 2, AL]

No similar provision appears in the European, American, or CIS regional instruments. This chapter will examine the right to self-determination in the light of the decisions of the United Nations Human Rights Committee and of other contemporary jurisprudence on the doctrine. The origin of the right will be traced before an examination of the right as a tool for securing decolonization. Brief consideration will then be given to some of the issues characterizing the current debate on the future of self-determination in the post-colonial era.

General Comment 12 on Art 1 of the International Covenant on Civil and Political Rights in 1984 deemed the right of self-determination to be of 'particular importance because its realization is an essential condition for the effective guarantee and observance of individual human rights and for the promotion and strengthening of those rights' (para 1). In spite of this, the right of self-determination (in the wake of decolonization) is one of the more controversial aspects of modern international human rights law.

17.1 **The right to self-determination**

The right to self-determination appears in Art 1(2) of the United Nations Charter as well as in both of the International Covenants. It is clearly of pivotal importance to the United Nations and thus to international human rights. To many commentators, the problem of self-determination lies with its beneficiaries—who are the people to whom the right ascribes? Hurst Hannum considers that:

no contemporary norm of international law has been so vigorously promoted or widely accepted as the right of all peoples to self-determination. Yet the meaning and content of that right remain as vague and imprecise as when they were enunciated by President Woodrow Wilson and others at Versailles. [p 175]

The right to self-determination is, without doubt, a group right. It is only exercisable by 'peoples'. As will be discussed, this in itself has given rise to jurisdictional problems when individuals have sought to bring communications before the international and regional bodies under the individual complaints mechanisms.

The meaning to be attributed to the concept of 'peoples' in the Charter was debated at the San Francisco Conference although no consensus was reached.

A people for the rights of people in international law, including the right to self-determination, has the following characteristics:

(a) A group of individual human beings who enjoy some or all of the following common features:
   (i)   A common historical tradition;
   (ii) Racial or ethnic identity;
   (iii) Cultural homogeneity;
   (iv) Linguistic unity;
   (v)   Religious or ideological affinity;
   (vi) Territorial connection;
   (vii) Common economic life.

(b) The group must be of a certain number who need not be large (eg the people of micro States) but must be more than a mere association of individuals within a State.

(c) The group as a whole must have the will to be identified as a people or the consciousness of being a people—allowing that groups or some members of such groups, though sharing the foregoing characteristics, may not have the will or consciousness.

(d) Possibly the group must have institutions or other means of expressing its common characteristics and will for identity' [UNESCO].

This definition represents a compromise on most commonly proposed definitions but remains essentially a working definition for the United Nations Educational, Scientific and Cultural Organization. There is still no universally accepted definition.

17.2 The origins of the right to self-determination

Self-determination has been an issue since the emergence of the nation State in Europe. Demands for autonomy and self-government grew as Austro-Hungarian, German, Russian, and Ottoman empires pursued increasingly assimilationist policies. Demands for local independence also increased. Even Lenin wrote a book on the subject. Self-determination is usually considered a form of the collective assertion of the population against any domination, the underlying theory being that ideally a Nation State is a one nationality State. Each ethnic grouping has its own State. Self-determination is thus a concept of liberation. Consequently, the invocation of self-determination, as the means to justify overthrowing an alien governing power, was traditionally considered to be a political, as opposed to a legal, tool.

17.2.1 After the First World War

The Peace Treaties drawn up after the First World War were designed to punish the defeated States and redraw the map of Europe in such a way as to achieve a permanent and lasting peace in the area. Consequently, the territory of the 'defeated' States was carved up with new States being created and old States enlarged in an effort to secure a lasting balance of power in the region. Self-determination was an obvious tool to be employed in the process—with the break up of the old empires, inevitably a number of smaller 'local' States would be created. Little attention was paid to physical boundaries which resulted in a somewhat artificial map with some States having no natural, defendable borders.

The consideration given to principles of nationality in delineating the frontiers of the new Europe is sometimes considered the precursor of today's concept of self-determination. Although Woodrow Wilson is often attributed with developing it, at no stage in his famous Fourteen Points plan is self-determination mentioned. President Wilson is considered an advocate of self-determination because he viewed the role of the victorious powers as liberators, dividing the defeated empires for the benefit of the populations concerned. Unfortunately, this view was not shared by all of the colonial powers—in their own jurisdictions overseas, the imperial powers (notably France and Great Britain) sought to retain their colonies. However, the Wilsonian doctrine had its roots in a number of historic ideas—for example, the concept that a government rules with the consent of the people and the idea of ethnic nationalism. It has been argued that understanding the Wilsonian theory of self-determination is the key to understanding the modern concept of self-determination and the interpretation placed on it by the United Nations. However, it is perhaps useful to examine the contemporaneous (to President Wilson) approach of the League of Nations.

17.2.2 The era of the League of Nations

The League of Nations considered the concept of self-determination in 1919 but it is not mentioned in its constituent Covenant. Later, when discussing the Aaland islands, in a special report to the League of Nations, the Committee of Rapporteurs stated:

The principle is not, properly speaking, a rule of international law … it is a principle of justice and of liberty … To concede to minorities, either of language or religion, or to any fraction of a population the right of withdrawing from the community to which they belong, because it is their wish or their good pleasure, would be to destroy order and stability within States and to inaugurate anarchy in international life. [League of Nations Council, The Report of the Committee of Rapporteurs, B7/21/68/106[VII]27–8]

In Europe, as States were divided and new States formed, national affiliations were considered, mainly through plebiscites and transfers of population. However, that in itself gave rise to problems. In Czechoslovakia, many Germans were automatically divested of their German nationality as they became members of the new State of the northern Slavs—Czechoslovakia. However, in the area of Schleswig, a plebiscite was held to allow the inhabitants to decide under which country's rule they wished to live—Germany or Denmark. The population of Schleswig therefore exercised their right to self-determination and the territory was divided accordingly.

Not all areas were treated in this manner by the Allied powers—the southern Slavs were forcibly united to become the then new State of Yugoslavia. Political considerations were paramount, the involvement of the 'people' almost incidental.

During the era of the League, self-determination evolved as a concept. In some situations, the views of the population were considered. In general, however, territory was allocated at the behest of the 'victorious' States, self-determination merely a political tool for justifying such decisions.

17.3 **The United Nations, decolonization, and self-determination**

Self-determination, as a principle, was expressly mentioned in international law for the first time in 1945—in Arts 1(2) and 55 of the Charter of the United Nations—albeit in the context of friendly relations between nations. Self-determination thereby entered into the realms of public international law and the guaranteed exercise thereof became a binding obligation on Member States. From a foothold in political thought in Europe, its application was globalized. Article 56 of the Charter contains a pledge by the High Contracting Parties to support the principles (including self-determination) enunciated in Art 55 of the Charter. Despite this, a right to self-determination was not included in the Universal Declaration of Human Rights. The imperative which crystallized self-determination as a right under the ambit of the United Nations was the desire to end colonization.

Article 1(3) of both the International Covenants renders the importance of self-determination to colonial peoples clear. In this respect, it also re-emphasizes the purposes of the United Nations itself. The 1960 General Assembly Declaration on the Granting of Independence to Colonial Countries (GA Resn 1514 (XV)) declared that all peoples have the right to self-determination (Declaration 2).

Discussion topic

Internal and external self-determination

In respect of the self-determination of peoples two aspects have to be distinguished. The right to self-determination of peoples has an internal aspect, that is to say, the rights of all peoples to pursue freely their economic, social and cultural development without outside interference. In that respect there exists a link with the right of every citizen to take part in the conduct of public affairs at any level, as referred to in article 5 (c) of the International Convention on the Elimination of All Forms of Racial Discrimination. In consequence, Governments are to represent the whole population without distinction as to race, colour, descent or national or ethnic origin. The external aspect of self-determination implies that all peoples have the right to determine freely their political status and their place in the international community based upon the principle of equal rights and exemplified by the liberation of peoples from colonialism and by the prohibition to subject peoples to alien subjugation, domination and exploitation. [Para 9, CERD General Recommendation XXI (1996), UN Doc A/51/18 (1996) 125]

Debate continues as to the nature of internal self-determination and the level of autonomy which can be demanded to satisfy that right, although some maintain that internal self-determination is not covered by the treaties.

However, there is also a reminder of the overriding principle of respect for territorial integrity (Declaration 7): the United Nations rarely separates the two principles. The duty to respect the right of peoples to self-determination was emphasized in the General Assembly Declaration on Principles of International Law Concerning Friendly Relations and Cooperation Among States in accordance with the Charter of the United Nations 1970 (GA Resn 2625 (XXV)) in which the General Assembly solemnly proclaimed the principle of 'equal rights and self-determination of peoples' which every State has a duty to promote through joint and several action. An enjoinder qualifies that nothing in the Declaration should be construed as authorizing any dismemberment or impairment of the territorial integrity or political unity of sovereign and independent States. To mark the fortieth anniversary of the Declaration on Decolonization, the United Nations General Assembly proclaimed that 2001–2010 should be the second international decade for the elimination of colonialism (8 December 2000).

No definition of the 'peoples' to whom the right ascribed was given in either instrument. However, in the context of decolonization, the main criteria appeared to be that the peoples dwelt in a colonized territory. This represents a swing from the League of Nations when the primary recipients of the exercise of self-determination were national groups: in many respects, the 'peoples' were less culturally homogenous than those of the former European empires; territory was the key criteria. The colonized territories were generally clearly defined enclaves with definable borders. The original intention was for the term to apply solely to States under colonial domination collectively exercising their right to decide whether to become independent. The international notions of 'State' and of 'People' are closely linked, though not synonymous. To quote Hector Gros Espiell, the special rapporteur on the subject: 'Self-determination of peoples is a right of peoples, in other words, of a specific type of human community sharing a common desire to establish an entity capable of functioning to ensure a common future' (para 56).

Indeed, it has been suggested that the right to self-determination for colonial peoples is now part of customary international law, and may even be considered *ius cogens* (*Advisory Opinion on the Namibia Case*, especially Judge Ammoun). Academics are divided on the subject. Professor Ian Brownlie and Gros Espiell both consider that self-determination may constitute *ius cogens*. Others are not convinced. The problem lies in the imprecision in definitions of 'peoples' and in maintaining the crucial balance between self-determination and territorial integrity.

Although self-determination became an issue of international prominence during the demise of the colonial period as promulgated by the United Nations (Art 76 et seq of the Charter), interpretation of the relevant provisions of the Charter (Art 73 et seq) was not uniform. Some States adopted what became the eventual view of the United Nations vis-à-vis self-determination, viz that dependent territories would, in time, exercise their right to self-determination and become independent territories. Belgium, however, proposed an alternative which became known as The Belgian Thesis which radicalized self-determination by insisting that it can apply to indigenous groups and minorities. The United Nations' response to this thesis was negative. As a result, in the order of the new world the function of the principle of self-determination, primarily as a lever for encouraging the practice of decolonization, was consolidated.

17.4 **Self-determination today**

The accepted view of self-determination is that it is a right exercised primarily by people living under colonial regimes, which could be exercised once and once only to remove the colonial regime in question. Essentially it was taken as referring to the right of a group of people, normally of one distinct territory, to decide collectively the manner in which they wish to be ruled or governed. The right to self-determination for all peoples is an apparently inalienable human right. However, it is not necessarily an absolute right. Most notably, its application to peoples living under non-colonial domination is not apparent.

Robert McCorquodale suggests that an approach less rigid that a strictly legal approach should now be taken to self-determination. Such a 'human rights approach' relies on the framework of international law but facilitates interpretation in the context of current State practice (p 857). Self-determination can, however, have a variety of meanings:

1. The right of a people to independence and to determine its international status.
2. The right of a State population to determine the form of government and to participate in that government.
3. The right of a State to territorial integrity and the right to non-violation of its boundaries and to govern its internal affairs without interference.
4. The right of a minority within or even across State boundaries to special rights including the right to economic and cultural autonomy.
5. The right of a State to cultural, economic, and social development.

It is the potential scope of self-determination outwith the traditional decolonization framework which is attracting interest today. Some of the salient issues are examined next.

17.4.1 **Examples of non-colonial self-determination**

In Czechoslovakia, the population voted to separate and become two States, the Czech Republic and Slovakia. The formal cessation occurred on 1 January 1993. This is a clear example of the peaceful exercise of self-determination on the part of the peoples concerned.

It may be argued that self-determination is one of the crucial issues in the crisis which destroyed the former Yugoslavia. The Croats, Slovenians, Macedonians, Bosnians, and Serbs exercised their 'right' to declare their own nation States, while Serbs within Croatian and Bosnian areas fought for the ideal of a Greater Serbia— Yugoslavia under a different, historical title. The southern Slavs were united after the First World War; they were not, technically, colonized. This demonstrates clearly the problem encountered when reconciling self-determination with territorial integrity and the principle of non-intervention in domestic affairs of States.

The policy has, however, had some notable successes in the post-colonialist era. South Africa eventually relinquished control over South West Africa, now the independent State of Namibia (albeit the mandate under which Namibia had been placed after the First World War should have been converted to a trusteeship under the United Nations and thus the issue should have been one of decolonization). The year 1994 brought the beginning of the partial transfer of power from the Israelis to the Palestinians—the Gaza Strip of Israel/Palestine was the first area to be redesignated. Further concessions have involved the West Bank Occupied Territories, including the transfer of Bethlehem to Palestinian rule in December 1995. Both the Israeli and Palestinian authorities recognized that this was a recognition of the right of the Palestinian people resident in Israel to self-determination. However, the tragic consequences of this are ongoing and the process of transfer of Israeli occupied territories is slow.

There are inevitably many inconsistencies in the practice of the United Nations. Hong Kong and Macau were accepted as belonging to the People's Republic of China without mention of the right of the inhabitants of those territories to self-determination. The treaty leasing the territories (or part thereof in the case of Hong Kong) to the United Kingdom and Portugal was taken as conclusive and the territory reverted to full Chinese ownership. Moreover, it took a long time for the peoples of East Timor to be given the opportunity to exercise self-determination after Indonesia took over the territory. West Irian remains in a more precarious position.

The *Western Sahara Case* in 1975 found the International Court of Justice discounting claims of Morocco and Mauritania to contested land. The land remains without definable borders and subject to dispute and counter claims twenty-five years later. Some examples of partition have been accepted, with the original land being divided between two sets of 'peoples', this despite the avowed respect for territorial integrity. When the Indian subcontinent became independent, the Muslim people were granted their own independent State in the north-east (Pakistan) whilst the Sikhs were placed with the majority Hindus in what is now India. Although an exercise of self-determination of both territory (decolonization) and of peoples (on religious affiliation), the resulting tensions continue over fifty years later.

Under the auspices of the United Nations itself, a number of plebiscites have been held, including West Irian and Togo. However, the United Nations does not have an entirely unblemished record vis-à-vis self-determination. In some instances it has been argued that the United Nations has compromised the doctrine of self-determination. For example, the people of the former Trust Territories of the North and South Cameroons were given only two choices: independence as part of Nigeria, or independence as part of the former French Cameroons. Becoming an independent State was not one of the proffered options. Consequently, the people of the North and South Cameroons once again found themselves under 'foreign' rule. Recolonization rather than decolonization was the result.

The right to self-determination as a group right applies to the people of a State wholly and not severally. Its application was clearly originally considered solely in relation to colonized areas. The 'peoples' concerned were the nationals of a colonized territory as a whole. The whole people of a territory achieved independence through the communal exercise of self-determination. United Nations' practice, as discussed *supra*, dictates that only 'classic' colonies—those 'Third World' nations under European domination—can exercise the right to self-determination. Self-determination is rarely used in relation to the so-called developed world despite claims in, for example, Canada and Australia and the ongoing problems in the Balkans. The advent of 'internal' self-determination, particularly for First Nations, is

> ### Discussion topic
>
> **The Republic of Kosovo/a**
>
> The Republic of Kosova was proclaimed in 2008. To many Kosovans this was an act of self-determination which was recognised by many States; to the government of Serbia (supported by many States) it was unilateral (illegal) secession.
>
> Kosovo was part of post-world-war Yugoslavia, following the implosion of which, it remained as part of Serbia. In 1990, a Republic of Kosova was proclaimed, contrary to the then prevailing Yugoslavian constitution and recognised only by Albania. Ethnic and political skirmishes and hostilities characterised the period after the 'Dayton accords' ended the Balkan conflict. In 1999, the UN officially took over administration of Kosovo (SC Resn 1244(1999)), with the objective of ensuring Kosovo autonomy within the Republic of Serbia. The territorial integrity of Serbia was thus assured, in accordance with the UN Charter. However, unrest continued in the region and discussions on the status of Kosovo failed to progress. On 17 February 2008, the Kosovar Assembly unilaterally and controversially proclaimed independence. Most of Kosova is now under the administration of the new Republic of Kosova, though North Kosovo remains under Serbian control. De facto and *de jure* recognition of the new administration (ie, an independent Kosovo) has followed.
>
> By General Assembly Resolution 63/3, the question 'Is the unilateral declaration of independence by the Provisional Institutions of Self-Government of Kosovo in accordance with international law?' was referred to the International Court of Justice for an advisory opinion. (Time limits for initial written statements and comments were fixed for 2009.) The opinion of the Court will undoubtedly illuminate the discussion of the scope of modern self-determination and its uneasy coexistence with respect for territorial integrity of states.

attracting growing support but challenges the traditional anti-secessionist United Nations' stand, pushing it to the limit.

17.4.2 Secession

Cohabiting with the United Nations' encouragement of self-determination is its strict practice of respect for the territorial integrity of a State—a policy deeply against partial or total interference with the territorial integrity of a State. Territorial integrity and respect therefore is enshrined in the Charter of the United Nations (Art 2(4)). The General Assembly, in Declaration 1514 on the Granting of Independence to Colonial Countries and Peoples in 1960, meanwhile, purported to exclude the exercise of self-determination by discernible groups in terms of Section Two: 'Any attempt aimed at the partial or total disruption of the national unity and the territorial integrity of a country is incompatible with the purpose and principles of the Charter of the United Nations.' To the contrary, support for the extension of the principle of self-determination to indigenous populations may be inferred from the powerful separate opinion of Judge Hardy Dillard in the *Western Sahara Case*. The judge opined that: '[i]t hardly seems necessary to make more explicit the cardinal restraints which the legal right of self-determination imposes. That restraint may be captured in a single sentence. It is for the people to determine the destiny of the territory and not the territory the destiny of the people'. This view is discussed at length by Rosalind Higgins. It could be inferred from this *dicta* that the 'people' must be of a whole territory and hence the judgment conforms to the traditional view of the United Nations. On the other hand, the use of the term 'territory' could be taken to mean that the land could be a part of an existing State.

This causes some problems for self-determination outwith the colonial framework where questions of secession arise. The issue of secession of Quebec from Canada was discussed by the Supreme Court of Canada in 1998 (*Re Secession of Quebec*). On the question of whether international law recognized a right to self-determination which could legally effect the unilateral secession of Quebec from Canada, the Court concluded that 'Canada is a "sovereign and independent State conducting itself in compliance with the principle of equal rights and self-determination of peoples"' (para 136); thus, the Quebecers had no recognized right to secede. Earlier in the judgment, the Supreme Court had recognized the right of a people to self-determination (para 114) and acknowledged that much of the Quebec population satisfied the criteria for determining what is a 'people'— they possessed a common language and culture, for example (para 125). However, the Court then distinguished between internal and external self-determination: the former being the accepted political development of a State and the latter only invocable unilaterally in extreme situations (para 126). The Quebecers were accorded internal self-determination insofar as their linguistic rights are recognized; they have a fair representation in national legislative, executive, and judicial bodies; and their culture is not threatened. The Court received many submissions on behalf of indigenous Canadians who argued also for their own territory and autonomy. This was not addressed by the Court because no application of the principle of self-determination was found as justified vis-à-vis Quebec. It should be noted that many Canadian native peoples enjoy considerable autonomy in the remoter regions of the State and exist in conformity with their own customary rules and regulations, exercising their traditional usufructory rights without State interference.

The scope of 'extreme' situations justifying external self-determination was addressed in the opinion of the African Commission of Human Rights in *Katangese Peoples' Congress v Zaire*. It was suggested that where a State denies a group participation in the Government process and violates their fundamental rights, the territorial integrity of the State may not be such a paramount consideration. This is an interesting argument and not without merit.

The spectre of secession continues to loom over the freedom of self-determination for all peoples. In the words of Martti Koskenniemi, 'The extraordinary difficulties into which an attempt at a consistent application of the principle leads stems from the paradox that it both supports and challenges statehood and that it is impossible to establish a general preference between its patriotic and secessionist senses' (p 245).

17.4.3 Different covenants, different rights?

The first Article in both of the International Covenants of 1966 postulates identical rights to self-determination: 'All peoples have the right of self-determination. By virtue of that right they freely determine their political status and freely pursue their economic, social and cultural development.' This has caused some discussion over whether both Covenants refer to the same right or variations thereon. The argument in favour of a distinction deems the Covenant on Civil and Political Rights to refer to a right of political autonomy, including independence as advocated during the colonial era. On the other hand, the Covenant on Economic, Social and Cultural Rights may be taken to refer to economic or cultural autonomy, not necessarily involving political autonomy.

17.4.3.1 *Political self-determination*

During the collapse of the communist regimes of the Eastern-bloc countries of Europe, one of the first actions taken by the post-revolutionary government in each State was to hold a referendum, a plebiscite, or an election to facilitate domestic approval of the new political regime. The purpose was twofold: the population could thus exercise self-determination in deciding upon the new government and, perhaps more importantly, such evidence of a democratic government is a prerequisite today for international recognition of a new regime. States and authorities were often recognized as de facto until the new regime was entrenched, then *de jure* recognition would be accorded—the distinction between *de jure* and de facto recognition is rarely employed today. The processes deployed for self-determination of New Caledonia, an overseas French territory, have been considered by the Human Rights Committee, albeit no violation of any right was upheld (*Gillot v France*).

17.4.3.2 *Economic self-determination*

Article 1(2) of both the International Covenants seems to point towards an element of economic self-determination, extending the right to securing a subsistence and independent disposal of natural resources. The 12th General Comment of the Human Rights Committee emphasizes the economic content of the right to self-determination, noting that it entails a duty on all Member States. Economic self-determination is often argued as an element of internal self-determination. However, the right of peoples to pursue their own economic, social, and cultural development is also accepted in international law through the right to development (see Chapter 23). From a political perspective, the right to economic self-determination in some ways is a freedom from State interference. This can be demonstrated more easily in the context of the right to freely dispose of natural resources and wealth. The peoples of Nauru argued that phosphate mining before independence violated the principle of self-determination. The case, *Nauru v Australia*, was brought before the International Court of Justice but settled and was discontinued; thus, no decision on the self-determination aspects was given. It should be noted that elements of the right to freely dispose of one's natural resources appear earlier in General Assembly Resolution 1803 (XVII) 1962 on Permanent Sovereignty over Natural Resources. Other reiterations appear in the documentation related to indigenous peoples.

Article 1(2) of both Covenants provides that people may not be deprived of their own means of subsistence. This has clear economic implications and overlaps with elements of the rights to housing and food, the right to an adequate standard of living, and even the right to life. The principal problem faced by groups seeking economic self-determination is separating the economic and political elements.

This is apparent when one examines land claims by indigenous peoples as the claimed land is often rich in mineral resources (Chapter 22).

17.4.4 Autonomy for minority and indigenous groups

Many minority groups claim the right to autonomy, an element of full self-determination. The Aaland islands have already been discussed. In northern Scandinavia, many rights of the Sami peoples are respected vis-à-vis their traditional pursuits. They enjoy a degree of autonomy. The Swedish-speaking minority in Finland has linguistic autonomy as do the various linguistic groups in Switzerland. In Canada and Australia, moreover, many indigenous groups enjoy a degree of autonomy over their societal structure and operation. This can be economic or cultural autonomy, but may go further.

However, some issues of sovereignty are pertinent to land as well as to the people. Many indigenous peoples are no longer a majority people in the land in which they live. Consequently, sovereignty is not easily achieved and 'the best advice [for indigenous groups] might be to stop talking in terms of sovereignty and to argue instead for self-determination' (Nettheim, G, p 118). Is possession of all the requirements of statehood a prerequisite for self-determination/self-determination by secession? International consensus would appear to dictate that it is. The Montevideo Convention of 1933 on the Rights and Duties of States is accepted as the modern statement of the criteria to be satisfied by an entity seeking recognized statehood.

Self-determination may yet become a reality for indigenous peoples, at least insofar as it represents a freedom of choice. Internal self-determination is less controversial as it occasions little threat to the territorial integrity of a State. In some areas, for example in the Amazon basin of Brazil's interior, much of the indigenous population is, in effect, self-governing due to the inaccessibility of the area. The same is true of some island interiors of Indonesia and of more isolated aboriginal settlements in parts of Australia, namely the Northern Territory, South Australia, and Western Australia.

For many indigenous groups, the actual realization of cultural, social, and economic internal self-determination alone would be gratefully received. At least, in such circumstances, the group's identity could survive. It is perhaps interesting to note that the General Assembly has indicated a shift in the focus of this debate to recentre on self-determination. Article 3 of the 1995 United Nations Draft Declaration on the Rights of Indigenous Peoples states: 'Indigenous peoples have the right of self-determination. By virtue of that right they freely determine their political status and freely pursue their economic, social and cultural development'. Such self-government and a limited degree of autonomy is the most likely interpretation of self-determination for indigenous peoples which would attract international acceptance.

17.4.5 Self-determination and the African Charter

Given the region's history, it is not surprising that the African regional instruments embody comprehensive provisions on self-determination, decolonization, and elimination of foreign economic exploitation. All peoples have the inalienable right to self-determination insofar as they can freely determine their political status

(Art 20(1)). All State Parties pledge assistance to peoples in 'their liberation struggle against foreign domination, be it political, economic or cultural' (Art 20(3)). The explicit reference to political, economic, or cultural domination is particularly interesting as it appears to involve more than the cultural and economic development of the peoples, raising the possibility of cultural and economic independence. In the decolonization scenario, such independence is feasible. However, the extension to minority groups elicits the potential for internal (cultural or economic) autonomy. This would still be in accordance with the duty of the individual to preserve the territorial integrity of his country (Art 29(5)).

Natural wealth and resources is another issue which receives detailed consideration under the African Charter (Art 21). Peoples cannot be deprived of the right to disposal of their wealth and natural resources. Dispossessed people have the right to the lawful recovery of their property and compensation.

17.5 Claiming self-determination

There are comparatively few issues raised by the right of peoples to self-determination in order to rid themselves of the shackles of colonial rule. Problems, as has been noted, arise with the extension of the right to other groups of peoples. The Human Rights Committee has been asked to consider the application of Art 1 in complaints raised before it under the Optional Protocol. However, the Committee has determined that Art 1 cannot be the subject of a claim by an individual. This view has been reiterated in views adopted on a number of communications. Chief Ominayak brought one of the earlier cases on behalf of the *Lubicon Lake*

Discussion topic

Self-determination and territoriality

Montenegro ceded from Serbia in 2006, becoming the newest member State of the United Nations. This was a peaceful transition of power when compared to the last State to achieve self-determination, East Timor. However, as the example of Kosovo (box above) illustrates, self-determination is often controversial and today usually involves an element of secession, the division of the territory of an existing state. Claims of self-determination are being made in respect of a number of regions including South Cameroons (in Nigeria), Ossetia and Abkhazia (regions of Georgia) and Palestine. Internal self-determination is not always acceptable to the peoples concerned and political and/or legal devolution is rejected as an option. In 1998, devolution measures were enacted in the UK to facilitate more formal evolution of power to Scotland, and devolution of legal power to Wales (and Northern Ireland, though this was revoked and later still reinstated). The independence of Greenland is relatively uncontroversial.

Modern forms of self-determination and reconciling self-determination with respect for territorial integrity are challenging to both international law and human rights.

Band v Canada. The communication raised various issues under the Covenant, including the application of the right to self-determination. However, the Committee observed that 'the author, as an individual, could not claim under the Optional Protocol to be a victim of a violation of the right of self-determination enshrined in article 1 of the Covenant, which deals with rights conferred upon peoples, as such' (para 13.3). The same argument was used to dismiss an application by *EP and ors v Colombia*, claiming that Colombia had violated their rights under Art 1(1) of the Covenant. The applicants all lived in islands forming an archipelago some 300 miles from the Colombian mainland and were overwhelmingly English-speaking. This would seem a situation in which elements of internal autonomy may be relevant though obviously there are political ramifications.

It is interesting that the African Commission on Human Rights has had no qualms over admitting claims to self-determination. In *Katangese Peoples' Congress v Zaire*, the Commission acknowledged that self-determination could be capable of being the subject of individual petitions. The Congress was seeking recognition as a liberation movement in furtherance of the goal of independence for Katanga and the removal of Zaire therefrom. The Commission held that self-determination could exist in various forms but was obliged to uphold Zaire's territorial sovereignty. The Katangese were thus restricted to exercising a 'variant' of self-determination and no issue arose under the African Charter.

An earlier case alleging infringement of the right to self-determination (ICCPR) of the peoples of Zaire was not upheld on the facts. The case of *Mpaka-Nsusu v Republic of Congo (Zaire)*, arose pursuant to a referendum by which the people had voted for a bipartisan constitutional system. Thereafter, the author had attempted to stand for president in accordance with Zairian law but his candidacy had been rejected. He had then been arrested and detained without trial and he fled into exile. This case potentially gave rise to many relevant issues but, in the opinion of the Committee, the disclosed facts did not justify a finding as to a violation of Art 1 (para 9.2).

The key to bringing issues of self-determination to the attention of the Human Rights Committee appears to lie in employing Art 1 in conjunction with other Articles, such as 27 (Minority rights—Chapter 21), as the Committee has reiterated that the provisions of Art 1 may be relevant in interpretation of other rights protected by the Covenant.

17.6 Conclusions

Self-determination is clearly acceptable for divesting States of colonial powers. The problems arise when groups not in solo occupation of a given defined State territory choose to exercise self-determination. Claims for ethnic, cultural, and religious self-determination are, in general, more problematic. Inevitably many modern States are reluctant to recognize self-determination outwith the extent necessary to secure decolonization. For example, in Africa, where many decolonized States lack cultural and ethnic homogeneity, self-determination is considered to have no role in the future. Territorial integrity is regarded as more important.

Some States have opted for variants of self-determination. Australia, for example, has facilitated autonomy for some of its indigenous peoples—land rights have been recognized with some State legislatures already having granted rights over specific tracts of land to the traditional owners. The Pitjanjatjara and Urangi peoples, for example, exercise custodial ownership over Uluru and Kata Tinggu (Ayers Rock and the Olgas as they were formally known). In terms of international human rights law, however, problems may arise as the treaty-monitoring bodies are reluctant to enter discussions on what 'peoples' means or the circumstances in which internal sovereignty can be removed (eg, *Diergaardt and ors v Namibia*).

Having virtually ended colonization, it is inevitable that attempts will be made to seek further redefinition of self-determination. The problem which has not been resolved arises when attempts are made to apply the rights to all 'peoples' as the ongoing debate on minority and indigenous peoples' rights illustrates. A clash with respect to territorial integrity is inevitable as few peoples occupy a whole territory under colonial or other foreign domination. The current solution appears to lie in granting limited internal self-determination, even personal autonomy as Klabbers (2006) advocates. This tendency towards semi-political autonomy is one of the evolutionary reincarnations of self-determination for the twenty-first century.

CASES

Advisory Opinion on the Namibia Case [1971] ICJ Reps 16.

Chief Bernard Ominayak and the Lubicon Lake Band v Canada, UN Doc CCPR/C/38/D/167/ 1984 (1990).

Diergaardt and ors v Namibia, UN Doc CCPR/C/69/D/760/1996 (2000).

EP and ors v Colombia, UN Doc CCPR/C/39/D/318/1988 (1990).

Gillot v France, UN Doc CCPR/C/75/D/932/2000 (2002).

Katangese Peoples' Congress v Zaire, Communication 75/92, 8th AAR (1995).

Mpaka-Nsusu v Republic of Congo (Zaire), UN Doc CCPR/C/22/D/157/1983 (1986).

Nauru v Australia [1993] ICJ Reps 322.

Re Secession of Quebec [1998] 2 SCR 21.

Western Sahara Case [1975] ICJ Reps p.12.

READING

Cassese, A, *Self-Determination of Peoples: A legal appraisal* (Cambridge: Cambridge University Press, 1998).

Craven, G, 'The Quebec Secession Reference: The law of politics or the politics of law?' (1999) 6(1) Murdoch University Electronic Journal of Law, accessible from www.murdoch.edu. au/elaw.

Espiell, H, *The Right to Self Determination: Implementation of United Nations Resolutions* (New York: United Nations, 1979).

Hannum, H, 'Self-determination as a human right' in R Claude and B Weston (eds), *Human Rights in the World Community: Issues and action* (Philadelphia: University of Pennsylvania Press), pp 175–84.

Heraclides, A, *The Self-Determination of Minorities in International Politics* (London: Frank Cass, 1991).

Higgins, R, 'Judge Dillard and the right to self-determination' (1983) 23 Virginia Journal of International Law 387.

Juviler, P, 'Are collective rights anti-human? Theories on self-determination and practice in Soviet Successor States' (1993) 11 Netherlands Quarterly of Human Rights 267–82.

Klabbers, J, 'The right to be taken seriously: Self-determination in international law' (2006) 28(1) Human Rights Quarterly 186–206.

Koskenniemi, M, 'National self-determination today: Problems of legal theory and practice' (1994) 42 International and Comparative Law Quarterly 241.

McCorquodale, R (ed), *Self-Determination* (Dartmouth: Ashgate, 2000) (this contains a variety of articles previously published elsewhere).

——, 'Self-determination: A human rights approach' (1994) 43 International and Comparative Law Quarterly 857.

Musgrave, T, *Self-Determination and National Minorities* (Oxford: Oxford University Press, 2000).

Nettheim, Garth, '"Peoples" and "Population": Indigenous peoples and the rights of peoples' in J Crawford (ed), *The Rights of Peoples* (Oxford: Clarendon Press, 1988).

Qane, H, 'The UN and the evolving right to self-determination' (1998) 47 International and Comparative Law Quarterly 537–72.

UNESCO Final Report and Recommendations of an International Meeting of Experts on the Further Study of the Concept of the Rights of People for UNESCO, 22 February 1990, Document SNS-89/CONF.602/7.

Rigo-Sureda, A, *The Evolution of the Right of Self-Determination: A study of United Nations practice* (Leiden: Sijthoff, 1973).

Tomuschat, C (ed), *The Modern Law of Self-Determination* (Leiden: Martinus Nijhoff, 1993).

Wright, J, 'Minority groups, autonomy and self-determination' (1999) 19 Oxford Journal of Legal Studies 605–29.

United Nations Human Rights Committee General Comment No 12 reproduced in UN Doc HRI/GEN/1/Rev.9 (Vol. I).

WEBSITES

www.un.org/issues/m-decol.htm—the United Nations and decolonization.

www.un.org/Depts/dpi/decolonization/Decolonization_brochure.pdf—United Nations online brochure on self-determination and decolonization.

18

Freedom of expression

Everyone has the right to freedom of opinion and expression. [Art 19, UDHR: see also Art 19, ICCPR; Art 10, ECHR; Art 13, ACHR; Art 9(2), ACHPR; Art 11, CIS; Art 32, AL]

Freedom of expression can take many forms, encompassing verbal, artistic, and physical expression. Freedom of opinion and expression is the cornerstone of any democratic society. However, it is a freedom which, as history attests, has been, and is, compromised in a number of States.

Due to the indivisibility of rights, the freedom of expression and opinion is linked to a number of other rights including linguistic rights, freedom of assembly and association, freedom of the press, right to privacy, and freedom from State interference in correspondence and personal property. It also overlaps minority rights, and rights related to health matters and education. The relationship with freedom of thought and conscience is most apparent when addressing issues arising from press and academic freedom and those concerning freedom of religion. In some instances, it also overlaps with the right to participation in public life, the right to vote, and the right to stand for election. The very Article number is the name taken by a principal NGO working to eradicate suppression of expression and press censorship—Art 19. Although the freedom of expression is, in essence, an individual's right, by definition there are also examples of it which are inherently communal in origin.

The origin of the rights-based concept of free speech can probably be traced to the seventeenth century when documents such as the 1688 English Bill of Rights provided for freedom of speech for legislators within the confines of Parliament. It was thus impossible for a Member of Parliament to be impeached for anything which was said during a Parliamentary debate. The same remains true today with many legislatures and parliamentary assemblies operating a similar policy. More general legal guarantees of freedom of speech appeared in Scandinavia in the eighteenth century before finally making their mark in the French and United States' instruments concluded in the closing years of the century. John Stuart Mill rationalized the freedom of speech in a classic formulation which is still being cited authoritatively within the courts of the United States.

The biggest challenge to (although also a major contribution to) the freedom of expression is now the World Wide Web and increasingly global Internet usage. There are very few countries without Internet cafés or other means of facilitating public access to the Internet. Information can be processed, reproduced, and disseminated in a manner and with a speed hitherto unimaginable. The incredible velocity with which viruses and chain emails spread around the world testifies to this. Information technology represents both a challenge to international human rights and a lifeline: a challenge insofar as there are major problems of jurisdiction and related issues regarding, inter alia, incitement to racial hatred and child sexual exploitation achieved through the Internet; a lifeline insofar as information, particularly on human rights and its abuses, has never been as easily accessible to millions of people.

Unlike many other rights and freedoms, the freedom of expression operates at both horizontal and vertical levels. The right is designed to protect the individual against arbitrary interference with the freedom of expression by both the State and other private individuals. States are obligated to ensure that national law protects the freedom of expression at both levels, providing appropriate safeguards and remedies in the event of infringement.

18.1 **Freedom of expression**

Freedom of speech can serve a multitude of functions: dissemination of information; expression of the will of the people (vis-à-vis elections, government policy, etc); generation of ideas, and so on and so forth. Today there are few States in the world which do not profess freedom of speech in their constitutions. Whether it is a freedom fully enjoyed by all peoples is another matter entirely. In the Cold War era, freedom of the press and freedom of expression entailed quite different rights in the communist and non-communist States yet all technically would claim to adhere to the Universal Declaration.

The United Nations did begin to draft a more detailed convention on the freedom in 1948 but this has never been adopted—the Geneva Conference resulted in only one convention: the Convention on the International Right of Correction. This instrument provides that contracting States may issue communiqués pursuant to any new dispatch 'capable of injuring its relations with other States or its national prestige or dignity' (Art 2). There must be an international dimension to the news dispatch and it must be false or distorted. The complaining State may submit its version of facts to the other States involved and the correspondent or information agency, which is expected to correct the news dispatch in question.

The right to hold an opinion and the right of free thought is absolute and almost impossible to control. Despite this, there are often allegations of 're-education' programmes used in some parts of the world which seek, in effect, to 'brainwash' individuals or groups in society. Human rights law really begins to enter play when the thought or opinion is expressed, particularly when it is expressed in public. The 1990 Report to the United Nations on the right to freedom of opinion and expression confirms this (Danilo Türk and Louis Joinet). The plight of 'prisoners of conscience', detained on grounds of their political beliefs has given rise to a number of cases. Clearly, such detention may also be contrary to other rights, such as the right to liberty and the freedom from inhuman treatment. The case of *Muteba v Republic of Congo* (*Zaire*) heard by the Human Rights Committee illustrates this. The victim was arrested, detained, subjected to ill-treatment, and deprived of the right to a trial or even judicial determination of the legitimacy of his detention. He was allegedly charged with attempts against the internal and external security of the State and the foundation of a secret political party. He was eventually released under an amnesty and left the country. The majority opinion of the Human Rights Committee was that Muteba had been arrested, detained, and subjected to ill-treatment for political reasons, being regarded as an opponent of the Zairian government. Article 19, among others, was thus held to have been violated. (Note that a minority of the Committee considered that, on the evidence before them, Art 19 was not infringed.)

The drafters of the United Nations Declaration envisaged freedom of expression as a means of securing the full exchange of information intra- and internationally. The International Covenant on Civil and Political Rights elaborates on this providing for the exchange of media and ideas regardless of frontiers (Art 19). Individuals are thus entitled to impart and receive information to/from individuals or groups in other States. This can entail communication by conventional methods as well as the use of modern technology. The circumstances in which States can interfere with the exercise of this right are narrowly prescribed.

Freedom of expression extends beyond the mere verbalization of ideas. Other types of expression are included: written word such as the press and, indeed banners waved in protest (*Kivenmaa v Finland*), as well as artistic expression (*Müller and ors v Switzerland*). All forms of manifestation of creative thought as well as verbal expression appear to fall within the ambit of the provisions.

Today Art 19 of the Universal Declaration is viewed as encapsulating a general freedom of expression and it is even arguable that parts of it are now accepted as customary law.

18.2 Freedom of the press and media

The absence of press censorship is often regarded as one of the overt manifestations of a free society in which individuals and groups may openly criticize the government in power and instigate debate on topics of national or regional interest. The right of the public to receive information was found to have been violated in the case brought by *Media Rights Agenda, Constitutional Rights Project v Nigeria*. Decrees had been issued proscribing the publishing of two magazines. Subsequent decrees proscribed additional publications. Moreover, a number of publications critical of the government were seized and a new system of registration was introduced by which owners, publishers, and printers of newspapers had to be registered and pay an appropriate fee. The African Commission upheld a number of infringements of Art 9 of the African Charter. These included the element of unilateral censorship integral to the registration process and the seizure of material although other actions (eg, libel) may have provided a more appropriate remedy.

18.2.1 State-owned media

State-owned media inevitably is open to allegations of bias as are other methods of exercising State control over media enterprises as the *Media Rights Agenda, Constitutional Rights Project v Nigeria* case illustrated. The key lies in the freedom accorded to the body in determining the content of any broadcasts or publications and the number and strength of other media enterprises. State-owned media is not per se problematic, the government in power has every right in terms of freedom of expression to circulate its own views. Problems arise when either the State-owned enterprise has a monopoly or when the State prevents other enterprises from operating or even from receiving information. Clearly, if a State limits access to information to its own media enterprise, other enterprises are at a disadvantage. Such a State monopoly on information infringes the idea of a free press. In Europe, freedom of expression is now accepted as meaning the end of monopolies in broadcasting (see, for example, *Informationsverein Lentia and ors v Austria*).

18.2.2 Regional developments

The American Convention is particularly concerned with freedom of the press; given the history of many member States of the OAS this is not surprising. Article 13(3) of the American Convention states that:

The right of expression may not be restricted by indirect methods or means, such as the abuse of Government or private controls over newsprint, radio broadcasting frequencies, or equipment used in the dissemination of information, or by any other means tending to impede the communication and circulation of ideas and opinions.

This provision of the American Convention would explicitly cover situations such as the State registration system adopted in Nigeria (above). Other human rights bodies simply imply a prohibition on indirect restrictions on media into the basic provisions on freedom of expression. This is essential to facilitate the proper functioning of democratic society.

18.2.3 Link to human rights education

As has been noted, the Universal Declaration requires that information should be exchanged without interference regardless of frontiers (Art 19). This links into the concept of transfrontier broadcasting which went through a period of judicial activity in Europe. Minority rights are also a relevant consideration. By way of illustration, consider the provisions of the United Nations Declaration on the Rights of Persons belonging to National or Ethnic, Religious and Linguistic Rights 1992, Art 2(5), or similar provisions in either the European Charter for Regional or Minority Languages or the Framework Convention on National Minorities. The desirability (indeed need) of minority groups to establish and maintain links with similar groups in other States is emphasized. This is particularly important from the perspective of preserving culture. It also links in to the right to education. Moreover, as will be seen in the chapter thereon, human rights education is heavily dependent on the dissemination of information in a truly global manner (Chapter 20). The role of the media in stimulating interest in international human rights has been acknowledged in the documentation on the present decade of human rights education.

18.3 Overlap with freedom of correspondence

Personal freedom of correspondence may be addressed both under the freedom of expression and, on occasions, under the umbrella right to privacy. The international

Discussion topic

**Internet and access to personal data - Human Rights Committee
General Comment 16 (1988): Article 17: The Right to Respect of Privacy,
Family, Home and Correspondence, and Protection of Honour and Reputation**

10. The gathering and holding of personal information on computers, data banks and other de-vices, whether by public authorities or private individuals or bodies, must be regulated by law. Effective measures have to be taken by States to ensure that information concerning a person's private life does not reach the hands of persons who are not authorized by law to receive, process and use it, and is never used for purposes incompatible with the Covenant. In order to have the most effective protection of his private life, every individual should have the right to ascertain in an intelligible form, whether, and if so, what personal data is stored in automatic data files, and for what purposes. Every individual should also be able to ascertain which public authorities or private individuals or bodies control or may control their files. If such files contain incorrect personal data or have been collected or processed contrary to the provisions of the law, every individual should have the right to request rectification or elimination.

In many countries, electronic databases represent a growing concern for advocates of privacy. Fingerprints, DNA and other biometric data, credit and debt scores, and taxa-tion and social security information are all held by government and related agencies. Balancing the right to hold the information with the need to protect privacy is yet to be achieved in many States.

instruments include it in Art 19 on expression whilst Art 17 of the International Covenant (Art 8 ECHR; Art 11 ACHR, etc) bestow rights to privacy and freedom from unnecessary interference with, for example, personal correspondence. Appli-cation to censorship of verbal and more tangible forms of correspondence have occurred. It is also raised in respect of interference with prisoners' correspondence. Many violations are found on the basis of the right to privacy or, in the case of prisoners, on rights associated with a fair trial—access to legal advice, for example.

18.4 **Exceptions**

As one may expect, the freedom of expression is not unfettered. Human rights instruments recognize a number of legitimate limitations on the exercise of the freedom of expression. It is these exceptions that lead to the freedom of expression meaning so many different things to so many different people, depending on the State and indeed situation in which one finds oneself.

In its General Comment 10 on Art 19, the Human Rights Committee (noting at para 3 that it is the interplay between the principle of freedom of expression and any limitations and restrictions which determines the actual scope of the individual's right) states that any restriction on the freedom of expression should not put the right itself in jeopardy. Essentially, restrictions on the freedom of expression are required to be prescribed by law and in furtherance of specified overriding aims. Unfortunate-ly, no definition of 'provided by law' or of exactly what restrictions are 'necessary' is provided. Many of these exceptions have been recognized for almost as long as the basic right itself. The principal exceptions relate to the need for recognition of the rights and freedoms of others. Others relate to national security although such exceptions can be open to arbitrary abuse. The African Charter merely provides that the expression and dissemination of opinions is a right 'within the law' though there is no attempt to define the legal restrictions which are permitted (Art 9(2)). Clearly, the law does not have an unfettered ability to restrict the exchange of opinions.

In most States, it is accepted that there can be limitations on the freedom of expression. The Universal Declaration provides for derogation when the exercise of the freedom would be contrary to the purposes and principles of the United Nations. In times of war or other public emergency derogation from the freedom of expression is often permissible (eg, ECHR, Art 15). Moreover, as the International Covenant on Civil and Political Rights specifies, the freedom of expression 'carries with it special duties and responsibilities' (Art 19(3)). Accordingly, it may be subjected to restrictions provided by law which are necessary for the respect of the rights or reputations of others and/or for the protection of national security, public order, public health, or public morals. Similar clauses are found in other international and regional human rights instruments. The protection of the rights and freedoms of others is perhaps the easiest to address as international human rights instruments chronicle what those rights and freedoms are. Considerable discrepancies arise in the scope of national security etc as the definition is a matter within the discretion of the State. Accordingly, in many States restrictions on freedom of the press is justified under such exceptions.

18.4.1 **Propaganda for war or national, racial, or religious hatred**

International law is explicit in its condemnation of any propaganda for war or propaganda which incites national, racial, or religious hatred. States are under an obligation to restrict the freedom of expression in these circumstances.

Propaganda for war was associated with incitement to crimes against humanity by the Nuremberg Tribunal. Article III(c) of the Genocide Convention prohibits incitement to genocide. The International Covenant on Civil and Political Rights furthers these measures: Art 20 decrees that any propaganda for war shall be prohibited by law and that any advocacy of national, racial, or religious hatred that constitutes incitement to discrimination, hostility, or violence shall be prohibited by law (see also Art 13(5) ACHR). This provision is unusual in that it does not, *ipso facto*, contain a right or freedom. However, its importance cannot be underestimated. It clearly acts as a restriction on the freedom of expression, a restriction of paramount importance to the realization of the purposes of the United Nations itself. Restrictions on freedom of expression when such expression is blatantly discriminatory to the extent of inciting racial hatred are legitimate. As Art 20 provides, all such restrictions should be prescribed by national law. Consider *Faurisson v France*, in which the Human Rights Committee opined that Art 19 of the International Covenant on Civil and Political Rights was not infringed by the punishment of an individual for making statements promoting anti-Semitism.

Article 4 of the International Convention on the Elimination of All Forms of Racial Discrimination requires State Parties to condemn all propaganda based on ideas or theories of superiority of race, colour, or ethnic origin. Dissemination of such ideas is to be prohibited and punishable by law (Art 4(a)). Interestingly, the United States

> ### 🔖 Key case
>
> *Jewish Community of Oslo and ors v Norway* **UN Doc CERD/C/67/D/30/2003**
>
> The 'Bootboys' held a march in Oslo, commemorating Rudolf Hess, a former Nazi leader from Germany. The authors of the communication alleged that this march prompted the establishment of a branch of the group in a nearby town and a number of violent attacks against blacks. The leader of the march was prosecuted under Norwegian law for 'threatening, insulting, or subjecting to hatred, persecution or contempt any person or group of persons because of their creed, race, colour, or national or ethnic origin'. However, the conviction was overturned by the Supreme Court which held that:
>
> penalizing approval of Nazism would involve prohibiting Nazi organizations, which it considered would be incompatible with the right to freedom of speech ... the statements in the speech were simply Nazi rhetoric, and did nothing more than express support for National Socialist ideology. It did not amount to approval of the persecution and mass extermination of the Jews during the Second World War. It held that there was nothing that particularly linked Rudolph Hess to the extermination of the Jews; noted that many Nazis denied that the Holocaust had taken place; and that it was not known what Mr Sjolie's [the accused] views on this particular subject were. The majority held that the speech contained derogatory and offensive remarks, but that no actual threats were made, nor any instructions to carry out any particular actions. [Communication, para 2.7]
>
> However, '[t]he Committee consider[ed] these statements to contain ideas based on racial superiority or hatred; the deference to Hitler and his principles and "footsteps" must, in the Committee's view, be taken as incitement at least to racial discrimination, if not to violence.' (para 10.4) and thus considered Arts 4 and 6 of the Convention of the Elimination of All Forms of Racial Discrimination infringed.

made a reservation to Art 4 of the International Convention on the Elimination of all Forms of Racial Discrimination upon ratification to preserve the perceived constitutional right of all citizens of the United States to speak freely regardless of content.

18.4.2 War/public emergency

Derogation in time of war or other public emergency is permitted for a number of rights (see Chapter 11). Any such public emergency must be declared and, usually, registered with an international body. The extent to which the freedom of expression is compromised must only be that necessary in the exigencies of the situation, ie the principle of proportionality must be considered. Consequently, the State cannot be unduly censorious and blame the public emergency.

More common than reliance on press censorship in times of war or public emergency is the reliance by States on arguments of protection of national security and maintenance of public order.

18.4.3 National security/public order

Inevitably, States reserve the right to restrict access to information and dissemination of some information on the grounds of national security, even outwith times of war and public emergency. This exception can be open to abuse, particularly as it can fall within the margin of appreciation open to States. Classification of any given material as a matter of national security is discretionary and there is little impact that international treaty bodies or even international opinion can have. In such circumstances, the international bodies will enjoy a supervisory function over the exercise of State discretion (terminology employed by the European Court of Human Rights). However, the treaty-monitoring bodies will only entertain this defence if it was the basis of the restriction on expression at the national level. National security was only raised as a defence by Belarus when a communication was considered by the Human Rights Committee in *Laptsevich v Belarus*, it had not formed part of the national proceedings in that case. An infringement of Art 19(2) was thus upheld.

National security as a defence is almost beyond reproach simply because States inevitably view it as part of their territorial integrity and sovereignty thus are unlikely ever to accept limitations thereon. All countries have intelligence bureaux and all thus have 'sensitive' information. National security arguments are employed in various situations: the gathering of 'intelligence', the publication of 'memoirs' of former intelligence personnel, and military information.

18.4.3.1 *The gathering of intelligence*

Some aspects of national security impact on the rights of others: for example, should a State reveal a source of intelligence information, the individual concerned (the mole) may then suffer violations of other human rights. Inevitably in such a situation morality comes into play as a 'traitor' may be viewed as a valuable intelligence source by one country but as a criminal by another.

18.4.3.2 *Publication of 'memoirs' of former intelligence personnel*

There has been a recent spate of former State employees deciding to write fictional books based on their experiences or indeed to write and publish their (factual) memoirs. In both situations, issues of national security may be raised. Some countries have express provisions to govern such situations. In the United Kingdom, the Official Secrets Act governs the activities of State employees both during their employment and after cessation of such employment. In many instances, the signatories of declarations under the Act have limited, if any, access to sensitive material. Conversely, there are a great many other people employed by the State who have access to data and information the publication of which could endanger the lives of others or precipitate security threats to the State.

In such circumstances, the general test that monitoring bodies employ is whether the information is in the public domain or, through other means, about to be so. Thus in the case of *Observer and Guardian v United Kingdom*, the fact that the memoirs in question had already been published and distributed in other countries (principally the United States of America) was deemed important. The maintenance of restrictions on publishing the material within the United Kingdom was not upheld under Art 10 of the European Convention since the material concerned could be lawfully purchased and imported into the United Kingdom.

18.4.3.3 *Military information*

Military information is inevitably precious to States and viewed as an integral part of their sovereignty. A State is rarely willing to release classified sensitive information on weapons capabilities to potential 'enemies' lest they lose any advantage they may possess. During the Cold War era, States went to extraordinary lengths to conceal details of weapons capabilities. Despite the shows of military strength which characterized national parades within communist States, little information was available publicly on weapons capabilities. The problems encountered in the 1990s by the United Nations' International Observers in attempting to ensure that all biological and chemical weapons in Iraq were disabled demonstrate this. Nuclear capabilities are in a similar position with weapons tests carried out in secret although technically banned—eg, the actions of the French in the South Pacific in 1996 and more recently of India, Pakistan and North Korea.

18.4.4 **Public health and morals**

Protection of public health and morals is perhaps an incongruous exception. Clearly the protection of children is one element of this—Art 13(4) of the American Convention permits States to censor public entertainment in order to regulate access thereto by children and adolescents for the purpose of their moral protection.

Most States operate a system of classifying cinematic and video images in an attempt to protect children. In many jurisdictions, television broadcasting, at least on public channels, is subject to scrutiny with, for example, a cut off time before which programmes containing excessive violence, swearing, sexual references, or other potentially disturbing material may not be shown. Clearly, this will not necessarily safeguard children as many have televisions in their own rooms which they watch unsupervised and the private use of video and DVD machines cannot be monitored by a State. Newer media such as the Internet and cable and digital television channels are also capable of being restricted with blocks on certain channels and sites enabling parents and guardians to restrict potential viewing by minors. In the main, these restrictions are acceptable to the majority of peoples and are in conformity with human rights norms.

What are more controversial are State restrictions on the basis of morality as regards adults. For example, in many Islamic countries media images are censored to prevent views of excess female flesh being transmitted. Domestic laws of blasphemy often work to restrict freedom of expression. In the absence of a State religion, blasphemy laws are more difficult to justify. However, there is an argument for employing them as part of the protection of the rights and freedoms of others. Now, issues such as the publication in Denmark and elsewhere of cartoons allegedly mocking the Prophet Mohammed, have polarized opinion on freedom of expression and respect for religious beliefs.

Public morals are in some ways ephemeral, evolving with changes in government and societal progress. There is no universal standard of public morality which is accepted though arguably child pornography comes close given the provisions in the Convention on the Rights of the Child and the Second Optional Protocol thereto proscribing the sexual exploitation of children in pornography and other materials. Consequently, there is a considerable margin of discretion accorded to member States in determining the parameters of the term. In *Hertzberg v Finland*, the Human Rights Committee refuted a complaint that Finland had violated Art 19 by imposing sanctions against participants in and/or censoring radio and television programmes dealing with homosexuality. The Finnish penal code proscribed public encouragement of 'indecent behaviour between members of the same sex'. The applicant had been interviewed on Finnish radio and asserted that in his opinion there was discrimination in the labour market on grounds of sexual orientation. The editor (not the applicant) was prosecuted in the Finnish courts. Other cases in the complaint arose out of censorship of materials on homosexuality. In this case, upholding public morality was an acceptable defence.

18.4.5 The rights and reputations of others

Given the universality, interdependence, and indivisibility of international human rights, there will always be occasions when rights and freedoms conflict. Freedom of expression is one of the more obvious examples of this. There are frequent examples of the clash between the freedom of expression and the right to privacy, particularly when combined with a free press. Inevitably, it is a question of balance—the State, courts, and ultimately the various treaty-monitoring bodies must decide whether this balance has been exceeded.

To illustrate, consider the communication brought before the Human Rights Committee in *Ross v Canada*. The author was a modified resource teacher for remedial teaching in Canada. He published and made controversial public statements during this time on conflicts between Judaism and Christianity. Following a decision of the School Board, pursuant to complaints, he was transferred to a non-classroom based post. The Human Rights Committee considered that restrictions on the author's freedom of expression were acceptable as they were for the purpose of 'protecting the "rights or reputations" of persons of Jewish faith, including the right to have an education in the public school system free from bias, prejudice and intolerance' (para 11.5). It should be noted that Canada did refer to Art 20 of the International Covenant in its submission to the Committee.

This links in with the right to reply in terms of which an individual who is subjected to an unwarranted attack on his or her reputation or is subject to defamatory or libellous acts may respond. Article 14 of the American Convention decrees that:

Anyone injured by inaccurate or offensive statements or ideas disseminated to the public in general by a legally regulated medium of communication has the rights to reply or make a correction using the same communications outlet, under such conditions as the law may establish. The correction or reply shall not in any case remit other legal liabilities that may have been incurred. [Art 14(1)–(2)]

As a consequence of this, the American Convention requires that every publisher, newspaper, motion picture, radio and television company has a person deemed responsible who is not immune from liability (Art 14(3)). In many respects this reflects the tone of the Convention on the International Right of Correction 1952 and thus an element of the right to reply is incumbent on many contracting parties to the International Covenant and the Universal Declaration by virtue of that instrument. For other States, arguably an element of the right to reply can be imputed into Art 19.

Article 3(c) of the Optional Protocol to the Convention on the Rights of the Child on the sale of children, child prostitution, and child pornography obliges States to extend criminal law to cover the 'producing, distributing, disseminating, importing, exporting, offering, selling or possessing' of child pornography. This Protocol goes some way to addressing the call for global criminalization of child

Discussion topic

Freedom of Information and National Security

Freedom of information legislation is being enacted in countries across the globe as the concept of transparent decision-making for governments and other bodies is demanded. However, states generally retain procedures for withholding sensitive information to protect national security, vulnerable individuals and interests of the state. Information has been made available on government expenditure, policy documentation, financial matters, and various 'facts and figures' in a range of countries.

Whilst facilitating access to official information may be desirable, a range of controversial cases have demonstrated the potential problems that may arise.

pornography by the 1999 Vienna International Conference on Combating Child Pornography on the Internet. Child pornography clearly is contrary to the basic rights of dignity and worth of the child. These rights supersede any claims of freedom of expression in terms of current international human rights law.

18.5 **Conclusions**

The scope of the freedom of expression is still evolving. International bodies have yet to rise to meet the challenge of coping with the information technology age and the ease with which information can be disseminated. The recent incidences of concerted opposition to the G8 summits and World Economic Fora provide evidence of the efficacy of the internet as a mode of communication. The use of small island states in the Pacific as bases for online paedophile rings and child pornography is a growing problem. The global hunt for the initiators of computer viruses provide vivid demonstrations of the problems facing the international community. Without some global jurisdiction (such as with international crimes) it is difficult to envisage any human rights systems which will fully prevent violations of rights from occurring through the internet. However, other modern developments such as satellite technology and transnational broadcasting have been addressed by the international community. In 1982 the General Assembly adopted Resolution 37/92 on Principles Governing the Use by States of Artificial Earth Satellites for International Direct Television Broadcasting while in Europe there have been many attempts to regulate transfrontier broadcasting.

The record of the United Nations on securing freedom of expression has been described as 'disappointing' (McGoldrick, D, p 470). With an ever-more globalized and interactive society, the international and regional organizations will sooner or later have to respond to technological advancement and perhaps in future instruments, cases, or comments will be able to define parameters for the operation of the principal exceptions to the freedom of expression.

CASES

Faurisson v France, UN Doc CCPR/C/58/D/550/1993 (1996).

Hertzberg v Finland, UN Doc CCPR/C/15/D/61/1979 (1982).

Informationsverein Lentia and ors v Austria, Ser A, No 276 (1993).

Kivenmaa v Finland, UN Doc CCPR/C/50/D/412/1990 (1994).

Laptsevich v Belarus, UN Doc CCPR/C/68/D/780/1997 (2000).

Media Rights Agenda, Constitutional Rights Project v Nigeria, Communications 105/93, 128/94, 130/94 and 152/96, 11th AAR, Annex (1998).

Müller and ors v Switzerland, Ser A, No 133 (1988).

Muteba v Republic of Congo (Zaire), UN Doc CCPR/C/22/D/124/1982 (1984).

Observer and Guardian v United Kingdom, Ser A, No 216 (1991).

Ross v Canada, UN Doc CCPR/C/70/D/736/1997 (2000).

READING

Article 19, *Virtual Freedom of Expression Handbook*, accessible from www.article19.org.

Barendt, E, *Freedom of Speech* (Oxford: Clarendon Press, 1996).

Dulitzky, A, 'Prior censorship in the American Convention on Human Rights' *Ko'aga Roñe'eta* Series VIII (accessible from www.derechos.org/koaga/vii/dulitzkye.html).

Gearon, L, *Freedom of Expression and Human Rights: Historical, literary and political contexts* (Brighton: Sussex Academic Press 2006).

Jones, TD, *Human Rights: Group defamation, freedom of expression and the law of nations* (The Hague: Martinus Nijhoff, 1997).

Mahoney, K, 'Hate vilification legislation and freedom of expression: Where is the balance?' (1994) 1 Australian Journal of Human Rights (accessible from www.austlii.edu.au/au/journals/AJHR/1994/1.html).

McGoldrick, D, and O'Donnell, T, 'Hate-speech laws: Consistency with national and international human rights law' (1998) 18 Legal Studies 453–85.

McGoldrick, D, *The Human Rights Committee: Its role in the development of the International Covenant on Civil and Political Rights* (Oxford: Clarendon Press, 1991).

Türk, D, and Joinet, L, 'The right to freedom of opinion and expression', UN Doc E/CN.4/Sub.2/1990/11.

Welch, CE 'The African Charter and freedom of expression in Africa' (1998) 4 Buffalo Human Rights Law Review.

United Nations Human Rights Committee General Comment Nos 10 and 11 reproduced in UN Doc HRI/GEN/1/Rev.9 (Vol. I).

WEBSITES

www2.ohchr.org/english/issues/opinion/index.htm—United Nations' Special Rapporteur of the Commission on Human Rights on the promotion and protection of the right to freedom of opinion and expression.

www.cidh.oas.org/relatoria—OAS Office of the Special Rapporteur for Freedom of Expression.

www.coe.int/T/E/human_rights/media/—Council of Europe Media division.

www.osce.org/fom/—OSCE Representative on Freedom of the Media.

www.article19.org—Article 19 NGO on Freedom of Expression.

19

The right to work

Everyone has the right to work, to free choice of employment, to just and favourable conditions of work and to protection against unemployment.

Everyone, without any discrimination, has the right to equal pay for equal work.

Everyone who works has the right to just and favourable remuneration ensuring for himself and his family an existence worthy of human dignity, and supplemented, if necessary, by other means of social protection. [Art 23(1–3), UDHR: see also, Arts 6–7, ICESCR; Arts 6–7, ACHR; Art 15, ACHPR; Art 14, CIS; Art 34, AL; European Social Charter (ESC)]

For a full appreciation of the rights discussed herein, it is necessary to have regard to the work of the International Labour Organization. In comparison with other rights and freedoms addressed in this text, international labour legislation predates the general international standard setting which has characterized the work of the United Nations in human rights. Within Europe, the European Social Charter and Protocols, the Revised European Social Charter (both of the Council of Europe), and the work of the European Community are included to provide a fuller picture of the scope of these rights. The provisions of the European Charter are particularly detailed, establishing standards possible in a relatively prosperous region.

19.1 The right to work

In itself, the right to work comprises a variety of related rights and obligations. It is not truly a single human right, rather it is 'a complex normative aggregate ... A cluster of provisions entailing equally classic freedoms and modern rights approaches as well as an obligations-orientated perspective made up of strictly enforceable legal obligations and political commitments' (Drzewicki, K, p 173).

The provision on the right to work attracted considerable debate during the drafting of the Universal Declaration. 'Work' is taken to mean the provision of a service for and under the direction of another in return for remuneration. There is no right to self-employment per se, though this can obviously be implied from the right to work and, perhaps even an extension of the freedom from compulsory labour. Given the economic crisis during the interwar period in Europe, a right to work was deemed important not only for economic reasons but also for civil peace and democracy. The drafters of the Universal Declaration were mindful of the role high levels of unemployment played in the rise of the Nazi regime in Germany and, indeed, in a number of other civil revolts.

19.1.1 **An absolute right?**

The right to work provides the individual with an element of human dignity as well as providing the remuneration so important to securing an adequate standard of living. However, it should be noted that there is no guarantee of employment. Clearly, this would be unenforceable and could ultimately lead to situations which might infringe the provisions on compulsory labour. Rather, international human rights law recognizes, 'the right of everyone to the opportunity to gain his living by work which he freely chooses or accepts' (Art 6(1) ICESCR). The *travaux préparatoires* of the International Covenant reveal that the exact wording of this right caused tension.

Given the correlation with the right of the individual to an adequate standard of living, measures within States to encourage those that are unemployed to accept viable offers of employment are not contrary to human rights. Some States do incorporate a strict right to work but these have proven to be effectively unenforceable. As a balance had to be struck between the guarantee of the right to work and free choice in employment, care must be taken not to cross the boundary into forced or compulsory labour (see Chapter 15). In spite of this, States are obliged to aim for 100 per cent employment within their jurisdiction. Article 6(2) of the International Covenant, for example, demands that States strive to achieve steady economic, cultural, and social progress in furtherance of full and productive employment under conditions safeguarding fundamental political and economic freedoms of the individual. The regional instruments make similar provisions. In the Americas, contracting States must adopt measures to make the right to work 'fully effective, especially with regard to the achievement of full employment' (Art 6(2), Additional Protocol ACHR). Within Europe, by virtue of Article 1(1) of the European Social Charter (1961 and 1996), States undertake to 'accept as one of their primary aims and responsibilities the achievement and maintenance of as high and stable a level of employment as possible, with a view to the attainment of full employment'.

19.1.2 **The duty incumbent on States**

Given the not inconsiderable economic implications of securing and maintaining high employment, the right to work is a goal which should be achieved over a period of time. Availability of work is governed by many factors, some external to the State. To produce appropriate employees, inevitably training and vocational courses may be required. The European Social Charter requires States to provide and promote, as necessary, 'appropriate vocational guidance, training and rehabilitation' (Art 1(4) of both 1961 and 1996 versions). Contracting parties may thus be required to assist in the retraining of employees in response to changes in work patterns and demands. For example, a State may support vocational programmes aimed at training former heavy industry employees in the necessary skills for high technology industries.

Economic stability is also vital in developing an environment conducive to employment and prosperity. Related provisions may be read as encouraging States to advance private sector growth and thus a more buoyant employment market rather than forcing States to expand public sector employment, a strategy deployed in many Communist States. In fulfilment of these objectives, States may draft employment policies which aim to reduce unemployment. Urban regeneration and financial aid to rural areas may assist in this. For example, within the European Community, improving employment within rural and marginal regions is one of the priorities for which money is available under the European Structural Funds.

19.1.3 **Components of the right to work**

Matthew Craven divides the right to work into three main elements: access to employment, freedom from forced labour, and security in employment (p 205). With respect to the notion of 'full employment', Craven notes that every State will have some element of unemployment. He categorizes unemployment as frictional, cyclical, and structural; the former (frictional) being a necessary consequence of worker mobility, referring as it does to those people between jobs. Cyclical and structural unemployment, on the other hand, are deemed to be of more serious concern: cyclical unemployment results from a 'deficiency of demand' for labour whilst structural unemployment occurs when there is a 'mismatch' between training and labour demands (Craven, M, p 206). Artificial deflation of unemployment statistics should be avoided, especially when the State elects to 'create' work in order to present more favourable statistics. In any event, given the vagaries of State systems, it is almost impossible to catalogue statistics of unemployment. In much of the world, the majority of the population is self-employed in subsistence and entrepreneurial work. It is difficult to quantify such work and render statistical information viable and accurate.

Essentially, the relevant provisions obligate States to adopt appropriate strategies and implement policies which aim at ensuring work is available for those who wish to be employed. It is these policies and the success or failure thereof that the Committee on Economic, Social and Cultural Rights scrutinizes when considering State reports.

The right to work embraces access to employment services including employment-finding services. The International Labour Organization first mooted this idea in its second Convention of 1919. The 1948 Convention No 88 concerning the Organization of the Employment Service elaborates on this. The international community has remained somewhat divided on the use of private fee-charging employment-finding agencies. The International Labour Organization imposes an obligation on those States supporting fee-charging agencies to ensure an appropriate system of supervision is in place. Article 1(3) of the European Social Charter (both 1961 and 1996 versions), in contrast, requires the establishment and maintenance of free employment services for all workers as part of the effective exercise of the right to work.

Given the problems associated with any kind of provision of a right to work, it is perhaps inevitable that more substance can be inferred into the rights to protection in the workplace and protection of employment itself. The former will be addressed in the section on health and safety in the workplace, the latter includes maintenance of the employment relationship and guarantees afforded to the employee on termination of employment. The Universal Declaration is unusual in that it appears to advocate a freedom from unemployment. This has been translated in subsequent instruments and in practice into legal remedies of review of dismissal, consultation in advance of redundancies and the establishment of social security schemes to assist former employees. The majority of such provisions aim at protecting workers following the unexpected termination of employment, they arguably do not adequately cover new would be employees and those wishing to re-enter the labour market. However, provisions on access to employment and provision of appropriate training to enable entry into the labour market may cover such people. In Europe, for example, the European Community has adopted measures on the protection of part-time and atypical workers. In this way, flexibility in working hours opens up the labour market to a greater spectrum of potential employees as well as allowing re-entry into the labour market for those who do not wish, or are not able, to work full time.

19.1.4 **Freedom from arbitrary dismissal**

The right to work encompasses as a corollary a freedom from arbitrary dismissal. Failure to include such would obviously deprive the right to work of its essential benefit. There is thus an element of security of tenure in employment which may be inferred into the right. Clearly dismissals from employment and even redundancy situations are inevitable in almost every State. These are not proscribed. Rather the onus lies on States to ensure that the law does not encourage individuals to hire and fire at will. Some kind of national legal restraint is required to protect the individual

---

🖊 Discussion topic

ILO Convention No 158 on Termination of Employment at the Initiative of the Employer

The provisions of the Convention (ratified by 34 States) are to be enacted in law unless 'otherwise made effective by means of collective agreements, arbitration awards or court decisions or in such other manner as may be consistent with national practice'. [Art 1] There are exceptions for those on probations, fixed term contracts etc (Art 2). In general a valid reason is required for termination, this excludes temporary illness/injuries and the following:

Article 5 (a–e)

(a) union membership or participation in union activities…;
(b) seeking office as, or acting or having acted in the capacity of, a workers' representative;
(c) the filing of a complaint or the participation in proceedings against an employer involving alleged violation of laws or regulations or recourse to competent administrative authorities;
(d) race, colour, sex, marital status, family responsibilities, pregnancy, religion, political opinion, national extraction or social origin;
(e) absence from work during maternity leave.

These exceptions are controversial in many States.

---

in this respect. Compensation or some other form of remedy has been advocated by the Committee of Economic Social and Cultural Rights to reimburse an individual arbitrarily deprived of the right to work. The International Labour Organization's Convention No 158 of 1982 on Termination of Employment at the Initiative of the Employer provides comprehensive protection for the worker, including a list of valid reasons for dismissal and procedures for appealing against the decision.

19.1.5 **Equality**

Of particular practical relevance to the right to employment is the prohibition on discrimination. Realization of the right to work implies equal access to employment, equal opportunities for promotion, and equality in terms and conditions of work. In many States, access to employment is not truly on the basis of merit. Women are discriminated against in, for example, some Islamic States as either they are admitted only to a few careers or they require the permission of their spouse or guardian to enter a profession. Protecting women from unsuitable employment and, *ergo*, exploitation was one of the original goals of the International Labour Organization. However, as discussed previously, this approach of the ILO may be regarded as unduly protectionist today. Women are now being afforded access to many careers previously regarded as male only. Perhaps this is most apparent with respect to the military. Many countries now allow women full access to careers in the forces although there may still be limitations in many States on women serving in the front line, serving at sea, and serving in submarines. Interestingly, the most progressive countries in this respect are often not those of the 'developed world' where a more paternalistic approach lingers. In those 'developing' regions characterized by protracted civil conflicts, often women have been left with little option but to accept a call to arms. Clearly, restrictions on employment of women is an evolving concept. Women also often suffer from indirect discrimination in access to employment. This issue is addressed in detail by the European Community.

Almost all systems recognize some exceptions in which an element of discrimination is permissible. For example, political belief and national origin may be a salient factor in vetting applicants for public service work. However, care should be taken to ensure that such restrictions are used sparingly and only when the exigencies of the post, on the basis on national and public security, so demand (see, eg, the European Court of Justice in *Sotgiu v Deutsche Bundespost*; *Commission v Belgium*). A related issue is that of 'closed-shop' style trade union arrangements when membership of a specified trade union is a *sine qua non* of access to a particular employment. In many countries, such closed-shop agreements are impermissible (see, eg, *Sigurjónsson v Iceland* in which the European Court of Human Rights condemned a closed-shop agreement). In most cases involving such arrangements, violations are considered under the provisions on freedom of association and right to trade union membership rather than a right to work. This kind of situation can be distinguished from essential requirements of membership of vocational professional bodies (eg, a Law Society or Medical Council or Teaching Body) which, as long as equal opportunities for membership exists, is legitimate. In some instances, compulsory membership of such bodies is essential for the realization of other rights—for example, requirements that all medical doctors are registered may contribute towards the healthcare rights enshrined in the Universal Declaration (Art 25) and elaborated on in, for example, Art 12 of the International Covenant on Economic, Social and Cultural Rights.

Population transfers can sometimes be a result of State interference in access to employment. The rights of migrant and alien workers are addressed in detail in specialist instruments as are the rights of refugees and asylum seekers: for example the Convention on the Protection of the Rights of All Migrant Workers and Members of their Families. A European Convention on the Legal Status of Migrant Workers has been adopted under the auspices of the Council of Europe.

The goal is clearly one of de facto equality in access to employment. As has been noted in the chapter on discrimination (Chapter 12), it is probable that affirmative action measures may be taken to remedy any imbalance in equality of opportunity. Remember, however, that any such measures must terminate when equality is reached.

Key case

Love v Australia, **UN Doc CCPR/C/77/D/983/2001**

The authors of the communication were pilots with Australian Airlines (now part of Qantas), a wholly State owned company. In terms of the company's compulsory retirement policy, the authors' employment contracts terminated the day before their sixtieth birthday. As no individual communications were competent under the Covenant on Economic, Social and Cultural Rights, a complaint was brought on ground of discrimination under the Covenant on Civil and Political Rights (Art 26). The Human Rights Committee noted that:

systems of mandatory retirement age may include a dimension of workers' protection by limiting the life-long working time, in particular when there are comprehensive social security schemes that secure the subsistence of persons who have reached such an age … [and] while the International Labour Organization has built up an elaborate regime of protection against discrimination in employment, mandatory retirement age does not appear to be prohibited in any of the ILO Conventions. [Para 8.2]

Moreover:

the aim of maximizing safety to passengers, crew and persons otherwise affected by flight travel was a legitimate aim under the Covenant. As to the reasonable and objective nature of the distinction made on the basis of age, the Committee takes into account the widespread national and international practice, at the time of the author's dismissals, of imposing a mandatory retirement age of 60. [Para 8.3]

There was thus no discrimination on grounds of age.

19.2 The right to just and favourable conditions of work and remuneration

Once more, the International Labour Organization pioneered much of the contemporary law, setting down basic standards of remuneration and conditions of work. A minimum standard of living is a precondition for all other workers' rights hence many of the elements of this right overlap with the provisions on it. The associated rights considered in this section attracted some controversy, not least with respect to whether a State can assume responsibility for the terms and conditions of employment within its jurisdiction.

19.2.1 Conditions of work

Just and favourable conditions of work is a multifaceted concept, encompassing maximum hours of work, holiday, vacation entitlement, and health and safety regulations. The ILO established a minimum standard for health and safety in Convention No 155 (1981) on Occupational Safety and Health. Unlike minimum wage requirements, the provisions on health and safety have no justifiable economic impact. As happens in some States, manpower is maximized by disregarding safety implications of work. The impact of such a policy, an 'expendable' workforce, is clear on the right to life and other civil and political rights. The evolution of technology and industry requires the constant re-evaluation of the health and safety implications of any given employment. Asbestos, for example, was once considered non-hazardous yet following on from multiple asbestosis claims, the use of asbestos is highly regulated throughout the world. Mining is another example. Over the years, regulation of mining has resulted in more stringent health and safety requirements. This has inevitably reduced production in some areas, though increased life expectancy. Thousands of people died in the early years of mining in Australia and the United Kingdom, for example, or laying railroads across the United States of America, northern Scandinavia, and the Union of Soviet Socialist Republics while even today miners in Bolivia and Sierra Leone encounter treacherous situations at work and there are regular incidents reported in China, despite substantial upgrading of facilities.

The most important aspect of health and safety legislation is implementation. Great care must be taken by a State to ensure that any standards specified in law are enforced in all non-exempt employment situations. States, of course, should progressively reduce the number of exempt spheres of employment. The International Labour Organization advocates Labour Inspectorates to oversee the implementation of the relevant legislation (eg, Convention No 81, 1947). It requires that inspectors are appropriately trained, are sufficient in number, and have sufficient powers to ensure that they are not a token body.

The European Community has paved the way with a comprehensive approach to health and safety legislation. From the outset, the European Community was concerned with productivity in the workplace and thus also with health and safety: minimizing health and safety risks would reduce occupational injury and accidents, *ergo* increase productivity and thus link back into the objective of bolstering national economies within the European Community. The Community initially focused on standardizing signs and prescribing technical limits for working with potentially hazardous materials. However, the approach of the Community evolved with the adoption of Framework Directive 89/391 containing general provisions on the prevention of occupational risk, the protection of safety and health, the elimination of risk and accident factors, and involvement of workers in the process (Art 1(2)). A Technical Adaptation Procedure enables the subsequent adoption of more specific technical requirements for any given sector. In such a way, the European Community can improve and harmonize working conditions throughout the region. The Directive applies to all sectors of employment although there is the potential for limited derogation for example in respect of the armed and defence forces or the police. The Framework Directive spawned a number of specific directives addressing specific risks: these include Directive 93/103 for health and safety aboard fishing vessels, Directive 89/654 on the layout of the workplace, or Directive 98/24 on chemical agents.

19.2.2 **Working time and rest periods**

In many respects, elements of this right link in to Art 24 of the Universal Declaration and similar rights in associated instruments: '[e]veryone has the right to rest and leisure, including reasonable limitation of working hours and periodic holidays with pay'. As an integral part of the evolution of just and favourable conditions of work, working time is also linked to health and safety legislation (for example, in the European Community, Directive 2003/88 on working time was adopted in the wake of earlier directives under the enabling health and safety Article of the Treaty—Art 118a (now 137)). The right to rest is not new—one of the earlier and more popular instruments adopted by the International Labour Organization provided for the regulation of rest periods (Convention No 14 on Weekly Rest In Industry, 1921 with over 110 ratifications). The ILO also adopted sector-specific conventions aimed at regulating working hours and rest periods in, inter alia, commerce (No 106, 1957), at sea (No 180, 1996) and in hotels and restaurants (No 172, 1991). In order to increase productivity and to afford workers an adequate standard of living, it is necessary to allow periods of rest within the working environment. Rest periods allow recuperation for the next period of work and also may be regarded as providing leisure time, though it should be noted that there is little consensus on the right to leisure per se. Rest time occurs within the framework of the working week and also the working day. It is thus linked to the provisions on the 'reasonable limitation of the working week'. The Committee on Economic Social and Cultural Rights has appeared to follow the lead of the ILO in this respect, referring in several observations to periodic reports on the ILO Conventions.

Although the International Labour Organization has strived to secure consensus on a standardization of working hours, it has not been particularly successful. Forty-eight hours per week was suggested in 1919 (ILO Convention No 1 Hours of Work (Industry), the first-ever ILO Convention) with a revision to forty hours in 1935 (ILO Convention No 47). Neither instrument attracted broad support. Working hours continue to be a matter of controversy in the international community with little consensus. The European Social Charter merely demands 'reasonable daily and weekly working hours' with a reduction in the working week achieved progressively to the extent that 'the increase of productivity and other relevant factors permit' (Art 2(1)). A number of issues impact on working hours including productivity levels, industrialization, computerization, and even the weather. In

Key case

Case C-520/06 *Stringer and ors v HM Revenue and Customs* and Case C-350/06 *Schultz-Hoff v Deutsche Rentenversicherung Bund*, ECJ ruling 20 January 2009

In response to references from national courts in England and Germany, the European Court of Justice ruled that employees who by reason of illness were not able to take paid annual leave in the year in which it was due could not be deprived of the right to paid annual leave at a later time or, in the case of employees who had been dismissed, to a payment in lieu of that annual leave. This ruling interpreted the Working Time Directive (EC Directive 2003/88) which gives workers four weeks annual leave. Leave can thus be carried forward if sick leave precludes the taking of annual leave within the normal leave year.

some instances, reducing working hours in a prosperous State will improve the standard of living and have the added bonus of possibly creating new jobs and thus lowering unemployment. Another related matter attracting some international attention, especially in the earlier years, was the protection of 'vulnerable' groups who required specific working times and conditions: the early example of regulating night work for women, arguably paternalistic in tone, and children (ILO Convs 89 and 90, 1948, respectively). The Council of Europe adopts a different slant on this theme, with a requirement for reduction in working hours or an increase in paid holidays for those workers engaged in 'inherently dangerous or unhealthy' occupations (Art 2(4), European Social Charters).

19.2.3 Holidays

The concept of a right to periodic holidays with pay is also controversial, especially for small enterprises in poorer regions. In many cases, it is almost an economic impossibility. The ILO attempted to set a standard in 1936 with a convention on holidays with pay (No 52) but was unable to secure universal support for it. As with working hours, the ILO has also adopted a series of sectoral conventions providing for holidays with pay in various sectors including agriculture (No 101, 1952) and seafarers (now No 146, 1976). According to the new general ILO Convention on holidays with pay (No 132, 1970), the minimum entitlement of a worker should be three weeks on completion of a year's service. (This clarifies and elaborates on the Universal Declaration which merely specifies 'periodic holidays with pay' (Art 24).) This remains a relevant standard today though many countries are now enacting longer minimum periods. It is interesting to note in this respect, the European Social Charter: in 1961, a minimum of two weeks' annual holiday with pay was specified (Art 2(3)); by 1996, the revised European Social Charter specified a minimum of four weeks' annual holiday with pay (Art 2(3)).

The International Covenant on Economic, Social and Cultural Rights goes further than requiring annual holiday periods. It requires that workers are paid for public holidays (Art 7(d); see also Art 2(2) of the European Social Charter). Naturally the number of public holidays varies from State to State and there appears no right to enjoy public holidays as days off work. In reality, most workers have some public holiday provision or accept days in lieu or overtime payments for working public holidays.

19.2.4 Remuneration

The International Labour Organization started the trend for specifying a minimum wage in 1928 with Convention No 26 on Minimum Wage-Fixing Machinery. In the aftermath of the two World Wars, minimum wage requirements were introduced in several European States. The requirements imposed by international human rights on fair remuneration link to the right of equal pay that is discussed *infra*.

Strict adherence to the Universal Declaration would suggest that the amount paid may take into consideration dependants and other factors impacting on the economic situation of the worker. Consequently, it could be perceived as legitimate to pay a single working mother more than a single man who is living with his wealthy parents. Authority for this can be drawn from the link between equal pay and the securement of an adequate standard of living through the right to work. The European

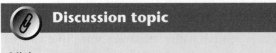

Discussion topic

Minimum wages

There is no specified amount for remuneration in international human rights:

- Argentina fixed 4 pesos an hour (800 per month).
- Australia fixed 13.74 Australian dollars an hour in 2007.
- Bangladesh distinguishes between categories of workers: 3.27 kilos of rice or equivalent money for agricultural labourers (introduced 2004) and USD 15.3 per month for workers in garment industry (fixed 2003), as examples.
- Cambodia requires USD 45 per month for regular workers in the textile industry (2000).
- China operates different levels for different provinces, thus Shanghai workers must be paid 750 yuan per month (fixed 2006) while those in Jianxi province only have 270 yuan per month (fixed 2005).
- Honduras imposes different levels depending on the size of the company and industry, from 54.50 lempiras a day for small companies rendering general services (under sixteen workers) to 112.23 lempiras per day for companies engaged in 'export and commercialisation of tobacco, coffee, seafood, bananas, melon; the reparation and maintenance of trains and ships; the refinery of oil and derivatives, electricity, gas and water' (2007).
- Norway ranges from 118 Norwegian kroner per hour for unskilled workers to 132.25 for skilled workers (2006).
- Senegal fixed minimum wages of USD 0.31 per hour for agricultural workers and 0.36 per hour for non-agricultural workers.

(Figures from the ILO, http://www.ilo.org/public/english/protection/condtrav/database/, database compiled November 2006.)

Minimum wages clearly vary from State to State. Defining criteria for fixing the levels continues to be controversial as is enforcing the minimum levels agreed.

Social Charter also makes this link with Art 4(1) recognizing the 'right of workers to a remuneration such as will give them and their families a decent standard of living'. Just and favourable remuneration does not carry with it any notion of transnational equality. The appropriateness of remuneration is dependent on the cost of living in a given State and includes reference to any associated 'perks' (non-pecuniary payments) of a particular job. Thus, education, housing, and medical benefits associated with a post will be considered. Many people in the armed and defence forces, for example, are provided with bed and board as well as a stipend. In terms of the International Covenant on Economic, Social and Cultural Rights, the minimum remuneration is required to be fair and thus reflective of the 'real social value' of the employment (Craven, M, p 232). Craven argues that the concept of fairness is dependent on the facts and circumstances of each job but should take into account a number of objective criteria including the level of skill required, the amount of responsibility, the value of the output to the local economy, the health and safety risks, and the disruption to family life (p 233). Workers may also be entitled to an increased rate of remuneration for overtime work (Art. 4(2) of the European Social Charter, for example, though certain exceptions are recognized).

Theoretically, it should be easier to implement a minimum wage in State-owned and controlled industries. However, note the problems in, for example, the former Soviet Union when many members of the military are owed substantial back payments by the State. The right to just and favourable remuneration links in to the right to social security (Art 23(3), UDHR; Art 6, ICESCR), as the goal is providing an adequate standard of living.

With respect to the overlap with the principle of equal pay, attempts are now being made to eliminate discrimination on any grounds with respect to pay.

19.2.5 Link to adequate standard of living

The international provisions on just and favourable conditions of work are often matched with provisions on the right to an adequate standard of living. United Nations research has demonstrated a link between the enjoyment of economic social and cultural rights and income distribution (Bengoa, UN Doc E/CN.4.Sub.2/ 1997/9). An adequate standard of living is, in itself, a right (Art 25, UDHR; Art 11, ICESCR; ESC, etc) which is integral to the notion of human dignity which underpins the entire modern international human rights system (see generally, Eide, A). The Committee on Economic, Social and Cultural Rights identified the most vulnerable groups as including landless peasants, rural workers, urban unemployed, migrant workers, and indigenous peoples. States are thus urged to ensure that the economic position and overall condition of these groups and other similarly vulnerable groups is improved. When reviewing State periodic reports, the Committee on Economic, Social and Cultural Rights examines the GNP for the poorest sector of the population of a State and the placing of the State on the Physical Quality of Life Index. This information enables the Committee to assess the relative standard of living in comparison to the previous report and chart any improvement or deterioration therewith.

19.3 The right to equal pay for equal work

That 'men and women should receive equal remuneration for work of equal value' is embodied in the Constitution of the International Labour Organization in Part XIII of the Treaty of Versailles 1919. It was recognized as a prerequisite to regulating labour conditions throughout the industrialized world. Although the idea was dismissed by some during the Great Depression of the 1930s, the United Nations, with its clearly specified basis of recognition of the equal rights of men and women (Preamble) paved the way for further development of the concept of equal pay for equal work. Europe has the most developed regional system with the work of the European Community being of particular note in this regard—Art 141 of the Consolidated Version of the Treaty establishing the European Community (formerly Art 119) imposes on member States an obligation to 'ensure that the principle of equal pay for male and female workers for equal work or work of equal value is applied'. The origin of the right lies not only with an intention to create fair working conditions, but also in the political field. For example, France had highly developed equal-pay provisions at the inception of the European Community and strived to include a clause on equal pay to prevent other member States from undercutting French industry by exploiting women in the workplace. Within the confines of human rights, the right to equal pay demands that remuneration received is proportionate to the value of the work carried out, the Universal Declaration's statement of 'equal pay for equal work' being augmented in subsequent documents to 'equal remuneration for work of equal value' (ICESCR). The terminology employed in the International Covenant is evocative of the International Labour Organization's Convention No 100 on Equal Remuneration in 1951. It represents a definite move away from the concept of payment according to necessity which appeared to fall within the ambit of the Declaration.

The provisions on equal pay for equal work are augmented by other instruments. The ILO has adopted a Convention on Discrimination in Employment and Occupation (No 111, 1958) which seeks to secure equality of treatment without discrimination on grounds of class, national origin, political opinion, religion, colour, sex, or race (Art 1). Other international human rights instruments specifically on discrimination include workers in their provisions. For example, Art 5(e)(i) of the International Convention on the Elimination of Racial Discrimination provides that, inter alia, the rights to work, to equal pay for equal work and to just and favourable remuneration shall be enjoyed by all 'without distinction as to race, colour, or national or ethnic origin'. Similarly, Art 11(1)(d) of the Convention on the Elimination of All Forms of Discrimination against Women provides for equal treatment in respect of work of equal value. This Convention also articulates basic standards of maternity provision for women and anticipates the current trend towards 'family friendly' policies (Art 11(2)). The International Covenant on Economic, Social and Cultural Rights extends the right to include equal opportunities for promotion on criteria only of seniority and competence (Art 7(c)) as well as applying equal pay for equal work across the rainbow of potential discriminations. A truly trans-industrial concept is envisaged which should help to prevent sectoral discrimination—eg, the growth in sectors of employment that are traditionally poorly paid and traditionally attract a section of society. Women in low-grade clerical and secretarial work are an obvious example.

Equality of pay requires a comparator and therein lies one problem with the right. It is not always possible to effect a direct comparison between two workers, one male, one female, in the same workplace, carrying out the same work. A system of objective appraisal of the work (as evinced by the ILO in Convention No 100) is essential to ascertain if the two employees are in comparable positions. In some instances, an appropriate comparator may be the predecessor or successor of the employee, in other circumstances, it may be an employee from a similar company. A direct male/female comparison may also prove problematic— what situation does a male experience which is comparable to pregnancy? Due to the difficulties in this, international human rights law has long recognized the right of women to special protection during pregnancy and whilst breastfeeding, although there is a fine line between protecting and patronizing. Within Europe, equality now extends to both parents being entitled to time off following the birth of a child (Parental Leave, Dir 96/34, OJ 1996 L 145/9). However, as such leave need not be paid, it is not a realistic proposition for many employees. In some States, for example the Netherlands, companies readily offer flexible working hours for new parents to accommodate their family responsibilities and ease the financial burden of childcare. Employees in other States are not so well provided for.

Equal pay has been deliberated at length by the Committee of Independent Experts and the Parliamentary Assembly within the Council of Europe, the principle is included within the framework of the European Social Charter. However, within Europe, the European Community undoubtedly leads the way with far ranging legal measures aimed at preventing discrimination on a wide variety of grounds at all stages of employment. Article 141 of the Consolidated Version of the Treaty Establishing the European Community consolidates the existing provisions on equal pay for equal work whilst providing a new basis to develop further legislation. Article 13 (amended by the Treaty of Amsterdam), on the other hand, extends the potential ambit of non-discrimination to include sexual orientation, racial or ethnic origin, religion, belief, or age. On this basis, Council Directive 2000/78 was adopted. This instrument establishes a general framework for equal treatment in employment and occupation within the jurisdiction of the Community aiming to combat direct and indirect discrimination on the grounds of religion or belief, disability, age, or sexual orientation as regards employment and occupation (Arts 1–2). Sexual orientation and religious discrimination were to be eliminated by 2 December 2003, with the possibility of member States enjoying a further three years' grace before securing the implementation of age and disability discrimination provisions. The European Social Charter requires the independence, social integration, and participation of persons with disabilities in the community and workplace (Art 15 of the 1996 Revised Charter which expands the provisions in Art 15 of the original). Separate measures have been drafted by the Community to combat race discrimination in the workplace. As these provisions relate not only to pay but also to access to employment, vocational training provision, and working conditions, their potential impact should not be underestimated. However, given the relative homogeneity and relative prosperity of member States of the European Union, it is perhaps only to be expected that such advanced measures can be adopted.

19.4 Conclusions

The right to work has clearly been incorporated into international human rights. At present, the ILO and regional organizations in Europe are the leading lights in articulating a framework within which conditions of work and pay are standardized with the European Community/Union achieving prominence in the area of equality in employment and the Council of Europe providing a comprehensive tabulation of the economic and social rights of all workers. In spite of this, the rights associated with the right to work remain difficult to isolate from other rights and freedoms. For example, the freedom of association, usually included in civil and political rights, is often used in the work scenario for trade union and other collective activities. Perhaps the right to work is best viewed as a freedom to exercise a degree of choice in the work undertaken to maintain one's standard of living in combination with a detailed set of safeguards which operate to ensure a dignified and fair system of working hours, holidays, and remuneration in the absence of discrimination. Termination of employment should be dealt with sensitively and in accordance with the relevant laws. While workers' rights are not absolute, the dignity of the worker is.

CASES

Commission v Belgium, Case 149/79 [1980] ECR 3881.

Sigurjónsson v Iceland, Ser A, No 264.

Sotgiu v Deutsche Bundespost, Case 152/73 [1974] ECR 153.

READING

Arnold, D, and Hartman, L, 'Worker rights and low wage industrialization: How to avoid sweatshops' (2006) 28(3) Human Rights Quarterly 676–700.

Barnard, C, *EC Employment Law* (Oxford: Oxford University Press, 2000).

Betten, L, 'At its 75th Anniversary, the International Labour Organization prepares itself for an active future' (1994) 12 Netherlands Quarterly of Human Rights 425–33.

Blainpain, R (ed), *Equality and Prohibition of Discrimination in Employment* (Leiden: Kluwer, 1985).

—— (ed), *Labour Law, Human Rights and Social Justice* (Leiden: Kluwer, 2001).

Craven, M, *The International Covenant on Economic, Social and Cultural Rights: A perspective on its development* (Oxford: Oxford University Press, 1995), pp 194–247.

Drzewicki, K, 'The right to work and rights in work' in A Eide, K Krause, A Rosas (eds), *Economic, Social and Cultural Rights* (Dordecht: Martinus Nijhoff, 1995), pp 169–88.

Eide, A,. 'Economic and social rights' in J Symonides (ed), *Human Rights: Concept and standards* (Aldershot: Ashgate/ UNESCO, 2000), pp 109–74.

Ellis, E, *EC Sex Equality Law* (Oxford: Clarendon Press, 1988).

Harris, D, and Darcy, J, *The European Social Charter*, 2nd edn (Transnational Press, 2001).

Nielsen, HK, 'Discrimination and lawful distinction in employment: The approach by the ILO' (1996) 14 Netherlands Quarterly of Human Rights 401–17.

Powell, B, 'In reply to sweatshop sophistries' (2006) 28(4) Human Rights Quarterly 1031–42.

Rodgers, G, Lee, E, Swepton, L and van Daele, J *The ILO and the Quest for Social Justice, 1919–2009* (Ithaca, Cornell University Press, 2009).

WEBSITES

www.ilo.org—The International Labour Organization.

www.coe.int/T/E/Human_Rights/Esc—Council of Europe European Social Charter.

europa.eu/pol/socio/index_en.htm—European Union Employment and Social Affairs.

20

The right to education and human rights education

Everyone has the right to education. [Art 26, UDHR: see also Art 13, ICESCR; Art 2, Protocol One ECHR; Art 13, Economic, Social and Cultural Rights (ESCR) Protocol to the ACHR; Art 17, ACHPR; Art 27, CIS; Art 41, AL]

Education shall be directed to the full development of the human personality and to the strengthening of respect for human rights and fundamental freedoms. It shall promote understanding, tolerance and friendship among all nations, racial or religious groups, and shall further the activities of the United Nations for the maintenance of peace. [Art 26(2), UDHR: see also Art 13(1), ICESCR; Art 7, CERD; Art 29(1), CRC; Art 25, ACHPR; Art 13(2), ESCR; Protocol to ACHR]

In many respects, the key to securing the universality of human rights lies in the right to education, hence this is a fitting topic to consider during the World Program for Human Rights Education (2005 onwards). According to the Vienna Declaration of the World Conference on Human Rights 1993, para 33, '[e]ducation should promote understanding, tolerance, peace and friendly relations between the nations and all racial or religious groups'. General Comment 1 (2001) of the Committee on the Rights of the Child considers education 'an indispensable tool for [each child's] efforts to achieve in the course of his or her life a balanced, human rights-friendly response to the challenges that accompany a period of fundamental change driven by globalization, new technologies and related phenomenon'. Education plays a pivotal role in disseminating information to people on their rights as well as promoting the Shangri-La of human rights—a world in which the right to be different is a *sine qua non*, a world in which all peoples 'practise tolerance and live together in peace with one another as good neighbours' (United Nations Charter, Preamble). This is certainly an optimistic, even idealistic goal, but it is by no means irrelevant. Indeed considerable progress has been made since the signing of the United Nations Charter.

This chapter will focus firstly on the right to education, the scope thereof, and the influence of parental views thereon. Eradicating illiteracy is a key goal. Attention will then turn to the more specific issue of promoting human rights through education. The rights to education and human rights education permeate through a variety of instruments. Neither the right to education nor the right to human rights education is restricted in application to children. The right to human rights education, in particular, applies to all.

20.1 **The right to education**

The right to education straddles the division of human rights between civil and political rights and economic, social, and cultural rights, embodying elements of each, according to Katarina Tomaševski, the former United Nations special rapporteur on the subject. Satisfactory completion of a prescribed education programme is an essential prerequisite for many employment opportunities, education is viewed as a gateway to success. Strong parallels can be drawn between the right to education and the development of respect for human dignity. Obviously, severe neglect of a child can result in a fit and healthy baby failing to be taught (and thus learn) the necessary skills of communication, hygiene, and social conduct. There have been many documented instances of this in orphanages and State homes in various parts of the world. One of the main challenges faced in educating the young, however, is balancing the rights of parents with the rights of children.

20.1.1 **Access to education**

The success of any right to education is dependent on the availability of that education and the conditions of access thereto. In accordance with general international human rights, there can be no discrimination in the provision of education: it is deemed as important for girls as boys. There are many factors implicit in a discussion of the accessibility of education including geography, cost, language, and the availability of teaching and learning resources. Moreover, education is not solely the prerogative of the young. International human rights law demands a basic level of education for all. This could place States under an obligation to extend educational facilities to adults seeking to obtain basic literacy and numeracy skills.

Two main features impacting on access to education are the costs of the education and the elimination of discrimination.

20.1.1.1 *Provision of free education*

In general, States are obliged to provide free education, at least at the elementary/ fundamental stages. Conformity with the Universal Declaration of Human Rights, Art 26, not only requires free education, but also compulsory education. This is one of the few explicitly positive obligations the Universal Declaration imposed on States. In contrast the First Protocol to the European Convention on Human Rights is one of the only instruments which phrases the right to education in the negative. The only justification is the age of the instrument. However, it was adopted after the Universal Declaration and Europe does claim to be one of the more developed regions as regards human rights, thus at least partially negating the age-based argument.

The Human Rights Committee has decided that parents who have elected not to avail their children of the free education provided by a State cannot then seek to claim any additional benefits that the State system provides by claiming discrimination (*Blom v Sweden*). There is discretion accorded to States as to what this free basic education is. According to Pentii Arajärvi, the fundamental stage of education should contain basic knowledge and social skills, while the overall category of elementary education includes literacy, fundamental mathematics, and basic civil education (Arajärvi, P, p 554). The Committee on the Rights of the Child states that education should reflect 'an appropriate balance between promoting the physical, mental, spiritual and emotional aspects, ... the intellectual, social and practical dimensions' with the overall objective of maximizing the child's 'ability and opportunity to participate fully and responsibly in a free society' (Comment 1, para 12). There appears to be agreement underpinning the various instruments that at least this first stage of education should be free. Arguably, children (initially through their parents) may have a corresponding duty to avail themselves of the free educational opportunities the State provides. Naturally, sending children (potentially excellent labourers) to school may cause economic hardship in some societies. This problem has been addressed by some States through careful scheduling of education—for example, education early in the morning, solely in the afternoon, or less education during harvest periods. Initiatives in many parts of the world aim at facilitating rural education and inner-urban education in deprived areas in a manner which is acceptable to all involved. In a similar vein, limiting the working hours of children through international human rights has the partial aim of facilitating the right to education.

Secondary education need not be free. However, parties to the International Covenant on Economic, Social and Cultural Rights recognize that secondary, technical, and vocational education should be generally accessible and available to all, thus States should strive towards progressively making such education free (Art 13(2)(b)). The Convention on the Rights of the Child also advocates the progressive achievement of free education for all, advocating a system of financial support for those in need where further levels of education are not free. Similarly, higher education should be progressively made available free to all, on the basis of capacity. This clearly raises some issues with respect to access to universities in some States.

Taking the concept of free education literally, not only should the actual schooling be free, so too should essential resources and ancillary costs. This would render a State liable for the cost of papers, pens, books, and potentially even any compulsory uniform as well as transport to and from the educational unit, at the very least for those in financial need at the primary level. Essentially, lack of financial resources on the part of the pupil should not justify non-attendance. In these situations, the State must strive to realize the positive obligations it has accepted on ratification of the salient instrument.

Arguably, levying costs on education could amount to discrimination based on wealth. However, there are many other grounds of discrimination which affect access to education.

20.1.1.2 Non-discrimination in the provision of education

The 1960 Convention against Discrimination in Education is concerned with eradicating discrimination in education. Although prohibiting discrimination at any level of the education process, Art 2 of this UNESCO Convention allows the maintenance of single-sex schools in certain circumstances and recognizes that different religious and linguistic groups within a State may be educated separately. It also permits the establishment and maintenance of private education institutions. In spite of this, States are obliged to ensure that standards of education are equivalent in all State institutions of the same level. This will ensure no discrimination results from any type of segregation or in respect of any given geographical area within a State. In terms of the Convention, equality of opportunity and treatment should be the object of national policy with particular encouragement for the education of those who have not received or completed primary education (Art 4). The need for non-discrimination in the training of the teaching profession is also highlighted. No reservations are permitted in respect of the provisions of the UNESCO Convention (Art 9).

Key case

DH and ors v Czech Republic, **Application 57325/00, European Court of Human Rights Grand Chamber November 2007**

European Roma children were systematically streamed into special schools in the Czech Republic, receiving a more basic form of education generally offered to those with special education needs. It was argued that Roma children were thus being discriminated against with respect to education on account of their ethnic or racial origin. A Chamber of the European Court of Human Rights held there was no infringement of the Treaty but the case was referred to the Grand Chamber which reached a different conclusion. Data from other Council of Europe bodies proved that most children in special schools were Roma and these schools were aimed at those with 'mental deficiencies' (para 16). A range of Council of Europe, European Union and UN materials were considered by the Court which stated that discrimination on ethnic origin was a 'particularly invidious kind of discrimination . . . with perilous consequences' (para 176). Roma people were identified in Europe as an especially vulnerable group. The difference in treatment between Roma and non-Roma children was not found to be objectively justified and there was thus a violation of Art 14 in conjunction with Art 2 Protocol 1.

This judgment contains an unusually detailed explanation of systems for establishing direct and indirect discrimination in international human rights.

The Committee on the Rights of the Child deems discrimination offensive to the human dignity of the child, possibly even 'destroying the capacity of the child to benefit from educational opportunities' (para 10). Children with disabilities and HIV/AIDS are singled out by the United Nations bodies as particularly heavily discriminated against. However, attention is now focused on indirect gender and religious discrimination with various countries banning religious clothing/symbols in schools and a number of cases challenging this (eg, *Sahin v Turkey, Hudoyberganova v Uzbekistan* and *Dahlab v Switzerland*; see box in Chapter 12).

The importance of prohibiting discrimination in education should be self-evident. Non-educated persons may be denied access to a variety of employment situations, may not be able to exercise democratic rights of public participation, and may, ultimately, become second-class citizens. It follows that denial of education is one of the most effective methods of circumventing rights. If education is necessary to allow States to develop, it is surely in the best interest of those States to ensure that all sections of the population receive that education and thus can contribute towards the development of the State.

In the *Case Relating to Certain Aspects of the Laws on the Use of Languages in Education in Belgium*, the European Court of Human Rights was called upon to decide a case brought by the European Commission of Human Rights on the right of parents to choose the language of instruction for State education. The applicants maintained that the provisions of Belgian law abrogated the right to education guaranteed in Art 2, Protocol 1 of the European Convention in conjunction with the provisions on non-discrimination (Art 14). The applicants lived in a Dutch unilingual area; thus there were no French-language schools. When one was established in the area it was denied public support and official recognition. By a narrow majority, the Court held that Belgian Law was discriminatory insofar as Dutch children living in the French unilingual area had access to Dutch-speaking schools in the bilingual communes around Brussels/Bruxelles while French-speaking children in Dutch unilingual area were denied a reciprocal right.

The sole ground for access to higher education should be merit. Students achieving the specified threshold required for access to a university should therefore not be denied a place on any other ground. Naturally, the State (and the higher-education institutions) retains discretion as to the academic requirements for entry into any given institute or any particular programme of study. Differences in entry requirements for different degree programmes are permissible and indeed, common.

20.1.2 **Nature of education**

The very scope and nature of education offered by a State may also be open to scrutiny. There is little guidance offered in the instruments. The most comprehensive provision in international human rights is found in the Convention on the Rights of the Child.

20.1.2.1 *Scope of education offered*

Article 26(2) of the Universal Declaration proclaims that education shall be directed towards the full development of human personality, the strengthening of human rights and fundamental freedoms, and the furtherance of the activities of the United Nations. The scope of education in furthering and promoting human rights is discussed infra. More detail can be drawn from other instruments. The need for tolerance and understanding, for example, can be gleaned from the various United Nations and UNESCO instruments prohibiting discrimination on specified grounds (in education itself in terms of the UNESCO instrument—Art 5). This sits alongside recognition of cultural values—Art 17(3) of the African Charter, for example, imposes a duty on the State to promote and protect the morals and traditional values of African society. The goal of eradicating illiteracy is deemed a binding obligation under Art 34 of the Arab Charter on Human Rights with other provisions relating to rights of religious education (extended to minorities).

Migrant workers' children and the children of asylum seekers or refugees have particular rights in respect of the language of the education provided. For example, the 1951 United Nations Convention Relating to the Status of Refugees requires refugees to be accorded the same treatment as aliens, vis-à-vis education and recognition of qualifications, while in Europe the 1996 Revised Social Charter (Council of Europe) requires the children of migrant workers to be taught, as far as practicable, in their mother tongue. Interestingly, the same Art (19) also requires the receiving State to arrange for the migrant workers and family to be taught the national language(s). This will clearly allow the migrant to at least partially integrate into society.

Minority education rights are fairly well documented and, arguably, follow naturally from the promotion of tolerance. More detailed provisions on the language of education thus appear in the European Charter for Regional or Minority Languages and the Framework Convention for the Protection of National Minorities. A similar stance is taken by the OAS, Art 13 of the Protocol of San Salvador (ESCR) demands education promotes respect for ideological pluralism, ultimately preparing everyone for participation in a democratic and pluralistic society. This corroborates the pre-requirement of education for enjoyment of rights of political participation.

The most detailed provision in international human rights which articulates the aims of education is to be found in the Convention on the Rights of the Child. Article 29 specifies five aims for the education of children, not least the development of respect for the natural environment. It also extends the idea of tolerance and plurality to respect for other civilizations and indigenous peoples, the latter is particularly interesting given the protracted history of developing rights for indigenous peoples under the auspices of the United Nations. The vast geographical area over which this instrument extends permits its provisions to be taken as reflective of international opinion.

From a variety of sources, Nowak concludes that there are four principal goals of education which have achieved broad universal consensus: to enable a human being freely to develop his or her personality and dignity; to enable a human being to actively participate in a free society in the spirit of mutual tolerance and respect for other civilizations, cultures, and religions; to develop respect for one's parents, the national values of one's country, and for the natural environment; and to develop respect for human rights, fundamental freedoms, and the maintenance of peace (p 251).

20.1.2.2 Influence of parents and guardians

The general principle is that education of children should be in conformity with the wishes of their parents or guardians. Article 26(3) of the Universal Declaration of Human Rights refers to the 'prior right' of parents to choose the kind of education to be given to their child. Clearly, this should be the case in respect of education the child receives in the home. However, the essence of the right to education implies that the child will also be educated in schools or equivalent where parents do not have an unfettered right of choice. Due to the compulsory nature of the right to education, a parent may not elect not to have a child educated at all. Similarly, it is not open to a parent to select a system of education which is contrary to norms of human rights.

Within the formal education environment, parents arguably have little or no control over the nature of the education. The law applies to allow parents to ensure that the education the child receives conforms to any salient parental convictions. This can cover aspects of religious education in schools, both the inclusion and exclusion of children in religious education. The greatest impact is probably found in respect of minority groups and indigenous peoples. Their children are entitled to an education but, as is noted in Chapter 21, cultural traditions (religious, ethnic, and linguistic characteristics) should be respected. This can cause problems for the State in the education environment. It is not practical in a pluralistic society for all children to be educated in accordance with all the convictions of parents. Therefore, a degree of balance will be sought. Ultimately, it will be for the treaty-monitoring bodies to decide if the parents' wishes should be respected. Freedom of conscience and religion, minority rights, and cultural rights may all overlap with the right to education in this respect.

In *Hartikainen v Finland*, the Human Rights Committee stated that a child withdrawn from religious instruction in response to parental convictions, must be given alternative instruction that is neutral and objective in deference to the agnostic views of the parents. This opinion was issued on the basis on Art 18(4) of the International Covenant on Civil and Political Rights which calls for the liberty of parents to be respected when ensuring that the religious and moral education of their children is in conformity with their own convictions. Within the European regional system, compulsory sex education in Danish schools was upheld despite complaints that it conflicted with the belief of parents (*Kjeldsen, Busk, Madsen and Petersen v Denmark*). In contrast, in the case of *Campbell and Cosans v United Kingdom*, the use of corporal punishment in Scottish schools was found to be contrary to the philosophical convictions of the parents. (The Committee on the Rights of the Child has consistently reiterated that corporal punishment does not respect the human dignity of the child—General Comment 8(2006).)

Key case

Leirvåg v Norway UN Doc CCPR/C/82/D/1155/2003 (2004)

[T]he Norwegian government introduced a new mandatory religious subject in the Norwegian school system, entitled 'Christian Knowledge and Religious and Ethical Education' … replacing the previous Christianity subject and the life stance subject. This new subject only provides for exemption from certain limited segments of the teaching. [Para 2.3]

The authors' demand for full exemption for their children from this subject was rejected. As stated previously in *Hartikainen v Finland*, Art 18 of the ICCPR extends to atheism and agnosticism. Education was found to involve not only religious knowledge but religious practice and applications for exemption had to give reasons. Some children enrolled in the 'exemption' programme nevertheless had to participate in Christmas celebrations.

The Committee concluded that Norway had to 'provide the authors with an effective and appropriate remedy that will respect the right of the authors as parents to ensure and as pupils to receive an education that is in conformity with their own convictions' (para 16).

20.1.3 Academic freedom

Concepts of academic freedom are often included in the right to education, although many aspects of academic freedom overlap with the freedom of thought and conscience, with the freedom of expression, or even with property rights. Academic freedom entails expression, opinion, dissemination of those opinions, and the publication of findings. There is a corresponding right to receive such opinions and information. Obviously the need to be educated is relevant to facilitate this. Parents and guardians, as well as the State, have duties in this respect.

Academics have often been subject to brutal oppression in times of public emergency and civil strife. History casts up many examples of this. Many academics draw on democratic theories and on principles underpinning the basic dignity and worth of the human person. As educated people, they may enjoy greater access to international documentation. This brings, as a corollary, duties.

Article 15 of the International Covenant on Civil and Political Rights requires States to respect the 'freedom indispensable for scientific research and creative activity' and to recognize the benefits derived from the encouragement and development of international contacts and cooperation. Article 36 of the Arab Charter embodies a right to be given an opportunity to develop intellectual talents. Arguably this tends towards academic freedom. No attempts to articulate international parameters of academic freedom have been successful although Art 13 of the Charter of Fundamental Rights of the European Union provides that academic freedom shall be respected.

States which systematically abuse human rights are less likely to condone the activities of academics who explicitly or implicitly advocate human rights. In these situations, academic freedom is often suppressed and problems ensue. This in itself has repercussions for the right to education of those the academics would otherwise teach as well as obvious repercussions for human rights education.

20.1.4 The United Nations special rapporteur on the right to education

In 1998, the United Nations Commission on Human Rights created the post of special rapporteur on the right to education (Resn 1998/33). Katarina Tomaševski was appointed with a mandate which included examining the obstacles impeding the realization of the right to education. She was succeeded by Vernor Muñoz Villalobos in 2004. In association with the Committee on the Rights of the Child and International Labour Organization's programme for the elimination of child labour, they have worked to address issues raised from the discrepancies between the minimum age for finishing compulsory schooling and the minimum age for working. The special rapporteurs have also worked with the World Bank to try and institute a policy of monitoring education lending to establish where primary education is still fee-driven. From the World Bank's perspective, education is the ticket out of poverty, and thus promoting education goes some way to achieving the goal of that organization—combating poverty.

The use of education as a tool for fighting war and conflict has also been of concern to special rapporteurs, as has its use in combating discrimination, especially on grounds of gender. The ten-year United Nations Girls' Education Initiative (launched at Dakar in April 2000) requires collaboration between the special rapporteur, the United Nations Development Programme, and UNICEF as well as State support. The initiative is a partial response to the Secretary-General's call for empowerment of girls, addressing amongst other issues protection against HIV/AIDS. The special rapporteur considers that there is often a gender bias, which discriminates against girl children, when it comes to education (eg, see 2006 Annual Report UN Doc E/CN.4/2006/45 on this topic).

In sum, the United Nations Rapporteur follows a '4-A scheme' for education advocated by Tomaševski and followed by her successor: to conform with their international human rights obligations, States should make education available, accessible, acceptable, and adaptable.

20.2 **The right to human rights education**

The Charter of the United Nations requires all States to promote and encourage respect for human rights (Art 1(3)). From this basis, many international human rights' instruments draw authority for the right to human rights education. As has been noted, the General Assembly Declaration, when adopting the Universal Declaration of Human Rights, called on the international community to widely disseminate the contents of the Declaration (Resn 217, Part D). Global knowledge and understanding of the proclaimed fundamental rights of all is still some way off. It is not only the less economically developed States which are at fault. Until the lead up to the passing of the Human Rights Act 1998 in the United Kingdom (which gave further effect to provisions of the European Convention on Human Rights within domestic law—the first international instrument on human rights to be accorded such status), large swathes of the population, including those with higher education qualifications, would have had difficulty listing the fundamental rights to which they are entitled. By contrast, in many so-called developing countries, there is a greater awareness of, if not enjoyment of, rights and freedoms: human rights education programmes are more developed and, with the active support of NGOs, more successful.

20.2.1 **Links to other human rights**

Human rights education is partially dependent upon the realization of the right to education. Human rights also apply to the uneducated and illiterate thus human rights education is also linked to obligations on States to disseminate human rights materials in appropriate form. Knowledge of human rights is a sine qua non of the exercise of those rights. Without knowledge, individuals and groups would not be able to demand their inalienable rights or seek redress for the violation or infringement thereof. At a more basic level, a lack of education can prevent enjoyment of other fundamental rights—for example, the rights relating to political participation. Full enjoyment of freedom of expression, the right to equal treatment at work, and various cultural rights require at least a basic level of education and often a degree of literacy. 'Human rights education is not only about good intentions and action plans' (Alfredsson, G, p 273).

20.2.2 **Achieving universal education on human rights**

In Part II of the Vienna Declaration and Programme of Action 1993, para 79, the World Conference on Human Rights calls on States and institutions to include 'human rights, humanitarian law, democracy and rule of law' as subjects in all educational curricula. This may link in to the 'civil society' element of basic compulsory education though arguably it could go further. Just as individuals need to know their rights in order that they can exercise them, the legislature and the judiciary need similar knowledge in order that national laws can conform to international obligations and the judiciary can ensure that basic rights and freedoms are enforced.

Accordingly, it is not sufficient to merely inform the beneficiaries of their rights and freedoms: '[t]he dissemination of relevant information, and human rights education as part thereof, are quite essential for bringing about the necessary knowledge of judges, other officialdom and all persons and groups coming under their jurisdiction' (Alfredsson, G, p 213). The World Conference on Human Rights in Vienna in 1993 reaffirmed that States are duty bound to 'ensure that education is aimed at strengthening the respect of human rights and fundamental freedoms' (Part I, para 33). Although the World Conference recognized that financial constraints may hinder the realization of this goal, States were urged to increase resources made available for human rights training, education and teaching (ibid, para 34).

Human rights education should be implemented at all levels. For this purpose, children's versions of the Universal Declaration and the Convention on the Rights of the Child are available. Cartoons and diagrammatic representations are regularly employed by NGOs, the United Nations, and other specialized agencies to assist with, for example, health education programmes and programmes designed to empower women in regions and States with a high illiteracy rate. UNICEF and other groups working with children have ploughed resources into developing accessible materials to inform children about their rights. At the other extreme, there are States such as Norway which pioneered dedicated ombudspersons for children: disseminating information on children's rights (not just international and regional human rights), acting as a forum for the airing of grievances, and feeding comments into the legislative process to ensure the interests of children are represented.

States may effect human rights education by enacting legislation, by policy implementation or, indeed, by example. State-owned or controlled media may be used to disseminate information on human rights. However, the duty does not rest with the State alone—academics, teachers, and researchers have moral obligations to the same effect (Alfredsson, G, p 222). This links in, as mentioned, to academic freedom issues.

In Europe, the work of the OSCE demonstrates the advantages of appropriate education. It adopted the Hague Recommendations Regarding the Education Rights of National Minorities which codify existing legal norms in furtherance of minority-education policy development. This instrument aims at diffusing ethnic tensions in States and regions through promoting education of both the minority and majority within the State.

20.2.3 Teaching non-discrimination

The right to education of all should, as has been noted, include the fostering of mutual tolerance and understanding. It should promote the principle of non-discrimination. Public education programmes aimed as dissipating intolerance are called for in various international instruments including the International Convention on the Elimination of All Forms of Racial Discrimination 1966, Art 7, the Convention on the Elimination of All Forms of Discrimination Against Women 1979, Art 5, and the Declaration on the Rights of Persons Belonging to National or Ethnic, Religious and Linguistic Minorities 1992, Art 4. Article 29(1)(d) of the Convention on the Rights of the Child demands that education is conducted in the spirit of understanding, tolerance, equality of the sexes, and friendship among all peoples; ethnic, national, and religious groups; and persons of indigenous origin. It also requires education on national history and values and those of the country of origin and other civilizations (Art 29(1)(c)). Comment 1 of the Committee on the Rights of the Child, para 16 states that promotion of such values is deemed 'even more important for those living in situations of conflict or emergency'. Education as a tool to eliminate prejudice is a common theme in the work of the International Labour Organization: Convention No 169 on Indigenous and Tribal Peoples (Art 31) or No 111 on discrimination in employment and occupation (Art 3), for example. Naturally the UNESCO Convention on Discrimination in Education also addresses the matter.

In November 2001, in Madrid, Spain, the United Nations special rapporteur on the question of religious intolerance convened an International Consultative Conference on School Education in relation to Freedom of Religion and Belief, Tolerance and Non-Discrimination. The Conference brought further calls for the development of cultural pluralism through education with an emphasis on international solidarity. It was noted that fundamental attitudes of peoples are generally formed during primary and secondary education. Therefore, to change attitudes in furtherance of the objectives of promoting tolerance and the principle of non-discrimination, the obvious place to start is the education system States are obliged to provide in accordance with international human rights law.

As the prohibition on discrimination underpins international human rights law, it is logical that educational resources of States are deployed to endorse this position. Education aimed at eradicating discrimination is clearly a key objective for human rights education.

20.2.4 **The United Nations Decade of Human Rights Education**

The Vienna Conference called for a decade of human rights education. The Commission on Human Rights endorsed this call and, by General Assembly Resolution 49/184 (1994), the United Nations Decade for Human Rights Education was declared with effect from 1 January 1995. The Decade was based upon the provisions of the international human rights instruments. Human rights education is defined as 'training, dissemination and information efforts aimed at the building of a universal culture of human rights through the imparting of knowledge and skills and the moulding of attitudes' (*Plan of Action for the United Nations Decade for Human Rights Education 1995–2004: Human rights education—lessons for life*, para 2). This education should be directed towards the strengthening of respect for human rights and fundamental freedoms; the full development of the human personality and the sense of dignity; the promotion of understanding, tolerance, gender equality, and friendship among all nations, indigenous peoples and racial, ethnic, religious, and linguistic groups; the enabling of all persons to participate effectively in a free society; and the furtherance of the activities of the United Nations for the maintenance of peace (ibid). Education is viewed as a constant factor in the multidimensional life of individuals and society (para 3).

The Plan of Action for the Decade had five principal objectives: assessing needs and formulating strategies; building and strengthening human rights education programmes at international, regional, national, and local level; developing educational materials; strengthening the role of the mass media; and globally disseminating the Universal Declaration of Human Rights. The latter is obviously aided by the compilation of over 300 language versions online at the website of the Office of the United Nations High Commissioner for Human Rights. However, the Plan of Action also required dissemination of the Declaration in other forms appropriate for various levels of literacy and the disabled (para 10). Not every person can access the World Wide Web so other, more traditional, modes of information delivery are also needed.

In furtherance of the aims of the Decade for Human Rights Education, States, international and regional organizations, and individuals have obligations. The United Nations itself hosted a meeting of experts to prepare Guidelines for National Plans of Action for Human Rights Education. Detailed human rights education is presently focused on students of relevant vocational courses, those requiring the knowledge for work (eg, police and judiciary), and lawyers. A cross-disciplinary approach is necessary to ensure that everyone enjoys the benefits of the international norms of rights and freedoms. In an attempt to target those responsible for human rights maintenance in States, under the framework of the United Nations Decade, Expert meetings were convened to develop Human Rights Training Packages for Prison Officials, a Human Rights Manual for Judges and Lawyers, and a Training Manual on Human Rights Monitoring for United Nations Field Operations. Practical teaching materials for conveying notions of human rights to primary and secondary children were also compiled and disseminated—the Internet proved a valuable tool in this respect.

Discussion topic

Draft Declaration on Human Rights Education and Training

The Human Rights Council Advisory Committee is undertaking research into a draft declaration on human rights education and training during 2009. This contributes to the World Programme for Human Rights Education. Inevitably, rights and freedoms cannot be enforced by those who do not know about them. Equally obvious is the fact that comprehensive training on human rights is required across a spectrum of government to ensure a high level of compliance with human rights' norms. The first phase of the World Programme (2005-9) seeks to infuse human rights in all educational processes while practising human rights within the national education systems of States. Quoting the UN OHCHR's key messages on human rights education:

Human rights education is an important strategy for achieving several important ends notably empowerment, participation, transparency, accountability, the prevention of conflict, conflict resolution, peacemaking and peace-building and the more effective protection and realization of all human rights for all, Human rights education, training and public information are essential for the promotion and achievement of stable and harmonious relations among communities and for fostering mutual understanding, tolerance and peace.
[From http://www2.ohchr.org/english/events/day2004/hre.htm]

The year 2009 is also being celebrated as the International Year of Human Rights Learning in an attempt to broaden and deepen human rights learning (GA Resn 62/171 (2008)).

In contrast to the rhetoric, many States do not fully incorporate human rights education into the curricula, perpetuating a cycle of ignorance and misinformation. Reasons vary from State to State and school to school, most are not convincing.

The emphasis for the decade was trans-institutional. Many specialist agencies of the United Nations and various regional bodies were involved. Human rights education is not an issue solely within the prerogative of any one institution or organization. Neither is it something which can be addressed at solely an international level. There is a limit to the implementation abilities of the United Nations; thus, regional and national bodies must take up the call for promoting human rights education. The International Decade provided the opportunity for all levels of society to work together towards the same goal. The result should be an improvement in conditions for all. As mentioned above, the Decade is followed by the World Programme for Human Rights Education (GA Resn 59/113 (2004)) which runs concurrent with the United Nations Literacy Decade 2003–12 (GA Resn 56/116 (2002)).

20.3 Conclusions

The promotion of ethnic, racial, and religious tolerance within States and between States would go a long way towards reducing tensions and dissipating violence. It would also develop truly pluralistic societies. Education is key to this. Without appropriate education, ignorance can breed contempt. In such situations, the right to education thus becomes even more fundamental. As ignorance of human rights and of human rights implementation machinery is all too often a major factor preventing the realization of human rights, human rights education is vital to inform individuals and groups of their rights. Full human rights education also acts as a deterrent on States and may help limit future abuses of rights and freedoms.

Everyone has the right to at least basic education. Such education must, by necessity, include information on human rights and aim at the realization of the principle of non-discrimination. Arguably, the right to education and the current push towards promoting the right to human rights education is the key to the advancement of the human rights movement and the continuation of the work of the United Nations and regional organizations in this respect. Realization of these rights will enable the protection and advancement of human rights to progress to a higher level. Given the increasing globalization of society, this is imperative.

CASES

Blom v Sweden, UN Doc CCPR/C/32/D/191/1985 (1988).

Campbell and Cosans v United Kingdom, Ser A, No 48 (1982).

Case Relating to Certain Aspects of the Laws on the Use of Languages in Education in Belgium, Ser A, No 6 (1968).

Dahlab v Switzerland, Application 42393/98, European Court of Human Rights.

Hartikainen v Finland, UN Doc CCPR/C/12/D/40/1978 (1981).

Hudoyberganova v Uzbekistan, UN Doc CCPR/C/82/D/931/2000.

Kjeldsen, Busk, Madsen and Petersen v Denmark, Ser A, No 23 (1976).

Sahin v Turkey, Application 44774/98, European Court of Human Rights (Chamber 29 June 2004) appeal (Grand Chamber 10 November 2005)

READING

Alfredsson, G, 'The right to human rights education' in A Eide, K Krause, and A Rosas (eds), *Economic, Social and Cultural Rights*, 2nd edn (Dordecht: Martinus Nijhoff, 2001), pp 273–88.
Arajärvi, P, 'Article 26' in G Alfredsson and A Eide (eds), *The Universal Declaration of Human Rights: A common standard of achievement* (The Hague: Martinus Nijhoff, 1999), pp 551–74.

Davies, L, *Citizenship Education and Human Rights Education: Parts 1 and 3* (London: British Council 2000) (accessed from www.british council.org/governance/cited.htm).

Henrard, K, 'Education and multi-culturalism: The contribution of minority rights' (2000) 7(4) International Journal of Minority and Group Rights 393–410.

Hodgson, D, *The Human Right to Education* (Aldershot: Ashgate, 1998).

Nowak, M, 'The right to education' in A Eide, K Krause, and A Rosas (eds), *Economic, Social and Cultural Rights*, 2nd edn (Dordecht: Martinus Nijhoff, 2001), pp 245–71.

Okafaor, OC, and Agbakwa, SC, 'Re-imagining international human rights education in our time: Beyond three constitutive orthodoxies' (2001) 14(3) Leiden Journal of International Law 563–90.

Tomaševski, K, *Annual Report of the Special Rapporteur on the Right to Education*, UN Doc E/CN.4/2001/52.

——, *Education Denied: Costs and remedies* (London/New York: Zed Books, 2003).

UNESCO, *The Right to Education: Towards education for all throughout life* (Paris: UNESCO, 2000).

United Nations, *Plan of Action for the United Nations Decade for Human Rights Education 1995–2004: Human rights education—lessons for life*, UN Doc A/51/506/Add.1, Appendix, 12 December 1996, para 2.

Wickliffe, C, 'Human rights education in the Pacific' (1999) 3 Journal of South Pacific Law.

WEBSITES

www.unhchr.ch/education/main.htm—site of the United Nations Decade for Human Rights Education and Training.

www.right-to-education.org—site established by the UN special rapporteur.

www.unesco.org—United Nations Educational, Scientific and Cultural Organization.

21

....

Minority rights

Everyone has the right freely to participate in the cultural life of the community, to enjoy the arts and to share in scientific advancement and its benefits. [Art 27(1), UDHR: see also Art 27, ICCPR (below); Art 14, ACHR ESCR Protocol; Art 17(2), ACHPR; Art 21, CIS; Art 41, AL]

In those States in which ethnic, religious or linguistic minorities exist, persons belonging to such minorities shall not be denied the right, in community with the other members of their group, to enjoy their own culture, to profess and practise their own religion, or to use their own language. [Art 27, ICCPR]

As Chapter 3 explained, the United Nations decided that the system of minority group protection advocated by the League of Nations had outlived its political expediency and elected to pursue a policy of universal human rights, rendering a separate system for minority protection superfluous. Minorities, however, did not disappear off the international agenda—the establishment of the Sub-Commission on the Prevention of Discrimination and the Protection of Minorities maintained a profile for relevant issues (now the Sub-Commission on the Protection and Promotion of Human Rights though its continuation is currently under review by the Human Rights Council). Moreover, international events have increasingly heightened awareness of the plight of minority groups. This chapter will return to the issue of minority rights, examining their scope and application today.

21.1 Background

Article 27 of the Universal Declaration restricted itself to establishing a 'right freely to participate in the cultural life of the community' despite detailed debates on the issue. The omission of a minority clause has been regarded as a 'mistake' (Capotorti, F, Preface). At the point of adopting the Universal Declaration, Resolution 217C demonstrates that the General Assembly had decided not to deal in specific provisions with the question of minorities, preferring instead to refer potential minority texts to the Economic and Social Council for further study under the auspices of the Commission on Human Rights and the Sub-Commission on the Prevention of Discrimination and the Protection of Minorities. The idea was that those bodies would make a thorough study of the 'problem of minorities' in order that the United Nations could subsequently take effective measures for the protection of racial, national, religious, or linguistic minorities. In 1950 one member of the Sub-Commission submitted a draft resolution (UN Doc E/CN.4 Sub.2/108), under which the Secretary-General would have been asked to circulate to the Sub-Commission a draft Convention, or a draft Protocol, to be attached to the International Covenants on Human Rights aimed at the protection of ethnic, religious, and linguistic groups. This proposal was subsequently withdrawn. In the end only one Article specifically addresses minority issues—Art 27 of the International Covenant on Civil and Political Rights 1966.

As a consequence, Art 27 is widely recognized as a real attempt in international law to promulgate the right of minority groups to preserve their special identity. The drafters considered the omission of such a provision in existing legislation a gap in the sequence of internationally recognized human rights (Nowak, M). That the Article was included in the Civil and Political Rights Covenant emphasizes its fundamentality: it is one of the rights which has to be given immediate effect (Art 2, ICCPR, although derogation is permitted under Art 4). Gradually, instigated by academic debate, the potential implications of Art 27 are being realized. In recent years, the provision has proven to be one of the more controversial of the Covenant especially when linked to self-determination issues. Minority rights are growing in prominence within the work of regional organizations too. Europe, with instruments concluded under the auspices of the various regional organizations, has the most-developed system to date. Its contribution will also be considered in this chapter.

As is often the case with a system of indivisible rights, there is a considerable overlap between minority rights and other rights: the interrelationship with the right to self-determination has been deliberated at length by the Human Rights Committee; rights of expression and freedoms of religion and assembly inevitably overlap with aspects of the manifestation of cultural identity; education, healthcare, and the working environment also have minority rights' dimensions when reflecting the culture of society. Culture manifests itself in various forms thus there will almost inevitably be a balancing act between different rights of different groups. Once more, the concept of proportionality is exercisable in this respect.

21.2 The need for minority protection

At the drafting stage of the International Bill of Rights, it was felt that the principal problem experienced by minority groups was lack of equality. Founding the United Nations on the principles of equality and non-discrimination (as discussed in Chapter 12) should have rectified this perceived, and in many instances actual, injustice. In spite of this, minorities have never disappeared from the international agenda. Indeed, a perusal of recent documented examples of international hostilities and events giving rise to 'threats to international peace and security' reveal that minority tensions frequently have dramatic repercussions. As was mentioned in Chapter 7, this has caused the Organization for Security and Cooperation in Europe to formulate detailed plans for addressing minority issues within Europe.

21.2.1 Rationalising minority protection

Conflicts rooted in cultural differences which have characterized international affairs in many respects realize the fears of many States vis-à-vis minorities, ie that any recognition of (even the mere existence of) minority groups can threaten the territorial integrity of a State. In many respects even recent history attests to these fears—the fate of the Union of Soviet Socialist Republics, Yugoslavia, and Czechoslovakia, for example. There are two principal schools of thought on minority treatment: assimilation and recognition (or fusion). The former entails the integration of minority groups into the life and culture of the majority of the population (this view predominated in Europe and the European colonies) whilst the latter entails the recognition and promotion of minority groups. Secessionist fears explain why assimilation was favoured in much of Europe—the process of decolonization addressed the external elements of this by 'unassimilating' the overseas colonies of the major powers through the exercise of self-determination. However, arguably globalization exercises an assimilationist influence on all States, particularly newer and developing States.

There was also considerable concern within the United Nations, and in academic circles, over whether minority rights were individual rights (vested in each individual by virtue of membership of a group) or group rights (exercised collectively). The United Nations clearly favoured individual rights as a concept thus proponents of group rights (including many aspects of minority rights) were sidelined in favour of the universal application of individual rights. The advantage of this to the individual is apparent when one recalls the problems encountered raising claims of self-determination before the Human Rights Committee.

21.2.2 The Universal Declaration and minority rights

It can be argued that the Universal Declaration covered minority rights insofar as many minority issues are included expressly or implicitly. To illustrate this, consider freedom of expression (Art 19) which does not limit expression to the official language of State; freedom of religion (Art 18) which includes the freedom to manifest religious beliefs in community with others; freedom of association (Art 20) which would facilitate meetings of minority peoples; and the prohibition of discrimination on grounds of race, colour, language, religion, national or social origin, birth, or other status (Art 2), all characteristics which may define minority persons within a State. However, the provisions of the Universal Declaration of Human Rights proved incapable of being used to protect minority groups in the manner they desired. Accordingly, the minority provision (Art 27) was included in the International Covenant on Civil and Political Rights.

21.3 Defining 'minorities'

One of the main problems associated with minority protection under international human rights law has been the lack of a universally accepted definition of what constitutes a minority. As has been mentioned (Chapter 17), similar problems have been experienced in defining the 'peoples' to whom the right to self-determination ascribes. To facilitate a realistic appraisal hereof, it is necessary not only to understand what is envisaged by the term 'minorities', but also to examine which specific minority groups are afforded the protection.

21.3.1 **Article 27 of the International Covenant on Civil and Political Rights**

Article 27 of the International Covenant is limited only to those States in which 'ethnic, religious or linguistic' groups are to be found. The selection of ethnic, religious, and linguistic groups is significant, as it is a narrower confine than that enshrined in non-discrimination instruments. In effect, by concentrating on ethnic, religious, and linguistic groups, the Covenant reiterates the criteria employed by the League of Nations in determining whether or not a group could be termed a minority and thus afforded the necessary protection. The substitution of 'ethnic' for 'racial' or even 'national' reflects contemporary practice though it may be noted that 'national' remains the preferred terminology in Europe (the 1995 Framework Convention for the Protection of National Minorities). It is arguable that 'racial' and 'ethnic' are interchangeable; any problem is ameliorated by the overlap in definition of the terms. The Sub-Commission decided, at its third session, that the cultural characteristics of minority status were adequately covered by the concepts of ethnicity, religion, and language.

It is clear that, in keeping with the spirit of universal rights, minority rights apply irrespective of the permanence of any given group in a State. Similarly, State recognition of the minority in question is not required. The drafting of Art 27 caused some problems, in particular with the ambit if its coverage: should all minorities be covered; what of immigrant groups; should the terminology be 'national minorities' or, as was eventually agreed, 'ethnic, linguistic and religious groups'? Irrespective of the terminology employed, it was not contested that the provisions would apply in addition to those contained elsewhere in the Covenant. Thus the minorities to whom the Covenant extends are afforded the benefit of an extra right, a degree (albeit limited) of specialist protection. (Additional groups benefiting from specific rights are considered in Chapter 22.) No limitations on this right were incorporated into the text. There was no public health, national security, or public morality derogation.

A State may or may not recognize all minority groups within its jurisdiction. Francesco Capotorti suggests that the phrase 'in those States' may be understood to mean that it is the responsibility of each State to recognize the existence of a minority in its territory (para 204). However, even should a State elect to ignore any minorities and refuse to recognize them in law, a group whose members can be distinguished from the majority population by one or more of the stipulated characteristics is entitled to rely on Art 27 of the Covenant. This line of reasoning can be seen in *Lovelace v Canada* (discussed in Chapter 12). The author of the communication, Sandra Lovelace, was born and registered a Maliseet Indian, but lost her rights and status as an Indian (in accordance with domestic law) when she married a non-Indian. Mrs Lovelace subsequently divorced and sought to return permanently to life on the reserve. As she remains ethnically a Maliseet Indian, the Committee opined that she could still be regarded as belonging to the minority group and thus invoke the rights which should accrue to her in terms of Art 27.

Capotorti refutes the idea that inclusion in Art 27 is dependent on the goodwill of States, arguing instead for inclusion on the basis of objective criteria. The term 'minorities' was abandoned in favour of the phraseology 'persons belonging to' minorities to ensure legal acceptance: minorities per se were not subjects of international law; persons belonging to such groups, however, could be defined.

Capotorti states that there are three reasons for using such terminology: historical—the Peace Treaties enforced by the League; to provide a coherent formulation of provisions—with the exception of self-determination, most rights are individual rights; and political—not attributing legal status per se should limit friction for States. The necessity for a group identity of a minority was reinforced by the inclusion of 'in community with other members of their group'. The rights enshrined in Art 27 are thus based on the interests of a collective group, the individual can exercise those rights solely on the basis of his or her membership of the group.

21.3.2 Tests employed to determine minority status

Discussion topic

Human Rights Committee General Comment 23 (1994):
Article 27: The Rights of Minorities

Article 27 confers rights on persons belonging to minorities which 'exist' in a State party. Given the nature and scope of the rights envisaged under that article, it is not relevant to determine the degree of permanence that the term 'exist' connotes. Those rights simply are that individuals belonging to those minorities should not be denied the right, in community with members of their group, to enjoy their own culture, to practise their religion and speak their language. Just as they need not be nationals or citizens, they need not be permanent residents. Thus, migrant workers or even visitors in a State party constituting such minorities are entitled not to be denied the exercise of those rights. As any other individual in the territory of the State party, they would, also for this purpose, have the general rights, for example, to freedom of association, of assembly, and of expression. The existence of an ethnic, religious or linguistic minority in a given State party does not depend upon a decision by that State party but requires to be established by objective criteria. [Para 5.2]

Does the problem of definition continue to impede the recognition of minority rights?

High Contracting Parties are permitted no discretion as to which groups benefit from Art 27. No provisions are made in the Covenant for the renunciation of membership of the group in question. Presumably it is thus a matter of interpretation for the State or group concerned. An individual should not be compelled to embrace membership of a minority group; it is possible to opt for assimilation into the majority of a State. (In *Kitok v Sweden*, the author, a member of a Sami family which had been actively involved in reindeer husbandry for a hundred years, had engaged in another profession for more than three years, thereby losing his inherited rights. Applying a test of proportionality, there was held to be no violation of the Covenant. The right to breed reindeer was, in effect, a once-only right, renunciation thereof being irreversible.) Conversely, individuals should be free to renounce membership of a group of their own free choice. This freedom of choice is, in itself, a right.

Both subjective and objective tests were employed by the Permanent Court of Justice in the *Greco-Bulgarian Communities Cases* (see box in Chapter 2). The objective test being the existence of facts and the subjective test, the 'sentiment of solidarity'.

This is probably the ideal position as a combination of many factors should give a clear indication of membership of a given group. Jules Deschênes, a Canadian member of the Sub-Commission proposed a definition in 1985:

a group of citizens of a State constituting a numerical minority and in a non-dominant position in that State, endowed with ethnic, religious or linguistic characteristics which differ from those of the majority of the population, having a sense of solidarity with one another, motivated, if only implicitly, by a collective will to survive and whose aim is to achieve equality with the majority in fact and in law. [UN Doc E/CN.4/Sub.2/1985/31, para 181]

Problems may arise when political ideologies become inextricably linked with culture, most predominantly, religion. One of the most established groups with linked political and religious ideologies are the followers of Judaism. Many States distinguish between Jews and Zionists in an attempt to separate the religious from the political ideologies prevalent in the Middle East. A similar situation is encountered necessitating distinctions between Arab and Muslim States, as well as different marked denominations of the latter.

A State counting minority groups among its population is obligated to adopt the legal and administrative measures necessary to enable the objectives of Art 27 to be achieved. States cannot fulfil their obligations by adopting a passive attitude (Capotorti, para 217).

It should be remembered that the rights pertain solely to persons 'belonging to' such minority groups. Group membership is thus a sine qua non of the enjoyment of the rights. 'The persons designed to be protected are those who belong to a group and who share in common a culture, a religion and/or a language' (General Comment No 23, para 5.1). Similarly, the rights can only be asserted in community with the other members of their group, ie collectively. This phraseology was incorporated to provide a legally ascertainable person to whom rights may be ascribed.

21.4 **The scope of the international provisions**

The role of the former Sub-Commission on the Protection and Promotion of Human Rights was viewed as twofold: the prevention of discrimination which required the implementation of the United Nations principle of equality; and the protection of minorities which required the achievement of equality with a caveat that those minorities who so desired may preserve cultural aspects of their race, nationality, religion, or language (E/CN.4/52 (1947)). Inevitably this would require negative and positive action on the part of States hosting minority groups.

A State's obligations to its minorities in terms of Art 27 of the International Covenant on Civil and Political Rights are threefold: enjoyment of culture; profession and practise of religion; and use of language. Each of these incumbent obligations/rights requires consideration. Note that the Covenant phrases the rights in the negative: 'shall not be denied the right'. Capotorti refutes the argument that States can thus take a passive approach to minority protection as he claims that would deprive the Article of its purpose (paras 211–17). The Human Rights Committee has recognized that positive measures of protection may be necessary under Art 27 to ensure that the rights of minorities are neither violated nor denied (General Comment No 23, para 6.1). The Human Rights Committee sums up the application of Art 27 by stating:

article 27 relates to rights whose protection imposes specific obligations on States Parties. The protection of these rights is directed to ensure the survival and continued development of the cultural, religious and social identity of the minorities concerned, thus enriching the fabric of society as a whole. [Para 9, General Comment]

The objective is thus clear, but what do the composite parts of Art 27 actually mean?

21.4.1 The right to enjoy one's culture

What is conveyed by the term 'culture'? The lack of a concise definition is one of the main stumbling blocks in this area of international law. The United Nations Educational, Social and Cultural Organization (UNESCO), by comparison, in a report by Michel Leiris entitled *Race and Culture*, defines culture as being inextricably linked to tradition:

As culture, then, comprehends all that is inherited or transmitted through society, it follows that its individual elements are proportionately diverse. They include not only beliefs, knowledge, sentiments and literature (and illiterate peoples often have an immensely rich oral literature), but the language or other systems of symbols which are their vehicles. Other elements are the rules of kinship, methods of education, forms of Government and all the fashions followed in social relations. Gestures, bodily attitudes and even facial expressions are also included, since they are in large measure acquired by the community through education or imitation; and so, among the material elements, are fashions in housing and clothing and ranges of tools, manufactures and artistic production, all of which are to some extent traditional ... [Leiris, M, p 21]

Distinctive clothing, standards of hospitality, language, religious rituals, social organization, ceremonial occasions, the performing arts, food, inheritance, marriage, and artefacts are all examples of aspects of the cultural life of a group. This list, although not exhaustive, demonstrates the broadening of the Covenant from its root civil and political rights to include matters that would fall, more correctly within the ambit of a document on economic and social rights. By way of contrast, the International Covenant on Economic, Social and Cultural Rights does not elucidate what is to be construed by 'culture'—the final rights enshrined therein (Arts 13–15) recognize rights to education and to take part in cultural life (Art 15) but no definition of what this may entail is provided.

'Culture' is a complex concept. It embraces all aspects of life in a community. It can be tangible, as in art and literature for example, or less physical, as in religion and customs. Social organization and laws governing the operation of a group are also included. Culture comprehends all that is inherited or transmitted through society. Institutional elements of culture are comparatively easy to ascertain: schools, museums, libraries, and religious buildings. What is more problematic is the influence of the less-tangible aspects on the rest of society, especially where the culture is of a minority. The use of a lesser-used language in public affairs may cause problems in law and administration; likewise with media coverage. Minority medical, religious, and educational practices could, conceivably, be unethical in the view of the majority of a State. To quote Boutros-Ghali, '[a] minimum of material well-being is necessary if the very notion of culture is to have the least significance' (p 73).

Key case

Mahuika and ors v New Zealand, UN Doc CCPR/C/70/D/547/1993

A number of Maori people claimed to be victims of violations of, inter alia, Art 27 (with Art 1 an aspect thereof) of the International Covenant on Civil and Political Rights. The 1840 Treaty of Waitangi concluded between some Maori peoples and the British Crown (then government of New Zealand), affirmed the rights of Maori people, including their right to self-determination and the right to control tribal fisheries. Following therefrom, in 1992 a fisheries settlement law was enacted. New Zealand acknowledged that Maori culture includes fishing and that the State had a positive obligation to protect this aspect of the culture. The Committee notes (paras 9.7–9.8) that under the terms of the enactment, Maori were given access to a great percentage of fishing quota, and Maori authority and traditional methods of control as recognised in the Treaty of Waitangi were replaced by a new control structure in which Maori share not only the role of safeguarding their interests in fisheries but also the effective control. Customary food gathering practices were protected and special attention was paid to the cultural and religious significance of fishing for the Maori. Despite the divisions caused within the Maori people, New Zealand had taken a number of steps to protect the culture of the Maori people and thus there was no violation of Art 27.

Any test of a State's compliance with Art 27 will, by its very nature, be objective. The physical realization of the rights will be most prominent: minority schools, churches, and museums. Positive or negative promotion of the culture by the State will be a key issue. Essentially, what is required is proof that a community's culture is not suffering from State oppression. The natural evolution of culture is something that cannot be stopped. Indeed, the Human Rights Committee has acknowledged that Art 27 allows for the 'adaptation of those [traditional] means to the modern way of life and ensuing technology' (*Mahuika v New Zealand*, para 9.4).

21.4.1.1 'Culture' through the case law

One of the earliest decisions impinging on Art 27 is that of *Lovelace v Canada*. Although discrimination on grounds of sex was the crucial aspect of the case (Indian men were not similarly denied Indian status), the Human Rights Committee contended that 'the major loss to a person ceasing to be an Indian is the loss of the cultural benefits of living in an Indian community, the emotional ties to home, family, friends and neighbours, and the loss of cultural identity'. The refusal of Canadian law to permit the realization of this natural cultural attachment was, in the considered opinion of the Committee, a breach of Art 27 of the Covenant. The case of *Lovelace* can be contrasted to that of the *Lubicon Lake Band* a few years later when the Committee appeared more willing to recognize the rights of indigenous groups without reservation.

Chief Bernard Ominayak of the Lubicon Lake Band, Canada, penned a Communication to the United Nations Human Rights Committee (167/1984 (1990)). The author alleged a violation of Art 1 of the Covenant—the right to self-determination. However, some aspects of the case were resolved with reference to Art 27 of the Covenant as the case concerned historical inequities and recent developments threatening the Lubicon Lake Band's traditional way of life and culture. Article 27, as exercised by a group of individuals all similarly affected by the events in question, could be distinguished from Art 1 (self-determination) which was deemed a collective right. There is thus potential for individual members of a linguistic, religious, ethnic, or indigenous group to bring an action citing Art 27 in preference to the declared group right of Art 1 even although the subject matter raised may be covered by either Article.

Although, the Committee was in no doubt that many of the allegations raised issues under Art 27 and that the life and culture of the band was threatened sufficiently to occasion a violation thereof, the government's proposals to remedy the situation were regarded as acceptable. One member of the Committee, Nisuke Ando, submitted an Individual Opinion on the application of Art 27 expressing reservation at the Committee's endorsement of the claimed violation of Art 27, submitting that:

the right to enjoy one's own culture should not be preserved intact at all costs. Past history of mankind bears out that technical development has brought about various changes to existing ways of life and thus affected a culture sustained thereon. Indeed, outright refusal by a group in a given society to change its traditional way of life may hamper the economic development of the society as a whole.

21.4.2 The right to profess and practise religion

In the international arena, religion, conscience, and belief tend to be linked together as an expression of one and the same concept. As early as 1956, the then United Nations Sub-Commission on Prevention of Discrimination and Protection of Minorities commissioned a study of discrimination in the matter of religious rights and practices. Subsequently, the General Assembly of the United Nations adopted its Declaration on the Elimination of All Forms of Intolerance and of Discrimination based on Religion or Belief 1981. However, even that specialist text does not provide a definition of what constitutes religion and comparable beliefs. Religion is essentially an overriding belief in something or someone which/who exists outside one's normal sphere. It prescribes a way of life and a set of rituals to be enacted by its followers. Arguably, atheism is also covered.

A principal problem in the guarantee by a State of freedom of religion, particularly for minority religions, is the historical interaction between a State and its religion. The Cairo Declaration on Human Rights in Islam reaffirms in its Preamble: 'the civilizing and historical role of the Islamic Ummah which God made the best nation that has given mankind a universal and well-balanced civilization in which harmony is established between this life and the hereafter and knowledge is combined with faith'. Many States have an accepted State religion from which holidays and the laws governing, for example, marriage and its dissolution evolve. Consequently, even a formal *de jure* separation between the State and religion does not guarantee true, de facto, separation. Religious beliefs influence too many aspects of life to be ignored. Even in atheist Communist States, a set of beliefs are instilled in the population and life revolves around their practice—observance of a day of rest and festivity on the anniversary of revolutions and of the births or deaths of revolutionaries.

Perhaps more than culture, religious freedom, by its nature, involves acts in community with others. Worship is not in itself a solo occupation. If conducted in private, it is unlikely that a State could have any bearing on the practice. However, when worship is in community with others, the wider community of the State may be influenced or disrupted by the worship and associated practices.

Once again, any test of a State's compliance with Art 27 of the International Covenant in this respect will tend towards objectivity. The provision or prohibition of religious instruction in schools, the existence of places of worship for the community, the absence of laws prohibiting rites and acts which form an integral part of religious life of the minority concerned, the merits of each are considered on a case by case basis. In itself, this may cause complications as an act which is essential to one set of religious beliefs may be repugnant to another. To an extent, the provisions of Art 27 in this respect overlap with those of Art 18 whereby '[e]veryone shall have the right to freedom of thought, conscience and religion'. Because religion and culture are related, in that religion prescribes a format of life and thus the culture of its followers, the terms may also be cross-referred within Art 27 itself, further strengthening the position of minority religions.

There is also an inevitable overlap with Art 26 as was demonstrated in *Waldman v Canada*, a case concerning State funding of certain secular schools. The Committee decided that the facts disclosed a violation of Art 26, with no additional issues requiring consideration under Art 27 of the Covenant.

21.4.3 **The right to use one's own language**

Minority languages may simply be the languages spoken by deemed minority groups or languages other than the principal language of the State. There is no universal consensus on the scope of 'language'. Is it generally restricted to languages which have developed to the extent of having a written form and a set script, or can languages which have not yet evolved into written form be counted too? Some of the languages of the South Pacific Islands, for example, have never been transcribed onto paper. Dialects and regional variations may be so far removed from the parent language that they become, in themselves, new languages. Ideally, each language and the approach of the State thereto should be resolved on a pragmatic basis.

Full and natural use of a language is complex. Not only does it necessitate the day to day use of the language in ordinary conversations, but it can extend to education being offered in the medium of that language, and the use of it in public and administrative services, judicial proceedings, and the media. Language impinges on all aspects of life and society.

It is perhaps interesting to note that linguistic minorities were a prominent concern of the then Sub-Commission on the Prevention of Discrimination and the Protection of Minorities. It recommended that, as an 'interim means of displaying its concern for minorities', the General Assembly should adopt a draft resolution on facilities to be provided for minorities, viz:

(1) the use in judicial procedure of languages of such groups;

(2) the teaching in state-supported schools of languages of such groups, provided that such groups request it and that the request in reality expresses the spontaneous desire of such groups. [UN Doc. E/CN.4/Sub.2/117, p 42]

Only the former was included in the International Covenant—Art 14 provides for the accused to be informed in detail in a language which he understands of the nature and cause of the charge against him (Art 14(3)(a)) and to have the free assistance of an interpreter if required (Art 14(3)(f)).

Key case

***Diergaardt and ors v Namibia,* UN Doc CCPR/C/69/D/760/1996**

The Reheboth Baster Community in Namibia occupy an area south of Windhoek, the capital, in which they essentially enjoy their own society, culture, language, and economy. The peoples claimed, inter alia, a number of land rights and cultural rights infringements, which they had pursued through the Namibian courts. Crucially, they were required to use English in all court proceedings and have all their documentation translated into English from Afrikaans. English is the official language of Namibia in accordance with the constitution:

The authors have also claimed that the lack of language legislation in Namibia has had as a consequence that they have been denied the use of their mother tongue in administration, justice, education and public life. The Committee notes that the authors have shown that the State party has instructed civil servants not to reply to the authors' written or oral communications with the authorities in the Afrikaans language, even when they are perfectly capable of doing so. These instructions barring the use of Afrikaans do not relate merely to the issuing of public documents but even to telephone conversations. [Para 10.10]

In the absence of explanatory evidence from Namibia, there was thus an infringement of Art 26 of the ICCPR on equality before the law without discrimination as to language.

Cases brought against France arguing preservation of minority languages have been inadmissible under Art 27 as France entered a reservation upon ratification which rendered Art 27 inapplicable (see, inter alia, *TK and MK v France*).

The State must seek to find a just equilibrium between the economic and practical interests of the State and the interests of the minority language users in its jurisdiction. Language can, however, naturally evolve and a minority language may, over time, become diluted with the majority language. What must be hoped for is the preservation of all languages to the extent required to enable their cultural aspects to be appreciated.

21.4.4 **Using the International Covenant**

Article 27 heralds progress for minority groups resident in the territory of Contracting States. However, the realization of the rights enshrined therein are often more idealistic than factual, being dependent on the will of the State. Primarily, a State can restrict the operation of the Article by imposing limitations on the concept of 'minority'. Thwarting the process of assimilation of minorities is viewed by some States as threatening the unity of the State. Minorities with a separate identity are often linked to separatist movements and thus perceived as a threat to the solidarity of the State.

The rights of minorities encapsulated by Art 27 are not absolute. Derogations are permissible in terms of Art 4. At no time during the term of the derogation, whatever the exigencies of the situation, may a State adopt measures or practices which involve discrimination 'on the ground of race, colour, sex, language, religion or social origin'. Consequently, even in such troubled times, the right of minority group members not to be discriminated against is guaranteed. However, Art 5 provides that nothing in the present Covenant may be interpreted as implying for any State, group, or person any right to engage in any activity or perform any act aimed at the destruction of any of the rights and freedoms recognized in the Covenant.

21.4.5 **The Declaration on the Rights of Persons Belonging to National or Ethnic, Religious and Linguistic Minorities 1992**

Progress on a more detailed codification of minority rights was slow. Political reality prompted a hastening of developments in the early 1990s. Ethnic tensions in, inter alia, Europe prompted the United Nations to adopt the Declaration on the Rights of Persons Belonging to National or Ethnic, Religious and Linguistic Minorities in 1992, the product of more than ten years of protracted negotiations and debate. The Declaration provides that 'persons belonging to national or ethnic, religious and linguistic minorities ... have the right to enjoy their own culture, to profess and practise their own religion, and to use their own language, in private and in public, freely and without interference or any form of discrimination' (Art 2(1)). The Declaration owes its existence to the inspiration provided by Art 27 of the International Covenant and aims at promoting peace and stability. The basic provisions of the declaration aim at prohibiting discrimination and, 'where appropriate' encouraging States to actively promote aspects of minority culture. The latter includes provision of minority language education, cultural and historical education for all, and political participation.

21.5 **Regional developments**

In the American system, there is a clear link to other rights—Art 16(1) provides for freedom of association for cultural purposes. The African Charter (Art 17(2)) provides that every individual may freely take part in the cultural life of his community. However, given the emphasis on 'peoples' rights' in the African Charter, it is inevitable that other 'minority rights' can easily be inferred in the provisions alluding to cultural and traditional values. Moreover, Art 29(7) of the Charter imposes a duty on all individuals to 'preserve and strengthen positive African cultural values'.

21.5.1 **European developments**

Europe, with a number of high profile ethnic conflicts (in history and present) has produced the most comprehensive regional criteria for preserving minority rights. There are instruments aimed at protecting and preserving minorities concluded under the auspices of the Council of Europe, the European Community/Union and the Organization for Security and Cooperation in Europe.

21.5.1.1 *Council of Europe*

There are no provisions in the European Convention on Human Rights which pertain directly to minorities. However, the Council of Europe has, as previously mentioned, adopted a Framework Convention for the Protection of National Minorities 1995. Article 1 declares that the protection of national minorities and minority rights form an 'integral part of the international protection of human rights'. The essence of the rights is similar to those in the International Covenant on Civil and Political Rights: preservation of religion, language, traditions, and cultural heritage (Art 5(1)). It should be noted that the underlying premise is the protection of European heritage to further stability, democratic security, and peace in the continent (Preamble). The Convention represents a reaction to the 'upheavals' in European history, and seeks to create a 'climate of tolerance and dialogue' to 'enable cultural diversity to be a source and a factor, not of division, but of enrichment for each society' (Preamble). Much of the Convention addresses issues of equality, tolerance, and mutual respect though various specific rights do appear: religious freedom, freedom of expression, participation in public affairs; and freedom of association. Provision is made for trans-frontier contact between persons sharing common cultural heritages with State Parties agreeing to facilitate the conclusion of bilateral and multilateral treaties, where necessary, in furtherance of this (Art 17–18). Education rights are deemed important—the State education system should foster knowledge of the culture, history, language, and religion of national minorities (and majorities) (Art 12). Private minority education systems should be permitted if the minority so desires (and can fund it). Language rights are also detailed in the Convention though, of course, the Council of Europe had adopted the European Charter for Regional or Minority Languages some three years previously. The implementation of the Framework Convention for the Protection of National Minorities is monitored by the Committee of Ministers of the Council of Europe. This applies even where the State Party is not a member of the Council of Europe. Reports are the primary method of supervision.

The European Charter for Regional or Minority Languages is also aimed primarily at national minorities—it expressly does not extend to immigrant languages. As with the Framework Convention, cognizance is given to the work of the Organization for Security and Cooperation in Europe. The object of the Charter is to protect those historical regional or minority languages 'some of which are in danger of eventual extinction' which contribute to Europe's cultural wealth and traditions (Preamble). The general objectives and principles to which all contracting States subscribe aim at the recognition, equality, and protection of all regional and minority languages within that State. All exclusions, restrictions, and preferences which endanger these languages are to be eliminated. States then select various provisions relating to education, judicial authorities, public services, the media, cultural, economic and social activities, and trans-frontier exchanges. Periodic reports submitted to the Secretary-General of the Council of Europe are examined by a Committee of Experts to ensure the application of the Charter in the territory of each signatory State.

21.5.1.2 *European Community/Union*

With the potential extension of the Community to the East, the plight of minority groups has attracted a higher profile. Attempts have been made to protect aspects of traditional identity in Europe. Again, the emphasis is on preserving the traditional cultural heritage of the region. No specific instruments have been adopted. However, Art 22 of the European Charter of Fundamental Rights of the European Union states that '[t]he Union shall respect cultural, religious, and linguistic diversity'. This will govern the operation of all Community institutions in the future.

21.5.1.3 *Organization for Security and Cooperation in Europe*

Discussion topic

Minorities and conflict

A High Commissioner for National Minorities was appointed by the Organization of Security and Cooperation in Europe with a mandate grounded in conflict prevention. He seeks to identify possible flashpoints and mediate through (usually closed) diplomatic activities. He also acts as a 'watchdog', 'flagging up' potential conflict situations to the OSCE. The mandate is thus one of short-term conflict prevention. As a region, Europe is the centre of some of the most deadly minority conflicts of the last hundred years, many pursuant to the redrawing of mainland Europe's territorial boundaries after major conflicts. Often the issue of secession and/or autonomy is a major factor. Recent (and ongoing) minority situations include the Roma/Sinti people in Central Europe; Georgia, the Russian Federation and the South Ossetians and Abkhazians; and Chechnya and the Russian Federation.

Much work remains to be done on identifying the cause of conflict in Europe and the mechanisms for protecting national minorities.

Probably the most significant contribution towards minority rights has been the work of the Organization for Security and Cooperation in Europe. As was noted in Chapter 7, the OSCE was prompted to add a human dimension to its work on regional security and expand it significantly as the Soviet bloc countries dissolved. Minority protection is at the forefront of these initiatives. Under the auspices of the OSCE, a system of guidelines has been adopted but there is no system of implementation or enforcement per se. The guidelines are on various aspects of minority rights including participation of minorities in public life, education rights, and language rights (in general and in the media).

21.6 **Conclusions**

Harmonious relations between minorities and majorities and between different minority groups within a State contribute greatly to the stability of that State as well as promoting multicultural diversity in an increasingly pluralistic world.

The heightened awareness of issues affecting minorities shows no signs of abating; thus, it is reasonable to assume that this is one area in which there may be further codification of the law, perhaps with the adoption of a more binding text on minority rights. The return to minority rights demonstrates that the assumption behind the original post-war documentation (that full recognition of individual rights obviates the need for group and minority protection) was inherently flawed. Certain claims of groups that relate to the preservation of their culture fall outwith the scope of individual human rights. Moreover, in minority protection, perhaps more than other rights, one of the fundamental problems with human rights is evident: that of the perceived Western bias of the norms. Through minority rights, the international community must reconcile the need to protect and preserve different groups with the need to avoid a protectionist, paternalistic approach. Diverse cultural traditions must be recognized. A response based on contemporary legal norms is unavoidable though the debate on cultural relativity and universality continues.

CASES

Chief Bernard Ominayak and the Lubicon Lake Band v Canada, UN Doc CCPR/C/38/D/167/1984.

Greco-Bulgarian Communities Cases, PCIJ Reps Ser B, Nos 17, 19, 21–3 [1930].

Kitok v Sweden, UN Doc CCPR/C/33/D/197/1985 (1988).

Lovelace v Canada, UN Doc CCPR/C/13/D/24/1977 (1981).

Mahuika v New Zealand, UN Doc CCPR/C/70/D/547/1993 (2000).

TK and MK v France, UN Doc CCPR/C/37/D/220 and 222/1987 (1989).

Waldman v Canada, UN Doc CCPR/C/67/D/694/1996 (1999).

READING

Eide, A, 'The non-inclusion of minority rights: Resolution 217C (III)' in G Alfredsson and A Eide (eds), *The Universal Declaration of Human Rights: A common standard of achievement* (The Hague: Martinus Nijhoff, 1999), pp 701–23.

Boutros-Ghali, B, 'the right to culture and the Universal Declaration of Human Rights' in *Cultural Rights as Human Rights* (Paris: UNESCO, 1970).

Capotorti, F, *Study on the Rights of Persons belonging to Ethnic, Religious and Linguistic Minorities* (New York: United Nations, 1991).

Fottrell, D, and Bowring, B (eds), *Minority and Group Rights in the New Millennium* (The Hague: Kluwer, 1999).

Leiris, M, *Race and Culture* (Paris: UNESCO, 1951).

Nowak, M, *UN Covenant on Civil and Political Rights: CCPR commentary*, 2nd edn (Kehl: Engel, 2005).

Pentassuglia, G, 'Minority protection in international law: From standard setting to implementation' (1999) 68(2) Nordic Journal of International Law 131–60.

——, 'The EU and the protection of minorities: The case of Eastern Europe' (2001) 12 European Journal of International Law 3–38.

Prott, L, 'Cultural rights as peoples' rights in international law' in J Crawford (ed), *The Rights of Peoples* (Oxford: Clarendon Press, 1988), pp 93–106.

Sohn, L, 'The rights of minorities' in L Henkin (ed), *The International Bill of Human Rights: The Covenant on Civil and Political Rights* (London: Stevens, 1981), pp 270–89.

Thornberry, P, *International Law and the Rights of Minorities* (Oxford: Clarendon Press, 1991).

Welhengama, G, *Minorities' Claims: From autonomy to secession—international law and State practice* (Aldershot: Ashgate, 2000).

Weller, M (ed), *The Rights of Minorities: A commentary on the European Framework Convention for the Protection of National Minorities* (Oxford: OUP, 2005).

Wheatley, S, 'The Council of Europe's Framework Convention on National Minorities' (1995) 5 Web Journal of Current Legal Issues.

——, *Democracy, Minorities and International Law* (Cambridge: CUP, 2005).

Wright, J, 'The OSCE and the protection of minority rights' (1996) 18 Human Rights Quarterly 190–205.

United Nations *United Nations Guide for Minorities* (2001), Office of the High Commissioner for Human Rights: Geneva (available online at www.unhchr.ch/html/racism/01-minoritiesguide.html).

United Nations Human Rights Committee General Comment No 23 reproduced in UN Doc HRI/GEN/1/Rev.9 (Vol. I).

WEBSITES

www2.ohchr.org/english/bodies/subcom/index.htm—former United Nations Sub-Commission on the Protection and Promotion of Human Rights.

www.osce.org/hcnm—OSCE High Commissioner on National Minorities.

22

....

Group rights

It is not only ethnic, religious and linguistic minorities who have benefited from additional protection under the international human rights system. One of the characteristics of the new international system is an evolving focus on providing protection for categories of peoples. Some examples have already been considered. The non-discrimination provision common to most instruments has had significant impact on racial groups and on narrowing the gulf between men and women (see Chapter 12) while minority rights have provided a remedy for many ethnic, religious, and linguistic groups on the verge of being consigned to history (see Chapter 21). Elements of these rights have promulgated a concept of group rights—rights which are extended to an individual on account of his or her classification as a member of an identified group. This chapter will focus on four groups which are currently beneficiaries of dedicated human rights' regimes: indigenous peoples, women, children, and refugees.

Indigenous peoples increasingly have been beneficiaries of rights evolved to challenge the threat posed by modern society, rights created to promote cultural diversity and to ensure fairness of treatment when addressing issues of natural resource development and dispossession of land. Although some suppose them to be minorities, many, including most importantly the peoples themselves, consider indigenous peoples to be a distinct category of peoples with distinct rights responding to their discrete needs. Women and children have also been singled out for particular attention: women because in most cultures they are subjected to an element of persecution, rendering true equality impossible; children because they are inherently vulnerable to the actions of adults. In each instance, the United Nations has been proactive in developing appropriate protective legal frameworks. Refugees are probably the category of people most overtly affected by the large numbers of conflicts which plague the planet. While refugees and displaced persons were a major issue in the aftermath of the Second World War when the United Nations was reformed, today almost one in three hundred people are of concern to the United Nations High Commissioner for Refugees. Refugees remain inherently vulnerable.

The rights and freedoms accorded to each group will be overviewed in this chapter. First, the particular needs of the group will be identified—why does the group require enhanced protection? Secondly, the evolving international, and where appropriate regional, framework will be outlined. A brief consideration of the salient provisions will follow—to what extent does the legal framework address the needs of the group in question?

To provide an appropriate context for this discussion, it is necessary to first consider why group rights have evolved in a system of human rights which, from the outset, was supposed to be universal.

22.1 Towards group rights

Given that all rights are universal, everyone is entitled to the minimum level of protection prescribed in the myriad of instruments outlined in the previous chapters. Sadly, there is no equality of enjoyment of rights, as Chapter 12 illustrates. Although considerable progress has been made towards articulating clear standards on equality and non-discrimination, particularly in respect of race and gender, discrimination remains. Recognition of particularly vulnerable and oppressed people has been prompted by a variety of issues but in most instances it has been apparent that the existing system of universal rights was in some way deficient. The identified group has been failed by the international system. Something more had to be done. A regime of specific legal protection is the obvious, though sometimes controversial, response of the international community.

22.2 Indigenous peoples

Indigenous peoples, although often distinguishable by virtue of their race, language or religion (like minorities), are a discrete group. First peoples around the world have been subjected to persecution and alienation. The claims of indigenous peoples have particular resonance in many regions: can historic wrongs yet be righted?

22.2.1 Historical issues

Although all indigenous peoples may have been persecuted to some extent, certain historical events represent watersheds in their history. For most groups, the 'golden age' of exploration and empires is a particularly large blot in their history. Colonization was usually a disaster for indigenous peoples: incoming colonial forces claimed large swathes of the globe with little regard for those previously residing in the locality. The concept of pre-existing territorial rights for indigenous people was rarely accepted. Recognition of the rights of indigenous peoples, the sanctity of their lives and culture were frequently obviated in the interests of empire expansion.

22.2.2 Claims of indigenous peoples

Many of the claims of indigenous peoples are particular to their historic situations. They reflect colonization, assimilation, and alienation of traditional ways of living. Not all indigenous peoples claim the rights discussed in this section. Many wish to assimilate with others in the State in which they find themselves. In accordance with contemporary international practice, it is up to each person to determine whether s/he wishes to be considered a member of the group in question. Such a policy of self-identification helps to obviate the problems caused by definitional issues.

22.2.2.1 Right to an existence

Of primary importance is, of course, the right to an existence (see Chapter 13). Many indigenous peoples were subject to treatment which today would fall within the jurisdiction of the International Criminal Court. Genocidal practices were rarely challenged during the empire-forming era as there were no war crimes tribunals. Today, the right to physical existence of indigenous groups is unassailable. What remains problematic is the continuation of their cultural traditions. There are some commentators who argue for recognition of cultural genocide (eg, Dunn). Indeed, earlier drafts of the Genocide Convention included cultural genocide: the brutal destruction of the specific characteristics of a group. With opposition from States such as the USA and France, the clause was dropped. The emphasis in the Convention is thus on political genocide, cultural genocide remains an academic discussion point. Indigenous people have the right to a physical existence, but what quality such an existence if their culture is under threat?

22.2.2.2 Autonomy

Self-determination is a popular claim of indigenous peoples. As discussed in Chapter 17, it was conceived as a mechanism by which colonized people could become independent of colonial rule: its extension to indigenous peoples remains problematic. However, an element of self-determination is almost synonymous with self-preservation for indigenous people (Turpel, M, p 593) particularly given the progressive erosion of aspects of the cultural identity of indigenous people. Of greater potential relevance to indigenous peoples is autonomy. Alternatives are thus being explored. It may be possible for indigenous peoples to achieve partial autonomy without threatening the territorial integrity of the State. It is essential not only that they participate in decisions affecting their destiny, but also that they can decide the direction of that destiny. Given that full self-determination is frequently mired in controversy and problems, perhaps internal autonomy represents a compromise. It would enable indigenous peoples who so desire to preserve their culture and live in accordance with traditional practices, customs, and laws, or to advance and develop those traditional practices in response to the evolving society in which they find themselves. Indigenous peoples need not be preserved, somewhat paternalistically, as a living museum piece. Rather they should be entitled to live their lives as they choose, in an atmosphere of respect for their heritage. The argument goes that permitting autonomy facilitates continuation of the culture of the peoples concerned while respecting the territorial integrity of a State in accordance with public international law.

22.2.2.3 Land rights

Land rights are particularly problematic for many indigenous peoples. This is especially notable when self-determination is not an option. Many indigenous peoples were dispossessed of their lands following colonization. Some indigenous peoples were forcibly removed from their lands, others ceded land under pressure. For example, some of the Maori peoples of Aotorea/New Zealand signed the Treaty of Waitangi, granting land rights to the 'invaders' while in the Americas, the land was regarded as *terra nullius*, literally empty land which was 'discovered' and occupied by Europeans.

Key case

Chief Bernard Ominayak and the Lubicon Lake Band v Canada, UN Doc CCPR/C/38/
D/167/1984 (1990)

This is one of the more famous early communications on indigenous peoples rights. On
behalf of the Lubicon Lake Band, Chief Ominayak argued the right of self-determination,
to determine freely its political status and pursue economic, social, and cultural development, as well as the right to dispose freely of its natural wealth and resources. As noted
in Chapter 17 of this book, self-determination cannot be invoked through the Optional
Procedure complaint process. However, the Committee noted 'no objection to a group
of individuals, who claim to be similarly affected, collectively to submit a communication about alleged breaches of their rights' (para 32.1). Thus indigenous people can use
the UN mechanisms to pursue alleged violations of their individual rights:

Although initially couched in terms of alleged breaches of the provisions of article 1 of the Covenant, there is no doubt that many of the claims presented raise issues under article 27. The
Committee recognizes that the rights protected by article 27, include the right of persons, in community with others, to engage in economic and social activities which are part of the culture of the
community to which they belong. [Para 32.2]

Historical inequities, to which the State party refers, and certain more recent developments threat-
en the way of life and culture of the Lubicon Lake Band, and constitute a violation of article 27 so
long as they continue. [Para33]

Canada offered a settlement package to remedy the situation. This was rejected by the
Band and negotiations collapsed around 2005. Canada officially claims to be offering
a satisfactory settlement. Lubicon Lake Band maintain the settlement is inadequate. As
of 2009, per the documents submitted by the Band during universal periodic review of
Canada by the Human Rights Council, an impasse remains.

The lack of identifiable (to the colonizers) systems of land ownership clearly caused
problems.

Although many indigenous peoples live a subsistence existence, and are nomadic, spiritual ties to land are strong. For many indigenous groups, traditional lands
are an integral part of their beliefs as well as essential to their existence due to
associated usufructory practices. The Australian aboriginal peoples' dreamtime
provides explanations of many geographic features in Australia. Attempts are now
being made to limit damage caused by tourism: Uluru (Ayers Rock) and Katu Tinggu (the Olgas) are no longer subjected to hordes of tourists climbing around and
over them. Usufructory rights have already been the subject of claims before the
international human rights bodies (for example, *Kitok* as discussed in Chapter 21).
The Inuit peoples of the subpolar region and multiple native Americans in North
America have been particularly affected by proposed and actual legal limitations on
their traditional hunting, gathering, and animal husbandry activities. With greater
awareness, many of these issues are being resolved at an individual national level.
Indigenous peoples frequently enjoy exemption from laws which may interfere
with their usufructory traditions (Inuit and seals, for example).

More recent and ongoing challenges to indigenous peoples arise through the exploitation of land and natural resources. In South America, many indigenous groups have seen their traditional lands eroded through mass deforestation. Mining and oil and mineral exploration are notable problems in large swathes of Africa. In Alaska, the Alaskan Native Settlement Claim Act 1971 was the largest Indian settlement in history, giving Alaska's indigenous people clear title to 40 million acres and cash of USD 962.5 million. This settlement paved the way for the trans-Alaskan pipeline which impacted heavily on traditional Inuit lands and affected natural migration routes of many indigenous species.

While land rights are clearly important to many indigenous peoples, multiple issues are associated with recognizing pre-existing claims to land. The political reality is that a return to the status quo ante is frequently impossible, neither Sydney (Australia) nor Vancouver (Canada) could easily be returned to their original occupiers in their original state. Other forms of restitution must then be considered. Foremost among these is financial compensation, though for many groups an official apology will suffice. In Australia, the issue came to a head in the famous case of *Mabo v State of Queensland*. In essence, the High Court of Australia recognized the pre-existing native title to land in the Torres Strait islands. The Native Title Act 1993 sought to rectify the 'historic wrong' creating a system for the formal recognition of native title and compensation for the loss thereof. Further developments in *Wik Peoples and ors v State of Queensland and ors* inferred a presumption of coexistence of property rights for native title claimants and those with State (or other) interests.

Key case

Hopu and Bessert v France, **UN Doc CCPR/C/60/D/549/1993/Rev 1**

Ethnic Polynesians claimed France, which administers Tahiti, had infringed a number of rights under the covenant. They argued their ancestors were dispossessed of their native land rights by the French authorities and that land upon which a hotel complex was to be built, represented:

an important place in their history, their culture and their life. They add that the land encompasses the site of a pre-European burial ground and that the lagoon remains a traditional fishing ground and provides the means of subsistence for some thirty families living next to the lagoon. [Para 2.3]

The construction work would thus destroy their traditional burial ground and decimate the fishing grounds. France has a declaration in place which effectively reserves Art 27 thus the committee is precluded from considering Art 27 per se. Nevertheless, the Committee found a violation of Arts 17 and 23 on privacy and family lives:

The authors claim that the construction of the hotel complex on the contested site would destroy their ancestral burial grounds, which represent an important place in their history, culture and life, and would arbitrarily interfere with their privacy and their family lives, in violation of articles 17 and 23. They also claim that members of their family are buried on the site ... cultural traditions should be taken into account when defining the term 'family' in a specific situation ... they consider the relationship to their ancestors to be an essential element of their identity and to play an important role in their family life. [Para 10.3]

22.2.2.4 *Cultural rights*

Indigenous peoples demand the right to enjoy their own culture unimpeded by restrictions. Culture includes religious practices, language, usufructory traditions, and other native practices. In many instances, cultural rights can easily be realized. However, some elements of cultural practices actually infringe international human rights—examples include female genital mutilation, a practice now condemned by the World Health Organization, and live sacrifices whether human or animal. Other traditional practices are more easily addressed. Linguistic and religious rights may benefit from the protection accorded under minority rights as may elements of traditional practices such as hunting and fishing (see Chapter 21). Even international instruments acknowledge traditional usufructory rights. For example, the international prohibition on whale hunting is not absolute; a limited amount of hunting by native peoples is permitted. Thus, in Bequia (St Vincent and the Grenadines), one or two humpback whales may be harpooned each year for local consumption in accordance with recognized custom.

22.2.3 **International developments**

The most significant problem which besets the international community is one of definition. Just as was discussed in Chapter 17 in the context of 'peoples' for self-determination, it is necessary to define who the beneficiaries are before rights can accrue. This is a crucial issue given that indigenous peoples' claims to self-determination are often rejected, albeit in favour of some form of semi-autonomy. The problems are similar to those encountered when delineating the parameters of minorities—section 21.3 (Chapter 21) addresses this in more detail. However, should indigenous peoples be recognized as 'peoples', there remains considerable concern among States as to what additional rights may ensue. Self-determination and compensation are the principal concerns.

The International Labour Organization led the way developing rights for indigenous peoples in the wake of its 1921 studies of indigenous workers. Convention No 50 on the recruiting of indigenous workers (1936) followed conventions on abolishing forced labour, a particular problem for indigenous peoples. Other conventions followed before the ILO produced two major conventions on the subject. Convention No 107 concerning the protection and integration of indigenous and other tribal and semi-tribal populations in independent countries and associated recommendations (1957) was the first international instrument completely concerned with indigenous populations. Essentially the convention aims at the progressive integration of the indigenous peoples into the society in which they live. Such an assimilationist overture was naturally viewed sceptically by many indigenous groups. Perhaps in mitigation thereof, a limited number of indigenous organizations were accorded observer status during the drafting process of the revised convention. Convention No 169 (1989) provides for self-identification of indigenous peoples (Art 1(2)) in accordance with a much less paternalistic definition. Land, employment, vocational training and rural industries, social security, and education are addressed. Despite the misgivings of many, Convention No 169 remains the most comprehensive legally enforceable instrument for indigenous peoples.

More recent developments have centred on the United Nations. A Draft Declaration on the Rights of Indigenous People has been adopted. The Human Rights Council adopted the Declaration in June 2006 but the General Assembly failed to adopt it in December 2006. The Draft Declaration covers a variety of issues, including linguistic, religious and cultural rights, land issues, and equality. Progress towards the Declaration was and is aided by the work of an open-ended working group on the matter (Commission Resn 1995/32). The sole purpose of the group is to elaborate the draft with the assistance of indigenous groups (co-funded by the United Nations Voluntary Fund for Indigenous Populations, as required). This working group should be distinguished from the more general Working Group on Indigenous Populations which was established in 1982. Its 22nd session in July 2004 was dedicated to the theme Indigenous Peoples and Conflict Resolution. Reconciliation is a key development in indigenous affairs (see for example, Australia). Many indigenous peoples actively contribute to the Working Group's annual sessions.

The advent of a Permanent Forum on Indigenous Issues (ECOSOC Resn 2000/22) indicates a willingness on the part of the international community to respond to the plight of this group. The Forum is expected to provide advice and recommendations on indigenous issues to the Economic and Social Council as well as contributing to the raising of awareness of issues, and preparing and disseminating information on indigenous issues. The Forum held its inaugural meeting in New York in May 2002. Its work should add further weight to the progress of the Draft Declaration on the rights of indigenous peoples, adoption of which was the major unfulfilled objective of the International Decade of the World's Indigenous Peoples (1995–2004). Indeed the Forum is critical of the further delays in adoption occasioned in the General Assembly in 2006. A special rapporteur on the situation of human rights and fundamental freedoms and indigenous peoples was appointed in 2001 (Commission Resn 2001/57). James Anaya, from the United States, is the current encumbent. He is focusing on 'thematic research' on issues impacting on the human rights situation and fundamental freedoms of indigenous peoples, country visits and communications with governments regarding issues of concern (www2.ohchr.org/english/issues/indigenous/rapporteur/). A previous 2006 report centred on constitutional reform, legislation and the implementation of laws regarding the promotion and protection of indigeneous peoples' rights and the effectiveness thereof. South Africa and New Zealand hosted recent country visits.

22.2.4 **Regional developments**

22.2.4.1 *Americas*

In the Americas, home to a substantial number of indigenous peoples from the Inuit peoples of Alaska and Canada to the Mapucho peoples of Southern Argentina and Chile, the plight of indigenous populations has long been of concern. There is a stark contrast between the impact of the European colonial culture on North American groups and those in less accessible regions of the continent such as the Amazon basin. It is perhaps not so surprising that the OAS has also developed a draft declaration on the rights of indigenous peoples. The text was drawn up by the Inter-American Commission on Human Rights in 1997. Indigenous people were encouraged to attend preparatory sessions and participate, at least indirectly, in the developmental process. Formal inter-State negotiations on the Draft American Declaration on the Rights of Indigenous Peoples began in November 2003 and a series of Meetings of Negotiation in the Quest for Points of Consensus are being held in 2007 in, inter alia, the United States and Bolivia. Progress is clearly being made. The Inter-American Commission on Human Rights has also been increasingly involved in indigenous issues. See for example, *Mary and Carrie Dann v United States of America*, notable not least for the fact this is one of the only fora before which complaints against the United States can appear.

Other developments in the Americas include recognition of native customs and practices in areas of Canada and the United States of America, and compensation for dispossession of land. In Central and South America, the evolution of society and progressive deforestation has resulted in ever greater interaction between remote groups and others. Meanwhile, land rights continue to be a major legal issue in, for example, Brazil as the pressure on natural resources increases.

22.2.4.2 *Africa*

Africa has perhaps a greater concentration of indigenous peoples in terms of numbers. With decolonization, some indigenous groups made significant gains in respect of political leadership. Multicultural understanding has become essential for the peaceful coexistence of peoples and States within the continent. The African Charter on Human and Peoples' Rights includes various provisions of particular relevance to indigenous peoples. Article 21 on disposal of natural resources and compensation for dispossession through spoilation and Art 22 on development are two such examples. The emphasis on peoples and society, rather than the nation State, in much of the African instrument further promotes indigenous ideals.

22.2.4.3 *Europe*

Within Europe, protection of indigenous peoples falls within the realm of the Council of Europe's Framework Convention on National Minorities and the European Charter for Regional and Minority Languages. Both these instruments aim at protecting indigenous culture.

22.3 **Women**

There is considerable debate over the separation of women's rights from universal human rights as, demographically, women are a huge group. Clearly, women are entitled to the enjoyment of all human rights and the breadth of women's rights exceeds the space available in the current text. To provide a flavour of the salient issues, this section will focus on elements of equality, family rights, violence against women, and the associated international and regional initiatives.

22.3.1 **Historical issues**

Pioneering work was undertaken by the International Labour Organization. In 1919, it adopted two landmark conventions on women's rights, Convention No 3 on Maternity Protection and Convention No 4 on Night Work of Women. Eighty-five years ago women regularly worked long hours for little money, and if they ceased work due to childbirth, their wages would stop. Essentially the modern system of social welfare did not exist, thus for many women working was an economic necessity, however oppressive the employer–employee relationship. As with indigenous peoples, the early work of the International Labour Organization was marred by a perceived paternalistic/protectionist approach to women's rights. Another area of activity in women's rights which received early attention is trafficking and exploitation. Women remain frequently subject to practices analogous to slavery thus the eighteenth- and nineteenth-century prohibitions on slavery remain applicable. Many of these issues are discussed in Chapter 15.

22.3.2 **Rights of women**

The United Nations paid particular attention to the rights of women, in accordance with the Charter provisions on equality. In 1945, there was considerable disparity throughout the world in the treatment and legal protection of men and women. Female emancipation was still ongoing: in many States, women had little legal recognition, no power to vote, and in general were inferior (in legal and political status) to men. Equality was the goal of the United Nations and the advancements made towards this have been remarkable. Initially international attention centred on political rights with a 1952 Convention on the Political Rights of Women demanding electoral powers for women. All women were to be entitled to vote, to stand for election, and to hold public office on the same basis as men. The period 1976–85 was declared the United Nations Decade for Women. The implicit Charter prohibition on discrimination against women was then elaborated in a 1967 Declaration on the Elimination of Discrimination against Women and the 1979 Convention on the Elimination of all forms of Discrimination against Women (see Chapter 12). In an attempt to secure equality of opportunity for the sexes, the Convention provides for equality in education, employment, healthcare, and law. Marriage and childcare were approached on an equal basis too. The Committee on the Elimination of all Forms of Discrimination against Women (CEDAW) was established to monitor the implementation of the Convention and work with other United Nations bodies for the advancement of women everywhere (discussed *supra*, Chapter 5).

Today the United Nations itself is pursuing a gender mainstreaming agenda, striving to meet the equality standard it espouses. The framework of the Beijing Platform for Action remains the benchmark for progression towards equality between the sexes. Equality of enjoyment of all universal rights and freedoms now sits alongside the goals of redressing the imbalance of power between men and women and neutralizing politics.

Equality, however, is not the beginning and end of the process. Women are routinely subjected to torture, mutilation, and mental abuse, practices analogous to slavery and dispossession purely on account of their gender. This adds credence to the demands for recognition of distinct women's rights. They have discrete needs to which the international community is gradually responding.

22.3.2.1 *Family rights*

There is little controversy surrounding the basic right to marry and found a family which finds expression in many instruments (Art 11, UDHR; Art 23, ICCPR; Art 12, ECHR; Art 17, ACHR; Art 18, ACHPR; Art 13, CIS; Art 38, AL). Some discussion arises with respect to the definition of family and the criteria for marriage. The former reflects religious and cultural norms, the latter raises issues of age, dissolution of marriage, remarriage, and whether marriage is restricted to a union between a male and a female. Both remain matters within the competency of States insofar as there is no discrimination. The issue of same-sex marriages and partnerships has produced polarized debate in many countries: the USA and the UK are among the most recent examples. However, a full discussion of these issues is beyond the scope of the present text.

In most societies, there was a traditional imbalance of power in family relations. Whether a patrilineal or indeed (as in some islands in the South Pacific) matrilineal structure is adhered to, the position of women is affected. For family rights, an added problem arises in that many of the issues are traditionally regarded as matters for internal law. This is particularly so with respect to taxation, nationality, and family relations. International law would thus appear to have no role and the first problem to be surmounted was articulating the rights in a manner acceptable to States. It has already been mentioned (Chapter 10) that the Convention on the Elimination of All Forms of Discrimination against Women has an excessively high number of reservations. Many of these reflect the clash between culture (as represented by national law) and the pro-offered international standards, family rights remain controversial.

Nevertheless, the United Nations has striven to set standards in family law. The United Nations Convention on Consent to Marriage, Minimum Age for Marriage and Registration for Marriages 1962 is an obvious example. This instrument requires marriage to be entered into with the full and free consent of both parties (Art 1). States should specify a minimum age for marriage (Art 2) and establish an appropriate system for registering marriages (Art 3).

When the United Nations adopted its Convention on the Nationality of Women 1957, many States still operated discriminatory practices. Women acquired residency rights based on their husband's nationality but not vice

Key case

Aumeeruddy-Cziffra v Mauritius, **UN Doc CCPR/C/12/D/35/1978 (1981)**

Before 1977, spouses of Mauritian citizens had residency rights in Mauritius. However, pursuant to the Immigration (Amendment) Act 1977 and the Deportation (Amendment) Act 1977, only wives of Mauritius citizens had residency rights. Foreign husbands were required to seek a residence permit and if rejected, would have to leave the country. Mrs Aumeeruddy-Cziffra was affected by this. Her husband's application for residency was pending for years—if rejected, she would be obliged to choose between moving abroad to live with her husband abroad and living apart from her husband to continue her public service career in Mauritius. The Committee noted that:

the principle of equal treatment of the sexes applies by virtue of articles 2(1), 3 and 26, of which the latter is also relevant because it refers particularly to the 'equal protection of the law'. Where the Covenant requires a substantial protection ... it follows from those provisions that such protection must be equal, that is to say not discriminatory, for example on the basis of sex. [Para 9.2]

A violation of the rights of those Mauritian women married to foreign husbands was thus identified.

versa (see Chapter 12 for cases). Moreover, in some systems women lost their own nationality in favour of that of their husband. The Convention prescribes independence of nationality for women (Art 1) but also requires that alien women should be able to acquire their husband's nationality through naturalization (Art 3).

22.3.2.2 *Violence and other abuse*

Women are frequently subjected to violence within the home. Statistics show that most domestic abuse is directed towards women and girl children. Clearly, those that are subjected to abuse and routinely degraded and belittled are less likely to enjoy the full range of universal rights. They are often less able to enjoy the freedom to choose their own destiny and the education to render dreams a reality. As this violence is frequently covert and may occur in the context of a home, women are also less likely to seek legal redress. Should they attempt to invoke the criminal law, many problems are encountered. For example, most societies were slow to recognize marital rape as a crime. In societies following Islamic law, rapes often must be witnessed which gives rise to a particular set of evidential problems for violence in the home.

The Declaration on the Elimination of Violence against Women 1993 was adopted by the General Assembly (Resn 48/104) to complement the provisions enshrined in associated instruments. Violence against women is defined as 'any act of gender-based violence that results in, or is likely to result in, physical or psychological harm or suffering to women, including threats of such acts, coercion or arbitrary deprivation of liberty, whether occurring in public or private life' (Art 1). Marital rape and female genital mutilation are explicitly prohibited (Art 2) and cannot be justified in terms of customary practice (Art 4).

22.3.3 **International developments**

International women's rights are, at present, very much steered by the agenda of the Beijing Platform for Action and the Beijing +5 and +10 reports. As the existing laws were deemed insufficient, the Beijing plan aims to provide a blueprint for the further advancement of women. Twelve critical areas of concern were highlighted: women and armed conflict; women and decision-making; women and economy; women and the environment; education and training of women; human rights of women; women and the media; women and poverty; violence against women; and institutional mechanism for the advancement of women and the girl child. Key issues were re-examined by the General Assembly in its special session Women 2000: Gender Equality, Development and Peace for the Twenty-first Century, otherwise known as Beijing 15. Commitment to the Beijing Platform for Action was reaffirmed, and further actions and initiatives were annexed to the resulting General Assembly resolution (UN Doc A/RES/S-23/3 (2000)). Work furthering these objectives is conducted under the auspices of the Commission on the Status of Women and the Division for the Advancement of Women. A commemorative meeting was held in Beijing in August 2005 following an Expert Group Meeting in Baku, Azerbaijan, on progress towards the Platform for Action and Millennium Declaration. The agenda is still being progressed and developments monitored.

22.3.4 **Regional developments**

22.3.4.1 *Americas*

The Inter-American Commission of Women (CIM) is one of the oldest intergovernmental agencies dedicated to promoting women's rights. It was established by the OAS in 1928. The Commission has been responsible for a number of Inter-American conventions including the 1933 Convention on the Nationality of Women, the 1948 Inter-American Convention on the Granting of Civil Rights to Women, and the 1948 Inter-American Convention on the Granting of Political Rights of Women. More recently, the prevalence of violence against women in the Americas, exacerbated by the fabled Latin American machismo, was tackled. The OAS adopted a Declaration on the Elimination of Violence against Women. The Inter-American Convention on the Prevention, Punishment and Eradication of Violence against Women (as discussed in Chapter 8) which followed was adopted in 1994, entering into force in 1995. Although adopted under the auspices of the OAS, the Convention is open to ratification by any State and currently has thirty-one ratifications.

Chronologically, the OAS has pioneered the tabulation of women's rights. The importance of its work cannot be underestimated.

22.3.4.2 *Africa*

Within Africa, one of the early acts of the new African Union was the adoption of a Protocol to the African Charter on Human and Peoples' Rights on the Rights of Women in Africa. It was adopted in July 2003 by the second Ordinary Session of the Assembly of the Union. As befits the region which adopted one of the most comprehensive and integrationist human rights instruments, this Protocol is notable for its broad approach to the subject. The Protocol provides for the elimination of discrimination against women (Art 2), the right to dignity for women (Art 3) and the elimination of harmful practices which 'negatively affect the human rights of women' (Art 5). Interestingly, there are comprehensive provisions on marriage. The minimum age for marriage is set at eighteen years (Art 6(b)); monogamy is encouraged (Art 6(c)); female independence of a spouse is acknowledged; and equality of right in case of separation, divorce, or annulment of a marriage is prescribed. Many other rights are included such as access to justice; participation in political decision-making; education and training; health and reproductive rights; and food, housing, and environmental rights. Women are to be protected in armed conflicts in accordance with prevailing international humanitarian law (Art 11). A notable novelty is the specific inclusion of widows' rights, protection of elderly women, and those with disabilities and special protection for women in distress including impoverished women and those in detention while pregnant or nursing. This is undoubtedly the single most detailed instrument on women's rights yet adopted. Although its real effect (in terms of bettering women's lives) remains to be seen, in international human rights terms, it is significant solely for the fact it was adopted.

22.3.4.3 *Europe*

In Europe, most work focuses on issues relating to equality of rights and eliminating discrimination against women. The European Union has been particularly proactive in this respect, developing substantially standards of care and equality of treatment for women in employment. This is discussed further in Chapters 7, 12, and 19. The Council of Europe seeks to promote women's rights and a balanced representation of men and women. Gender mainstreaming, violence against women, trafficking, and promoting women in decision-making are key areas on their agenda. A number of recommendations have been adopted in furtherance thereof.

22.4 Children

The development of children's rights has been one of the great successes of the United Nations. Children are inherently vulnerable and carry with them society's aspirations for the future. In the words of the Geneva Declaration on the Rights of the Child, mankind owes to the child the best it has to give.

22.4.1 Historical issues

There is almost universal consensus on the need for additional protection for children. Following the 1924 Geneva Declaration on the Rights of the Child (by the Assembly of the League of Nations), the United Nations took up the challenge. Children have particular needs, distinct from those of adults. Obviously, at an early stage they require intensive nurturing, being solely dependent on those around them for care. Nutrition, health and general well-being are key issues. Of course, children are often subjected to 'secondary violations' of rights—their standard of rights is dependent (to an extent) on that enjoyed by their carers. For example, a mother suffering from malnutrition is unlikely to be able to produce sufficient milk (quality and quantity) for her child. Similarly, a homeless carer living in northern Europe will struggle to ensure warmth and safety for his or her children. Improving the lives of parents and carers will therefore have a 'knock-on' effect on children. Securing respect for universal rights must remain a priority.

Environmental rights are of key importance to young people—they will live in the future created today. Issues raised at international fora such as the Earth Summits and the international conferences on climate change will have greater impact in years to come—future generations will reap the benefits or suffer the consequences of how the current power-brokers treat the environment.

The United Nations General Assembly proclaimed its own Declaration on the Rights of the Child in 1959. An International Year of the Child followed in 1979, spurring the international community into further action to prepare a binding charter of children's rights. The resulting 1989 Convention on the Rights of the Child has attracted almost universal ratification, entering into force in record time—just over nine months after adoption. It is based on recognition that childhood is entitled to special care and assistance and that every child should have the opportunity to grow up in a happy, loving, understanding family atmosphere in order to ensure the full and harmonious development of the child's personality (Preamble).

22.4.2 Children's rights and the United Nations Convention on the Rights of the Child

The Convention draws on a number of earlier declarations and instruments both on children, and on social and humanitarian law. In general, all persons under the age of eighteen are entitled to the rights and protection of the Convention. The rights, freedoms, and duties in this Convention are unusually diverse, with the best interests of the child a primary consideration at all times (Art 3). In the most comprehensive international human rights instrument to date, civil, political, economic, social, and cultural rights are prescribed for the child in a framework which recognizes the role of parents and legal guardians in developing the child. Although many rights accrue automatically to the child, there is clear recognition of the evolving role of the child in decisions affecting him or herself: as the child matures, the child is expected to participate in the decision-making process. In recognition of the indivisibility of rights, some commentators categorize the rights—protection, provision, and participation (for example, van Beuren). The child is thus protected from harm, provided with appropriate services and benefits and encouraged to participate in decisions affecting him or herself. Many of the rights in the Convention complement rights enshrined elsewhere, for example the right to education. However, the Convention does more than solely codify existing law.

There was nothing novel in the method of implementation of the Convention, a Committee on the Rights of the Child was established with power to review State reports. Yet the Committee can be distinguished from the other treaty-monitoring bodies in a number of ways, not solely concerned with the high number of participating States. The Committee seeks to actively involve all relevant specialized agencies of the United Nations, drawing on the expert knowledge and long experience of bodies such as the United Nations Children's Fund. It receives detailed non-governmental organization's (NGO) 'alternative' reports on States and works closely with UNICEF towards fulfilling its set plan of action. Moreover, reports to the Committee by States have tended to be disseminated more widely than other such documents. Today, children's rights are no longer a novelty—many newer States have incorporated children's rights into their constitutions (eg, the new South African Constitution). The Committee has taken a strong stance of many issues, for example developing the law to progressively limit corporal punishment of children. The Convention on the Rights of the Child is undoubtedly a watershed for the United Nations; in many respects, it almost represents the peak of the new United Nations era of international human rights law.

22.4.2.1 *Protection of children from harm*

Many elements in the Convention aim at protecting children, recognizing their inherent vulnerability. These rights clearly evidence the perceived need for a separate instrument on children's rights. Article 2 protects against discrimination on the status of either the child or the parent/guardian. The right to an identity of the child, of crucial importance in so many legal and social situations, is protected (Arts 7–8) as is the right to a family life (Arts 9–10). Abduction is proscribed under Art 35. This relates to the existing raft of measures on cross-country adoptions and child abductions: the Hague Convention on the Protection of Children and Cooperation in Respect of Intercountry Adoptions and the Hague Convention on the Civil Aspects of International Child Abduction, for example. Of particular concern is the abduction or sale of children for commercial gain.

The child trade is often linked with trafficking of women. Many young children are sold to 'employers' to satisfy parental debts or in the mistaken belief that the child's life would improve as a result of being moved to, for example, a major city.

While such activities may be deemed practices analogous to slavery, as with women, the victims are frequently not in a position to oppose their treatment. Sex tourism is widespread and all too frequently involves children. Sexual exploitation of children is prohibited under Art 34 of the Convention. The international community believes that a holistic approach is necessary to eliminate the sale of children, child prostitution, and child pornography, the latter of growing concern in the Internet era. Accordingly, an Optional Protocol to the Convention on the Rights of the Child on the Sale of Children, Child Prostitution and Child Pornography was adopted in 2000. The named practices are prohibited by Art 1, criminalized in national law in accordance with Art 2 and subjected to various provisions on jurisdiction and extradition. International cooperation should assist with the prevention, detection, investigation, prosecution, and punishment (Art 10) of those responsible for acts prohibited under the Protocol while care should be taken to protect the child victims (Art 8).

Economic exploitation of children is further proscribed in instruments adopted by the International Labour Organization. The International Labour Organization has been concerned with limiting working hours and restricting abusive working conditions for children since its inauguration. Two more recent instruments are included in the ILO's eight fundamental instruments: Convention No 138 (1973) on minimum age and the 1999 Convention No 182 on the elimination of the worst forms of child labour.

Children are also exceptionally vulnerable during armed conflict. Article 38 of the Convention provides that 'States Parties shall take all feasible measures to ensure that persons who have not attained the age of fifteen years do not take a direct part in hostilities.' States should not recruit younger people and when recruiting those between fifteen and eighteen years, should give priority to those who are oldest. Child soldiers, however, continue to be a major problem—not always through State recruitment, but sometimes through guerilla activities during civil conflicts.

Children orphaned by conflict may be especially vulnerable to recruitment. Another Optional Protocol to the Convention—on the Involvement of Children in Armed Conflict (2000) reinforces the international standard and increases the age limit. In accordance with the Protocol, members of the armed forces under eighteen years must not take a direct part in hostilities (Art 1) and there shall be no compulsory recruitment of those under eighteen (Art 2). More specific tests are laid down for ensuring that anyone volunteering under the age of eighteen does so

Key case

Prosecutor v Lubanga, **International Criminal Court (trial commenced January 2009) Child Soldiers**

Thomas Lubanga Dyilo, the first person to stand trial at the International Criminal Court, has been indicted on a number of charges related to the recruitment and maintenance of child soldiers: enlisting and conscripting of children under the age of fifteen years into the military wing of a Congolese rebel faction; recruiting, training and deploying children in hostilities fighting and as bodyguards; and of knowing and participating in these events in the Democratic Republic of Congo. Lubanga was a commander of the organisation concerned. Child witnesses have been called to give evidence. The trial is ongoing—see http://www.icc-cpi.int for up-to-date information.

with the consent of his or her parents and is fully aware of the consequences of such actions (Art 3). Non-national forces should also refrain from involving those under eighteen years in hostilities (Art 4). There are clear signs that the acceptable age for direct involvement in hostilities is now eighteen. The International Committee of the Red Cross/Red Crescent and the International Labour Organization (Convention No 182) both condemn the use of children in armed conflict. Moreover, the Statute of the International Criminal Court lists 'conscripting or enlisting children under the age of fifteen years into armed forces or groups or using them to participate actively in the hostilities' as a war crime (Art 8(2)(e)(vii)).

22.4.2.2 *Providing children with basic needs*

Clearly, merely to survive, a child requires some essential provisions such as food and shelter. Article 6 provides that every child has the inherent right to life and that States should secure the survival and development of the child to the maximum extent possible. Further requirements in the Convention make it clear that a holistic approach is being taken. Prenatal and postnatal maternal care should be provided as should primary healthcare to combat malnutrition and disease (Art 24). All the foregoing are particularly appropriate in the context of United Nations Millennium targets for slashing infant mortality rates. Children enjoy the right to an identity, a name, a nationality, and to know who their parents are (Arts 8–9). As children are deemed to develop best when with their parents, the Convention makes detailed provision for separation of the child from his or her parents. In all such situations, the best interest of the child is the determinative factor. Adoption is addressed in Arts 20–1.

Special consideration is to be given to the rights of children seeking refugee status and those who are mentally or physically disabled. However, all children are also entitled to the full range of universal rights. The Convention makes specific reference to many of these rights, focusing on inter alia, the juvenile justice system securing a fair trial for children, education, leisure time and play activities, cultural rights, social security, healthcare, and lawful detention of children. The right of every child to a standard of living adequate for physical, mental, spiritual and social development (Art 27) places responsibility on the parents/carers as well as the State, including payment of parental child maintenance where appropriate. The role of the media is facilitating development of the child is also recognized. The mass media is encouraged to disseminate a diversity of national and international sources aimed at the promotion of the social, spiritual, and moral well-being, and the physical and mental health of children (Art 17).

22.4.2.3 *Participation of the child*

Most of the Convention is underpinned by the notion that the best interests of the child is the deciding factor in any decision affecting the child (Art 3). This concept has already been adopted into many domestic legal systems—for example the Children (Scotland) Act 1995 (c36). In order to determine the best interests of the child, the view of the child may be considered. Indeed the child is recognized as having 'evolving capacities' (Art 5) in exercising the rights in the Convention. As a consequence, the concept of youth participation has evolved. Children are increasingly encouraged to participate in decisions affecting them. Children enjoy freedom of expression (Art 13) and have the right to have their views heard on judicial and administrative matters concerning them (Art 12). The right of the child to freedom of thought, conscience, and religion (Art 14) has proven more controversial (albeit that the rights of parents to guide and direct children is also included) as has the freedom of association (Art 15). Many attempts have been made to involve children in political decision-making. The European Youth Parliament and the United Nations mock Security Council and General Assembly meetings provide young people with a deeper understanding of politics. Other initiatives such as the new Scottish Youth Parliament can feed more directly into the political decision-making process, hopefully increasing electoral participation rates for the future.

22.4.3 International developments

The international developments on children's rights are generally related to the United Nations Convention on the Rights of the Child and associated initiatives, as discussed above. UNICEF and UNESCO are also heavily involved in these developments.

22.4.4 Regional developments

Perhaps it is due to the comparative success of the United Nations Convention, but regional attention has remained focused on universal rights and securing a functioning system of monitoring and enforcing the agreed regional instruments.

22.4.4.1 *Africa*

In Africa, however, progress towards children's rights has been more marked. An OAU Declaration on the Rights and Welfare of the African Child marked the International Year of the Child in 1979. However, the situation of most African children remained grave.

Accordingly in 1990, an African Charter on the Rights and Welfare of the Child was adopted by the then OAU. The Charter applies to all human beings below the age of eighteen, echoes many elements of the United Nations' instrument including the dominance of the principle of the best interest of the child (Art 4). Children enjoy a variety of rights including the right to life, survival and development; the right to a name and nationality; the right to freedom of expression, association, thought, conscience and religion; and the right to privacy, education, and healthcare. Children are to be protected from abuse, economic and sexual exploitation, harmful traditional practices, torture, armed conflict, apartheid, and trafficking. Refugees and mentally and handicapped children are singled out for particular care. All children are also entitled to have their opinions heard in matters concerning them in specified situations (Art 4(2)). In keeping with the ethos of the African Charter on Human and Peoples' Rights, children are also the incumbents of a series of duties. These include respecting their parents, serving the national community, preserving African cultural values, and contributing towards African unity (Art 31).

22.4.4.2 *Europe*

Europe subsequently also addressed (in a tangential manner) the issues of children's rights. In 1996, it adopted the European Convention on the Exercise of Children's Rights. This instrument did not seek to articulate children's rights. Rather, it endorsed the United Nations Convention and, in furtherance thereof, aimed at encouraging States to undertake appropriate legislative, administrative, and other measures for the implementation of the rights recognized in the United Nations Convention (Preamble, citing Art 4 of the United Nations Convention). Non-contentious resolution of disputes concerning families (Art 13), procedural rights of children to be involved in judicial proceedings (Art 3), and the role of judicial authorities to consider the best interest of the child and the child's own views in all decisions affecting children (Art 6) are all addressed.

22.4.4.3 *Americas*

Within the Americas, instruments have been adopted on Child Soldiers (OAS Doc AG/RES.1709 (XXX-O/00)) and on child trafficking (OAS Doc AG/RES.1948 (XXXIII-O/03)). The Santiago Summit in 2003 also adopted Resolution AG/RES.1951 (XXXIII-O/03) on the promotion and protection of human rights of children in the Americas. Many of the most serious issues facing children in the Americas are addressed in other human rights instruments, including those on disappeared persons.

22.5 **Refugees**

At the creation of the United Nations, as today, a great number of peoples were displaced, refugees, and seeking asylum. Conflicts, whether civil or international, frequently give rise to refugees, as do natural disasters of epic proportions. Mention has already been made of the League of Nations' attempts to cope with the aftermath of redrawing the boundaries in Europe. After the Second World War, the situation was equally confused—thousands of peoples had been displaced during the hostilities.

22.5.1 **Historical issues**

Refugees are undoubtedly an issue of global concern. From an estimated 1 million refugees in 1951 when the Convention was adopted, there are now over 20 million people within the remit of the United Nations High Commissioner for Refugees (currently António Guterres). Whether fleeing war, famine, floods, persecution, or earthquakes, refugees find themselves far removed from their homes, reliant on the host States for support. Frequently, refugees move in large exoduses rather than as individuals. Some 80 per cent of refugees today are women and children, further corroborating the need for protection of such groups. The plight of refugees ably illustrates the efficacy of an international response. A disaster in one State may produce a refugee emergency in adjacent States.

   A more recent phenomenon has been the rise in internally displaced people, those who are forced to leave their homes but remain in the same country.

22.5.2 **Refugees' rights and the 1951 Convention**

Refugees were a major issue of concern for the United Nations in the aftermath of the Second World War. Accordingly, in 1951, the Convention Relating to the Status of Refugees was adopted. This remains the key legal instruments for defining refugees and the protection and rights they are entitled to. It aims at consolidating and extending existing international law on the subject. It applies only to individuals who became refugees as a result of events occurring in Europe before 1 January 1951 and was designed to assist in the resettlement of persons displaced as a result of the Second World War. Given the continual growth in refugee populations around the world, the international community adopted a 1967 Protocol to the Convention which extended its ambit to all persons coming within the definition adopted by the original Convention without reference to the date of the events generating refugee status.

A refugee is a person who:

owing to well-founded fear of being persecuted for reasons of race, religion, nationality, membership of a particular social groups or political opinion, is outside the country of his nationality and is unable, or owing to such fear, is unwilling to avail himself of the protection of that country; or who, not having a nationality and being outside the country of his former habitual residence as a result of such events, is unable, or owing to such fear, is unwilling to return to it. [Art 1A(2), as amended]

Status as a refugee can be rescinded in specified circumstances. For example, if an individual has voluntarily re-availed himself of the protection of his country of nationality, has acquired a new nationality and enjoys protection by virtue of this or has voluntarily re-established himself in the country he fled (Art 1C). Similarly, those who are implicated in war crimes, crimes against humanity, or other acts contrary to the purposes and principles of the United Nations are excluded from the ambit of the Convention (Art 1F).

Refugees are entitled to the same protection aliens enjoy in a State (Art 7; for an overview of the law of aliens, see Chapter 2). Among the rights accorded to all refugees are access to courts (Art 16), the right to engage in wage-earning employment (Art 17), the right to education, housing, and food on the same basis as aliens and/or the population of the State. The right to food is based on the right to equal rations, given much of Europe was still operating rationing of food and essential provisions at the time of initial drafting. To assist with determination of status, refugee identity documentation should be issued by the host State (Art 27), expulsion should be regulated by law (Art 32) and 'as far as possible' States should facilitate the assimilation and naturalization of refugees (Art 34).

As a standard-setter, the Convention retains its original importance. The geographical extension of its provisions in light of the Protocol reinforce its importance. Today some 144 States are party to the Convention, 144 to the Protocol (though note both documents have slightly different State Parties).

Marking the fiftieth anniversary of the Convention, all contracting parties met in Geneva on 12–13 December 2001 for the first global refugee meeting. The then United Nations High Commissioner for Refugees, Ruud Lubbers, stated that the Convention had helped millions of refugees in the past fifty years but noted that the 22 million people the UNHCR was currently helping were 'products of political failure'. An examination of the root causes of displacement followed. This meeting was held against the backdrop of the refugee crisis in Afghanistan—the single largest refugee crisis in the world—a crisis which, in late 2001, was propelled once more into the international spotlight. The international community reaffirmed its commitment to the Convention and Protocol. A series of Global Consultations are in progress, examining ways to improve the implementation of the instruments, improve the protection of refugees and seek more permanent solutions for refugees.

At the time of writing, Afghanistan, Lebanon, Iraq, and South Sudan/Darfur/Chad were all experiencing considerable political turmoil and producing new refugees.

Other international instruments may be of additional benefit to refugees. For example, the fourth Geneva Convention relative to the Protection of Civilian Persons in Time of War, includes protection for refugees and other displaced persons. As with the Refugee Convention, this was adopted in the aftermath of the Second World War when protection of displaced persons and refugees was a major issue in Europe.

Two subsequent United Nations conventions relate to stateless persons—by definition, many stateless persons are also refugees. A 1954 Convention relating to the Status of Stateless Persons applies to those not considered to be a national by any State. Its *raison d'être* is to grant stateless people the security of legitimizing certain aspects of their residency thereby giving them a legitimate basis for living in a host State. This was followed by the 1961 Convention on the Reduction of Statelessness, which aims at ensuring a nationality to all those born within a contracting State and regulating the circumstances in which a State may remove nationality from any given individual. There are many people in the world who are stateless. For example, the Druze people living in the Golan Heights professed allegiance neither to Israel nor Syria during protracted territorial disputes. Many were effectively stateless. Elsewhere nomadic peoples may end up stateless with no nationality rights in any State in which they have lived. This problem proved acute during organization of the 1993 International Year of Indigenous People when passports and visas were required for indigenous representatives wishing to travel to the conference. In neither example are the people necessarily refugees. However, those divested of nationality may find protection in these instruments.

The only other instrument of potential use is the 1967 United Nations Declaration on Territorial Asylum which has yet to be translated into a binding convention.

22.5.3 The United Nations High Commissioner for Refugees

The United Nations High Commissioner for Refugees (established in 1950) is now one of the world's principal global humanitarian agencies, just as the Convention (and Protocol) is one of the main humanitarian instruments. General Assembly Resolution 319 A (IV) of December 3, 1949, established the office of High Commissioner. Initially the mandate was for three years, but has been routinely extended. Based in Geneva, the Office of the High Commissioner is represented in over a hundred countries. The role of the High Commissioner is to provide international protection to refugees and seek durable solutions for refugees by assisting governments to facilitate the voluntary repatriation of refugees or their integration within new communities (Art 1, Statute of the Office of High Commissioner for Refugees). Given the sensitivity of the mandate, the High Commissioner must be non-political, operating in accordance with emerging humanitarian and social needs. Ruud Lubbers is the current High Commissioner.

22.5.4 Regional developments

22.5.4.1 *Africa*

Given the huge number of refugees caused by natural disasters, famine, and conflicts in Africa, it is perhaps inevitable that there should be a regional instrument

---

Key case

US v Finland, UN Doc CAT/C/30/D/197/2002

Many of those seeking refugee status complain about (arbitrary) detention violating the International Covenant on Civil and Political Rights and the detention environment. However, there are also a large body of communications alleging deportation of an individual after a rejected asylum claim engages the treaties by subjecting the deportee to torture on his or her return. Lists of 'safe' countries' are maintained by many bodies.

The author of the communication was a member of the Peoples' Liberation Organization of Tamil Eelam (LTTE), an organization banned by the then Liberation Tigers of Tamil Eelam. He worked as a bus driver and travelled regularly between areas of Sri Lanka controlled by the Sri Lankan army and by the LTTE. He was repeatedly detained and interrogated by different bodies: the LTTE, the Sri Lankan army, and the Indian peacekeeping force and alleges he was tortured on several occasions. He escaped to Germany, had his claim for asylum rejected and then headed to France. French authorities arrested him, deported him to Germany and he was deported to Sri Lanka. On his return, he was again arrested and interrogated on a number of occasions by different bodies. He escaped through Russia to Finland and claimed asylum there. Once again his application was rejected, the rejection confirmed by appropriate court processes. A complaint was thus brought before the Committee Against Torture that 'the forced return of the complainant to Sri Lanka would violate the obligation of Finland under article 3 of the Convention not to expel a person to another State where there are substantial grounds for believing that he would be in danger of being subjected to torture' (para 7.2). The Committee was influenced by the fact that the events complained of had happened some time ago and that there was a peace process (in 2002) resulting in a ceasefire and there was an 'opinion of UNHCR of March 1999, according to which those who do not fulfil the refugee criteria, including those of Tamil origin, may be returned to Sri Lanka, and that a large number of Tamil refugees returned to Sri Lanka in 2001 and 2002' (para 7.7). Accordingly no personal and real risk of torture had been established and there was no violation of the treaty.

---

addressing the issue. The OAU adopted the Convention Governing the Specific Aspects of Refugee Problems in Africa in 1969. It was designed as a regional complement to the United Nations Convention and many of its provisions reflect the international standard. Indeed the preamble to the OAU Convention acknowledges that the United Nations Convention is 'the basic and universal instrument relating to the status of refugees' and encourages all States to accede thereto, noting that there must be close collaboration between the OAU and the Office of the High Commissioner for Refugees. The definition of a refugee complements that of the international document: the initial definition is almost identical to that of the 1951 United Nations Convention, however, Art I(2) continues that:

The term 'refugee' shall also apply to every person who, owing to external aggression, occupation, foreign domination or events seriously disturbing public order in either part or the whole of his country of origin or nationality, is compelled to leave his place of habitual residence in order to seek refuge in another place outside his country or origin or nationality.

This more generous definition brings many more Africans within the protective ambit of the regional instrument.

22.5.4.2 *The Americas*

Within the Americas, the first regional instrument on asylum was adopted in 1889 (the Montevideo Treaty on International Criminal Law which addressed the issue of asylum). A Caracas Convention on Territorial Asylum followed in 1954. Today, refugees and asylum seekers are dealt with in accordance with the provisions of the 1984 Cartagena Declaration on Refugees, a non-legally binding instrument which enjoys considerable support in the region. It was adopted in the wake of large scale civil strife in the region. The Summits of the Americas frequently exhort ratification of the 1951 United Nations Convention; see for example, the resolution on the protection of refugees, returnees and internally displaced persons in the Americas (OAS Doc AG/RES.1892 (XXXII–0/02)).

22.5.4.3 *Europe*

Europe was the initial focal point of international concern over refugees, prompting the development of the international standards. However, the Europe of the twenty-first century faces a different type of refugee crisis: asylum seekers from many areas of the world find their way to Europe in hope of sanctuary and a safer and better way of life. Considerable controversy surrounds the creation of 'fortress Europe', an area into which entry is regulated. Both the Council of Europe and the European Union have adopted a number of instruments concerning refugees.

Among the instruments adopted by the Council of Europe are the 1959 European Agreement on the Abolition of Visas for Refugees and the 1980 European Agreement on Transfer of Responsibility for Refugees. An intergovernmental committee, the ad hoc Committee of experts on the legal aspects of territorial asylum, refugees and stateless persons (CAHAR), works towards solutions to the legal problems in the field of refugees.

The European Union, on the other hand, has focused on developing a single internal market within which goods, services, people, and capital can move freely. With such a goal, it was inevitable that attention would centre on agreeing a common policy on refugees from outwith the Union. The Dublin Convention of 1990 addresses this, seeking to articulate the criteria within which States decide asylum cases. The Tampere European Council (1999) decided that a common European asylum system should be established, the first phase of this had an expected implementation date of 2004 and is known as the Hague Programme while the second-phase instruments are scheduled for adoption by 2010. Asylum issues are now brought within the ambit of the 'first pillar' and as such no longer require intergovernmental decision-making processes. This facilitates further developments on rights in this field.

22.5.5 **Developments**

Perhaps not surprisingly, the focus today is on preventing mass exoduses of refugees and securing the prescribed minimum standard of human rights for all. Improving international human rights situations should also ameliorate the position of the growing number of internally displaced persons. Violations of human rights within a State have been identified as a major cause of refugees and asylum seekers.

Convention Plus is an international effort under the auspices of the Office of the High Commissioner for Refugees. According to the High Commissioner, the plan is to produce 'special agreements aimed at managing the refugee challenges of today and tomorrow in a spirit of international cooperation'. In other words, the scheme should strengthen the operation of the Convention. Three main areas were identified as priorities: the use of resettlement as a tool of protection; the need for more effective targeting of development assistance; and clarification of State responsibility during 'secondary movements' (when refugees move from the initial state of refuge to another). Overall, the emphasis is on creating long-lasting solutions to the global challenges posed by managing refugees. It is hoped that these agreements will be multilateral, setting generic standards and commitments that can then be imported as solutions to particular situations as they arise. Canada, Denmark, Japan, South Africa, and Switzerland are facilitating the drafting process, each inviting other interested States to assist in the process. Forums are convened biannually to discuss progress. The first meeting of the facilitating States was held in February 2004; the first forum was held in March 2004. Agreements to date have included resettlement as a tool of protection and focusing on irregular secondary movements of refugees.

Alongside this the EC Strengthening Capacity Project aims to devise tools and approaches to strengthen the capacity of States to receive and protect refugees. The European Commission, Denmark, Germany, the Netherlands, and the UK are involved with funding, and pilot projects to date have included Kenya and Tanzania.

The process of ensuring refugees receive due care and attention from the receiving State is long and slow. Many receiving States lack the economic capacity to provide appropriate care while others few refugees and asylum seekers with suspicion, fearing they are in reality economic migrants or illegal aliens. Violence against refugees is becoming increasingly common in host States. While States have a duty to secure universal rights within their territories, thereby minimizing mass exoduses of refugees, all States have an obligation to offer emergency support to refugees, ameliorating their position before a proper determination of status can be made in accordance with the law.

CASES

Ato del Avellanal v France, UN Doc CCPR/C/34/D/202/1986 (1988).

Aumeeruddy-Cziffra v Mauritius, UN Doc. CCPR/C/12/D/35/1978 (1981).

Chief Bernard Ominayak and the Lubicon Lake Band v Canada, UN Doc CCPR/C/38/D/167/1984 (1990).

Kitok v Sweden, UN Doc CCPR/C/33/D/197/1985 (1988).

Lovelace v Canada, UN Doc CCPR/C/13/D/24/1977 (1981).

Mabo and ors v State of Queensland [No 2] 175 Commonwealth Law Reports (1991–1992) 1.

Mary and Carrie Dann v United States of America, OAS Inter-American Commission on Human Rights Report 75/02, Case No 11.140 (27 December 2002).

Wik Peoples and ors v State of Queensland and ors 187 Commonwealth Law Reports (1996) 1.

READING

Andrews, A, and Kaufman, N (eds), *Implementing the UN Convention on the Rights of the Child: A standard of living adequate for development* (Westport, Conn: Praeger, 1999).

Askin, K, and Koenig, D, *Women and International Human Rights Law* (New York: Transnational Press, 1999–2000).

Benedek, W, Kisaakye, M, and Oberleitner, G (eds), *The Human Rights of Women: International instruments and African experiences* (New York: Zed Books, 2002).

Brownlie, I, *Treaties and Indigenous Peoples* (Oxford: Clarendon Press, 1992).

Cook, R (ed), *Human Rights of Women: National and international perspectives* (Philadelphia: University of Pennslyvania Press, 1994).

Dunn, J, 'East Timor: A case of cultural genocide?' in GJ Andreopoulos (ed), *Genocide: Conceptual and historical dimensions* (Philadelphia: University of Pennsylvania Press, 1994), pp 171–90.

Fottrell, D, *Revisiting Children's Rights: 10 years of the UN Convention on the Rights of the Child* (Leiden: Kluwer, 2001).

Freeman, M (ed), *Children's Rights: A comparative perspective* (Aldershot: Dartmouth, 1996).

Goodwin-Gill, G, *The Refugee in International Law* (Oxford: Oxford University Press, 1996).

Jalal, PI, *Law for Pacific Women: A legal rights handbook* (Suva: Fiji Women's Rights Movement, 1998).

Lerner, N, *Groups Rights and Discrimination in International Law* (Leiden: Martinus Nijhoff, 1991).

Loescher, G, *The United Nations High Commissioner for Refugees: A perilous path* (Oxford: Oxford University Press, 2001).

Pritchard, S (ed), *Indigenous Peoples, the United Nations and Human Rights* (Federation Press, 1998).

Schabas, W, 'Reservations to the Convention on the Rights of the Child' (1996) 18 Human Rights Quarterly 472.

Turpel, M, 'Indigenous peoples' rights of political participation and self-determination: Recent international legal developments and the continuing struggle for recognition' (1992) 25(3) Cornell International Law Journal 579–97.

United Nations, *Fact Sheet No 9 (Rev 1) The Rights of Indigenous Peoples* (Geneva: Office of the High Commissioner for Human Rights, 1996).

——, *Fact Sheet No 10 (Rev 1) The Rights of the Child* (Geneva: Office of the High Commissioner for Human Rights, 1998).

——, *Fact Sheet No 20, Human Rights and Refugees* (Geneva: Office of the High Commissioner for Human Rights, 1997).

——, *United Nations Guide for Indigenous Peoples* (Geneva: Office of the High Commissioner for Human Rights, 2001).

Wilson, M, and Hunt, P (eds), *Culture, Rights and Cultural Rights: Perspectives from the South Pacific* (Wellington: Huia Publishers, 2000).

WEBSITES

www.cwis.org/wwwvl/indig-vl.htm—WWW Virtual Library Indigenous Studies.

www.unhcr.ch—United Nations High Commissioner for Refugees.

www2.ohchr.org/english/issues/indigenous/index.html—United Nations Office of the High Commissioner for Human Rights Indigenous Peoples site.

www.un.org/womenwatch—United Nations Women's site.

www.unicef.org—United Nations Children's Fund.

www.coe.int/equality—Council of Europe's Equality site.

23

Looking to the future

The foregoing chapters have provided the reader with an understanding of the scope and application of international human rights law and the role played by the regional organizations. A selection of rights and freedoms has been examined to provide a flavour of the universal rights and freedoms recognized under the principal international instruments. However, as has been noted, international human rights law is not static. In its present form, it is a relatively young legal system: the process of codifying rights and freedoms at the international, regional, and national levels is ongoing; means of achieving consensus between Member States on implementation are still being sought. Much has been achieved since the Universal Declaration of Human Rights was signed over sixty years ago, but work remains to be done.

So, what lies in the future for international human rights law? This chapter will provide a brief overview of a few of the issues which are likely to characterize the evolution of international human rights in the future.

23.1 Reform of the institutional procedure?

Given the issues addressed in Chapter 10 and the ongoing reform underway within the United Nations, it seems likely that there may be further streamlining of the United Nations procedures in the future. Perhaps moves will be made, under the auspices of the Committee of Chairpersons and with the backing of the High Commissioner, to simplify the State reporting system, preventing duplication of work. More interaction between the different United Nations treaty-monitoring bodies can only be advantageous. The various committees have already compiled guidelines for States; it is now up to the States to follow them and actively try and meet their reporting commitments. Without the active participation of the State Parties, the work of the treaty-monitoring bodies is somewhat limited. Clearly, the impact of concluding views adopted on an individual communication is less effective when the State has not submitted comments in explanation of its conduct—this has occurred in a number of instances involving not only the Inter-American Commission and Court on Human Rights but also the Human Rights Committee.

It is also possible that the current reporting procedures are reviewed with a view to streamlining the process for States with multiple reports to file. Easing the reporting burden on States should encourage conformity with reporting obligations by removing one of the perceived barriers. Promoting prompt, accurate, and appropriate reports is an important aspect of the work of the international community. This contributes immensely towards the efficacy of the process.

However, as more States ratify the principal instruments, so the backlog of reports awaiting observations and communications awaiting views will grow. The burden on the Committees at the international level will increasingly suggest the need for more frequent meetings or, given the resource implications, more effective use of Committee time. This may involve the use of smaller groups (subcommittees or chambers) to examine reports and communications. The European Court of Human Rights adopted Chambers and Committees as a tool to increase efficiency after it became permanent for example.

One possibility, which has increasingly been mooted, is the idea of a Universal Court for Human Rights or a single unified treaty body. This would facilitate not only a more efficient processing of State reports but also, perhaps, a more effective system for considering individual complaints.

23.2 **More effective enforcement of human rights?**

In 1968, the Proclamation of Tehran adopted by the World Conference on Human Rights noted that 'much remains to be done in regard to the implementation of those rights and freedoms' (Proclamation 4). Over three decades later, much more has been done to ensure implementation of the rights but many would argue the international system is still lacking in this respect.

At the regional level, there are clear moves towards developing greater enforcement measures for human rights. The European Court of Human Rights has paved the way for judicial supervision of State implementation of rights. The Inter-American system has adopted a similar procedure. Within Europe, the procedure itself has been simplified to encourage use thereof. The African authorities have now decided to go down the path of judicial settlement of disputes though many commentators question the wisdom of this initiative. Even should a Universal Court of Human Rights be established, it is unlikely that it will have significant powers of enforcement. However, the power of the Human Rights Council and its periodic review remains to be seen.

Naturally, the key to implementation lies with the States themselves. Due to the nature of international law, political and diplomatic support is essential to securing the goals of universal human rights.

23.2.1 **Spreading responsibility**

Complementing the role of States, there is increasing evidence of responsibility for the realization of human rights being extended outwith the tradition nation-State domain. Individuals, NGOs, and other organizations have responsibilities under human rights instruments, as previously noted. It is likely that non-State actors will become an increasingly prominent presence. Already NGOs regularly contribute to the discussions and monitoring arrangements of the international and regional treaty-monitoring bodies. This trend is particularly apparent in Africa and the Americas under regional arrangements.

In 1999, the Secretary-General announced the launch of the Global Compact, an initiative designed to engage major global corporations in the fight for human rights. It is a voluntary code, with companies agreeing to embrace a set of principles drawn from human rights, labour and the environment in furtherance of sustainable development and corporate citizenship.

23.3 **Greater popular awareness?**

The current campaign for human rights education will hopefully add further to the awareness of human rights on a global level. The situation has undoubtedly improved from the 1968 Proclamation of Tehran in which it was noted at Point 14 that there were over 700 million illiterates throughout the world. This obstacle has undoubtedly been reduced but there remain millions of illiterate people. Higher levels of education are essential to facilitate a variety of human rights as well as heightening awareness of rights and procedures for securing rights. Therefore, the need for promotion of international human rights and greater dissemination of State reports, etc, remains as relevant today. Naturally, a side effect of this may be an increase in the number of individual communications filed with the international and regional bodies fuelling the strain on the available resources.

Once more, States have a significant role to play in developing awareness of human rights. They should disseminate reports widely and render international rights more accessible to their population. Much of the onus for educating the population also lies with the State. However, non-governmental organizations and non-State actors increasingly contribute to the promotion of rights within States. Even individuals themselves have obligations: to obtain an education and to develop an awareness of their human rights.

The Office of the High Commissioner of Human Rights has already achieved much in furthering awareness of human rights; the website of the Office has greatly contributed towards the global dissemination of human rights. With increasing globalization of information technology, ever more use can and should be made of such resources.

23.4 **More rights?**

Since the adoption of the Universal Declaration in 1948, there has been an explosion in recognized human rights. For a term developed in intra and post-war theory, based deep in philosophy, human rights have been developed and codified to an incredible extent. As fundamental civil and political rights gain greater acceptance, attention has focused on economic, social, and cultural rights. At the international level, there now appears to be a greater emphasis on these rights, while in the African regional system they are deemed paramount.

Rights are developing in many areas. This in itself has given rise to concerns. In 1984, Philip Alston proposed a 'quality control mechanism' for creating 'new' human rights given his concern that the plethora of instruments increasingly

Discussion topic

Universal ratification

A number of commentators are examining why states ratify treaties and whether ratification makes a difference to the individuals living in the state. The evidence suggests
that for some states, ratification is prompted by political expediency or diplomatic
pressure. Without doubt the act of ratification serves primarily a political purpose, it is
the translation of the rhetoric of the treaty into reality in national law which gives full
adherence to international human rights.

See, for general analyses on this topic, Hathaway, O, 'Why do nations commit to human
rights treaties?' (2007) 51 Journal of Conflict Resolution 588–621 and 'Do human rights
treaties make a difference' (2002) 111 Yale Law Journal 1935–2042; Landman, T, 'Meas-
uring human rights: Principle, practice and policy' (2004) 26 Human Rights Quarterly
906–31 and *Studying Human Rights* (Oxford and New York: Routledge, 2006).

threatened the integrity of the entire process. Given some of the new rights which
have been proposed, some form of quality control for enforceable rights may well
be advantageous. The problem arises solely through the nature of human rights: the
traditional concept of the rule of law has been long overtaken by more expansive
written rights. However, as the full content of the rule of law was never codified, so
the full content of human rights has never been codified. In partial response, the
General Assembly, by Resolution 41/120 (1986), adopted guidelines to be followed
in developing new human rights. The need for broad international support, preci-
sion in wording, and implementation machinery is acknowledged. Debate continues as to whether it is more beneficial to draft new treaties protecting human rights
or to focus on making the existing treaties more effective, making the rhetoric
reality.

Two examples, development and environment, follow. Both are the subject of
dedicated United Nations programmes.

23.4.1 **The right to development**

The right to development is probably one of the newest accepted rights to emerge
from the international system. Various international bodies, including the General
Assembly and the Commission on Human Rights, for many years have asserted its
existence. The roots of development can be traced to the United Nations Charter,
Arts 55–6 of which urge States to cooperate for the achievement of higher standards
of living and economic and social progress. In accordance with these provisions and
in the spirit of the Universal Declaration, on 26 November 1957 the General Assembly opined that balanced and integrated economic and social development would
contribute towards the observance of human rights (Resn 1161(XII)). A decade later,
the World Conference on Human Rights in the Proclamation of Tehran (1968)
noted that the widening gap between the economically developed and developing
countries impeded the realization of human rights in the international community. The Development Decade had failed to reach its target. The following year,

the General Assembly adopted a Declaration on Social Progress and Development (GA Resn 2542 (XXIV)) with respect for human rights and freedoms mentioned. Prompted by the Commission on Human Rights, the Secretary-General undertook a study on the international dimensions of the right to development as a human right in relation to other human rights. The report was considered in 1979, ultimately leading to a global consultation on the right to development.

In 1981, the Commission on Human Rights established a working group to draft a Declaration on the Right to Development. Progress was slow and the matter was remitted to the General Assembly where in 1986, by Resolution 41/128, it adopted the Declaration on the Right to Development. The Resolution was approved by the majority of Member States, the United States objecting and eight States (including the United Kingdom, Japan, and Nordic States) abstaining. The Declaration considers the right to development to be 'an inalienable human right by virtue of which every human person and all peoples are entitled to participate in, contribute to, and enjoy economic, social, cultural and political development, in which all human rights and fundamental freedoms can be fully realized' (Art 1). The right to development was linked to the right to self-determination, which is discussed in Chapter 17. In terms of the Declaration, States recognize their duty to take steps to formulate international development policies in furtherance of creating national and international conditions favourable to the realization of the right to development. A number of aspects of the right to development were identified in the Declaration including non-discrimination, the maintenance of international peace and security and equality of access to education, health services, food, housing, employment, and the fair distribution of income. Popular participation was considered as key to the realization of the right to development.

The right to development was highlighted as one of the key areas for deliberation at the 1993 World Conference on Human Rights in Vienna. It was debated at length in that forum, the resulting Declaration reaffirming the right to development as a universal and inalienable right and an integral part of fundamental human rights, at para 10. Economic development of the least developed countries, the elimination of the illicit dumping of toxic and dangerous waste and the easing of the debt burden on developing countries are viewed as important in developing national and international systems for removing the obstacles to the recognition of the right to development. A working group was established under the auspices of the Commission on Human Rights to examine related issues. By Resolution 1998/72, the Commission established a third, but this time open-ended, working group on the right to development. The mandate of the open-ended working group includes monitoring and reviewing progress made in the promotion and implementation of the right to development; reviewing reports submitted by United Nations and other agencies thereon; and advising the Office of the High Commissioner for Human Rights regarding implementation of the right to development and associated technical assistance. The first session of this group was held in September 2000.

The Human Rights Council, in Resolution 1/14 (2006), reviewed the mandate of the Working Group and requested the relevant expert advice mechanisms to continue working on the right to development.

Simultaneous to these advancements in law, the United Nations Development Programme have instituted a series of Human Rights Development Reports analysing developmental progress.

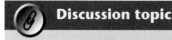

Discussion topic

UN Millennium Development Goals

The Millennium Development Goals were adopted in 2000 by the UN General Assembly (Resolution 55/2), setting time limits for realizing specific goals in eight areas: end poverty and hunger; universal education; gender equality; child health; maternal health; combat HIV/AIDS; environmental sustainability; and global partnership. Examples of the targets include halving the proportion of people whose income is less than USD 1 per day; ensuring full primary school education for all children everywhere; reducing under-fives' mortality rates by two-thirds; having halted and begun the reverse the spread of HIV/AIDS; having halted and begun to reverse the incidence of malaria; and halving the proportion of the population without sustainable access to safe drinking water and basic sanitation. The year 2015 is specified as the date for achieving the aforementioned targets. Progress is monitored regularly (see the September 2008 high level progress meeting - http://www.un.org/millenniumgoals/2008highlevel/) but debate continues as to how realistic these measures are and how effective they will be in ending world poverty.

The right to development remains unrealized. To quote one of its proponents, Roland Rich:

The right to development would be a positive force in involving Third World countries in human rights, including the less fashionable civil and political rights. The right to development acknowledges the importance of both the individual and the group. It would associate traditional human rights with the issue of greatest importance to developing countries—development. [p 54]

In spite of the passage of time, this argument is as compelling today as when it was written. By the same token, the right to development remains a source of friction and controversy in political and legal systems.

A high-level task force on the implementation of the right to development was established by Commission on Human Rights Resolution 2004/7, its mandate renewed by Resolution 2005/4. The right to development is recognized as important by the Human Rights Council, as mentioned above. The task force works alongside the working group to ensure the topic remains on the international agenda and to research practical ways of achieving development. Securing good governance practices in all States is one method of supporting the right to development and thus has been the subject of much debate in the United Nations. Good governance clearly relates to many civil and political rights but also impacts heavily on economic and social, especially as regards anti-corruption. The United Nations Conference on anti-corruption measures, good governance, and human rights was held in Warsaw in November 2006. Securing anti-corruption remains a goal of international and regional bodies—there is an Inter-American Convention Against Corruption 1996 and an Inter-American Democratic Charter 2001; the OSCE has undertaken relevant field work as part of its democratization projects under the auspices of the Office for Democratic Institution and Human Rights; and the Inter-Parliamentary Union has also examined the role of parliaments in strengthening democratic institutions and human development in a fragmented world (108th Inter-Parliamentary Union Conference 2003). As stepping stones to progressing development, democratization and anti-corruption are ever present. The right to development cannot be realized overnight; rather it is a matter of incremental changes, each advancing the cause little by little. Results are being achieved but progress remains slow.

23.4.2 Environmental rights

Environmental rights, originally restricted to the African Charter on Human and Peoples' Rights, are now gaining general international recognition. As the effect of modern society on the environment becomes ever clearer, calls for environmental rights gain weight. The right to environment is not protected in any universal instrument although Art 25 of the Universal Declaration articulates that everyone has a right to 'a standard of living adequate for the health and wellbeing of himself and his family'. What has developed over the years is a clear body of international (and indeed regional) environmental law. Many instruments establish regulatory frameworks for hazardous waste materials and pollution control, others address the use of natural resources (flora, fauna, and mineral). Clearly the result of this should be an improvement in the environment. However, contemporary debate is now centring on whether environmental rights exist and can be used to hasten ratification of international standards.

The 1972 Stockholm Declaration adopted by the UN Conference on the Human Environment stipulates that 'Man has the fundamental right to freedom, equality and adequate conditions of life in an environment of a quality that permits a life of dignity and well-being and he bears a solemn responsibility to protect and improve the environment for present and future generations' (Principle 1). Such a declaration is not legally enforceable. Arguably, parallels could be drawn with Art 25 of the Universal Declaration, given the similarity in the wording. The wording also echoes the tenor of the UN Convention on the Rights of the Child when it refers to improving the environment for future generations. The 1992 Rio Conference on the Environment and Development did little to progress environmental rights, stating in Principle 1 of the Rio Declaration that '[h]uman beings are at the centre of concerns for sustainable development. They are entitled to a healthy and productive life in harmony with nature'. More is needed to be done. The second and third conferences on the subject expanded on the concept of sustainable development with the Johannesburg 2002 conference producing a Plan of Implementation to further the declared and agreed political aspirations. Alongside these developments, the United Nations Framework Convention on Climate Change 1992 (opened for signature at the Rio Summit) and its 1997 Kyoto Protocol seek to regulate emissions damaging to the environment. Environmental sustainability is one of the Millennium Development Goals and a UN Climate Change conference met in Valencia, Spain in 2007 and in Bali, Indonesia in December 2007. The resulting Bali Road Map and Action Plan set the agenda for furthering negotiations on climate change. Other instruments such as those governing biological and chemical weapons, nuclear activities, and hazardous waste clearly have an effect on the environment too.

The regional systems have embraced some elements of environmental rights. Article 24 of the African Charter on Human and Peoples' Rights states that '[a]ll people shall have the right to a general satisfactory environment favourable to their development'. In the Americas, Art 11 of the Protocol of San Salvador provides: '[e]veryone shall have the right to live in a healthy environment and to have access to their basic public services'. Interestingly, it also explicitly imposes a duty on States to promote the protection, preservation, and improvement of the environment.

It would appear that environmental rights, if ever clarified, would be collective rights. The nature of the environment renders this unavoidable. As has been discussed, collective rights are still in their infancy.

Perhaps in contrast to the right to development, environmental rights have been enforced in certain circumstances through invocation of existing rights. There is an obvious overlap between environmental rights and the rights of indigenous peoples particularly where natural resources are involved. As cases discussed in Chapter 21 demonstrate, Art 27 of the International Covenant on Civil and Political Rights may provide an avenue for claims of certain groups. ILO Convention 169 (discussed Chapter 22) is further evidence of the link between land rights for indigenous peoples and the environment. The right to health may provide the monitoring bodies with an opportunity to examine some aspects of environmental rights. As indeed may some elements of the right to family and home life.

23.4.3 Beneficiaries of rights

Having established a universal benchmark for human rights, there has been a tendency towards specialization of protection, focusing on vulnerable groups. Children, women, and minorities have been discussed previously. As noted, the Permanent Forum for Indigenous Peoples was established in 2002. The rights of those living with AIDS/HIV are attracting ever more attention on the international stage, not least at the 2009 Durban Review conference in Geneva.

In recent years, post-conflict peace-building has assumed new prominence in the work of the United Nations (Secretary-General, para 120). This has entailed increasing coordination between the Office of the High Commissioner for Human Rights, the Office of the High Commissioner for Refugees and various other departments. As the situation in the Balkans corroborates, the United Nations may become involved in peacekeeping operations, humanitarian work, and even forge interim governmental arrangements. Both East Timor and Afghanistan experienced interim United Nations-sanctioned governance pending democratic elections. The United Nations may assist in the execution of such elections as well as being involved in human rights training for the police, defence forces, judiciary, and government elect. Emergency relief work, humanitarian aid, and post-conflict support will continue to occupy the resources of United Nations bodies and, inevitably, shape the development of associated human rights norms.

The relationship between peace and human rights, which characterized early enunciations of rights (post French Revolution and US War of Independence) is reappearing through the work of the United Nations and the OSCE. It indicates a growing need which international human rights must ensure is met in the twenty-first century.

23.5 **Conclusions**

International human rights instruments are living organs, enshrining non-static norms, evolving in response to global developments and political reality. Whatever the problems with the present system, and there are many, the mere fact that there are now instruments tabulating human rights and fundamental freedoms is, in itself, a success. Human rights are for the benefit of all; thus, through education and training, the goals must be achieved. The lawyers have played their role, drafting norms of rights, codifying a philosophy on the rights of the individual. It is now for the politicians, the governments of the States, to transform the theory into reality, the rights and freedoms into tangible norms enforceable before national courts and subject to international supervision.

READING

Alston, P, 'Conjuring up new human rights: A proposal for quality control' (1984) 78 American Journal of International Law 607.

Baxi, U, *The Future of Human Rights* (India: Oxford University Press, 2002).

Boyle, A, and Anderson, M, *Human Rights Approaches to Environmental Protection* (Oxford: Clarendon, 1998).

Claude, R, *Human Rights in the World Community: Issues and action*, 2nd edn (Philadelphia: University of Pennsylvania Press, 1995).

Espiell, H, 'The right of development as a human right' in R Claude and B Weston (eds), *Human Rights in the World Community: Issues and action* (Philadelphia: University of Pennsylvania Press, 1992), pp 167–75.

Henkin, L, and Hargrove, J (eds), *Human Rights: An agenda for the next century* (Washington DC: ASIL, 1994).

Mahoney, KE, and Mahoney, P (eds), *Human Rights in the 21st Century: A global challenge* (Leiden: Brill, 1993).

Megret, F, and Alston, P (eds), *The United Nations and Human Rights: A critical approach* (Oxford: Oxford University Press, 2004).

Rich, R, 'The right to development: A right of peoples?' in J Crawford (ed), *The Rights of Peoples* (Oxford: Clarendon Press, 1988).

Sano, H, 'Development and human rights: The necessary, but partial integration of human rights and development' (2000) 22 Human Rights Quarterly 734–52.

Secretary-General, 'Reviewing the United Nations: A programme for reform', UN Doc A/51/950, 14 July 1997.

United Nations, *Status of implementation of actions described in the report of the Secretary General entitled, 'Strengthening of the United Nations: An agenda for further change'*, UN Doc A/58/351 (2003).

Weston, BH, and Marks, SP, *The Future of International Human Rights* (New York: Transnational, 1999).

Zillma, DM, Lucas, A, and Pring, G (eds), *Human Rights in Natural Resource Development* (Oxford: Oxford University Press, 2002).

WEBSITES

unfccc.int—United Nations Framework Convention on Climate Change.

www.undp.org—United Nations Development Programme.

www.unep.org—United Nations Environment Programme.

www2.ohchr.org/english/issues/disability/index.htm—United Nations site on human rights and disability.

www2.ohchr.org/english/issues/hiv—United Nations site on HIV/AIDS and human rights.

www.unglobalcompact.org—Business and human rights.

www.un.org/millenniumgoals/—UN Millennium Development Goals.

INDEX